The HORSES of Monticello

EQUINE CULTURE IN THOMAS JEFFERSON'S VIRGINIA

BY

CARRIE BESS DOUGLASS

DEMENTI MILESTONE PUBLISHING

First Printing

Author
Carrie Bess Douglass

Publisher
Wayne Dementi
Dementi Milestone Publishing, Inc.
Manakin-Sabot, VA 23103
www.dementimilestonepublishing.com

Cataloging-in-publication data for this book
is available from
The Library of Congress.
ISBN: 978-8-9909631-6-0

Graphic design by:
Jayne E. Hushen
Dementi Milestone Publishing, Inc.

Official Presidential portrait of Thomas Jefferson (by Rembrandt Peale, 1800)

Printed in the USA

The HORSES of Monticello

EQUINE CULTURE IN THOMAS JEFFERSON'S VIRGINIA

BY

CARRIE BESS DOUGLASS

DEMENTI MILESTONE PUBLISHING

Table of Contents

Acknowledgements

For scholarly direction: Peter Hatch, Sandra Rebok, and Andrew O'Shaughnessy, and the Jefferson Foundation and the International Center of Jefferson Studies at Monticello. For my anthropological perspective: Fred Damon, and several twentieth-century anthropology mentors (Emile Durkheim, Clause Levi-Strauss, Marcel Mauss) and twenty-first century human/equine studies mentors (John Borneman and Donna Landry). For the reality of the printed book itself: Wayne Dementi, Julie Campbell, and Jayne Hushen. For readers and editors: Lydia Petersson, Jean Cooper, Christa Deirksheide, and especially Julie Campbell. To the horses I have partnered with since 1966: Playboy, Spook, Swift, Cider, and Yankee. To Becky Guercio at Trulily Farm in Albemarle County, Virginia, and her exquisite care of horses. To my maternal grandmother, Margaret Wallace Casteel Pickering (1894–1979), a child of a U.S cavalry officer, who drove ponies, brazenly rode horses with the cavalry recruits on the Army posts where her father was stationed, and competed in horse shows, winning trophies and prizes as a young woman. Finally, to Fernando, Philip, Peter, Camila, and Alicia, who bring me much joy, and who have learned more about horses and heard more stories about Thomas Jefferson than they ever imagined possible.

Dedication

To my father and mother,
John Jay Douglass (1922–2018) and Margaret Pickering Douglass (1921–2015),
who both, in their own ways, nurtured my life with horses,
my interest in history, my academic pursuits, and my home in Charlottesville, Virginia.
I am forever grateful to both.

chronology

Timeline of Jefferson's Life[1]

	Public	Private	Saddle Horse
1735		Peter Jefferson, Thomas Jefferson's father, patented 1,000-acre tract which became Monticello.	
1743		Thomas Jefferson born at Shadwell.	
1757		Peter Jefferson died.	
1760-62		Thomas Jefferson attended the College of William and Mary.	
1762		Began study of law with George Wythe.	
1764		Came into inheritance at age of 21.	
1767		Admitted to practice law before General Court.	
1768	Elected to House of Burgesses.	Leveling of Monticello mountaintop begun.	
1770		Construction begun at Monticello. Shadwell burned. Moved to South Pavilion at Monticello.	
1772		Married Martha (Wayles) Skelton. Daughter Martha born.	
1773		Graveyard at Monticello established with the interment of Jefferson's friend and brother-in-law Dabney Carr.	
1774	Wrote *A Summary View of the Rights of British America.*	Retired from legal practice. Inherited 11,000 acres of land and 135 slaves from his father-in-law. Laid off ground for kitchen garden. Daughter Jane Randolph born.	
1775	Elected to Continental Congress	Daughter Jane Randolph died.	The General
1776	Drafted Declaration of Independence. Elected to Virginia House of Delegates. Appointed to revise Virginia laws.	Mother Jane Randolph Jefferson died.	
1777	Drafted Virginia Statute passed by General Assembly in 1786.	Unnamed son born and died.	Caractacus
1778	Drafted Bill for the More General Diffusion of Knowledge.	Daughter Mary (Maria) born. Brickwork of first home (Monticello) completed.	
1779-81	Served as Governor of Virginia.		
1780		Daughter Lucy Elizabeth born. Began *Notes on the State of Virginia.*	
1781		British troops at Monticello. Daughter Lucy Elizabeth died.	
1782		Second Lucy Elizabeth born. Wife Martha died. First house substantially completed.	

1783	Elected delegate to Congress.		
1784-89	In France as Commissioner and Minister.		Sorrel riding horse
1784		Daughter Lucy Elizabeth died.	
1787	Published *Notes on the State of Virginia.*		
1790-93	Served as first United States Secretary of State.		Odin Tarquin
1794-1795		Began commercial manufacture of nails on Mulberry Row. Manumitted slave Robert Hemings. Sally Hemings 1st child, Harriet, born [1795]	
1796		Remodeling and enlarging of Monticello begun.	Darlington
		Manumitted slave James Hemings.	
1797-1801	Served as United States Vice President.	Sally Hemings 2nd child, William Beverley, born [1798]	
1797-1815	Served as president of the American Philosophical Society.	Sally Hemings's child, Harriet, born [1801]	
1800		Dome constructed on Monticello.	
1801-09	Served as United States President.		Wildair
1803	Louisiana Purchase concluded. Lewis and Clark expedition launched.		
1804		Daughter Maria Jefferson Eppes died. Sally Hemings' son, James Madison, born [1805]	Arcturus, Jacobin
1806	Lewis and Clark expedition concluded.	House at Poplar Forest begun.	
1807		Oval flower beds near Monticello laid out. Shadwell merchant mill completed.	Turncoat
1808		At Monticello, North Pavilion completed and South Pavilion remodeled. Winding walk and flower beds on West Lawn laid out. Sally Hemings's son, Thomas Eston, born [1808]	Celer
1809	Retired from presidency and public life.	Remodeling of Monticello and construction of dependencies largely completed. Vegetable garden platform completed.	
1812		Garden Pavilion constructed.	
1815	Sold 6,700-volume library to Congress.		1814 Bremo 1815 Tecumseh
1817	Cornerstone of Central College (later University of Virginia) laid.		
1822-25		Monticello roof recovered with tin shingles	1820 The Eagle
1824		Historic reunion with the Marquis de Lafayette at Monticello	
1825	University of Virginia opened.		
1826		Died at Monticello, July 4	

Prologue

"So Delightful and So Necessary": Jefferson's Daily Revival

> *I can assure you from experience that to old age the daily ride is among the most cheering of comforts. It renews the pleasurable sensation that we are still in society with beings and the things around us and so delightful and so necessary is this daily revival to me that I would wish to lose that and life together.*
>
> — Th. Jefferson [age eighty-one] to William Short, April 10, 1824[1]

Just before one o'clock on a sultry July day in 1817, Thomas Jefferson strode out of his private cabinet [Fig. P-1] and onto the terrace that adjoined his suite of rooms at his mountaintop home, Monticello. [Fig. P-2] He was in his riding gear: a doeskin overall that protected his finer breeches, and tall riding boots with spurs strapped on. A wide-brimmed round hat in hand, he descended the stairs from the terrace level to the ground and went directly to the tree where the big bay horse was tethered. A young enslaved boy jumped up from his resting position in the shade and skipped over to Mr. Jefferson, handing him his short whip, or riding crop. They exchanged pleasantries and comments about the horse, called Bremo, while Jefferson put on his round hat and looked appreciatively at the handsome animal, all tacked up and ready to go. His task now over, the youngster turned and disappeared toward the stable on Mulberry Row to await Jefferson's return a few hours later.

Fig. P-2 Actor-Interpreter Bill Barker, portraying Thomas Jefferson at Monticello, on the South Terrace, looking out over the Virginia Piedmont

Jefferson unhitched his horse and led him by the reins out to an open space. He steadied the eleven-year-old stallion with his right hand on the horse's muscled and silky, clean, dark brown neck, and then gathered the reins in his left hand and grabbed some black mane near the flat English hunt saddle. The seventy-four-year-old Jefferson, ever the patrician, stood facing the left side of the horse and lifted his left foot into the iron stirrup. Placing his right hand, still holding the riding crop, on the cantle at the back of the saddle and bouncing slightly on his right leg, Jefferson pulled his lanky, six-foot two-inch frame up the side of the horse, and leaning slightly over the saddle, let go with his right hand and swung his right leg over and around to the other side of the horse.

As the tall man sat down in the saddle, Bremo startled a bit, but Jefferson shortened the reins, sat back, and made the animal stand still while slipping his right foot into the other iron stirrup. Then, leaning over and patting the horse on the right side of his neck, the

Fig. P-1 *Left*, Jefferson's private cabinet at Monticello

Fig. P-3 Actor-Interpreter Bill Barker, portraying Thomas Jefferson at Monticello, on horseback in his riding apparel

rider squeezed his legs and touched a blunt spur to Bremo's side, and the equestrian team moved off toward Mulberry Row and the stone stables to the east. [Fig. P-3] As Jefferson passed the stables, as horse and rider disappeared down the Farm Road. [Fig. P-4]

Jefferson had proposed to ride down the Farm Road to check on the harvest of the wheat in the fields, or bottom lands, along the Rivanna River, across from Shadwell, his birthplace and boyhood home. Although he was in the process of handing over management of the plantation to his grandson, Jeff Randolph, Jefferson wanted to make sure himself that most of the wheat had been collected and stored and wasn't still exposed to the threat of late-afternoon thunderstorms that the dark skies looming over the Blue Ridge Mountains toward the west portended. Moreover, much of the Farm Road at the top of the mountain was carved through deep woods, and the shade would be a welcome respite from the midday sun. Jefferson's plan, after checking on the harvest, was to cross over the river at the dam next to River Field and continue his solitary ride upstream along the other side of the Rivanna, staying in the shade of the trees along the banks, toward Secretary's Ford and Charlottesville, and away from bustling shipping and commercial areas of the river downstream of the dam. He would return to Monticello by re-fording the river at Secretary's Ford and then head up the gully path to just before the Notch on the Thoroughfare. He would then catch the Second Roundabout and cut over through his Groves, going below the vegetable garden and the south orchard straight to the stable. Jefferson knew this would take him about

Fig. P-4 The stables at Monticello

two hours. He'd be home in plenty of time for dinner around four o'clock. [Fig P-5]

Despite temperatures only in the mid-eighties, the woods were dank with humidity. The creaking scrunch of the leather saddle competed with the wave-like vibrating crescendos of the katydid and cicada songs that filled the summer forest. [Fig. P-6] Bremo, gingerly picking his way down the rocky and rutted road at a walk, was already working up a sweat on his shoulders and around his girth. Jefferson started humming a tune, one he had picked up in Williamsburg in his student days. One of Bremo's ears flicked back momentarily before again joining the other ear pointing toward the direction they were going. The horse made several snorting sounds and shook his head in irritation at the flies gathering on his sweat. Jefferson flicked at the flies with his riding crop. He

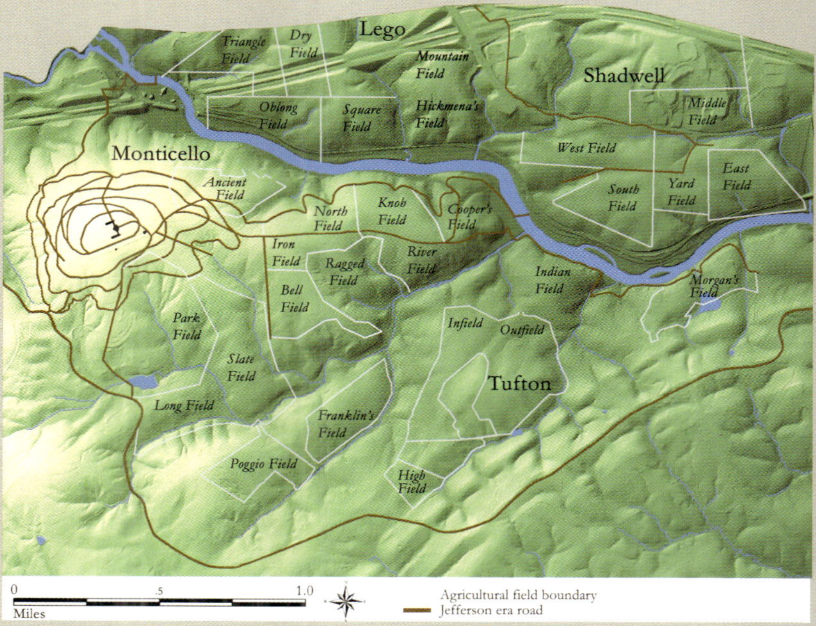

Fig. P-5 Map of Monticello and quarter farms, with Jefferson-era roads and roundabouts. Some current roads are also indicated

Fig. P-6 *Left*, Farm Road at Monticello

looked off into the woods toward a slave dwelling bordering the planted Knob Field: two people were moving about outside the dwelling. Suddenly, the rider stopped singing and lurched forward as Bremo slipped on a wet flat stone. Instinctively, Jefferson regathered the reins and leaned back. As the horse regained his equilibrium, the rider steadied him with a calm hand on his shoulder. Although Bremo was a blooded horse, he wasn't as tall and leggy as some of the Thoroughbreds that other gentlemen used mainly for racing. Usually very surefooted, Bremo served as a good mount on the hilly Albemarle plantation. After checking on the status of his crop, Jefferson crossed the Rivanna and put Bremo into a comfortable pacing jog upstream along the river. [Fig. P-7]

Humming a different tune now, Jefferson was working over in his mind the rationale for the Agricultural Society that he and his friend James Madison had

Fig. P-7 Moorman's River, which flows into the Rivanna River, in Albemarle, County, Virginia

just established in May. Already Jefferson was choosing more founding members in his mind. Certainly, he wanted to include John Hartwell Cocke, a nearby planter and friend, and Bremo's original owner.

Whoosh! A blue heron flew up from the low-running river, and this time Bremo didn't flinch. Jefferson talked to the bay horse, whose ear flicked back in response. With his legs, Jefferson urged the horse to keep going at his comfortable pace. They passed flowering phloxes and Queen Anne's lace, which dappled the green-laden riverbanks white. Every once in a while, bright yellow patches of black-eyed Susans splashed some color along the path; blue-winged dragonflies darted along the tops of the tall plants; frogs gave their throaty, twangy thump call and then scattered across the water as horse and rider passed by.

Later, after they recrossed the river and started back up the 875-foot mountainside of Monticello, again at a walk, the horse bobbed his head in the effort of the scramble up the mountain. Summer thunderstorms had made the earth muddy and slippery. Lather was appearing on Bremo's arched neck along the sweaty path of the reins. The trail, hardly visible in places, was strewn with fallen and rotting trees and was overgrown in spots with briars and vines. Bremo willingly forged ahead as his rider leaned out of the way of the fecund and drooping forest.

Jefferson stopped his horse at one point, letting him rest. Sitting straight on his steed, seeming almost to be part of the animal, the man looked up the mountain into the untamed woodland and up the trunks of the soaring majestic trees whose foliage formed a canopy above—white oaks, white pines, and the magnificent tulip poplars, which Jefferson called the Jupiter and the Juno of his Groves. Sunlight, filtered by the leafy cover, seemed to give up and disappear halfway down to the ground. Birdcalls echoed among the trees as the cicadas continued their roiling chorus. The rider let the now-damp reins slip through his fingers as the big horse lowered his head, searching, in vain, for any tufts of grass on the forest floor. The scratching noise of an animal, just a squirrel perhaps, sounded in the underbrush; Bremo looked in that direction but stayed still, only his black tail switching at the flies.

Fig. P-8 White-tailed deer

As they neared the top of the mountain and came out on the Second Roundabout, the strapping horse relaxed and caught his breath, nose flaring, while stretching out into a lengthened walk. Suddenly Bremo raised his head a bit higher and hesitated ever so slightly; he let out two puff-snorts while looking slightly to the right, but continued walking. The rider followed the horse's gaze and sure enough, in front of them to the right, three grazing white-tail deer raised their startled heads, [Fig. P-8] and then went bounding and leaping back toward the thick forest, white tails erect and wagging. Bremo swung his head back to the path and didn't seem fazed. Jefferson gave him the signal, and the horse picked up a collected, if weary, canter around the path, through the shady Grove, where the undergrowth had been cut out except for thickets of mountain laurel and rhododendron, already well past their bloom, and then suddenly out into the sunlight below the vegetable garden on the great terrace. Trees laden with fruit smelled of the heavy perfume of ripe peaches. [Fig. P-9]

Jefferson, firm and erect, flowed with the horse at the canter until the rider slowed him down with the stable in sight. As Bremo decelerated to a walk, he nevertheless started throwing and shaking his head in nervous excitement, and Jefferson reached down one more time with his steadying hand to mediate the eager dance to the stable.

Fig. P-9 Monticello (*left*), with views of Jefferson's vegetable garden (*center*) and orchard (*right*)

Thomas Jefferson often described himself as spending his days in a saddle, affirming that his daily ride was the "most cheering of comforts," a "pleasurable sensation," so "delightful" that he wished to "lose that and life together." Jefferson enjoyed his books, his gardens, his wines, his convivial dinners, his home, and his family, but one of his most cherished passions was a "good horse." He rode daily into old age.[2]

Our vision of this cerebral, contradictory, sometimes inscrutable man is sharpened by understanding his life with horses. Statues and portraits of George Washington place him on a horse, indicating his role as the Sword of the Revolution. Thomas Jefferson, as the author of the Declaration of Independence, is known as the Pen of the Revolution and is thus less associated in the popular mind with horses. Yet his family, friends, and associates—all those who knew him well—understood him to be a consummate equestrian, and many anecdotes place him on horseback.

The horse, for Thomas Jefferson, was not simply a utilitarian means of transport for work or travel. Nor was his favored saddle horse of the moment, always a stallion, merely a display of distinction, status, wealth, and masculinity, although he undoubtedly was that. Thomas Jefferson rode his horse every day, in the city or in the country, in Washington or in Paris, and although riding a fine horse for two hours every midday was a pleasurable pursuit available only to an affluent few, Jefferson also rode as his solitary escape, a vital necessity for both physical and mental health.[3]

In addition to being a respected equestrian, Thomas Jefferson was a breeder of horses and an admirer of horseflesh in any form. Surviving documentation provides a vivid picture of Jefferson's place in the equine world of Virginia in the late eighteenth and early nineteenth centuries. Although he was not necessarily one of the primary pioneers in the emerging creation of horse breeds (versus horse types), Jefferson was an enthusiastic participant.

Most of Thomas Jefferson's time in the saddle was spent riding on trails. [Fig. P-10] Although he never described a specific ride in such detail as imagined in the section above, Jefferson, like many of the Founding Fathers, left us copious records and evidence of both his political and domestic pursuits, enabling us to explore both his public persona and his private life. His written records, diaries, intimations in letters, and other archival information, taken together, allow us reasonably to conjure such a scene: the very horse, being tethered waiting for the morning stroll, Jefferson's seat on the horse, the roundabouts, the stables, the scenery, Jefferson's habit of singing, and his thinking and planning on his daily ride.

By exploring the many facets of Jefferson's life with horses, we expand our understanding of a pivotal time in animal-breed creation and reemphasize the role of the horse in the context of the lives of rural and urban Virginians during Jefferson's lifetime (1743–1826). Since to discover and understand Jefferson's equestrian life, we must also see him in the social context of eighteenth-century Virginia, drawing on the particular experience of Thomas Jefferson allows us to explore Virginia equine culture during the period.

If our vision of Jefferson is sharpened by understanding his relationship with horses, so is our understanding of equine culture clarified by examining the role it played at a critical period in the development of the United States. Throughout the nineteenth century, the horse population continued to grow as horses were bred to power the nation. In 1867, the number of horses in the US was estimated at nearly eight million. Early in the twentieth century, the horse's utilitarian role in society began to change as the internal combustion engine and motorized vehicles began to take over previously horse-powered tasks. Horses were no longer bred as cavalry mounts, to work in agriculture, or to pull public transportation vehicles. The number of horses in the United States peaked in 1915 at 26 million and then declined until the late 1960s, when only three million horses are estimated to have remained.[4]

Nevertheless, the horse, and particularly the saddle horse, has continued to have a place in American society. After the 1890s, horses were most commonly bred and used as pleasure or hobby animals. In the 1950s, the number of horses born began to increase again as "the horse entered new arenas as a pleasure animal." Equine numbers continued to grow rapidly in the twenty-first century, reaching a high of 9.2 million

Fig. P-10 *Left*, riding on the trails of Albemarle County

P-11 Jefferson's home in Albemarle County, Virginia: Monticello

by 2005, more than in 1867. In fact, the late twentieth century "witnessed a huge growth of interest in horses" for pleasure, recreation, and sport. Rather than "being a beast of burden, the modern horse enjoys a major role in recreation and organized competition." [5]

Although much of contemporary equitation activity in the United States has competitive ends, more people ride for pure recreation and pleasure rather than to compete in an organized sport, according to the American Horse Council. Often called hacking in the eastern United States, Great Britain, and Canada, and trail riding elsewhere, pleasure riding takes place in state and national parks, on private lands and ranches, and at public stables. [6]

Those of us who ride today are the inheritors of Jefferson's pleasurable sensation. Like Jefferson, we ramble in the woods, across streams and rivers, and up and down mountains and plains. We recognize and identify with Thomas Jefferson's description of this "most cheering of comforts," the pleasure of riding a horse.

In the early twenty-first century, scholarly interest and research into the relationships between humans and horses, and in the role and status of horses in (human) society, have blossomed in the context of the wide-ranging animal turn observed in the social sciences and humanities. Recent investigation into the biological and social continuities and relationships shared by humans and horses has resulted in new understandings of human-horse interactions that contrast with a sometimes very different mindset about animals that eighteenth- and early-nineteenth-century Virginians enacted in their relationships with horses. Yet recent understandings might also explain certain associations that those earlier Americans projected onto equine behavior beyond mere anthropomorphism, such as horses taking care of their riders, the strong attachment between Black hostlers and their horses, or the horse as doctor. [7]

It is impossible to discuss an equine culture without exploring the human social culture that has spawned it, and parallels between social and equine hierarchies are reflected in the structure of this book.

The introduction provides an overview of the book's major themes and interpretive framework.

Part I

On Their High Horses, is organized around the social hierarchy of Jefferson's Virginia. It includes a chapter describing what we know about Jefferson's riding habits and riding style; a chapter that explores Jefferson's equine-focused relationships with friends and neighbors; and a chapter devoted to the women, workmen, and enslaved people who rode horses at Monticello.

Part II

The Equine Hierarchy has chapters dedicated to each of Thomas Jefferson's four categories of horses (riding, carriage, breeding, and work horses) and a chapter on horses used for sport (foxhunting and racing), including Jefferson's comments on these activities.

Finally, readers who are eager to read about Jefferson's individual horses or just one type of horse (e.g., carriages and carriage horses) are urged to read the Introduction and then skip ahead to begin with the relevant chapter.

Introduction

Horses in Thomas Jefferson's World

Horses In The Colonies

In British America, prior to the American Revolution, colonists used horses for long-distance traveling, transporting goods, pulling farm plows, drawing coaches, and fighting wars. They used horses for exercise, for pleasure, and for sport. Colonists bred, trained, bought, sold, exchanged, bet on, hunted with, and in dire straits, ate horses.

Important as they were, horses were scarce during the first years of the colonies. Horses as a species had disappeared from the New World 10,000 years before European contact. Explorers from the Spanish Empire were the first people from Europe to reintroduce horses to the Americas in 1519, when Cortez landed in what is now Mexico. In 1539, Hernando de Soto brought horses to the present-day United States, when he landed on the coast the Spanish called Florida.

At the time of the first permanent English settlement in Virginia almost seventy years later, however, none of the surrounding Indian tribes as yet had horses. The first horses brought by English colonists to their New World arrived in Jamestown in 1609, two years after the founding of that settlement in the land the English called Virginia. Seven horses (six mares and a stallion) were hoisted down from the ships, sent to the colonists by the Virginia Company in hopes that they would prosper and breed and aid in the work and transport of the new settlers.

Those first years of the Virginia Colony were difficult, and survival was tenuous. During the winter of 1609–10, the native populations laid siege to the Jamestown fort, and the colonists, who dared not leave, ran out of food. During what they called the Starving Time, they ate all their animals—dogs, cats, and horses—down to their hides. It was not until the spring of 1611 that seventeen more British horses arrived. By 1649, about 200 English horses lived in Virginia.[1]

Reflecting the varying geographic origins of their immigrant owners, different horse types—not yet selected as intensively as breeds would later be—populated the regions and sections of colonial America. The first horses sent to Plymouth colony in Massachusetts arrived in 1625. They were small and stocky, typical of the general work animal that characterized the British Isles at that time. The Dutch sent horses, probably the bigger Flanders type, to New Amsterdam about the same time. Horses were expropriated from the French in Canada or brought over on ships in small numbers up and down the eastern seaboard. By the end of the 1600s, the imported horses were thriving, and further importation was halted.[2]

Until the end of the eighteenth century, farmers used oxen to work and plow the fields; horses were all-purpose animals, used to pull loaded wagons around plantations or pull gigs and chariots in town, but also used under saddle to travel long distances. There were no well-maintained road systems until late in the eighteenth century, so most travel was on horseback on Indian trails, rather than in wagons or carriages.

Colonists in the South, relying on the economic base of the plantation system and facing relatively longer distances between towns and farms, developed more of a saddle-horse culture than did their counterparts in the northern colonies. The Tennessee Walker and Kentucky Saddlebred breeds were both developed in the late eighteenth century within this context. Given the overwhelmingly rural quality of Virginia life in the early eighteenth century, even yeoman farmers and lower-class (white) farmers put a saddle on their work horses and rode them to church on Sundays. Indeed, visitors from England often commented on the Virginians' propensity to ride rather than walk.[3]

Here an English clergyman, who was serving as a professor at the College of William and Mary, wrote about Virginians:

> They are such lovers of Riding, that almost every ordinary Person keeps a Horse; and I have known some spend the morning in ranging several miles in the Woods to find and catch their Horses only to ride

two or three miles to Church, to the court House, or to a Horse-Race.

Both men and women—who rode sidesaddle—appreciated the smooth gaits of these early English horses.[4]

Match races, which pitted two horses in a mad dash down an often narrow path, was a recreational activity that took advantage of the speediness of these same comfortable, sturdy little work horses. In Virginia, records of match races in York County date from at least 1674. Horse racing was also popular in other colonies at the time. The colony of Rhode Island produced a kind of horse called Narragansett Pacers, and in that area Long Island became the principal place for horse racing, including trotting races, by 1665. Betting money on horses (gambling) was present at the origin of this American sport.[5]

Thomas Jefferson was born in 1743 into a revolutionary moment in equine culture in Virginia. In the 1740s, gentry in the Tidewater areas of Virginia, Maryland, and North Carolina began to import a new kind of horse. Attracted to the English style of horse racing, called course racing, in which groups of horses competed on elliptical tracks at distances of three or four miles, these men used their new tobacco-generated wealth to import a new kind of horse, a bigger, taller, faster animal, bred just for racing long distances. Although originally imported for the turf, or to produce racers, these new horses, at first called "blood horses" and later known collectively as the Thoroughbred, ended up being used as saddle horses, coach horses, and jumping or foxhunting horses, as well as military horses, and genetically influenced many breeds in the soon-to-be United States.[6]

During the second half of the eighteenth century, one key difference between the upper-class gentry and the commoner in Virginia was that the gentry could afford to maintain a variety of mounts, each dedicated to a specific activity. In contrast, the commoner's tough little all-purpose horse may have worked the fields at certain times of the year, drawn a wagon or chair to town, served under saddle when necessary, and then run in a match race on Saturday afternoon.[7]

Virginia gentry identified closely with their new tall breed of English horses, in the way that some people identify with expensive automobiles today. Ownership of one of these expensive "high horses" (meaning, literally, tall horses) was symbolic of high status, and to be seen riding one commanded admiration. Although as a young boy, Thomas Jefferson learned to ride on fat little Chickasaw mares, by the time he was a young adult, as a student in Williamsburg, he was infatuated with the high horses of the elite. After the Revolution, Jefferson rode only what we today call Thoroughbreds.

However, horses became much more than a status symbol for Jefferson. In fact, in this book, I argue that his lifelong management of horses played a significant role in the shaping of his own identity. Although the time and place in which he lived required equine interaction and expertise, he was much more personally engaged than was strictly required.

Some of this engagement helped him to find his place among his peers. Through horse trading and breeding, he mediated and sustained personal and financial relationships with the developing Virginia elites. Jefferson's involvement in horse breeding also reflects, and complicates, our understanding of Jefferson's worldview, which to twenty-first-century eyes can seem an odd mixture of the progressive and the conservative. He may have sought to improve the breed for intellectual purposes that were appropriate to his ambitions as a scientifically engaged landowner and gentleman, but his management records and interactions with others also clearly reflected an implicit breed hierarchy that paralleled his understanding of human social hierarchies. He recognized, one might say, that different breeds had different purposes, but that not all breeds and purposes were created equal.

However, Jefferson's relationship with horses evolved over his lifetime, becoming more relational and less transactional. He gave up horse breeding when he was still a relatively young man, for instance, but continued his daily ride until old age, seeking the "pleasurable sensation" of vigorous exercise combined with the opportunity for solitary reflection. Ultimately, I believe, we can identify with Jefferson as a horse lover while still recognizing that his relationship with horses reflected complicated social realities.

Social Hierarchy of Jefferson's Virginia

Male members of the gentry—a small group of landowners, very wealthy merchants, and financiers—were the upper crust of Virginia colonial society, dominating economic, social, and political life through much of the mid- to late eighteenth century.

They owned huge tracts of land, relying heavily on the labor first of indentured servants and then enslaved Africans. "Gentry men," or gentlemen, took it as their right and duty to govern others. They served as local magistrates, church vestrymen, burgesses, and councilmen. By the 1720s and 1730s, the gentry were well established and were erecting large, often magnificent, homes, mostly in the eastern Tidewater section of the colony, that dominated the landscape and symbolized their great power.

Although they clearly understood the market economy, the gentry preferred to see themselves as removed from and superior to physical labor and the commercial-exchange economy. Instead, they sought to portray themselves as men of leisure and generosity. Indeed, planters often sought to portray their relations with merchants as noncommercial in nature. Their lifestyle supposedly facilitated the cultivation of refined standards of personal conduct and cultural appreciation. This was visible in "the inordinate amount of time they devoted to visiting one another and to participation in gambling, dancing," and other fashionable pursuits.[8]

The First Families of Virginia originated with colonists from England who primarily settled along the James River and other navigable waters in the colony during the seventeenth century. They were not the first settler-survivors of the Jamestown colony, but rather were colonists who arrived after 1630, and set up plantations worked by enslaved African labor along the James River. Marriage among the FFVs helped seal their status and maintain a hierarchical society. In a society based on the possession of land and slaves, land was tightly controlled, and often passed between families of corresponding social rank. There was a propensity to marry within their narrow social scope for many generations. Jefferson became part of the landed gentry but was not an FFV, although his mother was. Thomas Jefferson was the son of a yeoman-type farmer, and later land surveyor, who was fortunate to marry into the powerful Randolph family, certainly one of the First Families of Virginia.[9]

In each of the social groups in colonial Virginia, males were considered to be the social superiors of women, although women shared in the social status of their wider group identities. "Gentry ladies," or gentlewomen, were at the top of social class and colonial fashion.

In contrast to the gentry, most white Americans during the eighteenth century lived and worked on small farms with the labor of only their own families—father, mother, and children—and perhaps one or two slaves or hired help. Soon, a new group, the "middling sort," gained a larger role in society and government. These men and women worked in trades—blacksmithing, silversmithing, printing, and millinery—or as professional lawyers or doctors, or owned stores.

The British American colonies also had a small but important population of free men and women of African descent. Though they did not enjoy the same rights as white citizens, these free Black men and women owned property, worked in a wide range of skilled jobs, and made significant contributions to their communities.[10]

Enslaved people were at the bottom of the social hierarchy, the descendants of Africans who had been kidnapped and eventually brought to America to work, mainly in agriculture. Slavery existed in all the British American colonies. However, the institution of slavery in eighteenth-century Virginia had its own normative hierarchy that emerged in practice. Some enslaved Africans worked as cooks, laundresses, manservants, blacksmiths, coopers, or in other skilled jobs. These men and women were generally considered better off than field slaves, but they still had little autonomy.

Some of these enslaved house servants had and retained surnames. In general, at this time in the case of slaves who retained an English last name, it meant they had a forebear who was white (a father, grandfather, or great-grandfather).[11]

In Virginia, however, most enslaved Africans were workers in the tobacco fields. In Jefferson's enslavement hierarchy, the lowest members were the unskilled field laborers. Men, women, and children worked from sunup to sundown, with only Sunday to rest. It was hard, backbreaking work. Field workers were often hired out or shifted from farm to farm as needed.

Jefferson's Equine Hierarchy

At Jefferson's Monticello, the social hierarchy of eighteenth-century Virginia was clearly the model for an equine equivalent. Based on his own documentation, Jefferson probably owned more than 135 horses in the sixty-five years between 1761 and his death in 1826. He owned, and was careful to distinguish among, horses belonging to several types; his hierarchy of categories incorporated use, pedigree, size, sex, price, and name.

Blood Horses: Significantly, Jefferson distinguished his blood horses from his work horses. "Thorough-bred" originally meant "pure-bred," and the term could be used for either a person or animal. Thoroughbred horses were, and are, pure-bred because they trace back to three stallions in England who had been imported between 1690 and 1730 from the Middle Eastern lands the English called "the Orient." A "high-bred" blood horse was the result of a closed breeding system, much like that of the aristocracy of England or of the planter elite of Virginia. Thus, pedigree became all-important. Jefferson, like many of his friends, was almost obsessed with his blood horses.

In colonial Virginia, only a few of the very wealthy Tidewater gentry could afford to import these expensive English racehorses. When they were retired from racing, these new blood horses stood at stud, and other planters brought their mares to them in order to get foals that would link the owners to the elite and their "high horses." The offspring were not necessarily racehorses but rather served mainly as saddle horses or carriage horses. To ride the new blood horses became a sign, or status symbol, of general gentry status, despite the implicit hierarchy between owners of the imported studs and the other planters (mare owners). Thomas Jefferson was one of the latter; yet all his horses (for his personal use: saddle/carriage/etc.) were offspring of the imported turf horses.

When we refer to Jefferson's horses, we usually mean a select group of about fourteen who served as his personal saddle horses, but Jefferson owned fifty-nine highly bred blooded horses over his lifetime. Most of these had names, and Jefferson carefully recorded their pedigrees, previous owners, age, color, height, markings, and price (always expensive and almost always bought on credit). These named horses can be further categorized in three ways: as his saddle horses, as his carriage horses, or as his breeding mares and their offspring. (Jefferson, unlike other gentry, did not have horses dedicated to sport—racing or foxhunting). These blooded horses, too, were arranged in a kind of equine hierarchy with respect to their relationship with Jefferson.

At the top of the hierarchy would be a stallion, designated as Jefferson's own saddle horse, the horse he preferred to ride every day. Several of these animals had important roles in Jefferson's biography. Family members and acquaintances remembered their names and connected them to events and places in Jefferson's life. Always blood horses, tall and elegant, commanding attention wherever they went, these horses were in many ways an expression of Jefferson himself. [Fig. I-1]

Fig. I-1 "Saddle Horse," as depicted in Mason, *The Gentleman's New Pocket Companion*

Below the saddle horses in status were the carriage horses. Although these horses could be used as saddle horses if necessary—Jefferson "broke all his horses to both ride and work"—their primary role was drawing Jefferson's several vehicles. These animals were always stabled at the top of the mountain, near the house, on Mulberry Row, and their elite pedigrees connected Jefferson to gentry across the state.[12] [Fig. I-2]

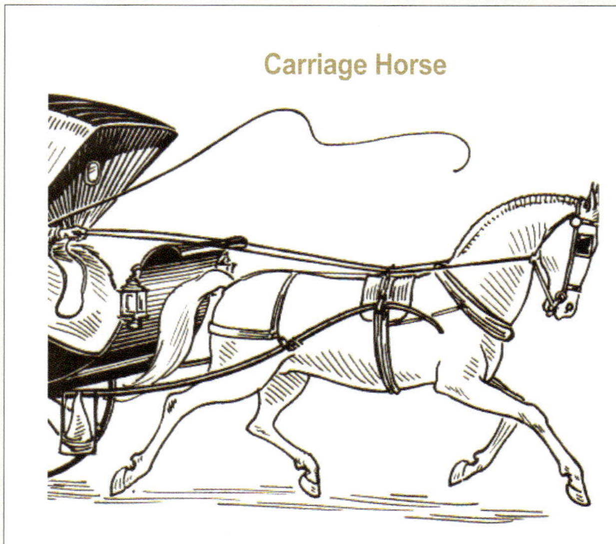

Fig. I-2 "Carriage Horse," as depicted in The Archives of Pearson Scott Foresman

Broodmares (females) were kept separate from stallions (males). Jefferson never used a mare in a carriage or under saddle. They were dedicated to breeding and were stabled far from the main house, sometimes at different farms. Stallions were kept in a stone stable near the main house. [Fig. I-3]

Fig. I-3 "Brood Mare," as depicted in Mason, *The Gentleman's New Pocket Companion*

These three groups of horses were all listed separately from the work horses and other livestock in Jefferson's *Farm Book*, the compendium of his agricultural assets. The animals are listed by name on the inside front cover and first pages of the book, with carefully recorded pedigrees that associate them with other breeders and Virginia gentry. The price of a blood horse in 1800 ranged between $300 and $500. In 1800, in Virginia, a young enslaved Black man cost about $400, or about the same as a blooded stallion.

Work Horses: For the first 100 to 130 years, until the 1740s, most of the horses in the British American colonies were the descendants of the small general-use horses, typical of England in the seventeenth century, referred to as Irish Hobbies or Scottish Galloways. In British America, horses were bred for different uses in diverse locales and consequently developed characteristics specific to the needs of each colony. Eventually, in the eighteenth century, horses bred and sold by Indians east of the Mississippi River made their way into the Carolinas and Virginia. These Indian horses, called Chickasaws after the tribes who traded them, were descendants of horses the Spanish had brought over in their conquest of Mexico and Peru. Described similarly to the Galloways and Hobbies, as hardy, active, and small, Chickasaws bred with their English cousins, resulting in the Virginia horse. (See Chapter 8.) These were Jefferson's work horses.

The work horses, or plantation horses, were always unnamed, rather inexpensive, and paid for in full at purchase, distinguishing them from Jefferson's highly bred riding, carriage, and breeding horses. Pedigree or previous ownership was never mentioned for the work horses. Between 1761 and 1826, Jefferson bought or owned about seventy-eight unnamed work horses (for plowing fields, pulling wagons, etc.). Jefferson also had mules and oxen for this kind of work. These animals lived far from the main house, on the quarter farms where they worked. In 1800, one work horse cost about $50. [Fig. I-4]

Jefferson's work horses or plantation horses, listed and counted along with the other stock in his *Farm Book*, equate in the social hierarchy to the enslaved people at Monticello (or specifically, those who worked in the fields with these animals). Significantly, men from that special group of house servants at Monticello were put in charge of Jefferson's blood horses (as hostlers), drove or rode Jefferson's carriage horses (as coachmen or postilions), or accompanied Jefferson as a manservant on a following horse (sometimes on Jefferson's own saddle horse). A few even owned a horse.

In general, the difference in status between a blood horse and a plantation horse was similar to that between a white person and a Black person. Moreover, the pedigreed blood horses

Fig. I-4 "Cart Horse," as depicted in Mason, *The Gentleman's New Pocket Companion*

were identity symbols of the Virginia gentry, while a nameless work horse, mere livestock, was associated with a field slave. In between these categories were various middlin' sorts. But it is clear that the human hierarchy served as the model for the equine one.

Jefferson's Evolving Relationship with Horses

During his youth and young adulthood, Jefferson seemed to be enamored of the status conferred by blood horses. He attended the course races where these newly imported English horses competed for money and trophies, and he participated in foxhunts with others in his social circles. Jefferson dedicated a decade to breeding his mares to imported studs, which wound him into tight relationships with their landed-gentry owners. He bought riding horses with impressive pedigrees. This was typical of the men of the planter elite in the mid-eighteenth century in Virginia. But in Jefferson's case, his equestrian interests were soon to go beyond merely performing status. His relationship with his riding horses was about to take an intense and passionate turn. I daresay that his riding horse was soon to change from merely an object of status to a subject, a partner—a subservient partner—but one with agency and influence on Jefferson's life and happiness.

On September 6, 1782, his young wife, Martha, died of the lingering effects of childbirth. For three weeks Jefferson kept to his room. When he finally emerged, Jefferson started to heal his grief and mend himself by riding his horse out on the mountain. It was after his wife's death that Jefferson began to ride daily, ritually, almost religiously. We know this because his family and friends, and he himself, describe him as doing so. He rode not only as a means of transportation or to oversee work in the fields like all plantation owners. That, yes. But it was something more essential for Jefferson. Above and beyond his errands on horseback, beyond his trips to the town, beyond the daily task of the plantation owner surveying his lands, Jefferson escaped on his horse every day of his life, in the middle of the day, for his own recreation. Jefferson jealously guarded this daily ritual, and he rode for the "pleasurable sensation" it afforded him, co-being with the horse, communing with nature and his own thoughts.

The horse became somewhat of a substitute, a physical relationship of sorts, an interlude of physical activity in his day. Note a slightly later description of the horse in a popular book in Virginia about horse care (first published in 1811) that Jefferson by then had in his library:

> If I were asked what were the two most beautiful objects in nature, I would answer that woman, lovely woman, before whose charms the souls of man bows with reverence and submission, stands unparalleled; next to this matchless paragon a beautiful horse displays nature in her finest polish and greatest perfection; his gay and cheerful appearance, proudly prancing and bounding; his elegance of shape, smoothness of limbs, polish of skin, due proportion of form, and gracefulness of action, united to a mild, soft, faithful and patient disposition, raise him far above the rest of brute creation.

Smoothness of limbs; polish of skin; proportion of form; gracefulness of action; a mild, soft, faithful, and patient disposition: all of these womanly characteristics were embodied in human form in the person of Martha for Jefferson, and lost to him at his wife's death (when he pledged never to remarry).[13] [Fig. I-5]

Fig. I-5 "A beautiful horse displays nature in her finest polish and greatest perfection," in the words of Mason, *The Gentleman's New Pocket Companion*, 14

There may well have been a sensual aspect to the widowed Jefferson's need for his daily ride and his loyalty to his favorite saddle horse. His grandson Jeff Randolph described it as a "recreation of body." Riding alone often in the deep woods and

IN 18TH CENTURY VIRGINIA		
SOCIAL HIERARCHY	**EQUINE HIERARCHY**	**GENDER HIERARCHY**
FREE/WHITE [13] Gentry Middlin'/ Farmer	**"BLOOD" HORSES** Saddle horses (racehorses) Carriage horses Breeding mares	MEN
ENSLAVED/BLACK House servants Field hands	**WORK HORSES/ LIVESTOCK** Galloways, Hobbies Chickasaws, Virginia horses Mules	WOMEN

uncharted paths around his home was a kind of physical retreat, like his intellectual retreat in his cabinet (study), which he called his *sanctum sanctorum*. It became a necessary part of his identity. He grieved, he found solace from periodical migraines, he mused, and he contemplated while on his horse. Again and again, Jefferson writes to friends, like George Wythe in 1795, "I live on my horse from an early breakfast to a late dinner, and very often after that till dark." Or to Benjamin Rush in January 1811, "From Breakfast, or noon at the latest, to dinner, I am mostly on horseback...which I find healthful to my body, mind and affairs." [14]

Riding was not simply a form of exercise for Jefferson; rather, it was a passion, an intimate part of his personality and a context for the pleasures of thought and song. His grandson noted, "Mr. Jefferson's daily rides were periods of relaxation... He said that on such occasions he would sometimes give utterance to his thoughts." Sometimes deep thought provoked a song. Edmund Bacon, Jefferson's overseer at Monticello for sixteen years (1806–1822), remembered, "I have rode over the plantation, I reckon a thousand times with Mr. Jefferson, and when he was not talking he was always nearly always humming some tune, or singing in a low tone to himself." And Isaac (Granger) Jefferson (1775–1849), who was enslaved many years at Monticello before gaining his freedom, concurred with Bacon: "Mr. Jefferson always singing when ridin' or walkin'; hardly see him anywhar outdoors but what he was a-singin'." [15]

Jefferson rode daily despite the weather. Many years later, a formerly enslaved woman in Charlottesville, known only as Aunt Polly, remembered Jefferson's visits to her then-owner's home:

> Mr. Jefferson would always go out in any kind of weather, never minding it in the least, winter or summer. Sometimes rain would be pouring down, or the snow would be blinding so that you couldn't see a yard ahead, yet he would order his horse to be brought to the gate and would mount and ride wherever he intended to go. [16]

Furthermore, Jefferson loved to go fast. Either riding or driving, he appreciated the fleet horse. Until old age, "he rarely drew rein for broken ground." With speed he was fearless, almost brash: "and when in haste, unhesitatingly dashed through the Rivanna, even when the usually quiet stream was swollen into a wide and rapid river by the rain." In another description of Jefferson's rush to get down to Charlottesville in 1819 to attend to his wounded grandson, his brash speed is noted: "He swept by the returning messenger like an arrow, and reached Charlottesville in a time that, over such ground, the boldest rider in Virginia might, without suspicion to his courage, have pronounced appalling." Riding across difficult terrain, at speeds that left others astonished at his boldness, reveals the trust and communication—oneness—between horse and rider. Riding fast, especially at an advanced age, is not just machismo; it reflects confidence in and partnership with the horse.[17]

Even broken bones and arthritis did not deter Jefferson from his daily and necessary habit. The following remembrance, by his great-granddaughter Sarah Randolph, refers to an accident at the close of 1822, when Jefferson broke his arm as he fell down a flight of steps leading to one of the terraces at Monticello: "Though debarred from his usual daily exercise on horseback for a short time after the accident occurred, he resumed his rides while his arm was yet in a sling."[18]

A description of the elderly Jefferson climbing into the saddle with a broken arm at age eighty-two again underlines the partnership and communication with his last riding horse, Eagle.

> His favorite riding-horse, Eagle was brought up to the terrace, whence he mounted while in this disabled state. Eagle, though a spirited Virginia full-blood, seemed instinctively to know that his venerable master was an invalid; for, usually restless and spirited, he on these occasions stood as quietly as a lamb, and, leaning up towards the terrace seemed to wish to aid the crippled octogenarian as he mounted into the saddle.[19]

Another characteristic of Jefferson's equestrian habits evidences his evolved relationship with horses, from using them as showy symbols of elite status to physical partner. Many contemporary commentators noted that Jefferson usually took his daily ride alone and that it was a way to satisfy his need for privacy. His grandson Jeff said, "He was fond of solitary rides and musing and said that the presence of a servant annoyed him." And much later Jeff repeated this. "He ... would never permit a servant to accompany him, as the presence of anyone annoyed him."[20]

Israel (Gillette) Jefferson, who in his youth had served as Jefferson's enslaved postilion for the landau, a kind of carriage, confirmed this later in his life as a free man: "He used to ride out to his plantations almost every fair day, when at home, but unlike most other Southern gentlemen in similar circumstances, unaccompanied by any servant." Jefferson rode the trails not to be seen, but to be private.[21]

Even in his final frailties, just weeks before his death, Jefferson still needed to be alone on his horse, and no servant was allowed to accompany him. Again, Randall relates: "When he was so weak that he [Jefferson] could not possibly mount him, except by getting *down* from one of the terraces into the saddle; yet, even then, he would not permit a servant to follow him." Eagle's temperament caused Jefferson's family great worry.[22]

Randall continues:

> These circumstances, and Mr. Jefferson's increasing debility, made his continued solitary rides sources of great apprehension to his family; and Mrs. Randolph finally besought him to allow himself to be accompanied by Burwell. His reply was that he had "helped himself" from childhood—that he had daily mused and conversed with nature alone—that the presence of a servant annoyed him—that it was too late to change the habits of a long life—that he would give up his rides if his family desired it, for his health was past remedy or preservation—but that if he rode, it must be *alone*.[23]

Jefferson's time alone on a horse, his daily ride, was also, besides reviewing his plantation at Monticello, ironically a way of relating with another creature, and a way into nature, into the forests and wilds wherever he lived. Jefferson wrote, "It renews the pleasurable sensation that we are still in society with beings and the things around us." He and his horse explored the environs of his beloved Monticello, other parts of verdant Virginia, or the surrounds, the parks, and countryside of wherever he was living, noting the changing vegetation of the seasons, and describing later in his letters and memorandum books the botanical and animal life that he saw.[24]

Horses, and human relationships with horses, signify different things in different places and at different moments in time. At least in the second half of Jefferson's life, his own saddle horses, with their individuating names and pedigrees, probably played several roles in his life. But from the few words he wrote about them, and from the observations of family members and others, we can be sure that Jefferson gained much pleasure from riding. That relationship seems to approximate current Euro-American studies that proclaim "horse human alliances...give pleasure to their human partners, and [it is possible to] summarize these benefits as a sense of connection, partnership and mutual trust [Fig. I-6] that arises in the shared embodiments of riding; feelings of happiness, relaxation, escape, freedom, transcendence, communion with nature and spirituality; a sense of community; and a sense of self-actualization and confidence"—all characteristics that inform Jefferson's equestrian habits.[25]

Fig. I-6. "Connection, partnership, and mutual trust," in the words of Davis and Maurstad, *Meaning of Horses*, 5

PART I

On Their High Horses

Gentleman on a Grey Horse, painting by George Stubbs,1781

Chapter 1

Jefferson in the Saddle

Thomas Jefferson used to tell his family that his "first memory was of being handed up to a slave on horseback and carried on a pillow from his father's frontier farm in Albemarle County, Virginia, to a far wealthier plantation fifty miles to the east near Richmond." If his first memories began on a horse, Jefferson also wished his last memories would be on a horse. At age eighty-one, just two years before he died, Jefferson wrote to William Short about the joys of riding on horseback: "so delightful and so necessary is this daily revival to me that I would wish to lose that and life together." This chapter provides a short survey of horse-related milestones in Jefferson's life, followed by a section devoted to Jefferson's horsemanship.[1]

Youth

As mentioned above, Jefferson's first memory of riding a horse was as a two-year-old in the arms of a mounted slave, traveling from Shadwell to Tuckahoe (near Richmond). On the vast rural plantations of Virginia, riding was something taught by older family members, or by enslaved African-Americans, to both the white young boys and girls. They in turn emulated older riders and friends. There were no riding academies or monumental riding schools, as in Europe, which taught classical *manège* (dressage) to the sons of the elite. In America, riding style emerged from the soil, so to speak.[2]

According to members of Jefferson's immediate family, he told them many times that it was his father who taught him to ride and to hunt. Peter Jefferson was a physically powerful man—a self-educated surveyor, woodsman, explorer, and planter—and his son Thomas seemingly adored him. One biographer claimed that "Jefferson liked to hike in the woods, but not to hunt. He was not graceful on his feet but he learned to ride boldly and wonderfully."[3]

By the age of eleven, young Tom was riding the woods and hills of Albemarle, as well as riding with his friends to his boarding school at Rev. Maury's, fourteen miles away from his father's house in Shadwell, and back home every weekend. "At Shadwell, his studies were very little interrupted by company. He usually took a gallop on horseback during the day, and at twilight walked to the top of Monticello."[4]

One also learns from one's peers, so we can imagine that young Tom also learned about horses from his friends at boarding school. Dabney Carr, especially, must have influenced Tom greatly. The best of friends, they wandered the woods of Albemarle together and rode up to the top of the mountain that would become Monticello. Dabney married Tom's sister, Martha, and grew even closer to Jefferson as a brother-in-law until Dabney's untimely death in 1773. One iconic story relates how the young Jefferson accepted with relish a challenge from his friend Dabney to a horse race. At the time, Dabney had a "fine racing horse," while Jefferson was riding a fat little old mare that his family could spare. It wasn't until later that anyone realized that Tom had set the date for the races on February 30.[5]

Since horses were the primary means of transportation in pre-revolutionary Virginia, during the early part of his life, Jefferson, like other colonists, used his horses mainly as a means of travel, to get from one place to another. Jefferson traveled back and forth to Williamsburg on horseback as a student and as a law reader at the College of William and Mary. As a student in Williamsburg, at least in the first years, the young Jefferson participated in the typical bachelor entertainment activities of attending horse races and fox hunting and the twice-annual horse races, along with all his buddies. Back at home in Shadwell, he guiltily admitted to his guardian that he had spent too much of his allowance on a "good Horse." In Williamsburg many of his school friends—Francis Willis, John Page, and William A. Dandridge—belonged to the Virginia gentry and later became owners and breeders of imported blooded horses.

Surely they, too, were brother equestrians and modeled horsemanship for each other.[6]

As a young lawyer, Jefferson rode several times a month from Monticello over the Blue Ridge Mountains forty miles to Staunton and back home again. Like many young men, he also drove horses in a small "chair" (a two-wheeled vehicle) and used the chair to make his first exploratory trip out of Virginia and up the East Coast to Philadelphia in 1766.

Marriage and Wife's Death (1772–1782)

When Jefferson married widow Martha (Wayles) Skelton, he soon after began trying to live the life of a gentleman planter at Monticello. Like other men of his class, Jefferson enthusiastically participated in the breeding of pedigreed horses, horses that would become the founders of the Thoroughbred breed today, crossing his mares with the studs of his gentry friends. (See Chapter 7.)

Soon after Jefferson married, he bought a four-wheeled phaeton for family transportation but continued to prefer to ride his horse rather than drive. He took the phaeton on his many trips to Philadelphia (to represent Virginia at the Continental Congress) in the 1770s, but he still had riding horses for his riding needs there. As governor of Virginia, he took his family to Williamsburg (and later to Richmond) in a carriage but rode his own horse in 1781 when retreating from the British siege of Richmond to Monticello (via Tuckahoe), and later from Monticello to Poplar Forest.

Martha's untimely death turned out to be pivotal in Jefferson's relationship with horses. Jefferson had spent several months attending to his beloved yet ailing wife before she finally died on September 6, 1782. Upon her demise, he was helped to his room, where he fainted. Jefferson's daughter Martha related that "he kept to his room three weeks," sleepless and restlessly walking both night and day. "When at last he left his room, he rode out, and from that time he was incessantly on horseback, rambling about the mountain, in the least frequented roads, and just as often through the woods." Jefferson found solace through riding.[7]

It was in these moments that his life-long ritual of solitary pleasure riding was established. From this point on, Jefferson was still entranced by fine pedigreed horses, but his saddle horse began to function first as his therapist, and later as the companion and intimate partner of his daily rides. Whether at home at Monticello or in the many cities in which he lived throughout his career, Jefferson tried to ride out for several hours after his morning paperwork and letter-writing. Late in life, Jefferson wrote that his horse was "to me the most sovereign of all doctors." Recent literature shows that "horses do bring healing benefits to humans." The horse as doctor is not empty metaphor in this case: Jefferson's riding changed, and it was after this emotional trauma that his daily ride at midday became such a necessary and engrained ritual in the ordering of his day, as a documented habit.[8]

Jefferson rode daily at the noontime hour in the Bois de Boulogne in Paris; he rode daily when he lived in Philadelphia; he rode daily as president in the then rural Washington City; and he rode daily during his retirement at Monticello. He generally left around one o'clock, to return to eat dinner around four o'clock in the afternoon. Moreover, there is evidence in letters and other correspondence that at certain times Jefferson may have ridden a second time, in order to ride with others or complete some errand. It is doubtful that in the heat and humidity of an Albemarle summer he chose to ride at one o'clock—an unbearable hour on hot summer days for both horse and rider. Isaac (Granger) Jefferson hints at this by saying, "If it was warm weather, he wouldn't ride out till evening." Lieutenant Anburey, a British prisoner-of-war held near Charlottesville between 1779 and 1781, noted that in summer "the heat of the weather is at present very intense, and renders travelling unpleasant, especially on horse-back, the rays of the sun are so very powerful in the middle of the day, that neither yourself nor your horse are able to withstand it, and you can only travel in the mornings and evenings."[9]

Despite his reputation as an excellent horseman, Jefferson fell from a horse several times during his lifetime. Some of his falls had life-changing consequences. For example, the first fall we know of was from his stallion Caractacus in 1781, toward the end of the Revolutionary War. The Jefferson family had taken refuge at Monticello, seventy miles west of Richmond, after the British had tried to capture Governor Jefferson and other members of the Virginia legislature. The British later pursued Jefferson to Monticello, and the family had to escape to another plantation home ninety miles to the south, Poplar Forest.[10]

A few days after arriving, while on their morning ride, Caractacus reared, and Jefferson fell and broke his left wrist. Unable to ride while his wrist mended, Jefferson confined himself to the house there and did not return to Monticello for six weeks. It was during this time that Jefferson began writing his first and only book, *Notes on the State of Virginia*. Although a result of an accident, and not necessarily planned, *Notes on the State of Virginia* has been called the "best single statement of Jefferson's principles, the best reflection of his wide-ranging tastes and talents." [11]

Paris (1784–1789)

Anxious to escape Monticello and the painful memories it held, Jefferson accepted a post in France as minister plenipotentiary for the recently independent United States. Jefferson left Boston by ship on July 5, 1784, with his eldest daughter, Martha, as well as enslaved servant James Hemings (who would learn French cooking), arriving in Le Havre, France, on July 31, 1784.

> His daughter described Jefferson's schedule this way:
>
> His habits of study in Paris were pretty much what they were elsewhere. He was always a very early riser and the whole morning was spent in business, generally writing till one o'clock, with the exception of a short respite afforded by the breakfast-table, at which he frequently lingered, conversing willingly at such times. At one o'clock he always rode or walked as far as seven miles into the country. [12]

Many references to his midday rides while in Paris appear in Jefferson's letters and notes. However, Jefferson did not buy himself a riding horse in Paris until 1786, after he had established himself in his house on the Champs-Élysées—the Hôtel de Langeac—which had its own stable. Those months without a saddle horse were the exception to his ritualistic noon ride. During that time, he walked daily to the parks and plazas of Paris. Recall that riding was not specifically an exercise for Jefferson. It was in Paris, before he bought his own riding horse, that Jefferson eloquently lauded walking as the best form of exercise. Note what Jefferson wrote to two of his protégées, first Peter Carr and then Thomas Mann Randolph Jr., back in Virginia, when walking was his main way of discovering the city, and comparing it to riding. [13]

> Walking is the best possible exercise. Habituate yourself to walk very far. The Europeans value themselves on having subdued the horse to the uses of man; but I doubt whether we have not lost more than we have gained, by the use of this animal. No one has occasioned so much, the degeneracy of the human body. An Indian goes on foot nearly as far in a day, for a long journey, as an enfeebled white does on his horse; and he will tire the best horses. There is no habit you will value so much as that of walking far without fatigue. I would advise you to take your exercise in the afternoon: not because it is the best time for exercise, for certainly it is not; but because it is the best time to spare from your studies; and habit will soon reconcile it to health, and render it nearly as useful as if you gave to that the more precious hours of the day. A little walk of half an hour, in the morning, when you first rise, is advisable also. It shakes off sleep, and produces other good effects in the animal economy. [14]
>
> If the body be feeble, the mind will not be strong—the sovereign invigorator of the body is exercise, and of all exercises walking is best. A horse gives but a kind of half exercise, and a carriage is no better than a cradle. No one knows, till he tries, how easily a habit of walking is acquired. A person who never walked three miles will in the course of a month become able to walk 15 or 20 without fatigue. I have known some great walkers & had particular accounts of many more: and I never knew or heard of one who was not healthy & long lived. [15]

Once he had procured his own riding horse, Jefferson returned to his midday exercise on horseback. He continued to ride alone, but he also frequently went out with his visitors and friends. Sometimes with his daughter and other women friends, Jefferson drove out in his cabriolet or chariot.

The Hôtel de Langeac was situated toward the far end of the Champs-Élysées (at the time) and thus quite near the Bois de Boulogne. Originally a royal hunting reserve, this park was two and a half times larger than Central Park in New York and almost three and a half times larger than Hyde Park in London. Several significant buildings were located there during the years of Jefferson's stay: the Château de Madrid, the Château de la Muette, and the Château de Bagatelle. During Jefferson's time, the woods were not yet landscaped as they would be by Baron Haussmann, the great city planner, in the nineteenth century. Even today this enormous park serves as an escape valve for greater Paris. The woods were made into a park much later by Napoleon.

Jefferson noted in letters that he went to the Bois de Boulogne every day to ride and marvel in this vast royal hunting reserve. The Bois de Boulogne is on the western side of Paris, but was quite accessible from Jefferson's house and stable for his riding horse and two carriage horses.

Jefferson often rode with friends and visitors, such as Gouverneur Morris (the Philadelphia lawyer, businessman, and senator). Sometimes he would ride across the woods and beyond to Mont Valerien (a monastic retreat of Catholic lay brothers under vows of silence), where he stabled his horse and took a cell to read and retreat from the world. [16]

Jefferson wrote to both Abigail Adams and Madame de Corny about his noontime rides to the Bois de Boulogne. On June 30, 1787, he wrote to Madame de Corny, "The Bois de Boulogne invites you earnestly to come and survey its beautiful verdure, to retire to its umbrage from the heats of the season. I was through it to-day, as I am every day. Every tree charged me with this invitation to you." [17]

Jefferson's second serious fall from a horse took place in Paris. On September 18, 1786, he attempted to jump a fence in a park on his new sorrel riding horse and fell, breaking his right wrist. The wrist healed badly, which inhibited him from playing the violin. Later in life his wrist stiffened so that even writing was painful. [18]

Philadelphia (1790–1793)

During these years as secretary of state under President George Washington, Jefferson lived in the center of Philadelphia, at Market and Eighth Street. As with all of his many homes, he extensively renovated it and added a carriage house, for three carriages and five horses. Jefferson suffered mentally and physically during these three years from his political feud with Alexander Hamilton for influence in Washington's government. Several times, he experienced tormenting migraines or tension headaches that lasted for weeks. He fought depression and migraines, and soon desired to quit his position and leave Philadelphia. He longed for family and Monticello. [19]

Isaac (Granger) Jefferson, the Monticello enslaved servant whom Jefferson apprenticed to a tinsmith in Philadelphia those years, recalled much later in an interview as a free man that "Mr. Jefferson used to ride out on horseback in Philadelphia." His daily rides out along the Schuylkill River must have assuaged his migraines and calmed his tensions. [20]

Monticello: First Retirement (1793–1797)

This period is known as Jefferson's "first retirement," when he returned home from Philadelphia after serving in President Washington's cabinet as secretary of state. Although he never really left the politics of Washington behind, Jefferson was quite busy during these years, implementing his plans for scientific agriculture at Monticello, and rebuilding Monticello itself. He tried to institute some money-making ventures on the farms at Monticello, such as a mill and a nailery, to supplement his agriculture. He wrote to John Adams, "I am on horseback half the day and counting and measuring nails the other half." [21]

These were the years when his daily ride might most often have coincided with overseeing farm work and, thus, his rides would have been mainly through and around the various quarter farms around Monticello (Lego, Tufton, Shadwell, and the base of Monticello Mountain).

Presidency (1801–1809)

Jefferson devised "a steady and uniform course" for his hard-working presidency, which included time in the saddle with his horse. "It keeps me from 10 to 12 to 13 hours a day at my writing table, giving me an interval of 4 hours for riding, dining and a little unbending," Jefferson wrote to Thomas Mann Randolph Jr. [22]

On the first day of the levee—a weekly reception to officially make the president available to the general citizens, usually a carefully scripted social ritual—Jefferson rode out at his usual hour of one o'clock, returning at three, and on entering the president's house, booted, whip in hand, soiled from his ride, found himself in a crowd of ladies and gentlemen fashionably dressed for the occasion. [23]

While president, Jefferson retained his habitual custom of taking regular daily exercise. He rarely, however, gave his Irish coachman, Joseph, the pleasure of sitting behind his four fiery bays, always preferring his saddle horse—the magnificent Wildair—which was the same horse he had ridden to the capitol and "hitched to the palisades" on the day of his inauguration. [24]

The president's house was not finished being constructed when Jefferson became president. Washington City itself was still in the design stage. Jefferson continued his daily midday rides, quickly getting beyond the muddy city streets, past Georgetown, and out into the countryside, up the Potomac and Rock Creek.

"[A]nd he sometimes stole away on secret solitary expeditions up the Potomac and into surrounding hills and woods," wrote Margaret Bayard Smith, a friend of Jefferson's through her husband, newspaper owner, Samuel Harrison Smith—and an important chronicler herself of the Washington social scene—in her diary. "Not a plant from the lowliest weed to the loftiest tree escaped his notice…He would [get off his horse and] climb rocks or wade through swamps to obtain any plant he discovered or desired and seldom returned from these excursions without a variety of specimens." All the trees along Pennsylvania Avenue were planted under his direction. "The willow-oak was among his favorite trees, and he was often seen standing on his horse to gather the acorns from this tree." [25]

Monticello: Second Retirement (1809–1826)

Jefferson returned joyfully to Monticello at age sixty-six and looked forward to the pleasures of domestic life. Upon arriving home after leaving Washington, the former president himself wrote to his successor, President James Madison, that weather had not stopped him:

> I had a very fatiguing journey, having found the roads excessively bad, although I have seen them worse. The last three days I found it better to be on horseback and travelled eight hours through as disagreeable a snow storm as I was ever in. Feeling no inconvenience from the expedition but fatigue, I have more confidence in my *vis vitce* than I had before entertained. [26]

During these years at Monticello, Jefferson exulted in his life on his horse and wrote about it in many of his letters. To Thaddeus Kosciusko in 1810, Jefferson wrote, "My mornings are devoted to my correspondence. From breakfast to dinner I am in my shops, my garden, or on horseback among my farms: from dinner to dark I give to society and recreation with my neighbors and friends; and from candle-light to early bed-time I read." [27]

At the age of seventy-one, Jefferson wrote to John Adams, "You and I have been wonderfully spared and myself with remarkable health, and a considerable activity of body and mind. I am on horseback three or four hours of every day; I visit three or four times a year a possession I have ninety miles distant [Poplar Forest], performing the winter journey on horseback. I walk little, however, a single mile being too much for me." [28]

Even at the age of seventy-five, he wrote to a friend in the spring of 1816, "I retain good health, and am rather feeble to walk much, but ride with ease passing two or three hours a day on horseback, and every three or four months taking, in a carriage, a journey of ninety miles to a distant possession, where I pass a good deal of my time." [29]

Certainly, Jefferson the plantation owner rode through his farms on either side of the Rivanna River to see how all of his plans were being implemented, from planting to the mill at Milton. Perhaps he would ride down the mountain and cross the Rivanna at Secretary's Ford and return home, crossing back over the river at Shadwell and come up the Farm Road to the house. [Fig. 1-1] Other days he might ride up to Montalto and survey the "sublimest of nature's operations" from on high; "our own dear Monticello, where has nature spread so rich a mantle under the eye?—mountains, forests, rocks, rivers. With what majesty do we there ride above the storms!" [Fig 1-2] Or he could ride down the Thoroughfare to Tufton, check the Indian Field, cross the Meadow Branch creek, saunter down the flood plain called Cooper's Field (later called the River Field), and return by the North Road, high up over the Rivanna River. [30]

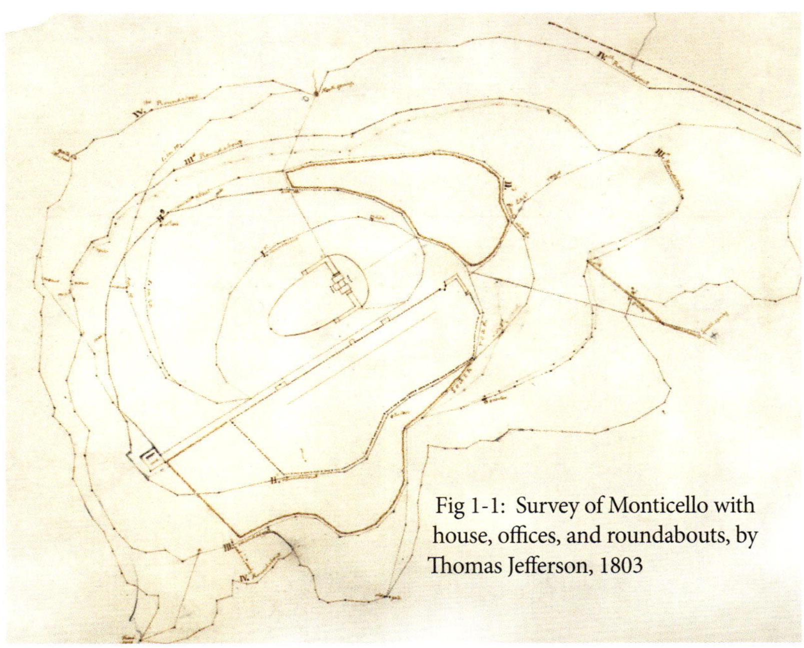

Fig 1-1: Survey of Monticello with house, offices, and roundabouts, by Thomas Jefferson, 1803

Fig. 1-2 Jane Pitford Braddick Peticolas, *View from Monticello Looking Toward Charlottesville*, 1827

Jefferson had his four roundabouts constructed specifically so he and his family could walk and ride about the mountain in all its natural splendor. Sometimes he escorted guests around the roundabouts in the phaeton. "Mr. Jefferson's daily rides were periods of relaxation of mind and recreation of body; he rode over fields and through forests." [31]

When Jefferson needed to go to Charlottesville on business, usually he rode to town. When he escorted the Marquis de Lafayette to the banquet at the Rotunda in 1824, they went down the mountain in the landau (a coach). But when Jefferson went alone, he rode his horse. In one incident, at age seventy-seven, he dashed down the mountain on his horse at a mad gallop, much to the chagrin of his family members, when he heard that his grandson Jeff had been seriously hurt in a fight near Court Square in Charlottesville.

Fig. 1-4 Frederick Edwin Church, "The Natural Bridge, Virginia," 1852

There were three paths to Charlottesville: one path led down the Thoroughfare Road, passing near Carlton (home of his granddaughter Anne Bankhead), crossing Moore's Creek, and coming up to Court Square through Belmont; another was called "the gutter," a more precipitous path down the gulch bed, again fording Moore's Creek a bit nearer the Rivanna River, then again coming up through Belmont. The final path was down the mountain toward Secretary's Ford on the Rivanna River, fording Moore's Creek there before it entered the river, and going up what today would be an extension of Market Street through the neighborhood now called Woolen Mills. This route took him through the countryside and past The Farm, the plantation owned by Colonel Nicholas Lewis, uncle of Meriwether Lewis and one of the first settlers in Albemarle. [32]

Fig. 1-3 The original bath building. Originally known as the Warm Springs Pools, its name was changed to the Jefferson Pools in the 20th century, and then was returned to the name Warm Springs Pools in 2021.

During his retirement years, Jefferson traveled only a little. In 1816, he took a health-related trip to the Baths in Warm Spring in Bath County, high in the Allegheny Mountains, of what was then still western Virginia. [Fig. 1-3] He also made the ninety-mile trip to his retreat in Bedford County, Poplar Forest, about twice a year. He rode there on his horse for many years, but later resorted to traveling there in his landau carriage (used for the first time in August 1814). Jefferson would travel with one or two of his granddaughters in the coach (driven by two enslaved postilions), and Burwell Colbert, his enslaved valet, would follow behind on Jefferson's saddle horse. At Poplar Forest, Jefferson continued his habit of riding daily before the three o'clock dinner. On one trip in 1817, Jefferson and two granddaughters decided to make an adventure and cross over the mountains to see Natural Bridge, in Jefferson's opinion "the most sublime of Nature's works," 215 feet tall, that had so enchanted him in 1774 that he had bought it and 157 acres. [Fig. 1-4] He probably also explored the Peaks of Otter, three mountain peaks in the Blue Ridge Mountains in Bedford County that fascinated him and that he thought were some of the highest in America. [Fig. 1-5]

Fig. 1-5 Edward Beyer, "View of the Peaks of Otter, Bedford County, VA," from *Album of Virginia*, 1852

Building the University

Jefferson worked diligently planning, designing, and founding the University of Virginia, which he called the *"hobby"* of his old age. He personally measured and marked off the first pavilion, built, and oversaw every detail of its construction. His use of the word hobby refers not just to a pleasant past-time, but to the easy-riding horses used in Virginia and the other colonies, called Hobbies (discussed later in Chapter 8), before the arrival of the high-bred blood horses. In the thirteenth century, *hobby* referred to a small horse or a pony. By the 1670s it came to describe a toy horse — a hobbyhorse. It's from the hobbyhorse that the word's modern sense of "favorite pastime" evolved after 1816. [33]

As Jefferson wrote to John Adams,

> "I am fortunately mounted on a hobby, which, indeed, I should have better managed some thirty or forty years ago; but whose easy amble is still sufficient to give exercise and amusement to an octogenarian rider. This is the establishment of a University, on a scale more comprehensive, and in a country more healthy and central, than our old William and Mary." [34]

During the construction of the University, Jefferson rode down to Charlottesville daily to direct the progress and help with the drafting of building plans. One enslaved woman noted, "When the university was being built, it was his habit to ride by my master's house (The Farm) and stop; though he might be covered with snow, or his umbrella might be soaked through, he would never listen to any urging to take shelter in the house." [35]

The Last Years

Jefferson enjoyed a vigorous life until the last few months before his death. His riding ritual was maintained to the end of his days. Yet Jefferson regretted it when he could no longer exercise by walking. Writing to Dr. Vine Utley, he noted, "except on a late occasion of indisposition, I enjoy good health; too feeble, indeed, to walk much, but riding without fatigue six or eight miles a day and sometimes thirty or forty." Or, later, writing to John Adams, "I am told you walk well and firmly. I can only reach my garden and that with sensible fatigue. I ride, however, daily." [36]

In 1824, in response to his protégée, William Short, who had just written Jefferson that he had sold all his horses and was extolling the virtues of travelling by rented coach, Jefferson wrote, "I hope you have not entirely unlearned the practice of riding on horseback. I can assure you from experience that to old age the daily ride is among the most cherished of comforts." [37]

Jefferson's final falls occurred from his last horse, Eagle. Once, the skittish stallion shied at a deer and put Jefferson on the ground. Finally, in 1822, when he was seventy-nine years old, Jefferson was riding Eagle with his left arm in a sling due to a broken arm. The horse and rider were crossing a stream on the way into Charlottesville when Eagle slipped going down the muddy bank into the creek and threw Jefferson over his head. Jefferson was able to save himself from drowning only by clinging to the bridle while Eagle dragged him ashore. [38]

Nevertheless, Jefferson did continue to ride till the end of his life, up and down the mountain to his University in Charlottesville, along his roundabouts, up to Montalto with his grandson, Thomas Jefferson Randolph (now manager of Monticello), still surveying "the prospect" he had "in rich profusion." "They had been riding together…a few months before [his] death…in the clear atmosphere of the Virginia mountains." [39] [Fig. 1-6]

His daughter Martha noted in a letter to her daughter Ellen, "He says he had derived great benefit from riding; he goes in a walk and never beyond the 2d roundabout but he had ridden 5 miles on them." [40]

Jefferson almost achieved his wish to lose the daily ride and life together. He rode daily until three weeks before he died, at age eighty-three, on July 4, 1826.

Jefferson's Horsemanship

In Jefferson's time, the upper classes in the English-speaking world saw the horse as an eminently noble animal. An eighteenth-century professor of horsemanship in England, Charles Hughes, wrote a treatise about the rules of the art of riding and made these admiring comments about the horse:

> There is not, among the whole Animal Creation, a beast of a more noble and generous nature than the horse, nor any one so capable of contributing to the ease and pleasure of mankind. In the horse, we know not which to admire most, the beauty of his form, the docility of his temper, or the various powers with which he is endowed. [41]

Riding a horse was described as "a manly sport" in eighteenth-century Virginia, and riding elegantly was a part of elite self-presentation. All young men who were, or aspired to hobnob with, members of the gentry, needed to acquire riding skills, and riding would have been an appropriate exercise for an otherwise shy, tall, gawky boy like Thomas Jefferson. Jefferson took to riding quickly, though, and learned to ride boldly and confidently. Although he once complimented George Washington by saying that Washington was "the best horseman of his age," Jefferson's own horsemanship was consistently lauded by his contemporaries, friends, and family, who said he was an uncommonly fine rider, master of his horse. [42]

Perhaps Jefferson partly modeled his horsemanship on riders he saw in equestrian performances that he attended. Carefully noted in his account books are the various shows of horsemanship that he went to see in Williamsburg, and in London, as well as closer to home. On June 12, 1826, less than one month before he died, Jefferson rode down to Charlottesville and paid $4.50 to watch a "shew of horsemanship." Most of the exhibitions featured trick riding, such as riding three horses at a time from a standing position. [43]

One can look in vain in Jefferson's libraries and catalogues of books for volumes devoted solely to equitation. Several influential tomes on equitation were in print by the eighteenth century, but Jefferson does not say that he owned them. Jefferson systematically categorized the many books in his libraries, and he had one category labeled Agriculture. In this section of the inventories, one can find books dedicated to animal husbandry. Many of these books have substantial sections on the care and housing of horses. Although many pages are devoted to how to choose a saddle horse, how and when to breed a horse, how to treat foals, how to cure diseases and ailments in horses, how to feed horses, and how to cure dung, these books do not include instruction about riding style. In 1812, Jefferson ordered a copy of one of the most popular books in Virginia in the early nineteenth century, Richard Mason's *The Gentleman's New Pocket*

Fig. 1-6 View from Montalto to the west

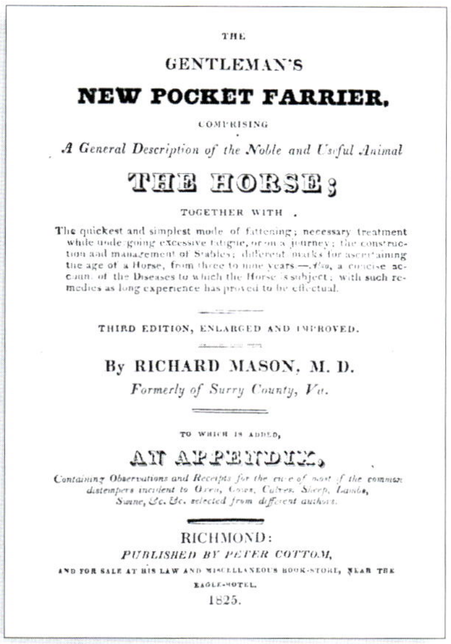

THE

GENTLEMAN'S

NEW POCKET FARRIER,

COMPRISING

A General Description of the Noble and Useful Animal

THE HORSE;

TOGETHER WITH

The quickest and simplest mode of fattening; necessary treatment while undergoing excessive fatigue, or on a journey; the construction and management of Stables; different marks for ascertaining the age of a Horse, from three to nine years.—*Also*, a concise account of the Diseases to which the Horse is subject; with such remedies as long experience has proved to be effectual.

THIRD EDITION, ENLARGED AND IMPROVED.

By RICHARD MASON, M. D.

Formerly of Surry County, Va.

TO WHICH IS ADDED,

AN APPENDIX,

Containing Observations and Receipts for the cure of most of the common distempers incident to Oxen, Cows, Calves, Sheep, Lambs, Swine, &c. &c. selected from different authors.

RICHMOND:

PUBLISHED BY PETER COTTOM,

AND FOR SALE AT HIS LAW AND MISCELLANEOUS BOOK-STORE, NEAR THE EAGLE-HOTEL.

1825.

Fig. 1-7 The front piece of Mason, *The Gentleman's New Pocket Farrier* (1848), first published in 1811 as *The Gentleman's New Pocket Companion*

Farrier, published in 1811, which included sections on grooming horses, appropriate conformation, and docking tails. [44] [Fig. 1-7]

When they were young, a friend described Jefferson as a centaur, [Fig. 1-8] and others later agreed. In Greek mythology, centaurs are creatures with the body of a horse and the torso, arms, and head of a man; the centaur image thus evokes a man sitting tall and firm in the saddle, looking as if he were part of the horse. Studies of the biocultural meaning of horses define the centaur as the "sum of intertwined capabilities of the horseperson and horse." Human-animal relations scholar Susan Keaveney has described the centaur complex as "communication … where rider and horse experience a feeling of togetherness in thinking, acting, feeling and movements." Others have employed the terminology of embodiment: "Embodiment and the shared act of riding bring a special dimension of sensorial experience to the horse human relationship. This relationship has been described as embodying the centaur." One cannot be sure what Jefferson's contemporaries in the eighteenth century meant by "centaur," but the mythological creature is the co-being of man and horse. [45]

Jefferson was not unique among Virginia gentlemen for his horsemanship, his confident seat, and his firm and upright manner in the saddle ("straight as a gun barrel"). Some English observers did not have kind words for other Virginia horsemen. Isaac Weld, an Englishman traveling through the United States in the late eighteenth century, described them in the following way:

> The Virginians are wretched horsemen, as indeed are all the Americans I ever met with, excepting some few in the neighborhood of New York. They sit with their toes just under the horse's nose, their stirrups being left extremely long, and the saddle put about three or four inches forward on the mane. As for the management of the reins, it is what they have not conception of. [46]

Fig. 1-8 Modern bronze copy of the type of the Young Centaur, Malmaison, 2006. It is a copy of a second-century BC bronze Hellenistic original, located in the Capitoline Museum in Rome since the late eighteenth century.

This position, or "seat," with feet out in front, describes well some of the jockeys seen in George Stubbs's equine portraits of English jockeys in the 1780s. (see facing page, Ch 1, p. 10) Jefferson, however, probably sat with his legs more under him, as George Washington is portrayed in statues made just fifty years after his death (and twenty-five years after Jefferson's). Note the seat of the rider in this 1819 print from an illustrated child's book, titled *Familiar Description of Horses.* [Fig. 1-9] The rider, in a coat with tails and a top hat (not Jefferson's preferred dress while riding), sits on an English saddle with feet directly under him. These descriptions show a longer stirrup than we are accustomed to seeing today in an English hunting saddle. Nevertheless, on his English saddle, Jefferson would have had a slightly raised stirrup, and had a bend in his knees, sitting up straight more than leaning back. [47]

Fig. 1-9 Note the seat of the rider in "The Saddle Horse," from a book for children, *A Familiar Description of Horses* (Philadelphia: E. and R. Parker, 1819).

Riding a horse—instead of traveling by coach—can be a very dirty affair, especially after three or four hours in the saddle. In a hot and humid Virginia summer, and among the hills and woods around Monticello, the horse does a lot of sweating. With the small, flat English hunting saddle, the rider's legs become covered with horse sweat (and smell). As an inveterate rider, Jefferson used a pair of overalls, called sherryvallies, still conserved at Monticello, that he pulled on over his pants to protect them from sweat, dust, and mud. [Fig. 1-10] The sherryvallies were made of doeskin. Since Jefferson typically wore knee breeches rather than pantaloons (trousers or long pants), even after the style had changed among the general public, the sherryvallies would have only reached to below the knee, to cover his more formal knee breeches. Jefferson adopted trousers only very late in life.

In some accounts, Jefferson is described on horseback as wearing a gray-colored round-about coat, which is a straight-bodied coat without tails. This was probably regarded as a plain, less formal, more democratic coat. [48]

Fig. 1-10 Sherryvallies

Monticello also conserves Jefferson's riding boots, which are tall boots (coming up to the knee) and look like riding boots still in use today in English equestrian circles. [Fig. 1-11] Jefferson also strapped spurs onto his boots. Jefferson in his later years wore gaiters, or half chaps. Gaiters cover the leg and the shoe or boot lacing, protecting the leg from brush and bad weather and horse sweat. Leggings, another term for gaiter, cover only the leg, not the ankle, footwear, and laces. Usually made of leather today, gaiters in the past were also made of cotton or canvas. [49]

Jefferson did not necessarily wear a hat for protection from a fall when riding, like our current English riding helmets. [Fig. 1-12] He probably wore his common round hat, with its wide brim for protection from the sun. In the late eighteenth century, the English gentry had adopted the common round hat from the working classes as a riding hat. It had also been popular in France during the Revolution as a symbol of republican sympathies. Like all his clothing styles, Jefferson kept his round hat long after it had gone out of style in the more elite classes. [50]

Fig. 1-11 Jefferson's riding boots

In 1822, S. A. Bumstead observed of Jefferson:

> He was mounted on an elegant horse going with speed—and he had no hat on but a lady's parasol, stuck in his coat behind, spread its canopy over his head … I am told he always rides in this manner during the summer without any hat.

Jefferson carried riding whips with him when out on his horse, and there are many entries in his account books for purchases of whips. [51]

Fig. 1-12 Jacques-Louis David, "Portrait of Pierre Sériziat," 1795, who is wearing riding accoutrements and a round hat

Tack: Equipment for Riding in the Eighteenth Century

At Monticello, Jefferson put certain enslaved workers in charge of the stables. Jupiter Evans was his first hostler, and later Wormley Hughes took over. (When Jefferson was president in Washington, D.C., from 1801 to 1809, the Irishman, Joseph Dougherty, was Jefferson's hostler). A hostler was the person in charge of the feed and care of the horses, and also in charge of the tack (saddles and bridles) and harness for the carriage horses. Jefferson bought the saddles and harnesses (they were not made at Monticello), but these servants took care of the tack, cleaned it, stored it, and knew when it needed repair. Only when he was traveling do we see

Jefferson paying for tack to be repaired. Tack was stored in a dedicated room in the stable, the tack room.

Although Jefferson rode almost every day of his life, we can suppose that he never wasted his time preparing the horse to ride, nor unsaddling it and cooling it down. His hostlers, or people working for the hostlers, did this.

Bacon, the overseer, mentions that "the boy who took care of his horse knew what time he started, and would bring him out for him, and hitch him in his place." So even though Jefferson was involved in buying the saddle, choosing the bits, or correcting a shying problem by using a blinder, someone else cleaned and saddled his horse for him. He was a stickler about grooming the horse, and woe be it if the groom had not done a good job. "When his saddle horse was led out, if there was a spot on him that did not shine as faultlessly as a mirror, he rubbed it with a white pocket handkerchief, and if this was soiled, the groom was reprimanded." [52]

Saddles: Saddles were made by expert craftsmen, who sold them in shops in major cities. [Fig. 1-13] Although handmade, they usually lasted a long time. Sometimes, a saddler had a small inventory of saddles, but usually they were made individually for each customer. The saddle frame was often made of wood and iron. The rest of the saddle was leather.

We know Jefferson bought a saddle in Richmond in 1780, while he was governor. Later he bought one (with bridle and bit and harness) while on a trip in England in 1786 with John Adams (during his appointment as minister

Fig. 1-13 A Colonial Williamsburg sign for a saddle store

Jefferson's Riding Costume

There are many comments on Jefferson's clothing and style.

Edmund Bacon, overseer at Monticello:
"He was always very neat in his dress, wore short breeches and bright shoe buckles. When he rode on horseback he had a pair of overalls that he always put on." (*Bear, at Monticello*, 74.)

"The President was out taking his habitual ride on horseback. On his return, being told that the public rooms were filled with ladies, he at once divined their true motives for coming on that day. Without being at all disconcerted, all booted and spurred, and still covered with the dust of his ride, he went in to receive his fair guests." (Randolph, *The Domestic Life of Thomas Jefferson*, 282.)

"His dress, when on horseback, is a grey straight-bodied coat, and a spencer of the same material, both fastened with large pearl buttons. When we first saw him he was riding; and, in addition to the above articles of apparel, wore round his throat a knit white woollen tippet [scarf], in the place of a cravat, and black velvet gaiters under his pantaloons. He wears a common round hat." (Randall, *The Life of Thomas Jefferson*, 3:505.)

"His dress was very plain, being of homespun cloth woven on his place, and of a slatishgray color. He wore a roundabout, coming down low as a coat … kneebreeches, gray stockings, low shoes with silver buckles, and a broadbrimmed dark hat.… The coat had brass buttons and wide pockets on the hips, and the breeches came only to the knees. After a deal of persuasion he laid aside kneebreeches to wear the more fashionable pantaloons. Over this suit, in riding, he wore his usual gray roundabout, in the place of the overcoat or cloak which were both then in use. Boots he never wore, but in winter always went out with woollen or leather 'leggings,' which were generally well spattered with mud when he came home at night from riding. He would sit down before the fire—a huge wood one—and take them off with his own hands, never allowing anybody to do it for him. He waited on himself a good deal. His clothes were always neat and well kept, tho." (Aunt Polly quoted in Daniel, "*Virginian Reminiscences of Jefferson*.")
"He was mounted on an elegant horse going with speed—and he had no hat on but a lady's parasol, stuck in his coat behind, spread its canopy over his head … I am told he always rides in this manner during the summer without any hat." (Bumstead, "*Appearance: Descriptions of Thomas Jefferson;*" MB1997, 1508.)

in Paris), and another in Paris in 1787. In Philadelphia in 1798, he paid for another. He bought yet another saddle and bridle set during his presidency in 1805. And in 1807, he bought plated stirrups. His saddles, like all those made for men in Williamsburg at the time (and portrayed in eighteenth-century American and English prints), were almost certainly early versions of the English hunting saddle.[53] [Fig. 1-14]

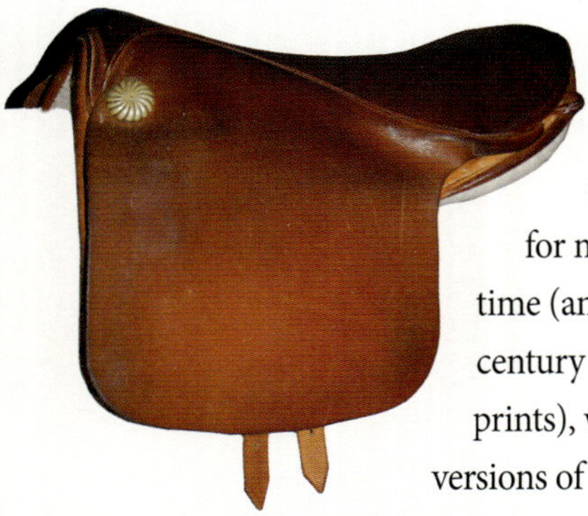

Fig. 1-14 Eighteenth-century English hunting saddle

Curiously, at one time Jefferson had a saddle cover made of "leopard or tyger's skin." Another saddle is described as having a "hogskin seat." Although Monticello has some of Jefferson's own paraphernalia for riding (overalls, riding boots, and perhaps a spur), as well as his phaeton seat, none of his tack was preserved.[54]

From today's perspective, the stirrups were placed too far forward on the hunt saddles. The place where the stirrup straps were attached to the saddle, the stirrup bars, was located much more forward than on contemporary English hunt saddles, and the bars stuck out, thus making it almost impossible for the rider to keep his legs underneath his body. This explains the practice, seen in equine paintings of the early eighteenth century, of a riding style with long stirrups and the feet pushed out in front. This English hunting saddle has changed over time as riding styles and "seats," or positions, have evolved, but it is still the model for all English-type riding saddles. [Fig. 1-15] Women riders of the eighteenth century almost always used the sidesaddle.

Still influenced by English design, another saddle type, the American plantation saddle, evolved in the Southern colonies. This saddle, with its wide sweeping cantle design, was used by Southern gentry (as they rode long distances from plantation to plantation) and by officers in the Revolutionary War era. The plantation saddle (later known as the Buena Vista style) was an adaptation to Southern gaited horses, like the Tennessee Walkers or Saddlebred types.[55]

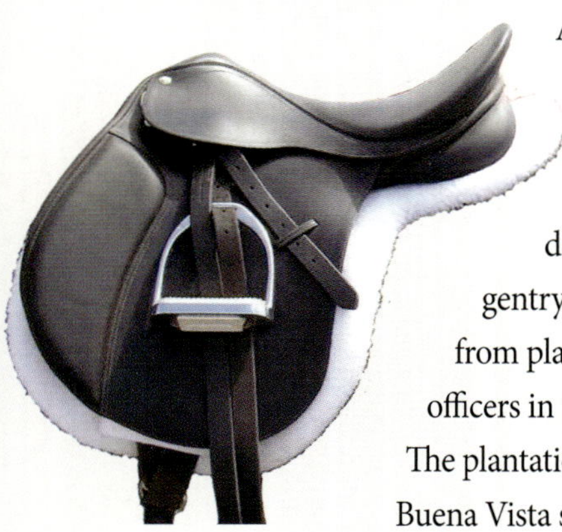

Fig. 1-15 Modern English saddle

Bits: As for bits (the metal mouthpiece held in place in the horse's mouth by the bridle), eighteenth-century prints and paintings of racing scenes and foxhunting scenes depict English bits of the direct pressure type (snaffle) [Fig. 1-16] or indirect pressure or leverage bits (curb). [Fig. 1-17] Both Colonial Williamsburg and Mount Vernon have collections of eighteenth- and early-nineteenth-century bits, commonly used in Virginia.[56]

Riding horses, racing horses, and hunting horses are shown wearing full cheek snaffles (wagon and cart horses are generally in snaffles as well). In the eighteenth century, these mouthpieces were called bridoons. Excavated snaffle bits were usually jointed in the mouthpiece, and the mouthpiece was narrower and longer than those we use today on what we think are larger horses (with larger heads and presumably larger mouths). Early examples of full cheek snaffles have smaller rings and longer cheeks than those we see today.

Fig. 1-16 Snaffle bit, as depicted in Latchford and Segundo, *The Loriner: Opinions and Observations on Bridal-Bits*

The use of curbs, or a combination of snaffle and curb (called a "full bridle," more commonly referred to in the period as "bitt and bridoon"), is seen and referred to mainly in military applications. [Fig. 1-18] The curb, because it is harsher than the snaffle, is used in order to have more control over a horse. The following example indicates its severity. Jefferson described using a bit and bridoon on a horse that he was trying out to possibly buy as a carriage horse. When Jefferson used that bit, he was riding the horse, and wrote later to the horse's owner that the horse must not have been used to a curb bit, and that the bit must have cut the horse's mouth "as I observed his mouth bled considerably after I got on him." Carriage horses were often depicted in curbs also, with slotted shanks to allow for more leverage, and thus more control. An ad for a runaway slave in the *Virginia Gazette* describes a curb bit that was stolen by the

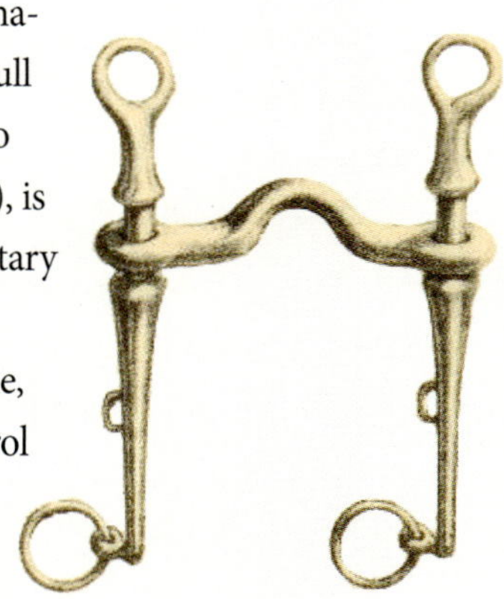

Fig. 1-17 Curb bit, as depicted in Latchford and Segundo, *The Loriner: Opinions and Observations on Bridal-Bits*

runaway: "The bit, very uncommon, made of steel, all in one piece, bent up in the middle, and a hole in it for a small chain to play in the horses mouth, with new rings and bar twisted." Sometimes ladies riding sidesaddle are depicted using curbs with full bridles, which was probably an effort to ensure more control over the horse by the woman (on the very insecure sidesaddle of that time period). [57]

Fig. 1-18 Curb bit and a bridoon (double bridle)

As an exception to his general norm of using bridoons and curbs, we know that one time, with a particularly difficult and fractious horse, Turncoat, Jefferson suggested to his son-in-law that they use a "mameluke" bit on that horse, who was too difficult to manage otherwise. A mameluke bit is a severe bit, even for the times, of the leverage type, that worked on both the inside and outside of the horse's mouth, applying pressure on delicate tissues, especially on the horse's nose. [Fig. 1-19] The thought was that in order to avoid the pain of the bit, the horse would behave. One year later, in October 1808, Jefferson asked his grandson Thomas Jefferson Randolph, at school in Philadelphia, to "get my Mamaluke bridle plated." [58]

Shoeing: Fifty-nine entries appear under the subsection "shod," under the section for horses, in the index of the edited *Memorandum Books*. Almost all entries refer to paying for horseshoeing while Jefferson was traveling or living in Williamsburg, New York, Philadelphia, or Washington, D.C. (there was no mention in the *Memorandum Books* of horse shoeing while Jefferson was in Paris). [59]

Traveling, especially, necessitated horseshoes. If a horse lost a shoe along the route, it was necessary to find someone who could make another shoe for the horse as soon as possible. A horse can quickly become lame if forced to walk unbalanced by the loss of a shoe, especially on rocky roads. In those times, there were few professional horseshoers, or farriers, as we call them today (the term *farrier* in eighteenth-century America referred to those who cared for and treated diseases in horses, including care of their feet).

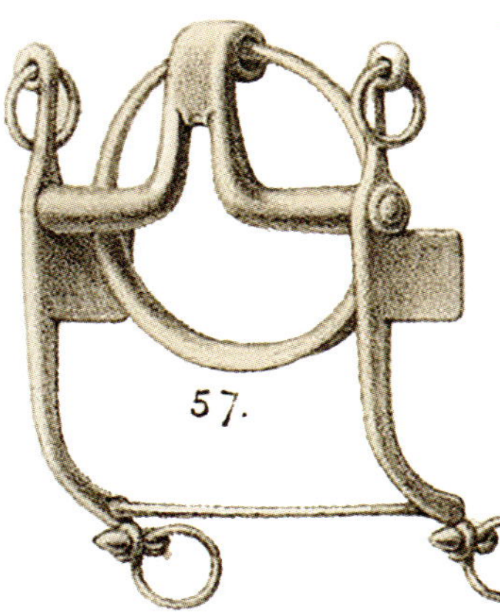

Fig. 1-19 Mameluke bit, as depicted in Latchford and Segundo, *The Loriner: Opinions and Observations on Bridal-Bits,*

In general, blacksmiths, who worked with iron, were responsible for shoeing horses with iron plates fitted to the hoof and designed to protect the horse's foot. Not all blacksmiths, however, were capable horseshoers.

At Monticello, the blacksmith forge was located across the river at Shadwell until the 1790s, when it was moved to Mulberry Row. It was staffed by a Jefferson employee or Monticello enslaved laborers. Jefferson set up the forge so that several nearby neighbors could also benefit and help pay for its use. During the Revolutionary War, in June 1781, when Jefferson had to escape from the British soldiers sent to capture him at Monticello, he had to send his horse off across the river to be shod at Shadwell before he could ride off after his family.

When Jefferson returned from France, the blacksmith shop was re-located on Mulberry Row. The enslaved Joseph Fossett served as the blacksmith (and continued to serve Jefferson's neighbors, thus earning himself some extra money) at Monticello after 1800. [60]

Much later, toward the end of Jefferson's life, a citizen of Charlottesville remembered, "Now and then, when passing through Charlottesville, his horse would cast a shoe, and thereupon he would go to a blacksmith's, and, while the horse was being shod, he would hold him by the ear in order to keep him quiet." This comment implies that Jefferson also used the blacksmith in Charlottesville. [61]

Jefferson's Treatment of Horses: Dominance

Horses, like humans, are social animals. In the wild, they live within communities of families, friends, bands, and herds. Bands consist of a stallion, several mares, and their offspring. Horses are very gregarious and cooperative in the band, where they form intense bonds and have preferred partners. Yet horses are creatures of instinct, and one instinct horses—wild or domesticated— have is to accept the authority of herd leaders. Dominance relationships thus characterize the herd. Since it is a natural instinct for horses to follow a leader, it means that horses are receptive to taking orders from humans, if humans can establish their dominance over the horse. Humans have taken advantage of this instinct to control these animals to make them work for humans, even though horses are bigger and stronger.

If humans can establish their dominance, a horse will instinctively submit. By controlling the horse's movements with ropes and fences, and separating it from the herd, a trainer can get the horse to accept him as herd leader and follow his instructions. Without a doubt throughout history, some trainers have controlled horses through brute force and intimidation. But by the eighteenth century, horsemanship in Europe and the colonies emphasized the relationship between rider and horse and took the horse's perspective into consideration. Yet among the gentry in eighteenth-century Virginia, when working with horses, the key was to make it clear who was in charge. If a rider was unsure, the horse would feel it and might ignore the rider's commands. Body language, although quite subtle, conveys dominance (or the opposite, insecurity). [62]

Some contemporary equestrians will look askance at the treatment of horses in Jefferson's time. Since the 1980s, a variety of horse training techniques, known by the term natural horsemanship, has grown in popularity and use in the United States and Europe. These techniques vary from trainer to trainer and from rider to rider, but collectively share several principles: developing a rapport with the horse, using communication techniques based on the observation of feral free-ranging horses (learning to "speak horse"), and rejecting abusive training methods. Natural horsemanship sees itself as a radical departure from traditional techniques, based on the use of unnecessary force and training though pain and fear. Critics of natural horsemanship say that working in sympathy with the horse to obtain its cooperation and using human body language to communicate effectively with the animal partner has been documented as far back as the Greek Xenophon, and that humane methods of horsemanship were practiced for centuries in French classical dressage and in the English riding disciplines.

Jefferson clearly believed that his job as rider was to dominate his horse. He often used expressions and metaphors that reiterate this idea. A horse is to be ridden. The relationship between horse and rider was a hierarchical one. The rider should lead. Again, grandson Jeff commented, "You saw at a glance, from his easy and confident seat, that he was master of his horse." [63]

However, as in all his hierarchical relationships, Jefferson probably preferred that this hierarchy be accepted graciously by the subordinate. Jefferson wanted a naturalized hierarchy. As one scholar described Jefferson's relationship with his enslaved servants and laborers, "He was a fair master but not uncomfortable in the role of master." Jefferson and his horse may have been partners, but Jefferson was the leader. [64]

There exist two recorded instances of Jefferson physically fighting with his horse and using the whip to bring it under control. These comments were by his grandson Jeff and his enslaved hostler, Wormley Hughes, two men who knew Jefferson, the horseman, intimately:

Jeff said: "The only impatience of temper he ever exhibited was with his horse, which he subdued to his will by a fearless application of the whip, on the slightest manifestation of restiveness." [65]

And Hughes said of Arcturus, a horse "Mr. Jefferson brought home from Washington":

> A crag of serpentine jutting into the narrow road, built high on the sides of a steep ravine, was selected by the fiery stranger horse as a shying butt—as if conscious that his rider would feel it dangerous to administer correction in such a spot. Mr. Jefferson tolerated this once or twice, but on its being repeated, punished the rearing and plunging animal with whip and spur until he was 'glad to put his fore feet on the rock and stand still.' [66]

While these are examples of Jefferson physically trying to intimidate his horse, it is unclear if they characterize his normal interactions with his steeds. Other scholars and authors have seen these examples as some kind of repressed violence in Jefferson. Many riders appreciate how important it is to sometimes struggle with a horse, and it is difficult and perhaps unfair to interpret these scenes. Jefferson is never described as being prone to violence in other contexts. Quite the opposite, he was often described as rather effete. With one or two exceptions, Jefferson discouraged his overseers from punishing the enslaved workers by whipping, nor does any evidence suggest that Jefferson himself ever raised a whip on any Monticello enslaved worker. [67]

We know that Jefferson's last riding horse, Eagle, was described as "fiery" and that while tied up, waiting for his master to take his morning ride, stood with "his ears back on his arched neck, pawing and stamping the ground with fiery impatience."

Eagle had another fault; he tended to shy (whirl around and bolt when startled). Eagle was difficult to handle, and there are plenty of examples of Eagle leaving riders on the ground, including Jefferson himself. [68]

On the other hand, we have no description of Jefferson reprimanding Eagle with a whip. And despite Jefferson's noted frailties, Eagle obviously accepted the elderly man, if not as the dominant one, as a trusted partner. Biographer H. S. Randall describes how Eagle immediately calmed down when Jefferson mounted him and how the horse moved off in a deliberate, careful manner "as if perfectly conscious of the necessity of discretion in his movements." [69]

Jefferson, of course, did control his horses, by various means. Like most horsemen of the time, Jefferson used spurs and whips. These are not necessarily always harsh instruments; both can be used to give cues quite subtly. The whip is a riding accouterment used for many tasks: opening gates, putting aside branches, as well as asking a horse to "give" to the side (step to the side). Jefferson also controlled his animals in other ways. In one description, when his horse was being shod at a blacksmith's, Jefferson "would hold him [the horse] by the ear in order to keep him quiet." [70]

A final consideration about dominance is that most of Jefferson's riding horses were stallions. As far as we know, as an adult he never rode a mare, nor were any of his coach horses mares. He did own some geldings, but these were mainly coach horses. Stallions, due to the hormone testosterone, have thicker, cresty necks and are somewhat bigger and more muscular than mares and geldings. Also due to their testosterone, stallions tend to be more aggressive (biting), especially with other stallions, and may be difficult to handle when around mares in heat (estrus). Usually, handlers separate stallions from other stallions, or they are left in breeding situations with harems of females. Owing to these difficulties, it is important that knowledgeable horsemen manage these animals. As with all horses, the key to working with stallions is to make clear who is in charge, who is the leader. [71]

Today it is uncommon for pleasure riders to ride stallions, and no one would put a child on one. Geldings are usually the preferred (male) horse, for their reduced aggressiveness and ability to live around other horses in stables. Even so, in some cultures today, especially in the Middle East, men always ride stallions. Moreover, the Spanish Riding School, in Vienna, Austria, uses only stallions in the performances, and most Thoroughbred racehorses are stallions. The temperament of stallions varies by breed and individual horse, and many riders today do ride high-performance, properly trained stallions in arenas with other horses. These animals can be marvelous athletes.

In the late eighteenth century, it was much more common for men from the planter society of Virginia to ride stallions. In many ways, a man's horse was a projection of his self, part of his planter-class identity. In this sense, riding, controlling, a virile high-bred stallion reflected the man's place, role, and status in planter society. But given that these men were riding stallions, it was important for them to make sure the horse knew who was in charge.

Most of the names Jefferson gave his horses were for heroic insurgents or revolutionary figures, as will be described in Chapter 4. Given his special identity with his horses, this may be the way Jefferson saw himself. It also, however, juxtaposes the rider upon the horse (above/below), as the dominating jockey upon the subordinate (but potentially revolutionary) horse (stallion), but in a (rational) relationship of acquiescence.

Portrait of George Washington Taking the Salute at Trenton *by John Faed 1856.*

Chapter 2

Brother Equestrians

As a member of the planter elite and Virginia gentry, Thomas Jefferson moved in horse circles. The Virginia gentry "not only rode horses and had them pull their coaches and carriages, but also bred them, traded them, bought and sold them, gambled on them, and talked about them incessantly." Horses were one of the many possessions that passed between family members and sealed relationships between friends. Blooded horses seemed like a natural medium of exchange. Like the exchange of plants and seeds, books and ideas, farming tips and architectural plans, the trade, exchange, buying, and selling of horses often retraced lines of relationship.[1]

The following vignettes describe several friends and family members in Jefferson's equine circles and the role that the horse played in their lives. Jefferson, the admirer of horseflesh, was like many of his friends and Virginia neighbors, from George Washington to James Madison, from John Hoomes to Thomas Mann Randolph, who often related to each other through horses. Although these men spoke of buying and selling their horses to each other, blooded horses were really used as links in their social relationships.

Friends and Neighbors

George Washington (1732-1799) —"The Best Horseman of His Age": Washington was a member of the House of Burgesses in Williamsburg when Jefferson arrived there as a college student. Born eleven years before Jefferson, Washington was already an established and well-known explorer, war hero, large landowner and land speculator, and local and Virginia politician. As colonial resistance to British rule evolved, with the Stamp Act crises Jefferson, then studying law, watched as others, including Washington, participated in the boycotts and maneuvering against the British. When Jefferson joined the House of Burgesses in 1769 from Albemarle County (by then as a practicing lawyer in western Virginia), Washington had already been there for a decade. By the time Jefferson was induced to attend the Second Continental Congress as a delegate from Virginia in June 1775, Washington had just been made commander in chief of the Continental Army and was preparing to go to the field. A year later, Jefferson wrote the stirring Declaration of Independence, while Washington was with his fledgling American army in New York.[2]

By 1778, George Washington was already lauded as the Father of His Country. [Fig. 2-1] At the end of the Revolutionary War, Washington returned to his home at Mount Vernon, while Jefferson was sent to Paris as minister to France. Jefferson was in Paris while delegates in Philadelphia struggled to write a new Constitution in 1787. In April 1789, Washington became the first president of the United States. When Jefferson arrived home from France (he thought temporarily) in December 1789, awaiting him was a request to serve as Washington's secretary of state. Jefferson accepted, with some hesitation, and headed to New York (later the temporary capital was moved to Philadelphia) to serve under President Washington. Finally, the intellectual pen and the pragmatic sword of the revolution were united in the same administration.

Fig. 2-1 Gilbert Stuart, *George Washington (Lansdowne* Portrait), 1796

In his four years in Washington's administration, Jefferson strove to impose his vision of government (later called Democratic-Republican until the 1820s) over those who became his political foes (called Federalists). Although Washington never declared himself a Federalist—he wanted to stay above the fray, and never endorsed political parties—he leaned toward and supported the ideas of Jefferson's arch-foe, Alexander Hamilton. It is in this emotionally difficult period for Jefferson that some animosity toward Washington built up. Jefferson resigned early from Washington's government and retired to Monticello in 1794 to return, he said, to life as a planter and farmer. Most historians consistently list Washington as our most popular president. Jefferson, too, recognized Washington's greatness of character and foremost place in American history. However, they did not correspond for the last two years of Washington's life due to a perceived insult to Washington by Jefferson.

When Jefferson retired from government the first time in 1794, he wrote Washington often in his role as farmer. Jefferson had visited Washington's home at Mount Vernon several times, on his way back and forth to Philadelphia or when he was in Alexandria. Both men were adherents of the new scientific agricultural movement aimed at improving farmland and livestock, read the same books on husbandry, and corresponded on this issue. Both men were also avid horsemen. Several years after Washington's death, when Jefferson was penning a eulogistic tribute to Washington, Jefferson famously declared that Washington was "the best horseman of his age, and the most graceful figure that could be seen on horseback." [3]

George Washington was a great admirer of horses. He loved horse racing and participated enthusiastically with friends in foxhunts near his Mount Vernon lands. He bred horses, housed them in a fine brick stable, owned elegant carriages, and was instrumental in the introduction of mules to agriculture in America. In his diaries, he often recorded the pleasures of riding and hunting.

Fig. 2-2 George Washington is depicted in front of his troops in December 1776 in *Washington at the Battle of Trenton*. Copy of engraving by Illman Brothers, 1931-1932, after E. L. Henry, c. 1870.

By all accounts, Washington was a fabulous rider. Not just Jefferson, but others noted his gracefulness on a horse. Humphreys stated that "all those who have seen General Washington on horseback, at the head of his army, will doubtless bear testimony with the author that they never saw a more graceful or dignified person." [Fig. 2-2] After General Washington's death, Wash Custis, his step-grandson, remembered, "He rode, as he did everything else, with ease, elegance, and with power." [4]

Washington was an avid horseman from boyhood. By the time he was seventeen, he owned a horse. He dedicated himself to his horses and horse breeding in the early part of his life, when he was first married. His marriage to the wealthy widow Martha Dandridge Custis in 1759 increased his property holdings and social status, which allowed him to indulge his passion for horses.

By November 1785, Washington owned a total of 130 horses. As a plantation owner, Washington divided his horses into those that tilled the fields, threshed the wheat, and pulled the wagons, and those that he rode daily, hunted with, raced, and rode to war. It is the second group of horses, of course, that distinguishes Washington as an equestrian.[5]

Washington experimented with breeding the newly imported blooded horses, like many planters of his day. By 1760, he kept a stallion for his own mares and also let the stallion cover (mate with) his neighbors' mares, too. The Virginia papers regularly advertised the services of various Washington stallions (with pasturage and guaranteed foal): Samson, Leonidas, Steady, Traveller, and Magnolia. His breeding and buying of horses connected Washington to all the other Virginia breeders. Two stallions, Leonidas and Magnolia, were especially significant. Washington bought both horses from his stepson, John Parke Custis (at Mount Airy, Maryland), after the British surrender at Yorktown.[6]

Leonidas was a blood bay stallion, a full 15 hands high, to whom Washington had sent his mares for several years before buying him. Custis had purchased Leonidas, foaled in 1774, along with his dam and another foal, from the former governor of Maryland, Horatio Sharpe. Both sides of Leonidas's pedigree were chock-full of imported highly bred horses. His dam's side was also the line contributing to Magnolia's tail line: Sharpe's Traveller mare, whose dam was Selima (1745) (a racehorse never beaten), and daughter of the Godolphin Arabian (1724). Leonidas stood at stud for several years (1777–1781) for Custis until Custis sold the horse to Washington for $300.[7]

The other horse Washington bought from Custis after the end of the war was Magnolia. He was thought to be one of the most beautiful horses in the colonies and was known as Washington's pride and joy. This horse commanded a price of $500, even higher than that paid for Leonidas. Magnolia (born 1780) was a half-Arabian chestnut horse, with flaxen mane and tail, 16 hands high, "finely formed, and thought by all who have seen him to be perfect. He was got by the Ranger Arabian, and his dam was by Othello son of Crab, her dam by Morton's Traveller and her dam was Selima by the Godolphin Arabian." Magnolia stood at stud at Mount Vernon from 1785 to 1788. [8]

Apparently, Washington tried to breed racehorses but was not successful. According to Custis's son, Magnolia ran a match race in Alexandria once, but lost. Others have carried on the persistent story that it was this horse, owned by George Washington, that raced against Jefferson's horse Tarquin and lost. If so, the race took place before Jefferson owned Tarquin. Jefferson bought Tarquin—an ex-racehorse to be sure—in 1790. In 1788, George Washington had already traded Magnolia to Colonel Henry Lee for 5,000 acres in Kentucky. Colonel Lee sent the horse to South Carolina to stand at stud.

The reason Washington traded Magnolia for land is instructive as to the cost of trying to breed horses in colonial Virginia. Washington decided that Magnolia was too expensive to keep and brought in few stud fees. As the Mount Vernon farm manager had written at the time of purchase, "If he [Washington] purchases them [Leonidas and Magnolia] he would hire Peter [an enslaved hostler], and give for him a liberal price. To keep such horses are expensive to the estate. They consume much corn; and hay, besides having Peter and a boy to attend to them." [Fig. 2-3] [9]

Magnolia may be most renowned for his sire, the Ranger Arabian, later called Lindsey's Arabian. Ranger was a white horse, 15 hands high, of the "most perfect form and symmetry ...with a gallant temper, which gave him a lofty and commanding carriage and appearance." Ranger's history is legendary in horse circles. It seems he was the gift from the Emperor of Morocco to the commander of a British frigate for some service rendered to the emperor's son. The captain took the colt, one of the best of the emperor's stud, on board the frigate and set sail for England, but somehow ended up at a port in the English West Indies for an extended period of time. The captain let the horse out for exercise on the nearby dock at a lumber yard. The horse, frisking around, fell on a pile of lumber and broke three

Fig. 2-3 Edward Savage, *The West Front of Mount Vernon*, c. 1787–1792. Everyday life at Mount Vernon is captured in this painting. In the foreground are George and Martha Washington, their grandchildren, and Major Pierre L'Enfant. Enslaved workers can be seen in the background.

of his legs. An American sea captain, also at port, was offered the horse if he could save him. The American skipper accepted the offer (and with Yankee ingenuity), got the horse on board his ship, and "secured him in slings and very carefully set and bound up his broken legs." The story always continues that by the time the sea captain arrived back in Hartford, Connecticut (around 1766), the horse was healed. The horse was bought by a Colonel Willis and called Ranger. He stood at stud, producing a slew of good runners, and "to all his stock he gave great perfection of form." [10]

During the Revolutionary War, General Washington noticed the superior horses ridden by the Connecticut cavalry when he took command of the Continental Army at Boston in 1777–78. Washington ordered Light Horse Harry Lee to find out where these horses were from. They proved to be sons and daughters of Ranger. A Captain Lindsey was sent to purchase the horse Ranger and did so. Ranger was then taken to Virginia (by ship) to William Lindsay's, of Port Royal, in Caroline County, and became known as Lindsay's Arabian. This horse continued to stand at stud in various places in Virginia and died in 1785 at twenty-three years of age. Magnolia was one of the first horses Ranger produced in Virginia.[11]

Virginians were understandably proud of American horseflesh. Note Mrs. Washington's comment in 1798 as recorded by an English visitor, Richard Parkinson, who had come to sell Americans English horses:

> I felt myself much vexed at an expression used at dinner by Mrs. Washington. When the General and the company at table were talking about the fine horses and cattle I had brought from England, Mrs. Washington said, "I am afraid, Mr. Parkinson, you have brought your fine horses and cattle to a bad market; I am of opinion that our horses and cattle are good enough for our land." I thought that if every old woman in the country knew this, my speculation would answer very ill: as I perfectly agreed with Mrs. Washington in sentiment. [12]

Washington, like many members of the gentry including Jefferson, was also a horse-racing fan. Although he never rode as a jockey in an official race, Washington did raise racehorses, and ran some of his horses in course races. Magnolia supposedly once ran for a purse, according to Martha's grandson, G. W. Custis. When he was in his thirties, before the Revolution and his life in politics, Washington was a racing devotee, traveling to all the important course races of the time in Virginia and Maryland and betting modestly. These races were quite the social scenes, including several days of accompanying balls and theater. Even after the Revolution, Washington continued to attend the socially prestigious races if he was nearby. [13]

Like all Virginia planters, Washington rode out every day on his horse to oversee his lands and the various farm tasks in progress. Nevertheless, there was also a leisure and sporting aspect to his riding: Washington had been passionate about foxhunting since his youth and needed horses that also had the stamina to race about the countryside and jump obstacles in the way.

In the 1760s, Washington built up a pack of hounds and worked on breeding them according to scientific principles as carefully as he did his horses. His favorite hunters were Blueskin and Nelson. Nelson had been a gift to Washington at Valley Forge in 1778, from Thomas Nelson Jr., then governor of Virginia and a signer of the Declaration of Independence. [Fig. 2-4] The dam of Allycroker, Jefferson's first broodmare, came from William Nelson, Thomas Nelson Jr.'s father, of Yorktown, who had also served as governor of Virginia. [14]

Blueskin was a light bluish-gray, not quite white. Nelson was a big-boned chestnut, 16 hands high, with white face and legs, sturdy enough to carry Washington foxhunting for many hours of riding. The details and escapades of many hunts appear in his diaries. Washington's last references to foxhunting were in

Fig. 2-4 John Ward Dunsmore, *George Washington and Lafayette at Valley Forge*, 1907

December of 1787 and January 1788. Washington assumed the presidency the next year and probably had little leisure time for such pursuits. Or perhaps he felt it wasn't dignified enough for the president. He broke up his kennels at this time and kept to more sedate riding after the presidency.

Furthermore, as a military commander, Washington took his riding horses to war with him. Having proven their stamina as hunters, both Blueskin and Nelson served Washington during the Revolution. Several of his mounts died from exhaustion under him during battle, but both Blueskin and Nelson survived the war. Blueskin didn't see as much action as Nelson, because he was more skittish around the cannon blasts than Nelson. But Nelson lasted the whole war, and was ridden from New York to the Carolinas.

Both these horses received their rewards and were well taken care of in their old age. John Hunter, an English visitor to Mount Vernon in 1785, makes the following reference to the horses in a letter to a friend:

> When dinner was over, we visited the General's stables, saw his magnificent horses, among them "Old Nelson," now twenty-two years of age, that carried the General almost always during the war. "Blueskin," another fine old horse, next to him, had that honor. They had heard the roaring of many a cannon in their time. "Blueskin" was not the favorite on account of his not standing fire so well as venerable "Old Nelson." The General makes no manner of use of them now. He keeps them in a nice stable, where they feed away at their ease for their past services.

Nelson died in 1790, at twenty-seven years of age. [15]

During his presidency, Washington rode two white horses, Jackson and Prescott. Prescott was 16 hands high and calmly withstood bands, flags and artillery fire during presidential parades. Prescott did have one annoying behavior, however—he was skittish at the approach of carriages.

As Father of His Country, as military commander and general during the War for Independence, as our first president, and eulogized by Henry Lee as "first in war, first in peace and first in the hearts of his countrymen," Washington is probably the subject of more statues than any other president. The vast majority of these statues have Washington mounted upon a magnificent steed. An equestrian statue is always a reference to a military hero (until the twentieth century), while at the same time underlining that aspect of the Founding Father. However, in the eighteenth century almost all rulers (military or not) were painted or sculpted on horses, as metaphors for hierarchy and dominance. [16] [Fig. 2-5]

Fig. 2-5 The equestrian sculpture of George Washington, at the center of Washington Circle, Washington, D.C.

The Virginia Washington Monument, in Capitol Square, Richmond, Virginia

Equestrian Statue of George Washington, 1856, by Henry Kirke Brown, Union Square Park, New York City

Probably due to Jefferson's role as the pen of the Revolution, there is not a single equestrian statue of Jefferson. Despite the fact that he rode every day until right before he died, Jefferson may not have wanted an equestrian statue due to his republican sympathies, given the hierarchical and grandiose implications of the mounted leader. He certainly had some uneasiness about a proposal for an equestrian statue of Washington by the Virginia General Assembly.

Washington supposedly broke and trained all his riding horses himself. Note what the French visitor De Chastellux wrote about a visit to Mount Vernon in the early 1780s:

> The weather being fair, on the 26th, I got on horseback, after breakfasting with the general—he was so attentive as to give me the horse he rode, the day of my arrival, which I had greatly commended—I found him as good as he is handsome; but above all, perfectly well broke, and well trained, having a good mouth, easy in hand, and stopping short in a gallop without bearing the bit—I mention these minute particulars, because it is the general himself who breaks all his own horses; and he is a very excellent and bold horseman, leaping the highest fences, and going extremely quick, without standing upon his stirrups, bearing on the bridle, or letting his horse run wild,—circumstances which young men look upon as so essential a part of English horsemanship, that they would rather break a leg or an arm than renounce them. [17]

Washington's papers describe several different kinds of horses that he owned: blooded horses, Narragansett, Andalusian, Chincoteague pony, Arabian, and draft horses. Washington was a big, imposing man, 6 feet, 3 inches tall and over 200 pounds, yet he seemed comfortable in the saddle of any horse. In his diary he notes regularly riding sixty miles in a day. In later life he rode quite tall horses, but even the relatively small horses of colonial times seemed to carry him easily. It is said that he "once rode his Chincoteague pony, Chinky, 147 miles from Mount Vernon to Williamsburg in a single day." [18]

According to one early historian, Washington:

> In his last days .... bought two of the easy-gaited animals known as Narragansetts... A peculiarity of these beasts was that they moved both legs on a side forward at the same time, that is, they were pacers. Washington's two proved somewhat skittish, and one of them was responsible for the only fall from horseback that we have any record of his receiving. In company with Major Lewis, Mr. Peake, young George Washington Custis and a groom, he was returning in the evening from Alexandria and dismounted for a few moments near a fire on the roadside. When he attempted to mount again the horse sprang forward suddenly and threw him. The others jumped from their horses to assist him, but the old man got up quickly, brushed his clothes and explained that he had been thrown only because he had not yet got seated. All the horses meanwhile had run away and the party started to walk four miles home, but luckily some negroes along the road caught the fugitives and brought them back. Washington insisted upon mounting his animal again and rode home without further incident. This episode happened only a few weeks before his death. [19]

Washington was also the foremost promoter of mules as work animals in the new United States, and he was one of the first Americans to attempt to raise mules. At the end of 1785, Washington received his first jackasses as gifts from the King of Spain, and a year later the French general Lafayette sent another jack and two jennets to Washington from the island of Malta. Washington found mules to be good workers, stronger than horses, and cheaper to keep than horses—they ate less. In fact, Magnolia's sale to Light Horse Harry Lee was due to the fact that Washington decided to concentrate on breeding mules at the expense of horses. As noted earlier, in 1785, Washington owned 130 horses but no mules. By the time of his death in 1799, he had fifty-eight mules and only twenty-five work horses. Jefferson also had begun to use and breed mules on his farms after the 1780s. [20]

Washington usually traveled around his farms by horseback, although he did own some wheeled vehicles, such as riding chairs, for quick trips into town (Alexandria) or for use in Williamsburg. In general, though, for many years, the roads around Mount Vernon would have prohibited the efficient use of a chair or coach. Upon his marriage to Martha in 1758,

Washington ordered his first coach from London. Although fashionable, it wasn't very sturdy. It was driven by postilions on horseback. Later, he had a second coach built in Philadelphia in 1780. This was the coach pulled by four impressive gray stallions that took Martha to Philadelphia when congress convened. The four grays were bred at Mount Vernon and were sons of Lindsay's Arabian.[21]

Washington's final coach was bought secondhand soon after he became president. Known as the White Chariot, it was a fine vehicle, with a cream-colored body and wheels, green blinds, and the Washington crest painted on the doors. His coachmen and footmen were dressed in white livery trimmed with orange. This coach, pulled by six horses, was the one Washington rode in as president, to and from Mount Vernon, and was for the personal use of Mrs. Washington while in Philadelphia. It lasted through many journeys.[22]

The "nice stable" where Blueskin and Nelson fed away to their hearts' content had a prominent place on the South Lane at Mount Vernon. The stable, built in 1782, was a lovely tripartite brick structure, fastidiously designed by Washington himself. Stables had stood at that same prominent place at Mount Vernon from 1733 on. The brick stable was built on the footprint of two previous stables of wood that had burned down. The brick stable had stalls for twenty horses and a center coach house. Behind the stable on a lower ground level was a sheltered space with open-tie stalls, for less important horses and mules. Across the small yard from the stable was a second coach house, where a replica of Washington's presidential coach now stands. These buildings proclaimed Washington's financial status as a horse breeder and member of the gentry class, and announced the role of fine horses in Washington's life.[23]

James Madison (1751–1836): Madison was Jefferson's philosophical and political soul mate. [Fig. 2-6] There is perhaps no one else who was so in tune with Jefferson and his political way of thinking for the fifty years of their friendship. Madison served in the Virginia state legislature (1776–1779 and again 1784–1786) and quickly became the protégée of Thomas Jefferson, eight years his senior. Madison helped revive Jefferson's Declaration of Religious Freedom (written but not passed in 1779), and finally guided the bill to passage in the Virginia General Assembly in 1786. Madison later served in the Continental Congress and gained fame and respect for his attention to detail, his work ethic, and his understanding of parliamentary procedure. It was Madison who persuaded Jefferson to return to civic life after the death of Jefferson's wife and later encouraged him to accept the position of minister plenipotentiary in France.

Fig. 2-6 James Madison, fourth president of the United States, 1816 portrait by John Vanderlyn

While Jefferson was in France, Madison wrote the plan for the US Constitution (and later the Bill of Rights), with its revolutionary three-branch federal system, and helped get it ratified. Thus, he is known as the Father of the Constitution.

Always in letter contact while Jefferson was in Paris, the two continued to support each other politically upon Jefferson's return. Madison served in Congress during the Washington administration. Jefferson and Madison opposed the supporters of Alexander Hamilton, who wanted a strong central government and who became known as the Federalists. Jefferson and Madison feared a strong central government as monarchical and created the Democratic-Republican Party. Madison served under Jefferson's presidency as secretary of state and helped orchestrate the Louisiana Purchase from France in 1803. When Jefferson retired from the presidency in 1809, Madison, with Jefferson's backing, was easily elected the fourth president of the United States.

Madison finally maneuvered on his own through politics as

Jefferson, now retired, became the so-called Sage of Monticello. Madison dealt with his own political issues and shepherded the United States to a victory in the War of 1812 (with Britain). After the British burned Washington in 1814, the Madisons lived in John Tayloe's house while in Washington. [24]

Madison grew up and lived almost all his life in Orange County, Virginia, just to the north of Albemarle County. He was educated at Princeton and later inherited his estate, Montpelier, and 5,000 acres from his father, and added on to the main house. Montpelier was a tobacco and wheat plantation, and Madison retired there, just twenty-eight miles from Monticello, and lived there with his wife, Dolley, until his death. During his last years, he suffered emotionally as his plantation, Montpelier, underwent financial collapse, like many of the Virginia gentry plantations, and specifically like that of his friend Thomas Jefferson. [Fig. 2-7]

The Madisons and Jefferson were constant visitors at each other's homes. One of the ground-floor bedrooms at Monticello was called the Madison Room because that is where James and Dolley stayed during their frequent extended visits. Jefferson often stopped at Montpelier on his way back and forth to Washington. [25]

Once again, horses were an important, significant thread in the woven tapestry of friendship between Madison and Jefferson. The two men shared many interests and a love for the Virginia countryside, gardening, and agriculture. They exchanged seeds, books, and ideas about architecture. Some of Jefferson's architectural ideas came to fruition at Montpelier. They also shared an interest in horses.

In September 1790, Madison sent Jefferson a horse to draw his phaeton in Philadelphia. Jefferson insisted that Madison have someone else (a "good judge") determine the price of the horse, because he was afraid his friend Madison would "think him of less than his real value." The next year, September 1791, on the way home from Philadelphia, Jefferson bought another carriage horse from Madison for £25 when he stopped by Montpelier before arriving at Monticello. The horse, however, took ill, and died a few days later. Both men were embarrassed and vied with each other (in letters) about payment for the horse (as usual Jefferson had not paid immediately). Later Jefferson insisted on paying for the animal—after all, it was total chance that the animal had died. Jefferson argued that the horse could have died years later and ended up giving Madison £12 more than he originally bargained for. Later Jefferson sold President Madison one of his own presidential carriage horses for $200 just as Jefferson left Washington for Monticello and as Madison was taking over in Washington, on April 19, 1809. [26]

Like others of his station, Madison admired fine horses and was an excellent rider. At Montpelier, Madison had a stable building south of the main mansion, but it must have been of log construction because it no longer exists. Paul Jennings, a former enslaved servant at Montpelier, said in an interview in 1865, "He [Madison] was very fond of horses, and an excellent judge

Fig. 2-7 Madison's home, Montpelier, Virginia, in 2011

of them, and no jockey ever cheated hm. He never had less than seven horses in his Washington stables while president." [27]

Like Jefferson and Washington and other planters, Madison ritually rode his horse, Liberty, around his plantation and over his lands every morning between nine and ten o'clock. Dolley Madison's niece Mary Cutts gave the following description of Liberty:

" 'Liberty,' which had grown old in his service, was petted, fed and stalled alone; he well deserved his name; not a gate which he could not open—nor, any outrage which cattle could commit was not, by the [slaves], ascribed to 'Liberty.' " Cutts continued, "Mr. Madison in his humorous way often repeated these amusing and generally false tales of his disused horse, but never curtailed his freedom." [28]

In 1818, Jefferson convinced Madison to be the first president of the Agricultural Society of Albemarle, an organization founded to promote scientific farming and husbandry in their part of Virginia and to serve as a practical, self-help organization in an effort to improve Southern farming. In 1822, the society took up a bond to send someone to Spain to buy an Andalusian stallion in order to improve the blood of the horse stock around Albemarle. They never found a horse that met the criteria set by the Agricultural Society, however. Nevertheless, the desire to go abroad to find a stallion to better the Albemarle stock demonstrates Jefferson's and Madison's continuing interest in horseflesh. [29]

Madison aided Jefferson in his last "hobby," which was the founding of the University of Virginia. Madison served on the Board of Visitors at the University along with James Monroe and John Hartwell Cocke (see below) and became its second rector upon Jefferson's death. The University was their last joint venture. A few months before Jefferson's death, he told Madison that he was relieved knowing he was leaving the University in good hands. "It is a comfort to leave that institution under your care." In this same letter, Jefferson again turned to his friend of fifty years, asking Madison to take care of his personal reputation. "To myself you have been a pillar of support through life. Take care of me when dead, and be assured that I shall leave with you my last affections." [30]

Fig. 2-8 John Hartwell Cocke (1780–1866) of Bremo in the 1850s

John Hartwell Cocke (1780–1866):

John Hartwell Cocke was Jefferson's neighbor, fellow progressive farmer, and another colleague on the University of Virginia project. Cocke shared many other interests with Jefferson. He was a noted Virginia planter and agriculturalist, a general in the War of 1812, a statesman, and a respected reformer against what he perceived as the great evils of his day: alcohol and slavery. Cocke was much younger than Jefferson (by almost forty years) and did not come to Jefferson's neighborhood until 1809, so their relationship developed after Jefferson's presidency. He was an important and innovative breeder of horses, and like the other men described in this chapter, bound himself to Jefferson in many ways, including through horses. [Fig. 2-8]

The original Cocke family plantation was Mount Pleasant in Surry, down in Tidewater, directly across from Jamestown on the James River. Cocke was orphaned as a young child but later inherited his father's land (which also included Bremo in Fluvanna County). Although young Cocke spent much time in Williamsburg when he was a student, he was often at Mount Pleasant for foxhunts. Early on, Cocke became interested in agriculture and managing the lands he had inherited. He started experimenting with

Fig. 2-9 Bremo Plantation, Fluvanna County, Virginia

plant agriculture in 1801. At Mount Pleasant, Cocke planted tobacco, but later he lost interest in tobacco because it ruined the land, and eventually became its chief critic. [31]

Cocke also was interested in managing the livestock that he had inherited. We can note his attention and participation in Virginia horse culture from his youth. Cocke's uncle (the executor of his father's estate) had had an active breeding program: "Richard Cocke VI sent two mares to William Stark, so that they could be bred with his stud horse, Wildair," and on several other occasions he sent mares out for stud service. For example, two of the Cocke plantation's mares were bred to a stud horse that was owned by "Mr. Ambler, in all probability John Ambler II of Jamestown Island." John Hartwell Cocke inherited an important horse from his uncle Richard, a Herod filly. Seemingly, Richard had several blooded horses to distribute at his death: a Boxor colt and an "old mare, pregnant with a colt sired by Cormorant." [32]

Cocke continued the family interest in blooded horses for the rest of his life. He bred his mares to imported stallions and bought blooded horses. "On July 4, 1800, he purchased a gray Medley mare and a Diomed filly from George Ruffin. A year later, he bought a horse from his uncle, William Taliaferro." At this point, Cocke must have caught horse-racing fever, because on April 20, 1803, Nicholas Faulcon, Cocke's brother-in-law, "sent word to John that his [John's] new filly had raced against Magnet, another mare he owned. Both horses had participated in races at New Market and in Norfolk and had 'run 'round the ground' there at Four Mile Tree." [33]

By 1801, Cocke had a herd of between fifteen to twenty horses and mules and owned a riding chair and a chariot. In 1808 and 1809, as Cocke was getting ready to move to Bremo, his brother-in-law wrote him about his horses, saying that "Diomeda and Key Hole and the Buzzard filly were in good shape, but that the Wonder filly and Magnet were thin." [34]

Cocke and his first wife, Anne, eventually decided to leave Surry County and move farther west to their lands in Fluvanna County. They conveyed their Mount Pleasant property to relatives and transported all their slaves, livestock, and household belongings to their Fluvanna lands, called Bremo. Other Cockes were already established in the area, in southern Albemarle County. James Powell Cocke, a cousin, had arrived by 1770, and lived in Edgemont (1797), a house designed by Jefferson. This family member was probably John Hartwell Cocke's introduction to Jefferson. Cocke was hopeful he could build up a stock of Merino sheep that Jefferson had introduced into the region. Eventually Cocke became one of the most successful planters in Virginia. [35]

Due to their shared interests, and Cocke's role as younger disciple, Jefferson and Cocke became friends and correspondents. Cocke must have shared Jefferson's architectural tastes.

Fig. 2-10 Bremo stables

Cocke's 1818 Palladian mansion at Upper Bremo was most certainly influenced by Jefferson, even if it was built by Jefferson's master builder, James Dinsmore (who also helped build the University and Madison's Montpelier). [Fig. 2-9] Moreover, by 1822, Cocke had built a fine brick and stone stable for his horses, which still stands at Upper Bremo. [Fig. 2-10] In fact, it was this stable that served as the model for the 1930s reconstruction of the Jefferson stables under the north terrace of Monticello. Cocke had earlier built a stone barn and stable at Bremo Recess, in 1806.

At Bremo, Cocke continued his interest in breeding fine horses. Despite his early interest in racing, Cocke was more interested in breeding and riding "excellent saddle horses." Thus, he was partial toward Quarter Running Horses, which, according to many, were dual purpose racehorses and saddle horses (runners that also paced and ambled but did not trot). He always had an interest in importing other breeds to correct for the deficiencies of the leggy Virginia racehorse that did not serve well under saddle. Cocke was involved in importing Spanish Andalusians, English hunters, and Cleveland Bays, and soon became a leading breeder of saddle horses in Virginia. [36]

In 1809, he advertised stud services for his horse Roebuck, and in the ad Cocke already lauds the horse's colts for their unrivaled uses as "Saddle, carriage and plantation business." In 1810, Roebuck I produced, with an English imported mare called Druid, a bay colt, Roebuck II (or Young Roebuck), that quickly became Cocke's favorite riding horse. Cocke described Young Roebuck as "incomparably the finest pacer" and "the most perfect model of a saddle horse I ever knew." This Roebuck served as Cocke's war horse during the War of 1812. In 1859, the most important equine portrait painter of the day, Edward Troye, painted General John Hartwell Cocke on his Roebuck as they would have looked at Camp Carter near Richmond in 1814. [Fig. 2-11] The painting is in the collection of the White House Historical Association. [37]

That Roebuck was General Cocke's favorite, there is no doubt. He often took Roebuck out and rode to Monticello (about twenty-eight miles away) to visit Jefferson before breakfast (about nine o'clock). When he arrived, Cocke would ask Edmund Bacon, the overseer, to take care of Roebuck at his house. (There was another stable at the overseer's cabin, south of Belfield.) Bacon remembered Roebuck as a "fine bay stallion."

Fig. 2-11 Edward Troye, *John Hartwell Cocke on Roebuck*, 1859

The portrait above of Roebuck (and General Cocke) is the only portrait that exists of a horse that we know was, at least at times, stabled at Monticello. Cocke's loyalty to Roebuck continued unto death. The Cocke family claims that when Roebuck died, Cocke had him buried in a standing position. [38]

Two other stallions that Cocke bred in 1833 out of Roebuck mares, and which later stood at stud at Bremo, were one called Cleveland and another called Utilitarian. Both were advertised in stud bills as pacers and as being the "best riding horses" for their "fine gaits." Cleveland, out of a Cleveland Bay stud, could "pace at ease, seven miles an hour." Utilitarian was definitely a highly bred horse, tracing to American Eclipse on his sire's side and out of a Roebuck mare, a Bedford mare (grand dam), and a Diomed mare (probably Cocke's own Diomeda) (great-grand dam) out of imported Janette. However, in Utilitarian's stud bill, Cocke again complained about racehorses: "The excessive and extravagant estimate put upon the qualities for the turf, (there can be but little doubt) has produced the present scarcity of fine saddle horses in Virginia." [39]

In the broadsheet, Cocke claimed that the "leading object

of breeding ought to be to produce a race of horse, the best suited to the useful and necessary purposes of life ...worthy of the patronage of such gentlemen as may desire to propagate that class of the noblest of our domestic animals—the sharer and companion of our sports—the aid in our healthful exercises—and the indispensible [sic] auxiliary in many of our most important labors—the saddle and harness horse." In 1814, a few years after John Hartwell Cocke moved to Bremo, he sold a horse to Jefferson. The horse, also called Bremo, was an eight-year-old tall dark bay, described as having a very "docile" character. Bremo was originally was used at Monticello as Jefferson's riding horse. Six years later, when Jefferson bought Eagle (his last riding horse), Bremo became one of the four carriage horses for Jefferson's landau. [40]

Payment for Bremo was, as usual for Jefferson, postponed several times, which I discuss below. Each time, John Hartwell Cocke responded graciously, in the Virginia gentry way, saying he was in no hurry for the money. Jefferson finally completed payment six months later.

In 1817, Cocke was asked by Jefferson to be on the Board of Visitors for the Central College (later the University of Virginia); thus he collaborated with Jefferson almost from the beginning. Cocke was on the building committee with Jefferson himself and helped supervise the construction of the Rotunda. When the University was finally chartered, Cocke became one of the four original people on the Board of Visitors (along with Madison, Joseph C. Cabell, and Jefferson—all have buildings named after them on Grounds). Cocke remained after all others had died. The University opened in March 1825 with only about thirty students. By 1852 there were 400 students per year.

After Jefferson's death in 1826, Cocke continued to pursue his several other progressive agricultural projects and reformist moralistic plans. He railed against the immoralities of alcohol and tried to convince his friends and workers to abstain. He founded and joined several temperance societies in Virginia. The second great evil of his time, Cocke believed, was slavery. Caught in the contradiction of not being able to farm without slaves, Cocke came up with many schemes for manumission. Cocke freed what he called some of his "most prepared" slave families, but (like Jefferson) did not think "Negroes" could live alongside whites, and so paid for their passage to Africa.

Turfmen

The original horse-breeding and horse-racing region of Virginia was the James River Tidewater area and the Northern Neck, bordered by the Rappahannock and Potomac Rivers, including the northern Virginia area. Later, by the end of the eighteenth century and the beginning of the nineteenth century, the center of breeding and racing had shifted to Southside Virginia and the area along the Virginia-North Carolina border, in the Roanoke River Valley. In each of these two areas, certain very wealthy planters made names for themselves as turfmen and came to dominate breeding, importing, and racing circles. In the so-called Northern Neck area were John Baylor of Newmarket (Caroline County), Colonel John Hoomes of Bowling Green (Caroline County), and Colonel John Tayloe II of Mount Airy (in Richmond County). Later, in the Southside area, Allen Jones Davie of Halifax, North Carolina; brothers John Goode of Mecklenburg County, Virginia, and Thomas Goode of Chesterfield, Virginia; General Allen Jones of Northampton County, North Carolina, and his brother Willie Jones of Halifax County, North Carolina; Colonel Jeptha Atherton of Northampton, North Carolina; John Randolph of Roanoke of Charlotte County, Virginia; and Colonel William Ransom Johnson (originally from Warrenton, North Carolina, but later transferred his residence to Petersburg, Virginia) stood out.

Jefferson, during his presidency, bought horses from both areas. His riding horse during his presidency, Wildair, was bought from Colonel Hoomes, while his four presidential carriage horses came from various owners in the Petersburg area where his son-in-law John Wayles Eppes resided. However, before his presidency, most of Jefferson's horses had come from friends and relatives on the James River or Northern Neck region, the center of horse importation and breeding at the time. During his ten years as a breeder, 1772–1782, Jefferson had favored sending his mares to Fearnought studs. Old Fearnought had been imported by John Baylor of Newmarket in Caroline County in 1764. Most of the sons of Fearnought that Jefferson used for his mares resided in nearby Hanover County.

John Hoomes (1755–1805): The Hoomes family had a long history in Caroline County, Virginia. The Hoomeses had come from the Tidewater region to the northern area of the York River (the Mattaponi branch) early in the late seventeenth century. They patented land in 1670, when the area was still a frontier. The family house was called Bowling Green, and racing had taken place on the mansion grounds since at least 1739, if not much earlier. Thomas Hoomes built an oval racetrack on the lawn in front of Old Mansion (the name of the house) almost right after he had built the house, supposedly the first horse-racing track in America. [Fig. 2-12] Caroline County soon became the "cradle of horse-racing in colonial Virginia." [41]

John Hoomes, born in 1755, was an important Virginia planter and large landowner; moreover, he owned 50,000 more acres of lands in Kentucky, where he proposed to raise racehorses. Like many of the gentry class, Hoomes served in politics. He was in the General Assembly as a delegate and senator from 1791 to 1803. More importantly, he was a sharp young business-man and entrepreneur. Hoomes was one of the first planters to imagine and realize a profit in speculating in horseflesh. After

the Revolutionary War, he became the paramount importer of Thoroughbred horses from England to the United States, and is best known as a horseman, breeder, and racer. [42]

Bowling Green was located within a few miles of the properties of other significant horse breeders. When Hoomes was only twenty years old, he began what became a long-term relationship with the Tayloe family (of Mount Airy in nearby Richmond County). Hoomes bought from John Tayloe II a young filly out of the imported turf stallion Yorick. With two fillies from this starter horse (called Sally Wright), Hoomes was on his way to becoming a breeder. John Baylor of Newmarket, who in 1764 had imported the celebrated racer Fearnought, lived just three miles south of Bowling Green.

The Revolutionary War took a great toll on the blooded horses of the United States. Many were used (and perished) in the war as mounts for cavalrymen and officers, while others

Fig. 2-12 A 1935 photograph of Old Mansion at Bowling Green, Caroline County, Virginia, by F. B. Johnston

were requisitioned for hauling and other duties. The British also took horses when they could, and killed stock too young to be used, in order to deprive the colonists of them. Moreover, racing had officially stopped during the war, and trade with England was on hold—so importation of horses had also stopped, thus further depleting the numbers available.

As soon as the war was over, Virginia breeders again began to import horses from England, and breed and race them on a scale much grander than before. John Hoomes became the foremost importer and breeder, and a leader in the racing scene. After the war, in 1788, Hoomes reorganized the Virginia Jockey Club, and established it at Bowling Green, where course-racing meets were held annually for a decade. There the horses of Tayloe, Baylor, Hoomes, and others would vie in speed. There were at least three tracks: the one on the mansion grounds and two more on the road leading south. The races went on for a week, and there were "Balls and genteel suppers every night during the meeting." [43]

Hoomes saw his importations as business ventures and was trying to turn a profit quickly by racing, selling, and breeding his horses. He became one of the first planters to make money as a turfman. In 1790, Hoomes made connections with James Weatherby of London, and soon began importing stallions and mares on speculation. In 1798, Hoomes, in partnership with John Tayloe III, inquired after a twenty-one-year-old, seemingly washed-up, ex-racing stallion named Diomed. When Hoomes and Tayloe asked their agent Weatherby about Diomed, he answered, informing them that the English had lost interest in this horse and "that the old horse was a 'tried and proven bad foal-getter.'" Not dissuaded, the two Virginians took a chance and imported Diomed in the middle of the mating season and put him right to work. [44]

Once the horse was in America, Diomed's fertility improved, along with the quality of his offspring. Diomed stood at stud at Bowling Green for eight years before he was sold, for six times the original investment, to breeders in Chesterfield County—the old racehorse region—where he was moved from farm to farm in the Roanoke Valley, as was the practice, producing a prodigious number of fine colts. Eventually he returned to Hoomes's Bowling Green, where he died at the age of thirty-one in 1808.

The racing historian John Hervey has said, "Had he never imported anything but Diomed, John Hoomes would have placed his name among the greatest of the American founder-breeders." However, Hoomes did import more horses, many more. In 1798, he imported from England another Derby winner, Spread Eagle, as well as Stirling, a King's Plate winner two times over. In the fourteen years between 1792 and 1805, John Hoomes imported nineteen different English stallions and thirteen different English mares, and made more than $15,000 in sales and stock. At his death in 1805, Hoomes left forty broodmares and four imported stallions, along with much young stock. Bowling Green was the "busiest breeding center on the continent." [45]

Many people, including John Hartwell Cocke and John Randolph, were very critical of Hoomes's massive importation and breeding of horses for speed. Critics believed that Hoomes almost personally caused the degeneration of the Virginia saddle horse. They claimed that the recent racehorses did not have the strong legs and comfortable pacing gaits of the Virginian quarter horses, and called Hoomes's horses "worthless." Others disagreed and cited the marvelous racers that the new bloodlines injected into racing history by John Hoomes's importations. [46]

John Hoomes was responsible for a further innovation with horses and transportation. Bowling Green was located on the road between the falls of the Rappahannock and the falls of the James River, which became the main highway between Richmond (the capital after 1780) and Fredericksburg, in northern Virginia. Hoomes, with his partner John Tayloe III, established a line of stagecoaches that carried passengers between Alexandria (near Washington, D.C.) and Richmond. Horses that did not do well in their development and training (for races) were sent to the stagecoach line. [47]

At the time, no commercial stage lines served the western parts of the state. So when Jefferson, who lived west toward the Blue Ridge Mountains in Albemarle County, wanted to take a stagecoach to Washington or farther north, he would take his own horses (sometimes riding them or sometimes riding in his own gig) to meet the north-south stagecoach trail. When he returned, Jefferson would give instructions to his slaves who rode the horses about where to meet him with his carriage or horse. From there, they would travel home together, usually through Orange Court House to Monticello. [48]

Hoomes was well known in the region for the quality of

his stud, and buyers looking for good horseflesh would inevitably inquire about the animals Hoomes might have for sale. When Jefferson was preparing for his presidency, he must have put out the word that he was looking for an impressive riding horse as well as a team of carriage horses befitting the presidency. Son-in-law John Wayles Eppes was searching and negotiating for both the riding horse and some carriage horses, the last of which he eventually found in Petersburg, Virginia. John Hoomes, however, contacted the soon-to-be president by letter: "I saw Mr. Eppes a few days ago who informed me you were in want of an elegant saddle horse, I have one to dispose of." Eppes said it was one of the finest horses in the state. Hoomes's horse was Wildair, a highly bred animal. Hoomes then went on to justify the horse's price, which he said Jefferson could have for $300 (although someone else had already offered him $400). Jefferson answered, as usual asking for a payment delay of ninety days, but added he would "accede to your proposition of taking him at 330. Doll." Jefferson ended his letter, "There may some difficulty in getting the horse brought here. But perhaps your connection with the stage may enable you to have him brought on through their [illegible] with safety." [49]

Hoomes sent the horse with his enslaved servant James and said, in the accompanying letter, "I should like to know whether the horse comes up to your expectation of him, & shall be very sorry if I am deceived in him." On April 17, Jefferson finally replied, sending payment for Wildair, and recording his reaction to receiving the horse as "extremely pleased with him." [50]

Wildair went on to become a well-remembered horse by Jefferson's family. The elegant big bay horse served as Jefferson's riding horse for his noontime rides around the still-rural Washington City for several years.

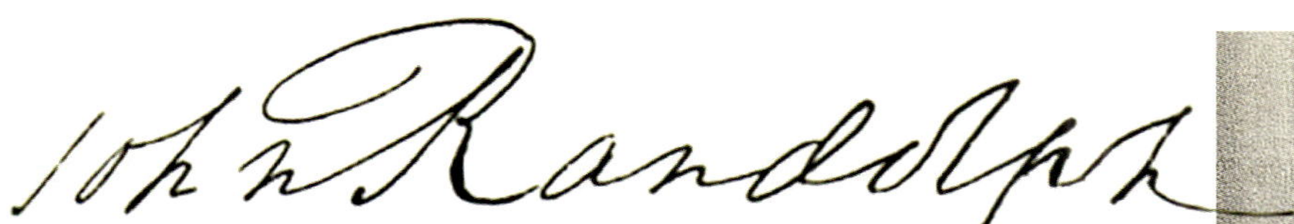

Fig. 2-13 John Randolph of Roanoke

John Randolph of Roanoke (1773–1833): Another member of the Virginia gentry, a charismatic orator, a feared debater, a member of the United States Congress and Senate, querulous yet powerful, snobbish yet charming, a superb horseman, and in 1820 the largest breeder of Thoroughbreds in the United States was John Randolph of Roanoke. [Fig. 2-13] Jefferson's mother was a Randolph, and John Randolph of Roanoke was a second cousin of Jefferson's. Originally from Bizarre in Cumberland County, near Farmville, sometime after 1810 Randolph moved to rustic Roanoke Plantation farther south in Charlotte County, Virginia, and he added the moniker "of Roanoke" to distinguish himself from others in his family. [51]

Much has been written about this rather odd character due to either his political or equestrian importance. Seemingly his physical presence was rather awkward; he was tall and lanky, with a strange high-pitched voice. While he could be charming, he was also off-putting. He suffered from ill health all his life. Aggravating his ill health were other eccentricities such as heavy drinking and his use of opium. He died of tuberculosis. [52]

Randolph was elected to the US Congress at a very young age in 1799 (he was twenty-six years old), after a rousing debate with the elderly Patrick Henry. He served almost continuously in Congress until 1825, when he was appointed to the Senate for two years (to fill a vacancy). In 1827 he returned to Congress. At the beginning of his political career, Randolph was a strong supporter of his kinsman Thomas Jefferson (about to be president) and his Republican policies. But in 1806, Randolph of Roanoke broke with Jefferson over the proposed Florida purchase and soon became his political nemesis, fiercely opposing Jefferson from the congressional floor with his fiery oratory and cantankerous style. Some rumored that he suffered from a mental disorder. He was a fierce champion of states' rights.

His appearance in Congress was always very flamboyant. Federalist William Plumer of New Hampshire wrote in 1803 of his theatrics: "Mr. Randolph goes to the House booted and spurred, with his whip in hand, in imitation, it is said, of members of the British Parliament." "Wearing a blue riding coat and buckskin breeches" he would stride into the House "accompanied by the jingle of silver spurs." He habitually appeared in Congress dressed this way, with his hunting dogs and slaves. "I am an aristocrat. I love liberty, I hate equality," he famously claimed. He became a permanent outsider in Washington. [53]

His personal belligerent style led him to challenge opponents to duels. In 1803, he challenged Jefferson's son-in-law, the thin-skinned Thomas Mann Randolph, also serving then in Congress, to a duel. President Jefferson was sorely afraid for his son-in-law's life (fearing his daughter's loss even more), and with some maneuvering the duel was avoided. Later, after the War of 1812, John Wayles Eppes, Jefferson's other son-in-law, won John Randolph's seat in Congress for one session from Virginia's 16th congressional district, serving from March 1813 to March 1815. Randolph charged that Eppes "was imported like a stallion, for the purpose of being run against him." Randolph took his seat back in 1815. In 1824, John Randolph of Roanoke was challenged to and fought a duel with the then speaker of the house, Henry Clay, due to an insulting remark he had made about Clay. Both men survived. [54]

Always the eccentric, and despite his aristocratic pretensions, John Randolph wrote in his will that his slaves were to be freed and left money to send them to Ohio (or some other state) upon his death. Despite Randolph's temperament, his importance was noted in many ways in his state; his name is memorialized in many buildings and institutions, such as Randolph-Macon College and Randolph-Macon Woman's College. [55]

Randolph's place in Virginia's horse history is unquestioned. As a youth, he "was the personification of freedom and indulgence in maintenance of fine horses to carry him where he wished to towns and tracks." Certainly he paid more attention to the turf at this time than civic matters. He was a recognized expert horseman and jockey. He rode his own horses in the quarter races he participated in as he went "riding from one race field to another." One of his overseers, Mr. Harvey, once recalled an anecdote about Randolph's fearlessness on a horse. "Randolph had his horse saddled in the dead of night to ride to a certain point in the plantation." Suddenly, Randolph's horse became frightened. "Mr. Randolph stuck the spurs deep in his side, and the horse plunged and reared at such a rate that Mr. Harvey became alarmed for the safety of the rider." But Randolph retorted with extreme confidence, "It was as easy to throw a new girth from a saddle as to throw him." [56]

John Randolph, like John Hartwell Cocke, was critical of John Hoomes and his imported racing horses for lowering the quality of horses in Virginia. In contrast, the quality of Randolph's Roanoke stud was unrivaled. Randolph bought his first mares in 1795, when he was just twenty-two years old. Between 1801 and 1823, John Randolph owned fifty-nine Virginia studs at Roanoke. During this time, however, he was not particularly successful as a racer of horses. Some have attributed this to his overreliance on the imported stallion Janus. (Janus produced superb quarter racers, but not distance racers. Randolph was breeding for course—distance—racing, popular with the gentry at the time.) Although still impressed with Janus crosses, Randolph later used Diomed and his most successful son, Sir Archie, in his breeding programs. Nevertheless, Randolph was a repository of knowledge about pedigrees and American blood lines. [57]

Book after book about John Randolph of Roanoke contain many anecdotes about Randolph and horses. One book on the Randolph clan starts off recounting a story about John Randolph sojourning at the springs at Warm Springs in 1826, where he called into question the "sanctity of the stud book," and the "truth of horse heredity" in the Old Dominion. Randolph regaled his audience of horse lovers with a tale about the pedigree of "the greatest Virginia horse of the time, Sir Archie." [Fig. 2-14]

Fig. 2-14 Sir Archie, as depicted in a painting by A. Fisher and engraving by Capewell & Kimmell, in Henry William Herbert, *Frank Forester's Horse and Horsemanship of the United States,* Vol. 1 (1857)

Randolph claimed that Sir Archie was not sired by Diomed, but rather that his dam, the blind Castianira, had been mounted first by the impatient teaser horse, an English racer named Gabriel. The bay horse Gabriel had passed on his color to Sir Archie (Diomed was a chestnut). Randolph swore he had been told this by "the white groom who had attended the mating." This was scandalous. Not even Randolph believed this, as his broadbill advertisements for his own stallion, Roanoke, announced that Roanoke was out of Sir Archie, out of Diomed. [58]

Another anecdote illustrates John Randolph's arrogance and self-regard as far as his horses were concerned:

> It was court Day and in the afternoon he offered for sale at public auction one of his best stallions. If I was not mistaken, it was Roanoke, by the celebrated horse Old Sir Archie, and out of Lady Bunsbury. For a considerable time after the horse was put up there was no bid made; but, at length, Hugh Wyllie, Esq., the owner of the celebrated racehorse Marske, bid fifty pounds. Mr. Randolph was very indignant at so small a bid; and turning fiercely on Mr. Wyllie, looking him full in the face, said: "Do you, Sir, bid fifty pounds for a horse that pushed Marske up to the throat latch?" There was a dead silence; no one spoke a word. The horse was led off the yard. [59]

Finally, John Randolph of Roanoke, along with the other leading turfmen of the day, attended the great match race, known as the race of the century, on May 27, 1823, on Long Island, New York. There, on a flat, oval racecourse, were pitted two horses against each other—American Eclipse, the best, if aging, racer from the North, against Henry, the best racer the South had to offer. [Fig. 2-15] Regional pride was at stake as people assembled to witness the winner of the three four-mile heats: Cornelius Van Ranst's horse from New York against William Ransom Johnson's horse from Virginia. Sixty thousand spectators from all walks of life traveled from far and wide to behold the race that would be American's first sports spectacle. Congress and the New York Stock Exchange closed down for the event. Randolph supposedly put down $500 on the Virginia horse, Henry, only to see him lose to Eclipse. But for Randolph, and no doubt for the other Virginians, their identity equated with the sectional pride of their beloved state and their beloved horses. It was who they were. The humiliating shock of their loss foretold later events. [60]

Jefferson's Sons-In-Law

Jefferson seemed genuinely fond of his two sons-in-law for most of their lives. Both were of the planter class and from elite families of Virginia. Both men lived on their plantations and yet also fulfilled civic duties. Both men followed Jefferson to Washington during his presidency to serve as congressmen. In general, they shared their father-in-law's political leanings. Jefferson obviously related to them not only as husbands of his daughters and fathers of his grandchildren, but also as agriculturalists and fellow horsemen. Through the exchange, trade, buying, selling, and gifting of horses, Jefferson wove a tight tapestry of mutual interests and obligation with these younger men. Horses were often the medium of relationship.

Fig. 2-15 Edward Troye, "American Eclipse, an undefeated American Thoroughbred racehorse," c. 1834

Thomas Mann Randolph Jr. (1768–1828): Jefferson was intimately related to the Randolph family, one of the important First Families of Virginia. His mother, Jane, was a Randolph, and Jefferson's father, Peter Jefferson, was close friends with her cousin, William, who lived farther southeast from Shadwell on the James River at Tuckahoe. [Fig. 2-16] When William died, Peter Jefferson became the guardian for his son, Thomas Mann Randolph (1741–1789). In fact, Peter Jefferson moved his whole family down to live at Tuckahoe for seven years, when his own son, young Thomas, was only two years old. As an adult, Thomas Mann Randolph took over the plantation at Tuckahoe, served in the Revolution, and married Ann Cary of Ampthill. [Fig. 2-17] He continued his relationship with Jefferson, buying land next to Shadwell (Edgehill). Randolph was quite a horseman, one of the early breeders of blooded horses, and an early promoter of course racing.

Fig. 2-17 Portrait of Virginia governor from 1819 to 1822, "Thomas Mann Randolph" (1768-1828) c. 1790. unattributed

Lt. Thomas Anburey, the British prisoner at Charlottesville, described Randolph and his horses thus:

> Colonel Randolph possesses that fondness for horses, which I observed was peculiar to the Virginians of all stations, sparing no trouble, pains, or expense, in importing the best stock, and improving the breed; and it was with no little

Fig. 2-16 Tuckahoe Plantation, Goochland, Virginia, view of the whole house, home of the Randolphs

> pleasure he shewed us a fine one, named Shakespeare, which he imported just as the war commenced. There was a stable built purposely for this horse, in which was a recess for a bed for the negroe who looked after it, that he might be with it at night. This horse is of a handsome dappled gray, about fifteen hands and a half high, with a most beautiful head and neck; as to any other points about him, it is impossible to tell, for the creature was so amazingly pampered and fat, and being of the race breed, his legs were so small and slim, that they appeared unable to support the weight of his body, exactly like horses that one see painted in old pictures; the best idea you can possibly form of his size, is by telling you, that from his withers to his tail, there was such a groove of fat, that you might pour water upon his withers, and it would run in a straight line down his tail; the horse is obliged to be kept in high condition, to enable him to receive the numerous visitors attending on him in the Spring. [61]

Colonel Randolph was well known for racing and breeding horses. The successful stud Partner stood at Tuckahoe for several years. Originally owned by Armistead Lightfoot of Brunswick County, Partner was sired by imported Traveler. By 1770, Partner was standing at stud at Tuckahoe and was owned by Randolph from 1772 to 1775, after which he was bought by Robert Skipwith. Partner's services were advertised in the *Virginia Gazette* during those years. Jefferson's father-in-law, John Wayles, had put his mare, Allycroker, to Partner in 1773, and of this union was born a colt, called Alfred (in spring 1774). By the time Alfred was born, John Wayles had died, and Jefferson and his wife, Martha, had inherited Wayles's land and stock from Elkhill, an estate at the confluence of the Rivanna and James rivers. The Jeffersons augmented their wealth through this inheritance but also became responsible for Wayles's debts. For example, five years later, on May 3, 1778, Jefferson's account books show that he paid "Colo. T. M. Randolph in full" £3 for "Mr. Wayles's estate for putting Allycroker to Partner" in 1773. Later, Allycroker became one of Jefferson's most important broodmares. [62]

Besides the studs Shakespeare and Partner, Randolph owned a high-bred mare known as T. M. Randolph's Young Kitty Fisher. This mare was out of (Old) Jolly Roger and Kitty Fisher, two early imports. Young Kitty Fisher was the dam of Syme's Wildair (bay colt, 1776, by Fearnought), who covered in Virginia from 1780 to 1799, and Randolph's Laburnum (chestnut colt, 1780, by Lath), who covered in Virginia from 1785 to 1788 and in Kentucky in 1789. [63]

Randolph's breeding program was quite a large enterprise. In 1780 he took out an advertisement in the *Virginia Gazette* offering a reward for a blood mare "heavy with foal" that had been "stolen" from Randolph's breeding program was quite a large enterprise. In 1780 he took out an advertisement in the *Virginia Gazette* offering a reward for a blood mare "heavy with foal" that had been "stolen" from a pasture. Then he added that lately "there has been 20 valuable horses stolen out of this neighborhood." All twenty horses may not have belonged to Colo. Randolph, but we get an idea of how these often unfenced pastures must have been tempting loot for thieves. [64]

Randolph's son Thomas Mann Randolph Jr. (called Mann Randolph), was a product of the marriage with Ann Cary. The younger Thomas Mann Randolph was a good student, attending William and Mary, and then continuing his studies in Edinburgh, Scotland, when Jefferson and his daughters were in Paris. Randolph visited the Jeffersons in Paris, where he met Jefferson's oldest daughter, Martha (Patsy). When Jefferson and his daughters returned to Virginia from Paris, and made their way up the James from plantation to plantation of old friends, the two young people met again at Tuckahoe in December of 1789. By February of 1790, they were married. Jefferson managed to convince the young couple to settle at Edgehill. Thus began a life near Monticello and the patriarch. [65]

Jefferson was very fond of young Randolph. One visitor said he seemed more like a son to Jefferson than a son-in-law. Randolph was tall, wiry, yet graceful, like Jefferson, but with a dark complexion. During the first years of Randolph's marriage to Jefferson's daughter Martha, Jefferson was in Philadelphia, and Randolph helped oversee Monticello from nearby Edgehill (inherited from his own father). [66] [Fig. 2-18]

Randolph was an adherent of the scientific agricultural

Fig. 2-18 Edgehill Plantation, Albemarle County, Virginia

movement and became a respected botanist. He also pursued a career in politics, serving as a Virginia delegate, senator, US congressman from Virginia during Jefferson's presidency (1803–1807), and governor of Virginia (1818–1822). As a congressman, Randolph was a loyal supporter of Jefferson and kept him company in Washington City (since daughter Martha stayed at Monticello during that time). Congressman Randolph almost got into a duel with another cousin, John Randolph of Roanoke, over his support of President Jefferson's policies (see above).

Randolph served in the War of 1812 at the rank of colonel, but when he returned to Monticello after that, his relationship with the elder Jefferson and his family (now consisting of Martha and eleven children) became conflicted. Martha and the children were then living at Monticello rather than Edgehill, and Martha served as her father's house hostess and manager, and oversaw the enslaved house servants. Either out of jealousy or an inferiority complex, Randolph took up drink; his financial affairs floundered, and he moved out of Monticello to live by himself. His service as governor was during this time. Although it is claimed that he reconciled with his family, his behavior was sometimes odd. He died at Monticello and is buried there.

Randolph was known as a splendid horseman, and was "one of the few Virginians who could outride Jefferson." There are all kinds of anecdotes about him as a rider. Typical of his "beguiling eccentricities" was to salute nonchalantly as his horse sailed over a fence. Longtime overseer Edmund Bacon said Randolph would do "the most strange and laughable things." [67]

Bacon remembered:

> Once going with him to Edgehill, his plantation, to look after the hands that were at work in the harvest field, cutting and putting up the wheat. He looked at the shocks, and a good many of them were not put up to suit him. He was riding Dromedary. Suddenly he dashed away and rode him right through a large number of the shocks, scattering them in all directions. We then rode on to where the overseer was engaged with the hands. After getting through with all his business with the overseer, as he was leaving he told him he thought the old bull must have been in the lot; he had seen a good many shocks torn down and scattered about as he came along. The overseer looked at me and laughed. He understood the matter perfectly. [68]

Underlining Randolph's eccentricities, Bacon went on, saying, "He would do strange things with that horse [Dromedary]. They were just suited to each other. I have often seen him take hold of his tail and run him up the mountain as hard as he could go." [69]

Another anecdote from Bacon was about Randolph's riding stamina: "Governor Randolph was a very hard rider. It was a very common thing with him when he was governor to start from Richmond after supper and ride Dromedary home by daylight next morning." Jefferson's biographer Randall said that Randolph's horses "fared as he fared, and they apt to look as he looked, gaunt and rough." Randall said that one of Randolph's best-remembered horses was Camel, "so called for withers which rose before the saddle like a camel's hump. To ride this powerful animal eighty miles a day, when the road were deep and sticky with mud—and then at nightfall, to take the Rivanna at full bank to save riding round by the bridge—were no uncommon feats with him." During his governorship, Randolph also served as the vice-president of the Richmond Jockey Club. [70]

The New York Times recorded an incident when Randolph was (mistakenly) arrested as a horse thief. (see p. 47)

Even his death, according to his family, involved "riding on horseback near nightfall, on a wet cold day." The story goes that the gallant Governor Randolph overtook an old man, without a coat and apparently suffering from the cold. "They were remote from any dwelling. Randolph, unsolicited, unbuckled his cloak, threw it on the old man, and rode on. He had a number

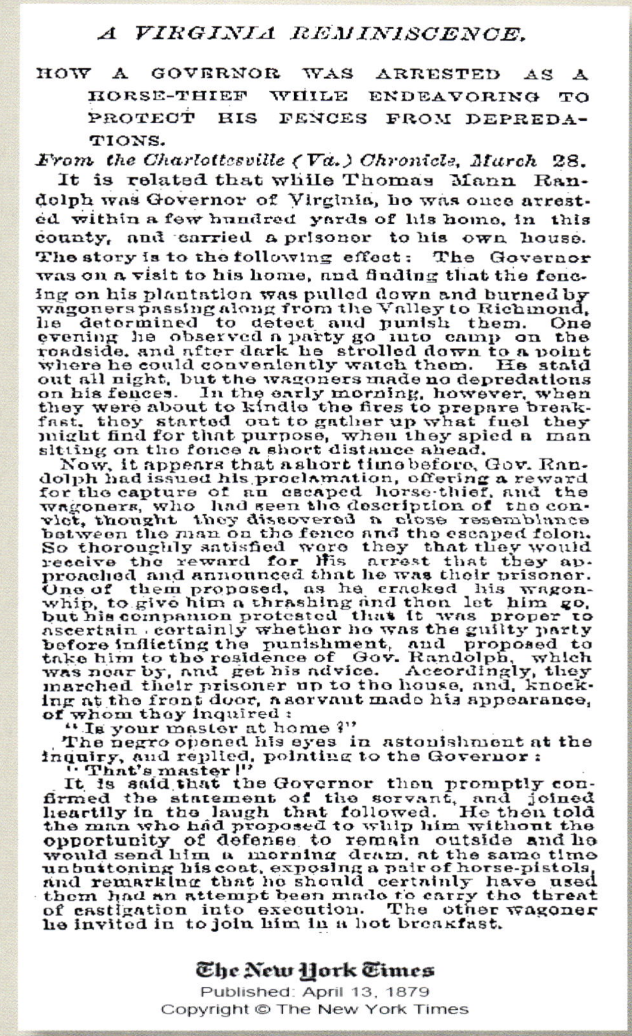

A VIRGINIA REMINISCENCE.

HOW A GOVERNOR WAS ARRESTED AS A HORSE-THIEF WHILE ENDEAVORING TO PROTECT HIS FENCES FROM DEPREDATIONS.

From the Charlottesville (Va.) Chronicle, March 28.

It is related that while Thomas Mann Randolph was Governor of Virginia, he was once arrested within a few hundred yards of his home, in this county, and carried a prisoner to his own house. The story is to the following effect: The Governor was on a visit to his home, and finding that the fencing on his plantation was pulled down and burned by wagoners passing along from the Valley to Richmond, he determined to detect and punish them. One evening he observed a party go into camp on the roadside, and after dark he strolled down to a point where he could conveniently watch them. He staid out all night, but the wagoners made no depredations on his fences. In the early morning, however, when they were about to kindle the fires to prepare breakfast, they started out to gather up what fuel they might find for that purpose, when they spied a man sitting on the fence a short distance ahead.

Now, it appears that a short time before, Gov. Randolph had issued his proclamation, offering a reward for the capture of an escaped horse-thief, and the wagoners, who had seen the description of the convict, thought they discovered a close resemblance between the man on the fence and the escaped felon. So thoroughly satisfied were they that they would receive the reward for his arrest that they approached and announced that he was their prisoner. One of them proposed, as he cracked his wagon-whip, to give him a thrashing and then let him go, but his companion protested that it was proper to ascertain certainly whether he was the guilty party before inflicting the punishment, and proposed to take him to the residence of Gov. Randolph, which was near by, and get his advice. Accordingly, they marched their prisoner up to the house, and, knocking at the front door, a servant made his appearance, of whom they inquired:

"Is your master at home?"

The negro opened his eyes in astonishment at the inquiry, and replied, pointing to the Governor:

"That's master!"

It is said that the Governor then promptly confirmed the statement of the servant, and joined heartily in the laugh that followed. He then told the man who had proposed to whip him without the opportunity of defense to remain outside and he would send him a morning dram, at the same time unbuttoning his coat, exposing a pair of horse-pistols, and remarking that he should certainly have used them had an attempt been made to carry the threat of castigation into execution. The other wagoner he invited in to join him in a hot breakfast.

The New York Times

Published: April 13, 1879

A Virginia Reminiscence — How a Governor was arrested as a horse-thief while endeavoring to protect his fences from depredations.[1]

It is related that while Thomas Mann Randolph was Governor of Virginia, he was once arrested within a few hundred yards of his home, in this county, and carried a prisoner to his own house. The story is told to the following effect:

The Governor was on a visit to his home, and finding that the fencing on his plantation was pulled down and burned by wagoners passing along from the Valley to Richmond, he determined to detect and punish them. One evening he observed a party go into camp on the roadside, and after dark he strolled down to a point where he could conveniently watch them. He staid out all night, but the wagoners made no depredations on his fences. In the early morning, however, when they were about to kindle the fires to prepare breakfast, they started out to gather up what fuel they might find for that purpose, when they spied a man sitting on the fence a short distance ahead.

Now, it appears that a short time before, Gov. Randolph had issued his proclamation, offering a reward for the capture of an escaped horse-thief, and the wagoners, who had seen the description of the convict, thought they discovered a close resemblance between the man on the fence and the escaped felon. So thoroughly satisfied were they that they would receive the reward for his arrest that they approached and announced that he was their prisoner. One of them proposed, as he cracked his wagon-whip, to give him a thrashing and then let him go, but his companion protested that it was proper to ascertain certainly whether he was the guilty party before inflicting the punishment, and proposed to take him to the residence of Gov. Randolph, which was near by, and get his advice. Accordingly, they marched their prisoner up to the house, and, knocking at the front door, a servant made his appearance, of whom they inquired:

"Is your master at home?"

The negro opened his eyes in astonishment at the inquiry, and replied, pointing to the Governor:

"That's master!"

It is said that the Governor then promptly confirmed the statement of the servant, and joined heartily in the laugh that followed. He then told the man who had proposed to whip him without the opportunity of defense to remain outside and he would send him a morning dram, at the same time unbuttoning his coat, exposing a pair of horse-pistols, and remarking that he should certainly have used them had an attempt been made to carry the threat of castigation into execution. The other wagoner he invited in to join him in a hot breakfast.

(Source: New York Times, April 13, 1879, copied from the Charlottesville (Va.) Chronicle, March 28, [1879].)

of miles to go, and the exposure proved fatal to him." [71]

During his lifetime, Thomas Mann Randolph Jr. continued his family's promotion of blooded horses. His farm, Edgehill, was stocked with many riding horses (and mules). He often bought and traded horses for Thomas Jefferson. Jefferson gave Randolph his horse Tarquin, a highly bred ex-racehorse, after Jefferson retired the horse back to Monticello from Philadelphia, where Jefferson was serving as secretary of state. Pleased that Randolph was delighted with Tarquin, Jefferson refused to take any money as compensation for the horse. Randolph also procured a horse for Jefferson's younger daughter, thirteen-year-old Maria, when she was learning to ride at Monticello. This horse, a mare, was also a blood horse from a racing lineage. It is clear that Randolph moved in breeding circles. [72]

Thomas Mann Randolph Jr. is intimately associated with the founding stallion of one breed, the American Saddlebred. Although the horse, Hiatoga, was brought to Virginia in 1798 by Thomas Mann Randolph's brother, William Randolph of Cumberland County, on the south side of the James River, the horse later stood at stud at Thomas Mann Randolph's Edgehill, in Albemarle County, between 1799 and 1803. [Fig. 2-19] An ad in the Richmond paper *Virginia Argus* described Hiatoga as a Chickasaw stallion. However, equine historian Fairfax Harrison describes Hiatoga as "pure Andalusian blood." Andalusian blood implies Spanish ancestry; Harrison says the horse was derived from west Florida (still in Spanish hands). Indians (the Chickasaw) were the brokers of the horses obtained from the Spanish and sold to the Americans. Hiatoga is described as 15 hands high (quite tall for a Chickasaw), with a lofty carriage and remarkable for his unusual chestnut roan coat. He was a gaited horse and natural pacer, "a fast racker and to ride after foxes." In 1803 Hiatoga was taken to Kentucky by the Rev. B. Bennett. Hiatoga's marvelous gaits were bequeathed to five generations of offspring, and particularly favored by Methodist circuit riders. Hiatoga died in Kentucky in 1814. Hiatoga's offspring may also have contributed to the Standardbred (harness racing) breed. [73]

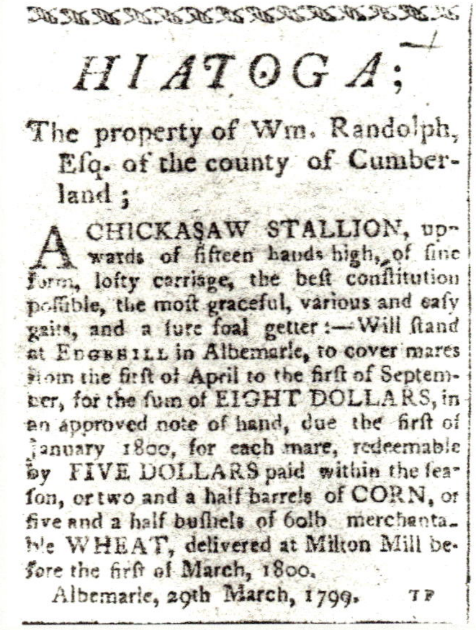

HIATOGA;

The property of Wm. Randolph, Efq. of the county of Cumberland;

A CHICKASAW STALLION, upwards of fifteen hands high, of fine form, lofty carriage, the beft conftitution poffible, the moft graceful, various and eafy gaits, and a fure foal getter:—Will ftand at EDGEHILL in Albemarle, to cover mares from the firft of April to the firft of September, for the fum of EIGHT DOLLARS, in an approved note of hand, due the firft of January 1800, for each mare, redeemable by FIVE DOLLARS paid within the feafon, or two and a half barrels of CORN, or five and a half bufhels of 60lb merchantable WHEAT, delivered at Milton Mill before the firft of March, 1800.

Albemarle, 29th March, 1799. TF

Fig. 2-19 A stud advertisement for Randolph's horse Hiatoga appeared in the May 24, 1799, issue of the Richmond newspaper *Argus*, p. 1

John Wayles Eppes (1773–1823): Jefferson's second son-in-law, John Wayles Eppes, was also a planter and politician. Eppes and his wife, Maria, Jefferson's younger daughter, visited Monticello often, but despite Jefferson's entreaties, the couple did not live near Monticello like the Randolphs did.

John Wayles Eppes [Fig. 2-20] was born in the heart of an old Virginia family at Eppington in Chesterfield County, Virginia, near Petersburg, south of the James River. His mother, Elizabeth Wayles, was a half-sister of Jefferson's wife, Martha. He was the youngest and only son of six children. Eppes attended college and studied law for several years in Philadelphia and graduated from Hampden-Sydney College in Virginia. Eppes began practicing law in Richmond a few years before he married his cousin Maria Jefferson in 1797, at Monticello. John and Maria spent much of their early married life at Eppington [Fig. 2-21] and at his maternal grandfather's estate, called The

Fig. 2-20 Saint-Mémin, Charles Balthazar Julien Fevret de, portrait of John Wayles Eppes, 1805

Forest. Their only surviving child, Francis Wayles Eppes, was born in 1801. By this time, Eppes had followed his father-in-law into politics. [74]

He served first in the Virginia House of Delegates (1801–1803), and then in 1803, under the Jefferson presidency, became a US congressman and served there for five terms. While in Washington, he lived in the White House with his father-in-law, Jefferson. His wife, Maria, fragile like her mother, died at Monticello two months after giving birth to her third child, in 1804. Eppes continued in Washington as a strong supporter of Jefferson policies, but after his wife's death, he moved his residence to an estate, Millbrook, in Buckingham County. Eppes remarried in 1809 and had more children with his second wife, Martha Jones. Jefferson became very protective and interested in his young grandson Francis's welfare and education and invited him to spend time often at Monticello. Eppes continued in Congress until he was elected to the US Senate in 1814. He resigned due to ill health in 1819 and returned to Millbrook. Despite his political career and its interruptions to agriculture, he ran a successful plantation. Eppes died in 1823, three years before Jefferson. [75]

Eppington, near Petersburg, was in the old racehorse region of Southside Virginia. Some claimed that the Newmarket Jockey Club course, one mile east of Petersburg in Prince George County, was "the most celebrated pleasure ground in the United States in the period between the Revolution and the War between the States." Racing and horse breeding both had long histories in this region, as it did in the Eppes family. A quarter race was held at Colonel Eppes's store at Bermuda Hundred in 1678. And both John Wayles Eppes's father (Colonel Francis Eppes) and grandfather (Colonel John Eppes) had been turfmen and avid importers of blooded horses. In this region, even during the Revolution, the races (and the attendant balls) continued. After the Revolution, Petersburg became the center of turf activities, with a week of racing in May and a week again in October. John Wayles Eppes was known as "a noted turfman as well as public man." In fact, Eppes's second wife, Martha Burke Jones, was a daughter of Willie Jones, from Halifax, North Carolina, a politician and planter and the most successful of all quarter-horse racers. Jones was notorious for the way he was able to get long odds on his winning horses. Jones would have been a ubiquitous figure at races around Petersburg and Southside Virginia. [76]

Fig. 2-21 Eppington, Chesterfield County, Virginia, home of the Eppes family. Built 1770-1790.

As with his other son-in-law, Thomas Mann Randolph, Jefferson wove himself closer to John Wayles Eppes, especially after Maria died, through horses. Eppes obtained Darlington (1796) and Jacobin (1805), two riding horses, for Jefferson. Eppes also bought Diomede through his brother-in-law Richard Thweatt in 1809, in Chesterfield. This horse was used as a carriage horse by Jefferson and replaced another horse called Diomede, bought from a Joseph Eggleston in Amelia County in 1808; it had taken the place of yet another horse, the aging Castor. Eppes had also obtained this first Diomede for Jefferson, and perhaps felt responsible for an unfortunate buy, because he assured his father-in-law that the second Diomede was "greatly superior" to Eggleston's Diomede. [77]

It was also Eppes who found Jefferson his most expensive horses. While waiting for the results of the presidential election of 1800, Jefferson had told Eppes to be on the lookout for carriage horses for Jefferson's newly commissioned ($1,200) chariot. Eppes had been trying to reach a deal on four horses for many months. He was in Petersburg at the end of April 1801 just before racing season and finally negotiated the sale of four fine, highly bred carriage horses (and Jefferson's only horses from Southside Virginia). Their owners, Mr. Haxall, Mr. Bell, and Dr. Shore, were such enterprising turfmen that they didn't need the status of selling to the president and had asked such high prices for their horses that it made the new president wince. With each of the sales, there was much correspondence between Eppes and his father-in-law. Jefferson ended up paying the scandalous price of $1,600 for the four. Finally, several months after receiving the horses, Jefferson wrote his son-in-law that he was "perfectly satisfied with them all." [78]

In racing circles, John Wayles Eppes was well known for

his own breeding program at Eppington. In this arena, his father-in-law was able to return a favor to Eppes, who many times had found horses for Jefferson to buy. In 1805, a Tunisian envoy presented to President Jefferson three horses (a stallion and two mares) from the stud of the Bei of Tunis (see Chapter 4 for more on these horses). In 1806, Eppes, a member of Congress at the time, ended up with one of the three horses—an African Barb mare, later known as Jefferson's Barb Mare. She eventually produced two foundational mares for the American Thoroughbred in 1805 and 1807.

Paying For Horses: Credit and Debt

All of the men in the vignettes above were intimate colleagues, friends, or family with Thomas Jefferson. They were all brother equestrians and admirers of fine high-bred horses. They reinforced their relationships by buying and selling horses to each other. Buying and selling horses in eighteenth-century and early-nineteenth-century Virginia gives insight into the social aspects of the plantation economy. Cash, much less full price, rarely directly passed hands in a horse transaction between planters. Rather, hands were shaken, agreements were recorded in account books, money was owed, payments postponed, later bonds were given, estates were credited, notes were passed, and debts were accumulated. Interest was not charged, years might go by, other horses were sold back, trades were made, and debts were voided or eventually paid off. Historian T. H. Breen has written on the role of credit and debt in his chapter "Mentality of the Great Tidewater Planters on the Eve of Revolution" in a book titled Tobacco Culture (1985). For the Tidewater planter society of eighteenth-century Virginia, credit and debt were a "form of communication," and owing money was a way of establishing and maintaining enduring social relations. Yet the old colonial elite was soon to be challenged in post-Revolutionary Virginia by a new class of market-minded capitalists. [79]

In their own Virginia world of Tidewater planters, these men competed not only for money and income but also, and more importantly, for honor, status, and social reputation. In eighteenth-century Virginia, honor was bestowed by one's social equals, and the values of honesty, generosity, hospitality, loyalty, and the pretense of not caring about practical economic matters produced honor and reputation. Money, naturally, was a measure of self, and a means of obtaining a high standard of living, which was the symbol of honor and pride. Without a doubt, the elite valued independence and autonomy as the ideal social conditions and planter masculine identity. But the external trappings of independence and social status—the great houses, the blooded horses, the sumptuous carriages, and other finery—cost money. Yet as symbols of status, these things seemed more like necessities than luxuries. Rather than pay for these luxuries with cash (which they may not have had on hand), the landed gentry extended each other credit and accumulated long-term debt. [80]

Moreover, extending credit and owing debts were two sides of the same coin in a local agrarian community. Planters were honor bound to repay debts, especially to their social equals, but time was not of essence. Debt over time merely kept the individuals mentally woven together and provided important personal links. "Indeed, beyond the members of one's own immediate family, credit offered a recognized means of structuring social relationships within the white community. Almost all the colony's freemen were involved in this vast, largely informal network of giving and receiving credit." Credit was considered a personal favor. Locally commercial relationships were personal relationships. [81]

Colonial Virginia was not a cash economy. Colonial Virginia literally did not have circulating money, and so the local economy ran on informal credit networks. There were no banks in the colonies, so colonists depended on the sale of their crops (once a year), or even the exchange of their crops, for goods. When crops failed or prices nosedived, debts were carried over for years. However, "cooperation and competition were two sides of the same economic culture." Since the community was tied together and mutually dependent, it was in no one's interest to call in debts precipitously. Better to bask in the web of relationships created by the debt culture, or as one historian called it, "a mesh of continuing loyalties." Part of the "code of gentlemen's credit" was a "willingness to help a deserving planter restore his personal honor … even if that act placed one's own finances in jeopardy." This was an expression of friendship in this agrarian economy. But in order to gain honor, and show wealth, planters often plunged themselves deeper in debt. On the eve of the war in 1776, many of Virginia's great planters, fifty-five members of the House of Burgesses, as well as George Washington and Thomas Jefferson, had large debts. [82]

Of course, the early Virginia tobacco-planter elites wanted

to maximize their incomes (not just their honor). Yet they were not quite yet agricultural capitalists on a par with the emerging British merchants with whom they were ultimately engaged in a global exchange. Virginians had convinced themselves that credit was an advance (to bridge the gap until receipt for payment of a tobacco crop). The Virginians projected their local values and mental categories onto their global commercial transactions, and were confused when right before the Revolutionary War in the 1760s and 1770s, they came out on the losing end as their debts were called in, their commercial "friendships" betrayed, and their (financial) independence lost. "They were dishonored." [83]

It is very difficult to follow the money trail of the horses that Thomas Jefferson bought from and sold to his friends, family, and acquaintances. This is because although prices were recorded in his account books, money may not have changed hands. Swift payment was not paramount. Long-term relationships were.

Sometimes Jefferson obtained horses in a barter situation. On December 27, 1813, Jefferson jotted down in his account book, "Bartered a gold watch with Sam Carr for a horse, got by Nosley, a red bay, 2 white hind feet, 6 years old." [84]

At times the price was bartered in produce. In January 1775, Jefferson bought from his friend John Walker the horse Le Fleur, for £35, "to be paid in wheat." However, we note in Jefferson's account book that the wheat did not yet exist. Jefferson went on to stipulate that the horse was to be paid for in wheat "in Richmond at the current price in April 1776" (one year later). However, Jefferson further protected himself (and inadvertently revealed Walker's obvious overriding concern for their friendship rather than his payment) by writing "if the stoppage of ports or other accident wheat does not sell tolerably, I am at liberty to withhold payment till it does only allowing 5 bushels percent ann. Interest from that time." [85]

Occasionally the price was paid in labor. For example, in 1799 Jefferson sold the horse Darlington to Richard Richardson, a Monticello overseer, for £60. The £60 was due in two installments of work: "to wit £36 this year and £25 next year." Early in his career as a lawyer, Jefferson himself had been paid in horses for legal work he had done over a period of several years in the Shenandoah Valley. His fee of £55 was paid by his two clients, by a horse of William Waterson's, worth £20, in September 1769, and by a horse of John Madison's, worth £35, in January 1770. [86]

Direct exchanges also supposedly took place, but they were almost always qualified so as to achieve true equity. Boot (extra) was paid if the quality of the animals was not equal. For example, in March 1773, Jefferson sold the horse Cuthona to Colonel Thomas Mann Randolph Sr. for a mule plus £15 boot. An exchange with boot was very common, and Jefferson bought at least ten horses this way, including during his presidency his riding horse, Jacobin (in 1805). In 1774, Jefferson exchanged with John Hylton his black horse for a sorrel mare (later called Everallin). However, Hylton thought the mare was with foal by young Fearnought, and if this was so, Jefferson was going to pay £3 "for putting her to horse." In this case, Jefferson seemed to have gotten the better part of the deal. Two days after the sale, Hylton came back and requested more money "to boot between our horses" because he was dissatisfied with their first bargain. There is no record that Everallin had a foal in 1774, but two years later, in December of 1776, Jefferson paid off the £5 balance of the boot for Everallin to Hylton. In 1780 in Williamsburg, Jefferson exchanged his three-year-old roan colt with his much-admired friend and mentor, George Wythe, for Wythe's sorrel horse (Thor). Nevertheless, the owners were sensitive to possible differences in value and agreed, in this case, to have the horses valued by "Jerm. Baler" ("at the old prices") and to pay the difference. Moreover, Jefferson was to have his roan horse "broke & delivered next spring [1781] unless sooner called for." Jefferson also thought that his friend James Madison had undervalued a horse he was buying from him, and requested that Madison "have [the horse] valued." Madison answered by letter the very next day, saying he would do that, but at any rate, the horse should serve as credit, for the "necessary set off against advances," which Jefferson made for him in France. [87]

Sometimes a complicated exchange would take place. In September 1783, Jefferson "received a horse" called Raleigh from Colonel Randolph in exchange for two horses, the General and Alfred, plus the promise to make the colonel a phaeton (a kind of carriage). Jefferson noted down in his account book that he didn't need to "find cushions or linings for the wings, etc., nor harness" for the phaeton. Moreover, in this exchange, Jefferson was relieved of the bond that he still owed on another horse, Sprightly, a blooded horse that he had bought from Randolph the previous May for £75 (that bond had not been due until May

1784). Older horses would have been worth less than similar younger horses, so the cost of the phaeton must have made up the difference in the horses' ages. [88]

In one case we know of, Jefferson refused payment for a horse and gave a horse to his son-in-law as a gift. The horse in question was called Tarquin, which Jefferson had bought in 1790, when he was on his way to be secretary of state in New York. However, upon making his plans for his return to Monticello in 1793, Jefferson was reluctant to take the horse back there, saying that his front feet were too tender for the rocky Albemarle trails. Jefferson offered the horse back to the original owner, who declined. In the end, Jefferson decided to send Tarquin back to Monticello anyway. Son-in-law Thomas Randolph took over the care of Tarquin in Virginia and soon wrote Jefferson that the horse had "mended so much" that Randolph asked to buy him. Jefferson immediately answered Randolph, insisting that he keep the horse. Randolph again offered to pay for the horse, and Jefferson underlined a second time that the horse was a gift and told Randolph to make "the most of him whenever you have good opportunity." [89]

When buying a horse, Jefferson rarely, if ever, handed over the full price when he took possession of a horse from a seller. In fact, in ninety-two recorded instances in Jefferson's account books of an exchange or a transaction of a horse, there is only one unambiguous time when the horse was completely paid for on the very day it was bought. This was when Jefferson purchased a handsome seven-year-old bay horse, which he called Tecumseh, from David Isaacs in Charlottesville. Jefferson didn't pay in cash, of course, but drew a note on his account at Gibson and Jefferson (in Richmond) in favor of Isaacs for $125 on June 14, 1815, the day he recorded buying the horse. Jefferson noted, "paid in full for the sd. Horse." Jefferson probably paid Isaacs in full because Isaacs was of a different social class than Jefferson's friends and neighbors with whom he usually bought and sold horses. Isaacs was not a planter, nor did he belong to the Virginia elite. Rather he was a Jewish merchant and shopkeeper with a general store on west Main Street in Charlottesville, who lived with and raised a family with a free woman of color, Nancy Ann West. Jefferson kept running accounts at the store for goods and food stuffs. (Actually, it was at David Isaacs's store that the string was bought to begin measuring off the foundations of the buildings for the future University of Virginia.) Whatever the reason, this transaction with Isaacs was unique. [90]

In the vast majority of the cases, Jefferson negotiated a future date for payment, often explicitly dependent on the sale of his crops, and carefully recorded his obligations in his account book. Especially in the last twenty-five years of his life, Jefferson bought almost all of his horses on credit (rather than by barter or exchange). Quite often, Jefferson wrote in his account book, along with the description of the horse, the price agreed upon and when it was payable. For example, Jefferson bought Brimmer from Carter Braxton on October 3, 1790. As usual Jefferson describes the horse: "5 yrs old last spring, got by Brimmer, who was got by Eclipse." Jefferson then added, "Gave him my note 116.2/3 Doll., paiable [sic] at Philadelphia Dec. 31 or Richmond Jan.15." On January 12, 1791, Jefferson sent Carter a note from his bank, "remitted under cover of Dr. Currie." Three months, four months, six months, or a year were common future due dates. [91]

In the case of Tarquin, however, the original seller, William Fitzhugh of Chatham, a fellow member of the gentry himself pressed for cash, wrote Jefferson four months after having Tarquin delivered, requesting some immediate payment. Fitzhugh said he was anxious to know about Tarquin, "having never heard a Tittle respecting him," since Jefferson's letter confirming delivery.

> I must beg leave to request of you, when disengaged from more weighty Concerns, to inform me whether he has answered your Purpose. It is possible his lameness may have returned, and that he has not been equal to the Business, for which you intended him. If it shoud be so, I am still willing that you shoud dispose of him, on my Account, for any thing you may think him worth; but if on the contrary he has proved a good Horse, and you can, with the most perfect Conveniency to yourself, contrive me the seventy five Pounds, by some safe Conveyance, you will do me a singular Favour.—The loss of my tobacco and Corn last year, had thrown me so much in Arrears, that even a tolerable Crop of Wheat will not relieve me.

Credit had its advantages as well as disadvantages. [92]

When paying for a horse, Jefferson never recorded using cash. Virginia agrarian society at this time was not a cash economy. Usually Jefferson gave his bond (which was a promise of future payment), or he simply waited and then wrote a note (like a check) on his account at his commercial accountant company. Sometimes payment went through a third party. For instance, in 1815 Jefferson bought a mare for $60 from a man called Cobb. Jefferson "drew on Archib. Robertson (his accountant) in favor of Jer. A. Goodman to be paid to Cobb. [93]

Often Jefferson had to request an extension on his payment due date. John Hartwell Cocke's reaction to this request was typical. At first (in April) Jefferson asked Cocke to wait until his flour was sold (one month hence—May). Later (in August) he asked for more time because his flour had not sold. Cocke, like most men of his class, feigned disinterest in the money. Each time John Hartwell Cocke responded in the gracious and honorable way, as anyone would to a national icon and from whom there are benefits in being a creditor: "I am sorry that you deemed it necessary to trouble yourself upon the subject of payment for the Horse, the understanding between us & the course of events prevents my expecting the money at this time, and be assured Sir, that I wish you to consult your convenience entirely about it in future." As noted in Breen, "it was the creditor, not the borrower, who made excuses." [94]

In most cases, at least with his horses, Jefferson did record final payment for the horse he bought on credit, albeit two or even three years later. In other cases, Jefferson arrived at another deal with the buyer before the amount was due. For example, Jefferson would sell the buyer a horse for the same price as the one he had contracted, thereby obviating his debt (it is not clear if money ever changed hands in these cases). A case in point is when Jefferson sold a horse called Ryno to his brother, Randolph Jefferson, for £35 on February 19, 1777. Six months later, on August 31, 1777, Jefferson noted in his account book, "bot Oroonoke of R. Jefferson & pd for him in full £36." Another instance of this is January 1, 1815, when Jefferson gave Pleasant German a note for $100 for a horse (called Bedford), payable in a year on January 8, 1816. On April 15, 1815, Jefferson sold German a mare called Hyatilda for $100 and "received back my note for $100." [95]

Most of the time we can assume no interest was charged when Jefferson bought these horses on credit. Once in a while, however, potential interest is noted: On October 9, 1783, Jefferson bought a sorrel mare and colt for S. Carr's estate by giving his bond. Jefferson noted the price was for £40-10 "if pd. By 1st of June 1784. If not, £41-16." Interestingly, Jefferson's last overseer, Edmund Bacon, charged Jefferson interest on horses he sold him (for example, for Traveller, bought June 3, 1817, for $120 with interest "from the first day of this month"). Again, as in David Issacs's case, Bacon, a paid workman and yeoman farmer, was not of the same social class as Jefferson, and had no qualms about charging interest to Jefferson, to whom he lent money. [96]

With these examples, it is easy to see that with horseflesh in Jefferson's time, "buying" and "selling," "bartering" and "exchanging," "giving" and adjusting "boot," "credit" and "debt," "postponing payment" or "payment in full," "bonds" and "notes" were much more about social relationships than merely financial accounting. Horses bought became equated with people—neighbors, kin, sons-in-law, colleagues, mentors, and friends. Consequently, it is a misreading of the historical record to reduce "buying" and "selling" blood horses among eighteenth-century rural Virginia planters to mere market transactions. Blood horses were inalienable objects, and their carefully recorded pedigrees conflated many local ideas about class and other relationships of solidarity among the FFVs.

The Virginia planter elite lived in a local economy that collapsed the moral and the material; commercial relationships were personal relationships. In the honor culture of the Tidewater and Piedmont planters, the flow of credit and debt existed outside the capitalist market and could not be reduced to economic rationality or self-maximization. A sale where money was exchanged immediately voided the enduring bond created through credit and debt. Examples show that Jefferson only paid cash when buying from men below gentry status. Buying (and selling horses) through credit and debt was like a gift exchange because it led to a mutual interdependence over time between giver and receiver. So besides obtaining an animal (a condensed symbol of a class), by supposedly "buying" a horse, the Virginia gentleman entered into a long-term relationship with the animal's previous owner.

"Sara Pierce Vick on Horseback", ca. 1842, Watercolor and cut paper, mounted on board, by William Henry Brown. The Historic New Orleans Collection, New Orleans.

Chapter 3

Others Who Rode on the Mountain: Women, Workmen and Overseers, Enslaved Servants

Monticello was like a small village. In Jefferson's time, many people lived there besides him and his family. Actually, he defined his family as more than just his wife and children. In 1776, Jefferson put the "number of souls in my family" at 117, which included, besides his wife and daughters, paid overseers and their families, other hired workmen, and eighty-three enslaved people. In the social hierarchy at Monticello, the Jefferson women were ranked lower than the planter men, followed by white paid workmen (and their wives), and at the lowest status were the enslaved men and women.[1]

After his retirement from the presidency (1809), Jefferson's surviving daughter, Martha, installed herself at Monticello with her (ultimately) eleven children. As the children grew up, some of them brought spouses to live at Monticello with their grandfather. And guests were always plentiful, including annual guests like Jefferson's sister, who stayed for several weeks at a time. The other permanent residents, such as the white overseers and enslaved people, lived in small dwellings and cabins with gardens, and workshops scattered all around. Since horses provided the only means of transportation (besides on foot) and were used to work the farm, many people besides Jefferson and his gentry friends had relationships with horses. Like cars today, the quality and use of the horse varied with a person's social position (and gender). Each of these groups—women, workers, and slaves— was lower on the social hierarchy than the gentry men, but most people understood the equine hierarchy and how to use it to emphasize or to raise their own social status.[2]

Women

Women on the mountain had to deal with horses, too. In the second half of the eighteenth century, horses were the principal means of transportation and field labor, and so were everywhere in the landscape and familiar to men of all social classes. But in Virginia, riding for sport, foxhunting, and attendance at horse races were associated with culture of the landed gentry, and among the gentry were enjoyed by both men and women. In towns and cities, travel in elegant carriages was also a sign of social status for both men and women. In the countryside, many young white girls learned to mount and ride alongside their brothers (enslaved African-American women are not described as riders). Not all women rode as a form of exercise or pleasure, and many may not have felt the need—they could be transported as passengers in carriages and wagons, if necessary. Nevertheless, given that horses were ubiquitous, most women probably knew something about horse behavior and how to act around one. In Jefferson's correspondence with his family, he referred to his blood horses by their names, so he must have thought his daughters were familiar with the individual horses and knew one from the other.

We know that the Monticello women were often passengers in carriages because if not, they were house-bound to the plantation. When he traveled, Jefferson most often rode his horse, or, if he went by carriage, had a servant follow behind leading his riding horse. When Jefferson tired of riding in the vehicle, or when road conditions were treacherous, he often mounted his saddle horse and continued on without the carriage. Women, however, are never described as traveling by horseback. Rather, they and the children were packed into a chariot, as when the family moved to Williamsburg when Jefferson took over as governor, or when Martha and the children escaped and were sent off ahead of the governor in the carriage when Lieutenant Colonel Banastre Tarleton's British troops tried unsuccessfully to catch Jefferson unawares at Monticello in June of 1781.

In other social classes, women drove horses in chairs or gigs, and perhaps even wagons and carts. [Fig. 3-1] But we do not have any notice of the Jefferson women driving these vehicles themselves at Monticello. Rather, Jefferson women were escorted around the countryside in chairs, gigs, carriages, and wagons on errands or visits to friends and nearby family, usually driven by a Monticello enslaved coachman. When Jefferson invited daughter Martha to visit him in Washington in 1803, he offered her his three Chickasaw horses for the journey but warned that he had "no gentleman to send for your escort." She would have to find her own escort, but Jefferson still offered her advice: "I think by changing horses half way, you will come with more comfort." Another example of needing a driver occurred when one of Jefferson's granddaughters, in a letter to her husband, explained her desire to go visit the Madisons for Christmas, saying, "if brother Jeff can spare his horses & driver, we will borrow his carriage to go in." [3]

Jefferson's granddaughters, Ellen, Cornelia, and Virginia, accompanied him to Popular Forest in the landau a couple of times a year after 1814. In a letter that young Cornelia wrote to her sister, Virginia, she described an accident the group (Jefferson, Ellen, and Cornelia; Gil and Israel were riding postilion) had with the landau and the horses on a bridge. Note the intimacy with which she spoke of Bremo, one of the four carriage horses:

> Then came our first misfortune in going over a high bridge one of the wheel horses broke through & sank nearly half way in the hole we all got out as quick as we could & found that the bridge was entirely gone to decay & not only several of the logs but one of the sleepers had broken down & that we had been in great danger of going down carriage & horses & all, the horses were all loosened & poor Bremo pull'd out by main strength, for he seemed so overcome by fright that he was incapable of assisting himself & and lay quite passive & let them do what they would with him, he was hurt in no other way than being much skin'd and bruis'd that as it was we were oblig'd now to walk up a long tedious red hill and thus pursued our journey in the carriage without any other accident, over abominable roads.[4]

Horses were everyone's connection with the world outside the plantation. Two years after Jefferson's death, one of his granddaughters, Virginia Randolph Trist, was still living at Monticello with her children; her husband, Nicholas Trist, was away working in Washington, D.C. In a telling moment, Virginia wrote her husband that since she had no horses up on the mountain, she had no way of sending their daughter down to the University (in Charlottesville) to "get the opinion of Dr. Dunglison" about an ugly inflammation surrounding the girl's eye. Her husband, Nicholas, responded immediately, asking why they had no way of sending her, and reminding Virginia that he had meant for her to keep Eagle (Jefferson's last saddle horse) at Monticello, "as long as there was a prospect of wanting him." Eagle apparently had already been taken to grandson Jeff's farm, Edgehill, across the Rivanna from Monticello, for board. Without a horse, women and children on plantations were literally stranded in the countryside.[5]

Fig. 3-1 In Colonial Williamsburg, character interpreter Nicole Brown, portraying Nation Builder Anne Wager, drives a riding chair on Palace Green past the Robert Carter House.

Riding Sidesaddle: Women riders of the eighteenth century almost always used the sidesaddle when they rode horseback. Cultural norms dictated that it was unbecoming for a woman (especially in the upper social classes) to straddle a horse while riding. Furthermore, women's fashions demanded long skirts, which were impractical and immodest if riding astride. Thus, sidesaddle was considered the only appropriate form of female riding. [Fig. 3-2] If a woman dared to ride astride, it was almost always commented upon in the correspondence of the day.

In the eighteenth century, the sidesaddle had only one fixed pommel, around which the lady hooked her thigh. The saddle had to be wide enough to accommodate the lady's (usually) right thigh and buttocks. Most saddles were designed so that the lady sat with both legs to the near (left) side. The sidesaddle only had one stirrup, worn shorter than in a man's saddle. Despite having both legs on one side of the horse, the lady faced forward with spine centered and weight evenly distributed. In general, this was a very precarious perch. Jefferson always warned his daughters to be careful when riding and to ride an easily managed horse. [Fig. 3-3]

Fig. 3-2 Example of an eighteenth-century sidesaddle in the saddlery shop in Colonial Williamsburg

Not until 1830 was the leaping horn (a second lower pommel) added to the sidesaddle. This second leaping horn (which acted as kind of a brace for the left leg in the stirrup) had revolutionary repercussions for a woman rider's security and freedom of movement. [Fig. 3-4] Now she could stay on at a gallop and participate in field sports like foxhunting and jumping, all the while conforming to societal expectations. So perhaps some of Jefferson's granddaughters took advantage of the new innovation on the sidesaddle, but that would have been after Jefferson's time.

Fig. 3-3 Interpreter Katharine Pittman, portraying Martha Washington, rides sidesaddle in the Colonial Williamsburg historic area in 2016.

Women Riding on the Mountain: We know that the white women who lived at Monticello did ride horses, at least sometimes, and mostly for pleasure or exercise (rather than mere transportation). Young Virginia women were described as especially fearless and passionate riders by contemporary observers. One of Jefferson's early biographers, Henry S. Randall, included the following anecdote in his three-volume *Life of Thomas Jefferson* about the lively and confident Virginia girls on horseback. It is worth citing at length:

> A Virginia woman ... rides like anything else than a dumb-jockey, or a city miss fresh from the riding academy; nay, if the road be shady, or the greensward looks temptingly elastic and says (as everybody knows it does sometimes say): "Come take a run over me," the Virginia woman does not always find it in her heart to refuse the challenge; but down goes the riding- whip, and the next moment her blood mare, with straight thin neck, broad red nostril, and eye lit to flame, is skimming like a low flying bird over the ground.
>
> It is difficult for one whose eye is accustomed only to females brought up at the feet of the

Fig. 3-4 The second leaping horn improved stability for women riding sidesaddle, as depicted in Theodore H. Mead, *Horsemanship for Women* (New York: Harper and Brothers, 1887).

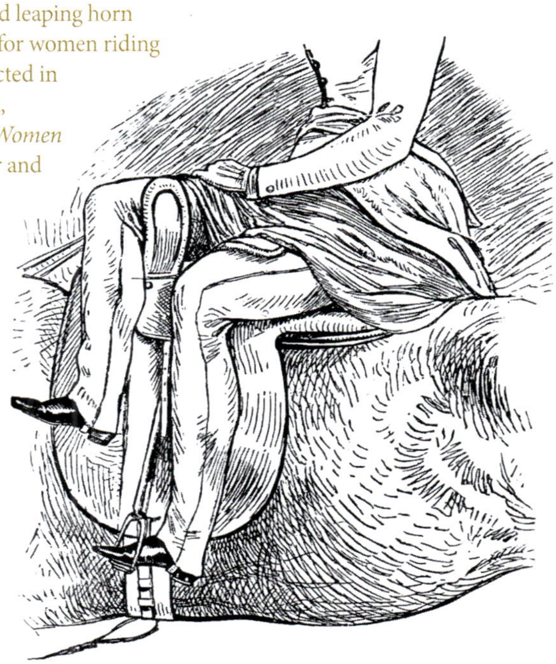

fashionable Fadladeens, to conceive the graceful and free movements of a highbred Virginia woman, when roused into full action, not in the ball room at Saratoga or Newport, but at home, with the turf of the Old Dominion under her feet, and the skies of the Old Dominion over her head. We once approached an old Virginia farm-house, with its owner, who had been for some days absent. A few hundred yards off, we suddenly stopped to gaze, for, at that moment, dashing round from the rear of the mansion, and darting like mad through the trees, came a troop of riders at full speed, all of them females but one. Sweeping round the house, they disappeared; but a circuit of a few moments again brought them in front, when, discovering us, they reined up for an instant; and then, affecting vast dismay, made a rush at a high carriage gate, on one side of the lawn, to escape. The foremost rider galloping past it almost without drawing rein, bent to one side, raised and dashed it open, and then, wheeling his horse, darted through with another rider, and went clattering down a rocky path, as the gate, made to swing shut, closed with a bang. Two more performed the same feat, and the last of the train made an effort to shoot through at the same time. This was a girl of perhaps a dozen years old, and she was mounted on by far the largest horse in the party. "There goes my horse whom I bade nobody ride!" exclaimed our companion, mock gravity very scantily hiding his expression of good-natured amusement. But the last rider was too late. The gate was shutting on her, and it appeared that it must inevitably catch her powerful horse between its head and the shutting-post. We held our breath. But a sharp, prompt, fearless pull on the reins of the heavy curb-bit suddenly arrested the horse, and it was done with such vigor and such a will, that the great animal threw his forefeet high in the air, and the gate *seemed* to swing under the uplifted hoofs, as it closed. In another moment, it was seized by the little rider, thrown open, and away she went with whip flying, to overtake her companions. We thought of the wild, fearless, graceful riders of the western plains, and wondered whether the blood of Pocahontas, which flowed in the veins of the merry party, had anything to do with the matter!

A day or two afterwards, we were walking with our friend in the neighboring highway. He picked up a horseshoe, gazed at it a moment curiously, and ejaculated with a smile: "I thought as much;" and then turning to us remarked. "That's ____'s." (naming a son): "I know his mark. Whenever the roads are passable, he tucks up his coat-tails, and then he'll take the hindmost until he throws at least two shoes! I believe," he continued "there must be something in our climate to make hard riders; our boys and girls can never rest with trotting a horse for a mile!" [6]

The highbred Virginia young woman, whip in hand, rode her blood mare, skimming like a bird over the ground, like "the wild, fearless, graceful riders of the western plains" in the above quotation. She mastered her horse with confidence and strength, and packs of young girls would race across the countryside with merry glee. Even riding her father's own horse, she more than kept up with her brothers.

If the mistress of the house was a known horsewoman, her skills were often noted by her contemporaries (just as her husband's were if his skills were out of the ordinary). It is said that Mrs. Washington shared George Washington's interest in riding and believed in riding as a form of exercise. Currently at Mount Vernon, a plaque testifies to Martha Washington's delight in riding with her husband, as well as her passion for participating in some of his foxhunts.

Wife, Martha (Wayles) Skelton Jefferson (1748–1782): Few descriptions of Martha exist, and they are summarized in Randall's 1857 *Life of Thomas Jefferson*, where she is described as a good dancer, a good harpsichord player, and a good rider. She "walked, rode, and danced, with admirable grace and spirit." Martha was the daughter of John Wayles, a plantation owner who made his home at The Forest in Charles City County near the James River. Wayles emigrated from England and outlived three wives. Martha was the youngest child of his first wife. By all accounts, she was a distinguished beauty and had "solid merit." Randall summarizes, "In person, she was a little above medium height, slightly but exquisitely formed. Her complexion was brilliant—her large expressive eyes of the richest shade of hazel—her luxuriant hair of the finest tinge of auburn ... sung, and played the spinet and harpsichord (the musical instruments of the Virginia ladies of that day) with uncommon skill."[7]

When Thomas met her, Martha had recently been widowed. She had married at eighteen, typical at the time, a young man named Bathurst Skelton, but he died only two years later. They had had a son, and Martha and the boy were living with her father's family at The Forest when Jefferson began courting her two years after Skelton's death. According to family lore, Thomas and Martha sang and played music together as he charmed her into becoming his wife, on January 1, 1772. Given Jefferson's reputation as a centaur and horseman at the time (during his law-reading days in Williamsburg) and her reputation as skillful rider, they may also have spent time courting on horseback.[8]

Jefferson's married life lasted only ten years before he, himself, was left a widower (in 1782). He always professed to have been madly happy and content with Martha. She was his partner in his domestic pursuits and in managing the farms. Most likely, since she was known as a fine rider, she accompanied Thomas as he rode around their properties.

Fig. 3-5 Thomas Sully, "Martha Jefferson Randolph," Thomas Jefferson's eldest daughter, 1836

Daughter, Martha (Jefferson) Randolph (1772-1836): Martha was Thomas and Martha's oldest child and the only one that accompanied him to the end of his life. Jefferson called her "the cherished companion of my early life, and nurse of my old age." Martha became Jefferson's companion when she was about ten years old, upon her mother's death in September 1782. Martha was the witness to Jefferson's grief; she attended to her father for months, "never a moment from his side," both in his room, and, "when at last he left his room," as he rambled over the mountains and through the woods on horseback in his heartache over his wife's death. Martha affirmed, "In those melancholy rambles, I was his constant companion."[9]

Thus, as a girl Martha rode horseback with her father. In Paris, there was probably little opportunity to ride horseback, although Patsy (her nickname) may have accompanied her father sometimes on his rides through the Bois de Boulogne when she was home from the convent school. Early in her marriage to Thomas Mann Randolph, future congressman and future Virginia governor, there is another allusion to Patsy riding. Randolph wrote his father-in-law in Philadelphia about a horse he was exchanging with Jefferson for another, and he implied that Patsy had ridden this very calm horse: "He is very gentle; enough so for Patsy to ride him without the least apprehension. We have driven him frequently in the chariot." Martha was only twenty-one at the time, and she probably continued riding through her young motherhood. When she was thirty-two, Jefferson proposed to "mount horseback" with her when he returns (from Washington) to Monticello for a visit. But later in life, after Martha became the mother of eleven children, we find little evidence that she continued using saddle horses. Carriages became her main mode of travel.[10] [Fig. 3-5]

Daughter, Mary (Jefferson) Eppes (1778-1804): Mary, called Polly as a child, was Jefferson's younger daughter and the second of the six children who survived infancy. Maria, as she was called after her years in France, learned to ride when she was about thirteen years old. Home from her years in Paris, she was living at Monticello at the time with her sister, Patsy, and Patsy's husband, Thomas Mann Randolph, who were overseeing work at Monticello.

Excitedly, Maria wrote her father, who was in Philadelphia as secretary of state, about her new horse, My Heart: "Mr. Randolph has bought a horse called my heart and a saddle for me to ride out on, also a pretty whip." There followed an exchange of letters between father and young daughter. As referred to above, Jefferson quickly responded: "My Dear Maria ... I am glad you are to learn to ride, but I hope your horse is very gentle, and that you will never be venturesome. A lady should never ride a horse which she might not safely ride without a bridle." "Bridle" here refers to the stronger curb bit; Jefferson wanted her to ride a horse that was easy to control and that could be ridden with just a snaffle bit. It's interesting to note that in the description above of the young Virginia girls on horseback, the fearless twelve-year-old rider "gave a pull on the reins of the heavy curb-bit suddenly" to stop her horse from charging the gate! One wonders if Jefferson the absent father knew about the reality of plantation girls.[11]

A few weeks later, Maria wrote her father: "I have began [sic] to learn botany and arithmetic with Mr. Randolph. The mare that he bought me is come. She is very pretty and is sister to brimmer. She can only trot and canter." This letter has three kernels of information. Brimmer was one of Jefferson's carriage horses in Philadelphia. A high-bred blood horse, Brimmer was bought from Carter Braxton of Richmond. Maria's mentioning that her new horse, that she called My Heart, was a "sister" to "brimmer" indicates the thirteen-year-old's understanding of horse pedigrees and horse relationships. Maria was aware of her father's horses by name and of their relationships with her horse. Furthermore, Maria told her father that her new mare could only "trot and canter." In other words, My Heart did not pace or rack, gaits that would be much more comfortable for a young girl riding sidesaddle than the trot or canter. Finally, My Heart is a mare, a female. In Jefferson's world, men rode horses (stallions); women rode mares. [12]

Although praised by all who knew her as quite beautiful, Maria was a very small and fragile woman, like her mother had been. Childbirth was especially difficult for her and recuperating to good health took a long while. In February 1804, Maria gave birth to her third child, but by March she remained gravely ill. President Jefferson planned to go home to see her, and wrote her sister, Patsy, "Tell my dear Maria to be of good chear [*sic*], and be ready to mount on horseback with us." After an illness Jefferson, himself, was always anxious to get back "on my horse, to me the most sovereign of all Doctors," so he probably thought it would be good for Maria to get out in the open air on a horse for a pleasant ride with her sister and father. Maria never had the chance for a last ride with her father. She died in April of 1804 from complications of childbirth. [13]

Randolph Granddaughters: After Jefferson ended his presidency and retired to Monticello in March of 1809, his daughter Martha Randolph left her home, Edgehill, across the river and took up residency on the mountaintop with her brood of children, where she effectively became the hostess of Monticello and caretaker of her father. Most of her eleven children grew up and three were born at Monticello; they were all intimates of their grandfather. Visitors often commented on his close relationship with his grandchildren and how he played vigorously with them outside. After Jefferson's death, several of his grandchildren penned memoirs about their grandfather and their lives at Monticello. The grandchildren are the sources of many observations about Jefferson's relationship with his horses. Jefferson took great interest in his namesake, Thomas Jefferson Randolph (known as Jeff) (1792–1875), as well as his Eppes grandson, Francis (1801–1881), but he was also close to several of the older granddaughters. Since both their father, Thomas Mann Randolph, and their grandfather, Thomas Jefferson, were avid horsemen, it is not surprising to find that, at least in their youth, these young country women, too, spent time on horses riding for pleasure. [14]

Anne Cary Randolph (1791-1826): Anne was Jefferson's oldest granddaughter; she became a fellow gardener with her grandfather. [Fig. 3-6] When he was in Washington as president, Jefferson counted on Anne to tell him what was happening in his garden. As she was living with her parents at Edgehill at the time, Jefferson would send her over to Monticello three miles away to check on things, which meant that she had to ride a horse or a mule. For example, one letter from Jefferson, when Anne was only twelve, says, "The figs also have been hurt? You must mount Midas and ride over to Monticello to inform yourself or collect the information from good authority and let me have it by next post." Midas (referring to the king with the ears of an ass) was probably a mule. Five years later Anne wrote her grandfather on the same topic and task, explaining why she couldn't get over to Monticello: "I am very anxious to go to Monticello to see how the flowers come on but Papa has not a horse that can be ridden by a lady with safety." Recall Jefferson's admonition to his own Maria, when she was a child, to never ride a horse that couldn't be safely ridden without a bridle (curb bit). The very fact that Anne referred to a horse being ridden by a "lady" is probably a clue reminding her grandfather that she was riding the horse sidesaddle. [15]

Fig. 3-6 William Coffee, "Ann Cary Randolph Bankhead" (1791–1826), Jefferson's eldest grandchild, c. 1818–1820

Ellen Wayles Randolph (1796–1876): Ellen was the second granddaughter, born while Jefferson was at Monticello during his first retirement (between being secretary of state under George Washington and being vice president under John Adams). Ellen, too, was an avid rider as a youth, and was encouraged in her habits by her equestrian grandfather. She wrote the following about his gift of a saddle to her:

> As child, girl and woman, I loved and honored him above all earthly beings. And well I might. From him seemed to flow all the pleasures of my life. To him I owed all the small blessings and joyful surprises of my childish and girlish years His nature was so eminently sympathetic, that with those he loved, he could enter into their feelings, anticipate their wishes, gratify their tastes, and surround them with an atmosphere of affection. I was fond of riding, and was rising above that childish simplicity when, provided I was mounted on a horse, I cared nothing for my equipments, and when an old saddle or broken bridle were matters of no moment. I was beginning to be fastidious, but I had never told my wishes. I was standing one bright day in the portico, when a man rode up to the door with a beautiful lady's saddle and bridle before him. My heart bounded. These coveted articles were deposited at my feet. My grandfather came out of his room to tell me they were mine.[16]

Fig. 3-7 Ellen Randolph (1796-1876), second granddaughter of Thomas Jefferson

Ellen, along with one of her other sisters, would accompany Jefferson on his thrice- yearly trips to his retreat at Poplar Forest (a three-day trip south of Monticello). [Fig. 3-7] There he continued his ritual of his daily solitary ride around the noon hour, but often the girls and he would take excursions into the countryside. One August in 1817 (Ellen would have been twenty-one years old), Jefferson decided to take Ellen and Cornelia to visit Natural Bridge, a geological phenomenon, an arch twenty stories high, carved from solid rock, located in the Shenandoah Valley, directly west over the Blue Ridge Mountains from Poplar Forest. The four days of tourism on horseback in the mountains required game and confident riders.[17]

Cornelia Jefferson Randolph (1799–1871): Cornelia, eighteen at the time, was the other participant in the excursion to Natural Bridge from Poplar Forest. She wrote her younger sister Virginia back home at Monticello about the journey on horseback. The three had started their adventure in the landau (guided by the enslaved postilions), but at one point they had to leave the landau at a woodsman's house at the foot of the mountains, unharness the horses from the carriage, and continue the rest of their journey on horseback.

> We left this place on horseback after having refreshed ourselves with ripe apples which they gave us & began to asend [sic] the mountain ... we rode three miles before we came to the top where we dined on cold bacon & chicken then descended three. Three more we had to go before we got to the place where we spent the night. The mountain was the wildest most romantic looking place I've ever seen the trees remarkably large & tall & no underwood so that you could see for a great distance around you.[18]

Cornelia learned mechanical drawing from her grandfather and helped him by making drawings of his plans for the University of Virginia. Cornelia seemed to be a natural teacher, helping the enslaved John Hemings learn to read. She, like her sisters, was a keen rider, who apparently was allowed to ride her grandfather's favorite saddle horse, The Eagle. This horse was described by everyone in the family as a spirited and fiery animal that was somewhat unpredictable. With everyone, including the elderly Jefferson, the horse often spooked and shied at deer and other animals. Cornelia's mother, Martha, wrote to sister Ellen in 1825, "Eagle started at a cow and placed Miss Cornelia on her feet in the road but she says took great care not to tread upon or jostle her and behaved well." Cornelia would have been a twenty-six-year-old woman at the time and was clearly not intimidated by her grandfather's horse. Cornelia never married; she lived with her brother, Jeff, and his family and eventually taught painting, drawing, and sculpture at a school for girls at Jeff's house at Edgehill.[19]

Virginia Jefferson Randolph (1801–1882): Virginia was the youngest of the granddaughters who were old enough to travel to Poplar Forest with their grandfather. Like Jefferson, Virginia had musical talent. She fell in love very young and had a long engagement with the son of a family friend, Nicholas Trist. They married at Monticello in 1824 and stayed there until 1828 (two years after Jefferson's death). While her husband worked in Washington, Virginia and her children lived at Tufton and then Edgehill with brother Jeff until the Trists moved to Havana, Cuba, when Nicholas was appointed consul there in 1833.

Virginia often wrote her husband about her pleasure rides in the company of friends, or alone. One September, six years after her grandfather had died, Virginia wrote about a ride in the crisp mountain air with her brother. She was already the mother of two children, a little boy and a little girl, and was then expecting her third child. Not only did she spend hours riding in the mountains and enjoying the views, but she also was riding old Eagle, Jefferson's hot-blooded stallion. Eagle must have tempered with age and lost his habit of "bounding and caracoling in the air," because no one would have risked a pregnant Virginia ending up "on the road" like Cornelia had a few years earlier:

> Yesterday I rode out on old Eagle, in company with Brother Jeff, [Fig. 3-8] and spent several hours very delightlyfully [*sic*] enjoying the beautiful views with which this neighborhood abounds, and the delightful autumnal weather which among the mountains is sweeter than anywhere else. My health is very much improved and my appetite like that of a visitor of the Sulphor [*sic*]Springs, I cannot help hoping that the beneficial effects of this journey on my own health, may make the expected a stronger, healthier baby than his brother or sister have been.
> The Dunglisons have sent me a message but are breaking a new horse to the carriage & have not been able to come yet.[20]

Fig. 3-8 Charles Vincent Peale, "Thomas Jefferson Randolph," 1808. Jeff (1792–1875) was the eldest grandson of Thomas Jefferson.

Another September, two years later, again Virginia enjoyed an autumn ride on Eagle: "Yesterday I rode old Eagle as far as Carlton. It was a sweet autumn day. I enjoyed the ride very much, notwithstanding the thousand tender and melancholic recollections it gave rise to in my mind."[21]

Guests

Guests arrived at Monticello on horseback, by private carriage, by hack from Charlottesville, and on foot. Supposedly, John H. Cocke often rode the twenty-four miles over from Bremo before breakfast on his horse Roebuck. Colonel Archibald Cary from Ampthill arrived in his carriage. The Madisons came by horseback and carriage. Visitors on their way to the springs in the summer would pass by Monticello in their coaches, so many that Wormley Hughes remembered the coaches being tied up under the tree off the coach rooms under the North Terrace.[22]

Overseer Bacon claimed they had room for thirty-six horses (perhaps including the stables down by his house), but that they at Monticello had need for only ten or so stalls at a time. The rest were often filled by guests' horses. Some guests were met by members of the Jefferson family and escorted by horse or by landau up the mountain (this is the case for General Lafayette, on his 1824 visit to Jefferson at Monticello). Other times, enslaved drivers were sent with a horse and gig to fetch family members or guests who lived at a distance.

The guests often arrived unannounced and stayed for weeks at a time. This resulted in a strain on the household budget, but the Southern code of hospitality to which Jefferson still adhered would not let anyone be turned away. We must remember that not only the guests but their horses had to be accommodated, cared for, and fed. Complaining about the economic burden on the plantation occasioned by visitors, Bacon said, "I finally told the servant who had charge of the stable to only give the visitors' horses half allowance." When Jefferson heard of this, he "countermanded [Bacon's] orders."[23]

Female Friends and Visitors: Most female friends and visitors arrived to Monticello by carriage. Martha wrote about dinner one evening when two carriages of women and children arrived, followed by four gentlemen on horses, totaling thirty-one people for dinner. Other friends may have arrived to a nearby postal station by public hack and then sent word to Monticello to come fetch them. In some family correspondence, there is an example of a servant and Old Eagle being dispatched to Everettsville to pick up a (rather stout) visitor, a Miss Elliott, who had to ride Eagle back to the house. Some friends and neighbors must have also ridden horseback for pleasure and to visit, like the white Monticello women did.[24]

As alluded to above, only when a woman rode astride do we find specific reference to her riding. One such rider was a temporary neighbor of the Jeffersons, the Baroness Riedesel. In the middle of the Revolutionary War in January 1779, Congress sent almost 4,000 captured British and Hessian troops as prisoners-of-war to an encampment near Charlottesville. The commanding officers were housed in socially more adequate surroundings at nearby plantations. General Riedesel, a Hessian baron, was offered the option to stay in Philip Mazzei's Colle, near Monticello, with his wife, the baroness. The Riedesels were in the area for only about a year, but the baroness made a deep impression on the gentry of Albemarle. They were frequent visitors to Monticello. Sarah Randolph, Jefferson's great-granddaughter, wrote, "The baroness,

Comments abound on the difficulties created by the guests and their retinue, including horses.

Edmund Bacon (overseer at Monticello): "After Mr. Jefferson returned from Washington, he was for years crowded with visitors, and they almost ate him out of house and home. They were there all times of the year; but about the middle of June the travel would commence from the lower part of the state to the Springs, and then there was a perfect throng of visitors. They traveled in their own carriages and came in gangs—the whole family with carriage and riding horses and servants; sometime three of four such gangs at a time. We had thirty-six stalls for horses, and used only about ten of them for the stock we kept there. Very often all of the rest were full, and I had to send horses off to another place. I have often sent a wagon load of hay up to the stable, and the next morning there would not be enough left to make a hen's nest." *(Bear, Jefferson at Monticello, 113–114.)*

Martha Jefferson Randolph to Ellen (Randolph) Coolidge: "This neighborhood is becoming a place of general resort during the summer season, many Parents who have sons at the University come to Charlottesville instead of going to the springs, and you know if a person has an acquaintance, particularly if there is the slightest degree of relationship it would be a slight to go to a public house if they can be accommodated at a private one at any possible inconvenience to the family. Poor Mr. Garrett has had William Bolling's family consisting of 6 white persons, 3 or 4 servants and 7 horses living upon him for a fortnight, although Mr. Garret is obliged to go back 4 generations and himself 3 before they come to the common stock." *(MJR to ERC, September 18, 1825, Jefferson Quotes & Family Letters.)*

Wormley (enslaved gardener and hostler at Monticello): "We once stood with him before the dilapidated pile of Monticello. The carriage-houses, three in number, were at the moment under our eye. Each would hold a four-horse coach.

"We inquired—'Wormley, how often were these filled in Mr. Jefferson's time?'

'Every night, sir, in summer, and we commonly had two or three carriages under that tree,' he said, pointing to a large tree.

'It took all hands to take care of your visitors?' we suggested.

'Yes, sir, and the whole farm to feed them,' was the concise and significant reply." (Randall, The Life of Thomas Jefferson, 3:332.)

Henry S. Randall, biographer: "The whole Monticello estate, so far as he had laborers to work it, did not in some years furnish a surplus of food sufficient for his guests, and their horses and servants. The general mode of traveling then in Virginia was on horseback; or by carriages drawn by at least two horses; and strangers who came from a distance, very generally took carriage from some Virginia town." *(Randall, The Life of Thomas Jefferson, 3:332.)*

James Madison (friend and neighbor): "When a friend commented on the circumstance that no less than nine strange horses were feeding in the stables at Montpelier, Madison remarked somewhat grimly that he was delighted with the society of the owners but could not confess to the same enthusiasm at the presence of their horses." *(Johnson, Jefferson and His Colleagues.)*

a warm-hearted, intelligent woman, from her immense stature, and her habit, was long remembered as a kind of wonder by the good and simple-hearted people of Albemarle." Others note that "tradition represents her as a cordial, warm hearted, highly intelligent and, withal, handsome woman, whose moderate pension for gossip, and not unfrequent blunders in talking and pronouncing English, only contributed to the amusingness of her lively conversation." But more than a handsome face and her height, the Baroness Riedesel was a striking figure because she rode horses astride instead of sidesaddle: "She rendered herself an object of wonder to the long-skirted and beplumed equestriennes of the neighborhood by riding in boots and astride, in what then was delicately called "the European fashion." Biographer Randall wrote, "Her Amazonian stature and practice of riding like a man, of riding on horseback *en cavalier* greatly astonished the Virginia natives." [25]

Other women in the neighborhood were also noted for riding astride. John Hartwell Cocke's second wife, Lucy, was known as an Amazon. All the women living at Cocke's home at Bremo on the James River, in Fluvanna County, took regular exercise by walking or riding morning and evening. [26]

Workmen and Overseers

More than 100 free white workmen were employed at Monticello and its quarter farms at various times during Jefferson's life there. Some were carpenters, joiners, gardeners, blacksmiths, millwrights, stonemasons, brick masons, joiners, roofers, stonecutters, and plasterers (free workmen). More than fifty of these workmen and artisans actually resided at Monticello throughout the years they worked there. Overseers were another category of employee that was necessary to run Jefferson's farms, especially due to his many absences throughout the decades of his public life. Sometimes Jefferson asked friends, neighbors, and family members to oversee his lands in his absences. But most of the time, he hired and paid wages to overseers for his Monticello and Poplar Forest lands. Some of these overseers had longer tenures than others. Overseers, too, resided at Monticello (or Poplar Forest) with their families.

Since horses were the only form of transportation, Monticello must have been the scene of the constant coming and going of horse traffic, as workmen who did not live up on the mountain came and went daily. Those horses would probably have been watered and fed and tethered with Jefferson's and any guests' horses. Meanwhile, those workmen that lived at Monticello during their work contracts did not necessarily own their horses. Horse ownership was very expensive. Jefferson and his hostlers would not have wanted to feed extra animals. An example of this is the following anecdote. Protecting Jefferson's economic interests, one overseer wrote Jefferson the following report: "Mr. Belt has a horse at the mill which I do expect you would be against staying thare [*sic*] or perhaps he got leave of you." Typically, the generous Jefferson replied that he thought Belt was "an honest man who would not apply our grain to his support." [27]

Some free workmen at Monticello did own horses, however. Davy Watson was a British deserter who came to work at Monticello in 1781 as a house joiner, wheelwright, carriage maker, and sometime cabinet maker. Jefferson valued his work (he was one of the people who taught carpentry to the enslaved John Hemings). Watson worked for Jefferson until 1784, when Jefferson went to Paris. He returned to work for him in 1793, when Jefferson came home from Philadelphia to supposedly retire from politics and take up farming at Monticello. Although his work was respected, Watson drank heavily and spent lots of money on whiskey. Watson lived at Monticello, and in August 1782 he paid to breed one of his own mares to Jefferson's stallion. Another workman, Richard Richardson, was a brick mason and sometime overseer who lived at Monticello from 1796 to 1801. In 1799, Jefferson sold Richardson his own horse Darlington for £60. Richardson would pay Jefferson for the horse in labor, £36 one year and £25 the next. [28]

Overseers needed horses in their daily work and often owned their own horses. The overseers were semiprofessional managers who ran the day-to-day production of the plantation, carrying out the orders (often written orders, in Jefferson's case) of the owner. They directed the enslaved work force, organized the various plantation projects of planting, building, and landscaping, marketed the crops, and kept account of payments and debt. Several of these men perhaps hoped one day to set up their own agricultural operations. The overseers at Monticello and Poplar Forest would have needed horses to move efficiently from one part of the plantation to another, and one quarter farm to another. They probably had reason to visit surrounding towns (Charlottesville and Lynchburg) on errands and other business. Although early on, in 1774, Jefferson wrote a contract for overseers or stewards that said they could not keep a horse ("not allowed to keep a horse"). With later overseers he made contracts, promising to find them a horse, as in the case of Samuel Biddle, overseer from 1793 to 1794. One overseer, however, stands out for his relationship with Jefferson through horses. [29]

Edmund Bacon (1785-1866): It is from Jefferson's long-time overseer (1806–1822), Edmund Bacon, [Fig. 3-9] that we know so much about Jefferson's love of horses. Bacon himself was quite an admirer of horseflesh. "Plants and animals, especially fine horses, were a source of delight to both." Bacon worked for Jefferson for sixteen years. Much of their relationship is evidenced in their written correspondence, which continued for several years even after Bacon left Monticello. (They exchanged 184 letters.) In 1862, the Rev. Hamilton W. Pierson, then president of Cumberland College, in Princeton, Kentucky, published a manuscript of material gathered during visits a year earlier with Edmund Bacon, on his farm in Trigg County, Kentucky, where Pierson interviewed Bacon about his recollection of life at Monticello. A neighbor had told Pierson, "Captain Bacon is enthusiastic and entirely at home on two subjects, and he never tires of talking about either. One is Thomas Jefferson, and the other is fine horses; and he easily passes from one to the other." By the time of Pierson's interview, Bacon, at age seventy-six, had become a respected, prosperous farmer and successful Thoroughbred horse breeder. As Pierson noted in the preface, "[Bacon] was certainly thoroughly Jeffersonian in his love for fine horses." In that interview Bacon spoke eloquently of Jefferson's life with horses. [30]

Fig. 3-9 Edmund Bacon, (1785-1866), Jefferson's long-time overseer

Edmund Bacon was one of several sons born to a "comfortable" yeoman farmer in Albemarle County, two to three miles from Monticello. Bacon claimed that his older brother, William, had been in charge of the estate while Jefferson was minister to France (although there is no record of this). When Jefferson was elected president the second time (1805), according to Bacon, Jefferson went to the Bacon family in search of another overseer. Although young, just twenty at the time, Bacon leapt at the chance to work at Monticello and convinced his father to let him go. Edmund went to live at Monticello October 8, 1806, and became Jefferson's longest-serving overseer. [31]

Bacon worked diligently, carrying out Jefferson's many plans and orders. When Jefferson was home, they often toured the grounds together on horseback. Bacon recalled, "I have rode over the plantation, I reckon, a thousand times with Jefferson." These rides would have been work-related, since Jefferson preferred to be alone for his daily midday ride, especially later in his life. [32]

Bacon took his young wife and two young sons with him to Monticello, and another son was soon born there. Bacon lived in the overseer's house, a half a mile from Jefferson's front door. Nearby was a stable, where he kept his own horses. In his interview with Pierson, Bacon described how General John Hartwell Cocke, a frequent visitor to Monticello, would send his prized bay stallion, Roebuck, down to Bacon's stable, rather than use the main stables on Mulberry Row. Bacon said, "He [Cocke] had rather trust him [Roebuck] with me than with the servants." Cocke had ridden Roebuck in the War of 1812; he was Cocke's favorite saddle horse. Very often the stables near the house were full of visitors' horses and the overflow was sent to Bacon's stable. [33]

The 1862 interview with Pierson included an entire chapter dedicated to "Mr. Jefferson's Blooded Stock." Although the first few pages dealt with sheep and cattle, Bacon stated "the horse was Jefferson's favorite. He was passionately fond of a good horse." Bacon also insisted that, in fact, Jefferson "would not ride or drive anything but a highbred horse." Bacon, as the overseer, was mainly in charge of obtaining and buying the simple work horses, Chickasaws, and mules for the various farms, but he also had an eye for the blooded horse and was a good judge of horseflesh. Bacon was often sent across the state to fetch Jefferson's new riding horses and get them into shape for their new owner (for example, Diomede in 1809). Other times, he claimed to be the one to find the horse and to make the deal, as in the case of Bremo (whom he bought from John Hartwell Cocke in 1814); Tecumseh (claiming he knew Tecumseh's stock well, Bacon negotiated for him with Davy Isaacs in Charlottesville in 1815); Wellington (whom he bought from a man in Augusta County in 1815; the man "didn't know his value," and Bacon got him for a low price); and finally, Jefferson's last riding horse, The Eagle, "the finest sort of riding horse," in 1820. Of Eagle, Bacon said,

"The last thing I ever did for poor Mr. Jefferson was to buy Eagle for him for a riding horse. The last time he ever rode on horseback, he rode Eagle; and the last letter I ever got from Jefferson, he described that ride and how Eagle fell with him in the river and lamed his wrist." In addition, Bacon also gave long descriptions of Jefferson's carriages and carriage horse teams.[34]

Bacon had his own horses while he worked at Monticello, no doubt housing them at his stable. He bought at least two riding horses from Jefferson: one for only $60 in May of 1816, and another described as a gray riding horse for $120 in 1819. This was a two-way street, however; Bacon sold a blooded horse called Traveller to Jefferson in June of 1817. This light bay three-year-old had an impressive pedigree (descended from the well-known horses Medley and Fitzpartner), and Jefferson paid $120 for him. As was typical with Bacon and his financial transactions, he charged Jefferson, who always postponed payment, interest on Traveller (for example, Traveller was bought June 3, 1817, for $120 with interest "from the first day of this month"). During those years Bacon also sold and exchanged horses with Jefferson's grandson Jeff.[35]

Bacon prospered at Monticello. He seemed to be one of the only people in the neighborhood that had money in cash. As noted above, he lent money at interest to those in the social stations above him, including Jefferson (in Jefferson's social class, gentlemen hardly ever charged interest on loans to each other). But it soon became clear that "the desire to do best by my family" meant that Edmund Bacon should become master of his own destiny and buy his own land.[36]

Land in Virginia at this time was still rather expensive, so starting in 1818, after more than ten years of dedication to the Monticello farms, Bacon took temporary leave of his duties there to make several trips west in order to explore places of possible settlement for his large extended family. When Bacon headed for Kentucky on that trip, he rode a mare that was a granddaughter of "imported Diomed" (probably sired by Jefferson's Diomede). Bacon claimed she was "one of the best animals ever backed." Explaining that there were no bridges on their route, so that they had to swim all the smaller streams, he lauded his Diomede mare, saying "she would swim almost like a fish. She would seldom wet me above the knees."[37]

Bacon seemed to know that financial ruin for Jefferson's Monticello was a certainty, explaining "it was not a profitable estate; it was too uneven and hard to work." Finally, in 1822, Bacon and his family left Albemarle County in Virginia and settled in Trigg County, Kentucky, where he lived on an "immense plantation," becoming a successful farmer and breeder of blooded horses, a man of "wealth and character."[38]

Pierson wrote the following description of his visit to Bacon's farm:

> Captain Bacon insisted that we should go to his stable and see his horses. He had two of them brought out and exhibited for our gratification. They were magnificent specimens of that noble animal. Their pedigrees for an indefinite period backward were at his tongue's end, and he showed a knowledge of blooded horses that I think would have astonished an old Virginia connoisseur in that time ... He had taken the leading stock journals of the country for more than fifty years and seemed to know all about all the most noted horses there had been in the country in all that time. Like Mr. Jefferson, he had never patronized nor in any way encouraged horse racing.[39]

Pierson's comment above about Bacon taking "the leading stock journals of the country" must refer to, among others, the *American Farmer,* established in 1819, and *American Turf Register and Sporting Magazine*, established in 1829, both published in Baltimore by John S. Skinner. If Bacon had taken these magazines "for more than fifty years," it meant that he began taking them while overseeing at Monticello. There is no record of Jefferson taking these magazines, but he was certainly familiar with Skinner. In 1818, Jefferson and James Madison had been instrumental in founding the Agricultural Society of Albemarle in an attempt to update agricultural and husbandry techniques in the area. John S. Skinner, the *American Farmer* editor, had volunteered to go to Spain to buy a stud for the society (eventually, an unsuccessful endeavor). As overseer, perhaps Bacon had access to the very person, as well as the publications, of Skinner.[40]

It was common for breeders and buyers to register (and advertise) their stock in the *American Turf Register*. In February of 1839, for example, Edmund Bacon of New Design, Kentucky (in Trigg County), registered his purchase of four blooded mares between 1837 and 1839 under the sub-title "Stud of Mr. Edmund Bacon." He described the color, age, and pedigree of each animal (as well as the history of their offspring), noted that each was "heavy with foal," and named the sires. Two of these mares were mated with "the imported horse, Philip," which probably belonged to Bacon's stud at New Design. Studying these pedigrees, what stands out is Bacon's continued reliance on and confidence in the blood of the most important stud from his early days in Virginia: the imported horse, Diomed. Several of Jefferson's last horses were of Diomed blood (including two he called Diomede). Each of the mares recorded in the journal had sires that were sons of Diomed. One of the mares, Minerva, had several Diomed crosses as well as Fearnought blood (like Jefferson's last horse, The Eagle). [41]

In the same article, Bacon also recorded five fillies and a colt "foaled at New Design—1837 and 1838." Each animal's color and pedigree was carefully elaborated. All had the same sire: Stockholder, which must have also belonged to Bacon himself. In the article, Bacon said Stockholder was "by Sir Archy," the most distinguished son of imported Diomed. Five of the six had dams that were also Diomed blood. Two mares, Kitty Fisher and Virginia, produced two foals each with Stockholder (one in 1837 and one in 1838) and obviously belonged to Bacon's breeding operation. Both were double Diomed crosses (Diomed was both in the line of the sire and the dam). Like the animal on which Bacon rode out to Kentucky in 1818, and that he called "one of the best animals ever backed," both Virginia and Kitty were granddaughters of imported Diomed through a son, Diomede. Kitty's dam was a Peacemaker mare. Peacemaker (out of imported Diomed) belonged to the preeminent turfman and Virginia breeder John Hoomes. Jefferson also had a horse, also named Peacemaker, from this line, which he bought in 1819 from Fielding Lewis. [42]

Hoomes, back in Virginia, may have been the source of many of Bacon's breeding stock. John Hoomes (see Chapter 2) had imported the original Diomed in 1790. *The American Studbook* notes that one of the foundation stallions of the emerging American Thoroughbred breed, Duke of Bedford, was brought to Kentucky by Captain Edmund Bacon. Duke of Bedford, a bay horse foaled in 1800, had been bred by John Hoomes at his plantation, Bowling Green, in Virginia, out of the imported horse, Bedford (imported 1796). (Jefferson also had a Bedford horse that he bought in 1815). Duke of Bedford was called a fine breeder by Bruce, author of the *Studbook*, and "some of the most celebrated horses in America descend from his daughters." Duke of Bedford "got" (sired) the American Thoroughbred matriarch, Mary Bedford. [43]

At Monticello, Bacon was a paid overseer, an employee. But once he left Jefferson's shadow and moved to Kentucky, with horses bred at Monticello and bought from Jefferson as well as from others, Edmund Bacon became master of his own plantation and an eminent stockman and breeder of the new Thoroughbreds, without losing his ties to the Virginia horse world.

Enslaved Men

There is no single definition of the slave experience in the United States. Certainly, the institution of slavery, as nefarious as it always was, varied in intensity through time, across states, from rural to urban contexts, and from owner to owner. Furthermore, the lived experience of one enslaved person was rarely equal to that of another, even on one plantation, even under one owner. The ideology of slavery was barbaric, but the embodied reality of an enslaved person—the humiliation, the self-autonomy, the ability to move freely, the sense of defeat versus a sense of agency, or ownership of self—varied by age, by gender, by family, by skills acquired, by locale, by year, by genetic relationships with whites, by owner, by personality, and by luck. Looking at their relationship with horses can convey some of the different realities experienced by enslaved individuals. Without doubt in Virginia, slaves as a class were at the bottom of the social hierarchy and were thereby most usually associated with the bottom of the equine hierarchy: work horses and mules.

The number of enslaved people at Monticello varied by year. In 1776, there were eighty-three. Other years there would be an average of 200 slaves working and living on Jefferson's various farms. It is disconcerting, distressing, and confusing to witness Jefferson's relationship with people he called slaves, some of whom were his own biological children. Horses often mediated these relationships. Some "servants" (the term Jefferson often used for the enslaved domestics) at Monticello had daily access to horses and the freedom of movement and social status afforded by them. Others did not. [44]

Just as Jefferson had a hierarchy of horses, he had one of people. "The lowest members of Jefferson's slave hierarchy were the field laborers, with no skills other than to do manual farm work," writes biographer Jack McLaughlin. "These were the anonymous field hands, men and women, who appear on Jefferson's slave rolls only as names and birth dates." They equate in many ways to Jefferson's work horses or plantation horses, and mules, listed and counted along with the other stock in his *Farm Book*. Work horses, although noted in the *Memorandum Books* when bought, did not merit names, cost very little, and lived on the quarter farms where they worked. (See Chapter 8.) [45]

On the other hand, a special group of enslaved people lived and worked (and learned skills) near the main house at Monticello. Although still listed in the slave rolls, several of these slave families seemed to have a special relationship with Jefferson and notable agency in their lives. Jefferson often referred to them by name in his letters, and a few knew how to write and corresponded with Jefferson when he was absent. He seemed to consider them part of his "family." Living at Monticello were several extended slave families with surnames, the Hemings family being the most well-known. The only slaves freed during Jefferson's lifetime were Hemings descendants. Some of the people in these families did indeed have a genetic relation to either Jefferson's wife, Martha (through her father John Wayles), or to Thomas Jefferson himself. Some were his own children (through the enslaved Sally Hemings). [46]

Similar to the status hierarchy between house slaves and field slaves, Jefferson's blooded riding horses also had a very different role in his life from the work horses. His expensive riding horses were listed in their own separate list at the beginning of the *Farm Book*, and carefully described by height, color, and pedigree. Many maintained the name of their previous owner or their imported stud or dam. By the 1790s, these horses were stalled in sturdy log or stone stables near the main house. Physically, these blooded horses were taller and more elegant than the shorter, stodgy work horses. While field slaves may have used work horses for plowing the fields, Jefferson would have ridden by on his high horse of the elite.

Finally, Virginians often went to biblical heroes or classical Rome for the names of both the slaves they purchased and their blooded horses. "Jupiter, Samson, Hercules, Pompey, Caesar, Minerva and Juno were common slave names" at that time. Jefferson didn't name any of the slaves he owned, but he did own saddle horses and carriage horses named Tarquin, Romulus, Remus, Castor and Diomede. [47]

Slaves as Horsemen in the Context of Colonial and Post-Revolutionary Virginia: Although it was never illegal during Jefferson's lifetime to teach enslaved people to read and write, there was pervasive white opposition to instructing slaves in their letters. Whites feared that if educated, blacks could no longer be kept in subjugation. On the other hand, the knowledge and skill of horsemanship, at least for some enslaved men in Virginia, despite it being a potential avenue for escape and other acts of freedom, was necessary in a culture powered by horses. Many black men knew how to ride and were admired and depended upon for their skills. A number had roles as equestrians, such as riding servant, hostler, coachman, postilion, or racing jockey. Some enslaved men won their freedom due to their riding skills (such as racing jockeys). [48]

Others must have been quite familiar with horses, worked around them, fed them, shod them, cleaned them, led them out to the master, hitched them up to carriages, plowed with them, or drove them in carts and wagons loaded with goods. In fact, the horse industry, or plantations that bred blood horses for the turf and/or to sell to the gentry, would have been impossible without the enslaved labor to undergird these operations. Other wealthy whites who owned slaves (only about 20 percent of Southern whites owned slaves) probably assigned them to, among other things, care for their several horses (certainly, the owner did not clean stalls or groom horses). Some of these horses that the enslaved men would have worked with would have been the small work horses called Chickasaws, while others were the high-strung blooded horses used by the master for riding and drawing carriages. It is not surprising that many whites believed that their slaves had a special bond with horses, and whites described the strong attachment slaves had to the animals. [49]

Enslaved women were never mentioned as riders, and, of course, did not work with horses. No mention of an enslaved woman or girl on a horse on the mountain has been found, and there is only one mention in the records of Monticello of a female slave rider. Adam Hodgson, a visitor from England, wrote of his visit to Jefferson and Monticello in June 1820. When he left Monticello on the way to Richmond, he stopped at Powell's Inn for breakfast on the second morning, not far from Richmond. There he breakfasted with "an opulent tobacco planter and his wife," also on their way to Richmond in a carriage. Hodgson noted, "The lady's maid rode on horseback behind." He further opined, "I suppose nothing would induce them to admit her into the carriage." We must assume the maid was riding sidesaddle. [50]

The gentry's blooded horses, however, were often better cared for than the enslaved caretakers themselves, a fact commented upon by foreign visitors. Those high-bred animals were housed in buildings and barns (sometimes made of stone or brick) finer and more substantial than the slaves' wooden cabins. The horses were kept well-fed and immaculately clean. Slaves often attended a master's favorite horse, sleeping in the stall next to it. For example, Colonel Thomas Mann Randolph had an imported horse, called Shakespeare, for whom he built a special stable "in which was a recess for a bed for the negroe who looked after it, that he might be with it at night." [51]

It must have seemed that many owners valued their horses more than their slaves. Toward the end of the War for Independence, General Cornwallis set up his headquarters on Thomas Jefferson's farm, called Elkhill, in Goochland County, where he and his men systematically destroyed crops, fences, and barns, and plundered the storehouses and livestock. When Cornwallis left, he took with him nine of Jefferson's fabulous blooded horses, killing several young (valuable) high-bred foals (which were useless to Cornwallis). Jefferson also accused Cornwallis of carrying off thirty slaves. (More likely, they "fled with the enemy." The British offered freedom to those slaves who left their American masters and escaped to the British camps.) For the rest of his life, Jefferson spoke of the "spirit of total extermination with which [Cornwallis] seemed to rage over my possessions." Although most of the slaves died of disease in the British camps, some were eventually returned to Monticello. The horses were not. For Jefferson, the two kinds of possessions seem conflated. [52]

Thomas Jefferson grew up in a world where the majority of men, Black and white, were horsemen. Recall that his first memory was of being handed up to a slave on horseback to ride from his father's frontier farm in Shadwell to Tuckahoe near Richmond, where he would live for seven years with his family. At that point in his young life (about age two), there was no serviceable road from Shadwell to Tuckahoe, so riding in a carriage was out of the question. But the fact that a slave carried the young boy on a horse attests to the servant's riding skills.

How did enslaved men attain their riding skills? Who taught them to ride? Perhaps those boys destined to become the manservant of a young master, often near the same age as the white boy, even playmates during their youth, learned to ride right along with their adolescent owner. Others, who served as groomsmen and stable boys under the watchful eye of an experienced hostler, learned while exercising their charges. In some cases, it may have been these servants who taught the young white children, both boys and girls, how to ride their first horse.

As we contemplate the landscape of eighteenth- and early-nineteenth-century Virginia, it is sometimes surprising to see Black men riding alone, or occasionally with companions, across Virginia, night and day. Many of these men were "trusted" and "faithful" servants on errands for their masters, riding workhorses or mules, but in many cases riding their masters' blooded-horses. Sometimes the records show that enslaved men even owned their own horses, as was the case with at least one of Jefferson's slaves. The horse Isaac (Granger) Jefferson rode may have been his own. Later in his life, Jefferson refers to the value of half a colt left to Isaac by his father, George Granger, the enslaved headman and overseer. Like driving a car today, riding a horse across country implies a certain autonomy and sense of independence. [53]

Jefferson's letters are full of references to his slaves sent on various errands everywhere in Virginia and beyond on horseback, sometimes for weeks at a time—errands such as delivering money, finding doctors, or just going to the post office. Some were sent to fetch friends or family members and bring them to Monticello. A poignant example was July 1774, when Jefferson was on his way to Williamsburg for the Virginia Convention. Suddenly, he was struck by illness and had to turn back home. He gave Jupiter Evans, who was accompanying him as his riding servant, copies of *A Summary View of the Rights of British America* to deliver to the convention. Evans continued on to Williamsburg to hand over the papers, returning alone later to Monticello. Ironically, at the end of the Revolutionary War, in 1781, Martin Hemings, the enslaved Monticello butler at the time, was sent to Williamsburg and later to the coast in search of Jefferson's slaves that had been scattered (or escaped) from Elkhill by the British army as it had advanced through Virginia. Martin found at least one of those slaves because George Wythe, Jefferson's law professor in Williamsburg, wrote, "I desired Martin to take the roan horse then in good plight to assist him in carrying home the servant he recovered in my neighborhood." One slave on horseback, bringing back another to slavery! [54]

Many examples illustrate Jefferson's slaves traveling alone across Virginia. Once in 1793, when Jefferson was working in far-off Philadelphia, he requested by letter that a slave be sent to Georgetown (on the Potomac River) with an extra horse recently purchased by his son-in-law, in order to exchange for the horse Jefferson would send down with another slave from Philadelphia. The Philadelphia horse (Tarquin) would return home to Monticello. So Jupiter Evans on a mule, leading a horse, set out on the three-day trip to Georgetown to meet Jefferson's coachman, Lapsely, there, riding south from Philadelphia, leading the soon-to-be retired Tarquin. [55]

Sometimes a slave was sent with a second horse to meet the public stage at Fredericksburg, where Jefferson would get off— there was no stage route west to Albemarle in those years. Jefferson would then ride the rest of the way to Monticello with his slave. In later years, these slaves would drive with Jefferson in a carriage or the phaeton to the stage line and then return home alone (or vice versa, they would drive over to Fredericksburg in the carriage at the assigned time to pick Jefferson up in order to return him home). These men made one part of the journey on their own. This was a common occurrence. For example, Jefferson's friend and neighbor, John Hartwell Cocke, had two enslaved coachmen, Jesse and Phil, who were also trusted to travel alone, "transporting Cocke to and from long-absenting trips, collecting the children from [boarding] school, guests from their house, and mail from nearby towns." Many other plantation owners also sent their male slaves alone across country on errands. Jefferson tipped Wilson Cary Nicholas's servant a dollar for bringing his newly bought horse Darlington to Monticello (on June 23, 1796). Presumably the slave then returned home, with the dollar in his pocket, to southern Albemarle. [56]

Other times slaves were chosen to deliver, or collect, large sums of money while riding alone back and forth across the countryside. One time in 1798, Jupiter Evans was sent to collect from a Jefferson debtor "any sum you may have in readiness for me." Whites liked to brag about the loyalty of their enslaved servants, riding about, far from home on a horse and with a pocket full of money. [57]

Phil Evans, Jupiter's son, consistently proved his loyalty throughout his lifetime. Once in 1819, Phil was sent off in the night across county lines on a horse to find a doctor and convince him to come to the aid of his young master, Jefferson's grandson, who had been dangerously wounded in a brawl with his brother-in-law. Earlier in his life, Evans had accompanied Jefferson's son-in-law Thomas Mann Randolph to Lake Ontario in New York to fight the British in the War of 1812. At one moment, Phil had found himself left behind with three horses. "Instead of taking the advice of the local New Yorkers to sell the horses and seize his freedom, he set off alone to lead them to his master at the army's winter quarters over a hundred miles down the St. Lawrence." [58]

The danger (for plantation owners) of allowing, even encouraging, some Blacks to master the art of riding, was that some men would ride out on their own journeys, a kind of freedom through mobility. For example, it was known that enslaved people used horses to visit from plantation to plantation at night, or in their free time. A plantation owner from the Northern Neck, Landon Carter of Sabine, noted several times in his diaries of catching slaves riding his "plow horses in the night" or "on the gray Colt." Sometimes the evidence was a muddy or worn saddle found the next morning in the tack rooms. Men would steal off to nearby plantations to visit lovers or wives, or perhaps just to go fishing in order to bring in more food for their families. Slaves sent off the plantation on some task (either on horseback or on foot) usually carried a pass or a document of permission stating their destination. After work hours, during their time (free time), traveling under cover of dark obviated this requirement. Using a plantation horse, one could cover more ground and return before dawn. [59]

In 1818, Joel Yancey, Jefferson's overseer at Poplar Forest, dashed off a note to Jefferson at Monticello about two enslaved laborers showing up at Poplar Forest on horseback around the Christmas holiday to visit friends, supposedly with Jefferson's permission but without passes. Yancey's note underlined that the greater offence was the fact that two white men showed up a week later in pursuit of the "Boys," Dick and Moses, accusing them of having stolen their horse and saddle. One of the young men admitted to riding the horse but argued that it was a stray, and that he had been trying to find the owner. That young visitor agreed to take a whipping from the men rather than go before the justice of the peace. Yancey feared that both horses had been stolen, but the pair assured him that the second horse was Jefferson's. Yancey would wait to hear from Jefferson about the horse before sending the two young men back to Monticello with it. [60]

> Dr. Sir
>
> Your two Boys Dick & Moses arrived here on Monday night last both on Horse-back without a pass, but said they had your permission to visit their friends here this Xmass. Yesterday two men came in pursuit of them for stealing their Horse and Saddle,

they found the horse here and Dick acknowledged that he road it from albemarl, but that it was a stray, and that he was endeavouring to find the ow[n]er, Moses has made his escape, and Dick agreed to take a whiping, which I thought was better than takeing them before a justice of the Peace, which the men were determined to do unless they got some satisfaction, the owners of the horse William Hamner & son both from your County, after getting their Horse was content to give him a very light whipping indeed not near sufficient in my opinion to deter him from commiting a like offence, I have thought it probable they may be runaways and that both Horses is stolen, the other Horse, they say is yours, which I have, and shall have taken care of until I here from you or the owner comes, should I not here from you before next Tuesday I send them down with the Horse. In haste with great respect I am yr. mo. Obt. Joel Yancey. [61]

Not all surreptitious travel by slaves was for visits to friends or family. Many enslaved people ran away in hope of reaching freedom. Most probably escaped on foot. For the most part, the few Jefferson slaves who tried to run away permanently did so on foot. Some, however, escaped on horseback. [62]

In 1769, when Jefferson was twenty-six years old, he put a notice in the *Virginia Gazette* (a newspaper published in Williamsburg) announcing a reward for a runaway, a mulatto slave called Sandy. [Fig. 3-10] The man was described as a shoemaker with an addiction to drink. Jefferson wrote that Sandy

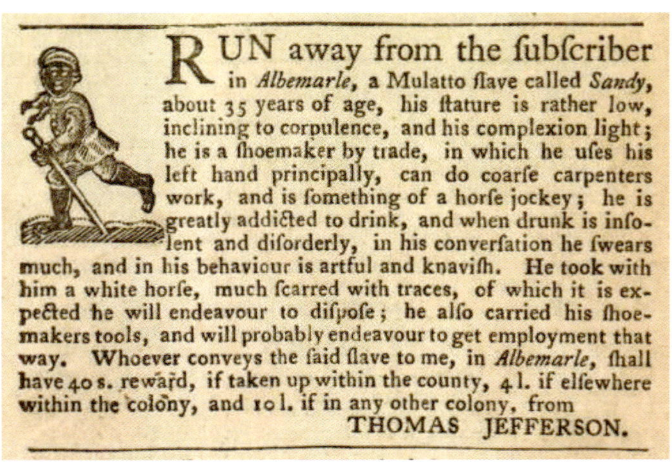

RUN away from the ſubſcriber in *Albemarle*, a Mulatto ſlave called *Sandy*, about 35 years of age, his ſtature is rather low, inclining to corpulence, and his complexion light; he is a ſhoemaker by trade, in which he uſes his left hand principally, can do coarſe carpenters work, and is ſomething of a horſe jockey; he is greatly addicted to drink, and when drunk is inſolent and diſorderly, in his converſation he ſwears much, and in his behaviour is artful and knaviſh. He took with him a white horſe, much ſcarred with traces, of which it is expected he will endeavour to diſpoſe; he alſo carried his ſhoemakers tools, and will probably endeavour to get employment that way. Whoever conveys the ſaid ſlave to me, in *Albemarle*, ſhall have 40 s. reward, if taken up within the county, 4 l. if elſewhere within the colony, and 10 l. if in any other colony, from

THOMAS JEFFERSON.

Fig. 3-10 Jefferson placed this advertisement for a runaway slave in the Virginia Gazette, September 14, 1769.

"took with him a white horse, much scarred with traces [harness and pole marks], of which it is expected he will endeavor to dispose." So Sandy, at least, absconded on a cart horse. Despite having the horse for transportation, Sandy was returned, and sold three years later. We do not know about the horse. Many other advertisements in the *Virginia Gazette* also imply that men took off to freedom from other owners on horses. In some cases the enslaved person took with him ("stole") the gear to ride a horse: a saddle, saddle cloth, and bridle. [63]

Horse Jockeys: In the 1769 advertisement of the mulatto slave called Sandy (above), Jefferson described him as "something of a horse jockey" besides being a shoemaker and sometime carpenter. "Horse jockey" referred to a man who rode atop the horses in races, and this was another line of work for young slaves.

Fig. 3-11 Sam Savitt, *Match Race at Tucker's Quarter Path*, 1983, depicts a quarter-mile race with Black jockeys. From Mackay-Smith, *The Colonial Quarter Race Horse.*

During Thomas Jefferson's lifetime, two kinds of horse racing characterized Virginia: quarter racing and course racing. (see Chapter 7 for more on these forms of racing.) Quarter racing, present almost from the start of the colony, matched two horses sprinting down a path through the woods, or on a street through a town, for a quarter mile. Although originally, in the seventeenth century, owners (from the gentry) rode their own horses, soon, probably due to all the jostling and whipping of the opponent jockey, owners substituted the young slave boys for themselves, and the owners concentrated on waging large sums of money on their horse. [Fig. 3-11]

After the 1740s, quarter racing moved to the frontier, and course racing became a main focus of social life for the gentry. These races pitted the newly imported English blood horses and their offspring against each other on long oval race courses.

These distance races (the winning horse had to win two out of three four-mile heats) required horses with more endurance than the smaller quarter-mile racers. Under these circumstances, the jockey's weight was an issue, and young boys, especially young slave boys, raced these blooded horses. [64]

In 1796, Isaac Weld, a visiting Irishman, attended races near Petersburg, and he noted that "the horses are commonly rode by negro boys." Weld added that some of the Black young men were "really good jockeys." It was one of the few contexts where an enslaved man was a protagonist (along with the horse). [65]

Many enslaved persons beside the jockeys attended these races, some as attendants to their masters and mistresses, but others were able to attend the race days on their own. They even wagered bets, all the while cheering on their favorite contestant. At the end of one Virginia horse race, witnesses described the enslaved attendees "in particular hallooing, jumping and clapping their hands in a frenzy of delight, more especially if the horses had happened to jostle and one of the riders been thrown off with a broken leg." Enslaved African-Americans were obviously enthusiastic participants at horse races. [66]

Some jockeys achieved such notoriety and respect and money that they were able to achieve their freedom. A few bought their way out of slavery, while others were manumitted by their grateful owners. One of the first Black jockeys to achieve his freedom through horse racing was a mulatto slave jockey named Austin Curtis, who rode in both quarter races and course races. He consistently won almost every race he rode in. Later, after his racing days were over, he trained and bred horses for his owner, Willie Jones, an important planter and politician from the old racehorse region in North Carolina. Together they developed a formidable stable of racehorses. Curtis and Jones had a unique relationship. Jones gave Curtis responsibilities unheard of for a slave in the eighteenth century. Curtis was often sent off alone, crossing state lines, in order to prepare for various races. During the invasion of British troops in 1778 and 1779, Curtis hid Jones's blooded horses so they would not be confiscated by the invaders. Curtis won his freedom in 1791. When he died, his obituary appeared in a Raleigh, North Carolina, newspaper, at a time when few deaths of Blacks were recognized in print. The obituary characterized Curtis as "well known for many years past as a keeper of racehorses. His character was unblemished; his disposition mild and obliging. He possessed the esteem of many—the respect and confidence of all who know him." [67]

Fig. 3-12 Isaac Granger Jefferson (1775–c. 1850), an enslaved artisan who was a blacksmith, at Monticello. He obtained his freedom by 1822, and then lived and worked in Richmond until his death. This daguerreotype was made c. 1845.

Others of these ex-jockeys may have become trainers. Isaac (Granger) Jefferson, [Fig. 3-12] the former Monticello slave, in an interview in 1847 at age seventy-two as a free man, mentioned a trainer named Pompey, who worked for Colonel Thomas Goode of Chesterfield. Goode was an important importer and turfman, who, according to Isaac, used to visit Jefferson occasionally at Monticello. Goode must have brought Pompey with him on these visits, because Isaac (Granger) Jefferson seemed to know him. [68]

Riding Servants, Hostlers, Postilions, Coachmen and Wagoners:

Riding servants would accompany their master during travel, take care of horses at night and at tavern stops, pay ferry fares, and probably carry luggage cases (called portmanteau). Before the advent of passable roads, nearly all travel was on horseback rather than by wheeled vehicle. Most of young Jefferson's trips to Williamsburg before the Revolution were in the saddle of his own horse. His riding servant, Jupiter Evans, rode a second horse alongside or behind him. If the master drove a chair or gig, the riding servant would follow behind on a horse, sometimes leading another extra horse (the master's saddle horse). If the traveling party was a carriage with a coachman driver, a riding servant often rode behind nevertheless. Once they had stopped for the night or reached their destination, the riding servant doubled as a manservant (to dress and shave the master).

Obviously, these riding servants had to have been more than adequate riders, with an excellent knowledge of horses.

Jupiter Evans was Jefferson's first enslaved valet, from at least 1764, when they both turned twenty-one, until 1774, when Jupiter assumed the new duties of hostler and coachman. Both born at Shadwell, Jupiter and Tom shared a childhood. Jupiter may have followed Tom on horseback down to Williamsburg when Jefferson attended the College of William and Mary, and served as his enslaved valet while there.[69]

In 1774, Jupiter Evans's duties were transferred to the Monticello stables, and a young boy, twelve years old, whom Jefferson had inherited from his father-in-law's estate, the light-skinned Robert Hemings, took over as personal servant. From 1775, Robert Hemings rode behind Jefferson wherever he went (to Williamsburg, Philadelphia, and Annapolis) and escorted him (and daughter Martha) up to Boston when they embarked to France in 1784. Robert then had to return alone back to Virginia with the three blooded horses in his care. Robert's brother, James Hemings, also became (briefly) Jefferson's traveling attendant. James sailed to France with Jefferson and his daughter and first served as Jefferson's personal attendant until he was charged with learning the art of French cooking. But when Jefferson returned to the United States, James Hemings assumed his old role as riding valet when Jefferson toured New England with James Madison for a month in 1791.[70]

One of Robert's and James's nephews, Burwell Colbert, became Jefferson's enslaved valet after the presidency. Colbert was more generally the head butler at Monticello; nevertheless, he always followed behind Jefferson's landau on Jefferson's riding horse (Bremo, and later, The Eagle) for the three or four annual trips to Poplar Forest, the retreat in Bedford County, or wherever else Jefferson went in the landau. This way, Burwell Colbert was there to help if anything went wrong with the carriage, but also Jefferson's saddle horse would be available if Jefferson tired of the landau. He could mount his horse and ride on. It also spared the saddle horse Eagle the effort of pulling the landau so that he was fresh for Jefferson's daily rides once they arrived at their destination. The Eagle was a difficult horse to ride (due to his shying), so Colbert's horsemanship must have been up to Jefferson's standards.

Hostlers were those people in charge of the stables and coach houses—either at taverns or at plantations like Monticello. Hostlers did not accompany the owner on travels. They were in charge of housing, feeding and watering, shoeing, cleaning, and perhaps exercising the horses, as well as maintaining in good condition the various vehicles, or coaches used to travel, in addition to the upkeep of the tack and harness.

In 1774, Jupiter Evans stopped traveling with Jefferson, and became the chief hostler and coachman. It is not clear if Jupiter was happy about giving up his role as riding servant, but later he protected his new turf quite assertively.[71]

Several years after Jefferson's death, his grandchildren related to his biographer a colorful anecdote about an exception to Jefferson's "unruffled temper" involving Jupiter Evans and his charges, the carriage horses:

> On [one] occasion, Mr. Jefferson directed one of his servants to take a horse and go to the Charlottesville post-office for his letters and papers. The boy replied that there was not a horse out of use but those belonging to the carriage. "Go, then," said Mr. Jefferson, "and tell Jupiter [the colored coachman] to lend you one of his horses." The boy soon returned, saying "old Jupe" sent back word that nobody could have his horses for that business. Mr. Jefferson looked amused, and told the boy to go again to Jupiter and tell him that the case was urgent, as he was expecting important letters. The sable Olympian, however, replied flatly that "neither of his horses should go for anybody." "Tell Jupiter to come here," said his master, evidently in a passion. The pampered coachman soon arrived to meet a look and hear a tone never before or after-wards witnessed at Monticello—never witnessed by any member of Mr. Jefferson's family, except by Martha in the boat. Jupiter at once prudently took in a good deal of sail, but he firmly declared that he must not be expected to keep the carriage horses in the desired condition, if they were to be "ridden round by boys." Mr. Jefferson admitted this, but he told his coachman that he had better never again take quite so blunt a method of "telling his mind." And here the matter ended.[72]

As head hostler, Evans felt very proprietary about the Monticello carriage horses. Evans replied flatly that "neither of his horses should go for anybody." Moreover, Evans was the coachman; he trained and cared for the team of driving horses. He firmly declared that he must not be expected to keep the carriage horses in the desired condition, if they were to be "ridden round by boys." Such was his self-confidence that Evans "had dared to cross an invisible line, stepping outside his subordinate station to challenge ... authority." Finally, underneath this anecdote of Jefferson's little-seen rage is the description of these boys grabbing a "blooded" horse to ride to Charlottesville (three miles away) to pick up Jefferson's letters at the post office, i.e., an eagerly sought, youthful adventure, off the plantation, into the town, on a horse! A young slave boy, trusted with a horse, off on his own! And what a privilege and status-marker to ride into Charlottesville on one of Jefferson's treasured blooded horses![73]

In Washington during his presidency, President Jefferson hired an Irishman, Joseph Dougherty, to take charge of his horses and stables and drive his biggest carriage (the chariot) (President Jefferson brought very few of his slaves to the President's House). Meanwhile, back at Monticello, Wormley Hughes took over (after Jupiter) as chief hostler of the stone stables on Mulberry Row until the end of Jefferson's days. Hughes had several duties at Monticello (he was also the principal gardener at that time), but as hostler he was in charge of the care and provisioning of the horses. Jefferson's biographer Henry S. Randall spoke to Hughes while visiting Monticello in 1851. The biographer described Hughes, then seventy years old: "Like most of his color, he had a strong attachment for horses," and further noted, "He could distinctly remember, and describe the points, height, color, pace, temper, etc. of every horse as far back as Arcturus, which Jefferson brought home from Washington."[74]

It is not surprising that many nineteenth-century white Virginians thought that "most of his [Hughes's] color . . . had a strong attachment for horses," as cited above. However, in some respects, this statement seems to equate, perhaps inadvertently, the enslaved groomsmen with livestock and other animals. Yet recent research confirms that, like humans, horses are also social animals, and in the wild, horses themselves live in communities of families and friends and herds. "They form intense bonds and have 'preferred partners' with whom they spend extra time, follow, and co-groom, and these best friends can be members of other species." Enslaved hostlers and groomsmen, who were assigned to care for these animals, feed, clean, groom, saddle and tack them up, and sometimes even sleep in adjacent rooms, would inevitably have had special relationships of mutual trust and even affection for many of their horses, equal to or possibly even superior to those of some of the white gentry riders.[75]

These hostlers also probably controlled a bevy of enslaved stable workers who actually cleaned and groomed the horses. Jefferson's horse was brought out to him each day for his daily ride by a young boy. If Jefferson wasn't ready to go quite yet, the horse was tied up to a nearby tree. This was also probably the same groom responsible for keeping Jefferson's tack and saddle spotless and dust free. Two biographical accounts mention "the white handkerchief test." Supposedly, when he was younger, Jefferson was "finical" in the treatment of his "magnificent horses" and very exacting of his groom, demanding that his horses be "beautifully kept." "It was his habit, when his riding horse was brought up for him to mount, to brush his white cambric handkerchief across the animal's shoulders and send it back to the stable if any dust was left on the handkerchief," and the young enslaved groom was scolded.[76]

Fig. 3-13 The man on one of the front horses is a postilion. "A Coach with Two Extra Horses, Ridden by a Postilion," after an etching by Rowlandson, 1793, in Fairman Rogers, *A Manual of Coaching* (London: J.B. Lippincott Company, 1900).

Postilion: A postilion was someone who rode the near (on the left) horse of a pair in order to guide the horses pulling a carriage [Fig. 3-13] (a carriage without a coachman). It was probably while he was minister to France, from 1784 to 1789, that Jefferson acquired his custom of using postilions. In France, the norm was for carriages to be guided by a postilion rather than a coachman sitting on the vehicle. In his long-distance travels in France. Jefferson had to pay the postilions separately from the rent for the horses who pulled his carriage. (On a long trip in France, one started with one's own horses, but stopped at a stage, sent one's own horses home, and rented horses from stage to stage from then on. One set of horses would not have lasted a long trip.)

Upon his return to the United States (after 1790), Jefferson sometimes continued with the custom of using postilions. He didn't seem to trust any other driver than himself. Thus, when Jefferson didn't drive his own gig or phaeton, often the vehicle was guided by postilions (i.e., by riding the horses). His landau, which he used continuously after 1814, was pulled by four horses and always ridden by two postilions (siblings James and Israel Gillette).[77]

These riders, as well as the riding servants, clearly had to be competent horsemen. Usually the postilions were younger (lighter) boys, whose weight would not tire the horses. They also had to have the stamina to endure the faster gait of the coach horse, the trot. The posting trot developed from the necessity for postilions to be able to ride the trot of the Thoroughbred horses. There were special postilion saddles (we have references to President Jefferson's having two postilion saddles made in Philadelphia along with his presidential chariot in 1801), which had shortened stirrups so the boys could rise up and down in the trot: i.e., to post. Jefferson mentioned the two postilions in his maiden voyage of his landau to Bedford in 1814. He wrote to his daughter, "My journey was performed without accident. The horse and postilions performed well. James will be an excellent driver and Israel will do better with more strength and practice. You will always be perfectly safe with their driving." His reference to Israel needing more strength and practice probably referred to his getting used to posting, or rising to the trot of the blood horses.[78]

The Gillette siblings, Israel and James, along with their brother Gill, served as both house servants and postilions. All three accompanied Jefferson on his two or three annual visits to his retreat at Poplar Forest during his retirement years (1809–1826). Israel (Gillette) Jefferson said in an interview with a newspaper in Ohio in 1873 that "sometimes Mr. Jefferson rode less ostentatiously, and the leaders were left off. Then but one rider was needed. Sometimes brother Gilly acted as postilion; at other times I was employed." After Jefferson's death, Israel was able to buy his freedom in 1841 from the man who had bought him, Thomas Walker Gilmer, and soon made his way to Ohio with his wife and children. He returned several times to Monticello to visit family before he died sometime after 1873.[79]

Coachmen and Wagoners: Jupiter Evans took over as hostler and coachman at Monticello in 1774, but his service as coachman was not for Jefferson (Jefferson either drove himself or used postilions). Jupiter drove the chariot for Mrs. Jefferson and the young children. Driving horses in harness and traces takes knowledge, skill, and practice. First of all, the horses need to learn how to be driven in the various kinds of vehicles, sometimes as a single horse, sometimes in teams of two or four horses. This often took several days, if not weeks, of training and accustoming the horse. Furthermore, the coachman was in charge of maintaining and repairing all the harness and collars, as well as supervising the hitching up of the coach horses. Driving with passengers was a great responsibility, especially since we have constant references to coaches falling over, getting stuck in the mud, or going down in rivers and streams. Some enslaved men specialized in driving. One advertisement offering a reward for a missing "Negro man" described him by saying "he considers himself an excellent driver and manager of Horses." The man had lived three years away from "home," presumably using this skill.[80]

Several adult Monticello enslaved men were asked to drive women or run other errands in carriages over the years. This implies that they were proficient and trusted drivers as well as experienced around horses in general. Phil Evans was often asked to taxi Jefferson's sister, Mrs. Marks, in a one-horse chair, or Jefferson's phaeton, back and forth to Monticello from her home in Louisa County for her summer visits. One time during Jefferson's presidency, John Freeman was accompanying the president back to Washington when the carriage was slowed down due to mud. The second day of the journey, Jefferson "left John with the carriage and mounted my horse" and forged on to Washington alone. We assume John drove the carriage back to Monticello or onto Washington later. Wormley Hughes, the Monticello hostler for the last twenty-five years of Jefferson's life, also drove the coach for family members, ferrying Mrs. Marks or driving horses in the gig on one errand or another. After Jefferson's death, many of the grandchildren stayed on for several years at Monticello. A driver they called Uncle Titus cared for the horses and taxied the women from site to site (to the Madisons for holidays, to Charlottesville to the doctor).[81]

Wagoners were those men that drove the mules, oxen, and work horses in the wagons. Wagons were bulky vehicles, without springs, made entirely of wood (including the four wheels and axles) that were not meant to transport people over any distance. Wagons carried loads at a very slow pace, although it is telling that sometimes enslaved women and children would travel long distances in a wagon (as when the family moved to Williamsburg when Jefferson became governor). Wagons were used on the farms to haul tobacco to the port, dung from field to field, cargo from Milton on the Rivanna River to the mansion, and limestone from the Hardware River. They were most likely stationed in the barns at the quarter farms (Tufton, Pantops, Lego). Oxen, mules, and work horses each have different personalities and characteristics that the wagoners had to be familiar with. Also, their nutrition requirements as work animals were different from each other's, as well as different from the riding and carriage horses. Driving a wagon is a different skill from driving a carriage.

Overseer Bacon spoke about the three wagons he took up to Washington to bring Jefferson home from the presidency in 1809. Two of them, loaded with boxes, were six-mule teams, while the third was drawn by four sorrel Chickasaw horses and loaded with shrubbery from a place near Washington called Maine's nursery; the servants also rode on the wagons. Bacon drove the carriage horses and carriage (Jefferson was driving his one-horse phaeton). Undoubtedly, the three wagons were driven by Monticello wagoners. One of them would have been David Hern (also known as Wagoner Davy), who had made same trip twice a year for three years using a two-mule cart. Hern would return to Monticello with "letters, crates, even horses, as Jefferson purchased new ones and retired 'decayed' ones." Toward Monticello went seeds, trees, animals for Jefferson's breeding experiments, and fittings for the house. Sometimes the turn-around time in Washington extended to more than a week.[82]

However, in March 1809, upon Jefferson's retirement to Monticello at the end of his presidency, the slow-moving caravan got caught in a dreadful late winter snowstorm on the road home, and was not able to continue. The wagon caravan arrived to Monticello several days after Jefferson, who had left his snow-bound phaeton in Culpeper and mounted his horse for the final leg of his journey through the blizzard. All told, the wagoners must have spent at least two weeks driving, feeding, watering, and caring for their animals, on the way up and the way back for that final journey home from Washington.

Historical interpreters portraying a jockey and a racehorse owner at Colonial Williamsburg. The jockeys were almost always enslaved boys, thus reversing the usual roles. The enslaved jockey is on the gentry's "high horse," while the white gentry owner is down below, on the ground.

PART II

The Equine Hierarchy

Blue Ridge Mountains in background. Hores in foreground. Wahoo Photos

Chapter 4

The Equine Gentry: Thorough-Bred, Jefferson's Saddle Horses, 1766–1826

All who knew him well knew that Thomas Jefferson was "passionately fond of a good horse." But for Jefferson, a good horse was a high-bred horse, and "he would not ride or drive anything else." Jefferson's contemporaries consistently described him as sitting ramrod straight, effortlessly containing and constraining the nervous energy of an explosively fast stallion.[1]

From one perspective, the story of Thomas Jefferson and his horses is the story of the American Thoroughbred breed. It was invented in England during the late seventeenth and early eighteenth centuries by aristocrats who wanted to raise long-distance racehorses—racehorses for the Sport of Kings. Within an equine generation or two, prime examples of that new kind of horse arrived in the colonies, especially in Virginia. Jefferson never owned an imported English horse, but from his young adulthood on, the horses he bought and bred to were the offspring of these spectacular equines, the American foundation stallions and matriarchal mares of the breed we call Thoroughbreds today, the racehorse par excellence.

The term Thoroughbred, however, was not applied to a breed of horses until late in the nineteenth century. In the eighteenth century, people referred to these horses as blood horses, or high-bred horses. Jefferson called them "high blooded." At that time, the term *thorough-bred* could apply to other animals, and humans as well. It referred to purity of pedigree. Jefferson's blooded riding horses were at the top of the equine hierarchy for the landed gentry in Virginia. In many ways, these horses were equated with the gentry men themselves.[2]

Origins: "Oriental" Horses

In seventeenth-century Europe, few true horse breeds existed. Rather, we can refer to horse types, which were naturally selected groups of animals that shared certain physical characteristics (phenotype, or appearance) or purposes. The animals had adapted to a specific and limited geographical location. Today there is much debate and little consensus over the definition of a horse breed. In general, a breed is a population of horses that has been selectively bred; usually, the pedigrees of the animals have been recorded in a breed registry. For an animal to be considered a member of that breed, both lines (parents) for several generations back must be recorded in the registry.

During the 1600s, types of horses known as Turks (from the eastern Mediterranean), Barbs (from North Africa and Morocco), and Spanish jennets were imported into England and bred with the native Galloways and Hobbies (originally from Scotland and Ireland)—small but fast running horses. These Hobbies were the native British racehorse. Hobbies were described as short but with heavy muscling and a stocky, short back, broad chest, round back and rib cage, and powerful loins. They had lateral gaits that made them extremely comfortable to ride.[3]

By the early eighteenth century in England, a new breed of horse was being developed and subsequently exported to the colonies. Besides the Turks, Barbs, and Spanish horses, Arabian-type horses had become available and had been imported into England between 1650 and 1750. "Arabian" was the name given to a certain regional type of horse native to the Arabian Peninsula, Yemen, the Levante, Syria, and Egypt, what we call the Middle East today, but then known (in English) as the Orient. Arabians are thought to be one of the oldest horse types, and their genes are in many other bloodlines.

Horses in the Arabian Peninsula were not used for travel (camels were), but rather for war, and were valued for their endurance. Given these requirements, they were not bred to promote comfortable gaits. One significant difference between the Arabian and the English horses was that Arabian horses were diagonal trotters, not lateral pacers. In place of comfort, however, British breeders were looking for notable speed and "bottom" (endurance) to produce faster racehorses at longer distances.

In the equine literature on this topic, we often find the adjective "Oriental," or the gloss "Arabian," whether the horse came from the Arabian peninsula, Morocco, Persia, Syria, Egypt, Turkey, the Barbary Coast (north Africa), or even southern Spain, Andalusia. So for several generations this emerging breed was described as coming from "Oriental" stock, or having "Oriental" blood. Those horses were Arabian types, but all had different regional provenance (in general, "the Orient") and were definitely the progenitors of the Thoroughbred breed, passing to them their speed and endurance.

The irony is that an original hybridization between the exotic "Oriental" sires and local English Hobby mares would soon generate a closed breed. After the mid-eighteenth century, the English blood horse itself produced a racing horse superior to all other types or crosses. It no longer needed the input of "Oriental" stock. The appearance of the *General Stud Book* in England in 1791, with its pedigree data assuring purity of all the animals listed, effectively sealed the breed from further outside influences, and led to official registration for recognition as a Thoroughbred. Yet for these racehorses, the owner had to be able to prove that both sides of the horse's pedigree traced back to one of the originating three "Oriental" studs. In this sense the English royalty and aristocracy, those in control of the racing stables and breeding, projected their own marriage rules and rules about membership in the aristocracy onto the high-bred blood horse. [4]

The conformation (shape) of the new blood horse, the Thoroughbred, was quite different from that of both its English and "Oriental" ancestors. The English mares (Galloways and Hobbies) were short, almost pony size, and quite compact yet quite hardy. [Fig. 4-1] The Barb from North Africa was a fast

Fig. 4-1 Scottish Galloways, now extinct, as pictured in Oliver Goldsmith, *A History of the Earth, and Animated Nature*

Fig. 4-2 The Barb horse, from North Africa, during a *tbourida (fantasia)* in Morocco in 2019. Fantasia is an equestrian art form prominent in Morocco and other North African countries.

horse with great stamina. It had high withers (shoulders) and short back, with a sloping croup (back hips), and carried its tail low. [Fig. 4- 2] Traditionally the Arabian horse's head was characterized by its dish-shaped profile, broad forehead, with large wide-set eyes, large nostrils, and small muzzle. Other breed characteristics are its arched neck and high tail carriage. Arabians have a compact body with a short back, and well-angled hip and shoulder. Arabians are small, usually standing between 14.1 and 15.1 hands high. [5][Fig. 4- 3]

Fig. 4-3 George Stubbs, *Warren Hastings on his Arabian Horse*, 1796

The first several generations of the new blood horse were short in height like the "Oriental" horses and may have been rather compact. But by the end of the eighteenth century, this new kind of horse was a perfect racing machine. The blood horse, soon to be called Thoroughbred, had gained height and length, and was characterized by its high withers, deep chest, and short back. It could measure well over 16 hands high. Its body was lean, with long muscles and long, delicate legs. Its well-chiseled head was carried on a long neck. [6] [Fig. 4-4]

Fig. 4-4 An early Thoroughbred horse depicted by George Stubbs, *Molly Long-legs, racehorse owned by Frederick St John, 2nd Viscount Bolingbroke, 3rd Viscount St John,* between 1761 and 1762

The Foundation Sires

For more than two centuries, it has been put forward that all Thoroughbred horses trace their bloodlines back to three dominant stallions imported into England from those areas called the "Orient." Each of the three horses has its own almost mythical story about how it was brought to England somewhere between the years 1690 and 1730. There they were bred with native Galloway and Hobby and other English racing mares. Their offspring eventually produced the breed originally known as the "English horse," later the "blooded" horse, and finally the "Thoroughbred." The Thoroughbred is a breed known the world over, first for its sustained speed over long distances, but also for its elegance and nobility. [7]

Fig. 4-5 John Wootton, *The thoroughbred horse Byerly Turk and a saluki dog*

The first of these foundational stallions to arrive in England was the Byerley Turk, around 1690. [Fig. 4-5 } It is not clear how this dark brown stallion came into the hands of Robert Byerley—either captured in battle in Hungary or bought from a Dutch officer who had seized him in the Battle of Vienna. Later the horse served as Byerley's own war horse in the Battle of the Boyne in 1690 in Ireland. Today it is believed this horse was probably "a breed called Akhal-Teke from Turkmenistan." Eventually this horse wound up in Yorkshire, the center of racing and racehorse breeding in England. [8]

Fig. 4-6 Another of the foundation sires of the Thoroughbred breed, depicted by John Wootton, *The Darley Arabian*

The second horse, the Darley Arabian, was a strikingly beautiful and refined colt, a horse "of exquisite beauty," discovered among the tents of Bedouin herders in the desert outside of Aleppo, in Syria, by an English merchant, Thomas Darley. [Fig. 4-6] He arranged to buy the yearling from Sheikh Mirza II, but then found out that the Sheikh had reneged on the deal, so Darley had the colt smuggled out through Smyrna. The fine, young, dark bay horse arrived in England in 1704, and was sent directly to the Darley family estate in Yorkshire. Thomas Darley knew nothing of the horse's speed, of course, when he smuggled him out of Syria, but the "Arabian" horse covered mares until 1719, producing a great number of good runners. Research shows that 95 percent of modern Thoroughbreds can trace their Y-chromosome back to this horse. [9]

Fig. 4-7 George Stubbs, *Godolphin Arabian*, before 1806

The most romantic of the Thoroughbred equine histories belongs to the third foundation sire, the Godolphin Arabian (or Godolphin Barb), imported into England in 1730. [Fig. 4-7] The horse is often called an Arabian, and much controversy persists over his origin. Sometimes he is referred to as a Barb because his country of origin was thought to be Tunisia, on the so-called Barbary coast of north Africa. One author has him coming from Yemen. Others call him a Turkoman. In his portraits and descriptions, he appears to be a classic Arabian, with his arching, high-carried tail, wide-set eyes, and dish-shaped face. He was imported into England from France by Edward Coke in 1729. How this horse got to France and what happened to him in France before he was bought by Coke is the stuff of several children's stories, the first one being the Frenchman Eugene Sue's *The Godolphin Arabian*, first published in 1846. [10]

Supposedly the horse was a gift of the Bey of Tunis to the king of France. His headstrong temperament soon resulted in his being kicked out of the royal stables, and purportedly he wound up abused and pulling a cart on the streets of Paris, where Coke found him. In 1731, he was crossed with a mare of "Oriental" blood, Roxanna, and they produced the first of three colts that soon became racing legends (Lath, Cade, and Regulus). Upon Coke's death, his friend, the Earl of Godolphin, inherited his stables, which is how the "Arabian" became known as the Godolphin Arabian. He continued to stand at stud until 1753. As well as his sons, several of his daughters also proved very influential on the track and as breeders of turf horses. [11]

Although, as stated above, 95 percent of modern Thoroughbreds trace to the Darley Arabian in the male line, "most horses have more crosses to the Godolphin Arabian (13.8 percent) than to the Darley Arabian (6.5 percent) when all lines of descent (maternal and paternal) are considered." Certainly the Godolphin Arabian was overwhelmingly represented in the bloodlines of the English turf horses imported into Virginia in the eighteenth century. Thomas Jefferson owned thirty-four horses whose pedigrees could be traced back two, three, or four generations to the Godolphin Arabian. Three of the most important bloodline sires for Jefferson's horses, Janus, Fearnought, and Diomed, were grandsons or great-grandsons of the Godolphin Arabian. [12]

Blooded Horses in America

By the late 1730s, several of these new blooded horses were introduced to the colonies. They were bred with the Hobbies, Galloways, and Chickasaws already in Virginia with the stated intention of "improving the blood," which at first meant racing speedily for long distances. Some of the colonial horses already in Virginia were quite fast, and this had encouraged the popularity of quarter racing, a match between two horses down a straight trail or through the center of town for a quarter of a mile. In contrast to quarter races, course races, transplanted from England, catered to the new "Oriental" blooded horses, and consisted of four-mile heats. The new blooded horses had bottom (endurance) and could maintain high speeds longer than the Virginia quarter horses. Thus arose a whole new industry around breeding these blooded horses for these new kinds of races. (See Chapter 6.) [13]

Buying, importing, maintaining, racing, breeding, and selling these remarkable horses became the purview of the landed gentry. Importing a winning racehorse from England was an extremely expensive affair and could only be attempted by the most wealthy and successful members of the Virginia landed gentry. [Fig. 4-8] The cost of such a horse would include the expense of sending an agent to England to find a retired turf winner whose owner was willing to sell. Then arrangements had to be made to send the horse to the colonies by ship. The Atlantic crossing sometimes took three months. Sufficient quantities of fresh water and food had to be available to the horse, and the stall had to be kept clean of manure during the whole voyage.

Fifty-nine blooded horses were imported from England to the colonies between 1730 and 1776. Most went to Virginia. Course racing in Virginia quickly became an important social event and form of entertainment for all social classes in colonial Virginia, although the racehorses were owned and bred by only a small number of upper-class planters. Soon breeding racehorses became another product, like tobacco, raised for profit on the extensive plantations of Tidewater Virginia. [14]

Before the Revolutionary War, these imported horses, the sires and dams of subsequent American offspring, were all proven racehorses on the English turf, so there is no question that the planters who imported them were interested in breeding them for distance racing. However, in those first twenty-five years (1740–1776), they were also sought to improve the blood of the gentlemen's riding horses and carriage horses as well. Perhaps the refinement of form and pedigree mimicked the planter's same preoccupations. [15]

Owning several blooded horses for use under saddle, for riding and foxhunting, and as carriage horses, not just to race them, quickly became a symbol of the aristocratic-aping gentry classes in Virginia. The imports were taller and perhaps more elegant than the smaller plantation horses already in use in Virginia, as well as faster for longer distances. As riding horses, however, they may have been less comfortable and practical than the Virginia quarter horses because they were trotters, not pacers (riding the trot can be quite bumpy and jarring and exhausting unless one "rises to the trot," a later riding-style innovation). However, as a symbol, owning and riding these horses trumped comfort.

Fig. 4-8 Unloading horses from a ship upon arrival in the Americas as depicted by William Wilson, *It All Began Here in Annapolis*. It shows Maryland Governor Samuel Ogle observing the arrival of the first pair of imported British thoroughbreds—Queen Mab and Spark—at the Annapolis City Dock in June 1747.

All of the imported horses oozed status, but inevitably some horses produced more offspring (get) or more valued offspring, including race winners, than others. Three especially well-known imports were Janus, Fearnought, and Diomed. Those three stallions appear in many of Jefferson's horses' bloodlines.

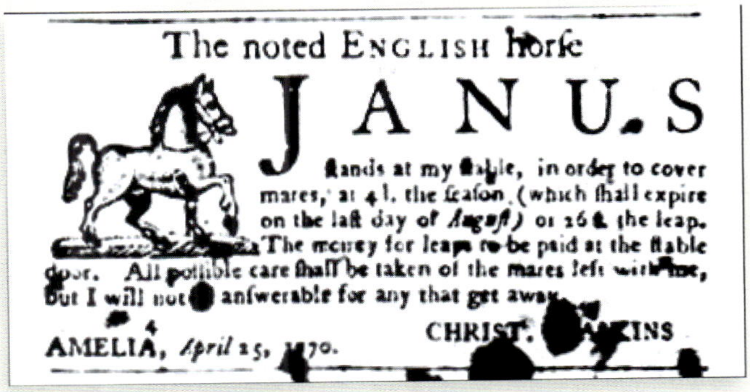

The noted ENGLISH horſe

JANUS

ſtands at my ſtable, in order to cover mares, at 4 l. the ſeaſon (which ſhall expire on the laſt day of *Auguſt*) or 26 s. the leap. The money for leaps to be paid at the ſtable door. All poſſible care ſhall be taken of the mares left with me, but I will not be anſwerable for any that get away.

AMELIA, *April* 25, 1770. CHRIST. [illegible]KINS

Fig. 4-9 Ad for Janus as stud in the May 24, 1770 issue of *Virginia Gazette*

Janus: Janus, even in Jefferson's time, was already a legend. An early import, Janus was a prodigious sire and bred wonderful saddle horses and quarter horses of tremendous speed. Foaled in England in 1746, Janus, a short (14.1 hands) chestnut grandson of the Godolphin Arabian, was a somewhat successful but not impressive distance (four-mile) racer from 1750 to 1752, after which he stood at stud from 1753 to 1756. In 1756, Janus was imported to Virginia by the planter and merchant Mordecai Booth, in Gloucester County, Virginia, near Yorktown. The next spring, at eleven years old, Janus won a race against one of William Byrd III's horses and was promptly stood at stud. [Fig. 4-9] From then on, Janus was moved literally every year all over Virginia and the Roanoke River valley of North Carolina, an area known as the old racehorse region of North Carolina, to stand at stud. His fertility was amazing, producing legions of offspring. In 1780, after twenty-four seasons in Virginia and North Carolina (when he was thirty-four years old), Janus died on his way back to Virginia to yet another owner. [16]

Although Janus was imported to improve the blood of distance runners, his get did not have the bottom for racing over long distances. Although his pedigree was seven-eighths "Oriental," he didn't sire distance runners or trotters. Ironically,

Janus, a Thoroughbred import, produced amazing sprinters that excelled in the quarter-mile races still popular on the frontier (see Chapter 7), especially when crossed with the small American "common" (not blooded) mares. In fact, today Janus is considered one of the founders of the American Quarter Horse breed. [17]

Despite many detractors, Janus had his vociferous supporters. Janus seemed to pass on two characteristics that other imported horses did not. First, Janus colts were pacers, not trotters. Among many plantation owners, however, the gaited horses (those that pace and rack) were valued as comfortable and durable saddle horses. Additionally, Janus's conformation was universally described in glowing terms: "Janus, from his shoulders back, was considered the most perfect formed horse ever seen in Virginia, by the most skillful connoisseurs. He was remarkable for roundness of contour, strength of articulation, and indicating great powers and stamina in his whole conformation." The descriptions of Janus certainly sound more like those of a modern American Quarter Horse than the longer and leggy Thoroughbred. "More good saddle horses and harness horses have sprung from [Janus stock] than from any other." Another breeder added, "Janus' colts were horses of fine constitution, long lived and performed well on the road. Their action in all their paces, was short and quick." [18]

Fearnought: Fearnought was larger than Janus at 15 hands, 3 inches tall. Sired by Regulus, son of the Godolphin Arabian, Fearnought was a bright bay colt, foaled in 1755 in England. Fearnought was praised as "a King's Plate winner, and won four-mile heats under high weights and so was considered the most desirable of specimens for importation to improve the small, sprinting types prevalent at the time in the Virginia Colony." [19]

Virginian colonel John Baylor, of Newmarket in Caroline County, an important breeder and the chief importer of Thoroughbreds in the colony before the Revolution, sent a very specific order to his agent in England for the kind of stallion he was looking for. He asked for "a most beautiful strong bay at least 14.3 hands high, as much higher as possible, provided he has beauty, strength and sp't with it, and one that had won some Kings plates with a pedigree at full length and cert. of age under a noblemen's hand as most of the list belong to noble'n." Baylor's agent wrote back that Fearnought fit the description perfectly. Fearnought was imported to Virginia by Baylor in 1764 at the age of nine. After Baylor's death, Fearnought stood more seasons in southern Virginia, dying at age twenty-two. He is often known as Old Fearnought or Imported Fearnought, or Baylor's Fearnought. [20]

All the early commentators on American turf horses laud the value of this horse for the legacy of his blood. One said, "Fearnought left the most numerous and valuable stock of any horse that was ever stood in Virginia and North Carolina before the days of old Diomed; there are few well bred horses in either state that do not trace to old Fearnought; his stock was the largest and handsomest on the continent, while their success on the turf left them almost without competitors." Fearnought "injected much needed size, stamina and courage into American breeding programs." Many of his sons served as horses in the Continental Army (and were lost or killed during the war, as we shall see later). Many Fearnought mares were taken to Kentucky, and five are among the matriarchs of the American Thoroughbred breed. His stud fee was five times the amount charged for other good sires, and he was the most important sire in America until Diomed was imported after the Revolution, in 1799. [21]

Diomed: Diomed was legendary. Foaled in 1777, he was chestnut with a white star and two white feet. He had an Arabian-like dished face and stood 15 hands, 3 inches high. His bloodlines on both sides have many crosses of all three of the foundation stallions. In England, Diomed had been the very first Epsom Derby winner, in 1780. Although a great winner in his youth, Diomed peaked early. His racing career foundered. When he stood at stud in England, his get proved problematic and temperamental, and he had a reputation as a bad foal-getter. His fertility declined with age.

Nevertheless, John Hoomes of Virginia was looking to invest in blood horses and imported him to America in the spring of 1798, when the horse was already twenty-one years old. Hoomes put Diomed immediately into stud service and liked the results. The horse was later purchased by Thomas Goode and stood at stud in Chesterfield County. Then, as we have seen before with Janus, Diomed moved from farm to farm in the Roanoke River valley in Southside Virginia before eventually returning to John Hoomes's plantation, Bowling Green, where he died in 1808.

Fig. 4-10 John Nott Sartorius, *Diomed*, 1780, depicts the Epsom Derby winner.

The effect of Diomed's blood on his American offspring was nothing more than revolutionary. Diomed sired some of the most famous horses in American turf history, and could be called the grandfather of all fine racing stock in America. Perhaps his most famous and successful offspring was Sir Archy, from Tayloe's mare Castianira. Sir Archy was considered America's first great racehorse, and he also produced a long line of winning colts. Some have claimed that his blood was disseminated throughout the entire blood-horse structure to such an extent that his name occurs in the pedigree of every modern Thoroughbred. In fact, it is possible to trace the pedigree of every horse that has won the Kentucky Derby for the past ten years back to Diomed, including the Triple Crown winner American Pharaoh. [22]

When Diomed died at age thirty-one, one historian reported, "There was as much mourning over his demise as there was at the death of George Washington." Diomed is one of the first American founding stallions of whom we have a George Stubbs portrait. [23] [Fig. 4-10]

Thomas Jefferson also sought Diomed offspring. In 1809, toward the end of his presidency, his son-in-law John Wayles Eppes procured for his father-in-law a son of imported Diomed, which Jefferson also called Diomede, and used as a carriage horse. Several of Jefferson's last horses were also of old Diomed blood: Peacemaker, bought in 1819, was a seven- or eight-year-old chestnut, got by old Diomed. A six-year-old (unnamed) bay of "Diomed blood" was bought in 1822 (the last horse Jefferson bought). Eagle, Jefferson's last saddle horse was also got by old Diomed.

Jefferson's Saddle Horses

When contemporaries refer to Thomas Jefferson's fondness for a "good horse," they imply that he preferred to use the new blood horses arriving in Virginia as his personal saddle horses. Jefferson, like other many Southern plantation owners, took more pleasure in riding these horses than racing them.

Although Jefferson kept horses on his farms for breeding, harnessed horses in his gigs and carriages for travel, and used horses to work his plantations, it was with his saddle horses that he most closely identified. Several of them became important named characters in his biographies. Riding out alone every day on his favorite saddle horse became a central part of Jefferson's self-definition. His letters to friends are full of references to his solitary riding. To tell the story of Thomas Jefferson's horses is also to tell the story of Jefferson's life. After 1772 (when Jefferson was twenty-nine years old) and until his death in 1826 (when he was eighty-three), Jefferson described and referred to thirteen (maybe fourteen) favorite riding horses. When someone asks about Jefferson's horses, or what kind of horse he rode, the answer is these fourteen horses. This chapter discusses the social history of each of Jefferson's saddle horses in chronological order. It was on these blooded, highly bred horses that he did his pleasure riding and spent the middle part of his day. [24]

The General: Jefferson left no physical description of this horse, a retired racehorse, who was six years old (foaled in 1769) when he acquired him.

Lineage: Jefferson noted down later in his *Farm Book* that The General "was got by Janus." Janus was the very important turf horse imported to Virginia from England in 1756, who left hundreds of offspring. As Janus colts were valued for their comfortable gaits, many became saddle horses rather than racehorses. Horses Jefferson bought were above all general-purpose horses. He used them for riding, as well as in harness when convenient. The General was an example of that. The retired racehorse became a saddle horse. [25]

Social connections: Jefferson bought The General from Alexander Spotswood in Spotsylvania County on June 14, 1775. Alexander Spotswood (1751–1818) was the grandson of Alexander Spotswood (1676–1740), the governor of Virginia from 1710 to 1722. The grandson would serve in the Revolutionary War and held the rank of general. He was a close friend and neighbor to George Washington. Spotswood was an avid

Jefferson's Significant Saddle Horses				
DATE PURCHASED	NAMES	DOB	COLOR	OTHER MARKINGS
1775	The General. 1769			
1775	Caractacus	b. 1775		
1788	Odin	b. 1778	sorrel	
1786	Sorrel riding horse		sorrel	
1790	Tarquin	b.1780	roan	
1796	Darlington	b. 1789		
1801	Wildair	b. 1794	bay	16 hands
1804?	Arcturus			
1805	Jacobin			
1807?	Turncoat			
1808	Celer	b. 1802	bay	
1814	Bremo	b. 1806	Dark bay	star
1815	Tecumseh	b. 1808	Bright bay	Few white hairs in forehead
1820	The Eagle	b. 1814	Fine bay	16 hands, 2 hind feet white, star

horseman and breeder and may have had several magnificent animals to offer the young Jefferson besides The General.

Jefferson paid Alexander Spotswood £25 for The General and then gave him an order for £25 more, the payment of which was not completed until May 1778, three years later. In September 1783, Jefferson traded the now fourteen-year-old General, along with another horse, nine-year-old Alfred, to his friend and fellow horseman, Colonel Thomas Mann Randolph, for Raleigh, a "five- or six-year-old" chestnut sorrel, and the promise to make Randolph a phaeton (carriage).

Social History and Role in Jefferson's Life: The General was only the fourth horse listed on Jefferson's list of horses on the first page of his *Farm Book*. Jefferson was traveling from Williamsburg in his two-horse phaeton (a kind of carriage), on his way to Philadelphia, to attend the Second Continental Congress as a delegate from Virginia, when he had stopped at Spotswood's for the night. [26]

Many years after Jefferson's death, family members and slaves still included The General in the list of favorite Jefferson saddle horses. Since Jefferson bought this horse quite early in his career, The General must have been an impressive horse to stay in the family memory for so many years. [27]

Caractacus: One of Jefferson's favorite and well-remembered riding horses from early in his career was Caractacus, foaled in 1775 at Elkhill. Unfortunately Jefferson gave no physical description of this fine horse either. Most likely he was a bay (like his grandsire, [Old] Fearnought), a much-admired horse color of the time and Jefferson's preferred color for the rest of his life. We know nothing of this horse's markings or his height. The social connections inherent in Caractacus's pedigree were more important for Jefferson to record than his physical description. [28]

Lineage: Hand-drawn meticulously by Jefferson himself, Caractacus's vaunted pedigree is found on the inside front cover of the *Farm Book*. [Fig. 4-11] As a matter of fact, Jefferson may have inaugurated his *Farm Book* with his notes on this horse. Caractacus was got by the well-known (stud) Dandridge's Young Fearnought on the highly bred mare (dam) Allycroker. The rest of the pedigree was elegantly drawn in Jefferson's own hand on the "tail side" (female line) up four generations.

Caractacus was also used as the stud for at least one of Jefferson's mares and for the mares of many of Jefferson's neighbors in Albemarle County in the years between 1779 and 1782. Jefferson bred Caractacus to his own iron-gray mare Silvertail to produce Silveret (number 27 in the *Farm Book*).

Social Connections: Jefferson carefully recorded the names of the owners of other horses in Caractacus's sire and dam lines. Through the sire, Young Fearnought, Jefferson reinforced connections with owner William A. Dandridge, a friend since student days at the College of William and Mary and a cousin of George Washington's wife. Dandridge was married to Ann Bolling, daughter of Colonel John Bolling, who also imported running horses and owned a mare in Caratacus's dam's pedigree. Young Fearnought's sire and dam are also noted by Jefferson: Young Fearnought was out of Old Fearnought, imported in 1764 by an important turfman, John Baylor of Newmarket. The dam was an oft-cited mare, Calista, owned by William Byrd III of Westover, of one of the First Families of Virginia.

Caractacus's dam, Allycroker, had been inherited from Jefferson's father-in-law, John Wayles. Allycroker's sire Silver-eye was an imported horse (1756), owned by Samuel Duvall, who was involved in Virginia politics before the Revolutionary War, and an important investor in land and mines. Allycroker's dam's line was even more thoroughly recorded for the relationships reified in her pedigree. Her dam, Patty Banister, was by Spanker, a stud imported in 1740 by William Nelson, governor of Virginia in 1770–1771. Spanker was crossed with Jenny Morris, owned by Colonel John Bolling, related in marriage to William Dandridge (see above). This mare was by another imported stud, Beau, owned by Secretary Carter, a member of one of the wealthiest and largest land-holding families in colonial Virginia. Jenny Morris's dam was another imported mare owned by Colonel Eppes, a neighbor of Colonel Bolling. By 1772, the Eppes family was related to Jefferson through marriage, and in fact, one of Jefferson's daughters would marry an Eppes much later.

Social History and Role in Jefferson's Life: Caractacus's name is significant: A few weeks before this colt had been born, on May 7, 1775, the British had marched out of Boston and killed American militiamen at Lexington and Concord, resulting in heavy casualties. America was at war with its mother country. The news would have taken a week or so to arrive at Monticello, just before Allycroker's colt was born. Jefferson named the colt Caractacus—the name of the Celtic king of the Silures, who had fiercely resisted the first-century invasion of Britain by imperial Rome. Certainly, the American Jefferson identified with the Silures and the brave defense of their homeland from the invading Roman Empire.

Jefferson was governor of Virginia toward the end of the War for Independence, when in January 1781 British troops managed to attack and invade Richmond, the capital of Virginia. It was on Caractacus that Jefferson as governor had escaped

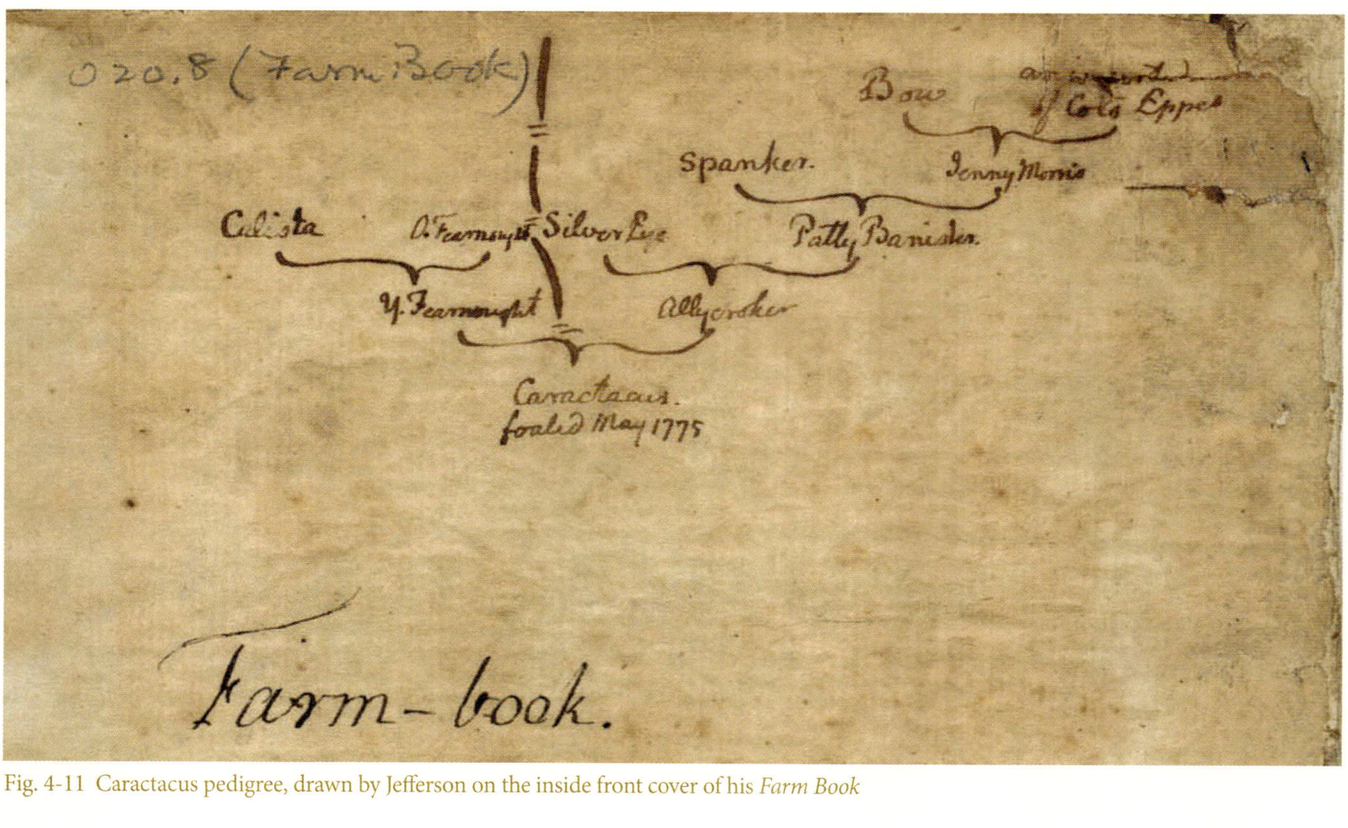

Fig. 4-11 Caractacus pedigree, drawn by Jefferson on the inside front cover of his *Farm Book*

from the British troops in Richmond in January 1781 and went west to rejoin his family at Tuckahoe before going on together to Monticello in Albemarle. And it was Caractacus that on June 4 took Jefferson through the woods on Carter's Mountain, shod with his horseshoes on backward, as Jefferson avoided at the last moment the English troops of Colonel Banastre Tarleton who came looking for the governor at Monticello. When Jefferson later reconnoitered with his family (sent on ahead in a carriage) in southern Albemarle, they headed southwest to his home Poplar Forest in Bedford County, where they spent the next six weeks. Although technically Jefferson's governorship had ended two days earlier (June 2), the escape from Monticello on Caractacus caused searing accusations of cowardice to be directed at Jefferson. Although officially absolved of cowardly actions later by the General Assembly, these accusations tarnished Jefferson's reputation and haunted him for the rest of his life. [29]

After his wife's death in 1782, Jefferson soon left Monticello on various governmental assignments and eventually was sent to France in August 1784. Although Jefferson took his phaeton to France with him, he did not take any of his horses. Caractacus was obviously left behind. Since Jefferson and his daughters did not return from France until almost 1790, we are left to wonder what happened to Caractacus, who would have been only fifteen years old by then.

We have one hint. In February 1790, just back from France and attending to business at Monticello before joining President Washington's government in New York City, Jefferson wrote to his brother-in-law Charles Lilburne Lewis (married to Jefferson's sister Lucy). The letter is dated February 22, 1790, one day before Jefferson's eldest daughter, seventeen-year-old Martha, was to marry her second cousin, Thomas Mann Randolph Jr., at Monticello. Jefferson says he is sending Lewis "the pedigree of Caractacus" that he had requested, along with two books for Lewis's son. Besides marriage ties, Jefferson had kinship ties with Lewis. At the time, Lewis lived in Albemarle, so it is probable that while Jefferson was in Paris, he had left Caractacus with this man who had such close links with the family. Lewis must have continued standing Caractacus at stud and needed the pedigree recorded in Jefferson's Farm Book. Probably due to the horse's age, Jefferson would no longer have wanted him as a saddle horse for the long trip to New York. Both men seemed to be wrapping up business details before Jefferson was soon to leave the area again. [30]

Odin: Foaled in April of 1778, Odin was a sorrel horse that stood 4 feet, 11 inches high (not quite 15 hands).

Lineage: Odin was another colt from the get of Dandridge's Young Fearnought, whose dam was one of Jefferson's mares, a bay at Willis Creek (land across the river from Elkhill).

Social connections: As Odin came from one of Jefferson's own mares (inherited from his father-in-law, John Wayles), social connections in this case came through the owner of the sire, William Dandridge, discussed above.

Social History and Role in Jefferson's Life: Odin must have remained at Monticello and been used there during Jefferson's absence in France. According to Isaac (Granger) Jefferson, in the 1847 interview when he was a free man, Odin was a riding horse that Jefferson took from Monticello to Philadelphia (via New York City) as secretary of state sometime after 1790. [31]

Sorrel Riding Horse in Paris: After being appointed minister plenipotentiary to France by the new American government, Jefferson, with his oldest daughter, Martha, and his slave James Hemings, left Boston by ship on July 5, 1784, arriving in Paris in early August. [32]

For more than a year, the Jeffersons resided in temporary quarters until they finally moved to their permanent residence, the Hôtel de Langeac, on the Champs Elysées, in September 1785. [Fig. 4-12]

For the first two years in Paris, Jefferson did not have

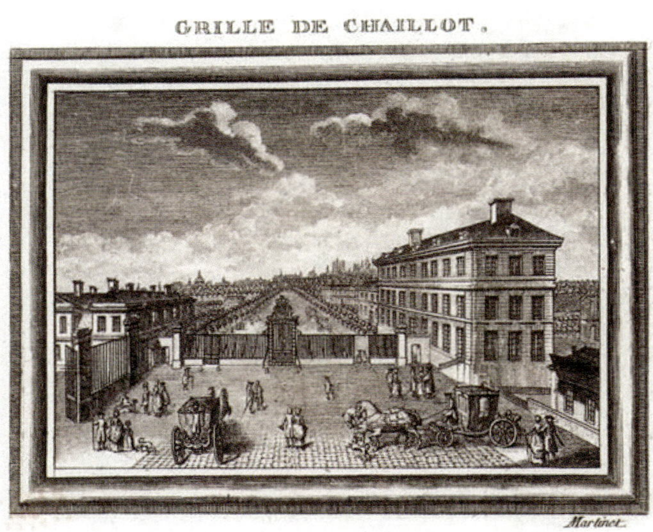

Fig. 4-12 Jefferson's residence in Paris. François Nicolas Martinet, "The Hotel de Langeac on the Champs Elysees," in *Description Historique de Paris,* 1799.

Fig. 4-13 Grand Stables (Grandes Ecuries), built 1719 outside Paris, in Chantilly

a riding horse, and he walked or used a carriage for travel. Parisian fashion would have demanded that one arrive clean and unsoiled to appointments and dinners, so Jefferson would have used a carriage rather than ride. In general, it seemed that Jefferson explored the city on foot. Certainly, it is during these years that he extolled the virtues of walking in his letters and maintained that walking was the best possible exercise. [33]

The Hôtel de Langeac had stables, but Jefferson did not buy his own horses until May 1786—two horses to draw his carriages. Jefferson had hoped to buy a riding horse in England on a trip he made there with John Adams in March and April 1786 and had written to friends in England to help him procure one, but to no avail. Finally, when he returned to Paris, in August 1786, Jefferson bought what he called his "sorrel" riding horse. [34]

We know very little about this horse. Jefferson always and only referred to it as his sorrel horse, as did others. Sorrel refers to a color of light reddish brown, including the same color of mane and tail. However, in Virginia at that time, when one spoke of a sorrel horse, it usually meant that the horse was not a blood horse (not a Thoroughbred). Sorrel in Virginia probably referred to the small, stocky, colonial all-purpose horse used before English turf-horse imports arrived. Jefferson recorded that the French sorrel was six years old when he bought it.

Lineage and Social Connections: This riding horse cost almost twice that of each of the two bay carriage horses (1320 francs vs. 720 francs), which must indicate something about the perceived quality of the horse. Yet there is no comment about the horse's bloodlines or breed. His sorrel horse was probably not a Thoroughbred (or it would have deserved a name and pedigree description). Jefferson paid a Mr. Kendrick for the sorrel riding horse but did not seem to have any other relationships with Mr. Kendrick.

Fig. 4-14 Horse in courbette. Ludwig Koch, *Die Reitkunst im Bilde/The Art of Riding in the Picture*

Fig. 4-15 Spanish bullfighter on horseback (*rejoneador*)

Social History and Role in Jefferson's Life: Although he hadn't been able to buy a horse in England on his trip with John Adams in the spring of 1786, Jefferson did buy a saddle and bridle, along with boots and whips. The fact that Jefferson bought an English saddle probably underlines the difference in equitation styles between France and England at the time. By the mid-eighteenth century, the English had distinguished themselves from the continental riders in accoutrements and style with the development of the new English Thoroughbred breed for racing and sport in England.

French riding style was characterized by *manège,* or what we today call dressage. For more than a century, French nobility had sent their youth to royal equitation academies to train (*manège*) in military horsemanship and other virtues. Just north of Paris are located the Grand Stables (*Grandes Écuries*) of Chantilly, built in 1719 by the order of Louis-Henri, Duke of Bourbon. [Fig. 4-13 see p. 89] These mammoth stables, considered an eighteenth-century architectural masterpiece, housed more than 240 horses, as well as 500 hounds. Hunting took place daily all year round. The stables were the site of royal breeding programs and an academy for *manège*. Sumptuous dinners, which the king attended, were held under the stable dome. Chantilly is very near the royal palace in Versailles, so Jefferson would have been well aware of these Grand Stables. [35]

Fig. 4-16 Example of a western saddle as depicted in *The Horse Wrangler,* 1910

Dressage trained horse and rider for military maneuvers, culminating in the *haute école* (high school), of the "airs above the ground" of the *levade, courbette,* and *capriole,* moves consisting of the horse rearing, leaping, and kicking out backward in place. [Fig. 4-14 see p. 89] Even then, the *haute école* was likened to dance and seen as a courtly art. The saddle used (high pommel and high cantle) and the bit used (the curb) were meant to collect the horse. Collection is when the horse lowers its hindquarters, and the weight of the horse shifts back on to its hind legs; it is "forward-going energy contained." The horse submits to the control of the man on its back. The rider sits straight and tall and back in the saddle, legs long, high boots up over the knee. [36]

Fig. 4-17 English flat saddle. John E. Ferneley, *Portrait of James Ogilvie Fairlie of Coodham,* c. 1840, with his grooms John Jennay and Cooper, and his hunters Spicey, Wing, and The Little Mare.

This saddle was based on a model used for mounted combat, because its high pommel and cantle provided support to the rider. For those same reasons, this saddle was used in Spain and Portugal for bullfighting and cattle work, as well as long-distance travel generally. We can still see this saddle in use today at the Spanish Riding School in Vienna, as well as in Spain [Fig. 4-15] and elsewhere. The western saddle in the United States is a descendant of the Spanish saddle and continues to have a high pommel and cantle. [Fig. 4-16]

Fig,4-18. Galloping across the countryside: Freedom. John E. Ferneley, Sr., *The Quorn Hunt in Full Cry*, 1825.

The horses used in these academic maneuvers were the big, strong, stocky Neapolitan, Andalusian, or Frisian types—what we call "warm bloods"—still used today in dressage. In France at that time, riding in a saddle was still an aristocratic prerogative and was about control and restraint.

In England, on the other hand, by the mid-eighteenth century, a new style of riding had evolved in tandem with the new blooded horses being bred there with bottom (endurance) and speed for racing and riding across country in pursuit of a fox, jumping all obstacles they met. Now, instead of collection and control, free forward movement of the horse and minimal interference by the rider were the objective of riding. The saddle was now flat, with little or no padding and with a low cantle and pommel so as not to get in the way when the rider leaned back upon jumping or forward at the gallop; the saddle gave the rider close contact with the horse. [Fig. 4-17] In England, not only royalty and nobility rode horses, but also the rural gentry, who rode over hill and dale in their symbolic pursuit of status. For Englishmen, the English hunting seat—this free forward movement of horse and riders with a minimum of restraint—became a metaphor for liberty and for Englishness itself. [37][Fig. 4-18]

Although Jefferson was often accused of loving all things French, he inherited his riding style and preferences from the English. He enthusiastically rode English blooded horses all his adult life, and used the flat English hunt saddle, the only one available in Virginia. He did not even buy the saddle horse in Paris until he had bought a saddle and other equitation accoutrements in England, thus rejecting the French aristocratic style of riding and choosing "liberty" over "control."

As soon as he had finally bought his sorrel riding horse, Jefferson was able to return to his tradition of a two-hour noontime ride before the afternoon meal, most often through the nearby Bois de Boulogne, a practice that Jefferson continued throughout the rest of his stay in Paris. According to his daughter Martha, Jefferson never missed a day. Jefferson often took American guests and visitors out riding with him through the royal forest.

The acquisition of his sorrel horse came at the beginning of Jefferson's quasi-courtship of Maria Cosway. One afternoon in September 1786, when Cosway and Jefferson were out together in the Tuileries Gardens, Jefferson took a fall when trying to jump a fence and broke his right wrist. Although his daughter Martha implied that Jefferson had been out for a walk, his bookseller and the man who acted as his secretary while he recuperated, Mr. Goldsmith, recalled that his fall that day was from a horse. Jefferson had only had his riding horse for a month when the fall occurred. Perhaps the horse was still skittish and may have shied. The horse must have had a tendency to throw its head, because Jefferson had purchased a martingale for him the day he bought the horse. Jefferson's wrist never healed correctly, having now been twice broken, and was permanently disabled and misshapen. [38]

William Short, Jefferson's personal secretary while in Paris, wrote Jefferson when Jefferson traveled to southern France to assure him that his horses back in Paris were being well taken care of and were getting exercised. Jefferson's valet and later butler, Adrien Petit, seemingly helped exercise the horses but would only ride the "saddle horse." Short further wrote, "On the day of the review, Colo. Smith mounted one of your carriage horses, my servant followed us on the other, and I had your sorrel." [39]

When Jefferson and his family left France to return to the United States in late 1789, his sorrel horse was lame and stayed at Hôtel de Langeac. William Short stayed behind in Paris to tend to Jefferson's affairs. Short eventually sold the sorrel to the Compte de Langeac for 300 livres as credit on the house rent still owed. [40]

Tarquin: Foaled in 1780, Tarquin was a ten-year-old retired racehorse when Jefferson bought him in March 1790.

Tarquin was well known by turfmen due to his unusual roan color. [41]

Lineage and Social Connections: Jefferson bought Tarquin from William Fitzhugh, of Chatham, located across the Rappahannock from Fredericksburg. Fitzhugh was an important planter, horse racer, and breeder, and good friend and later neighbor of George Washington. Fitzhugh's daughter married Washington's (adopted) grandson. Fitzhugh's wife, Ann Randolph, was a second cousin of Jefferson's.

Jefferson noted that Tarquin's sire was Eclipse. If Tarquin was actually ten years old, his sire was probably John Harris's (of Powhatan) Eclipse, a son of Old Fearnought. Tarquin's dam was a roan mare owned by Peyton Randolph (Jefferson was his first cousin once removed). Randolph was a member of the House of Burgesses, attorney general of Virginia, and the president of the First Continental Congress. Randolph was also an important mentor to Jefferson in Williamsburg, who later replaced him at the Continental Congress. [42]

Fig. 4-19 Roan-colored horse. The color of this American Quarter Horse is described as "red roan" or sometimes "bay roan."

The roan dam came from a famous line of horses: Monkey, Othello, and Dabster. Monkey (a grandson of the Byerley Turk), a bay colt born in 1725, had been on the turf in England and was imported by Nathaniel Harrison of Brandon, in Prince George's County on the James, in 1737. Thus, he was one of the first English imports. (He covered in Virginia from 1738 to 1749). Monkey is the only horse in America before 1776 whose portrait is known, and which was painted before he left England. Nathaniel Harrison was related to the Randolphs in Jefferson's family.

Othello (b. 1746) was another horse imported into Maryland in 1755 and brought to Virginia a bit later (1761), again by Nathaniel Harrison. He was a beautiful black horse that left many offspring. Dabster, a chestnut colt (b. 1736), had also been on the turf in England before being sent to Virginia in 1741, and was in the Carter and Byrd studs on the James River in Charles City from 1743 to 1761.

Social History and Role in Jefferson's Life: Jefferson bought Tarquin in Alexandria on his way up to New York City to be secretary of state under George Washington in March 1790. (Jefferson was asked to join Washington's government soon after returning from France with his family.) When the government moved to Philadelphia, Jefferson took Tarquin there as his riding horse (thus supplanting Odin). Tarquin was an exception to Jefferson's general preference for bay horses; he was a roan, and a retired racehorse. Isaac (Granger) Jefferson, in the 1847 interview, declared that Tarquin was the only roan racehorse he had ever seen. In fact, when racing, Tarquin was known as the "Roane colt." [Fig. 4-19] As a racehorse, Jefferson wrote in his account book, "he excelled in 2.mile heats 140 lb." [43]

Although Jefferson used Tarquin in Philadelphia as a saddle horse (for his daily rides), he thought that Tarquin's front legs and hooves were not strong enough to endure the rocky trails of Albemarle County and decided not to take him home to Monticello upon his (first) retirement in 1794. Because the horse's feet were too tender, Jefferson said, "I should not use him myself, because of his awkwardness in going down hill, that is to say half the time one is on him, as all is either up hill or down hill with us." Jefferson offered to sell Tarquin back to William Fitzhugh, but Fitzhugh said he couldn't use him at that point: "I am much obliged to you for the offer of Tarquin, & should if I was a young Man again prefer him to any Horse I know, but at present I am provid'd with two most excellent riding nags of smaller Size." Therefore Jefferson made plans to have the horse taken back to Monticello, and another horse brought to Philadelphia in his stead. The horse was to be led to Georgetown on the Potomac and exchanged for a horse that his son-in-law had procured for him in Albemarle. There was an involved series of letters back and forth between Randolph and his father-in-law about the adequacy of the substitute horse, but nevertheless, on September 4, 1793, the horses were exchanged at Georgetown. Tarquin returned to

Albemarle with a Monticello slave, and the substitute continued on to Philadelphia. [44]

At Monticello, Tarquin was put in the care of Thomas Mann Randolph, Jefferson's young son-in-law, who was living nearby (at Edgehill) and overseeing work at Monticello. After a couple of months, Randolph had the horse in such good shape that he offered to buy him from Jefferson. Tarquin had "mended so much that I must beg to have the preference at 120 Drs. If you are determined to part with him." Jefferson immediately answered Randolph, insisting that his son-in-law keep the horse:

> I am happy that you think Tarquin will suit you, and insist on your acceptance of him. This is no sacrifice to me, because my sole motive for having thought of parting with him was that he is unnecessary for me, as I must keep carriage horses, which will do to ride. I insist also as a condition, that you feel yourself perfectly free to part with him whenever he ceases to answer your end or you can by parting with him have your end better answered. From this moment then he is yours, and I am much happier in it than to have turned him over to any other person. [45]

Randolph again offered to pay for the horse, and a second time a month later Jefferson underlined that the horse was a gift: "I must repeat and insist that you take Tarquin, and on the express condition of making the most of him whenever you have good opportunity." Tarquin must have been quite a striking and magnificent saddle horse, because correspondents remembered him more than a decade later. [46]

Darlington: This riding horse was seven years old when he became Jefferson's saddle horse. Unfortunately, we have no physical description of Darlington.

Lineage and Social Connections: Jefferson did not record anything about Darlington's pedigree. He received this riding horse from John Wayles Eppes, soon to be Jefferson's (second) son-in-law, but note that Eppes was already relating to Jefferson through horses. Eppes paid himself directly out of the estate of John Wayles (Jefferson's wife Martha's father) and told Jefferson to credit Mr. Wayles's estate £65. [47]

Social History and Role in Jefferson's Life: Jefferson used Darlington as a riding horse for several years during his first retirement at Monticello and then during his years as vice-president. At one point in 1798, Jefferson decided he had to give Darlington a "long rest" because the horse was given to "dullness, stumbling & weakness." Jefferson attributed this to "sickness" but was confident that if "his health becomes firm he will be highly valuable to me." The rest was to give the horse time to recover. Jefferson told his son-in-law Thomas Mann Randolph that he was welcome to use Darlington "the half of year" that Jefferson was away from home. "I would rather you should keep and use him for your own riding in the neighborhood than leave him at Monticello. He must now be as well as rest can make him. I wish you therefore to take him till wanting for my journey." [48]

Randolph responded later in the month:

> With pain I mention Darlington: anticipating your kindness I took him early in the Winter to ride being absolutely on foot—he had not been long at Belmont before he came in the way of my Dun horse (tho' I kept him always chained; he unluckily got loose) & rec'd. a bite from him on the middle of the neck which was very near killing him and had greatly injured his appearance—he is quite well now & in far better plight & health than I ever saw him—I keep him still and as the depression in his neck will not spoil him for me, I beg you to take Meriwethurs horse in exchange for him: I can have him at a short warning. Darlington will always be dull and a stumbler, he needs keen spurs & heavy Bridle but with those is the finest riding horse I know & except the bite an elegant Animal. I am sorrier for the accident as I fear you cannot get a better one just now notwithstanding his failings. [49]

Darlington's bite on the neck is due to an attack by another stallion (Randolph's Dun horse), a consequence of keeping stallions near each other. Randolph said he kept the dun chained, but that the horse had escaped. When stallions challenge each other for supremacy, they often attack by biting the neck of the other. Interestingly, although Randolph thinks Darlington is a superb riding horse, he was worried that his appearance (with the bite) would make him inapp2ropriate for his father-in-law. Darlington was sold to Richard Richardson, a Monticello workman and overseer at the time, in the summer of 1799 for £60 worth of labor. [50]

Jefferson and the Jockey

Jefferson's favorite exercise was riding. He was a good judge of a horse, and rode a very good one.

One day, during his presidential term, he was riding somewhere in the neighborhood of Washington, when there came up a cross road, a well-known jockey and dealer in horse-flesh, whose name we will call Jones.

He did not know the President, but his professional eye was caught, in a moment, by the noble steed he rode.

Coming up with an impudent boldness characteristic of the man, he accosted the rider, and forthwith began talking in the slang of his trade, about the horse, his points, his age, and his value, and expressed a readiness to 'swap' horses.

Mr. Jefferson gave him brief replies, and civilly declined all offers of exchange.

The fellow offered boot, and pressed and increased his bids, as the closer he looked at the stranger's steed, the better he liked him.

All his offers were refused with a coolness that nettled him.

He then became rude, but his vulgarity made as little impression as his money, for Jefferson had the most perfect command of his temper, and no man could put him in a passion.

The jockey wanted him to show the animal's gait, and urged him to trot with him for a wager. But all in vain.

At length, seeing that the stranger was no customer, and utterly impracticable, he raised his whip and struck Mr. Jefferson's horse across the flank, setting him off in a sudden gallop, which would have brought a less accomplished rider to the ground.

At the same time he put spurs to his own beast, hoping for a race. Jefferson kept his seat, reined in his restive steed, and put an equally effective rein upon his own temper.

The jockey wondered; but impudently turned it off with a laugh, and still keeping by the side of his new acquaintance, began talking politics. Being a staunch Federalist, he commenced to launch out against "Long Tom," and the policy of his administration.

Jefferson took his part in the conversation, and urged some things in reply.

Meanwhile they had ridden into the city, and were making their way along Pennsylvania Avenue. At length they came opposite the gate of the presidential mansion.

Here Mr. Jefferson reined up, and courteously invited the man to enter. The jockey raised his eye-brows, and asked—

"Why, do you live here?"

"Yes," was the simple reply.

"Why, stranger, what the deuce might be your name?"

"My name is Thomas Jefferson."

Even the jockey's brass turned pale—when, putting spurs to his nag, he exclaimed—

"And my name is Richard Jones, and I'm ok!"

Saying which, he dashed up the avenue at double quick time, while the President looked after him with a smile, and then rode into the gate.

(Source: Ellis, Thomas Jefferson: A Character Sketch, 62–64.)

Wildair: Wildair was a charismatic, big bay horse, 16 hands high, who was seven years old when Jefferson bought him.

Lineage and Social Connections: A highly bred animal, Wildair had lineage through John Syme's Wildair (1776), whose sire was Colonel John Baylor's Old Fearnought. Syme, the half-brother of Patrick Henry, was a breeder in Hanover County along with Jefferson's friend, William Dandridge (Syme's brother-in-law). The dam of Syme's Wildair was Thomas Mann Randolph Sr.'s Young Kitty Fisher (1764). This Thomas Mann Randolph, an important horse breeder, cousin, and lifelong friend, was the father and namesake of Jefferson's son-in-law. [51]

Jefferson bought Wildair from John Hoomes of Bowling Green in Caroline County, by then the preeminent breeder of turf horses in post-revolutionary Virginia. John Hoomes was a large landowner, great planter, and importer of Thoroughbred horses. (See Chapter 2.) He organized the Virginia Jockey Club in 1788 and made the town of Bowling Green the busiest breeding center on the continent. Between the years 1792 and 1805, he imported nineteen different English stallions and thirteen different English mares "whose influence on the American thoroughbred breed was incalculable." His most famous and important import was Diomed, founder in this country of one of the greatest dynasties of racehorse sires and dams in the United States. [52]

Social History and Role in Jefferson's Life: Jefferson bought Wildair from Hoomes in February of 1801 as he passed through Caroline County on the way to the District of Columbia to be inaugurated as the third president in March. Hoomes assured Jefferson that Wildair was the "the finest horse I know in the State, he is 7 years old, near 16 hands high, a very fine presence, gay, but perfectly gentle, & his color bay. If I rightly recollect the roan horse you formerly rode, this is his equal if not his superior." The roan horse referred to the retired racehorse, Tarquin, that Jefferson had bought ten years earlier, in 1790. Homes said Jefferson could have the horse for $300, although he was worth much more. Hoomes justified the price, and continued: "I have rode him but a very small distance never more (perhaps) than half a mile on a good road, that I can only say he trotted & galloped that distance, extremely well, all who saw him are delighted with the horse, & suppose he would answer well your purpose." Jefferson answered, "I have no hesitation on your judgment that the horse you propose to me is equal in form to old Tarquin (the roan) to accede to you price." [53]

Hoomes asked Jefferson to let him know if the horse came "up to your expectation of him." Four months later, Jefferson finally responded to Hoomes in a letter, saying, "The first view of the horse did not impress me equal to his merit. I soon, however, became sensible of it, am extremely pleased with him, & attached to him as a riding horse, & am thankful to you for having thought of me on the occasion, & furnished the opportunity of procuring so fine a creature." Jefferson went on to add, "I was offered the same money very soon after receiving him: but had already become too much pleased with him to part with him." (Note the anecdote in the box above, "Jefferson and the Jockey.") [54]

Jefferson family lore, as recounted by great-granddaughter Sarah Randolph, says that the magnificent Wildair was the horse Jefferson rode to his inauguration and tied to the palisades, as described by an English traveler who was in Washington at the time. Sarah describes him thus: "His dress was of plain cloth, and he rode on horseback to the Capitol without a single guard, or even servant in his train, dismounted without assistance, and hitched the bridle of his horse to the palisades." An early print of Jefferson with a horse (made later) shows him riding to his inauguration and tying a gray horse to the palisades. In reality, however, Wildair was a bay. [55] [Fig. 4-20]

The story of Jefferson riding a horse to his presidential inauguration in 1801 turns out not to be true. He walked to his inauguration, but this version of events was convincing to family members who knew him. Jefferson continued his daily rides while president. Washington, DC, was still very rural, and the White House was near the countryside. President Jefferson

Fig. 4-20 Jefferson tying his horse to the Palisades at his inauguration, 1801, Washington D.C., as depicted by Matthew Tucker

would daily meander through what is today Rock Creek Park in the wilds of the countryside near Washington from one to three o'clock in his lifetime routine of solitary rides. At least four stories are told of strangers who, coming upon Jefferson on his daily ride, and not recognizing him as the president, struck up conversations with him. Usually these strangers were his "enemies," i.e., Federalists, or some such political enemy. The story always ends in the shock of the stranger, charmed by Jefferson's simplicity and lack of pretense, when Jefferson turns to go in the White House. These are apocryphal stories that underline Jefferson's supposed democratic nature, but it is significant that these stories usually have him riding his horse off in the countryside.

Arcturus: Arcturus is another saddle horse that Jefferson used during his presidency. We do not find specific mention of Arcturus by name in Jefferson's account books, so it is difficult to know when he bought this horse. Nor do we have any physical description of him.

Social History and Role in Jefferson's Life: The first mention of this horse was in 1804 in a letter from Monticello to son-in-law John W. Eppes, when Jefferson spoke of the possible acquisition of a bay horse that would "do" with Castor or Fitzpartner (to draw a chariot). Eppes must have offered his father-in-law a horse, because Jefferson wrote that he knew of no finer horse than Eppes's own horse, but that he was "much too fiery to be trusted in a carriage—the only use I have for him while Arcturus remains." By this comment, it is clear that since Arcturus was Jefferson's riding horse, any new horse would be used to drive. In 1806, Arcturus must have been again at Monticello, because Jefferson wrote his overseer telling him "to dispose of Arcturus as soon as possible," suggesting a price of $150 (considerably more than a mere work horse). If Arcturus was then worth $150, perhaps he is the unnamed horse Jefferson bought in 1797 for $100 from a Mr. William Farris. That price indicates a riding horse, not a work horse, which in those years only cost $30 to $50. [56]

Arcturus was not sold, however, and at some point, went back to Washington, because Wormley Hughes, the hostler at Monticello after 1800, said that Jefferson brought Arcturus home from Washington when he retired from the presidency in 1809. In Hughes's conversation with Jefferson's biographer, he described how Arcturus's habit of shying at jutting rocks caused Jefferson to lose patience with the animal and resort to the whip. Perhaps this is why Jefferson was anxious to sell the horse because, in general, Jefferson tried to avoid conflict. [57]

Jacobin: We have no physical description of this horse, who served as Jefferson's riding horse during the later years of his presidency. The horse's politically charged name, Jacobin, is a sardonic reference to Jefferson's sympathy for French egalitarianism and democracy.

Social History and Role in Jefferson's Life: Jacobin was another riding horse Jefferson obtained through an exchange of horses and boot (something given in addition, especially to equalize an exchange) with John Wayles Eppes during his White House years. The exchange was recorded in Jefferson's account book on May 27, 1805. By this date, Jefferson must have been bereft of a good saddle horse, because he wrote Eppes that he "was never better pleased with a riding horse. It is now really a luxury to me to ride." Jacobin thus had replaced Arcturus as a saddle horse. [58]

Turncoat: Turncoat was a horse Jefferson owned in his second term as president, but very little else is known about this horse.

Social History and Role in Jefferson's Life: We know that when Turncoat was used as a saddle horse, he was difficult to control. Jefferson wrote his son-in-law Thomas Mann Randolph, in May of 1807, to discuss how to control this restless and nervous horse. The president wrote saying that "[Turncoat] cannot be managed with a common curb" and proposed that they use a mameluke bit on him. A mameluke bit is much more severe than a "common curb," but was the norm in Spanish America at the time. [59]

Celer: Celer was another bay horse, six years old, when President Jefferson acquired him in August of 1808 as a riding horse for his last months in Washington, DC. Family members recalled Celer as one of Jefferson's "superb horses." [60]

Lineage and Social Connections: Celer was a highly bred horse, and Jefferson wrote that this horse was out of Fitzpartner on a Celer mare. The sire, Fitzpartner (or Meade's Fitzpartner), was a bay horse got by Old Partner (Partner was an important stud that had stood at Thomas Mann Randolph's Tuckahoe plantation and had been bred to Jefferson's broodmare Allycroker). The dam was a Celer mare, which meant that her sire was Celer. Celer (or Meade's Celer) was considered to be the "best son of Janus." Janus was the imported horse that bred quarter horses of blazing speed and wonderful saddle horses. His son, Celer, also produced one of the American Thoroughbred foundation mares (#13). Both Fitzpartner and Celer were owned by General Everard Meade from Amelia County in Virginia. The dam of both these horses, Meade's Fitzpartner and Meade's Celer, was the same gray mare, Brandon. [61]

President Jefferson purchased this Celer in August 1808 from a Mr. (Richard) Durrett, another planter and neighbor, who lived near Earlysville (in Wakefield) in Albemarle County.

Fig. 4-21 Oaklands (Malvern), Route 708, Albemarle County, Virginia

Social History and Role in Jefferson's Life: As was typical of those times, Jefferson called the horse after its most famous ancestor (see also Wildair, Diomede). Also, as was noted above, Jefferson wrote down this horse's name as "Seelah" in his notes. "Seelah" would be the pronunciation of "Celer" in a Southern accent, current even today. Jefferson used this spelling (as he pronounced it) every time he referred to a Celer. For example, much later in November 1822, Jefferson bought a six-year-old blood bay mare, Stella, from John Flood, the owner of a tavern on the way to Poplar Forest, for $80. Jefferson noted that the mare was "of Janus and Seelah blood." Janus's most famous offspring, of course, was Celer. Moreover, early Jefferson biographer Henry Randall listed Jefferson's important saddle horses as remembered by his family and included the horse spelled as "Celer." [62]

Bremo: Overseer Bacon described Bremo, another favorite saddle horse, as "a horse of fair size, full, but not quite as tall as Eagle," i.e., not quite 16 hands, and added that Bremo was a good riding horse as well as excellent for the harness. A splendid dark bay, with a white star, and eight years old when Jefferson acquired him in 1814, he was not as tall as his sire, Knowsley, either. It was impressive Bremo that Jefferson was mounted upon in his midday ride that I imagined in the preface of this book. [63]

Lineage and Social Connections: Bremo's sire, Knowsley, was imported into Virginia in 1801 by William Lightfoot (from Sandy Point in Charles City), another turf breeder, after having been on the turf in England for two years. Another bay colt, and 15.3 hands high, Knowsley ended up at stud at William Woods's farm in Albemarle County, Oaklands, [Fig. 4-21] from 1805 to 1807. (Dick Woods Road in Albemarle County still bears one brother's name.) The Woodses were also breeders (acquiring horses from the stud of John Randolph of Roanoke) and turfmen, and active members of the Albemarle Agricultural Society. Knowsley covered 940 mares in Albemarle and Charlotte Counties. Fairfax Harrison, the equine historian, says his stock was "highly esteemed for durability of service, i.e., chiefly as saddle horses." Given what we know about John Hartwell Cocke's interest in breeding comfortable riding horses, not racing horses (see Chapters 2 and 7), and this description of Knowsley offspring as "saddle horses," Bremo was most likely a smooth riding pacer. Surely he fulfilled for Jefferson on his daily ride what Cocke described as the "sharer and companion of our sports, the aid in our healthful exercises." [64]

Jefferson bought Bremo from John Hartwell Cocke, his neighbor and fellow planter, who lived in nearby Fluvanna County, southeast of Monticello at Bremo. Although a generation younger than Jefferson, Cocke helped found the University of Virginia and was on the Board of Visitors until his death in 1866. Cocke shared many interests with Jefferson, including an appreciation of fine horses, and was a frequent visitor to Monticello (see Chapter 2).

Social History and Role in Jefferson's Life: In April 1814, Jefferson's grandson Thomas Jefferson Randolph had seen one of Cocke's horses and recommended him to Jefferson. The horse was named after Cocke's farm, Bremo. Jefferson wrote to Cocke that he was looking for a carriage horse and wondered if he could try Bremo out for a week. Cocke replied that the horse:

> answered the description they have given of his qualities as a carriage & riding Horse. I have driven him chiefly in double Harness, he has been seldom in a gig but when tried performed very well & I am sure from his docile character may be trusted without risk. You are at liberty to take him on your journey to Bedford and return him when you get back if you find that he does not suit you. [65]

However, at this point in his note, Cocke warned Jefferson about a slight defect in the horse: "He has been occasionally subject to a spasmodic affection something like the Thumps which I once thought alarming but am now induced to believe that it is nothing more than Hickup, as it always succeeds a hearty meal or draught of water." Jefferson rode Bremo for six years until he got The Eagle (in 1820). Then Bremo became a carriage horse, one of four that pulled the Jefferson in his landau. [66]

Tecumseh: Tecumseh was a handsome, bright bay horse with a few flecks of white on his forehead. He was foaled in 1808. Jefferson bought him in 1815.

Social History and Role in Jefferson's Life: Although Jefferson may have bought Tecumseh as a riding horse, Bacon said he worked better as a carriage horse and thus became part of Jefferson's landau team. Tecumseh is described as a carriage horse (see Chapter 5).

The Eagle: Eagle was a fine bay and the last horse of Jefferson's life. Eagle was six years old when overseer Bacon bought him for Jefferson in 1820. A tall (16 hands), fiery bay with white hind ankles with a white spot on his nose, "the finest sort of riding horse" according to Bacon, Jefferson rode him for six years until the final weeks of his life. [67]

Lineage: Eagle was from the get of the famous Diomed, imported by turfman John Hoomes, and his dam was a Spread Eagle mare of Fearnought blood. This means that her sire was Spread Eagle, while her dam was sired by Fearnought. Spread Eagle, a bay colt born in 1792, was a turf horse imported into Virginia in 1798, also by John Hoomes. After 1802, Spread Eagle was sent to South Carolina and later to Lexington, Kentucky. Recall that Fearnought had been imported by John Baylor much earlier (1777). Thus, Jefferson's last horse combined the blood of two of the most important English imports for the American Thoroughbred breed: Fearnought and Diomed.

Social Connections: Bacon bought The Eagle for Jefferson from Captain John Graves of Louisa. Graves had previously lived in Albemarle County, and several of his children were born there. He had served in the militia in the War of 1812. Captain Graves sent his son to the same school for boys that John Hartwell Cocke's son attended, so Graves may have belonged to the same social circles as Cocke. Note that this last horse, The Eagle, establishes one new relationship, with Captain Graves, while reaffirming some older, more commercial ones with the Hoomes and Baylor families.

Social History and Role in Jefferson's Life: Dr. Robley Dunglison, Jefferson's medical doctor the last years of his life, referred to Eagle as "his excellent and gentle horse." "But Eagle had his one fault," said family members. Eagle had a tendency to shy and bolt. Henry S. Randall, Jefferson's 1857 biographer, shows the immediacy of these stories received from Jefferson's family. [68]

> If suddenly and very severely frightened, he [Eagle] would whirl about to fly with suddenness which no firmness of seat was proof against. He thus once (when an antlered deer suddenly started up from behind a pile of brush immediately in his path) threw Mr. Jefferson, when greatly stronger than now.

Despite Eagle's nervous temperament, Jefferson let others, even his grandchildren, ride the horse. They, too, found it a challenge to contain the spirited and easily startled horse.

> Yet this animal was so spirited, that when a young kinsman of Mr. Jefferson's rode him with a company to meet Lafayette, at his visit to Monticello in 1825, the brave old horse became so ungovernably excited by the approaching roll of drum and trumpet—bounding and caracoling in the air—that the young rider was fain to fairly turn tail and retire. [69]

Granddaughters also tried their hand with Eagle, with the same results. In a letter to her daughter Ellen, Martha Jefferson Randolph wrote how "Eagle started at a cow and placed Miss Cornelia on her feet in the road." Nevertheless, Eagle did not seem to be a devious horse and was considered ultimately honest and trustworthy. Martha continued in her letter, "but she says [Eagle] took great care not to tread upon or jostle her and behaved as well as possible." [70]

Randall relates another incident where Eagle almost provoked a calamity but ended up saving his rider:

> On a recent occasion, when the latter [Mr. Jefferson] was riding down into a ford on Moore's Creek, where the bank was rather steep, the fore feet of the horse stuck in a new-formed bank of mud, and Mr. Jefferson was pitched over his head into the stream. His broken left arm was in a sling, his right wrist without strength, the water high, and he would have been drowned had he not in falling clung to the bridle, or grasped it, while Eagle was extricating himself, and thus been dragged ashore. [71]

Notwithstanding these incidents, Jefferson implicitly trusted Eagle. For example, supposedly it was Eagle who took the aging Jefferson down the mountain at a gallop in the dead of night one February to attend to his wounded grandson. Randall relates that occasion:

> When Jefferson was old and decrepit—after the last accident to his wrists—a messenger arrived to inform him that a grandson had met with a disaster, and lay seriously injured at Charlottesville. The weather was dark and lowering, night was setting in, and he was more than usually feeble. He directed Eagle to be brought to the door. His family entreated him not to set out, at least on horseback, at such a time; but his order was repeated in a tone which brooked no further opposition. The moment he

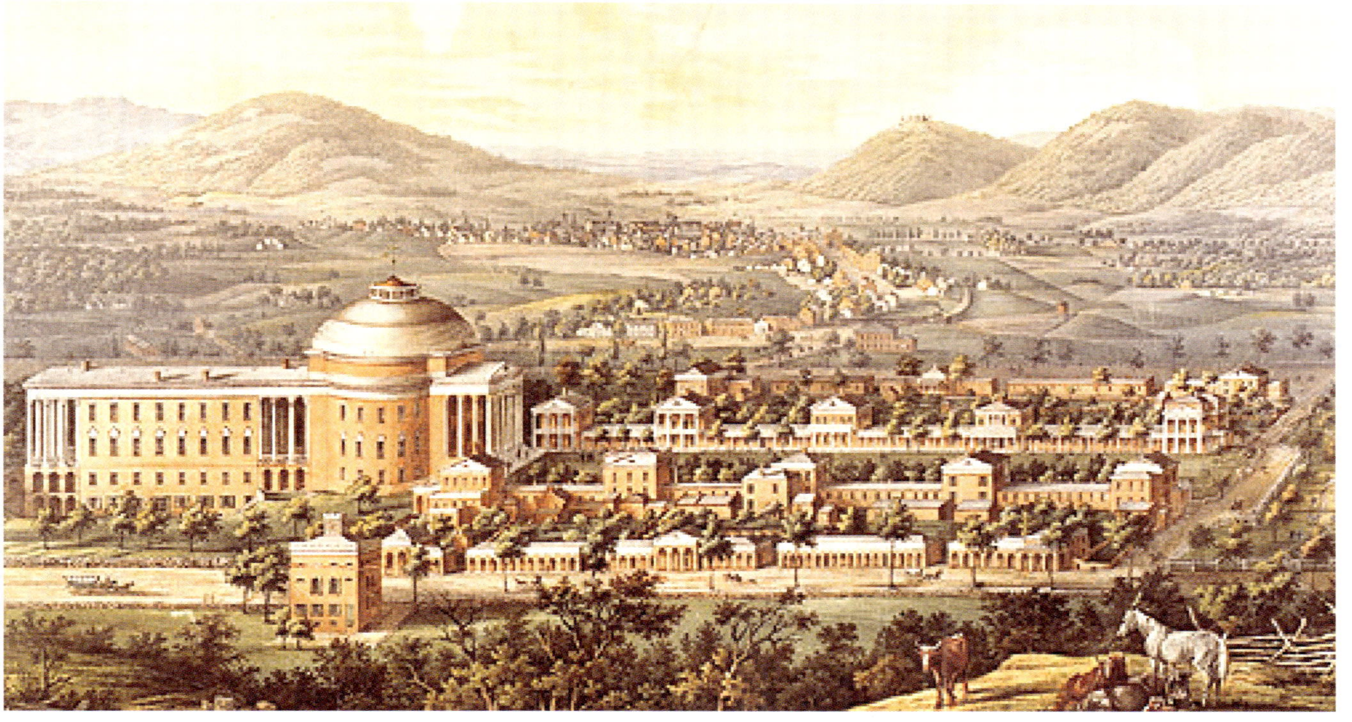

Fig. 4-22. Edward Sachse, *View of the University of Virginia, Charlottesville & Monticello,* taken from Lewis Mountain, 1856

> was in the saddle, he struck the noble horse, which bounded forward at full run. His family held their breath with suspense, expecting he would draw bridle at the "notch," where the mountain begins to descend abruptly. But the clatter of hoofs from the rocky passes showed them that the fearful race was continued. He swept by the returning messenger like an arrow, and reached Charlottesville in a time that, over such ground, the boldest rider in Virginia might, without suspicion to his courage, have pronounced appalling. [72]

Many further endearing stories abound about The Eagle taking care of the by-then elderly Jefferson:

> Old Eagle, like his master, was well stricken in years, but he retained the fire and almost the swiftness of the monarch bird whose name he bore. It was a sight to see him brought out curvetting from the stable for his master's ride. If the latter was not quite ready, a hook and staple in a Persian willow, marked Eagle's place in the mean time; and there he stood with his ears back on his arched neck, pawing and stamping the ground with fiery impatience. But when led to the terrace to be mounted, he stood as immovable as a statue; and when, the reins were disposed in the crippled hands—as ineffectual as an infant's to curb his strength—he moved off with slow and stately gravity, as if perfectly conscious of the necessity of discretion in his movements. [73]

I have stressed throughout these descriptions that the Jefferson family knew the Monticello horses as individuals, with their own personalities and traits. The Jefferson descendants and extended family could tell detailed stories about Jefferson's preferred saddle horses, especially the ones they knew intimately, like his last horse, Eagle. They attributed all kinds of purposeful behavior to Eagle in his relationship with Jefferson: Eagle had a fiery impatience yet stood as still as a statue in order to let the infirm and elderly Jefferson mount him, leaning against the terrace in order to "aid" the eighty-year-old to get into the saddle, and moved with a slow gravity "as if perfectly conscious of the need for discretion." Eagle saved Jefferson from drowning in Moore's Creek; he was not devious; and when granddaughter Cornelia fell off him, he took "great care" not to step on her or jostle her. Attributing agency to Eagle (care, aid, protection) seems like the Jefferson family was guilty of anthropomorphism, something science has tried to avoid until recently. But it is instructive that the Jeffersons, like others of their time, attributed resolve and willpower and choice to Eagle. [74]

Current research on human-horse relations proposes that "through riding both beings entrain to one another, fostering feelings of connection, boundary loss, and joined identity. This strengthens the human-horse bond and creates a mutually apprehended and co-created world. Within this space, horses can come to adopt a 'protective, possessive attitude toward the rider' that motivates them to them to 'think well and bravely'—they will disadvantage themselves to help their riders. Riders and well-treated horses take care of one another." Jefferson, perhaps without realizing it, and his mounts, especially The Eagle, are an example of this caretaking. [75]

Despite his age and infirmities, Jefferson rode his stallion Eagle to the University of Virginia Board of Visitors meetings [Fig. 4-22 see p. 99] those last months of April and May of 1826 (before Jefferson died in July), down the mountain, across Moore's Creek near Secretary's Ford, and up Market Street through town to the University. According to family members and Bacon, Jefferson rode Eagle to "within three weeks of his death."

What happened to Eagle? Was he sold with the furniture, tack, stock, and slaves in the January 1827 auction? [Fig. 4-23] Or did he, like some, receive special treatment? At first, Eagle was kept at Monticello for the use of the family that was still there, specifically for granddaughter Virginia Randolph Trist, while her husband, Nicholas P. Trist, was working in Washington, DC. Later, it seems Eagle went to nearby Edgehill with Virginia Trist when she moved there to live with the Thomas Jefferson Randolph family. [76]

Fig. 4-24. Bay horse with white markings

Eagle continued in the service of the family, with various mentions of him in family letters. In 1841, a great-granddaughter then residing in Mississippi wrote her seven-year-old brother, Wilson Cary Randolph at Edgehill, asking about Old Eagle. The letter writer said, "I suppose he is Louis horse now, and that you can ride chink, and papa's horse." Eagle would have been twenty-seven years old. We don't know how much longer he lived, but that is the last reference to Eagle that we find. [77]

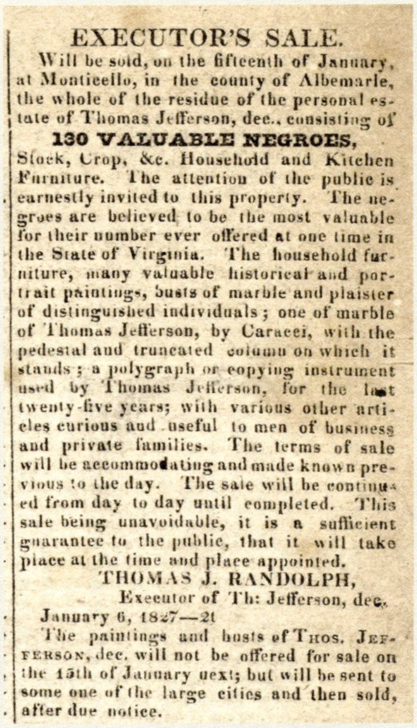

EXECUTOR'S SALE.

Will be sold, on the fifteenth of January, at Monticello, in the county of Albemarle, the whole of the residue of the personal estate of Thomas Jefferson, dec., consisting of

130 VALUABLE NEGROES,

Stock, Crop, &c. Household and Kitchen Furniture. The attention of the public is earnestly invited to this property. The negroes are believed to be the most valuable for their number ever offered at one time in the State of Virginia. The household furniture, many valuable historical and portrait paintings, busts of marble and plaister of distinguished individuals; one of marble of Thomas Jefferson, by Caracci, with the pedestal and truncated column on which it stands; a polygraph or copying instrument used by Thomas Jefferson, for the last twenty-five years; with various other articles curious and useful to men of business and private families. The terms of sale will be accommodating and made known previous to the day. The sale will be continued from day to day until completed. This sale being unavoidable, it is a sufficient guarantee to the public, that it will take place at the time and place appointed.

THOMAS J. RANDOLPH,
Executor of Th: Jefferson, dec.

January 6, 1827—2t

The paintings and busts of THOS. JEFFERSON, dec. will not be offered for sale on the 15th of January next; but will be sent to some one of the large cities and then sold, after due notice.

Fig. 4-23 An ad for the executor's sale of Monticello, November 3, 1826, *Richmond Enquirer*

Color, Age, And Sex

Throughout his life, Jefferson rode horses of several different colors: sorrel, roan, and bay. After 1800, all of his saddle horses were bays. Overseer Bacon stated in an interview that for Jefferson, "Bay was his preference for color. He would not have any other." Bay is a color terminology that has been very stable in the English language, almost always referring to horses. A bay horse can be many shades of brown: reddish or blood bay, copper, mahogany, auburn, or very dark brown (almost black). Jefferson also described a "bright bay" (Tecumseh) and a "light bay" (Traveller). Stella was a "blood bay" and Bremo was a "dark bay." But a bay always has black points (legs, muzzle, mane, and tail, and the tips of their ears are black). [Fig. 4-24] Many bays also have white markings on their lower feet and face. Jefferson's preference for bays was typical of the times. In a book on horse husbandry owned by Jefferson, the author says, "Colour should suit the taste of the purchaser, though a mahogany bay is certainly the best colour." [78]

Jefferson, like all horsemen, tried to match his driving horses, both in size and color. Depending on the vehicle, Jefferson used teams of two or four horses. Bacon implied that these, too, had to be bays. The team of four expensive blooded horses that drew his presidential coach was matched bays, as was the team of four that drew his landau in his later final retirement.

In the decade that Jefferson devoted to breeding horses (1774–1784), his mares produced foals of many colors: bay, black, iron gray, chestnut, roan, sorrel. The color sorrel did not seem to be held in high esteem. Son-in-law Thomas Mann Randolph once described it as a "bad color." [79]

If Jefferson bought a horse to use as his saddle horse, the animal was usually between five and seven years old. Training a horse under saddle did not begin until he was three or four years old. This means that a five- or six-year-old horse was fully trained and at his peak fitness. Note this comment from Mason's Pocket Farrier: "Horses that have not arrived at three years of age, are unfit for use, and those that are more than nine, decrease in value with great rapidity." When Jefferson bought a six- or seven-year-old horse, he was looking for physical maturation, and a well-trained, settled, and proven mount. [80]

All of Jefferson's riding horses were referred to as "horses," that is, stallions. Geldings (neutered horses) were always noted as such. None of Jefferson's saddle horses (nor carriage horses) was a mare (female). [81]

Gaits

Readers may be surprised to learn that in Virginia, when Jefferson learned to ride as a youth, he probably learned to ride on horses that were pacers rather than trotters. Today we call these horses "gaited horses," because they have some extra gaits, intermediate between the trot and the canter, i.e., pacing horses, with the amble and rack. [82]

These gaits are very comfortable for the rider to sit (and not be bounced around) for

Horses' Gaits

Walk, trot, canter, and gallop are called "natural" gaits because they are seen in wild horse populations and occur in all horse breeds.

- **Walk:** The walk is a four-beat gait that averages about 4 miles per hour (mph). When walking, a horse's legs follow this sequence: left hind leg, left front leg, right hind leg, right front leg, in a regular 1-2-3-4 beat. At the walk, the horse will always have one foot raised and the other three feet on the ground, except for a brief moment when weight is being transferred from one foot to another. A horse moves its head and neck in a slight up-and-down motion that helps maintain balance.
- **Trot:** The trot is a two-beat diagonal gait of the horse where the diagonal pairs of legs move forward at the same time. There is a moment of suspension between each beat. A trot can vary in speed but averages about 8 mph. A really slow trot is sometimes called a jog. Nevertheless, the trot (and the amble, see below) is the travel gait for a horse, as it can be kept up for a long time.
- **Canter:** The canter is a controlled, three-beat gait. It is a natural gait possessed by all horses; it is faster than most horses' trot but slower than the gallop, and is used by all riders. Depending on the length of the stride of the horse, the speed of the canter can be between 10 and 17 mph. A very slow canter, called a lope in western riding, clocks no more than 8 to 12 mph.
- **Gallop:** The canter and gallop are related gaits, as the rider simply makes the horse gallop from the canter by urging it to lengthen its stride until it is four-beat, rather than three-beat. When the stride is sufficiently lengthened, a canter becomes a gallop. The gallop is the fastest gait of the horse, averaging about 25 to 30 miles per hour.

However, other gaits, such as the amble and rack, occur naturally in some breeds (in other words, they are inherited), but individuals in these breeds often must be trained to perform these gaits.

- **Amble:** The amble (also known as the pace) averages about 9 miles an hour and is thus a faster gait than the trot. It is a two-beat gait, right hind and right front striking the ground at the same time, followed by left hind and left front, also at the same time. Therefore, two legs on the same side of the animal move forward together.
- **Rack:** The rack (or single foot) is a four-beat gait, right hind, right front, left hind, left front, and extended gait at regular intervals.

(Sources: "In the diagonal trot the horse's back rises and falls, but in the lateral amble and rack it remains relatively level, swaying slightly from side to side."—Harris, *Horse Gaits, Balance and Movement*, 32–50. When sitting on the back of a horse, the amble and the rack are much more comfortable gaits than the trot, especially over long distances.—Mackay-Smith, *The Colonial Quarter Race Horse*, 9.)

long periods and, thus, these horses became the basis for the first authentic American horse breeds in the rural South: horses that could reliably carry riders over long distances at a fast, yet comfortable, clip. [83]

A surprised Englishman tried to explain the pace and amble in American horses in the following way:

> A scientific English agriculturist named Parkinson, who came over in 1798, tells us that the American horses generally "leap well; they are accustomed to leap from the time of foaling; as it is not at all uncommon, if the mare foal in the night, for some part of the family to ride the mare, with the foal following her, from eighteen to twenty miles next day, it not being customary to walk much. I think that is the cause of the American horse having a sort of amble: the foal from its weak state, goes pacing after the dam, and retains that motion all its life." [84]

Eventually, however, toward the last quarter of the eighteenth century, as Jefferson began to buy and breed the offspring of the blooded horses being imported into the colony, he would have encountered horses that did not pace, but rather only trotted. Thoroughbreds do not pace. To go faster than a walk, for a long distance, they trot. For a rider, the trot is a much more jarring gait to sit and exhausting in the long run.

Trotting long distances was not as comfortable as pacing, unless the rider learned to ride the trot by rising in the stirrups, or to post. As British Lieutenant Anburey noted in 1777, "In travelling on horse-back, you must either walk or gallop your horse, as the motion of trotting is too fatiguing for yourself and the beast." Virginians still preferred the smooth gait of the pace and/or rack despite their infatuation with the new high-bred trotting horses. [85]

One English traveler to United States in 1795–1797, Isaac Weld Jr., wrote the following description of horses and their gaits during his visit to Petersburg, Virginia, in 1796:

> A trot is odious to them, and they express the utmost astonishment at a person who can like that uneasy gait, as they call it. The favorite gaits which all their horses are taught, are a pace and a wrack [*sic*]. In the first the animal moves his two feet on one side at the same time, and gets on with a sort of shuffling motion, being unable to spring from the ground on these two feet as in a trot. We should call this an unnatural gait, as none of our horses would ever move in that manner without a rider; but The Americans insist upon it otherwise, because many of their foals pace as soon as born. These kinds of horses are called 'natural pacers', and it is a matter of the utmost difficulty to make them move in any other manner; but it is not one horse in five hundred [in England today] that would pace without being taught. In the wrack, the horse gallops with his forefeet, and trots with those behind. This is a gait generally devoid of grace with the other, and equally contrary to nature; it is very fatiguing to the horse; but the Virginian finds it more conducive to his ease than a fair gallop, and this circumstance banishes every other consideration. [86]

In England, riders may have begun rising to the trot, copying the riding style of the postilions who guided the post-coaches (or stagecoach), but evidence indicates that in Virginia many riders resisted this maneuver. Even as late as 1820, one author wrote about the "quality in the saddle horse of which our country [Virginia] people are very fond," the rack, where a horse can travel "14 or 15 miles an hour." The question is, did Jefferson adapt to the signature trot in the new blooded horses by changing his seat, by rising to the trot (i.e., posting), or did he continue to try and sit the trot? [87]

Early on, in the 1760s and early 1770s, Jefferson's horses would have been pacers. He rode with his father in the woods and later inherited horses from his father. He rode horses to boarding school as a young boy, racing with his friends for fun. He rode his horse to Williamsburg and back as a student and law reader from 1760–1766. And he rode a horse back and forth to Staunton as a young lawyer; he was even paid with a horse as part of a law fee. But none of these horses was named, or pedigreed. They were probably generic Hobbies or Chickasaws. They paced. Jefferson's first blooded horse was Allycroker, inherited upon the death of his father-in-law, in 1773. After that, all his saddle and coach horses were high-bred Thoroughbreds. [88]

There was one exception to the fast and sleek blooded horses with the jarring trot. As discussed above, one British turf (distance) winner and stud, imported into Virginia in 1756, had a profound influence on the American Thoroughbred as well as the modern Quarter Horse, yet he did not produce trotters: Janus. Most of his get (offspring) were pacers, and thus were sought after as riding horses as well as racing horses. Janus's fertility was legendary, and his blood runs in the pedigrees of many outstanding contemporary racers. But his offspring was also known for their comfortable lateral gaits as riding horses. Many praised the "good saddle horses" that came from Janus stock. [89]

Significantly, several of Jefferson's blooded saddle horses were Janus offspring. Recall that in 1775, on his way to Philadelphia, Jefferson bought a retired racer called The General (1769), a son of Janus. Jefferson used The General as a riding horse and carriage horse. Later, in 1783, Jefferson bought a light chestnut sorrel called Sprightly, by a Janus mare. In 1808, President Jefferson bought a riding horse called Seelah (or Celer). In 1815, Jefferson bought another horse called Seelah (Celer), which was used as a riding horse before he became a coach horse. Both these Celers had Janus blood. In 1822, when Jefferson was seventy-nine, he bought a horse from John Flood, who kept a tavern on the way to Jefferson's retreat, Poplar Forest, in Bedford County. This horse, named Stella, was described as having "Janus and Seelah (Celer) blood." Since all of these horses had Janus blood, most likely all of these were pacers, and continued the earlier Virginia tradition of the ambling and the racking horse for long journeys, for business, and for social visits along early roads, when water transportation wasn't available. [90]

Jefferson's later and more well-known blooded horses—for example, Caractacus, Odin, Brimmer, Tarquin, Wildair, Jacobin, Tecumseh, and The Eagle—were mostly of Fearnought and Diomed blood and surely were trotters. These trotting horses were especially difficult for women to ride. In 1791, Jefferson's younger daughter was learning to ride at Monticello, while her father was in Philadelphia. This difficulty was alluded to in an earlier-described exchange of letters with her father (see Chapter 3), when Maria complained that the new horse that her uncle had bought for her, named My Heart, which she noted was a sister to Brimmer, "can only trot and canter." She sounded disappointed that My Heart did not have the comfortable intermediate lateral gaits like the pace. Blood horses (the Thoroughbreds), like Brimmer, were bred for speed, bred for the turf; they were born trotters, not pacers. Although posting to the trot makes riding these horses more comfortable, as a woman riding sidesaddle, she could not rise to the trot, which is why blood horses were

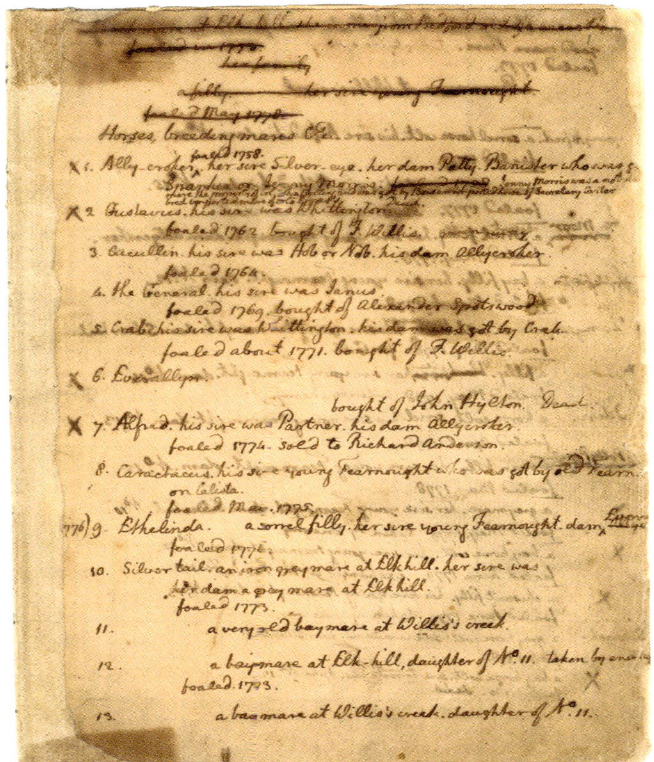
Horses, breeding mares &c.
1. Ally-croker, her sire Silver-eye. her dam Patty Banister
foaled 1762. bought of F. Willis.
3. Cucullin. his sire was Hob or Nob. his dam Allycroker.
foaled 1764.
4. the General. his sire was Janus
foaled 1769. bought of Alexander Spotswood.
foaled about 1771. bought of F. Willis.
6. Eversalloper.
bought of John Hylton. Dead.
7. Alfred. his sire was Partner. his dam Allycroker.
foaled 1774. sold to Richard Anderson.
8. Caractacus. his sire young Fearnought who was got by old Fearn.
on Calista.
9. Ethelinda. a sorrel filly. her sire young Fearnought.
10. Silvertail. an iron grey mare at Elkhill. her sire was
her dam a grey mare at Elkhill.
foaled 1773.
11. a very old bay mare at Willis's creek.
12. a bay mare at Elk-hill, daughter of No. 11.
13. a bay mare at Willis's creek. daughter of No. 11.

Original manuscript from The Coolidge Collection of Thomas Jefferson Manuscripts at the Massachusetts Historical Society.

Fig. 4-25 A list of named (blood) horses on the first page of Jefferson's *Farm Book*

not as comfortable to ride sidesaddle as the smaller and more stocky, smooth-pacing Chickasaws. [91]

John Hartwell Cocke, Jefferson's friend and neighbor, was a severe critic of the riding qualities of the very specialized turf horses imported into the United States at the end of the eighteenth century. Cocke, recall, was quite a horse breeder himself, and insisted that constantly breeding blood horses only for speed, only for racing, had been devastating to American bloodlines. Cocke promoted horses that served as fine saddle horses, which usually meant they were pacers. [92]

One minor anecdote from Jefferson's life reveals that he rode trotting horses at least occasionally. Toward the end of his life, Jefferson began to suffer from what we would call irritable bowel. Sometimes he would refer to it as "a slight indisposition." However, he wrote a letter to Henry Fry of Madison County, Virginia, indicating that "a trotting horse *strengthens the bowels* [italics added] and would aid Fry in arresting his diarrhea, adding that he used the treatment himself, suggested by the British physician, Dr. Thomas Sydenham, and believed it had cured him." Jefferson was never cured of his "indisposition" (many believe it was what led to his death), but it does help explain why he thought his horse was his best doctor. After an illness, he was always anxious to get back "on my horse, to me the most sovereign of all Doctors." Jefferson obviously got much relaxation and relief from stress while riding, but his comments highlight the difference in effort between riding a pacing horse and a trotting horse. [93]

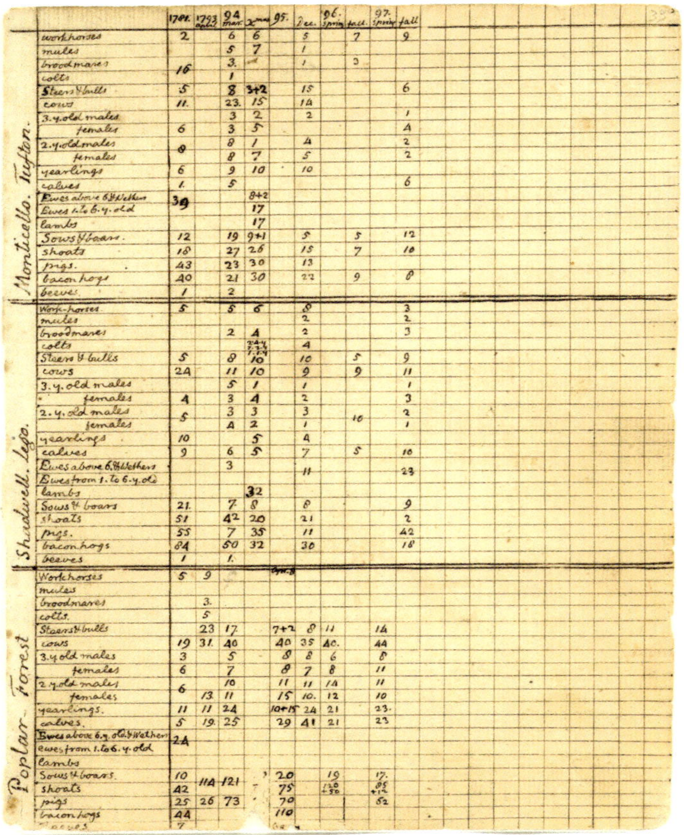

Fig. 4-26 Horses without names were listed with other livestock on p. 33 of Jefferson's *Farm Book.*

Names

Names implicitly convey identity. [Fig. 4-25 see p. 103] In human society, names identify who we are. Different aspects of our identity conflate in them: gender, age, social relationships, ethnic groups, even culture and religious tradition. Most importantly, names individuate as well as connect people. The names people give to animals also tell us many things. First, they tell us what categories of animal merit names. In Jefferson's time, dairy cows and workhorses might have been given familiar and affectionate names by those who worked with them. Beef cattle, for example, were not given formal names and certainly do not appear in Jefferson's account books. But some horses were given formal recorded names. Second, in the Anglo-European cultures, humans maintain distance from the animal world by not giving animals human Christian names. Finally, an animal's name often tells us more about the owner (or namer) than about the animal. Although names usually reflect the sex of the animal, they also are often an extension of the owner. In Jefferson's case, the names he gave his horses reflect his own personality and interests.

One general theme predominates in the names Jefferson gave his horses. Starting about 1774, a bit before the beginning of Revolution, Jefferson reached deep into his knowledge of classical literature and poetry to pull out names of earlier native heroes from Anglo-Saxon and other ancient cultures, leaders of insurrections and uprisings against more powerful forces. In this way, his horses' names serve as insight into Jefferson's mind and a projection of his personality. The names were metaphors for Jefferson's concerns.

Jefferson had many horses that were not named, at least on paper (in his account books). These were generally his (relatively inexpensive) work horses, or plantation horses, or Chickasaws (always just called "my Chickasaws"). [Fig. 4-26] These animals may have had names given to them by the people who worked with them daily, the slaves and field laborers, but those names were not recorded. Oddly enough, many of the mules that lived and worked at Monticello did have names that appear in the letters and account books. On the other hand, almost all Jefferson's (expensive) riding horses and carriage horses were referred to by name. The only riding horse that never received a name was his "sorrel riding horse" that he bought in France in 1786, nor did the two carriage horses that Jefferson had there merit names.

Fig. 4-27. "The Capitoline she-wolf with the boys Romulus and Remus." Thirteenth-century AD, with figures of Romulus and Remus added in the fifteenth century.

We can only guess who named the horses Jefferson recorded in his account books or referred to in letters to family and friends. Horses that he bought from others may have come with their names (such as the General, Tarquin, and Eagle). As was the case in eighteenth-century equestrian circles, the horse's name might refer to its (male) progenitor, or sire (such as Wildair, Diomede, Seelah

Fig. 4-28 Nicolai Abildgaard, "Ossian Singing His Swan Song," between 1780 and 1782

[Celer], or Bedford) or its human owner and progenitor (for example, Dandridge's Fearnought, Gay's Fearnought—two studs to which Jefferson bred mares). On the other hand, Crab, a horse Jefferson bought in 1778, was sired by the admired imported turf horse Whittington. Crab's name came down through his dam (mother), owned by John Syme, whose own sire was called Crab (thus the dam is referred to as a "Crab mare"). Traveller, a three-year-old light bay acquired in 1817, was described as a "Medley & Fitzpartner horse out of a Traveller mare" (meaning Traveller was the dam's sire). Jefferson's last riding horse, Eagle, was got by the famous Diomed (sire always mentioned first) on a Spread Eagle mare. Spread Eagle was not as significant as Diomed but was a valued stud imported from England in 1798 by John Hoomes.

Moreover, it is possible that once they were in his possession, Jefferson may have named horses that he bought nameless, or, like horsemen of every epoch, he may have changed their names to ones he preferred. In Philadelphia in the 1790s, Jefferson had two carriage horses named Romulus and Remus. It was typical of horsemen of the era to name horses after personages in Greek and Roman mythology. There is no evidence that these horses were related or came from the same source, but the names Romulus and Remus would have continued Jefferson's preference for indigenous culture heroes—like the twin founders of Rome. [Fig. 4-27] Later, in retirement at Monticello, Jefferson had two coach horses (acquired around 1815 or 1816) named Wellington and Blucher. Both these names were for generals (from England and Prussia, respectively) who helped defeat Napoleon at the Battle of Waterloo in 1815. Since Jefferson didn't buy the horses until 1815, it was probably he who gave them their names.

Fig. 4-29 King Alfred

Jefferson himself surely named the horses he bred and raised on his own plantations. He chose these names with much obvious care and personal significance. After 1774, when he inherited land, slaves, and stock upon the death of his father-in-law, John Wayles, and began to organize these properties in his *Farm Book*, Jefferson enthusiastically took over the horse-breeding programs at Elkhill and Willis Creek. Until he left for France in 1784, Jefferson carefully bred mares (and his stallion Caractacus). During this decade, he named and recorded all the foals born to his mares with the names of insurgent heroes of Gaelic and Irish, Icelandic, and Anglo-Saxon times (Cucullen, Cuthona, Fingal, Ryno, Alfred, Orra Moor). This began a theme that extended throughout his life—naming his mounts after revolutionary indigenous heroes.

Fig. 4-30 *Caractacus, King of the Britons*, from Thomas Mante, *The Naval and Military History of the Wars of England, Including, the Wars of Scotland and Ireland*, etc., vol. 1, 1880

Several of Jefferson's horses born in the 1770s were given names that come from a cycle of poems authored and narrated by Ossian, supposedly a third-century Celtic

Fig. 4-31 Gustavus Adolphus, king of Sweden, depicted in *Gustav II Adolph at the Battle at Breitenfeld*, seventeenth-century painting, unknown artist

bard. In 1761, the Scottish poet James Macpherson claimed to have found Ossian's poems and translated them from the ancient Scots Gaelic. The epic poem about the hero Fingal was translated in 1762. These poems, with their incipient Romanticism, were soon admired on the Continent and in America and influenced many writers of the time. [Fig. 4-28 see p. 105] Ossian was considered the Celtic contribution to classical literature, equivalent in value to Homer and the Greeks. Jefferson was particularly enamored of Ossian's poetry, with its "cult of masculine gallantry," embedded in its "dark and mysterious heroic tale." "The images of Ossian never entirely receded from Jefferson's imagination." Although he discovered Ossian during his student days in Williamsburg, again and again Jefferson recites lines from these poems to family members and beloved friends, even through old age. In the 1770s, when Jefferson was a young man in his thirties, he gave names to his horses from characters in the Ossianic tales: Fingal (the principal hero of the Ossian epics and king of Morven), Cucullin (a giant of exceptional strength who confronted Fingal), Cuthona (lover of Conlath, raped by Toscar, died of grief), Everallin (wife of Ossian, courted by him at the lake of Lego), and Ryno (Fingal's son). [94]

Fig. 4-32 This figure possibly represents Odin. It's part of a helmet, made of pressed bronze plate, 540–790 AD, depicting a Swedish Vendel Era figure.

Other names he gave his horses in these years indicate Jefferson's profound knowledge of literature and the classic epic tales. Most of these other names indicated Jefferson's awareness of his and the colonies' role in the historical moment, as insurgent upstarts against a powerful empire, the British, and no longer taking cues from eighteenth-century Britain: Alfred, the king of Wessex (849 A.D.-899 A.D.), [Fig. 4-29 see p. 105] resisted the Danes and drove them out of England. Caractacus, a chieftain of the Silres, an indigenous people of Britain in the first century A.D., resisted the Roman invasion. Tradition places Caratacus's last stand at British Camp in the Malvern Hills. [Fig. 4-30 see p. 105] In 1759, William Mason published in London a book titled *Caractacus, A Dramatic Poem*, thus disseminating the legend of Caractacus. Gustavus, known as the "Lion of the North," founded the Swedish Empire in the early seventeenth century and was widely regarded as the ideal model of a European king at the time and revered as one of the greatest generals in all of history. [Fig. 4-31] Historians have attributed the Golden Age of Sweden to his rule. Odin, a Norse god, was an ambivalent deity, associated with both poetry and war and madness, and closely connected with a horse and spear; he was portrayed as the leader of

Fig. 4-33 *Oroonoko kills Imoinda*. Handout for a 1776 performance of Thomas Southerne's theatrical play *Oroonoko* (1776).

Fig. 4-34 Owen Staples, *Tecumseh, Shawnee chief*, 1915 watercolor. Attributed to Staples, based on Lossing's 1868 engraving.

Fig. 4-35 *Jacobin Club*, Paris. January 1792, satirical print

the dead. [Fig. 4-32] Thor, son of Odin, was the much-revered Germanic and Norse god of thunder. Orra Moor, an Icelandic hero, was the protagonist of a love poem in the *History of Lapp Land*, published in London in 1712. And two names of insurrectionary Black characters from theatrical plays of the epoch, Oroonoko (the enslaved Black prince in Suriname from a short novel by that name, published in 1688, later a stage tragedy by Thomas Southerne) [Fig. 4-33] and Zanga the Moor (a Black character in a 1721 play called *The Revenge*), are also given to blood horses. [95]

Three of Jefferson's horses carried names of important Native American leaders: that of Arontyoony, an Iroquois chief (of the Onondaga tribe), who signed a 1742 treaty with the British in Philadelphia (Jefferson had this horse before 1773), and Tecumseh, a well-known Shawnee leader (1768–1813) [Fig. 4-34] who rallied various Native American groups in defense of their lands.

Fig. 4-36 *Beggars Opera*, British, 1728, design formerly attributed to William Hogarth, anonymous

Tecumseh died in the War of 1812 (on the side of the British). Nevertheless, Americans of the time recognized Tecumseh for his heroism and honored him by naming towns and warships and even children after him. Jefferson also admired Tecumseh. A visitor once described seeing "the belt and shot pouch of the famous Tecumseh" in the entrance hall (museum) at Monticello. It is not clear how these items came to Jefferson, but it is clear that Jefferson admired Tecumseh. Jefferson bought his horse named Tecumseh in 1815. A third horse had the name Assaragoa, which was the Iroquois name for the governor of Virginia (meaning Big Knife) in the Treaty of Lancaster 1744. [96]

Another horse Jefferson owned whose name continues the revolutionary theme is Jacobin. He was a horse that Jefferson's son-in-law John Wayles Eppes bought for Jefferson during his presidency, in the spring of 1805. The Jacobin Club was a political club during the revolution in France, formed during Jefferson's stay there. [Fig. 4-35] A Jacobin in politics is someone who holds extreme left-wing revolutionary views. In smear campaigns against Jefferson in the run-up to the presidential election of 1800, Jefferson was dubbed "the great arch priest of Jacobinism." Since Jefferson called his election to the presidency the "Revolution of 1800" (because it was a return to republican values), he was probably satisfied with this slightly subversive name. If Jefferson didn't give the horse this name, he at least did not change it! [97]

Fig. 4-37 John Lewis, *Portrait of Margaret 'Peg' Woffington*. She was an Irish actress. .

Although Jefferson only rode and drove male horses (mainly stallions), during the early part of his marriage, he owned a herd

Fig. 4-38 Eighteenth-century violin, made by Tomasso Balestrieri, Mantua, Italy, of spruce, maple, ivory, and fruitwood

of broodmares. He gave names to some of these mares, although he used them only for breeding. Some of the names came from the Ossian poems, but others came from one of his favorite diversions in Williamsburg in the 1770s: theatrical plays (a somewhat scandalous context for female actresses). Two were Polly Peachum and Peggy Waffington, two little fillies (females) born in the spring of 1778, got by Young Fearnought on two mares at Elkhill. Polly Peachum was a character in *The Beggar's Opera*, an influential and long-running satirical play using some of the conventions of opera. [Fig. 4-36 see p. 107] The lyrics of the play were set to well-known folk tunes and church hymns, and the play is often said to be the ancestor of the modern musical. The satirical theme of the opera dealt with the double standards the aristocracy imposed on the rest of society, playfully comparing low-class thieves with their aristocratic superiors. This play opened at the Old Theatre near the Capitol in Williamsburg, June 3, 1768, which Jefferson surely attended (as he did many other performances at the Old Theatre) when he was in Williamsburg that spring. Jefferson was an accomplished violinist, and amongst the sheet music that he owned was the music for *The Beggar's Opera*. Peggy Waffington (a misspelling of Margaret [Peggy] Woffington) [Fig. 4-37 see p. 107] was the English actress who as a child played the part of Polly Peachum in *The Beggar's Opera* in Dublin in the 1720s. [98]

Allycroker, Jefferson's most important broodmare during his early married years at Monticello (1774–1784), was inherited from his father-in-law, and may not have been named by Jefferson. The name "Ally Croker" is the name of a tune written and music composed by Lawrence (Larry) Grogan of Johnstown Castle, County Wexford in Ireland, who was renowned as a "gentleman piper" and composer of Irish airs. It is Grogan's most famous composition. Both the air and song date from 1725, according to Crofton Croker, with single sheet editions of the song from 1730 and 1740. The lyrics describe the vagrancies of a disappointed suitor of Miss Alicia Croker, the sister of Edward Croker, High Sheriff of County Limerick. The song quickly found favor and was adopted by ballad singers and was soon introduced into Sam Foote's comedy *The Englishman in Paris.* [99]

This play opened in Williamsburg on May 1, 1771. Jefferson was there and bought a play ticket that day. Playgoers in colonial Williamsburg often bought sheet music for the songs they heard in the theater, to play and sing in their own homes. Such performances were a common diversion among the gentry, many of whom were taught early to play a musical instrument. Jefferson was an avid fiddle player. All that spring and summer of 1771, the young Jefferson was back and forth to The Forest (the Wayles plantation, near Williamsburg), courting his soon-to-be wife, Martha. It is easy to imagine the suitor, young Jefferson, playing his fiddle to her harpsichord and singing this very tune. [100] [Fig. 4-38] [Fig. 4-39]

In sum, the names Jefferson chose for his high-bred Thoroughbred horses were thoughtfully given and probably projected an identity Jefferson wanted to capture and nurture for himself, that of a revolutionary patriot. Although he wasn't a military hero like George Washington, known as

Fig. 4-39 Spinet made by William Harris, London, England, 1764

the Sword of the Revolution, Jefferson was always acknowledged as the Pen of the Revolution.

Thomas Jefferson died July 4, 1826, a few weeks after regretting by letter that due to illness, he could not attend the celebrations of the fiftieth anniversary of the Declaration of Independence that he so eloquently had authored. It was the first achievement he wanted to be remembered by, and had it engraved on his tombstone. [Fig. 4-40]

Fig. 4-41 The Great Seal of the United States, 1782

So it is not without significance that Jefferson's last riding horse, which he rode daily until weeks before his death, was named The Eagle. The American bald eagle [Fig. 4-41] was made the American emblem in 1782 for the Great Seal of the United States because of the eagle's great strength, long life, and majestic appearance. Thought to be native to the United States, the eagle came to represent freedom because it was known to fly at great heights in unlimited liberty. Eagle would have served well as a name for the last horse of a man who wanted to be remembered as a founding father the United States of America and author of the Declaration of Independence, and who staved off death until the exact day of the fiftieth anniversary of that declaration, July 4, 1826. [101]

Fig. 4-40 Thomas Jefferson's tombstone at Monticello, with epitaph wrote shortly before his death

Wide view of the Coach house on the northwest side of the Stables at Mount Vernon, the home of George Washington, in Virginia. The coach is a replica.

Chapter 5

Carriage Horses, Carriages, and Roads

Jefferson not only rode horses, but he also often drove them in carriages (chairs, gigs, sulkies, chariots, cabriolets, phaetons, landaus). Jefferson's horses were specialized as either riding horses or carriage horses, but not usually both at the same time. In general, in those days, carriage horses in America were smaller and shorter than what we would expect today. Most gentry tried to match their carriage horses both in size and color, as well as in temperament and pace. Carriage horses required a different training and practice in harness and gear from a riding horse. Still high-bred (Thoroughbreds), still quite expensive, and still stabled near the house, these horses symbolized Jefferson's relationships and connections with other people, but Jefferson did not use them daily. Especially as a young man, riding in a carriage seemed a bit effeminate to Jefferson. Women generally traveled by carriage. Consequently, the horse that pulled the carriage merited a secondary place in the equine hierarchy for Jefferson.

As a member of the Virginia gentry, Jefferson owned wheeled vehicles early on in his professional life, but his principal use of them was in cities or for long-distance travel. Around and near home, he still preferred to ride his horse. But a carriage keeps one cleaner, if that mattered. It wasn't clear with Jefferson—he met guests in his riding clothes as president. A carriage takes more than one passenger (as well as luggage for travel); it also can protect one from the weather. Moreover, many horses travel better in a carriage trace. If the vehicle is light and well-balanced, and the road is in good condition, the animal effectively feels about a fifth of the weight as when a rider is on its back. This way the horse can go faster for longer distances than it can carrying a rider. Therefore, of course, Jefferson used carriages.

Jefferson had his own definite personality as a driver and was used to driving himself in a carriage. "He liked few things better than to gallop off on a good mount or go for a breakneck drive in his two-seat phaeton with a 'pair of keen horses.'" Isaac (Granger) Jefferson, the enslaved blacksmith and longtime Monticello resident, testified to Jefferson's habit of taking the reins, even when he had brought along a driver: "Whenever he wanted to travel fast, he'd drive; he would drive powerful hard himself." [1]

Besides going extremely fast, Jefferson did not like anyone else to have the reins, except himself. For example, if he did not want to drive himself, he preferred postilions (riders) to a coachman, although as president he used a coachman for his chariot. The fact that he liked to drive himself explains his clear preference for two-wheeled gigs and chairs (and cabriolets), even throughout his presidency. These vehicles were passenger-driven and usually did not have room for more than one person. Jefferson also owned several phaetons, which were four-wheeled vehicles and thus a bit more stable than the two-wheeled ones, but with space for only one or two people, and were also most often passenger-driven. He always preferred, until the very end, to be in control. This need for control also explained his preference for using his saddle horse over a carriage.

Moreover, especially before the Revolutionary War, wheeled vehicles created many inconveniences for Jefferson and others. They were not always the obvious choice of the Virginia landed gentry.

Carriage Horses and Their Carriages

What horses were used to draw these vehicles? Some of the horses Jefferson bought were specifically to draw a carriage, others were just for riding. Some served first one, then the other function. Always they were blooded horses whose names and pedigrees were carefully recorded by Jefferson. Sometimes a saddle horse was demoted to be a carriage horse as Jefferson "trained all his horses to both ride and work." Jefferson spent significant amounts of money when buying carriage horses, but they certainly were not as identified with him as much as his saddle horses were. There was more social distance between Jefferson and these animals, perhaps because they were used in pairs or in teams of four, perhaps because of Jefferson's clear preference to be in the saddle. The teams of carriage horses were identified more with the vehicle they pulled than with their driver. Nevertheless, Jefferson's family, overseers, and slaves knew these horses as distinct personalities and could recall them by name when discussing Jefferson. As usual, when discussing horses in Jefferson's time, one ends up discussing pedigrees and ownership lines, i.e., the social relationships that the horse represents.[2]

Although Jefferson often used the generic term "carriage" to refer to any and all of his vehicles, he also distinguished them all by kind, or style. Most scholars agree that the eighteenth century was the height of carriage production, at least as far as the numbers of vehicles and the variety of types. Any perusal of eighteenth- and early-nineteenth-century American carriage collections shows us that there is a wide diversity of styles and models within so-called types. Names changed and were invented rapidly as types of carriages went in and out of fashion. Once we cross the Atlantic, the two places that Jefferson visited in depth during his years abroad (France on the Continent and England) each had its own styles and favorite types of carriage. Moreover, styles of carriage used varied by gender, social class, and economics. Each of these horse-drawn vehicles, like

JEFFERSON SIGNIFICANT CARRIAGE HORSES

DATE BOUGHT	NAME	DOB	COLOR	OTHER MARKINGS
Dec. 1772	Gustavus	b. 1763		
June 1775	The General	b. 1769		
May 1786	Chariot horse in Paris	b. 1778	Blood bay	High star
May 1786	Chariot horse in Paris	b. 1780	Blood bay	
Oct. 1790	Brimmer	b. 1785		Two white feet
1790?	Romulus			
1790?	Remus			
April 1801	Bell	b. 1794	bay	
April 1801	Wildair	b. 1796	bay	
April 1801	Castor	b. 1793	Blood bay	
April 1801	St. Louis	b. 1793	Blood bay	
April 1814	Bremo	b. 1806	Dark bay	star
Dec. 1808	Diomede	b. 1803	Dark bay	Left hind foot white
May 1815	Wellington	b. 1809	bay	Few white hairs in foretop
June 1815	Tecumseh	b. 1808	Bright bay	Few white hairs in forehead
Jan. 1815	Bedford	b. 1809	Bright bay	Blaze face, right hind foot white
April 1815	Hyatilda			

contemporary motorized vehicles today, had their own purpose or function. Within the car world there are sedans, two-door and four-door cars, sports cars, station wagons, economy cars, luxury cars, Jeeps, racing cars, vans, trucks, sixteen-wheelers, buses. Imagine all the possibilities for carriages.[3]

Gustavus: Isaac (Granger) Jefferson, in his reminiscences, listed Gustavus as one of Jefferson's coach horses. Like many of Jefferson's early horses, no color is recorded. Gustavus was nine years old when Jefferson bought him in December 1772. [4]

Lineage: Gustavus's sire was Whittington (chestnut, foaled 1743), a grandson of the Godolphin Arabian, which means Gustavus was a third-generation blood horse (or Thoroughbred).

Social connections: Jefferson bought Gustavus from Francis Willis, from Gloucester Country in the Northern Neck, with whom Jefferson had been friends since their student days at the College of William and Mary. The sire, Whittington, had been imported to Virginia in 1759 by John Syme of Hanover County (dam not listed). Whittington's get was spread all over Virginia among important breeders, and his mares had particularly good reputations. [5]

Jefferson later bought another Whittington colt for £65 from Francis Willis, again, in Williamsburg in January 1778. This was seven-year-old Crab. In 1783, Jefferson paid Colonel Thomas Mann Randolph at Tuckahoe £75 for four-year-old Sprightly, a light chestnut sorrel, from "Sprightly on a Whittington mare from a Janus mare." Jefferson thought that Whittington blood got fine horses. [6]

The General: Again, Jefferson does not record much physical description of this horse. The General was a six-year-old when Jefferson bought him in 1775 (foaled in 1769). The General was described earlier (in Chapter 4) as one of Jefferson's riding horses, but like many of his mounts, The General also served as a driving horse for the gig or phaeton.

Lineage: In his *Farm Book* Jefferson wrote that The General "was got by Janus." Janus was another grandson of the Godolphin Arabian, which makes The General, too, a third-generation blood horse.

Social connections: Jefferson bought The General from Alexander Spotswood in Spotsylvania County on June 14, 1775, when he passed by on his way to Philadelphia to attend the Second Continental Congress as a delegate from Virginia. The Spotswood family had a deep history in Virginia, and Alexander Spotswood had important political connections in Virginia and later would serve in the Revolutionary War. Like many of the hereditary gentry, Spotswood was a horse breeder and turf man. The General had recently been retired as a racehorse. [7]

Carriages for Gustavus and The General:

Williamsburg and Beyond: Thomas Jefferson spent his early years going back and forth to primary school on horseback, boyishly challenging his friends to races. Later he attended college at age sixteen in the colonial capital, Williamsburg. He rode down to Williamsburg on his saddle horse, followed by his enslaved manservant Jupiter Evans on another one. As a young practicing lawyer, Jefferson went back and forth to Staunton (over the Blue Ridge Mountains and into the Shenandoah Valley) to meet with law clients, by horseback. He never mentioned riding in a vehicle.

Chair: The first notice we have of Jefferson driving a vehicle, rather than mounted upon his horse, was of his first trip north to Maryland and Pennsylvania in 1766, when he was twenty-three (recently graduated from the College of William and Mary and waiting to be admitted to the bar), in a one-horse riding chair. [Fig. 5- 1]

Fig. 5-1. At Colonial Williamsburg, character interpreter Ron Carnegie portrays George Washington driving a one-horse riding chair down Duke of Gloucester Street.

A chair is a light, open, simple two-wheeled vehicle. It looks like a captain's chair or a Windsor chair set on a platform, perched between two wheels, although some travelers used a bench (which fit two people). The chair could be outfitted with a portmanteau (a kind of suitcase, or trunk) for Jefferson's change of clothing and other necessities. Moreover, rather than riding on the sweaty back of a horse in the sultry summers of lowland Virginia, one could keep drier and cleaner on a leather seat in a chair.

Many chairs were imported from Europe but "Williamsburg had its own riding-chair makers." With only two wheels and one horse, riding chairs were ten to fifteen times cheaper than coaches. They were taxed less and "cost less to operate and maintain." For example, the governor's elegant four-wheel coach needed to have four or six horses to pull it. Along the way, one would need feed for all those horses, plus need to find places for them to stay. A driver (or postilion) and other servants would be needed to drive and care for the passengers. All these animals and people, plus the vehicle, took up space upon arrival at a destination. In a chair, on the other hand, the passenger was the driver. It was small and convenient to store. There is absolutely no protection from bad weather, but it was easy to handle, easy to maneuver, and functional. For these reasons it was used by the more common (middlin') folk in Williamsburg. Yet George Washington, as well as Thomas Jefferson, drove to the House of Burgesses in a chair. [8]

Although the riding chair was typically owned and driven by men, its simplicity and ease of handling also appealed to women. Women favored using chairs for the same reasons as men. It was a very common vehicle in America in the eighteenth century, and Jefferson preferred some version of a chair until he was nearly eighty years old. Most probably it gave him a sense of independence and efficiency, which he always valued. Money matters may also have played a role in the size vehicle Jefferson preferred. By the middle of the eighteenth century, tax was proportionate to the number of wheels on a vehicle. Thus, owners paid less tax on two-wheeled vehicles than on four-wheeled ones. [9]

Fig. 5-2. Example of a doctor's phaeton, from Charles Lewis Flint, et al., *One Hundred Years' Progress of the United States* (Hartford, Connecticut: L. Stebbins, 1871)

Early marriage: Phaeton: When Jefferson got married in 1773, he brought his new wife, Martha, almost all the way home to Monticello on that snowy January evening in a phaeton. [Fig. 5-2] A phaeton refers to a kind of four-wheel open sporting vehicle. The phaeton became very popular in America after the 1760s because it had several advantages over other vehicles. They were lighter than other four-wheeled vehicles, but more comfortable and safer than the two-wheeled vehicles. The phaeton often had a folding hood or bonnet over the seat, as can be seen in the illustrations. However, Jefferson's last phaeton did not have this feature (see illustrations), [Fig. 5-3] so we do not know if his earlier ones did. Generally, phaetons accommodated only two passengers, but so-called double phaetons carried four passengers in two rows. [10]

Fig. 5-3. A reconstruction of Jefferson's last phaeton at Monticello, from "The President's Phaeton," *The Carriage Journal* 14, no. 2 (Autumn 1976)

Another popular feature in democratic-leaning America was that the phaetons were owner-driven; there was no driving seat. This allowed "the owner the satisfaction of handling his own carriage and horse, a factor contributing immensely to its popularity as a sporting vehicle." Knowing what we do about Jefferson's driving habits—that he preferred to drive himself—we can understand his predilection throughout his life for this kind of vehicle. The term "phaeton" refers to a character in mythology,

Phaeton, who drove the Chariot of the Sun so recklessly that Zeus struck him down with a thunderbolt. [11]

The term phaeton could refer to both large and small carriages, drawn by one or more horses. Jefferson sometimes drove his phaeton with two horses, for example, when he arrived to Philadelphia in 1775. Over the many years of its popularity, many styles and forms evolved, but Jefferson remained rather conservative in his tastes, as confirmed by his drawings for the phaeton he had built by 1805. [Fig 5-4]

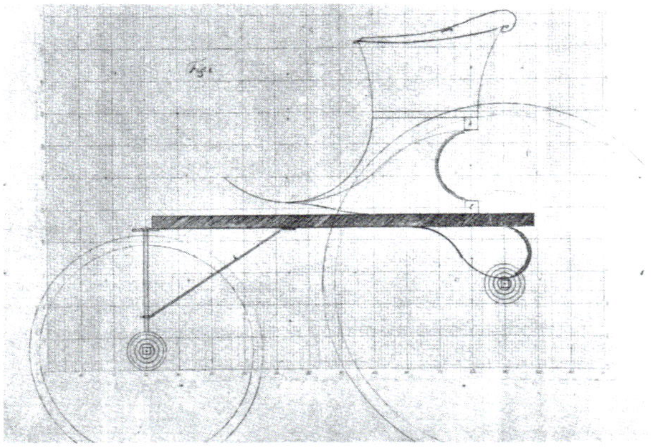

Fig. 5-4. Jefferson's 1806 drawing plans for his last phaeton

Fig. 5-5. Colonial Williamsburg coachman Edward Merkley drives the Wythe Chariot with a pair of carriage horses at Great Hopes Plantation.

Chariot: In June 1773, soon after Jefferson was married, he bought his first enclosed carriage, a four-wheeled vehicle called a "chariot." [Fig. 5-5] He traded his phaeton plus boot for it in Williamsburg with Everard Meade, who was later to be quite an important horse breeder, before driving it home to Monticello. Jefferson probably thought that he needed to transport his new wife in a more appropriate and protected vehicle. [12]

THE EIGHTEENTH-CENTURY COACH

One of the earliest forms of carriage was the **coach**, the standard to which all other types were compared. Developed in the sixteenth century for royalty, a coach is an enclosed four-wheeled carriage, hung from springs, in a bombé shape, that sits four people, two facing forward, and two facing back. A main characteristic is its roof, which forms part of its frame. The coach's roof contrasts with other vehicles that have "folding tops or canopy tops supported by rods and pillars."

A coach was usually drawn by two or more horses harnessed as a team. The coachman drove with long reins from a raised coach box in the front, or the coach was controlled by postilions. Postilions drove coaches or chariots by actually riding the horses. In the case of two horses, one postilion would sit on the left (or near) horse. In the English tradition, horses are trained to be mounted from the left (near) side. In the case of a coach-and-four (four horses), a double team, there would be two postilions, one for each lateral pair of horses. Footmen stood on a platform behind.

Often, the body of the coach serves as a canvas for elaborately painted decoration and a coat of arms. The interior can be richly appointed. A fine coach was almost always a sign of European royalty in the eighteenth century.

George Washington had a coach made for himself with his coat of arms on it, during his presidency. Appropriately, Lafayette, on his reunion tour of the United States in 1823–1824, was given John Hartwell Cocke's coach to travel in from Richmond to Monticello.

If someone you know would never own a Lincoln Town Car because it is too large and pretentious a vehicle, perhaps that explains why Thomas Jefferson never bought himself a coach, with all its intimations of royalty.

(**Source:** Berkebile, *Carriage Terminology,* 94.)

A chariot was a member of the coach family. It looks like a coach that is cut off in front of the doors, and is, thus, sometimes called a half-coach, or in French, a *coupe* (meaning "cut"). In England it became known as a post-chaise. The front is closed by a panel below and a glass window (with two panes) above. The sides and back of a chariot most often had glass windows also. The interior of the chariot was lined in fine material, the window protected by venetian blinds or curtains, and the owner's coat of arms was often painted on the sides. Much heavier than chairs or phaetons, chariots were drawn by two- or four-horse teams. Most chariots have an undercarriage of a single perch, but the body is suspended on four steel springs. Appearing in America by 1700, the chariot, although not as imposing as a coach, was still a symbol of rank and wealth. An important difference for Jefferson between the chariot and the phaeton was that in the chariot, passengers sat inside the vehicle, chatting and conversing, and protected from the weather. The owner was assumed to be a

Fig. 5-6. Colonial Williamsburg interpreter Mark Schneider rides postilion on a team of carriage horses pulling the Wythe Chariot through the woods.

passenger and was not driving the carriage. Rather, he was driven. A driver, called a coachman, would sit outside (unprotected) on a separate perch. However, most often in Jefferson's case, postilions guided the vehicle. Jefferson, when ceding the driving to another, always preferred to use postilions (over a coachman) till the end of his life. [13] [Fig. 5-6]

Berkebile in his *Carriage Terminology* says, "The carriage [frame] was like that of a coach, but shorter. The single seat inside held two or three passengers [facing forward], and some had a small folding seat in front to accommodate children. A detached driver's seat was ornamented with a hammercloth, and the vehicle was attended by footmen." Basically, a chariot for Jefferson seemed to be something for his family (note he bought

Fig. 5-7. Two-horse phaeton with folding bonnet in George Stubbs, *Lord and Lady in a Phaeton*, 1787

his first one just after he married). When the family moved to Williamsburg (1779) and then to Richmond when Jefferson was governor, he went down in his phaeton, while the family was in the chariot and his slaves in a wagon. [14]

By the time. Jefferson went to Philadelphia for the Continental Congress (1775), he was back driving a light two-horse phaeton again. [Fig. 5-7] Recall that these phaetons were not grand things, more like little sports vehicles versus the painted and plated chariots and coaches, with linings and venetian blinds, and coats of arms painted on their sides. Jefferson, as usual, preferred the vehicle where he had control of the reins and whose style proclaimed it was democratic, or less pretentious.

All these various carriages were always custom-made or bought secondhand. There was no standing inventory for any horse-drawn vehicle until later in the nineteenth century. In two instances, Jefferson gave detailed instructions when he ordered new chariots, as we shall see. Jefferson had a new phaeton made sometime in 1782, at the end of his governorship. It was built at Monticello from Jefferson's own design by hired workmen: Davy Watson, the house joiner (who had deserted from the British army), and William Orr, the smith. Several of Jefferson's neighbors were impressed with the functional elegance of this design and asked him to make them one just like it. [15]

France: Hired Horses: Thomas Jefferson went to Paris, France, in summer 1784 as the new minister plenipotentiary for the United States. Jefferson, accompanied by his daughter Martha and the enslaved nineteen-year-old James Hemings (who was to be trained in the art of French cooking) arrived at the port of Le Havre on July 31, 1784. Although no horses accompanied him, Jefferson brought one of his own carriages (a phaeton) along with him on the ship. Once they had disembarked, Jefferson had his phaeton mended, and as was the custom, he hired some post horses with postilion, had them harnessed to his phaeton, and began his drive to Paris. It took the American travelers five days to reach Paris, changing horses and postilion at each stage along the way. [16]

For their first year in Paris, the family lived in temporary lodgings. Although he had his phaeton, he soon bought a chariot and hired horses to drive it about town when necessary. A year later, in September 1785, the family moved to a permanent residence, the Hôtel de Langeac. That year Jefferson paid a Mr. Gouyon promptly the first of every month 300₣ "for horse hire." We have no description of these hired horses. We do not know if they were a matched pair, although most likely they were. Jefferson continued paying horse hire until the following June 1786.

France: 2 blood bays: Jefferson did not buy his own two carriage horses until May 1786. Jefferson noted in his account book that he had paid for two carriage (chariot) horses:

> June 20, 1786 Pd 720 Π for a bay chariot horse 8 yrs old, 5 pi-1½ po (pies-pouce). High star in forehead
> June 21, 1786 Pd Richard 720 Π for a bay chario horse 6 yrs old 5 pi-1½ po. High [17]

Later, in August, Jefferson bought himself a saddle horse (a five-year-old sorrel horse). It is worth pointing out that these carriage horses merit more descriptive details than the riding horse; for example, we know their height. They are perfectly matched blood (red) bays (except one has a star), same height (5 feet, 1.5 inches), and same price (720 livres). There is no information on their pedigrees, however. Consequently, we must imagine that they were not Thoroughbreds but rather warm-blood continental types.

Jefferson used his chariot horses often: while escorting his daughter to Abbaye Royale de Panthemont where she attended a convent school, exploring the city and visiting with women friends, and while dressed for business or formal presentations at court. Later in 1787 Jefferson's younger daughter, Mary (later called Maria), arrived from Virginia with her "nurse" (or nanny), the enslaved fourteen-year-old Sally Hemings (James's sister). These two young Jefferson daughters would also be escorted around the city in these vehicles with the matched bays. The butler, Adrien Petit, as well as William Short, Jefferson's secretary, could drive the horses in various vehicles. When necessary, others used these horses for riding. [18]

Like the saddle horse, Jefferson left the carriage horses in Paris when he returned to the United States in late October 1789. William Short, left behind to attend to Jefferson's affairs, eventually sold the matched carriage horses in 1790 for much less than they originally cost: 432 livres. [19]

France and England: Post-horses: When Jefferson made long trips outside of Paris, he hired teams of post-horses, along with a postilion rider, to carry him from stage to stage (or segment) of the journey each day. At the end of each stage were post-stations, where passengers could get out and stretch while the horse teams were changed. Sometimes Jefferson hired the carriage also; other times he took his own vehicle. The number of horses per vehicle and the prices per stage were officially controlled and published. For example, on a trip to the south of France it was necessary to use three horses for Jefferson's chariot for the first leg of the journey from Paris until Lyon. After Lyon, he had to hire four, sometimes five, horses. [20]

Before the trip to southern France, Jefferson had taken a trip to England, with John Adams, in March and April of 1786, in carriages driven by post-horses. Jefferson then traveled to southern France the next year in spring 1787 (February to June), and to Holland and Germany in spring 1788 (March to April). For all of these long-distance trips, Jefferson hired post-horses, as was the custom in Europe. [21]

Carriages for Travel in France

Phaeton: Jefferson had brought on board the ship to France, along with his other baggage, the 1782 phaeton made by his Monticello craftsmen, described above. After Jefferson disembarked from the ship, he had his phaeton mended, and then he hired horses for the drive to Paris. According to the Italian Philip Mazzei, friend and neighbor of Jefferson, and a fellow vintner in Albemarle County, the design of this phaeton was supposedly much admired in France. However, after his first year, Jefferson did not use his phaeton much in the streets of Paris. He bought and preferred to use several French carriages, as we will see. [22]

Chariot: Just seven months after arriving in Paris, in March of 1785, Jefferson bought a chariot, an enclosed vehicle, probably more appropriate for young Martha to travel about town in than the phaeton. Later, in September 1785, Jefferson and his family moved into their permanent quarters, the Hôtel de Langeac, a small urban palace with its own stables, yet they were still using hired horses.

Before Jefferson left Paris definitively in the fall of 1789, he had bought two more chariots. One he custom ordered, through his friend, the painter John Trumbull, who was living in London at the time. Trumbull facilitated Jefferson's contact with a young carriage maker in London, John Kemp. This English chariot took almost six months to be finished and delivered to Jefferson in Paris (in January 1789), only months before he and his family returned to Virginia. Jefferson shipped this chariot with him back to Virginia, as he said he had ordered it mainly for his daughters' use. The style elements of the English chariot must have pleased him, because many years later, when he commissioned a new chariot as president of the United States, he requested some of the same details.

While Jefferson had waited for his English chariot to arrive, he bought another secondhand chariot to use in the meantime. He now owned three chariots, along with several other vehicles.

Cabriolet: In June of 1786, Jefferson finally bought the matched pair of chariot horses. In October of that same year, Jefferson bought a cabriolet. He now had three different vehicles: the phaeton, the chariot, and the cabriolet.

Jefferson seemed to like this last sporty little vehicle—all the fashion in Paris—because he immediately bought yet another one the following month. "Cabriolet" refers to a two-wheeled vehicle drawn by a single horse, which was apparently all the rage in Paris in the last half of the eighteenth century, when Jefferson was there. The name comes from the Italian word for "kid" or "goat," due to the capering or goatlike motion the vehicle made when swinging between its long shafts. The cabriolet's shape, an "exaggerated comma or nautilus shell," relates it, like the chariot, to the coach family because of its cut-down coach body. The wheel spokes were brightly colored, and the seat was shaded by a shiny black leather hood that could be raised and lowered. [Fig. 5-8] Many coincide in saying that the cabriolet was "an elegant, easy-running, two-wheeled vehicle with a light body" that evolved from the gig (or chair). It was occupant-driven. It is no wonder that Minister Thomas Jefferson found these vehicles to his liking. He, too, said a cabriolet was what "we call a chaise or chair." [23]

Apparently, all the dandies in Paris had colorful cabriolets, too:

> In higher-class houses not only the young master but also the head steward and the majordomo had their own cabriolets. The gentlemen of the robe, businessmen, dentists, dancing-masters and fencing-masters use the same type of vehicle to go about their tasks as the dandies did to show off. Even ladies could be seen driving cabriolets. [24]

There were so many cabriolets on the streets of Paris in those years that they actually posed a danger to pedestrians:

> It being a light and fast carriage, its owners tried to overtake and cut in on all carts, wagons and cabs, and even on stately *berlines* and coaches, just for the sheer fun of it. They drove past between them so recklessly—without heeding the side-walks which at that time were still level with drive-ways—that the pedestrians were all but run over before they knew where they were. Frightened they pressed themselves against the wall to let the cabriolet dash past. [25]

One imagines that both Jefferson's

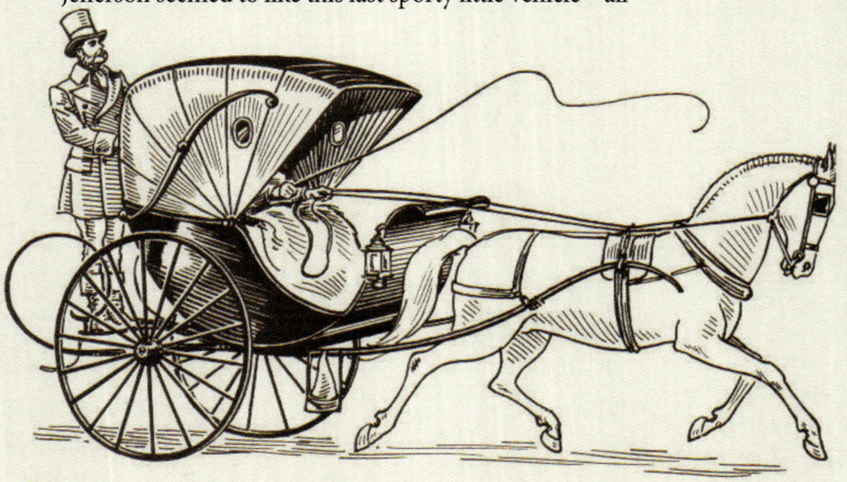

Fig. 5-8. Cabriolet with groom on footboard behind the covered seats

personal secretary, William Short, and the butler, Adrien Petit, had use of the cabriolets, to run errands and to accompany Jefferson's daughters to school and home again.

Fig. 5-9 Post coach, or stagecoach, depicted by James Pollard, *Mail Changing Horses, at the "Falco." Walthamstowe*, nineteenth century

Post-coach and diligence: In early spring of 1786, Jefferson went to England upon the request of the newly appointed American ambassador to England, John Adams. Jefferson had gone to England to join Adams on official United States business, but while there, Jefferson and Adams managed to tour the southern English countryside together and visit some English gardens. As was the custom on the Continent, Jefferson hired a cabriolet from Paris to Calais, paying for post-horses and postilions along the way. Once in England he was able to travel, in the English custom, by post-coach (or stagecoach).

By this date, post-coaches carried both the mail and paying passengers on the post roads that connected all of England. These vehicles, expressly built to carry from four to eight passengers, sped from stage to stage, carried along with teams of four or six big horses trotting the whole time. At the end of each stage were post-stations, where passengers could get out and stretch while the horses were changed. Travel was very rapid, and in the case of long-distance destinations, the coaches went continuously throughout the night. Price was calculated by posts, or stations (in England five English miles equaled one "post-stage," but stages where horses were changed were usually between ten and fifteen miles apart). In these vehicles the horses were not driven by a coachman, but rather were ridden by postilions. [26]

In the middle of the eighteenth century, in England, with the development and spread of this new way of travel—post coach (or stagecoach)—there was also a revolution in riding style of the postilions. The Thoroughbred blood horses and bigger warmbloods (crosses with Thoroughbreds) that pulled the post-coaches were trotting horses, not pacing horses. The postilion boys who guided these horses by riding them spent many long hours at the trot on the flat and skimpy little postilion saddle. Although there are references to rising to the trot as far back as the seventeenth century in England, it seems it was the postilions on the post-chaises who learned to raise their stirrups up quite high, and who began to systematically rise to the trot with the beat of the horse, thus avoiding being bounced and jostled in discomfort for miles and miles along the roads. Posting to the trot, especially a fast trot, leaves the rider much less tired, and much more comfortable. [27]

Jefferson noted in his *Memorandum Book* that he paid for post horses for some destinations. But after two weeks in London, when Adams and Jefferson started their private touring, they paid for a month-long hire of a (semi-private) carriage (chariot) for a month and chariot horses (and sometimes a coachman, sometimes a postilion) to travel from post to post, or from destination to destination, as they visited gardens and other sights in southern England. [28]

France, also, had excellent roads by the 1770s, and the public stagecoach (or diligence) and coach travel in general in France was quite advanced. [Fig. 5-9] When Jefferson traveled on the Continent, to southern France and later to Holland and Germany, he traveled in his own chariot (the custom-ordered one from England), using post-horses for the whole trip. On the southern France trip, when he crossed over the Alps for a short foray into Italy, Jefferson was forced to abandon the chariot at Nice and switch to mule travel, since there were no passable roads over the Alps. [29]

At one point, Jefferson took the wheels off his chariot and stored it on a barge as he traveled for several days more than 200 miles along the canal of Languedoc. Jefferson loved this portion of the trip, writing to his secretary, William Short, back in Paris:

> Of all the methods of travel I have ever tried this is the pleasantest. I walk the greater part of the way along the banks of the canal. When fatigued I take

> seat in my carriage, where, as much at ease as in my study, I read, write, or observe. My carriage being of glass all around, admits a full view of the varying scenes thro' which I am shifted. [30]

Leaving France: During the five years he was in Paris, Jefferson bought three chariots (one ordered and meticulously designed from England) and two cabriolets (two-wheelers). Thus, when Jefferson and his family quickly made plans to leave Paris and return to the United States in late 1789—it wasn't clear for how long—Jefferson had six vehicles he had to make decisions about: his original phaeton, two cabriolets, and three chariots. In the end, Jefferson packed and sent the English chariot (which he planned to leave in Virginia for his daughters' use), the secondhand chariot, and one cabriolet. He took his old phaeton back on the ship with his family, and he used it to get from Norfolk to Monticello, borrowing horses from friends all along the way. The other vehicles were left in France, and eventually William Short sold them in 1790, along with the three horses.

Brimmer: In October 1790, on his way home to Virginia from New York City, where he was serving as secretary of state, Jefferson passed through Richmond and there bought Brimmer for use as a carriage horse. Jefferson described him as five years old (foaled 1785), not very tall, "high blooded, a most excellent creature and I believe perfectly sound." He had two white feet, but no other color description. [31]

Lineage: Brimmer was another expensive high-bred horse and an ex-racing horse, like The General and Tarquin. Jefferson wrote in his *Account Book* that the horse was got by (Goode's) Brimmer, who was got by (Harris's) Eclipse. Eclipse was got by (Old) Fearnought. Thus, Brimmer continued Jefferson's proclivity for Fearnought horses.

Social connections: Jefferson bought the horse from Carter Braxton, a Virginia gentleman planter, who had been very involved in American independence, and was a signer of the Declaration of Independence. [Fig. 5-10] He knew Jefferson from his days in Williamsburg as a student. Before the Revolution, Braxton had been an important importer and breeder of blooded horses. By 1790, however, Braxton had lost his wealth and estates and was living in Richmond city.

Fig. 5-10 Carter Braxton, a Continental Congress member from Virginia and signer of the Declaration of Independence. Albert Rosenthal, *Carter Braxton*, 1901, after a miniature by an unknown artist.

A second connection Braxton had with Jefferson was through Jefferson's young daughter, thirteen-year-old Maria. In May 1791, Maria was living at Monticello with her now-married sister, Martha, and Martha's husband, Thomas Mann Randolph, while her father was serving as secretary of state in New York City. Dutifully, she wrote her father often. She had wheedled permission out of him to learn to ride. Randolph bought a mare from Carter Braxton for Maria's use. This mare was from the same sire and dam as Jefferson's Brimmer (thus, she was a sister).

Jefferson used Brimmer the three years he lived in Philadelphia as secretary of state. He sold this horse to Samuel Clarkson, a Philadelphia merchant, for $120 in February 1793, before he returned home to Monticello. Jefferson wrote Clarkson a note about the horse:

> You may be glad of information respecting the horse which may be relied on, I take the liberty of mentioning that I purchased him in Oct. 1790. For 5. Years old the preceding spring, and I gave 116 2/3 Doll. For him in Virginia. ...He [goes well?] in a carriage, for which purpose I bought him, and I now sell him for no reason but that the horses I have since purchased for my set, render it necessary to get a larger in his stead. [32]

Romulus and Remus: Romulus and Remus were two carriage horses that Jefferson owned in Philadelphia during his term as secretary of state (1790–1794), along with Brimmer. We do not know when Jefferson bought these horses, nor any of their distinguishing characteristics.

Lineages: We know nothing of their pedigrees. However, they may have been a related pair of horses that Jefferson brought with him to Philadelphia from Monticello. We assume they were a paired set because Jefferson and others spoke of them together, and their names refer to the legendary twin founders of Rome. Isaac (Granger) Jefferson also mentioned these two horses together in his reminiscences.

Social connections: Although in 1791, Jefferson thought Remus was going to die from some lingering illness, it seems that he did not. Much later, in 1801, while president,

Jefferson wrote that Martha should send at once for Mrs. Marks (Jefferson's own younger sister). He said, "Remus and my chair, with Phill as usual, can go for her." For thirty years, Jefferson sent his carriage and horses to southern Virginia for Anna Marks to spend the three or four months of the sickly season (summer) with the family at Monticello. Phil Evans, an enslaved Monticello driver, would fetch Mrs. Marks in Jefferson's small one-horse chair. In the case cited above, the horse was Remus, still alive and still drawing a carriage.[33]

Carriages for Brimmer, and Romulus and Remus: After he had returned to the United States from France, Jefferson drove to New York City and Philadelphia in his old phaeton, and by 1794, he had only his phaeton. Back home (in his supposed retirement after leaving President Washington's government) at Monticello, he again acquired a chair, by 1797. At this point Jefferson was commuting back and forth to the centers of government as vice president under President John Adams and using Romulus and Remus with the chair and phaeton.[34]

Presidential Carriage Horses: Thomas Jefferson was elected president, and inaugurated on March 4, 1801. He took over from John Adams, under whom Jefferson had served as vice president for four years. Before leaving the presidency, Adams wrote Jefferson a letter saying he would leave him seven horses and two carriages:

> In order to save you the trouble and Expense of purchasing Horses and Carriages, Which will not be necessary, I have to inform you that I shall leave in the stables of the United States, seven Horses and two Carriages with harness the Property of the United States. These may not be suitable for you: but they will certainly save you considerable Expense as they belong to the stud of the President's Household.[35]

The House of Representatives was irate that Adams had used funds approved for furnishings to buy these horses. The House passed an act approving of the sale of the horses and carriages to refund the United States Treasury.[36]

Thomas Jefferson, on the other hand, had spent several months searching for suitable horses to take with him for a presidential carriage, if he should actually win the election. Despite his famous democratic leanings, in questions of horseflesh, only the best would suffice. In contrast to Adams, Jefferson spent his own private money on these (extremely expensive) horses. He had already bought a spectacular saddle horse, Wildair, from John Hoomes in February. Once inaugurated president in March, even before he had carriage horses, he ordered a custom-made "handsome" chariot through Enoch Edwards in Philadelphia to have ready by May.[37]

Son-in-law John Wayles Eppes had been on the hunt in the Petersburg region for months to find four "capital" horses, a matching team, suitable to draw a presidential chariot. In January, Jefferson had told him to "keep your eye on those horses, or any others equal to them, in case I should want them." Two of the horses Eppes finally bought were two he had been attempting to buy since the previous July. Jefferson and Eppes exchanged many letters about these horses, discussing their (elevated) prices and plotting their options. Eppes wrote Jefferson, "I think there are no other horses in this part of the state ... whose figure & size would please you."[38]

Finally, on April 20, 1801, President Jefferson noted in his *Memorandum Book*:

> April 20. Recd from J. W. Eppes the following horses
> bought for me
> from Bell 300. D. paiable June 16 8.yr old last spring
> 2. from Shore 800.paiable July 128. Do.
> From Haxhall 500 paiable July 16.6. do. Wildair[39]

Bell, Haxall, and Dr. Shore were all well-known turfmen from the old racehorse region and members of the Petersburg Jockey Club, perhaps the most important racing center at the time, in Petersburg, Virginia. None of them was willing to come down on his price, not even for the president of the United States. Jefferson named Bell's horse Bell, after his former owner. He called the one from Haxall, Wildair, and the two horses from Dr. Shore he did not name specifically. Castor was probably one of those horses, and perhaps another carriage horse, St. Louis, referred to in family letters, is the other.[40]

Eppes admitted that the prices were "excessively high" and he could "scarcely justify myself for having given" such. Clearly feeling guilty, he justified these prices by saying that they were all "horses of fine form gentle well broke and steady.... I thought a few hundred dollars more than the real value would be well bestowed upon such as were gentle and steady." All four horses were bays. Given the high prices and the seller's connections with the Petersburg Jockey Club, all four horses were certainly blood horses (Thoroughbreds). [41]

Bell: This bay horse was eight years old when Eppes bought him. No information on his pedigree exists.

Social connections: Bell's horse was one Jefferson had been interested in for a long time. Eppes became attracted to this horse when a visitor had borrowed it from Mr. Bell to ride over to Eppes's nearby home for a visit. Eppes thought the horse Bell, "though different in colour would appear well in harness with Shore's being of the same height & having the same marks." For a long time, owner Bell had promised to get a match for this horse for Jefferson, but when it finally arrived, Eppes was so disappointed in it as a match ("so far inferior") that he "refused" him. He didn't dare buy an inferior horse for the president. [42]

Apparently, Bell had a weak eye when he first arrived at Monticello. He was led to Washington, but soon became blind in both eyes for ten to fourteen days. Then they mended. Because the horse's eyes remained weak, Jefferson decided not to use him. In fact, by June, Jefferson asked Eppes to look for a replacement for Bell. Since Bell was a horse Jefferson had had his eye on for quite a while, this must have been a significant disappointment. Bell was probably retired, because there is no further mention of him.

Wildair: The five-year-old bay Wildair (b. 1796) was unusual in Jefferson's stable in that he was a gelding (Eppes called him "the first gelding in the state"). In fact, this Wildair is the only gelding recorded among Jefferson's horses. Although a gelding was usually cheaper than a stallion, Dr. Haxall was asking $500 for this horse. Eppes said nothing less "would induce him to part with him." Jefferson said he was willing to give $500 for Haxall's horse as a riding horse, but that it was much too much for a carriage horse (note the different status). Eppes wrote Jefferson that he thought Haxall's horse would serve as a parade horse and that "from his gentleness and beauty would be equal to any that could be purchased." Later Eppes confirmed that Wildair performed well in harness and was a match for Bell. In June, Jefferson wrote Eppes that Haxall's horse was surely "the finest gelding in America." [43]

Lineage: Given the custom at the time to name horses after either their previous owner (i.e., Bell) or after an important horse in its pedigree, it is likely that Jefferson named this horse Wildair because it had the same blood as his recently bought saddle horse, Wildair (by Syme's Wildair, by Baylor's Old Fearnought).

Social connections: Dr. Haxall was Mr. Bell's brother-in-law, an important breeder, and the racemaster (steward) for the Petersburg races. Haxall later brought the celebrated Sir Harry to Virginia from England in 1804. Sir Harry stood at stud in Virginia from 1805 to 1816 and produced several important sons: Sir Alfred (from a Diomed mare), Sir Hal, and Haxall's Moses.

Dr. Shore's Horses (Castor and Another [St. Louis?]): John Wayles Eppes said that he had examined Dr. Shore's two horses and had even driven them several miles. Both horses were eight years old (b. 1793). Eppes described them as "fine blood bays upwards of 16. Hands high well made spirited & active." He was stunned, however, at their price. Shore was asking $1000 for them, "far beyond anything I have ever heard of." Supposedly Dr. Shore had already turned down $800 for the pair. President Jefferson wrote back saying that he was willing to pay $800 for them if he could get Haxall's (Wildair) for $500. He asked Eppes to confirm that Dr. Shore's horses matched Mr. Bell's in color. Eppes assured him they were "considered the finest in the state" and a "first rate pair for Service—They match well both in appearance and spirit and carry themselves finely in harness." He confessed, however, that they were not quite equal in form to Bell and Wildair. [44]

Jefferson scholars believe that Castor was one of Dr. Shore's horses. A tall blood bay, Castor is mentioned often as a carriage horse for many years, both during Jefferson's presidency and after retirement. There is nothing known about his pedigree, but Jefferson valued him as a driving horse. In 1801, he asked Eppes to find a match for him, "another fine horse." Eppes wrote back saying he was having a hard time finding one in the Petersburg area to match Castor because they all lacked height. Note that Dr. Shore's horses were 16 hands high, which was tall for the time. [45]

Later, Jefferson often mentions having problems with Castor on the roads, back and forth to Monticello and Washington. When the roads were deep with mud, Castor refused to draw the carriage, and Jefferson had to leave him at a friend's house in Fauquier County and mount his saddle horse (as usual being led

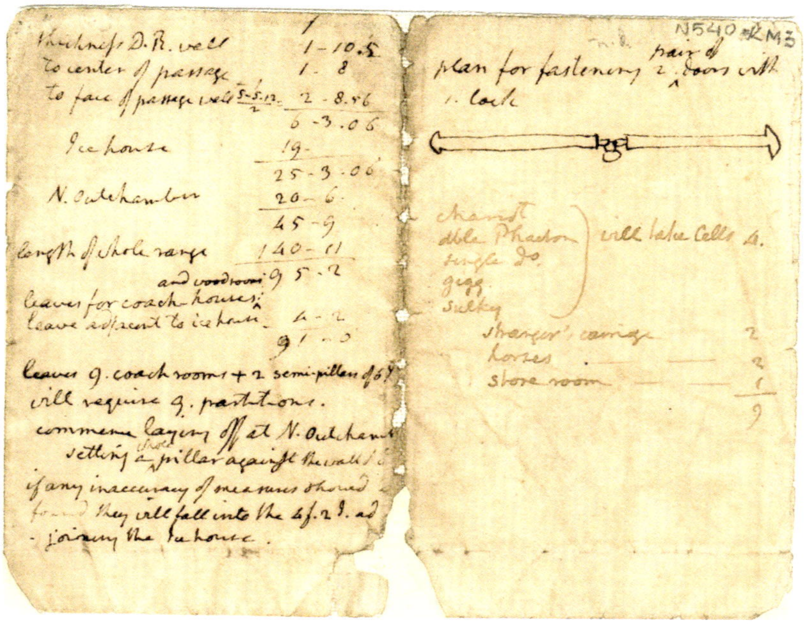

Fig. 5-11 Notes and plans for carriages in the North Terrace. Jefferson's *Account Book*

behind the gig) to ride the rest of the way to Washington. Several years later, in October 1807, again on their way back to Washington, DC, Castor almost drowned in the Rapidan River when he lay down in the water. [46]

In general, Jefferson seemed to use Castor in his one-horse vehicles, especially the gig. Castor lasted as a carriage horse until fall of 1808, when John Wayles Eppes bought Jefferson a substitute for the "aging Castor" (Castor would have been fifteen at the time). The substitute horse was Diomede, another blooded horse from the Petersburg (Chesterfield) area (see below).

On the whole, President Jefferson professed to be extremely pleased with these four carriage horses. Upon receiving them, Jefferson said he was "perfectly satisfied with them all, & they completely answer my expectations; they are dear certainly, but horses less perfect, however cheaper would not have answered my purpose at all." He did slightly complain that they were not ready to be driven (over April spring roads) in the phaeton, back to Washington, without several more days of practice. He decided to have them led behind his gig to Washington, where he would have them "broke…under more favorable circumstances." [47]

A couple of months later, Jefferson again reassured Eppes (and the previous owners) that the horses, with a little practice, were now going fine in the phaeton:

> Doctr. Shore need not be in the least uneasy about his horses having proven restive. On new ground, with new persons about them, unacquainted with them or their manner of going, I saw when they first approached the Phaeton that they would not touch it. One of them however soon came to, and is now I think the finest horse I ever saw in a carriage. The other being more fractious, I left him to be broken here, and after 10. Days driving in the stage, he took the Phaeton freely and now draws well with his companion. Haxall's horse is the finest gelding in America; & I think Bell nearly equal to him. So that tho' they were rather dear (except Bell) I am most perfectly satisfied with them all. [48]

"The finest horse I ever saw in a carriage," "the other … draws well with his companion," "Haxall's horse is the finest gelding in America," "I think Bell nearly equal to him," "I am most perfectly satisfied with them all"—all comments of unconditional approval. Only later in the letter did Jefferson mention Bell's eye weakness.

Carriages During the Presidency: For Bell, Wildair, Castor, and St. Louis: Once elected president and installed in the president's house (as yet still unfinished), Jefferson acquired several different kinds of carriages over the next three or four years: a gig, a sulky, a new chariot, a double phaeton, and back at Monticello, another phaeton. In fact, at Monticello, Jefferson had his enslaved and hired white workmen begin work on the coach rooms in the North Terrace and planned space for these five vehicles. [49] [Fig. 5-11]

Gig and Sulky: Both the gig [Fig. 5-12] and the sulky [Fig. 5-13] were light, two-wheel, one-horse vehicles that were owner-driven. In many ways they were similar to a chair. In the eighteenth century in America, the sulky was a vehicle with room for but one passenger, and it was from this aloofness of the

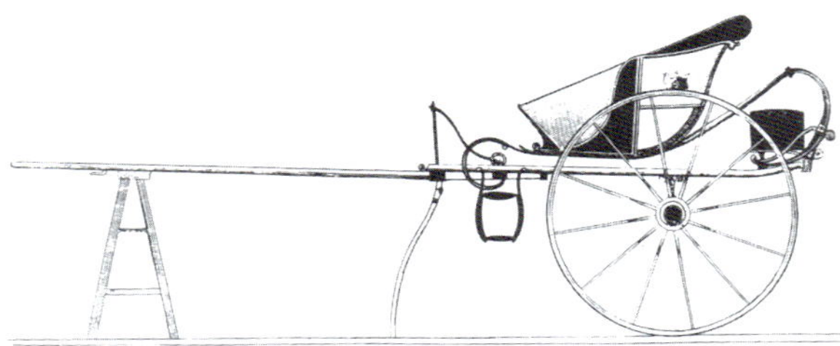

Fig. 5-12 A gig, as depicted in Phineas Jones & Co.'s *Illustrated Catalogue of Fine Carriages*, 1883

Fig. 5-13 A sulky, as depicted on a gilt Harris-style weathervane

rider that came the application of the adjective "sulky" to the vehicle. "It was used almost exclusively by men, which caused such annoyance to some American ladies that they called the vehicle a SELFISH." Both these vehicles underline Jefferson's attempt to play the role of a democrat (i.e., lack of pretension and lack of need for display as president) after the Revolution, in contrast to the British aristocracy, despite the fancy horses he used to pull the vehicles. [50]

Chariot: As described above, at the very beginning of his presidency, Jefferson ordered from Philadelphia and paid for with his own money an impressive, custom-built chariot. A bit later, he bought the four, matched, very expensive blooded horses to pull it.

The chariot was going to be his state coach. Jefferson applied to a friend, Enoch Edwards, in Philadelphia, where the best carriages were still made, for help in ordering the chariot: "I wish a handsome chariot to be made for me in Philadelphia … wishing always to have as many enjoiments [sic] for my money [as it will procure] … I, of course, wish to get things as cheap as I can. Therefore it may be proper not to say for whom the carriage or harness is, till prices are fixed." Jefferson went on to enclose a separate sheet with quite detailed instructions for the carriage maker and added at the close of his letter, "I am not fond of splendid things; but of chaste neatness. This is as applicable to the harness as to the carriage." Edwards and Jefferson corresponded several times about these details. [51]

The chariot was made by Conrad Hanse and finally delivered to the president at the end of September 1801 (six months after he began his presidency). The "plain, well-finished chariot, with plated harness for 4 Horses, and 2 postillion Saddles" [Fig. 5-14] cost a total of $1,200. The new president may have wanted to get the chariot as cheaply as possible, but, as with the horses he bought to draw this carriage, in the end he was willing to spend what it took to get what he wanted. When Jefferson left the presidency and retired to Monticello, he sold this presidential chariot. It was not something that would be useful at Monticello. [52]

It is clear that the president's house coachman, the Irishman Dougherty, was never able to drive this chariot much, unless Jefferson's daughter Martha and her children were in Washington, DC. When Jefferson's daughter did not visit often, Dougherty seemed "particularly chagrined," because as President Jefferson said, "I suppose he wishes to have an opportunity of shewing himself on his box, which with me he has never had." Jefferson went to great lengths to have a carriage worthy of a president, but he preferred to tool around town in his gig or the sulky. Mostly, of course, he rode on his horse rather than ride in any carriage, continuing his daily two- or three-hour rides to Rock Creek and beyond. [53]

Double phaeton: During these years, besides the gig, sulky, and chariot, Jefferson had what he called a double phaeton. The body on a phaeton was generally a single seat that accommodated no more than two people—the driver and a passenger. A double phaeton was built to carry four persons—two rows of forward-facing seating. [Fig. 5-15] However, in a letter Jefferson wrote to Enoch Edwards at the beginning of his presidency, he made a small sketch in the margins of a carriage

Fig. 5-14. Chariot (or post- chaise) about 1770, probably similar to Jefferson's Presidential chariot. From and by Edwin Tunis, *Wheels: A Pictorial History* (New York: Crowell 1977).

Fig. 5-15. Double phaeton

body that he calls a landau, but which he said is "in fact a [double] Phaeton, the two tops closing together, when desired." [Fig. 5-16] In the sketch, the seats of the double phaeton face each other, like in a landau. [54]

To Enoch Edwards

DEAR SIR Washington July 9. 1801.

Your favor of the 3d. is duly received. I have not suffered for want of the carriage: and even now mr Hanse may take his own time, for I shall shortly set out for Monticello where I shall pass the months of August & September. he may finish it off therefore at his leisure; and whenever it is ready a line from him or yourself notifying it to me will find me at Monticello, and will suffer but a delay of one week more for the distance. I will immediately order the person from hence who will have been previously engaged to go for the carriage with a pair of horses, and will direct mr John Barnes, here, (who [acts] for me in all private business) to remit the amount as shall be desired. I suppose the only cover necessary for the carriage on that journey will be a chemise of coarse linen. the oilcloth cover is [a] thing of no value [or] discretion. it is to be brought only to this place. the harness I suppose can be secured within—I thank you for [the] prices of the coachees. but I think were I to indulge myself in another carriage of luxury, it should be a Landau, which in fact is [a double] Phaeton, the two tops closing together, when desired, in the following [manner].

I am not certain but that mr Hanse might tempt me by good work at low prices to indulge in such a cap[rice.] could he say what the body of such a carriage would cost by itself, and what the carriage part separately? or whether it might be fixed on [the][1] carriage of the chariot he is making, as they would never be [used] together. I shall be glad to hear from you on the subject of [. . .] as I had no friend at N. York I could charge with the enquiry. being too [poor to] pave the streets of our great city, we are making gravel turnpikes, which [I] believe will be found sufficient for our state of population & more agreeable. we hope to do it at 1000. D. a mile and to shew to all towns of the 2d. & 3d. [. . .] what they may do to advantage. present me respectfully to mrs Edwards and accept yourself assurances of my esteem & respect.

TH: JEFFERSON

PrC (DLC); faint; at foot of text: "Dr. Edwards"; endorsed by TJ in ink on verso.

[1] TJ here canceled "[back?]."

[530]

Fig. 5-16 Jefferson drew his idea for a "double phaeton," or landau, in a letter to Enoch Edwards on July 9, 1801.

New phaeton: By 1802, President Jefferson began to make drawings for a new phaeton, which may not have been built until 1805 or so. [Fig. 5-17] Paid white workmen at Monticello made this phaeton. The wooden parts were made by James Dinsmore, the Irish joiner, while William Stewart, a blacksmith, made the iron parts. The chair, or seat, for this phaeton still exists and was on display at Monticello. [Fig. 5-18] In the 1950s, Monticello (owned and operated by the Thomas Jefferson Foundation) took Jefferson's designs (drawings) and reconstructed this phaeton (stored away now). [Fig. 5-19] Recently a new reconstruction of the phaeton has been made. It was in this vehicle that one visitor, Margaret Bayard Smith, on a visit to Monticello in August 1809, rode with Jefferson, and out of which she jumped during a ride on the roundabouts, afraid it was going to overturn. Although the seat usually accommodated two people at most, three of them were jammed into the phaeton that day: Ellen, Margaret, and Jefferson (see the anecdote later in the chapter).

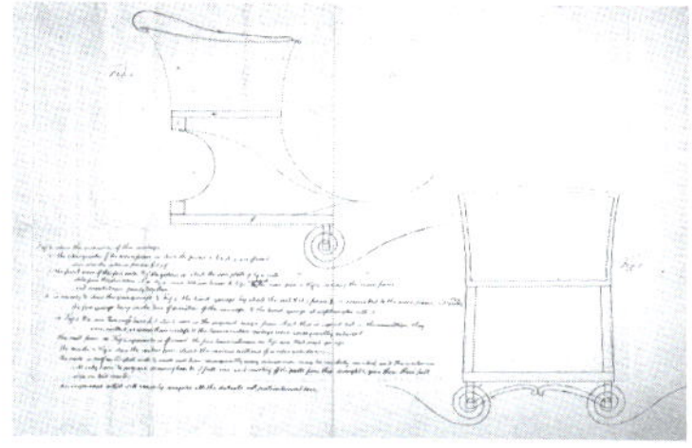

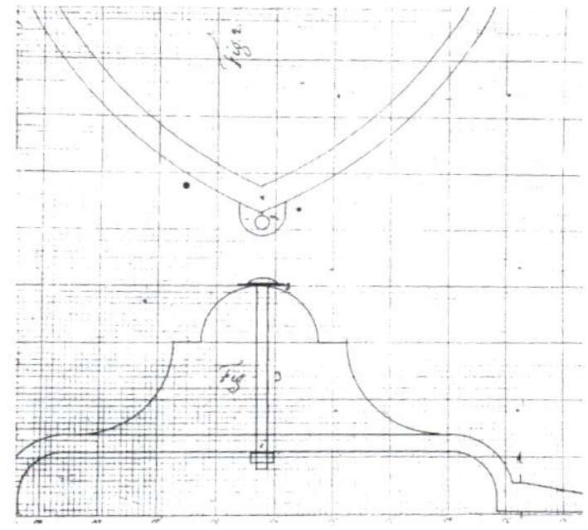

Fig. 5-17 More Jefferson drawings of his last (1802) phaeton

Fig. 5-18 Original wooden seat of Jefferson's last (1805) phaeton

Fig. 5-19 Jefferson's phaeton, restored in 2020

Retirement at Monticello: Bremo, Diomede, Wellington, and Tecumseh: In his later years, Jefferson used his landau exclusively when he traveled by carriage. This distinctive handcrafted vehicle was pulled by a team of fine, highly bred, perfectly matched bay horses: Bremo, Diomede, Tecumseh, and Wellington.

Bremo: Bremo, a dark bay with a white star, 15.3 hands high, and eight years old, was bought in 1814. Bacon described Bremo as "a horse of fair size, full, but not quite as tall as Eagle," i.e., not quite 16 hands, and added that Bremo was a good riding horse as well as excellent for the harness. As Bremo was Jefferson's riding horse for many years, he is described more thoroughly in the chapter about Jefferson's saddle horses. (See Chapter 4.) It was only after 1820 when Jefferson bought Eagle, his last saddle horse, that Bremo began to be used exclusively for driving and served as part of Jefferson's landau team. Bacon described him as excellent for the harness. [55]

Lineage: Bremo was out of Knowsley, imported from England by William Lightfoot in Charles City in 1801. In Albemarle County, Knowsley stood at stud at William Wood's farm, Oaklands, from1805 to 1807.

Social connections: Jefferson bought Bremo from John Hartwell Cocke, a friend and neighbor who lived just nineteen miles from Monticello on his own plantation called Bremo, on the James River. Younger than Jefferson, Cocke was a progressive planter and horseman and helped found the University of Virginia with Jefferson. (See Chapter 2.)

Diomede: In September 1808, John Wayles Eppes bought a five-year-old bay horse called Diomede. Eppes thought Diomede resembled the horse they had bought from Mr. Bell (called Bell), except for his height, only about 14.5 hands high. Eppes had worried about Diomede's height from the beginning but hoped it was just because he was still a young horse. They were looking for a tall horse because Jefferson needed a reliable horse to replace the "aging Castor" in the gig and one-horse phaeton (Castor had been quite tall). But according to Eppes, Diomede was well broke, gentle, and high-spirited. Eppes acknowledged that Diomede was "not fit for the saddle as he trots hard & gallops badly." But Eppes had told Jefferson from the beginning that he would "find him a fine carriage horse," and that he did. Overseer Bacon went to Chesterfield to get the horse. He said that when he "got him home, he was poor, but [he] had him in fine order when Jefferson got home" from Washington. According to Bacon, "he was a fine high-formed bay horse, not as good for riding as the others, but a fine harness horse." [56]

Jefferson's problem using this horse at first is illustrated in the following letter written from Montpelier to daughter Martha, just three weeks after he received the horse: "My new horse is perfectly gentle, but so fractious and ill-tempered in difficult roads that I fear he will not answer." Later Diomede must have settled down, because he had a long career pulling Jefferson in his carriages. Although Diomede seemed to serve reliably on the landau team till the end of Jefferson's life, the horse "became blind, poor fellow," said Bacon." [57]

Lineage: Diomede was a high-bred blood horse, the son of imported Diomed. Diomed was related to all three foundation stallions and was the great-great-grandson of the Godolphin Arabian on both sides (see Chapter 4 for more on imported Diomed). Jefferson paid $250 for Diomede.

Social connections: Eppes procured this horse in Chesterfield County from Richard Thweatt, who was the brother of Eppes's brother-in-law (from Eppes's second wife, whom he married after Marie Jefferson had died).

Jefferson's Diomede seemed to be used as a stud at least a couple of times. When Bacon left Monticello to explore Kentucky in 1818, the horse he took with him was the granddaughter of imported Diomede, and Bacon claimed she was "one of the best animals ever backed." Imported Diomed blood was in three of Jefferson's other horses (Diomede, Peacemaker, and The Eagle). [58]

Wellington: Wellington was a match for Diomede. This

horse, which Jefferson bought in May 1815, was a six-year-old bay. Jefferson noted that he had "no white but a few white hairs in his foretop. He had a lump on the left side of the neck." Overseer Bacon said he was a large horse, and that Wellington was a better saddle horse than Diomede but not as good as "the other two" (meaning Bremo and Tecumseh). [59]

Social connections: Jefferson wrote that he bought Wellington from Elias Wells for $120. However, Bacon said he, Bacon, had bought the horse from a Dutchman from Augusta County named Imboden for £60. [60]

Tecumseh: Tecumseh, a seven-year-old bright bay (b. 1808), with a few white hairs in his forehead, first served as a riding horse, and later pulled Jefferson's landau, along with Diomede, Bremo, and Wellington. Tecumseh tended to shy or scare at rocks and birds, so Jefferson devised a blind that "cured him" of this habit.

Lineage: Bacon claimed to know the horse and his stock well, and Jefferson sent him to buy the horse. There is no recorded mention of his pedigree.

Social connections: Jefferson saw this horse several times in a field as he was riding into Charlottesville. In June of 1815 he told Bacon to make some inquiries about him. The horse belonged to David Isaacs, "a Jew who owned a store in Charlottesville." David Isaacs was married to Nancy West, a free woman of color. Their daughter married Eston Hemings (a son of Sally Hemings and Thomas Jefferson) in 1832. Tecumseh was the only named horse Jefferson bought and paid for in full immediately. [61]

The above four horses—Bremo, Diomede, Wellington, and Tecumseh—must have made quite a stately sight as the elderly Jefferson and his granddaughters made their way down to Poplar Forest and back a couple of times a year. Four impressive bay horses, harnesses jangling at the trot, mounted by two postilions in livery, would deliver their important cargo to Jefferson's retreat far south of Albemarle.

The Carriage for Retirement at Monticello: By 1814, Jefferson, now retired and living at Monticello, paid taxes only on a phaeton and a gig. Yet Jefferson was not finished with carriages. That very year, he designed and had built at Monticello a new vehicle, called a landau. Many years earlier Jefferson had mused, "I think were I to indulge myself in another carriage of luxury, it should be a Landau." He went on to call it a "caprice." [62]

Landau: The landau has been called Jefferson's only true coach. In shape, its bottom half certainly resembles the structure of a coach. However, a landau differed from a coach in that its top was divided into two separate leather folding half-hoods, that when put up would lock together in the middle but could also be folded down (accordion-like) behind the back- and front-facing seats (for four passengers). In other words, it was a convertible. [63] [Fig. 5-20]

Jefferson drew up the plans for his landau and gave them

Fig. 5-20. English landau—convertible (about 1760). From and by Edwin Tunis, *Wheels, A Pictorial History*, (New York, Crowell 1977).

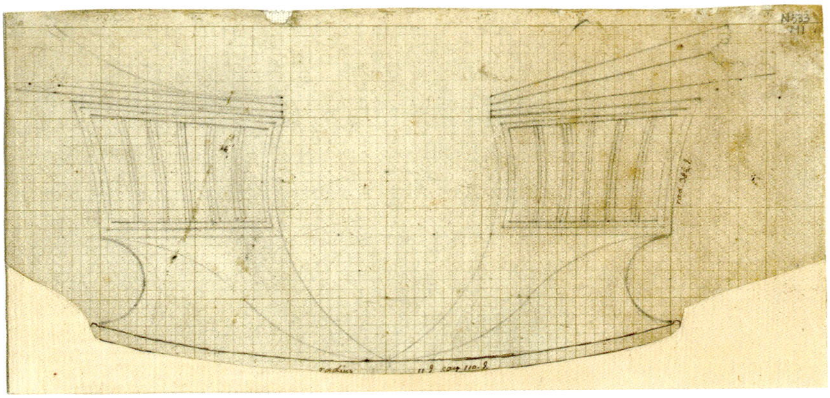

Fig. 5-21 a. and b. Jefferson's plans for his landau, 1802

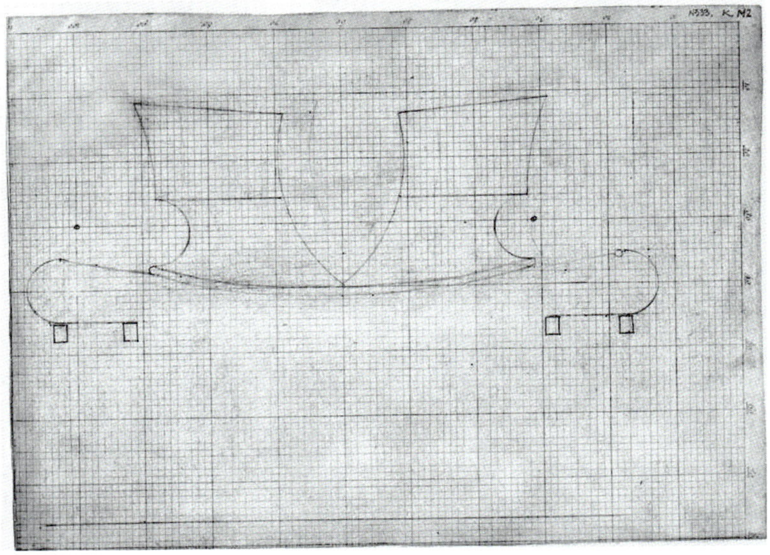

over to be realized by the current joiner, John Hemmings (trained by Dinsmore) and the smith, Joe Fosset (trained by Stewart), aided by Moses, all enslaved Monticello workers. Burwell, Jefferson's enslaved manservant, was also the painter at Monticello and painted the landau. [Fig. 5-21 a, and b] Jefferson attended to the interior décor and bought scarlet rattinet for the lining of the carriage. Many years later, one family member recalled, "When the weather was pleasant the occupants could enjoy the open air; when it was rainy, they were protected from it by the closing of the covering, which fell back from the middle." [64]

It was in this vehicle that Jefferson and his granddaughters would ride down to his retreat at Poplar Forest (after he stopped riding his horse there). This big, bulky, open coach-like carriage was pulled by the four horses described above, with two slaves—James and Israel Gillette—riding postilion on the near pair; Burwell Colbert, then Jefferson's valet, always followed on horseback on Jefferson's saddle horse, Eagle. That way Jefferson would have Eagle for his daily ride once they arrived at his retreat at Poplar Forest. If they were just going about the neighborhood, Colbert could go for help on Eagle if the landau broke down. For example, one time the landau fell through the rotted-out slats of a bridge flooring, and the horses got stuck in the water below. The carriage was not damaged, and eventually the party was able to continue on, but such accidents must have been common. [65]

By 1817, Jefferson, at seventy-four years of age, had given up the one-seated gig due to the exhaustion of driving it, and either rode in the landau or rode on his horse. In 1824 the Marquis de Lafayette, the French hero of the Revolutionary war, who had come to Monticello on his reunion tour of the United States, and three presidents (Jefferson, Madison, and Monroe) were conveyed down from the mountaintop to Charlottesville in the open landau pulled by Bremo, Wellington, Diomede, and Tecumseh (and their postilions). From the landau, Lafayette was greeted by the citizens of Charlottesville at Jefferson's new University, where a dinner was given in his honor.

Bedford: On January 1, 1815, Jefferson bought a six-year-old (b. 1809) bright bay with a blaze on his face and a white right-hind foot. This horse, bought several months before Wellington and Tecumseh, may have been meant to be a match for the landau team; he was a bay carriage horse like Bremo and Diomede. Bedford died, however, in late March of that year, just three months after Jefferson bought him. A month later, Jefferson bought Wellington and then Tecumseh. [66]

Lineage: Jefferson, in his Memorandum Books, called this horse "a Bedford," which implied that he was a blooded horse whose sire would have been the well-known stud Bedford. (Jefferson then referred to this horse as Bedford, too, as seen in other correspondence). [67]

The famous stud Bedford, foaled in England in 1792, was imported by turfman and breeder John Hoomes to his

Virginia stud farm, Bowling Green. On the turf in England, this horse had "won a match at Newmarket and a plate at Bedford—whence he derived his name after he left the turf." In 1796, Bedford was advertised as "high bred horse Bedford, fine bay, 15.3 high, 4 years old." After two years at Bowling Green, Bedford, like so many of the imported studs, was passed around from breeder to breeder in Virginia and the Carolinas. Harrison, the equine historian, says that Bedford was "much esteemed in Virginia also for the beauty, spirit and docility of the saddle horses of his get." Edmund Bacon, when he retired as Jefferson's overseer, took a horse called Duke of Bedford (by Bedford) to Kentucky with him in 1822, which got the American Thoroughbred matriarch Mary Bedford. [68]

Social connections: Jefferson bought the horse from an Albemarle neighbor named Pleasants German for $100 (payable in a year).

Hyatilda: Hyatilda must have been one of Jefferson's all-purpose horses. There is no other information on her. Perhaps she was one of Jefferson's Chickasaws. Jefferson called her a "draught animal," but it is not clear if that meant she was a work horse. Grandson Jeff was using her as a saddle horse. Bedford (discussed above) had died just as he had been hitched with another horse to take Jefferson's sister, Anna Scott Marks, south to Snowden in the gig. Jefferson quickly wrote his grandson Jeff, who was visiting his new bride and her family at Warren, that he was sending his hostler Wormley Hughes to exchange horses with him to bring back Hyatilda. Jeff must have ridden Hyatilda to Warren. Hughes took Celer (Seelah) for the switch. Jefferson needed a carriage horse; he described Hyatilda as "an excellent draught animal, and with a match I have for her at Tufton will carry the girls very well; only that it is sometime since she was in geer [*sic*], it will be advisable to drive her in the wagon two or three days." Due to Hyatilda's lack of practice in the gig, Jefferson decided to hitch her to a wagon. He was also trying to find a way to get two of his granddaughters, Ellen and Cornelia, safely to Warren to visit their brother's new family. [69]

At any rate, Hyatilda is one of the few mares we ever hear Jefferson mention using, perhaps because her passengers were young girls. Nevertheless, she was sold almost as soon as she arrived back to Monticello. In April of 1815, just two weeks after Bedford died, Jefferson sold the mare, Hyatilda, back to Pleasants German, from whom he had bought Bedford, for the same price as Bedford, $100. Jefferson noted in his account book, "received back my note of 100D. ante Jan. 1 in payment." [70]

Jefferson's Use of Carriages

To summarize, for most of his life, if he used a carriage, Jefferson drove his own vehicles, and they were small one- or two-horse vehicles, like the two-wheeled chair or gig, or the four-wheeled, and safer, phaeton. He owned chariots (larger enclosed vehicles) at certain times of his life, but always seemed to prefer the smaller vehicles for himself. When he became president in 1801, he used his own funds to have a carriage made and bought four fabulous blooded bay horses to draw it. His son-in-law John Wayles Eppes helped him find these very expensive horses (the most expensive he ever bought) down near Petersburg during the racing season. With the impressive new chariot, these fine horses made a grand scene. However, because Jefferson didn't use this fine carriage much, his coachman, the Irishman Dougherty, was always anxious for Jefferson's daughter Martha and the children to come to Washington so he would have an excuse to take it out. The president preferred driving his gig or sulky. When he could no longer drive his gig, he traveled in his Monticello-made landau. Jefferson bought fine horses to draw his carriages, but the best and most highly bred horse in his stable at all times was always his personal saddle horse. [71]

Care of Equipment

Preparing Jefferson's gig or phaeton or landau to drive was a laborious and time-consuming process. Like they did for his saddle horse, the hostler and his crew got the horses and coach ready for Jefferson and probably brought the vehicle round for him to mount from the house. The harness sets and traces that were used for carriage horses could be quite complicated and

Fig. 5-22. Harnesses and collars in the tack room at Mount Vernon

JEFFERSON'S CHARIOT INSTRUCTIONS

Jefferson's drawings of the designs for his phaeton and landau are preserved. Presumably, he gave these drawings to his workmen to follow as they worked on the vehicles. However, we know that Jefferson commissioned two chariots from carriage makers, one in London in 1788, and the other in Philadelphia in 1801. It is informative to look at the instructions he conveyed to the carriage makers for these two elegant carriages. Basically, he asked the Philadelphia carriage maker to repeat the same details he had requested thirteen years earlier from the London carriage maker—another indication of Jefferson's conservative tastes.

London: In the summer of 1788, Jefferson corresponded with John Trumbull in London, requesting that Trumbull procure for him a second-hand crane-neck chariot. This would be Jefferson's second chariot in Paris. There were two kinds of chariots as defined by their undercarriage: perch and crane neck. A perch was a straight or slightly bent single pole, whereas a crane-neck consisted of two parallel iron rods bent in such a way as to allow the front wheel to pass under them. Although a perch was light, a crane-neck carriage let the vehicle turn in narrow streets.

Trumbull (1756–1843) was the famous artist who had painted the Declaration of Independence and other important portraits of Revolutionary heroes. In 1785, he had worked with Jefferson in Paris. Later, he went to London to study under Benjamin West. He replied, "Perch carriages (which won't do for you) abound. But the crane neck is not so much us'd tho infinitely more in demand; so that I don't really find any second hand thing for which I should dare give the price which is ask'd." Trumbull suggested that Jefferson order a new one built by a young carriage maker that Trumbull knew and trusted, John Kemp. Jefferson liked the idea and decided the price was right. He wrote Trumbull with the carriage details he wanted:

"I would wish it to be 3 feet 8 inches wide within, a strapontin [foldaway seat] to unship and ship as may be wanting, the steps to shut within, a box to take in and out, coachman's seat to ship and unship readily, mortise locks, venetian blinds, spring curtains and vallons, a large oval back light of 2 feet diameter lengthwise to let down and up, crane neck. I would wish a mantle painted in front, flanks &, without either arms or cipher. The carriage to be hung half way between the old fashion and the new, that is to say lower than the new, and somewhat high for the old fashion. It is intended for America, where you know our roads do not admit a high carriage with safety. I shall carry it there with me next spring, and shall probably leave it there for the use of my daughters ... The taste in painting, and finishing I will leave to you."

This began a series of detailed exchanges between the two men. Trumbull responded that three details in Jefferson's description would significantly add to the price: the Venetian blinds ("not much us'd here"), the large back light, and the strapontin. He then goes on to question one aspect: "The Vallons is what I do not understand. I do not find the word in my French dictionary and the Coachmaker knows as little as I do. There is a part of the common finishing of a Carriage known by that name here, but I suspect you to mean festoon curtains." Trumbull asked if Jefferson wanted two trunks for traveling and an imperial, a luggage case for the top of a coach. He also wanted to know:

"When you say you shall want two Setts of Brass harness: do you mean a Harness compleat for four horses in the same Carriage, or two harnesses for two Horses, as there is a difference in the length of Traces Reins & &.—the Coachmaker objects to your using brass Harness with the Chariot He means to send you because the mouldings, Handles of the Doors && are to be plated, and He thinks the Harness should correspond. Of that which you are to use in Paris, I am of his opinion for the brass and Silver will certainly not look well together."

Trumbull also discussed the difference in price according to the quality of material:

"You will judge from the prices, which are for a pair of Horses with brass trimmings plain and good in every respect, Nine guineas—you may go as low as Seven.—For do. Plated trimmings plain and good, Fifteen to sixteen guineas, and may be as low as Thirteen:—but in case of the cheap one, you will find the leather is both bad and the plating so thin that with good care it shall show the copper in the first year..—For the first price you are sure of the best leather, and the plating so thick as to wear with equal care, three years at least. If you have a Cypher, or which is most common a Crest engraved on the Harness trimming, it may be a Guinea difference."

Jefferson responded that the Venetian blind was absolutely essential in the hot climate of Virginia, that he did not want an imperial, and he wanted only one trunk to go behind. As for the harness, he was adamant about the brass, noting that he already had plated harness, and that these would be for the country. He wanted the brass to be "plain, and substantially good. Neither cipher nor crest on them."

The plated harness arrived in Paris in October of 1788, but the English carriage (chariot) did not arrive until January 1789, only a few months before Jefferson ended up returning to the United States. The total cost of that chariot was £171-5. Jefferson left the carriage in Paris.

Philadelphia: Many years later, in 1801, just after Jefferson was inaugurated as president of the United States, he decided to buy a carriage worthy of the head of state. He applied to a friend in Philadelphia, where the best carriages were still made, for help in ordering a "handsome" chariot. Jefferson then listed on a separate sheet of paper his instructions for the carriage, yet yielding to Enoch Edwards (and his wife) all questions about "colour, form, and every thing about it which is taste." The new president said he would not need the carriage until after the first of May because he would be in Virginia until then. (It did not arrive until August.) It should be added that at the time of the request, the president did not yet have carriage horses for a new chariot. Finally, Jefferson reminded Edwards, "I am not fond of splendid things; but of chaste neatness."

The following are the enclosed instructions:

Instructions for a carriage

A handsome chariot for both city & country use, consequently to be made very light, and to be hung absolutely low, without any regard at to the modern fashion, as low as they came in former times, which the dangerous roads of the country absolutely require.

- A very large semicircular light behind.
- Quadrantal lights in each hind quarter.
- Venetian blinds and glasses to all the lights, & spring curtains
- Calico lining
- Qu? Plated caps to the hubs of the wheels.
- A driver's box to be taken off or on easily. By 4. screws.
- No lanterns.
- Plated beads & cipher.
- A light boot to be off or on at pleasure. In this, have no regard to the ridiculous fashion of enormous boots.
- 2 pr. Plated harness, with both pads & postilion saddles, to be easily changed.

Jefferson justified the use of calico: "The calico is to be over a cloth lining [...] because it can easily be taken out, [...] & kept clean. It has a cooler look too in summer." As for the shape of the carriage house itself, Jefferson agreed with Edwards, saying, "the beauty of the body depends mainly on the sweep of the stern, & that being too square is the worst extreme. The other extreme is more [tolerable] as it leads to lightness."

The chariot was finally ready for delivery at the end of August, but many preparations were necessary to transfer the carriage from Philadelphia to Washington. Edwards wanted to make sure it was covered so that Jefferson would receive it "spotless and beautiful as it really now is" and so as to prevent "the Eyes & Fingers of the curious from doing it an Injury, on its journey."

Then, adequate horses had to be found and a "sober driver" to fetch it. Eventually, Jefferson's Irish coachman at the president's house convinced Jefferson to let him hire "a pair of Steady horses," and he set off from the White House stables with a letter for a Mr. Hanse. The harness was sent by ship ("water"), as it was too bulky to fit inside the carriage, and an old pair of harness lent for the trip. The new chariot finally arrived at the end of September.

Comparing the notes on the two carriages, although they were thirteen years and two continents apart, one can notice many similar details that Jefferson wanted included on both: a large oval back light, venetian blinds, spring curtains, a driver's seat to be taken off or on easily, and two pairs of plated harness. His English carriage must have served him well and comfortably, as he repeated many aspects of it in his presidential chariot.

(Sources: Tarr, The History of the Carriage, 241; John Trumbull to TJ, August 15, 1788, in PTJ, 13:519; TJ to John Trumbull, August 24, 1788, in PTJ, 13:445; Trumbull to TJ, September 2, 1788, in PTJ, 13:563; TJ to Trumbull, September 10, 1788, in PTJ, 13:597; TJ to Enoch Edwards, March 30, 1801, April 18, 1801, in PTJ, 33:500-502, 609; Edwards to TJ, August 20, 1801, in PTJ, 35:115; John Barnes to TJ, September 7, 1801, in PTJ, 35:224.)

consisted of many parts. [Fig. 5-22] Jefferson said he preferred a collar rather than a breast plate because it allowed the horse to pull without getting chafed.

> Collars are greatly preferable to breastplates. The latter [gall] the horse immediately & then by [...] the motion of his breast under [these] they cha[fe?] [...] the gall & set the best horse to [kick]ing. I have had [...] experiences travelling with collars, and never yet had a [horse] [galled?] by them. [...] they would lie so dead on it, as (after the [...] out) to press only like a tight [harness?] [72]

The metal parts of the harness (buckles and rings) could be made of brass or silver plate. [Fig. 5- 23] In Paris, Jefferson ordered from England a pair of chariot harness "plated, not foppish but genteel," as well as one for a cabriolet. Later, in 1788, he ordered a brass harness for his new English-made chariot. Jefferson saved the plated harness for use in the city but preferred to use brass harness at home at Monticello. [73]

Fig. 5-23. A buckle for Jefferson's carriage harness

Coachmen and Postilions

Like those who served all gentlemen of the day, Jefferson's coachmen and postilions were dressed appropriately when driving in public. Isaac (Granger) Jefferson, in his reminiscences, said the postilions Jupiter Evans and John Hemmings wore "caps & gilded bands." Two descriptions of Jefferson's postilions in the later retirement years at Monticello coincide in noting that they wore short gray roundabouts (a kind of short coat). One qualified this by saying, the "postilions [were] clad in gray roundabouts, without any brass buttons, though their caps had a large band of lace and buckles in front." [74]

As to riding style, it is not clear if Jefferson's enslaved postilions at Monticello rose to the trot like their counterparts in England and France. If Jefferson did not post to the trot, it is unlikely that his postilions did.

The coachmen did not always ride postilion, however. Several of Jefferson's enslaved servants sat in the driver's seat and were adept at driving his vehicles, the phaeton and gig as well as wagons. Sometimes these coachmen were sent off across the countryside in the phaeton to pick up Jefferson from a stop on the stagecoach route or to pick up family members from far-off plantations to bring them to Monticello for their annual visits. They were often commandeered to drive the white Jefferson women to others' homes, such as the Madison's Montpelier, or to visit the president when he was in Washington, DC.

Coach House

Jefferson probably had storage space for his carriages (a coach house) as part of the stables at his permanent home in Paris, the Hôtel de Langeac. Later, when he was in Philadelphia as secretary of state, his home had a stable for his horses and probably space for his carriages. When Jefferson lived at the White House, the complex was still under construction (and he was intimately involved in its design). The president's house (the White House) had stables and rooms for coaches soon after it was ready to be lived in. [Fig. 5-24 a, and b]

Many of the private plantation homes in Virginia at the time had finely built stables and separate coach houses to store the owners' various vehicles. At George Washington's Mount

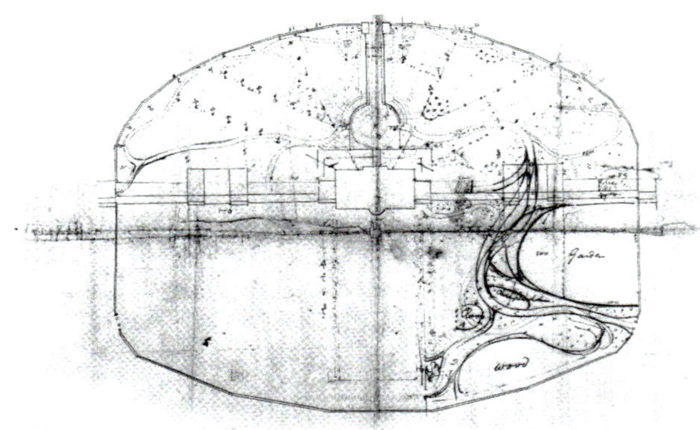

Fig. 5-24 a. and b. a. "Sketch plan for landscaping the grounds of the President's House," c. 1802-1805. Attributed variously to Benjamin Latrobe, Robert Mills, and Thomas Jefferson. b. Stables situated to the left of the president's house

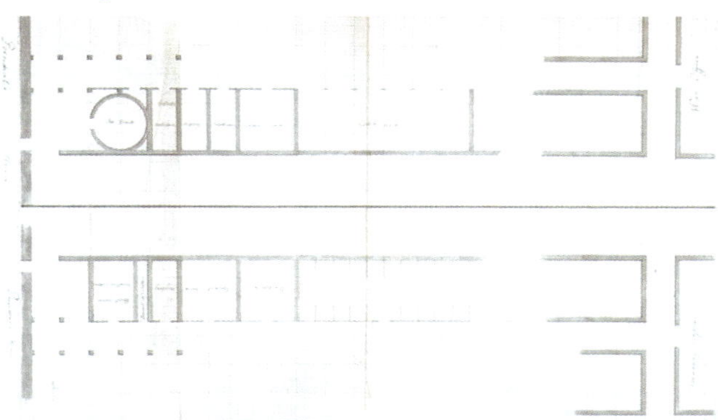

Fig. 5-25 Coach house at Monticello, north wing

Vernon, the coach house was across the yard from the brick stable. At Monticello, no formal coach houses were built until 1803 (with instructions sent from Washington, DC, and oversight during visits), when the "offices" under the North Terrace were completed. Although in some of his earliest plans for Monticello, Jefferson had planned for stables to be located under the North Terrace, when he finally ordered construction on this area after 1803, it was organized with enough spaces or cells to house the five carriages he had as president at the time: the elegant chariot, his gig and his sulky, the double phaeton, and his single phaeton. [Fig. 5-25] Under this same terrace were two spaces to stable visitors' horses, as well as a saddle room. Many years after Jefferson's death, Wormley Hughes recounted how in summer, many visitors would come to Monticello. The carriage houses beneath the North Terrace did not have enough spaces for all the visiting coaches, and two or three visitor's coaches would spill over and be parked under the tree outside. [75]

State of the Roads

For the first 150 years of English colonization in Virginia (1607–1760), rivers were the preferred means of travel and transporting goods. Three large rivers transversed the Tidewater area from west to east (emptying into the Chesapeake Bay): the Rappahannock, the York, and the James. These rivers, with their many tributaries, were easily navigable until the fall line, where cargo had to be carried beyond the falls (rocky cascades as the rivers dropped from higher elevation down to the Tidewater) in order to continue using river transportation. The higher terrain from the fall line west to the first mountains, the Blue Ridge Mountains, became known as the Piedmont. The rivers running across this vast territory were often low and impassable. Thus, horses and roads were necessary to open the West. [76]

Land transportation down in the Tidewater region existed more in theory than in fact. Saddle horses were the only means by which a land trip could be taken. At first, old Indian trails were used to crisscross the peninsulas and move west. "Moving in single file along the narrow trails called 'tote-roads,' 'pack-roads,' or 'horse-ways,' was the horse traffic between the western frontier and older towns." Roads were mandated early on, but during the wet season (three months a year), the roads were muddy, and for wheeled vehicles, impassable, "hopeless seas of mud with archipelagoes of stumps." Vehicle traffic was all but impossible for the first century and a half. Not until the close of the Revolutionary War and in George Washington's administration (1789–1797) was there a plan to develop transportation routes for wheeled vehicles to the West.

In towns, especially in Williamsburg, the colonial capital, the elite soon used private coaches. For example, the royal governor, Sir William Berkeley, possessed one in 1677. Quickly, more horse-drawn vehicles appeared and grew in number. The wealthy Tidewater gentry wanted the same luxuries and possibilities to display status as their English cousins. According to one historian, by 1722 most "families of note in Williamsburg had a coach, chariot, Berlin or chaise." During his law student days in Williamsburg (1762–1769), young Jefferson used a gig, or chair, a simple, open, two-wheeled vehicle pulled by one horse, for travel around the area. But beyond Williamsburg, few people owned carriages. [77]

Jefferson was born in 1743 in what would become Albemarle County, in the western Piedmont, near the Blue Ridge Mountains—what was essentially the frontier at the time. He built Monticello just across the Rivanna River from Shadwell, his birthplace. What roads connected Shadwell to Williamsburg? Beginning at the falls (in Richmond) of the James River and extending by different routes into Albemarle County were two main routes, which first had been Indian trails and later became full-fledged roads. Three Notch'd (or Three Chopt Road) and River Road both probably carried Thomas Jefferson down to Williamsburg, Richmond, and beyond all his life:

> I will repeat that the three horses & chair are to go, and my saddle & bridle also on one of them. The harness should be looked to in time & repaired, as also the chair if it wants any thing. If the three notched road is in order, they had better go along that & cross James river at Goochland courthouse. If the three notched road is not in order, they had better go by Dungeoness. [78]

Three Chopt Road, which may have been surveyed in the 1730s by John Lewis, was a significant east-west route; it continued west, past Charlottesville and over the Blue Ridge Mountains, into the Shenandoah Valley. By 1761–1765, there were petitions to the legislature to improve several roads (among them Three Chopt), but the so-called French and Indian War and later the Revolutionary War intervened. Money would not be spent on road building and upkeep at that time. When Jefferson commuted to the Staunton Court House in the Shenandoah Valley for legal work as a young circuit lawyer from 1767 to 1774, he traveled on horseback. No wheeled vehicle could yet cross the mountains. It was not until 1782 that carriages were finally able to cross the Blue Ridge by Rockfish Gap in Albemarle County. Soon, all over Virginia, as the heavy traffic caused dirt roads to become all but impassable, especially in winter, the necessity for adequate thoroughfares became evident. After 1802, turnpikes (toll roads) were constructed (Rockfish Gap 1808). The tolls paid were used for upkeep on the roads. [79]

In contrast to the west, roads going north and south along the Atlantic seaboard were constructed early on to connect Boston, New York, Philadelphia, Alexandria, Fredericksburg, Petersburg, and farther south. Along these routes, public transportation soon became available. By 1786, "slow stagecoaches were [already] lumbering southward from Alexandria to Petersburg. These vehicles, covered with mud from top to wheel, rattled along, sometimes overturning, frequently sinking into bogs and always uncomfortable." [80] [Fig. 5-26]

After the 1790s, Jefferson often caught the public stage at Fredericksburg or Culpeper in order to go farther north to Philadelphia, or later, Washington, DC. He would either ride northeast to Fredericksburg with an enslaved riding servant, who would then take his horse home or follow him behind the stage, or he would have his slaves meet him upon his return at the stage with his phaeton or other vehicle to make the rest of the way home through Orange Court House on unreliable roads. On more than one occasion, however, due to miserable weather and road conditions, Jefferson would leave his vehicle

Fig. 5-26 "Stage stuck in the mud," Ball Knobs, Floyd County, Indiana. Photo by Heimberger & Son, New Albany, 1898.

with his riding servant, mount his horse, and get home long before his carriage.

In fact, this is how he came home from the presidency in March 1809, leaving his vehicle in Culpeper and riding through a snowstorm. Several other examples follow.

This description is of Jefferson's trip from Virginia to New York City as George Washington's newly appointed secretary of state:

> I arrived here on the 21st instant, after as laborious a journey of a fortnight from Richmond as I ever went through, resting only one day at Alexandria and another at Baltimore. I found my carriage and horses at Alexandria, but a snow of eighteen inches falling the same night, I saw the impossibility of getting on in my carriage, so I left it there to be sent to me by water, and had my horses led on to this place, taking my passage in the stage, though relieving myself a little sometimes by mounting my horse. The roads through the whole way were so bad that we could never go more than three miles an hour, sometimes not more than two, and in the night not more than one. [81]

The following letter was written upon Jefferson's return to the capital after a visit home to Monticello during his presidency:

> I arrived here last night after the most fatiguing journey I have experienced for a great many years. I got well enough to Orange C. H. the first day. The 2d. there was a constant heavy drizzle through the whole day sufficient to soak my outer great coat twice, and the road very dirty and in places deep. The third the roads became as deep as at any season, and as laborious to the horse. Castor got into ill temper and refused to draw, and we had a vast deal of trouble and fatigue with him and obliged to give him up at last. I was from day light to sunset getting from Fauquier C.H to Colo. Wren's where I left John with the carriage, mounted my horse and arrived here at 9. Oclock in the night more sore and fatigued than I ever remember to have been with a journey. With the circuitous route I was obliged to take it made about 55. Miles, of as deep and laborious roads as could be travelled. [82]

Simply crossing water in a carriage could be risky and provoke an accident. One of Jefferson's biographers cites a letter to John Page, a friend from student days, about an accident suffered on Jefferson's way north to Maryland and Pennsylvania after he had finished his studies and was waiting to be admitted to practice law: "As he forded the Pamunky River in a one-horse carriage, it almost overturned 'in water so deep as to run over the cushion as I sat on it'." [83]

Another later example occurred when President Jefferson was heading back to the District of Columbia in a carriage from a visit to Monticello, and his vehicle overturned in a river, almost drowning the horse (Castor).

> My journey to this place was not as free from accident as usual. I was near losing Castor in the Rapidan, by his lying down in the river, where waste [sic] deep, and being so embarrassed by the shafts of the carriage and harness that he was nearly drowned before the servants, jumping into the water, could lift his head out and cut him loose from the carriage. [84]

Often, daughter Maria could not return to Monticello to visit from her homes, Eppington or The Forest, because of the state of the roads (and her fragility). Her husband commented in a letter to Jefferson: "The badness of the roads prevented our reaching Millers last evening. We arrived here at an early hour after being overset once with out receiving the smallest injury. The carriage went down so gradually that the glass windows which were up received no injury." After one spring journey to Poplar Forest in 1821, Jefferson's granddaughters reported that "the roads for the greater part of the way were so bad that Gill once stopped and said he thought if he ventured any farther we should certainly be upset, and once Burwell was obliged to dismount and hold up the carriage to prevent its going over." [85]

Merely getting up and down the 868-foot Monticello mountain on the Thoroughfare (Charlottesville to Milton) in a carriage was somewhat of an ordeal. The roads suffered, like other Virginia roads, during the rainy season. There are several accounts of the family returning home and the horses not being able to get up the mountain due to the mud and gullies. Family members had to get out and struggle up the mountain, women in their long dresses, men in perhaps-inappropriate shoes. When Jefferson and his family returned from France in December 1789, as they approached Monticello the struggling horses were

Margaret Bayard Smith gave this charming description of Monticello and her fear of the roundabouts, as Jefferson had kindly invited her out for a ride in the phaeton on the rather rough roads.

Monday morning—I again rose early in order to observe the scenes around me and was again repaid for the loss of sleep, by the various appearances the landscape assumed as the fog was rising. But the blue and misty mountains, now lighted up with sunshine, now thrown into deep shadow, presented objects upon which I gaze each morning with new pleasure. After breakfast Mr. J sent E[llen] to ask me if I would take a ride with him round the mountain; I willingly assented and in a little while I was summoned; the carriage was a kind of chair, which his own workmen had made under his direction, and it was with little difficulty that he, Ellen and I found room in it, and might well be called the sociable. The first circuit, the road was good, and I enjoyed the views it afforded and the familiar and easy conversation which our sociable gave rise to; but when we descended to the second and third circuit, fear took from me the power of listening to him, or observing the scene, nor could I forbear expressing my alarm, as we went along a rough road which had only been laid out, and on driving over fallen trees, and great rocks, which threatened an overset to our sociable and a roll down the mountain to us. "My dear madam," said Mr. J., "you are not to be afraid, or if you are you are not to show it; trust yourself implicitly to me, I will answer for your safety; I came every foot of this road yesterday, on purpose to see if a carriage could come safely; I know every step I take, so banish all fear." This I tried to do, but in vain, till coming to a road over which one wheel must pass I jumped out, while the servant who attended on horseback rode forward and held up the carriage as Mr. J. passed. Poor Ellen did not dare get out. Notwithstanding the terror I suffered I would not have lost this ride; as Mr. J. explained to me all his plans for improvement, where the roads, the walks, the seats, the little temple were to be placed.... We returned home by a road which did not wind round the mountain but carried us to the summit by a gentle ascent. It was a good road, and my terror vanished and I enjoyed conversation.

(Source: "Margaret Bayard Smith's Account of a Visit to Monticello.")

unhitched from the carriage, and the slaves pulled the phaeton up the hill. Then "joyfully" they passed Jefferson himself over their heads to his doorstep. [86]

Seemingly many bridle paths wandered through the woods and up and around Carter's Mountain, but carriage roads were quite something else. Jefferson constructed four roundabouts at Monticello for the family to walk upon or to enjoy for horseback riding or carriage rides. Even on the roundabouts, guests were unnerved by the bumpy inclines and rocky roads. The overturning of a carriage was always a possibility in their minds, as we can see in Margaret Bayard Smith's reminiscence. [87]

Despite the "terrors" on the groomed roundabouts, the other roads that Jefferson had his workmen make connecting the many parts of Monticello, such as the Farm Road, the North Road, and the South Road, were even less carriage-friendly. Riding a horse up the Farm Road from the river in August 2007 took me half an hour on a very rocky and gullied road.

Two Colonial Williamsburg interpreters riding in a chair. The woman is driving, as the chair was an appropriate and common vehicle for a gentry woman driver.

"Racing in the Colonies" depicts Benjamin Tasker admiring his mare Selima capturing a win at the racecourse in Gloucester, Virginia in 1752. By William Wilson.

Chapter 6

Sport: Foxhunting *and* Horse Racing

Some Virginia gentry, besides caring for their saddle horses and carriage horses, were able to keep other high-bred horses dedicated only for sport: foxhunting and horse racing. Thomas Jefferson eschewed participating in these sports, and did not assign any of his equines to these categories.

While president, Jefferson wrote a letter of advice to his oldest grandson and namesake, Thomas Jefferson Randolph, with whom he was very close. In this letter, we glimpse Jefferson's attitude toward foxhunting and horse racing, two popular equine sports among the gentry of Virginia. Jeff, as the family called him, was studying in Philadelphia. His grandfather himself had suggested that Jeff go to Philadelphia to continue his studies at age sixteen, and had given him letters of recommendation to friends and scholars resident in that city.

> Your situation, thrown at such a distance from us and alone, cannot but give us all great anxieties for you. As much has been secured for you by your particular position and the acquaintance to which you have been recommended as could be done towards shielding you from the dangers which surround you. But thrown on a wide world, among entire strangers, without a friend or guardian to advise, so young too, and with so little experience of mankind, your dangers are great, and still your safety must rest on yourself. A determination never to do what is wrong, prudence, and good humor, will go far towards securing to you the estimation of the world. When I recollect that at fourteen years of age, the whole care and direction of myself was thrown on myself entirely, without a relation or friend qualified to advise or guide me, and recollect the various sorts of bad company with which I associated from time to time, I am astonished I did not turn off with some of them and become as worthless to society as they were. I had the good fortune to become acquainted very early with some characters of very high standing, and to feel the incessant wish that I could ever become what they were. Under temptations and difficulties, I would ask myself what would Dr. Small, Mr. Wythe, Peyton Randolph, do in this situation? What course in it will ensure me their approbation? I am certain that this mode of deciding on my conduct tended more to its correctness than any reasoning powers I possessed. Knowing the even and dignified line they pursued, I could never doubt for a moment which of two courses would be in character for them. Whereas, seeking the same object through a process of moral reasoning, and with the jaundiced eye of youth, I should often have erred. From the circumstances of my position, I was often thrown into the society of horse-racers, card-players, foxhunters, scientific and professional men, and of dignified men; and many a time have I asked myself in the enthusiastic moment of the death of a fox, the victory of a favorite horse, the issue of a question eloquently argued at the bar or in the great council of the nation, Well, which of these kinds of reputation should I prefer? That of a horse-jockey? A fox-hunter? An orator? Or the honest advocate of my country's rights? Be assured, my dear Jefferson, that these little returns into ourselves, this self-catechizing habit, is not trifling nor useless, but leads to the prudent selection and steady pursuit of what is right. [1]

Thomas Jefferson's father died when the boy was just fourteen and still a student at Rev. Maury's school. His mother, with eight young children, was left to run the farm at Shadwell, but was obviously expecting help from her oldest son. Nevertheless, two years later, at age sixteen, Jefferson convinced his guardian, John Harvie, that the College of William and Mary in Williamsburg was the only place he could continue his studies. He persuaded Harvie that this would be a good use of his inheritance from his father. Jefferson arrived in Williamsburg in March of 1760 and lived at the college for his first year.

Although a good student and dazzled with learning and the intellectual company of the scholars and leaders of the capital city, Jefferson probably spent most of his time with his many friends and peers, the other students, many of whom were sons of the Tidewater elite. Many of these young men, future political leaders, also were or became horse breeders: Francis Willis, John Page, William Dandridge, John Ambler, Thomas Mann Randolph, and John Bolling. These young men certainly studied, but they knew how to have fun too. Many of these youths pulled numerous pranks, and some of them were certainly wags. Frank Willis, for example, would get drunk and keep his horse in the basement of the Wren building (where the students lived at the college). Seemingly, there was a lot of drinking and cavorting and flirting with the unattached young women at dances in the Apollo Room at the Raleigh Tavern. Williamsburg had many temptations, such as gambling and card playing, that beguiled a student away from his studies—so many temptations that Jefferson began calling Williamsburg "Devilsburg." Among these temptations were also the activities of horse racing and foxhunting.

In his 1808 letter to his grandson, Jefferson implied that he had enthusiastically attended horse races and participated many times in foxhunts, but he said that these were "vices" of his youth. After his first year at the College of William and Mary, Jefferson returned home to Shadwell and sheepishly went to his guardian, admitting that he had spent too much of his inheritance on "foolish" things—among other things, a "fine horse." His guardian answered that his expenses had been harmless and that his inheritance was still intact. Young Jefferson resolved to spend his time more "wisely." We aren't sure if this means that Jefferson, the student, completely forswore the diversions of foxhunting and days spent gambling at horse races, but certainly his young friends did note that Tom spent less time with them and more time with his studies after that first year. According to his friend John Page, Jefferson "could tear himself away from his dearest friends, to fly to his studies." [2]

After those early student years in Williamsburg, there is no record of Jefferson participating in foxhunts on horseback. George Washington, on the other hand, like other Virginia horse owners, kept certain horses expressly for this sport. Washington often noted in his diary that he went foxhunting with friends and neighbors day after day, for several hours a day, in the years before the Revolution. Jefferson's memorandum books are silent about this activity. Moreover, there were no hunt clubs in the county of Albemarle until the twentieth century. Foxhunting was a diversion of the great plantation owners in the Northern Neck and Tidewater area more than the uplands of Virginia. At any rate, Jefferson seemed to think they were a supreme waste of time. He would rather ride alone singing, musing, thinking, and contemplating nature than thrilling in the company of others at the death of a fox. To cite William Shenstone, the English poet, who wrote in 1760, "The world may be divided into people that read, people that write, people that think, and foxhunters." This seems to sum up Jefferson's opinion on foxhunting after his first year in college. [3]

Horse racing, however, was a different matter. What Jefferson gave up in his youth was betting on horse races. Nor did Jefferson race his own horses. However, we know he often attended the course races in his neighborhood. As president in Washington City, he attended the annual races of the Washington Jockey Club a couple of days in November of 1802, 1803, 1804, and 1805. He complained in letters to family when illness prevented him from attending. Horse races were large social gatherings, and were held twice a year in several of the major towns up and down the Eastern Seaboard. What Jefferson eschewed was putting money on a horse. He never gambled. Nor did he raise horses for racing, a practice taken up by several planters full time after the Revolution. But attend races he did. [4]

Although Jefferson always used his own horses for pleasure riding, they may have raced previous to his ownership. For example, on his way to Philadelphia for the First Continental Congress in 1775, Jefferson stopped at Alexander Spotswood's and bought a retired racehorse, called The General, a Janus colt. Later, while in Philadelphia as secretary of state in the early 1790s, Jefferson owned two ex-racehorses (horses past their racing days) that he used for riding and for the coach. Both these horses, Tarquin and Brimmer, had impressive racing pedigrees, but it is not known how successful they were on the turf.

John Hervey relates in his book, *Racing in America: 1665–1865*, that George Washington's stallion Magnolia was beatenat the races in Alexandria by a roan colt owned by Thomas Jefferson. If this is true, it attests to Tarquin's success on the turf. Some data coincide—Jefferson had indeed bought a roan racehorse, Tarquin, in 1790, in Alexandria. However, Washington had sold Magnolia in 1788, and the horse had been sent to South Carolina. Perhaps Tarquin did beat Magnolia in a race in Alexandria at some point, but it must have been before Jefferson became the owner of Tarquin.

Fig. 6-2 John Frederick Herring Sr., *Foxhunting: Over the Gate*, 1839

Foxhunting in Virginia

Foxhunting is, simply, hunting foxes on horseback with hounds. Before hunting on horseback, people hunted all kinds of vermin with hounds and followed the pack on foot. The first person to have a pack of hunting dogs in the colonies was Englishman Robert Brooke, who arrived in Prince George's County, Maryland, on June 30, 1650, with his wife, children, servants, and hounds. Lord Baltimore had given Brooke a 2,000-acre piece of land to develop into a plantation. Brooke's hounds had probably been all-purpose hunting dogs (harriers) back in England and were not brought over expressly to chase foxes. For many centuries in Europe, hounds had long been used to hunt stag, boar, and hare, as well as vermin like rats, weasels, and foxes. [Fig. 6-1] Although the earliest record of hunting a fox with hounds was in 1534, the first packs of hounds to hunt specifically foxes are recorded in England in the 1600s (1666, 1690, 1698). In the colonies in the second half of the seventeenth century, hounds were used to hunt such pests as opossums, wolves, raccoons, and foxes. Yet until the eighteenth century, hunters followed their hounds on foot for the most part. [5]

Fig. 6-1 George Stubbs, *Hound Coursing a Stag*, c. 1762

Back in England, with the passing of the Enclosure Acts (the laws requiring the fencing and enclosing of open fields, thus doing away with common grazing lands) after 1750, the deer population declined (the deer forests disappeared) and hunting deer, originally a royal prerogative, became much more difficult. At that point in time, foxes were overrunning the countryside and invading chicken coops, and they were despised by farmers. The landowning gentry, still in the countryside while the landless masses were now moving to the cities, took up foxhunting on their newly developed breeds of warm-blooded hunting horses (the new Thoroughbred race horses crossed with the heavier, native, military draft-type horses). Moreover, the new fences separating (enclosing) the fields became obstacles to jump and thus an important part of the eighteenth-century rural English foxhunting tradition. [Fig. 6-2]

Crashing across country, brashly jumping fences, hedges, ditches, and everything in sight, it was as if these new horses "demanded to be ridden differently." The so-called English hunting seat had the rider shortening his stirrups somewhat (making standing in the stirrup possible), turning down his boots in order to let the knee bend, and being ready to sit forward and bend at the waist. This new kind of riding required a new kind of saddle. The old saddle was awkward for hunting. Until the late nineteenth century, riders would lean back in the saddle over a fence, and the high cantle would get in the way of the rider, while the high (front) pommel banged painfully against the rider as he went over jumps. The new saddle was flat, low in front and back, with little padding, giving the rider much contact with the horse but very little support. The snaffle bit was substituted for the curb bit so that the jockey would ride "lightly," thus helping the horse to balance itself to the terrain. [6]

English horsemen claimed this new style of riding as their own defining English style. What came to be known as the "English hunting seat" developed in response to this cross-country riding and contrasted radically to the more formal French, or Continental, style of *ménage,* or what today we call dressage. [7]

Over in Virginia and Maryland, the wolf was the first animal hunted with hounds and horses, "probably because it was easier for a person on horseback to keep up with the hounds. When the wolf population became depleted in the eighteenth century, the fox was the natural replacement." By 1714 in New Jersey and 1723 in New York, however, there were already bounties on the red fox. After the 1730s in Virginia and Maryland, as newly prosperous planters began importing English turf horses, they discovered that the bottom (endurance) of these horses and their offspring served well for hours of sportive riding to hounds. As explained in Chapter 4, the English hunting saddle, evolved specifically in response to the practice of foxhunting in England, with the low pommel and low cantle, was soon adopted in the American colonies by the Southern planters. [8]

Furthermore, people began breeding hounds expressly for foxhunting, crossing and mixing strains to create the foxhound. [Fig. 6-3]. In fact, one of the earliest people to maintain a private hunting pack of foxhounds was Dr. Thomas Walker of Albemarle County in Virginia. He founded the Castle Hill Hounds in 1742 with imported hounds from England. Dr. Walker was friends with Peter Jefferson (and later became one of Thomas Jefferson's guardians upon his father's death), and young Tom may have learned to hunt with these dogs. Later, other important Virginians bred foxhound packs, including George Washington. Especially between 1759 and 1774, Washington oversaw the breeding of his hounds and gave them such names as Mopsey, Tipler, Tarter, Cloe, Chaunter, Forester, and Rockwood. Washington evidently inspected his kennels twice a day and hunted with them several days a week. [Fig. 6-4] In fact, hunting hounds became so associated with the horses of the hunt that nineteenth-century painters often portrayed horse and hound together in stable scenes. [9]

Fig. 6-3 William Ward, *Fox Hunting: Raby Pack / The Earl of Darlington's Fox Hounds in Their Kennel,* 1814

Fig. 6-4 Horse and hounds together, George Stubbs, *Bay Hunter with Two Spaniels,* 1777

George Washington is probably the best-known foxhunter of colonial times. He was introduced to foxhunting when he was just a teenager by Thomas, sixth Lord Fairfax, who settled in Virginia in 1747 (on his inherited lands), bringing both his horses and his hounds. Lord Fairfax initially settled at Belvoir, which is but a few miles south of Washington's estate, Mount Vernon. Fairfax first met Washington in 1748. Washington was only sixteen at the time, but Lord Fairfax was so impressed with Washington's talents that he employed the young man to survey his vast lands west of the Blue Ridge, in the Shenandoah Valley (Fairfax owned more than five million acres). Supposedly

FAIRFAX FOX HUNTING WITH WASHINGTON

Fig. 6-5 Washington Irving, *Washington and Fairfax: Field Sports*, c. 1850

the first organized hunt for the benefit of a group (rather than a single patron) was started by Fairfax. Washington, in the company of his mentor, became an ardent hunter, spending days dedicated to this (still highly informal) activity. [Fig. 6-5] As noted above, Washington bred a pack of hounds and kept horses dedicated to the sport. Two of his favorite horses, Blueskin and Nelson, were both well-honed foxhunters.

Washington's diaries are full of references to foxhunting with Fairfax and other friends and neighbors. They rode in all kinds of weather, even with snow on the ground. Usually Washington noted in his diary if they "started" a fox or not, how many they "catchd," and how long they "ran him." It was common to run for three to four hours but, for example, on March 2, 1768, they caught a fox "after 7 hours chase in wch. Most of the Dog's were worsted." [10]

In an *American Heritage* article about foxhunting, Caroline Jones wrote:

> Washington cut a dashing figure in the field astride his favorite hunter, Blueskin. He possessed a wardrobe, as described by social historian Foster R. Dulles, of "riding frocks, waistcoats of superfine scarlet cloth and gold lace … elegant buckskin breeches … all specially made in England." Martha, when she occasionally joined him, also wore scarlet.
>
> Washington gave up the sport at the onset of the Revolution, of course. Afterward he tried to pick it up again; Lafayette even sent him a pack of French staghounds in 1785, although these proved unsatisfactory for foxhunting. But more urgent matters forced him to break up his kennels and give away all his dogs in 1787. [11]

Many other important Virginians and Marylanders were avid foxhunters. Some, however, could not afford their own pack of hounds and so joined organized hunting clubs (where the club owned and maintained the pack). Probably the first hunting club established was near Philadelphia in 1766—the Gloucester Foxhunting Club. This club included prominent Philadelphians, and in 1774 they adopted a uniform that consisted of a dark brown coat with "lapelled dragoon pockets, with white buttons and frock sleeves, buff waistcoat and breeches, and a black velvet cap." In 1768, a hunt club was established in 1768 on Long Island and 1783 in Brooklyn. [12]

By 1775, foxhunting had become a somewhat organized sport. After the Revolution, when the citizens of the new United States could return to their traditional forms of diversion and entertainment (suspended during the war), foxes were hunted quite regularly "by the wealthy landowners in Pennsylvania, Maryland, and Virginia. A pack of hounds became as integral a part of a gentleman's assets as his 'horse, slaves, and guns,'" noted Jones in *American Heritage*. A history by the Masters of Foxhounds Association said, "On one occasion, while Congress was in session, hounds ran near the capital. Many congressmen ran outside to watch the hounds and some jumped on their horses and joined the chase." [13]

However, it was not until the mid-nineteenth century that organized hunts became established. By 1904, there were seventy-six clubs in all of North America. After the 1907 establishment of the Master of Foxhounds Association of America, hunting became much more regulated. The hunting season takes place from September to March. There are more than 168 registered packs in the US and Canada, and currently more recognized foxhunting clubs in Virginia than any other state, with twenty-five according to the Masters of Foxhounds Association and Foundation. The earliest hunt club in Virginia, the Piedmont Foxhounds, was formed in 1840, and continues in existence today. The Blue Ridge Hunt (of Virginia) hunts today on much of Lord Fairfax's former territory. There are two hunt clubs based in Thomas Jefferson's Albemarle County: Farmington, founded in 1929, and Keswick, which dates back to 1897. Nearby Nelson County (to the south) hosts the Oak Ridge Hunt. [14]

As foxhunting became more ritualized over time, different

human participants fulfilled different roles in the organization and management of the hunt. The most prominent role is the master (or mistress) of the hunt (abbreviated as MFH). The huntsman directs the hounds in the course of the hunt, while the whipper-in assists the huntsman. The kennel man is in charge of the hounds in the kennels, while the secretaries are two volunteers who collect the money (cap) to pay for the hunt. [15]

As foxhunting became associated with the privileged social classes, dress was used to underline their distinctiveness. Tailors were engaged to make the traditional hunting attire. The scarlet coats often worn by huntsmen, masters, whippers-in, and other officials are sometimes called "pinques." [Fig. 6-6] These colors help them stand out from the rest of the field. Various theories about the derivation of this term have been advanced, ranging from the color of a weathered scarlet coat to the name of a purportedly famous tailor. The expression "in the pink" comes from the foxhunt, meaning feeling healthy. If you were "in your pink," you were ready to go. Note the description of George Washington above, dressed in his waistcoat of superfine scarlet cloth and gold lace. [Fig. 6-7] Martha, too, wore scarlet. The rest of the field, if not leaders of the hunt, usually wore black, gray, or tweed jackets, a white ascot-like scarf, with tan jodhpurs (tight pants at the calf, flared at the thigh), with tall riding boots and leather gloves. [16]

Fig. 6-6 Pinques, as depicted in Henry Thomas Aiken, *Fox Hunting. Going into Cover*, 1821, for *British Sports*

The hunt itself is driven by the hounds. The hunting begins when hounds are "cast" or directed toward:

> rough or brushy areas called "coverts," where foxes often lay up during daylight hours. If the pack manages to pick up the scent of a fox, they will track it for as long as they are able. ...The hounds pursue the trail of the fox and the riders follow, by the most direct route possible. ...' The hunt continues until either the fox evades the hounds, *goes to ground* (that is takes refuge in an underground burrow or den) or is overtaken and usually killed by the hounds. [17] [Fig. 6-8]

Fig. 6-7 John Ward Dunsmore, *The First Gentleman of Virginia, George Washington elegantly sailing over a snake fence on his horse Blueskin, hard on the heels of running hounds and his long-serving Huntsman Billy Lee*, 1909

Since 2005, foxhunting with hounds in England has been banned, while in the United States it continues to be legal and enjoy a loyal following. Some parts of the United States have clubs that hunt other animals than foxes (the coyote, for example). At any rate, North American foxhunting claims to be distinct from the British tradition, most obviously due to the fact

Fig. 6-8 John Frederick Herring Sr., *The Kill*, c. 1850

that in America the emphasis is on the chase rather than the kill. If the fox goes to ground (enters a hole in the ground), American foxhunters can still revel in the scenery, the companionship, the exhilaration of the ride, and the enjoyment of watching the hounds. Jefferson's disgust at the "moment of the death of the fox" has been superseded by American foxhunters who merely claim to enjoy the thrill of the chase. [18] [Fig. 6-9]

Fig. 6-9 Contemporary fox hunting, Blue Ridge Hunt, 2008

Virginia equestrian historian Alexander Mackay-Smith summed up the American foxhunting ethos in the following way:

> Fox hunting in North America is a sport about the chase, not the kill. The true foxhunter rides across country behind a pack of hounds in order to hear and watch how, with the help of their huntsman, hounds follow the twisting and turning trail of a hard-running fox (or coyote) until he goes to ground or the scent fails. The contest between fox and hounds is "level." We don't mar it with practices especially designed to kill foxes, such as bolting and digging out foxes, stopping earths, or closing refuge holes.
>
> Because they can end the chase whenever they please, foxes and coyotes aren't afraid of fox hounds. They frequently run from half an hour to an hour and a half before calling it quits. Unless they make a mistake, which rarely happens, foxes live to run another day. The accidental death of a straight-running fox is a calamity.

Fig. 6-10 Hunt Races at James Madison's Montpelier, November 2023

Due to the athletic skill involved in foxhunting on the part of both the horse and rider, foxhunting is the origin of the other equestrian field sports such as the steeplechase and other contemporary cross-country field events. [19] [Fig. 6-10]

Horse Racing in Virginia

Virginians inherited their passion for horses and horse racing from the English. Jefferson was born and grew up at a time when there were two competing kinds of horse races in Virginia: quarter races and course racing. Quarter racing had been invented by English, Irish, and Scottish settlers along the Atlantic Seaboard and had been present almost from the inception of the colonies, while the other form—course racing, or distance racing—had been imported later from England, after the 1730s. During the Revolution, all forms of diversion and gambling were frowned upon as an inappropriate waste of resources, and so horseracing (along with card games, cock-fighting, theater) was suspended. By the time these activities were taken up again around 1783, one kind of racing—quarter racing—had been eclipsed by the other—long-distance course racing with the new imported Thoroughbreds. By then, the less affluent tended to favor quarter racing, while the gentry tended to promote course racing. Quarter racing remained popular on the frontier, and so it migrated to Southside Virginia along the border with North Carolina, and then out to Kentucky with settlers in search of new lands and new horizons. Soon after Jefferson's death (1826), however, Kentucky again replaced Virginia as the home of horses bred for distance racing. [20]

Fig. 6-11 Depiction of a quarter race in Burlington, New Jersey. The judges stand at the end to decide the winner. Detail from "Birth Record for Samual Asay," c. 1830.

Quarter Racing in Virginia: The quarter-horse match race was an all-out blazing sprint between two horses over a quarter-mile straight dirt track that came to be known as a "quarter path." This kind of horse racing had no antecedents in England and is probably indigenous to Virginia. The earliest record we have of a quarter horse race in Virginia is in 1672, but surely they had been popular long before that. At first, these races took place down the main street of a town or village (sometimes the only street). [Fig. 6-11] When racing through town was later prohibited by legislation, two narrow parallel paths were hewn out through the forests and woods, possibly near a crossroads and around which ordinaries (or taverns) sprang up (or vice versa). [21]

At first, in the late seventeenth and early eighteenth centuries, these quarter races were exclusive to the landed gentry. Moreover, the horse owner was the jockey. A race was the result of a challenge and a wager between the two proud, competitive, and daring planters who were willing to risk large amounts of money or goods (tobacco) on their race. In 1674, a York County court declared racing "a sport only for Gentlemen." But as time went on, quarter racing changed from a gentry ritual to something more proto-democratic. By the mid- to late eighteenth century, yeoman farmers and laborers now had access to these fast horses and were willing to challenge others in the hopes of winning the seductive wagers. The center of raising horses for blinding speed moved from the Northern Neck and James River area of Virginia to the southern Virginia-North Carolina border, and later out to the democratizing frontier in Kentucky. In addition, the planter-owner was no longer the jockey. Young boys, and especially young enslaved boys, became the jockeys. And the public—and the gambling—became more colorful. [22]

As one equestrian historian wrote, "Nothing in regular racing has ever approached it in its picturesque and vivid *mise en scène,* the raciness and dramatic quality of its protagonists, or the variety of its incidents." [23]

Note the following description on the frontier aspect of the later quarter races:

> In the assemblage surrounding the starting place and packed along each side of the path the most extraordinary contrasts prevailed. Here was an exiled Cavalier, member of a noble house, mounted upon his blooded saddlehorse, accompanied by his richly dressed lady, riding her soft-paced ambler; attending them a Negro slave, not long from the Guinea Coast. Nearby was one of the sporting parsons, almost as frequently to be encountered in Old Virginia as at a fox-hunt in an English shire. Wilderness hunters, garbed in deerskin and with mink and beaver caps, elbowed indentured artisans and laborers of purest Cockney strain, come

over from London to work out their terms of servitude and then become free men and landholders.

Maids from the homes of the rich planters aired their scanty finery and were ogled by midshipmen on shore leave from brigs and merchantmen anchored in the James nearby, or that had adventured up the river from Hampton Roads to see what this strange New World might look like. Members of the Council saluted officers of the militia. Traders down from New Amsterdam, in quest of the tobacco of which the Hollanders had become extravagantly fond, gazed curiously at the crowd, so different from that to be seen at home along the Bouweries.

Here and there even a stern New England Puritan, drawn to the godless Stuart colony by the allurement of gain which was always coupled with his piety, gazed from under frowning brows at the unregenerate company in which he found himself. Swarthy privateers from the Caribbees jostled bravos from New France. Hovering about on the outskirts stalked chieftains of the Powhatans, the Potomacs, or the Appomattox, their towering stature and head-dress of feathers lifting them above the rest of the throng, their skins of ruddy bronze and savage physiognomy, wild and furtive, their scarce dissembled pride and hatred of the pale-faces that had come across the Big Water to deprive them of their patrimony, adding to the motley pageant, the lurid touch of danger and romance.…

At the starting end of the path, booths were set up for the sale of eatables, drinkables, and gewgaws; peddlers and venders hawked their wares about; itinerant healers and magicians put up improvised platforms from which to proclaim the wonders that they worked; fortune tellers plied their trade; and "freaks" exhibited themselves and their deformities. It was like a one-day fair, to which the entire countryside turned out. [24]

From the beginning, quarter races (like the later course races) were sites for gambling. Historians emphasize that most of the early planter society was addicted to all forms of gambling. Whereas cards, cockfighting, and other games of chance were accessible to the lower classes, horse racing could only be performed by those who owned horses, fast horses, horses bred for speed. At the beginning this was only true of the gentry, whose horses were a kind of extension of their owners. [25]

There were two levels of wagers. The main bet was between the contestants themselves (or the horse owners). Considerable and irrational sums were bet. Of course, this wagering was not only due to the confidence the planter had in his horse, but due to the planter's very honor. Then there are side wagers, made between the spectators or the spectators and a contestant. By the eighteenth century, even the slaves, who attended massively to urge on the Black jockeys, were laying wagers. [26]

Given the immense sums often wagered on these races, the outcome of the race was frequently challenged. The start of the race in particular was very contentious and contested. Certainly, given all that was at stake, these quarter races were "wild, no-holds-barred affairs." Although the gentlemen made formal and elaborate agreements in front of several witnesses to "fair Rideing," the races were full of jostling, whipping, and kneeing the opponent. Fans for one rider would jump onto the track to spook or scare the other horse. Foul play was the name of the game. Consequently, the loser often recurred to the courts to help him win. [27]

Many court cases give evidence to the fractiousness of quarter racing. Indeed, in 1698, a recorded court case shows a dispute about a quarter-horse race, involving a horse owned by Thomas Jefferson's grandfather, who was also called Thomas Jefferson. The match race occurred at a "race-ground commonly called the Ware" in Henrico County. Jefferson owned a mare called Bonny that ran against a horse called Watt, owned by the commissioner and justice of Charles City, John Hardiman (in this case the owners were not the jockeys). Although the mare was given "five horse Lengths" (10 yards) advantage, the wager was that the mare need only come within five horse lengths of the horse Watt. Apparently, witnesses confirmed that Bonny did out run the horse and "came in first between the poles" and that the race was "fairly run." The jury found for Mr. Jefferson's mare, "Wherefore the afores'd pl't't saith that the afores'd Mare, Bonnie, with fair Running & Riding according to agreement, did beat the s'd horse Watt and that—he, the s'd plaintiff, hath won the Wager." [28]

Visitors from England were fascinated with this lively American form of racing. Thomas Anburey, a captive British officer during the Revolutionary War, describes a quarter race he attended near Charlottesville, in Jefferson's Albemarle County, in May 1779:

> A few days ago, I went with several officers to see a diversion peculiar to his country, termed quarter-racing, which is a match between two horses, to run a quarter of a mile in a straight direction, and near most of the ordinaries, there is a piece of ground cleared in the woods for that purpose, where there are two paths about six or eight yards asunder, which the horses runs in, this diversion is a great favorite of the middling and lower classes, and they have a breed of horses to perform it with astonishing velocity, beating every other for that distance with the greatest ease. I think I can, without the least exaggeration, assert, that even the famous Eclipse could not excel them in speed, for our horses are sometime before they are able to get into full speed, and these are trained to set out in that manner the moment of starting. It is the most ridiculous amusement imaginable, for if you happen to be looking another way, the race is terminated before you can turn your head; notwithstanding which, very considerable sums are betted at these matches. We stayed and saw several. [29]

Another English visitor concurred:

> In the southern part of the colony, and in North Carolina, they are much attached to quarter-racing, which is always a match between two horses, to run one quarter of a mile straight out and they have a breed that perform it with astonishing velocity, beating every other, with great ease; but they have no bottom. However, I am confident that there is not a horse in England, nor perhaps the whole world, that can excel them in rapid speed; and these likewise make excellent saddle horses for the road. [30]

Contemporary Quarter Horse Racing: Whistle Stop Cafe finishes first during the 2020 running of the All-American Futurity at Ruidoso Downs Race Track & Casino, Ruidoso, New Mexico. Sep 8, 2020.

Breeding quarter-racing horses in Virginia continued until the later eighteenth century, when the industry was eclipsed by course racing, and it moved westward with the pioneers. Eventually, through crosses with many other kinds of horses, these quarter-racing horses became the American Quarter Horse. Although the American Quarter Horse stud book was not established until 1940–1941, most breeders believe this is our oldest native breed of racing horses.

Many Quarter Horse pedigrees run back through the extraordinary stallion named Janus, imported into Virginia in 1756. (See Chapter 4.) This English-imported grandson of the Godolphin Arabian consistently sired "horses of blazing speed over short distances" for twenty-five years. His get was prodigious. Printer, of Janus blood, foaled 1795 in Kentucky, is "the earliest horse to be designated a Foundation Sire by the American Quarter Horse Association, and appears in the pedigrees of most present-day Quarter Horses." [31]

Quarter Horses today, with their muscular, compact bodies, continue to be fine riding horses and have a long tradition, due to their speedy maneuverability, of working with cattle. In contrast with the tall, long, lean, and lanky Thoroughbred horse of distance racing, the American Quarter Horse is short and stocky, with a short, refined head, broad chest, and powerful, rounded hindquarters. The general public has long associated Quarter Horses with cowboys and with their performance in Western rodeo competition. In recent years, Quarter Horse racing has returned in popularity. There are American Quarter Horse associations, which promote these races of a quarter mile for the "fastest horse in the world." Quarter

Horses have been clocked up to fifty-five miles per hour and can cover a quarter of a mile in less than twenty-one seconds. The most important American Quarter Horse race is the All American Futurity, run at Ruidoso Downs in New Mexico. [Fig. 6-12]

Course Racing in Virginia: In 1732, a Virginian planter, Samuel Gist of Hanover County, in an effort to "improve the blood of American stock," imported the first Thoroughbred horse from England, Bulle Rock. He was descended from the Darley Arabian and a Byerley Turk mare, and thus genetically connected to two of the three stallions of "Oriental" origin (horses that some people, like Thomas Jefferson, also referred to as "Arabians") that produced (when crossed with native English mares) a new breed of horses, that the early colonists called blood horses but by the late nineteenth century came to be called Thoroughbreds. (See Chapter 4.) Bulle Rock soon bred with many Virginia mares, and the stock of the colonies improved immediately in several qualitative and quantitative ways. Specifically, the English form of distance-course racing would now take root in the colonies.

Fig. 6-13 Course races. Theodore Gericault, *The Epsom Derby*, 1821.

The 1730s inaugurated an expansive economic time in the Southern colonies. The Tobacco Act controlled the quality of tobacco, promoting it as a medium of exchange, and the Virginia planters came into a time of great wealth and prosperity. They were now able to indulge their desire for and interest in course racing, or distance racing, by importing horses coming off the turf in England. The new English blooded horses, infused with "Oriental" blood, had much more bottom (endurance) than the American quarter-racing horses. This endurance proved helpful for the plantation owners of saddle and hunting horses. Even more significantly, the imported horses changed racing. These blooded horses (who were also trotters, not pacers) could maintain their speed for the four-mile heats typical of the course racing practiced in England. [32] [Fig. 6-13]

The first distance race around an oval turf (grass) track by more than two horses took place in October 1737, in Virginia near Hanover County, according to an announcement in the *Virginia Gazette.* The advertisement proposed that "20 Horses or Mares do run around a Three Miles Course" for a prize of £5. The race was to take place at the Old Field near Capt. John Pinkerton's. From this point until just before the Revolution, with the importation of more and more English racehorses, course racing became more fashionable in the northern part of Virginia (and quarter racing shifted to the Southside and the frontier). Eventually course racing consisted of horses running three and even four four-mile heats. The winner was the horse that won the best of two out of three heats (or three out of four). Usually, there was only a half an hour between each heat.

Clearly, these horses needed a lot of bottom. [33] Horses (males), as well as mares, competed together. Each horse had to carry the same weight (usually determined in "stone," for example 10 stone). The horses were at least four years old. Today three-year-olds are considered the fastest racers, but in those times three-year-olds were not considered strong enough yet to race those distances. Jockeys were no longer the owners, but rather other young men, often enslaved boys.

Although in general no emphasis was put on the jockeys and we know few of their names, some gained fame and renown (and their freedom) at the time. The "negro jockeys" were said to be "really good." [34]

The purses in these distance races were made up by subscription, composed of membership and entry fees. All the owners whose horses participated put in money, as well as the general public, and the winner took all. Betting and wagering among the general public was, of course, endemic. Other activities sprang up around the tracks, usually situated right outside of a town. Races were held two times a year, in the fall and in the spring. Whereas quarter races had been rather local affairs, course racing brought people from all over the region, and eventually had entrants that hailed from New York to South Carolina. These races facilitated networking among the elite. In Williamsburg, the races became part of the Publik Times, when the colony's courts were in session and markets and fairs took over the streets of the capital. People came to attend from all over Virginia. [35]

An English visitor described these races:

> There are races at Williamsburg twice a year; that is every spring and fall, or autumn. Adjoining to the town is a very excellent course, for either two three or four mile heats. Their purses are generally raised by subscription and are gained by the horse that wins two four-mile heats out of three; they amount to an hundred pounds each for the first day's running, and fifty pounds each every day after; the races commonly continuing for a week. There are also matches and sweepstakes very often, for considerable sums. Besides these at Williamsburg, there are races established annually, almost at every town and considerable place in Virginia; and frequent matches, on which large sums of money depend; the inhabitant, almost to a man, being quite devoted to the diversion of horse-racing.
>
> Very capital horses are started here, such as would make no despicable figure at Newmarket; nor is their speed, bottom or blood inferior to their appearance; the gentlemen of Virginia sparing no pains, trouble, or expense in importing the best stock, and improving the excellence of the breed by proper and judicious crossing. Indeed nothing can be more elegant and beautiful than the horses bred here, either for the turf, the field, the road, or the coach; and they have always fine long, full, flowing tails; but their carriage horses seldom are possessed of that weight and power, which distinguish those of the same kind in England. [136]

Emphasizing the status of the course races, Thomas Anburey, the British soldier cited above on quarter races, continued:

> These races [quarter races] are only among the settlers in the interior parts of this Province for they are much laughed at and ridiculed by the people in the lower parts, about Richmond and other great towns; at Williamsburg is a very excellent course for two, three, or four mile heats, where there are races every spring and fall; they run for purses are generally raised by subscription, and the horse that wins two four-mile heats, out of three, is entitled to the prize, which is one hundred pounds the first day's running, and fifty pounds every other day, and these races commonly last a week. [37]

Between the importation of Bulle Rock (in 1737) and the American Revolution, 117 stallions and 64 mares were imported into the colonies from England. The real wave began in the 1750s with the importation of Jolly Roger, Childers, and Morton's Traveler. Most of these horses had proven themselves on the turf in England. In the colonies, wealthy planters were willing to spend large sums of money and stake their reputations to import the best and most promising horses they could that would serve to infuse American stock with new blood and produce fabulous long-distance runners. [38]

What started as a drip soon became a flood. Buying, breeding, and racing blooded horses quickly became a sign of belonging to the landed elite in the South, especially in Virginia, where the majority of imported horses arrived. By the time of the Revolution, there were twenty-seven stud farms along the James, York, Rappahannock, and Potomac Rivers. On the racetrack, it soon became apparent which of these horses were the most successful studs. Probably Fearnought, imported in 1764 by John Baylor, was the greatest early distance sire. In the 1770s, when Jefferson was breeding horses, most of his mares were bred to first-generation offspring of Fearnought. [Fig. 6-14] In Virginia, early on, John Baylor at his home in Caroline County, named Newmarket (after the English racing center), John Hoomes at Bowling Green, and two generations of the John Tayloe family (II and III) at Mt. Airy were all significant breeders and important turf men in Virginia. [39]

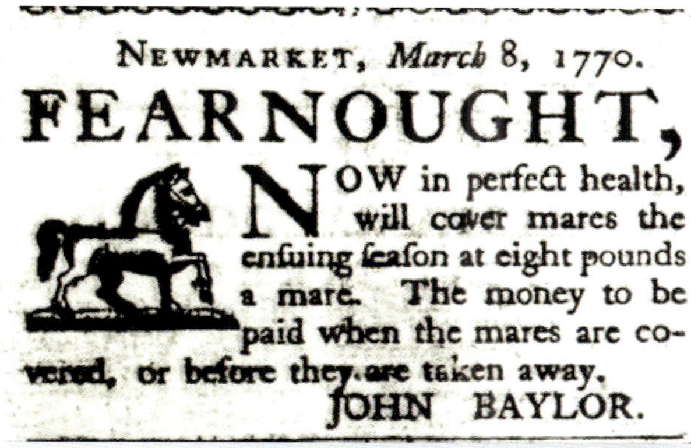
NEWMARKET, *March* 8, 1770.

FEARNOUGHT,

NOW in perfect health, will cover mares the enſuing ſeaſon at eight pounds a mare. The money to be paid when the mares are covered, or before they are taken away.

JOHN BAYLOR.

Fig. 6-14. A Fearnought stud advertisement in the *Virginia Gazette*, March 22, 1770

Soon in towns up and down the Eastern Seaboard, outposts of the Jockey Club were established to govern distance racing. Of course, jockeys did not belong to these clubs; rather, they were for the horse owners and social elites. Charleston, South Carolina, claims to have had the first Jockey Club, established in 1734, but the clubs of Annapolis and Williamsburg were the first true centers of racing in the upper South. Later clubs were founded in Fredericksburg, which quickly became an important center (1773), and Petersburg, Leedstown, Yorktown, and Gloucester in Virginia. Some of these places experienced a racing craze. Edward Carter, who owned Blenheim in Albemarle County (a home that several times played an important role in Jefferson's life), moved from his Albemarle plantation to Fredericksburg so that his horses could participate in the races there. Although racing activities and the importation of horses stopped during the Revolutionary War, by 1783 it began to pick back up again. [40]

Entrepreneurs decided it was lucrative to set up a track and charge entrance fee for racegoers. Intercolonial races between Virginia and Maryland and Virginia and New York sprang up. Within a few years after its founding, Washington City also had its own Jockey Club. President Jefferson attended the fall races there in November when he could (entry charge $1 for attendees in carriages).

During the Revolutionary War in Virginia, many of the blood horses were impounded by the two armies, and the breeding stock was quite depleted by the military effort. British Colonel Banastre Tarleton was infamous for his plundering of the colonists' horses. All over the South, breeders tried to hide their blooded horses and other livestock from both armies. In Virginia, Jefferson was governor at the time (1779–1781). At one point, he specifically tried to protect the stallions and broodmares on the stud farms of Virginia from impressment by American military troops. Jefferson argued with Gen. Steuben of the American forces about what kind of horses could be borrowed from the Virginians. The governor had authorized the military to seize horses if needed for battle from local citizens but, when one militia commander took thirty-two horses, Jefferson ordered the return of stud horses or mares "kept for breeding." This was not just an attempt to save potential racehorses. During the hostilities of the Revolution importation from England had come to a halt, and the only way to get good new horses was to breed them in the colonies. [41]

Later, during the English invasion of Virginia in the summer of 1781, the British general, Cornwallis, made his headquarters on Jefferson land at Elkhill on the James River, where his breeding horses were located. Besides using or destroying all of Jefferson's crops and livestock, when Cornwallis left, he took the mares to use and killed the foals. This effectively ended Jefferson's breeding program, exactly what he had been trying to prevent by his orders as governor.

When once again, after the Puritan pause during wartime, racing was reorganized, breeding had to, in effect, start all over again. Some of the pre-Revolutionary planters and merchants managed to convert totally to turfmen, importing large numbers of bloodstock into the United States, breeding, and selling, as well as racing, horses. During this time Colonel John Hoomes, with his neighbor and partner, John Tayloe III, imported the first Epsom race winner, Diomed (age twenty-one years) in 1798. The importance of this horse cannot be repeated enough. Diomed never raced in America, but he stood at stud in Virginia, and his get was very successful (on the track and off). His bloodlines run in most American racehorses today. Several horses that Jefferson bought with Diomed blood have been described earlier (See Chapter 4). [42]

After the war, the center of racehorse breeding shifted from northern Virginia to Southside and the Roanoke Valley

Fig. 6-15 Triple Crown winner American Pharoah wins the Kentucky Derby, May 2, 2015.

along the Virginia-North Carolina border to what became known as the old racehorse region. Two men from this area were especially significant in promoting Thoroughbred breeding and racing, John Randolph of Roanoke (a cousin of Thomas Jefferson's, a US senator, and Jefferson's political nemesis) and William Ransom Johnson. (See Chapter 2.) The races at Petersburg (in Southside Virginia) became an important social scene, as well as the site for horse sales. President Jefferson's son-in-law John Wayles Eppes, who lived near Petersburg, bought Jefferson four very expensive carriage horses from there at the beginning of his presidency. (See Chapter 2.) But by the nineteenth century, Thoroughbred breeding and racing were drifting out the Cumberland Gap to the bluegrass region of Kentucky and Tennessee.

More and more, the descendants of Virginia's imported turf horses were taken out to Kentucky to stand at stud and leave their offspring farther west. The race courses became shorter, and dirt tracks substituted for turf. Speed became an obsession. The War of 1812 took another harsh toll on Virginia and North Carolina racing traditions, and by 1830s the bluegrass region reigned supreme, crowned by the famed Kentucky Derby, a race for three-year-old Thoroughbreds at a mile and a quarter, founded in 1875. Yet Virginians have bred or owned nine Kentucky Derby winners, including Cavalcade, Exterminator, Genuine Risk, Go for Gin, Kauai King, Pleasant Colony, Riva Ridge, Sea Hero, Reigh Count, and Secretariat.

The Kentucky Derby is one of three races that together are known as the American Triple Crown. [Fig. 6-15] The other two races of the American Triple Crown were actually founded earlier: the Belmont (at a mile and a half) in New York in 1867 and the Preakness (at a mile and three-sixteenths) in Baltimore, Maryland, in 1873. These races were patterned after three English classic races of similar lengths: the Epsom Derby (1780), the Epsom Oaks (1779), and the Doncaster St. Leger (1776).

Probably the most successful and the best-known Thoroughbred race horse of the twentieth century was the Virginia-bred Secretariat. In 1973, as a three-year-old, Secretariat won the Triple Crown, and set a track record in each of the three races. Secretariat's stakes records still stand today for two of the three races.

Secretariat's pedigree, like all recent Kentucky Derby winners, traces back many generations to the early Virginia studs, the imported English blood horses used by Jefferson and the eighteenth-century Virginia gentry to produce their distance racers and saddle horses: Fearnought and Diomed. [Fig. 6-16]

Jefferson and Racing

Jefferson lived at a time (1743–1826) when he would have been a spectator at both kinds of horse races, quarter races and course races, especially in the eighteenth century. Albemarle County and the little village of Charlottesville were rustic backwaters for many decades after their incorporation (1741–1742). We know there were quarter races around Charlottesville through the 1770s at least. In August of 1769, Jefferson paid to go to the races in Charlottesville. Jefferson also worked as a lawyer over the Blue Ridge in Staunton, in Augusta County in the Shenandoah Valley—which was truly the frontier—and could have enjoyed quarter racing there. [43]

Williamsburg was an early convert to course racing. By the time young Jefferson was a student there (1760–1762), course racing had a long history. Visitor descriptions depict three or four days of races in the fall and spring. The race course lay just southeast behind the Capitol of the little city, at the intersection of the present-day Lafayette and York Streets. Race days were the scenes of much student carousing. Later, Jefferson continued attending course races, and as mentioned above, attended the annual meetings of the Washington Jockey Club while president. In 1802, the racetrack was just west of the president's house. Later, it moved to a track near the present-day Columbia Road, between 14th and 16th streets. Although he rarely, if ever, bet money on a horse, and disparaged betting in his 1808 letter to his grandson, Jefferson would not miss the social scene. [44]

Fig. 6-16 Secretariat, late 1970's

Mares and colts: Valiant, a new Cleveland Bay foal, frolicking in the pasture by the Governor's Palace at Colonial Williamsburg with his mother, Fudge

Chapter 7

Breeding Horses (1772-1782) Improving the Breed

Besides his riding horses and carriage horses, which were all mostly stallions, many mares appear in Jefferson's detailed lists of horses and other stock. Never used by Jefferson for riding or pulling carriages, these mares were the basis of his decade-long breeding program that he established early in his career as planter. They were recorded as "breeding mares" in his *Farm Book*. (Their offspring, frisky little colts and fillies, were tallied under the category "colts.") Although only a few plantation owners were able financially to import the new English race horse, those planters soon recouped their monetary outlay by standing the stallions at stud, or selling the offspring of the imported horses to others. Individuals one rung down in status were eager to use the stud services of these horses, especially the most renowned horses, to produce their own Thoroughbred racing or riding horse, in order to have their own symbol and verification of status.

Thomas Jefferson bred his mares to the second generation of these blooded horses. Jefferson was always dedicated to improvement in animal husbandry and was aware of the possibilities of selective breeding. His interest in these horses most likely sprang from his participation in the science of the Enlightenment in general, and the eighteenth-century scientific agricultural movement in particular.

Jefferson projected his human social categories upon horses, and even though many of his broodmares were blooded horses, they occupied a category further down his equine hierarchy due to their sex and status as breeders. Their lower status was paralleled by their physical distance from Jefferson; they did not live at Monticello, but rather farther east on the Rivanna River, miles away at Elkhill.

Two tragedies caused Jefferson to give up his own breeding program, yet he continued to be interested in improving the stock of American horses and, especially, in promoting the new blood horses in Virginia. Jefferson investigated the herds of mustangs out West, advertised the potential of stock gifted to the United States by North African leaders, formed local organizations dedicated to improving animal husbandry, and sought to import a horse "of the best race" to improve the breed generally.[1]

Left, Valiant, a new Cleveland Bay foal, frolicking in the pasture by the Governor's Palace with his mother, Fudge.

Marriage, Status, and the Thoroughbred in Early Virginia

The breeding of blooded horses in colonial Virginia in many ways mimicked marriage, in that it joined families and linked names of prestigious members of the gentry. Marriage (and kinship) weaves together the fabric of society. Certainly, this was true in colonial Virginia.

The First Families of Virginia (FFVs) originated from those first colonists from England who settled along the James and other Tidewater rivers in the seventeenth century. They were the leading families of Virginia—although not necessarily the first chronologically—socially prominent, wealthy, large landowners, overly represented on the colonial council. Many were second sons of aristocrats in England who were granted large tracts of land by the king, and who often transplanted family ties to the Virginia colony. Others rose from modest beginnings. In a society based on the possession of land and slaves, land was tightly controlled, and often passed between families of corresponding social rank.[2]

Consequently, there was a tendency to marry with their social equals for generations, and certain surnames became common in the growing colony. In Virginia, many of the FFVs claimed relation to Pocahontas, a daughter of Chief Powhatan,

Fig. 7-1 A member of the gentry on his high horse. John Wootton, *Portrait of a Man on Horseback*, c. 1740.

In eighteenth-century Virginia, men of the landed elite exchanged many things besides women: books, architectural ideas, seeds and plants, social visits (hospitality), enslaved men and women, and political responsibilities, among them. After the 1720s, the emergence of a gracious lifestyle produced a spate of mansion building, marked by many symbols of elite status. One of the most important icons of elite status at the time, which passed back and forth and often retraced marriage ties, were the new and expensive blooded horses imported from England into Virginia after the 1730s. These horses, tellingly, were also referred to as FFVs. Like their elite owners, these horses were bred only to each other. They were thorough-breds, pure-breds. Mimicking the English royalty, the FFVs took their own marriage rules and ideas about membership in the gentry elite and copied them in their breeding practices with the new racehorses. Comments from contemporary observers underlined, sometimes in surprise, the identification and almost fetishization that the gentry men had with their horses. Planters would identify their horses with the same genealogical terminology as they would themselves. One visitor to the Carter plantation of Nomini Hall in 1774 noted in his journal the "loud disputes concerning the Excellence of each other's Colts—Concerning their Fathers, Mothers (for so they call the Dams), Brothers, Sisters, Uncles, Aunts, Nephews, Nieces, & Cousins to the fourth Degree!" [4]

leader of the native peoples during the first ten years of English settlement, which began at Jamestown in 1607, due to her marriage to the Englishman John Rolfe. Marriage among the FFVs helped seal their status and maintain a hierarchical society. From 50 to 140 names have at various times been proposed as FFVs, including Ball, Berkeley, Beverley, Bland, Bolling, Burwell, Byrd, Carter, Cary, Custis, Digges, Eppes, Fairfax, Fitzhugh, Gooch, Harrison, Isham, Landon, Lee, Madison, Mason, Nelson, Page, Randolph, Spotswood, Taliaferro, Tayloe, Warner, Washington, and Willis. Of all these family lines, perhaps the Carters and the Randolphs have produced the greatest number of distinguished and politically significant names in Virginia. All were closely related through intermarriage, a veritable skein of relationships, and spouses were often distant kin. Thomas Jefferson and his wife, Martha, were third cousins. [3]

Virginia gentlemen spared no expense on their prized horses, and portraits of the successful racehorses and the prolific stud adorned the walls of the plantations, in gilded frames, just like the portraits of family progenitors. The same visitor mentioned above, Philip Fithian, noted that in Colonel John Tayloe's dining room hung "twenty-four of the most celebrated among the English Race-Horses, Drawn masterly, & set in elegant gilt Frames." [5]

Even more significantly, blooded horses in colonial Virginia were valued because they were non-alienable objects. Previous owners were as important as the animals themselves. Although horses were bought and sold, it was common for payment to be postponed for months and years. This debt owed between families simply retraced the attachment of the horse to the previous owner. (See Chapter 2.) Annotating the pedigree of the horse, where the name of the animal often included the previous owner, underlined the economic connections, strikingly similar to the marriage connections of these families. [6]

The imported horses, infused with "Oriental" blood, held themselves in a more aristocratic way than the smallish workhorses. These horses, whom we would call "hot" (excitable) today, pranced and danced, holding their heads high and, appropriately, became the high horses of the elite, a kind of metaphor for the gentry's own self-image. The high-bred, blooded horse became identified with and represented its (male) owner. Thomas Jefferson would not ride anything else. [Fig.7-1]

Thomas Jefferson as Horse Breeder

During the ten years between 1772 and 1782, Jefferson, besides serving in the Virginia House of Burgesses and Continental Congress, writing the Declaration of Independence, helping with the Virginia Constitution, rewriting Virginia's laws, and serving as governor of Virginia, worked to establish himself as a progressive landowner and horse breeder. Jefferson married, left his law practice, and dedicated himself to planting and raising children with his wife, Martha. In May of 1773, Jefferson's father-in-law, John Wayles, died, and the following year, the Jeffersons inherited lands, slaves, other livestock, and horses. [7]

This inheritance drastically changed the Jeffersons' financial prospects. It doubled the amount of land that Thomas Jefferson possessed, and he suddenly became the owner of 135 enslaved workers. Through this inheritance, Jefferson acquired lands at Elkhill, Willis Creek, and Poplar Forest. On the Elkhill and Willis Creek lands, Wayles had left a dozen mares and their offspring, some with fine blooded pedigrees, including several mares in foal by imported studs from elsewhere. This group of broodmares became the nucleus of Jefferson's breeding program; they are listed on the first pages of his *Farm Book*. Some are provided with names (Allycroker, Silvertail, Cacullen), and others are simply described and numbered (i.e., "#12 bay mare at Elkhill"). In the almost ten years that Jefferson dedicated to breeding, his mares were always located down river at Elkhill. Those lands were much flatter and more open than the wooded mountainsides of Monticello. [8]

Jefferson soon seemed to be caught up in the shared enthusiasm of Virginia gentry for horseflesh. Horses and horse breeding seemed to dominate the conversations of the planter elite. During the decade, he expanded his own breeding operation, using the offspring of imported English racehorses who belonged to friends and neighbors as studs, in hopes of producing a herd of fine, high-bred horses. Yet Jefferson was not raising horses to race. His horses were for riding or driving, not for racing. Meanwhile, at least ten Albemarle neighbors brought their mares to Monticello and paid Jefferson to breed them to one of his prize stallions. We know that after 1774, Jefferson's riding horses and carriage horses would now be called Thoroughbreds, their pedigrees tracing back to the founding sires of all Thoroughbreds today. (See more in Chapter 4.) Furthermore, we can see in the pedigrees of his horses, which he carefully recorded in his *Farm Book*, that he used horses to retrace kinship and marriage lines, as well as to cement other important social relationships with Virginia's eighteenth-century elite families. [9]

Like many planters in colonial Virginia, Thomas Jefferson kept detailed notebooks and account books in an attempt to rationalize, organize, and document his farming activities. Jefferson's *Farm Book*, a bound manuscript volume, is a veritable gold mine of information on agriculture, husbandry, and slavery at Monticello and his other properties, and also serves to illuminate the late-eighteenth and early-nineteenth-century plantation economy of Piedmont Virginia in general. The volume spans the years 1774–1824 and includes "Diary" entries (Jefferson's term) arranged by date, detailing his plans for plowing, sowing, planting, and cutting activities, as well as providing inventories of his livestock and slaves and a section titled, "Aphorisms, Observations, Facts in Husbandry." Along with his *Garden Book* and *Memorandum Books* (or account books), Jefferson's *Farm Book* helps to provide a portrait of Jefferson's interests in agriculture and animal husbandry.

The important role horses had for Jefferson at this time is underlined by the fact that his *Farm Book* begins with a list of his horses. Most tellingly, just inside the front hard cover of the *Farm Book*, before the first pages, we find a hand-drawn pedigree [see Fig. 4-11, p. 87] of one of Jefferson's favorite saddle horses at the time: Caractacus (foaled in May 1775).

This pedigree was probably drawn after Jefferson wrote in the first pages of the *Farm Book*, for there he lists the horses in his possession (his own, and those inherited from his recently deceased father-in-law), probably as of January 1774. This list included his broodmares, as well as his riding horses and carriage horses. The list does not contain his plantation horses or work horses; they are included in other inventories in the book. Most of the twenty-eight horses in the list are named, described by color, age (year foaled), location (which farm), and pedigree. Significantly, the previous owners of the horse's dam and sire are noted. [10]

Looking at the pedigrees of some of the horses Jefferson used for breeding, we can see the various social relationships that are conflated in each horse. When Jefferson records in the *Farm Book* the names of a horse's owners in several generations of its pedigree, he does so because the owners are in some way part of the horse. Their names matter, i.e., those relationships give social value to the horse and are important to Jefferson and to others of his social class. Some of the "breeding mares" (as he called them) and "horses" (referring to stallions) included in the program are noted below.

Jefferson recorded the births of twenty foals from his own mares between 1772 and 1782. He sold or exchanged many of these Elkhill-bred colts and fillies with friends or family members. Jefferson sold several animals to Colonel Thomas Mann Randolph; in June 1774, he sold Fingal "to Colo. Randolph for £35 and 200 pounds of wool." In 1777, Jefferson sold Ryno to his brother, Randolph, but several months later, he bought Oroonoko from Randolph. He also exchanged #25, a bay colt, with Randolph in 1779. Zanga, an iron-gray colt, out of Fearnought and Silvertail, was bred expressly for Jefferson's intellectual mentor in Williamsburg, George Wythe. Later in 1780 Jefferson exchanged Thor, a three-year-old sorrel, with George Wythe for a roan horse. [11]

Allycroker (b. 1758 – d. after 1779): We have no physical description of Jefferson's top broodmare, although her sire was sorrel, and there were grays and a chestnut within her known ancestry. Allycroker was already sixteen years old when Jefferson inherited her from his father-in-law John Wayles in 1777, but she remained a reliable broodmare until at least 1779, producing three more foals for Jefferson.

Lineage: Jefferson's notes in the *Farm Book* emphasize Allycroker's male ancestry, an emphasis that remains in modern Thoroughbred pedigrees. In those days, the dam's lineage, or "tail line," was considered weaker and had to be justified more. Allycroker's male line was indeed impressive. Her sire was Silver Eye, grandson of Godolphin Arabian (through Regulus). [12] [Fig. 7-2]

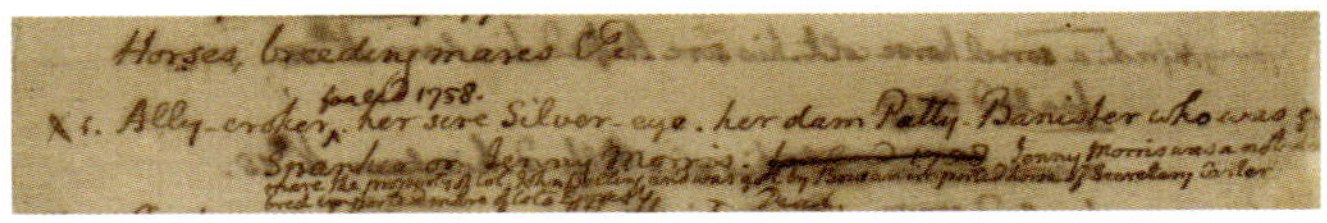

Fig. 7-2 A notation for Silver Eye in the *Farm Book*

Silver Eye was a pale sorrel horse with light blue eyes, imported to the colonies in 1756 by Samuel Duvall, from Henrico (Richmond). Duvall was a member of the House of Burgesses and attended the first and second Virginia Conventions in 1774 and 1775. Duvall had income-producing lands (mines and coal) and built the first brick house in Richmond. Some of Silver Eye's offspring (his get) later arrived in Kentucky, where they founded many matriarchal pedigrees of the later Thoroughbred breed. [13] [Fig. 7-3]

Jefferson tells us in his *Farm Book* that Allycroker's dam was Patty Banister out of Spanker, an Andalusian horse owned by William Nelson from Yorktown. (George Washington got his well-known bay war steed named Nelson from the same source.) William Nelson, an important planter, was governor of Virginia between royal governors (1770–1771), and his son, Thomas Nelson Jr., signed the Declaration of Independence and also served as governor of Virginia during the Revolution. Spanker was imported from southern Spain in 1740.

My *Engliſh* horſe

SILVER EYE

COVERS mares, at my houſe in HENRICO county, at twenty ſhillings each cover, three pounds the ſeaſon, or four pounds to enſure a colt; for ready money, or tobacco. Good paſtures for the mares, *gratis*.

SAMUEL DU VAL.

Fig. 7-3 An ad for Silver Eye in *Virginia Gazette,* April 4, 1766

Patty Banister's dam was a gray mare, Jenny Morris. Jefferson wrote in the *Farm Book*, "Jenny Morris was a noted [running] mare, the property of Col. John Bolling, and was got by Bow [Beau] an imported horse of Secretary Carter's, [and by] an imported mare of Col. Eppes's." Colonel Bolling was from Cobbs, in Chesterfield near Petersburg, and his son had married Jefferson's sister, Mary Jefferson, in 1760 (i.e., he was Thomas Jefferson's brother-in-law). These Bollings were directly related to Thomas Rolfe, and thus Pocahontas. [14]

Fig. 7-4 Shirley Plantation

Jenny Morris's sire was Beau, a chestnut horse, who was one of the earliest horses imported from England to Virginia, in 1740 by Secretary John Carter to the impressive plantation Shirley on the James in Charles City County. [Fig. 7-4] Secretary Carter explored Albemarle County and owned almost the entire mountain known as Carter's Mountain. Secretary's Ford, which crosses the Rivanna to Charlottesville near Monticello, is named after him. Beau had been on the turf in England from 1736 to 1740, winning two King's Plates.[15]

Carter's horse Beau was crossed with an imported gray mare owned by Colonel Eppes of Eppington in Chesterfield, thus near Bolling. Colonel Eppes married a Bolling and was the father of Francis Eppes, Jefferson's brother-in-law through his wife, Martha Wayles (and thus, her cousin); he was also the father of Jefferson's own son-in-law many years later. Jefferson's second daughter, Mary (Polly), married John Wayles Eppes, son of Francis Eppes and Elizabeth Wayles. Again, if Jefferson mentioned the names of the owners of the horses back several generations, it is because they matter. They are part of the horse.

Offspring and social connections: Jefferson was quite partial to Fearnought blood, but before Jefferson owned her, Wayles had bred Allycroker with two other stallions, and Jefferson had also inherited those offspring. Cacullen (1764) was got by Hob & Nob (1751) on Allycroker. Hob & Nob, another grandson of the Godolphin Arabian, was brought to Virginia in 1760 by Archibald Cary, of Ampthill in Chesterfield County. Cary's wife, Mary Randolph, was a cousin of Jefferson's mother. Cary's eldest daughter, Anne, was the first wife of Thomas Mann Randolph, another cousin of Jefferson's and father of Jefferson's later son-in-law. Colonel Cary, as he was known, was a frequent visitor to Monticello. [16]

Just before he died, Wayles had also put Allycroker to a stud called Partner. The result was Alfred, foaled in 1774. Four years later, in 1778, Jefferson paid a note of £3 from Wayles's estate to Thomas Mann Randolph for that stud fee. [Fig. 7-5] Partner was originally owned by Armistead Lightfoot of Brunswick County and had been sired by the imported horse Traveler. By 1770, Partner was standing stud at Tuckahoe, Colonel Randolph's home. Thomas Mann Randolph owned Partner from 1772 to 1775, [Fig. 7-6] and then sold him to Richard Skipwith, a brother-in-law of Jefferson's wife, Martha. [17]

Partner

STANDS at *York*, where he covers MARES at twenty ſhillings the leap, and two ſhillings and ſixpence to the groom: four pounds the ſeaſon, or ſix pounds enſurance. The money to be paid at the ſtable door.

ARMISTEAD LIGHTFOOT.

Fig. 7-5 Ad for Partner, *Virginia Gazette,* April 18, 1766

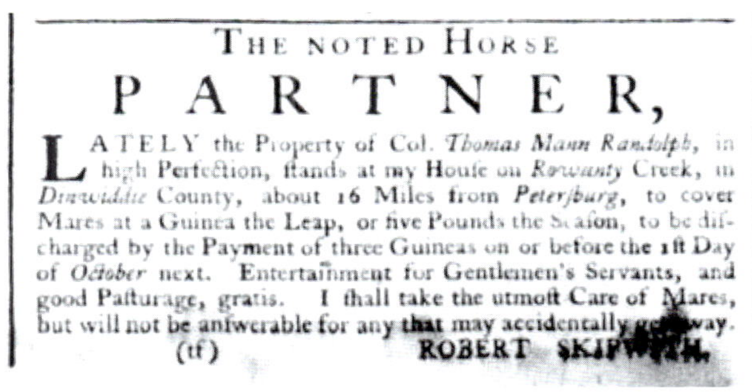

THE NOTED HORSE

PARTNER,

LATELY the Property of Col. *Thomas Mann Randolph,* in high Perfection, ſtands at my Houſe on *Rowanty* Creek, in *Dinwiddie* County, about 16 Miles from *Peterſburg,* to cover Mares at a Guinea the Leap, or five Pounds the Seaſon, to be diſcharged by the Payment of three Guineas on or before the 1ſt Day of *October* next. Entertainment for Gentlemen's Servants, and good Paſturage, gratis. I ſhall take the utmoſt Care of Mares, but will not be anſwerable for any that may accidentally [illegible] away.

(tf) ROBERT SKI[illegible]

Fig. 7-6 Ad for Partner, *Virginia Gazette,* April 16, 1766

Allycroker was Jefferson's top broodmare because of the several prized foals she produced for him. One in particular, Caractacus, became Jefferson's favorite riding horse in the years before he went to Paris. So remarkable was Caractacus, in both conformation and performance, that others requested his stud services. Caractacus's sire was the horse called Dandridge's Young Fearnought, son of John Baylor's imported Fearnought. Two years after Caractacus was born, Jefferson bred Allycroker to Young Fearnought again to produce a chestnut filly he called Orra Moor (born May 1778).

Dandridge's Young Fearnought (b. 1768): William Dandridge's Young Fearnought was a chestnut stallion who became one of Jefferson's favorite studs, although he never owned him. Jefferson bred Allycroker and at least nine other mares during the 1770s to Young Fearnought.

Fig. 7-7 Westover plantation, in Charles City County, Virginia, is the homestead of the Byrd family, established c. 1730–1750.

Lineage: Young Fearnought was a son of the famous imported turf horse Fearnought (described in Chapter 4). The sire was referred to in the contemporary literature as Old Fearnought or Imported Fearnought. Young Fearnought's dam was an oft-cited mare called Calista, owned by William Byrd III at Westover (a lovely plantation on the James River, with an impressive library) in Charles City. [Fig. 7-7] This Young Fearnought was acquired from the Byrd stud by William A. Dandridge II of Hanover County. [18]

Offspring: Young Fearnought covered in Hanover and Cumberland Counties from 1775 to1782. The box below contains the names of all foals produced by Young Fearnought and Jefferson's mares, as named or listed in the *Farm Book*. All of the mares and their foals were located at Elkhill or Willis Creek (land across the river from Elkhill).

Social Connections: William Dandridge had a long relationship with Jefferson through horses. Dandridge married Ann Bolling (of Cobbs in Chesterfield, see above), whose father, John Bolling, also had an offspring of old Fearnought. William Dandridge, himself, was a cousin of Martha Dandridge Custis, the wife of George Washington (her second marriage). William knew Jefferson as a student at the College of William and Mary. Young Jefferson stopped often at the Dandridge family place, which was on Allen's Creek in Hanover County, about twenty-five miles from Jefferson's Elkhill, on his way back and forth from Williamsburg. One time Dandridge, Jefferson, and Patrick Henry famously played the minuet together there during a visit. William A. Dandridge II later served in the Revolutionary War and was the commissary for troops in Yorktown.

	Horses from Jefferson Mares Bred to Dandridge's Young Fearnought
1774	Everallin
1775	Caractacus (dam Allycroker)
1778	Orra Moor (dam Allycroker)
	Peggy Waffington (bay, dam #12)
	Zanga (dam Silvertail)
	Odin (bay, dam #13)
	Polly Peachum (roan, dam #15)
	#21 bl. Filly (black, dam #14)
1779	#24 gray mare (dam Silvertail)
	#25 bay colt (bay, dam #12)
	#26 chestnut filly (bay, dam #13)

Jefferson remained impressed with the (Imported) Fearnought blood throughout his life. During those early years at Monticello, Jefferson bred not only to Dandridge's Young Fearnought, but also to other Fearnought colts owned by other nearby friends and neighbors. These horses also advertised their owner's name as well as their sire's; for example, John Bolling's Fearnought (who sired Ethelinda, 1776) or Gay's Fearnought (sire of Raleigh and a sorrel mare, bought in 1783). Several of the horses Jefferson later bought had (Imported) Fearnought in their pedigrees: Assaragoa, Tarquin, Brimmer, Wildair, and even Jefferson's last riding horse that he bought in 1820, The Eagle, was of the Fearnought line. [19]

Fearnought had been imported to America for his speed and racing victories; the hope was that he would pass his speed on to his offspring. It is important to emphasize, however, that Jefferson was breeding riding horses, not racing horses. I noted above that his contemporaries all said Jefferson never raced a horse (nor is there any record of such action), although he often attended the races. But unlike some other Virginians, Jefferson was breeding horses to ride, i.e., saddle horses. Jefferson mentioned the speed of these new horses but also stressed their beauty: "their fleetness and beauty will recommend them." Rather than merely fleetness, Jefferson was looking for stamina, carriage, and comfortable gaits to travel around his extensive farms and back and forth to the seats of government, in Williamsburg, Philadelphia, and Richmond, and for his daily pleasure riding. Moreover, perhaps Jefferson just wanted a well-bred horse, and the personal connections that came with those horses. [20]

Jefferson's Stud: In general, in Virginia before the end of the Revolutionary War, there was a hierarchical relationship between those wealthy members of the Tidewater gentry (the FFVs) who imported and owned studs and those who bred their mares with the imported stallions in the hopes of bettering their American stock. The gentry who imported the English racehorses were higher on the social (and economic) hierarchy than other planters who took their native Virginia mares to breed with the imported horses in hopes of producing their own turf champions and, later, high-bred studs. For the most part, Jefferson took his mares to the studs of other gentry to breed, such as with William Dandridge's Young Fearnought, the particular favorite mentioned above. Young Fearnought sired at least eleven Monticello-born foals. [21]

Only at the end of the decade that he devoted to horse breeding and raising did Jefferson reverse the direction of breeding, but in that case only within Albemarle County. [Fig. 7-8] Jefferson experimented with a couple of his own American-bred stallions, Alfred and Caractacus, as potential studs, crossing them with his own mares to try and produce higher-quality stock. Jefferson used Alfred as a stud as a two-year-old, with two of his own mares, producing colts in 1777 (young

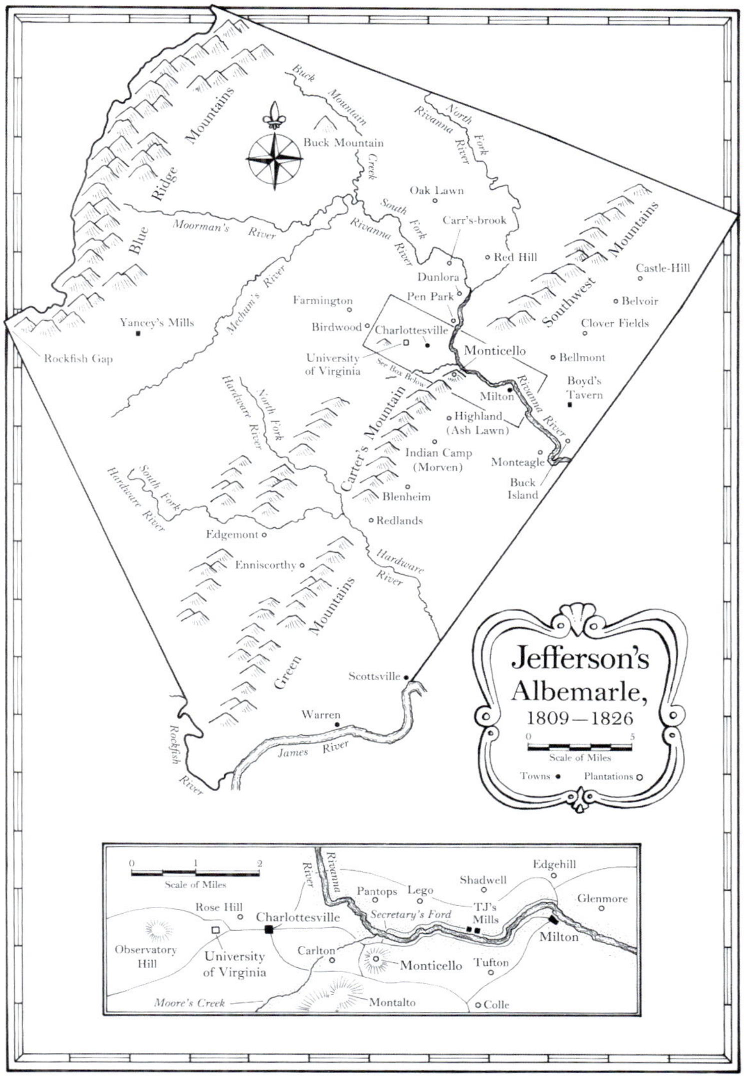

Fig. 7-8 Jefferson's Albemarle County

Alfred and a roan colt), but eventually sold Alfred to Richard Anderson. Caractacus produced two colts with Jefferson mares in 1780: a bay colt with #12 as dam and a gray colt with Silvertail as dam. But only with one of the stallions, Caractacus, did Jefferson reverse the direction of breeding. [22]

Apparently Caractacus was impressive enough as a riding horse that many of Jefferson's neighbors paid to put (breed) their mares with him between 1779 and 1782. The following gentlemen paid for a leap (one time) or a season (several months boarding at Monticello) with Caractacus. Thomas Garth, who served as overseer and then steward for Jefferson in Albemarle County from 1772 to 1782 later owned thousands of acres along Ivy Creek and was a magistrate and served as sheriff. Colonel John Harvie, whose father had been one of Jefferson's guardians after his father, Peter, died, owned the Barracks, Pen Park, and Belmont, and was a lawyer and member of the House of Burgesses and the Continental Congress. Dr. Gilmer, a physician, served as sheriff and was a member of the House of Delegates. He bought Pen Park from Harvie and made his home there. James Jones had acreage on Old Lynchburg Road near Dudley's Mountain. William Turner was another customer. Charles Goodman had land on the south fork of the Rivanna River, west of the mouth of Ivy Creek. James Powell Cocke, a relative of John Hartwell Cocke of Bremo, came to Albemarle sometime after 1770, and at least once supplied fish to stock the pond at Monticello. (It is almost certain that Jefferson designed James Powell Cocke's house, Edgemont, built around 1797 between Keene and Scottsville.) Benjamin Norell made the list. Claudius Bustard had 300 acres on the north fork of the Hardware River and kept a tavern. And Davy Watson, a house joiner by trade, who went to work for Jefferson in 1781 (after deserting from the British army), was a carriage maker at the time at Monticello.

Jefferson may have been a member of the FFAs (First Families of Albemarle), as evidenced by the direction of breeding in Albemarle, but he was not an FFV, nor did he come from the Tidewater elite. When his father, Peter Jefferson settled in Albemarle, it was considered the frontier. Thomas Jefferson became a planter, but he never had the wealth to import an English horse. By putting his mares with the studs of others, he acknowledged his secondary (and relatively new) status relative to the old guard.

The End of Jefferson's Breeding Program: By 1782, Jefferson had stopped his breeding program. He continued to admire fine horseflesh and always recorded buying only fine and well-bred mounts, but never again do we see evidence in his *Memorandum Books* or *Farm Book* or other papers of blooded foals being born at Monticello (or at Jefferson's other farms), or blooded mares being covered, or his horses used as studs. Why? What happened to make Jefferson give up the pursuit of his fellow gentry? Two catastrophic events most likely account for the end of horse breeding for Jefferson: the British invasion of Virginia in 1781 at the end of the Revolutionary War, and the death of Martha Wayles Jefferson. [23]

Fig. 7-9 Sir Joshua Reynolds, *Portrait of Sir Banastre Tarleton* (1754-1833), 1782

"British horse came to Monticello": Jefferson's entry in his memorandum book for June 4, 1781, dispassionately noted one of the most noteworthy moments in his noteworthy life. In the spring of 1781, General Charles Cornwallis, the British commander in the southern colonies during America's War of Independence, began moving his army north from North Carolina in an attempt to seize Virginia by force. Upon realizing what the British were about to do, General Washington sent the Marquis de Lafayette to Richmond, capital of Virginia, to bolster the militia. Thomas Jefferson was governor of Virginia at the time but was in the last months of his term (which concluded at the end of May). In January of 1781, Richmond had already come under a surprise attack by a British force under Benedict Arnold, and Governor Jefferson had tried to organize a last-minute defense of Richmond, but ultimately retreated to Tuckahoe plantation, a few miles west of Richmond on the James River, where he had sent his family on ahead. Although after the January raid, Arnold had retreated from Richmond to a fortified position, by April, General Cornwallis was threatening Richmond again. In early May, due to the military threat, Governor Jefferson and the Virginia legislature decided to leave the capital city and reconvene two weeks later in Charlottesville. [24]

By the end of May, however, General Cornwallis had occupied Richmond and then continued to chase the revolutionary forces into the heart of central Virginia. It was at this point that Cornwallis sent Lieutenant Colonel Banastre Tarleton on his infamous and legendary raid to Charlottesville to "to disturb the Virginia General Assembly" and to attempt to capture the governor at his home at Monticello. The subject of Lieutenant Colonel Tarleton introduces another important equestrian escapade. [25]

Lieutenant Colonel Tarleton was a British cavalry officer who served under various generals, earning a ferocious reputation among the Americans. He was known as a gifted leader and gifted horseman. In fact, he is responsible for importing an important blooded mare, Dian, to America during the war (1779). He was also known for his ruthlessness, especially in the campaigns in South Carolina, where he led his Tarleton's Raiders in several brutal massacres against Francis Marion and the American militias, such as Waxhaw Massacre in May of 1780. In one incident, Tarleton's men torched the houses and crops and killed the livestock on the estate of a deceased American general, then dug up his corpse and made his widow serve him a meal. The American breeders of blooded horses in the region hid their stock from his troops because the British troops had orders to confiscate all adult horses for the British war effort. The reputation of these depredations went before Tarleton on his way into Virginia in the spring of 1781. [26] [Fig. 9]

Tarleton and his men marched into Virginia with General Cornwallis in March 1781, and Tarleton was sent on several small expeditions by the general while there. One was the raid he made on Charlottesville, a small village near Monticello, in the attempt to capture then-Governor Jefferson and disrupt and capture the assemblymen of the Virginia legislature who had taken refuge there. Hoping to catch the Virginians by surprise, Tarleton and his more than 180 dragoons and 70 cavalrymen, many on blooded horses confiscated from Americans, moved swiftly, and even at night, clattering brazenly down the roads toward Charlottesville. At one point, on the evening of June 3, about forty miles from Charlottesville, the British troops stopped to rest and eat at a tavern in the adjoining Louisa County. Outside the tavern was a young Virginia militia member, the strapping six-foot-four Jack Jouett, soon to become known as the "Paul Revere of the South." [27] [Fig. 7-10]

Jouett was from Charlottesville, and his father ran the Swan Tavern there, where the governor and Virginia assemblymen had been meeting for the last several days, so he quickly guessed what the British troops' destination was and who they wanted to capture. Thus began Jack Jouett's ride to carry a warning to Jefferson and the legislature, which just may have prevented the British from defeating the Americans in their bid for independence. At about ten o'clock in the evening, Jack mounted his blooded bay mare, Sallie, and with a full moon to guide his way, took off over the countryside, determined to warn Governor Jefferson and then ride on to Charlottesville. [28]

Fig. 7-10 Silhouette of Jack Jouett, only known portrait from life, before 1827

Fearing detection on the main road, Jack made a beeline to Monticello on the back roads. Jefferson later commented that Jouett knew the "byways of the neighborhood, passed the enemy encampment, rode all night, and before sunrise the next day [June 4] called at Monticello." [29]

Historian Virginius Dabney wrote his version of the ride in a 1928 article:

> The unfrequented pathway over which this horseman set out on his all-night journey can only be imagined. His progress was greatly impeded by matted undergrowth, tangled bush, overhanging vines and gullies .... his face was cruelly lashed by tree limbs as he rode forward and scars said to have remained the rest of his life were the result of lacerations sustained from these low hanging branches. [30]

Jouett arrived first to Monticello, plunging through woods from Milton at 4:30 a.m., and was able to warn Governor

Fig. 7-11 John Singleton Copley, *Charles Cornwallis, 1st Marquess Cornwallis*, c. 1795

Jefferson and his guests. Taking only a few moments rest for his mare (and fortified by a glass of Madeira offered by Jefferson), he spurred Sallie on down the mountain toward Charlottesville to alert the others. There, after much insistence, he was able to convince the assemblymen to flee over the Blue Ridge Mountains to the small town of Staunton.

As is well known, Jefferson quickly sent his wife and two young daughters off in a carriage, with a promise to meet them later at a friend's house. Then with all deliberate speed he gathered his papers, ordered a servant to take his horse, Caractacus, to be shod and then to be led to the road to await him. After observing through his telescope the British troops entering Charlottesville three miles below his mountain, Jefferson finally mounted his sturdy and trustworthy six-year-old stallion and, in order to avoid being detected, "plunged into the woods of the adjoining mountain," as Jefferson later described it, on trails he must have known well, skirting the side of Carter's Mountain heading south, until he intersected the road his family was traveling on. Although it took them several days, staying with friends along the way, the couple made their way down to Jefferson's property in Bedford County, about 100 miles away. Jefferson's term as governor had ended at the end of May, but he did not think it prudent to return to Monticello with his family for almost two months. [31]

General Cornwallis at Elkhill: In the meantime, Cornwallis and his forces encamped at Elkhill, Jefferson's inherited home and income-producing lands at the confluence of the Rivanna and James rivers (Point of Fork), for the first few weeks of June. [Fig. 11] Although Tarleton's men had, notably, not touched anything at Monticello when they arrived (to find that Jefferson, forewarned, had already left), Jefferson accused Cornwallis of destroying his possessions at Elkhill in fury and wrath. The general had his men destroy all the crops of corn and tobacco. He burned the barns and all that was stored within, as well as all the fences, and he fed his army with the cattle, sheep, and hogs there. According to Jefferson, Cornwallis also helped to flee or carried off up to thirty slaves from Elkhill. But just as grievously, Cornwallis "carried off all the horses capable of service. Of those [horses] too young for service, he cut the throat." Jefferson lost nine horses that day (most of Jefferson's horses at Elkhill were the mares he bred to Young Fearnought) and several colts. In a sense, they were irreplaceable. [32]

News of this scorched-earth policy had preceded the British, as noted above, and Jefferson was not the only property owner to lose his prized blooded horses. All throughout Virginia, the British captured "horses, saddles and bridles … whatever provisions they wanted," noted one colonist in his diary. Residents everywhere fled "dreadfully alarmed & sending off their families, Horses & most valuable effects." Governor Jefferson had written the Virginia House of Delegates in early May that the British had been able to assemble a very formidable cavalry because they had stolen "some of the most valuable Horses in the Commonwealth." There were more blooded horses in Virginia than anywhere else in the colonies, and the British were taking advantage of that fact, which explains why the British cavalry by then vastly outnumbered Virginia's force. [33]

Fig. 7-12 Joseph-Desire Court, *Portrait of Gilbert Motier the Marquis De La Fayette as a Lieutenant General*, 1791, commissioned 1834

General George Washington, quartered in New York, had sent

the young French general Lafayette to defend Virginia. [Fig. 7-12] Lafayette knew he had to assemble a larger cavalry force in order to defend Virginia, but the Virginia planters also resisted giving up their horses to the American cause. The House of Burgesses was full of the First Families of Virginia, many of whom were interconnected through the activities of breeding and buying imported blooded horses. Reluctantly, they agreed to allow Lafayette to impress some horses, but Governor Jefferson nevertheless wrote to Lafayette, "Stud horses and broodmares will always be excepted, because to take them would be to rip up the hen which laid the golden eggs." Stud horses and broodmares could only be confiscated if they were not hidden from the enemy, Jefferson told Lafayette. Now the Virginians were caught in a web of their own contradiction; this policy only served to encourage horse owners to hide their hens and golden eggs, their blooded stock. It is clear that Governor Jefferson had known the risks of his unguarded treasures at Elkhill. [34]

Poplar Forest and the "Arabian Horse":

Jefferson never seemed to have recovered from the humiliation of Cornwallis's destruction of Elkhill and, most significantly for Jefferson's horse breeding, the carrying off of his horses. He spoke bitterly of this until the end of his life. It is only in retrospect, however, that we can say that these events marked the end of Jefferson's breeding of the new Thoroughbred horses. At the time he fled to his retreat in Bedford, Poplar Forest, to avoid the British, he did not yet know about Elkhill. Some of what Jefferson wrote while at Poplar Forest seemed to imply that his agricultural and animal husbandry pursuits would go on as usual. To see the evidence for this, it is necessary to review again how that summer in Poplar Forest, Jefferson ended up writing about the profits of breeding these new kinds of horses, with their beauty and speed.

One morning early in his stay at Poplar Forest, Jefferson had Caractacus saddled up and went out for a ride. That day, his horse, who had served him so well under fire and in the dead of night in the defense and then retreat from Richmond in January, and later equally well during Jefferson's escape from Monticello in his last days as governor, reared up and shied at perhaps a deer, and his rider fell to the ground. Instinctively, Jefferson stretched out his left arm to break his fall, and "shattered his left wrist" in the process. It would be six weeks before he could ride again. [35]

To take advantage of his down time at Poplar Forest, Jefferson decided to begin work on a project that would eventually become his first and only full-length book, *Notes on the State of Virginia*. When Jefferson began, he was responding to twenty-six questions posed about Virginia by François Barbé-Marbois, then secretary of the French legation in Philadelphia. Although not published until 1784 (in Paris), this book is often said to be one of the most important American books published before 1800. It is a compilation of the scientific descriptions and data on the geography and flora and fauna of Virginia. However, Jefferson also promulgated several philosophical agendas in this work, from outlining his ideas about the political, legal, and constitutional principles that lead to a good society, to refuting the theory that plant life, animal life, and human life all degenerate in the New World in comparison to the Old World. Counter to the degeneration theory, Jefferson sought to demonstrate the large size and vitality of American natural life. [36]

In chapter twenty of the book, "Subjects of Commerce," and in answer to one of Barbé-Marbois's queries, Jefferson listed the pre-war Virginia exports (tobacco, wheat, corn, pork). He discussed tobacco and explained why wheat must and should take its place as the main crop of Virginia. One of the reasons he gave for planting wheat was to enlarge available pasture lands, which in turn would make the breeding of "Arabian" horses very profitable. "The culture of wheat, by enlarging our pasture, will render the Arabian horse an article of very considerable profit." Here again was reference to the hen that laid the golden eggs.

Jefferson then wrote about the "Arabian" horse and its adaptation to Virginia's climate without any degeneracy:

> Experience has shewn that ours is the particular climate of America where he may be raised without degeneracy. Southwardly the heat of the sun occasions a deficiency of pasture, and northwardly the winters are too cold for the short and fine hair, the particular sensibility and constitution of that race. Animals transplanted into unfriendly climates, either change their nature and acquire new fences against the new difficulties in which they are placed, or they multiply poorly and become extinct.

Jefferson continued extolling the virtues of these "Arabian" horses, which already existed in great numbers in Virginia; they suffered the heat well and could serve not only as saddle and carriage horses for the elite, but also could pull the plow and

Fig. 7-13 An Arabian horse today: La Mirage, purebred Arabian stallion, by Salaa El Dine out of Bint Mangani

wagon. Their beauty and speed had already created a "preference for them among the people":

> A good foundation is laid for their propagation here by our possessing already great numbers of horses of that blood, and by a decided taste and preference for them established among the people. Their patience of heat without injury, their superior wind, fit them better in this and the more southern climates even for the drudgeries of the plough and wagon. Northwardly they will become an object only to persons of taste and fortune, for the saddle and light carriages. To these, and for these uses, their fleetness and beauty will recommend them. [37]

When Jefferson used the term "Arabian horse," he was not referring to the breed we call Arabian today. [Fig. 13] Rather, when he wrote in the *Notes on the State of Virginia* of the "great numbers of horses of that blood" already in Virginia, Jefferson was referring to both the recently imported English racehorses and their offspring, offspring produced when the imported studs were put to the local Virginia mares, resulting in horses that were tall, spirited, and could run long distances like the wind, and yet also serve as elegant saddle horses. These new horses (soon referred to as blood horses, or blooded horses, or high-bred horses) were then bred to others with the same pedigree to maintain these preferred characteristics. Soon a closed stud book or closed registry (1770 in England, 1863 in the United States) restricted membership of the breed to those animals that could trace their pedigree back to the foundational sires. They were pure-bred or thorough-bred, a name adopted for the breed by the end of the nineteenth century. [Fig. 7-14]

Jefferson most certainly knew that these coveted blooded horses in Virginia were themselves the descendants of (genetic) crosses between the small sturdy English and Irish mares and three foundation stallions imported into England from 1680 to about 1750 from various kingdoms in the Middle East (see Chapter 4). This area of the world, called "the Orient" in Jefferson's time, was dominated geographically by the Arabian peninsula, and, with the spread of Islam, the area was influenced culturally and linguistically by Arabia. And there is no doubt that the various breeding programs throughout the Middle East produced locally differentiated Arab-type horses (Turks, Barbs). This may be why Jefferson and others sometimes used the term "Arabian" for horses from this part of the world.

By the mid-nineteenth century, with the establishment of stud books and registries, the Arabian horse was recognized as a true closed and pure breed (as distinguished from merely a type) that originated in the Arabian peninsula and which had more than 3,500 years of selective breeding. It is now considered one of the oldest and most influential breeds in the world, with

Fig. 7-14 A Thoroughbred, the fastest horse breed

a distinctive head shape and high tail carriage. Today it is also one of the most desired horse breeds globally. Arabian blood did indeed help develop many other horse breeds. However, with one or two exceptions in colonial times, the Arabian horse did not come to the United States until 1888, when a small breeding program was begun. Further interest in the breed was inspired when forty-five Arabian horses were exhibited at the 1893 Columbian World's Fair.

Jefferson, when he bred his mares to Dandridge's Young Fearnought, was producing fifth-generation pure-bred, or blood horses (i.e., five generations from one of the foundation stallions, the Godolphin Arabian, whose origin was the Barbary Coast of north Africa, or Tunisia, not Arabia). In his *Notes on the State of Virginia*, Jefferson may have referred to "Arabian" horses in Virginia, but he really meant the blood horses, which today we would call Thoroughbreds. The two breeds phenotypically look very different, even if Arab-type horses from various places in the Middle East helped create the Thoroughbred breed in England in the early eighteenth century.

It is clear from Jefferson's *Notes on the State of Virginia* that at least in the summer of 1781, he probably planned to continue breeding the profitable "Arabian" (or blooded) horse. Later, when the reality of his loss at Elkhill made itself felt, he may have begun to reassess. However, another, more tragic reason ended definitively Jefferson's breeding program.

Martha's Death: The second catastrophe that changed the direction of horse breeding at Monticello was the death of Jefferson's wife, Martha, in September 1782, one year after the British invasion. This loss, in his words, of "the cherished companion of my life, in whose affections, unabated on both sides, I had lived the last ten years in unchequered happiness" was an especially searing experience for Jefferson. The poignant descriptions by family members of the young husband's sorrow are still heartrending. A moment before her death, Jefferson was led out of the room by his sister "in a state of insensibility," to his library, where he fainted. He remained unconscious for so long that family members feared he would not revive. Seemingly he expressed "violent" grief. [38]

His daughter Martha described her father's reaction to his wife's (her mother's) death:

> He walked almost incessantly night and day, only lying down occasionally, when nature was completely exhausted, on a pallet that had been brought in during his long fainting fit. My aunts remained constantly with him for some weeks. [39]

Jefferson himself spoke of a "stupor of mind" that took almost three months to dissipate. During that time, he wrote, he had been "as dead to the world as she whose loss occasioned it." I refer to this incident repeatedly because it was at this dark moment that the young widower began to find solace by riding hours in the woods around his home, a habit he ritualized for the rest of his life. "The horse," Jefferson later declared, was "to me that most sovereign of all doctors." [40]

Monticello now held too many raw memories of his former happiness for him to remain there during those initial months after Martha's death. Thus, Jefferson effectively fled from Monticello to escape his grief, fulfilling political posts in Philadelphia, Annapolis, and Richmond before he was eventually sent as minister to France (a post he had previously turned down due to his wife's fragile health) in 1784. Little did he know how long he would be gone from his beloved home on the Mountain.

Accompanied by his oldest daughter, Martha (known as Patsy by the family), and the enslaved cook, young James Hemings, Jefferson arrived in France at the end of June 1784. Jefferson and his family did not return to Virginia until December 1789. Upon disembarking from the ship in Norfolk, Jefferson learned that President George Washington had asked him to become his secretary of state. Thus, after only a few weeks back at Monticello, Jefferson was on his way to New York City and later Philadelphia, where he spent the next four years residing, in the service of the new country he had helped to found.

Except for brief sojourns back to Virginia, until he left Washington's government for what he called his (first) retirement from public life, Jefferson had not been a farmer or planter for more than twelve years. Monticello was in a sorry state, and Jefferson was anxious to return to his beloved home on the Mountain, and his agricultural life. He re-dedicated himself to replanting his fields (according to the newest scientific methods) and redesigning and rebuilding his house. He never, however, returned to breeding horses.

Fig. 7-15. Mustang in Wyoming, 2007

Mustangs

Once back in the United States from his years in France, Thomas Jefferson pursued his interest in improving the stock of horses in the new United States. Jefferson had heard about the herds of wild horses that inhabited the plains past the Mississippi River and was quite interested in them, for both scientific and economic reasons. In March 1798, when the Polish poet and statesman Julian Ursyn Niemcewicz (1758–1841) dined with Vice President Jefferson and others, Niemcewicz noted in his journal that Jefferson had spoken of wild horses "on the other side of the Mississippi." Jefferson had explained that the inhabitants of Kentucky go "in to this country expressly in order to catch them." Niemcewicz went on to explain that the horses were "Spanish runaways, agile, excellent in all respects, and very long lived." Jefferson had confirmed that one of those horses in Virginia had supposedly lived for 47 years. [41]

Mustang is the term used to refer to the herds of wild horses that first appeared on the plains of North America at the beginning of the eighteenth century. Although these animals have traditionally been called wild, they all descended from domesticated horses first brought to the Americas by the Spanish and other Europeans in the sixteenth century. As horses escaped or were stolen from their Spanish owners, they propagated profusely and lived in free-roaming herds. Therefore, the more correct term is "feral" horse. The word *mustang* is an English corruption of the Spanish word *mesteño* or *mesteña* (feminine), which in medieval Spanish meant "wild, stray, ownerless." Spanish speakers referred to the herds of wild horses that spread over the landscape in several ways: *Caballada mesteña* or *mesteñada* (mustang horse stock) or *bestia mesteñas* (mustang beasts or animals). The word moved through a Mexican-Spanish form: *mestengo/ mestenga*, before Americans appropriated it as "mustang." The first written use of mustang was during the explorations by Zebulon M. Pike in his journal, June 20, 1807: "passed through several herds of mustangs or wild horses." [42]

Most of the free-roaming mustangs that today have legal protected status in parts of the United States are not pure strains of Colonial Spanish stock. [Fig. 7-15] For the first few centuries after these herds appeared, all mustangs were descendants of the Iberian horse. The Indians of North America got their horses directly from the Spanish and not from the wild herds. Since few if any Spanish horses survived the Spanish expeditions in the southeast from Florida to North Carolina to Mississippi, most of the herds of mustangs that appeared on the North American plains came up from Mexico through Texas after 1680. Within 100 years after that, all Indians in North America had acquired and were using horses, but Native American horse culture would last only 100 more years. Certain Native American groups bred their own herds and selected for certain features, such as color or size. The Chickasaw obtained horses, bred them, and sold their well-respected stock (known as Chickasaws) throughout the English colonial Southeast during the eighteenth century. [43]

The Colonial Spanish stock that became mustangs multiplied ferociously, and millions of horses soon populated the plains. Those horses looked like their Barb-type ancestors: they were small (most mustangs today vary between 13 to 14.2 hands high) but exceptionally hardy, with good bone structure and small but healthy feet. Their heads have a straight to concave profile, with a straight or convex nose. [44]

Another striking characteristic of the mustangs is the variety of colors that distinguished them from the Thoroughbred and Arabian type horses known in England:

> A full range of solid colors including black, bay, brown, chestnut, sorrel, grullo, zebra dun, red dun, buckskin, palomino, and cream. Other solid colors such as the champagne colors, and even silver dapple occur. In many horses these base colors are combined with white hairs or patches to result in gray, roan, paint (tobiano, overo, and sabino types), pure white, and the leopard complex of blankets, roans, and dark spots usually associated with the Appaloosa breed. [45]

The image of the Native American on his spotted pinto or paint pony comes from the Spanish heritage of those horses. [Fig. 7-16]

In June 1798, in his capacity as president of the American Philosophical Society, Vice President Jefferson had written to Philip Nolan. Nolan (1771–1801) was a horse trader and later called a filibuster, or someone who led an unauthorized expedition into Spanish-held territory (Texas). When Jefferson wrote him, Nolan had already made three trips into Texas from New Orleans—illegally—to trade with Indians and in search of mustangs (1791, 1794, 1797). On each trip, he had brought back hundreds of horses; the last trip he had returned with (variously estimated) "between 1300 and 2500 western horses" for prospective buyers in the East. He was catering to the market for working ranch horses for the growing cattle industry in Louisiana. [46]

In Jefferson's 1798 letter, however, he asked for scientific data on the vast herds of horses that roamed Texas:

> It was some time since I have understood that there are large herds of horses in a wild state in the country West of the Missisipi [*sic*] and have been desirous of obtaining details of their history in that state. Mr. Brown, Senator from Kentucky, informs me it would be in your power to give interesting information

Fig. 7-16 A member of the Crow tribe, Spotted Rabbit, c. 1905

> on this subject, and encourages me to ask it. The circumstances of the old-world have, beyond the records of history, been such as admitted not that animal to exist in a state of nature. The condition of America is rapidly advancing to the same. The present then is probably the only moment in the age of the world and the herds above mentioned the only subjects, of which we can avail ourselves to obtain what has never yet been recorded and never can be again in all probability. I will add that your information is the sole reliance, as far as I can at present see, for obtaining this desideratum. You will render to natural history a very acceptable service therefore, if you will enable our Philosophical-society to add so interesting a chapter to the history of the animal. I need not specify to you the particular facts asked for, as your knowledge of the animal in his domesticated, as well as his wild state, will naturally have led your attention to those particulars in the manners, habits, & laws of his existence, which are peculiar to his wild state. I wish you not to be anxious about the form of your information. The exactness of the substance alone is material: and if, after giving in a first letter all the facts you at present possess, you could be so good, on subsequent occasions, as to furnish such others in addition as you may acquire from time to time, your communication will always be thankfully received. If addressed to me at Monticello & put into any post office of Kentucky or Tenissee [*sic*], they will reach me speedily & safely, and will be considered as obligations on Sir. Your most obedt. & humble servt Th: Jefferson. [47]

Jefferson asked about "manners, habits, & laws of his [the horse's] existence, which are peculiar to his wild state." He did not ask about buying or receiving any of the horses. Nevertheless, Nolan planned to meet with Jefferson at Monticello during the summer of 1800 and to make him a gift of an excellent paint stallion. But the stallion and Nolan never arrived to Monticello. Nolan sold the stallion in Lexington, Kentucky and returned to the frontier to plan his next (and final) expedition. Due to the previous unauthorized expeditions, the Spanish suspected him of being a spy. In 1801, when Nolan re-entered Texas territory near the Brazos River, where he put up a corralling station for mustangs, he was surrounded and killed by Spanish military forces. [48]

Jefferson's relationship with Nolan simply underlined the interest in the already huge bands of mustangs in the West. Lewis and Clark were soon going to be able to supply more information to Jefferson on the horse in lands past the Mississippi. The fact that Nolan had chosen a paint stallion pointed to the lack of such spotted horses in the east. A paint stallion would certainly have added exotica to Jefferson's stable of bay and sorrel horses. [49]

Jefferson's Barb Mare

Even after the demise of his equine-breeding program at Elkhill, Jefferson remained passionately interested in improving the blood of Virginia horses, just as he keenly participated in the eighteenth-century scientific revolution in agriculture in general. Jefferson promoted new techniques in planting and farming, and contributed enthusiastically to the transglobal exchange of seeds and seedlings in gardening, as well as experimented in animal husbandry with different breeds of sheep and mules. His curiosity about mustangs was part of these interests.

When Jefferson was president, he took great advantage of an opportunity to improve the horse stock of his young country. Ironically, an opportunity to improve the American horse stock came as a diplomatic gift. It was during Jefferson's presidency that the United States had decided to confront the Barbary pirates (1801–1805). Jefferson had been outraged at the constant capture of merchant ships off the coast of North Africa and the demand for ransom for captured civilians. The pirate states, off the Barbary Coast (autonomous provinces of the Ottoman Empire), also demanded annual tribute to ensure against further seizure. Finally, in 1803, US Navy ships seized Tunisian vessels and blockaded Tripoli, and in response the bey (king) of Tunis decided to send an ambassador to Washington to negotiate a settlement of claims and to barter for tribute. [50]

The envoy, Sidi Soliman Mellimelli, arrived in November 1805 and stayed for six months in Washington, until May 1806. He came laden with gifts for Jefferson, among them three spectacular examples of North African Barb horses (recall that horsemen along the Eastern Seaboard were anxious to import so-called "Oriental" horses to "improve the blood" of American stock). Mellimelli presented to President Jefferson one black Barb stallion and two mares. Originally, Jefferson planned to sell the horses and repay the US Treasury to compensate for Mellimelli's stay. Jefferson soon decided to use the stallion to improve the blood of horses in America.

On April 24, 1806 the following ad appeared in the *Universal Gazetteer:*

> The superb barb Black Sultan will stand the ensuing season at Petworth, the farm of John Tayloe III, Esq. near Rock Creek Church, and within two miles of the city of Washington. This Royal present being one of the most choice animals of the Regency of and Tunis and a full 16 hands high, a desire has prevailed that so valuable a race should be extended as much as possible and it has there fore been directed that he be placed at a low price [of $20]. Chester Bailey (manager Th. Jefferson, Esq.). [51]

Six months later, the horses were put up for sale:

> For Sale: On the second day of the Washington races, which are to commence on Thursday the 28th, there will be offered for sale at auction the elegant Barbary horse and two mares, which were brought from Tunis by his Excellency the Tunisian Ambassador and intended as a present to the Executive of the United States." [52]

Although Jefferson was probably in attendance at these races, the horses did not sell. Two months later another announcement appeared in the *National Intelligencer:*

The horse Black Sultan and the two mares will be disposed of in a private sale. Both the mares are in foal to the horse and all three are in good condition. Application to be made to the subscriber at the office of the Secretary of State. [53]

There is no evidence of any sale.

Eventually, Black Sultan was bought by a member of Congress and sent to South Carolina. One mare, in foal to Black Sultan, was bought by another member of Congress and sent to Louisiana (she produced Beau Laquaise c. 1807). The other mare, known as Jefferson's Barb mare, went to Jefferson's son-in-law John Wayles Eppes, also a member of Congress. (See more on Eppes in Chapter 2.)

Jefferson's Barb mare, also with foal by Black Sultan, produced the filly called Sultana (1807), who eventually became a Thoroughbred foundation mare (tap root of Family #A25). Eppes later bred Sultana to Sir Archie to produce an important breeder (Lady Burton). Eppes bred Jefferson's Barb mare again, this time to Citizen (imported by Thomas Goode, standing at stud in Chesterfield in 1808) to produce another filly, called Araline. This mare, half-sister to Sultana, also became a foundational mare, and is known as The Citizen Mare (and is the tap-root of Family #A30). Both these fillies ended up in the stud of Hutchins Gordon Burton (1774–1836) of Halifax County, North Carolina, racehorse breeder and governor of North Carolina, as well as brother-in-law of John Wayles Eppes through his second wife. Little did Thomas Jefferson know how much the gift horses from Tunis, with the help of his son-in-law, would improve the blood of American horses. [54]

The Albemarle Agricultural Society

During his post-presidency retirement years at Monticello after 1809, Thomas Jefferson remained concerned with improvements to agriculture and animal husbandry in his country. In general, he worked locally, although he communicated by letter with leaders and intellectuals in Europe and the United States. While far past his horse-breeding days, Jefferson continued to sustain an interest in this activity.

In 1817, Jefferson and about thirty of his illustrious friends and neighbors founded the Albemarle Agricultural Society. The mission of the society was to educate Virginians about the most innovative and scientific farming and husbandry practices. Jefferson convinced his good friend and fellow farmer, James Madison, fresh from his own presidency, to be the society's first president. Together they wanted to promote a "rural and republican virtue in country life." [55]

A little over one year into the life of the society, its members decided to take up a bond to purchase an Andalusian horse from Spain, in order to "improve the breed" in Albemarle County. [Fig. 7-17] The society was "impressed with a belief that the Horses of [Virginia] would be much improved by the introduction of the Andalusian stallion from Spain." [56]

A resolution was adopted (March 2, 1818) to appoint a committee:

> [To] open a correspondence with the government of Spain, through our minister at Madrid and the Spanish minister accredited to the United States, for the purpose of ascertaining whether a person acting

Fig. 7-17 Andalusian horse, 2006

> under the authority of its society will be permitted to purchase in Spain, and transport to the United States, a horse of the best race of that country with the view to improve the breed in our own. [57]

Interest in importing an Andalusian stallion continued despite little progress toward the goal. It was first necessary to obtain the special permission of the king of Spain to export any Andalusian horses (or even any jennies or jacks for mule breeding). President Madison was able to secure royal permission, but then came the issue of actually finding and buying a suitable animal. Eventually, in 1819, the society procured the help of John S. Skinner of Baltimore, editor and publisher of the agricultural journal *The American Farmer* and honorary member of the Albemarle Agricultural Society. Skinner had volunteered to intercede in Spain on the society's behalf and to place a credit in Spain "to the amount of whatever sum might be necessary to procure a pair of that breed of Horse." Skinner was clear about the purpose: "in order that the breed, if as valuable as represented, might be perpetuated in this country." He went on: "From Andalusia in Spain, a stock might be procured to meliorate the breed of our saddle horses, which, when of best quality afford the most pleasant and healthful mode of travelling and exercise." [Fig. 7-18] Skinner transferred the task of actually going to Spain to search for the requested animal to Commodore Jacob Jones of the *USS Constitution*, on duty in the Mediterranean area. [58]

Jones, however, wrote back to Skinner in September 1822 that he would have been happy to carry an "Andalusian Horse and Mare" back to Baltimore, but that the "best that could be found here, would be but little valued in the U. States." He went on to state that he "did not see, from Cadiz to Seville, a horse, which in our country, would bring $200; not a mare which could be sold at $50." Jones continued telling Skinner that "an *Arabian* horse was not to be found this side of Egypt." Furthermore, according to Jones, the "best Barbs are to be had in Morocco," but the Moroccan Barbs were too expensive: "the price is from 600 to $1000, besides a high duty for exportation." Obviously Commodore Jones was not impressed with the steeds of Andalusia and the Moroccan horses were too expensive! And so ended the saga of the Andalusian stallion for Albemarle. [59]

Fig. 7-18 A Spanish horse depicted by Cornelis van Caukercken, after Abraham van Diepenbeeck, *Welbeck Le Superbe Cheval de Spanie*, engraving from the first Duke of Newcastle, *A general system of horsemanship in all its branches* (new edition printed for J. Brindley, bookseller to His Royal Highness the Prince of Wales, in New Bond-street, 1743)

Weedy Horses

One of the drawbacks with creating a breed, or type of horse, and then continuing the breed by propagating only with those horses registered in the *Stud Book*, is that the conformation, or shape of the horse, is exacerbated. In eighteenth- and early-nineteenth-century Virginia, the speedy high-bred horse tended to be tall and lanky, sometimes called "weedy." And like in the Thoroughbred horse today, the hoof is small in relation to the overall weight of the horse. This led to leg problems when used on the "frequently deep state, and irregular surface of our roads." Thomas Jefferson was already complaining of this issue with an ex-racehorse horse he bought in 1790. Jefferson decided to give the horse away rather than try and ride him around Monticello, because he stumbled going down hills. [60]

By the time the Albemarle Agricultural Society was searching for a Spanish Andalusian stallion, a general dissatisfaction over the saddle-horse quality in Virginia was apparent on the part of many admirers of horseflesh. If the Albemarle planters were intent on importing an Andalusian stallion to improve the breed, it was because many felt the Virginia saddle horse had deteriorated in quality. Significantly, one of the most strident voices in this discussion was Jefferson's friend, neighbor, and fellow planter, John Hartwell Cocke. (See Chapter 2.) In fact, as a member of the Albemarle Agricultural Society, he had been one of the prime movers in the search for the Andalusian import. However, around the same date, Cocke was gathering money from another set of friends to import an English hunter. [61]

Indeed, Cocke participated in an ongoing debate about the effects of post-Revolutionary War importation of racing studs to the United States. As we have seen, the war had caused the loss of many of the offspring of the first imported blood horses. After the end of the war, great numbers of English racing horses were again imported and course-racing mania flourished, especially in the South. (See Chapter 6.) Horses were bred primarily for speed, and, in fact, some planters converted to turfmen and invested themselves solely in this new form of speculation. John Hoomes, the important Virginia turfman (importer of Diomed and Spread Eagle) came in for special criticism due to the influence of his imports. (See Chapter 2.)

Cocke railed against the pernicious effects of having bred horses to race only:

> The taste and passion for racing so far from contributing to has retarded the progress of improvement in our horses—Upon this subject few, perhaps have had more experience than the author of this communication [Cocke], having labored under the racing mania for a term of years that almost reduced him to a race of worthless garrons, though none of their distinguished dams cost him less than a hundred guineas apiece, and were certified for through an uncontaminated succession of famous English ancestors down to the Godolphin Arabian. Fortunately, however, about twelve years ago, I became convinced of my delusion, and since I have been endeavoring to get back to the well known old stocks, and breeding exclusively with a view to useful qualities, the result has answered my most sanguine hopes. [62]

Cocke believed that the best Virginia horse had been the third- and fourth-generation horses of the early imports, such as Fearnought, Jolly Roger, and Janus. They were "less tall, bulkier and stronger jointed, with thicker and coarser coat," for they had been fed the more nutritious maize and exposed to the weather, instead of, as in England, pampered in warm stables. The new racehorse type, bred only for speed and serving only to race, was "tall (not less than 16 hands) thin-skinned, long-legged and apt to slouch and stumble." [63]

Cocke wrote the following letter about the same time the Albemarle Agricultural Society was taking up the bond for the Andalusian stallion in order to improve the blood of the "weedy horses" in Albemarle County.

Note his negative description of these "spindly-legged" horses:

Fig. 7-19 a and b Contrast of racehorse versus saddle horse. Prints from Mason, *The Gentleman's New Pocket Companion.*

> The essential points of the turf horse are, a thin and deep shoulder, narrow breast, delicate clean legs, long in the pasterns, a broad or wide hock well let down, and a thigh or haunch more remarkable for length than bulk; a long back more common than a short one, and a body oftener flat sided than round—and finally the taller the better, but not less than sixteen hands for the first rate courser. This carcase and set of limbs is covered by a skin so thin and an coat of hair so fine as to express the very veins as well as the muscles beneath the delicate integument—Equally disqualified by the nature of his skin is he for the harness—the slightest pressure producing a gall—and as unsuited are his long legs and limber pasterns to the frequently deep state and irregular surface of our roads. [64] [Fig.7-19 a and b]

Cocke then goes on to describe his more preferred saddle horse:

> A horse of compact form and nimble movements, will always be found more lasting and serviceable—less tall with more bulk, shorter and stronger jointed, more active and sprightly in its movements and better able to stand the vicissitudes of our climate. The noble animal to be cherished as the companion of our manly pleasures and glorious achievements should be of the form for power, docile and courageous in his temper, quick, firm and clear in his movements. These properties are found for the most part connected with roundness of contour and strength of articulation; with a texture of skin and strength of coat which will bear the pressure of the saddle and the friction of the harness; —it is rare that you find a horse of this description exceeding fifteen hands and a half high." [65]

The illustrations of a Virginia racing horse and a Virginia saddle horse are from a book titled *The Gentleman's New Pocket Companion*, by Richard Mason of Surry County. This book became known as *Mason's Farrier* and was first published in 1811, but went on to have twenty-two further editions (from 1814 to 1883). Its influence was very widespread. It was published in Petersburg, the heart of the old horse racing region at the time. John Hartwell Cocke was one of Mason's financial backers. The prints conform to Cocke's descriptions of the two kinds of horses he described in the letter to the *American Farmer.* [66]

In his letter, Cocke said that his conversion to breeding saddle horses (versus racehorses) came about in 1811. However, in 1809, he advertised stud services for his horse Roebuck, lauding the horse's colts for their unrivaled uses in "Saddle, carriage and plantation business." In 1810, Roebuck I produced, with an English imported mare called Druid, a bay colt, Roebuck II (or Young Roebuck), that quickly became Cocke's favorite riding horse. [Fig. 20] Cocke described this Roebuck as "the most perfect model of a saddle horse I ever knew." In 1814, Cocke sold Jefferson a horse named Bremo, who became one of his favorite saddle and carriage horses. [67]

John Randolph of Roanoke, was also critical of the post-Revolutionary imported horses and what their blood had done to Virginia stock. And like Cocke, Randolph disparaged John Hoomes's imported racing horses for lowering the quality of horses in Virginia.

> The true, serviceable horse is the quarter horse, being active, sure-footed, speedy and capable of breaking down the fashionable stock in a hard ride of fifty, or even five and twenty miles. His feet are of the old horny and cupped description that distinguished the Virginia horse before Col. Hoomes inundated our country with worthless stallions, and introduced the flat, thin-soled, weak-crusted foot that can hardly hold a shoe, and cannot travel five miles without one. Our old-fashioned horses never required shoeing except in hard frosts, or hard work on stony ground. A more hardy and thrifty race of horses never existed. He will keep fat upon what only will hardly keep alive the leggy, long-backed garrons that are now all the rage. It is only in a race of more than a mile-that the longbacked horse can be successful competitor against the quarter horse. He [the former] is a stumbler and breaks down with his own unwieldy weight. [68]

Randolph was partial to Janus blood lines. Janus, as described earlier, is known as the progenitor of the American Quarter Horse breed, fast at a quarter mile, but shorter and stockier than the tall refined Thoroughbred and more active and sure-footed than the later imports. As Randolph insisted in the quote above, "A more hardy and thrifty race of horses never existed."

Jefferson was always and only interested in saddle horses; it is important to repeat that he never bred a horse to race. Over the years, Jefferson's horses got taller, but like his friends John Hartwell Cocke and John Randolph of Roanoke, Jefferson preferred a smooth-pacing traveler to a delicate racer. And for most of his adult life, Jefferson dedicated much time and thought to improving the breed of the American saddle horse. [69]

ROEBUCK.

A BEAUTIFUL bay, fifteen hands and a half high, in the prime of life, and poſſeſſing a degree of beauty, fine bone, and ſtriking ſymetry that will decidedly eſtabliſh his claim with all good judges to rank among Horſes of the firſt order—But this Horſe's higheſt recommendation does not conſiſt in his fine colour, good ſize and powerful form: The judicious and reflecting breeder would naturally enquire what is the reputation of his ſtock? How have his colts turned out? and it is upon this ground that ROEBUCK ſtands peculiarly recommended as a covering Horſe.—Many of his colts are now in ſervice in the neighbourhood from which he came, and for the various purpoſes of the Saddle, Carriage, and plantation buſineſs, are unrivaled in t ir good qualities,—Several of the beſt riding Horſes in the lower part of the ſtate are of Roebuck's get,—From the known reputation of his ſtock for their fine gaits, hardy characters, and docile manageable diſpoſitions the preſent proprietor of Roebuck was induced to purchaſe him chiefly as a Brood Horſe upon his own eſtate.—As a ſure foal getter, Roebuck has proved himſelf inferior to no Horſe.

THE above Horse will ſtand the enſuing season, (to commence the 20th of March, and end the 10th of Auguſt) ~~at my ſtable in~~ New-Canton, ~~four days in each week,~~ and two days at upper Bremo, and will be let to Mares at the very moderate price of Six Dollars the Seaſon—Ten Dollars to enſure a Mare to be in foal, payable at any time before the 1ſt of November next—Three Dollars the ſingle Leap, to be paid at the time of ſervice—In every inſtance a quarter of a dollar to the groom. Produce will be received in payment, delivered at New-Canton, or the Virginia Mills, at the current prices at thoſe places.—Mares going to the Horſe will have no ferriage to pay at New-Canton.

JOHN ANDERSON.

New-Canton, 1ſt March, 1809.

PEDIGREE.

ROEBUCK was got by Powell's Selim one of the beſt bred Sons of the celebrated old Selim—Powell's Selim was as much celebrated for the number of fine Horſes of which he was the Sire, as any other Stallion ever known in the lower Southern Counties of the State. The blood of Roebuck's Dam I have never enquired into the particulars of in purchaſing him being influenced entirely by what I knew of his colts and always having underſtood that he was a well bred Horſe on the Dam ſide.

JOHN H. COCKE.

STAR-OFFICE.

Fig. 7-20 Handbill advertising John Hartwell Cocke's horse, Roebuck. From MacKay-Smith, *The Colonial Quarter Race Horse.*

Wild horses (Mustangs, with protected status) near Pilot Butte, Wyoming. *Credit: Photo by author*

Chapter 8

The Livestock: Work Horses, Chickasaws, and Mules

When people said that Jefferson was "passionately fond of a good horse," a "good" horse meant a high-bred horse, not a common Hobby or Chickasaw, and certainly not one of the work horses or mules that tilled the fields and provided power for the mills at Monticello. If we think of Jefferson and his horses, we imagine him on one of his high-bred stallions on his daily ride. And although that stallion would have been what we now call a Thoroughbred, the young Thomas Jefferson would have known and ridden many other types of horses. And the elder Jefferson would have owned many more work horses than high-bred riding horses.

In his *Farm Book*, Jefferson separated his list of named blooded saddle horses (and their pedigrees) from lists of his work horses. We know that Jefferson owned at least 135 horses in his lifetime, probably more. More than seventy-eight of the recorded horses were horses to work his farm, animals that literally supplied the horsepower for the plows and wagons and threshing barns that defined Monticello as a plantation and farm, as well as "hauling produce of all kinds, hitched to wagons and carts, to haul wood, rocks, manure, earth." Sometimes. Jefferson called these animals work horses, sometimes plantation horses, sometimes Chickasaws. [1]

In many ways, these work horses (livestock), the lowest horses in the equine hierarchy, symbolically paralleled the low-status enslaved field hands that lived and worked on the quarter farms. However, not only horses worked the plantation fields under the hands of the enslaved laborers, or worked the farms of poor and middling whites as well, but mules and oxen also toiled as draft animals there.

The Virginia Horse

Reflecting the varying geographic origins of their immigrant owners, different horse types populated the regions and sections of colonial America. In Virginia, prior to the first arrivals of the blood horses from England in the 1740s, horses were general all-purpose animals descended from Anglo-Irish Hobbies and Galloways, and Spanish Barb-type horses called Chickasaws. These horses may have served under saddle or drawn a chair or chariot in towns, as well as worked the fields

Fig. 8-1 Connemara pony family, with Tully Mountain in the background, Galway, Ireland

certain times of the year. In New York, Rhode Island, or Pennsylvania, different types and mixes would have predominated.

Hobby horses and Galloways: The first horses arrived in Virginia at Jamestown in 1609, although none of them survived the "starving times" of that first settlement. But later ships arrived, bringing the sturdy little horses common in Great Britain at the time, disembarking both mares and stallions so they would reproduce in the new lands. These first English horses were the Irish Hobbies and Scottish Galloways, smallish-sized horses (often ponies by today's standards), native to the British Isles. Although both these breeds are now extinct, the modern counterparts of the Hobbies are Irish Connemara ponies, and of the Galloways, the British Fell pony. [Fig. 8-1] [Fig. 8-2] The Hobbies and Galloways were both laterally gaited horses; they paced, or ambled, instead of trotting, and their smooth gaits were always noted in their descriptions. Quite strong, they originally served as light cavalry mounts. Quick and agile, the two types were also used in racing in the sixteenth and seventeenth centuries and were considered extremely fast. Over the centuries, they had been bred with stallions from other parts of Europe, imported by English royalty to better the blood of English horses. As a result, by the seventeenth century these English horses already had genes from crosses with many types: Spanish Jennets, Barbs, Turks, and Italian coursers. Then in the seventeenth and early eighteenth centuries, it was these native English mares that were crossed (mated) with the "Oriental" stallions, which produced the new course-racing blood horse. [2]

Fig. 8-2 British Fell Pony

When first brought to the English colonies, these rather generic, hardy little British horses were sometimes crossed with offspring of horses that had been brought over by the Spanish. Later, after the 1740s, planters took their fastest Virginia mares and put them to the newly imported English racing stallions in an effort to improve the blood of the Virginia horse, thus (eventually) creating the American Thoroughbred. [3]

Even until the end of the eighteenth century, however, people still referred to some horses that they kept as Hobbies. In 1792, Thomas Jefferson inquired of John Syme about a horse, Romeo, which Syme owned and that might be for sale. Syme wrote back explaining that Romeo was one of a pair "that Mrs. Syme and the Girls are Very fond of, and who Carrys them to Richmond, Very Comodiously" and that the women were unwilling to part with the pair. Syme offered Jefferson the pick of some of his other horses, but not the "Hobby Horses of the Ladys." Because of their size and smooth ride, a "Hobbie" was not generally a work horse. At least among the gentry, Hobbies became associated with women riders and drivers. By then, gentlemen almost always rode the bigger, more prestigious blood horses. [4]

Recall that in another reference to Hobbies, Jefferson called his plans for founding the University of Virginia the "hobby" of his old age. When Jefferson used the word "hobby," he was playfully referencing the Irish Hobbies, these eighteenth-century easy-riding horses. "Hobby" in English already characterized a pastime done for pleasure, but Jefferson wrote about being "mounted on a hobby" with its "easy amble" to describe his designing and overseeing the construction of his University. So although we in the twenty-first century understand hobby to refer to an activity done for pleasure, usually during leisure time, or a hobby horse, a subject that one talks about all the time (if not a toy composed of a stick with a horse's head on it that a child pretends to ride), for Jefferson, the Hobby was the gentle and ambling or pacing mount, giving exercise to ladies and eighty-year-old men. [5]

Spanish horses: When the Spanish arrived on the continent of the Americas in 1519, there were no horses. So the Spanish, too, had shipped over mares and stallions of the various types that were native to the Iberian peninsula. The Spanish settlers' horses thrived first in the Caribbean Islands and later on the pampas and plains areas (that the Spanish colonized) in the Americas. The Spanish conquistadors and their soldiers brought two main types of horses to the Americas: the Spanish Horse, also known as Andalusians, which is the part of Spain from

Fig. 8-3 Andalusian horse performing flamenco in southern Spain

which they originated, and Spanish Barbs. Examples of the first type had already been exported to England and other parts of Europe in the late Middle Ages. [6]

Both the Andalusians and Barbs probably evolved from the earlier Spanish horse known as the Spanish Jennet, a short horse with an ambling gait. It was a compact and well-muscled saddle horse, with a reputation for a good disposition. The Jennet was an especially flashy horse, with a proud carriage, coming in all sorts of brilliant colors and patterns. [7]

The Andalusian horse was probably a mixture of the heavier European war horse and the lighter Spanish Jennet, already selected by monks in the south of Spain (Andalusia) to breed for the king's royal stud by 1400, and was specifically created by a royal decree of the Spanish king, Philip II, in 1567. [Fig. 8-3] Bred as a war horse, the Andalusians became utilized for classical dressage, and were exported all over Europe to be used in royal stud farms and palaces. Later, Arabian and Barb bloodlines were introduced to improve the breed. In Spain, besides being used for both riding and driving, Andalusians were also used as stock horses, especially with the Spanish bulls, and were the horses used in mounted bullfighting. A closed breed today, modern-day Andalusians have a short back and high-set arched neck, and measure between 15.11⁄2 to 16.2 hands. They have a convex profile (or Roman profile) in the face. Other characteristics are a long flowing mane and tail, a deep barrel, and heavy bones, giving them an air of strength and nobility. They, too, were taken to the Americas to be used in the conquest. Later stud farms in South America were set up to help promote this very athletic horse in the Spanish territories. [8]

The Spanish Barb supposedly resulted from the crossing of North African horses with horses native to the Spanish peninsula, after the Moorish invasion of 711. Current DNA results imply mutual influences back and forth across the Straits of Gibraltar between the horses from the north African Barbary Coast (the Barb) and the Iberian horses. Barbs were shorter than the Andalusians. Another horse with lateral gaits, many Barbs, too, crossed the Atlantic Ocean with the Spanish to conquer America. Contemporary gaited breeds in Spanish America are considered Spanish Barb descendants: the Argentinean criollo and the Paso Fino are two. More important for our story, the Spanish Barb is represented in the mustang, as well as the American Quarter Horse. They were especially hardy animal specimens and survived well under often harsh (often legendary) conditions. [9] [Fig. 8-4]

Fig. 8-4 A chestnut Paso Fino

Individuals from these two horse types eventually populated the plains of North America. By the end of the seventeenth century, some Native American groups had traded or stolen or inherited (from unsuccessful Spanish expeditions and settlements) small numbers of these horses directly from Spanish explorers. As noted earlier, numbers of them escaped later to become feral horses and reproduce in the wild, forming huge herds of horses that became known as mustangs (Chapter 7). It is questionable if any horses from sixteenth-century Spanish expeditions (De Soto, Ponce de Leon, Ayllón) on the East Coast of North America survived to be encountered and captured by the Native American groups. Currently, certain equine associations promote the idea that small remnants of feral horses that exist in isolation on some of the Outer Banks of North Carolina, the marshes of the Carolinas and Georgia, and in the cow country of Florida (now called Florida Crackers, but earlier called Chickasaws) are of Colonial Spanish heritage. [Fig 5] Samples of DNA are being tested to look for bloodline relationships with the early Spanish imported stock. [10]

Fig. 8-5 A Florida Cracker horse depicted by Frederick Remington, "Cracker Cowboy," from "Cracker Cowboys of Florida," *Harper's New Monthly Magazine* 91, no. 543 (August 1895)

Chickasaws: English colonists on the Atlantic Seaboard had a different understanding of how the Spanish horses became mixed with their own sturdy little Hobbies. Native American groups from the Southeast dedicated themselves to being the brokers of the Spanish horses and mustangs obtained from other groups beyond the Mississippi, such as the Caddo in Texas. The Chickasaw (one of the five "civilized" tribes from the Southeastern regions), as well as other groups like the Choctaw, obtained horses and bred their own herds to later sell or trade to the English settlers. In eighteenth-century Virginia, all these Indian-traded horses—small, strong, fit—became glossed as Chickasaws, which denoted their provenance. As to type, Chickasaws were similar to the Spanish Barb, short (about 13.2 hands), but well-muscled, and an all-around utility animal, known for their hardiness. Like their Barb ancestors and the

Fig. 8-6. Chickasaw horse, Orange County, Virginia

English Hobbies, Chickasaws were laterally gaited horses, and so were smooth-riding saddle horses. Their tractability and strength also made them good draft horses, for both the plow and wagon or carts. [Fig. 6] The Chickasaw became very popular with planters and others in the Southeastern colonies, but with cross-breeding, the true Chickasaw eventually began to disappear. [11]

When Jefferson referred to "my Chickasaws," he was referring to purpose more than breed of horse. Chickasaw came to signify a generic work horse, or plantation horse, in contrast to his saddle horses. Their hardiness and trustworthiness were characteristics of these horses. While president, Jefferson wrote his daughter about his arrangements for her upcoming visit to Washington and asked if her own carriage could bring her halfway. "I think my Chickasaws, if drove moderately, will bring you well that far." He told her that his overseer would know that she would want them and "could add a forth." He went on to add, "I think that by changing horses half way, you will come with more comfort." When Jefferson left Washington at the end of his presidency in March 1809, his overseer at the time brought up three wagons from Monticello to pack with Jefferson's things to return to Virginia: "two six mule teams loaded with boxes and the other four sorrel Chickasaw horses and a wagon loaded with shrubbery." [12]

Virginia Quarter Horse, or F.A.Q.R.H. (Famous American Quarter Running Horses): As described in another chapter, early Virginia colonists were passionate about racing, and they regularly pitted good sprinters against each other down villages' main streets or on quarter paths hewn through the forests. Selecting for speed, the Virginia colonists eventually created a type of horse known as the Virginia Quarter Horse, or F.A.Q.R.H. (Famous American Quarter Running Horses). [13]

It is generally accepted that the Virginia Quarter Horse is the ancestor of the American Quarter Horse, but ancestry of the Virginia Quarter Horse itself is less certain. Some contend that the Chickasaw, with its Barb extraction, is its true ancestor, while others believe that the blazingly fast Virginia Quarter Horses were crosses between many types: the Chickasaws (the offspring of Indian-traded Spanish Barbs), early Anglo-Irish Hobbies, and some early imported Thoroughbreds, specifically Janus and later Sir Archie. [14]

Janus (mentioned several times in previous chapters), a blooded horse, grandson of the Godolphin Arabian, was imported to Virginia in 1756 to sire long-distance racers. But crossed with local mares, he produced quarter racers. Descriptions of Janus's conformation always approximated the future American Quarter Horse rather than the tall Thoroughbreds being produced by other imported sires at that time: "a chestnut horse of low stature, about 14 hands ¾ of an inch high. Janus had great bone and muscle, round, very compact, large quarters and very swift." "Janus stamped his foals with speed over short distances, as well as the ability to pass that speed through successive generations. Compactness of form, strength and power" were the traits associated with the get and progeny of Janus. [15]

Whatever its extraction, the Virginia Quarter Horse was bred to race down quarter paths at breakneck speed. They were quick, tough, and hardy, serving both as saddle horses and racehorses on race days, and seemed especially suited to life on the frontier. These horses eventually moved west with the frontiersmen, then to Texas and out on the Great Plains, where they met up and crossed with mustangs (the feral descendants of the Spanish-introduced Barbs). There the Quarter Horse's athletic skills were translated into working with cattle.

Once the blooded Thoroughbred became the fashion among the gentry for racing and riding, the fleet Virginia Quarter Horse moved west to the frontier, and the other Virginia horses became mere "work horses."

Work Horses at Monticello

The difference between Jefferson's list of saddle horses, carriage horses, and broodmares and his lists of work horses could not be starker. The difference in status is clear. Beginning on the first page of the *Farm Book*, the first list of twenty-eight horses was of the blood horses. Most animals had a name, a physical description (height, color, distinguishing marks), sex, year foaled, the name of the previous owner, usually something about the animal's pedigree, and cost (and when the full price was due). After 1780, Jefferson did not continue his list of blooded horses in the *Farm Book* (perhaps because he had not left enough pages to continue expanding the list), but rather he jotted down the description of the horses he bought in his *Memorandum Book*. For example, for Tarquin, he wrote on March 11, 1790, in Alexandria: "Re'cd here Mr. W. Fitzhugh's horse Tarquin 9 or 10 yrs old, got by Eclipse out of Peyton Randolph's roan mare who was of blood of Monkey, Othello, Dabster. £75, Excels in 2. Mile heats 140 lbs." [16]

On the other hand, the lists of work horses are buried deep in his *Farm Book*, in the charts with the other livestock. The numbers of work horses, mules, steers and bulls, cows, ewes, lambs, shoats (young pigs), pigs, bacon hogs killed, "beeves" (cattle) killed were listed in columns by years (see lists below). The years 1781 and 1793–1797 are on page 33; the years 1809-1822 appear on page 132. In other words, these work horses were mere livestock. [17]

While all of Jefferson's riding horses had carefully assigned names, not one of the work horses had a name recorded anywhere. Probably the various workmen and slaves who cared for and used the horses on the quarter farms called them by names, but Jefferson might have been unaware of them. Occasionally a riding horse may have been demoted from saddle horse to carriage horse to farm horse. Perhaps this was the case with Arcturus, a horse Jefferson used as a saddle horse while president and later took to Monticello. In a letter to his overseer in 1806, Jefferson wrote:

> If Arcturus has not been exchanged to Mr. Smithson's mare, I wish him and the Chickasaw mare to be disposed of immediately. I think $150 might be expected of him, and $100 for her; but I would take a fair wagon horse or mule for either, rather than keep them. For Arcturus we ought certainly to get a first-rate wagon horse or mule. I would prefer a mule to a horse in both cases, provided they were large and docile.

In this note, Arcturus is equated with a Chickasaw mare and/or a mule! [18]

Likewise, a work horse may have been elevated to a carriage horse. Perhaps that was the case with the mare Hyatilda, which Jefferson thought could substitute for Bedford in the gig, a least temporarily after Bedford suddenly took sick and died. It was unheard of for Jefferson to use a mare to draw a carriage, but this was an emergency. In his letter to his grandson Jeff, he said Hyatilda would need a few days training to be able to go, and that he would put her with a horse he had at Tufton. [19]

Furthermore, Jefferson's riding horses' notations all had lengthy and involved physical descriptions of the animal, including the age, height, and distinguishing markings. For example, Peacemaker was a seven- or eight-year-old chestnut sorrel, got by Old Peacemaker out of Old Diomed, standing 5 feet, 2 inches tall, and bought from Fielding Lewis, costing $125. Peacemaker had two white left feet and a star on the forehead. Horse straying and horse thieveries were common in the eighteenth century, so an accurate description of an expensive animal was helpful in retrieving it. This was especially true before the advent of secure fencing. Hundreds of advertisements for strayed horses in the *Virginia Gazette* testified to this situation. Owners who paid for the ads included a detailed description of the horse and often offered a reward. [20] [Fig. 8]

STRAYED or STOLEN from *Richmond*, on *Sunday* the 22d of *April* laſt, a middle ſized black horſe, about 4 feet 7 inches high, with a hanging mane and bob tail, low in fleſh, has a mealy mouth, two ſaddle ſpots, and a ſmall ſtar in his forehead. Whoever brings the ſaid horſe to Mr. *Iſaiah Iſaacs*, ſilverſmith in *Richmond*, ſhall have [illegible]s. reward.

Fig. 8-7 A notice of a strayed horse, *Virginia Gazette*, May 24, 1770

By the end of the eighteenth century, the owners of the blooded horses were building substantial stables, not only to house and protect their animals from the elements but also to insure themselves from loss due to straying and thievery. On the other hand, Jefferson's work horses get minimal description, and no housing.

Beyond designating the sex of the work animal by the label "horse" (stallion) or "mare," only sometimes was the color mentioned. These undervalued, laboring creatures were often the ones stolen by runaway slaves. When Jefferson advertised for the "run away" Sandy (1769), he claimed that Sandy "took a white horse," covered in scars from the traces and harness from pulling carts. [21] [Fig. 12 in Ch. 3: see p. 115]

Whereas the precisely named and treasured Thoroughbreds (the blood horses) were all stabled at Monticello, in a stable built of logs after 1793 and in a stone stable after 1806, the work horses were divided out to the quarter farms and were kept where they worked (in fact, the lists are divvied up by farm: Tufton, Monticello, Lego, Poplar Forest). At night, the work horses may have been kept in the barns on each farm, where the machinery, tools, and the crops were stored and dried, or they may have been tethered nearby. The only true building dedicated to horses was the stable near the house at the top of the Mountain at Monticello. But tethering would have let the laborers collect and take advantage of the manure the animals produced. Allowing the work horses to roam freely in the woods was an inefficient way of resting the horses. Manure could not be collected, and one of the slaves would have had to go looking for the animal every day. At any rate, work horses needed grain supplement in their feed to keep them healthy. Jefferson counted on ten barrels a year of corn for "plough horses," much of which was not supplied by the Monticello fields and had to be bought. [22]

Price was another aspect that separated the blood horses from the work horses. The price of any animal was always duly noted, as well as to whom the payment must go (the seller). However, work horses were always much cheaper than blood horses. In June 1796, Jefferson paid £65 to John W. Eppes, his soon-to-be son-in-law, for a seven-year-old riding horse, Darlington, yet a few months later he paid Joshua Burras £11 for a "white horse" (no further description, no age). [23]

Price is almost all one needs to know as to whether the horse was a work horse or a saddle horse. For example, in 1810, Jefferson bought several work horses; he seemed to be stocking up his farms with work animals after his retirement from the presidency and return to the farm life of Monticello. In January, Jefferson bought a light bay plow horse from John Butler for $30 and a sorrel Chickasaw mare (eight years old) from the sheriff for £6–10. Later in June he bought a mare for $17.15 from Thomas Trevilian. However, the month before he bought the above-mentioned plow horse and sorrel Chickasaw mare, in December 1809, Jefferson had paid $250 to Richard Thweatt for a five-year-old bay horse, called Diomede, "out of imported Diomed, 4 ft. 11 in. high, left hind foot white." Diomede was one of Jefferson's four bay carriage horses and cost eight times more than the plow horse. [24]

Jefferson's breeding program for his blood horses had effectively stopped after 1782. The destruction of his herd by General Cornwallis at the end of the Revolutionary War, and Martha's death one year later, led Jefferson to leave Monticello for almost twelve years. He never again systematically engaged in breeding the blood horse, like so many of his contemporaries were doing. He did, however, maintain some mares on some of his farms for many years to help supply his work-horse needs. From 1794 to 1797 (when Jefferson was home at Monticello during his first retirement from public life), he listed three broodmares shared between Monticello and Tufton, two to four across the river at Shadwell and Lego, and three mares one year (1793) down at Poplar Forest. After Jefferson returned home from his own presidency in 1809 for his final retirement, he continued listing the numbers of his livestock until 1823, when his list stops. He recorded only two years (1811 and 1812) with (one and two) breeding mares at Monticello. No other property had breeding mares in its inventory of livestock. For each farm, workhorses show up on the inventory, but we no longer see any breeding mares. [25]

What kind of work did these horses do? Work horses were employed, along with oxen and mules, in plowing the fields. One of the innovations in the eighteenth-century agricultural revolution was the use of horses, instead of oxen, for plowing fields, encouraged by Jethro Tull in his 1731 book, *Horse-hoeing Husbandry*, a later edition of which Jefferson owned. Tull had perfected the seed drill and had made design improvements to the plow, as well as having invented a horse-drawn hoe, which purportedly helped control weeds. The use of the horse in the fields was considered a modern innovation. [26] [Fig. 8-8]

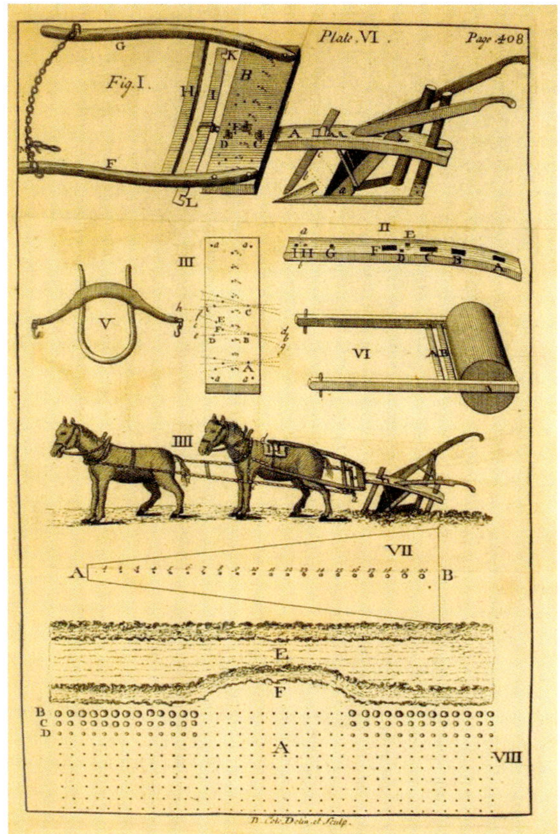

Fig. 8-8 Seed drill, 1762, from Jethro Tull, *The Horse-hoeing Husbandry* (fourth edition)

Horses also treaded the grain in the barns to help with the threshing. Barns were located in the fields where the wheat was harvested. Horses were driven round and round over the harvested wheat to "tread out" or trample on the wheat to break the grain off the straw and separate the wheat from the chaff. After the 1790s, Jefferson used a threshing machine. The horses were also hitched to all kinds of wagons and small carts for hauling, a never-ending task on the mountainside plantation. Building material—rock, timber, and earth—was hauled from lower lands near the river (many goods were delivered by river at Milton, a town several miles away on the Rivanna River). Horses hauled manure as well to be spread on the agricultural fields that were not near stables. Water, for stock, was hauled from the springs and from the river up to the house. [27]

Fig. 8-9 In Colonial Williamsburg, two young boys help their father load firewood into an ox cart.

The hauling was done with wagons or carts made completely of wood, including the wheels, on the premises at Monticello. [Fig. 8-9] Depending on the time of year, roads conditions could be deplorable. The main house at Monticello and the work space on Mulberry Row were up the mountain at an elevation of almost 900 feet. The approach was on

Fig. 8-10 A Shire draft horse

constantly eroding roads and trails. Some jobs were deemed better done by oxen, or later, mules. When the president retired to Monticello in 1809, the number of mules increased, as these animals were deemed more economical and hardier than the smallish work horse in Virginia. The large draft horse breeds that later came to define farm labor, such as the Shires, Percherons, Clydesdales, or Belgian drafts, were breeds invented later in the nineteenth century. [Fig. 8-10]

As mentioned, horses were not the only animals used to work in the fields and draw the carts. Work horses were often equated with those other animals: oxen and mules.

Draft Animals

During the eighteenth century in the colonies, much debate took place among farmers and planters as to the advantages and disadvantages of using oxen, mules, and horses for farm labor. Each animal had its partisans. Different aspects were weighed and argued against each other: animal strength and endurance, expense or cost (feed and maintenance), and speed under plow.

Oxen (steers): Thomas Jefferson's slaves used oxen to plow fields and pull wagons, along with the work horses. [Fig. 8-11] Oxen are castrated male cattle used as draft animals. Jefferson called them steers in his livestock lists and had several on each of his farms. He advised breaking the steers at three years old "so that when an ox is fatigued, you may have others to relieve him," adding, "This costs nothing as you feed oxen only when you work them." Citing the English agriculturalist Logan, Jefferson noted that "oxen should be fatted & killed at 10. Years old; not sooner." As he did with his horses and mules, Jefferson noted how many oxen it took to pull a heavy load: "4 oxen & a horse brings in a cart from Milton 28. Bundles of nailrod = 1568 lb." [28]

Fig. 8-11 Farmers plying historic trades at Colonial Williamsburg plow a field at Great Hopes Plantation using a team of oxen.

For much of the eighteenth century in agricultural and husbandry circles in England, the debate was over the advantages and disadvantages of using specifically oxen versus horses as the power source for wagons and plows. Formerly, horses had been few in number and had been used primarily for road transport and in warfare. This debate about horse power versus ox power was spelled out in the many books on agriculture and animal husbandry at the time.

Typical was the argument found in *The Gentleman Farmer: Being an Attempt to Improve Agriculture, by Subjecting It to the Test of Rational Principles*, by Henry Home, Lord Kames, first published in 1776. (Jefferson owned a 1799 edition.) Home was one of the leaders of the Scottish Enlightenment and a promoter of the agricultural revolution. Home insisted, "There is not in agriculture any other improvement that equals the using oxen instead of horses." According to Home, oxen were just as tractable as horses but less expensive. An ox required no oats or corn; in summer he existed on grass and in winter on hay. It was with the issue of fodder that the ox was proved the superior beast for farming. Furthermore, their dung supposedly made excellent manure. "Horse dung, on the contrary, burns where it falls." Additionally, the price for a work horse was double that of an ox. The horse needed more care (curried, combed, and rubbed); then there was the expense of shoeing; finally the horse had to be replaced every ten years while oxen "last for ever; or, which comes to the same, they can be sold to the butcher." [29]

For Home, the only reason to prefer a horse was the problem of bad roads. When roads were impassable for carts in winter, he said, produce could be carried to market on horseback. But since roads had improved (by 1776) in England, there was no longer the pretext of bad roads. Typical of these books, several pages of charts were included "shewing how much a farmer saves by employing oxen instead of horses." [30]

It was true that oxen could pull heavier loads for longer periods than a horse could. And oxen were especially useful in opening new, hard ground with the plow. What facilitated this was the use of the yoke, adapted as it was to the neck and shoulder of the ox. But their pace of plowing was extremely slow, only about 2 mph. On many farms, horses were still often hitched to loads with a breast collar, meaning they had to pull a load with their weaker front legs and could not compete with the strength of the ox. But when the horse collar finally came into generalized use, it allowed horses to push forward from behind with their strong hindquarters and begin to equal oxen in draft-load weight. At that point, horses were able to work about 50 percent faster than oxen and pull 50 percent heavier loads, which helped create more agricultural surplus. Jefferson stated his preference for a horse collar ("collar") over a breast collar ("breast plate)" in an 1801 letter to his Philadelphia carriage and harness maker, Enoch Edwards. [31]

Although oxen had been used for centuries by farmers, between 1800 and 1840 they almost completely disappeared from use and were substituted with the faster horse and new and improved plows. As noted above, the many editions of Jethro Tull's book *Horse-hoeing Husbandry* (1731) and his innovative seed drill and plow designs encouraged many farmers to switch from oxen to horses. [Fig. 8-12]

Fig. 8-12 Alan Slavick plowing with Noah, a Belgian gelding. From Lynn R. Miller, "Plowing with the Single Horse," *Small Farmer's Journal* website.

Around 1788, while in France, Jefferson himself had designed a plow, called the "moldboard plow of least resistance," which helped facilitate the substitution of horses or mules for oxen. The moldboard was the wooden part of the plow that lifted up and turned over the earth. Jefferson wanted to make a more efficient moldboard, so that the lifting and turning process encountered the least resistance possible. In 1794, Jefferson began using his plow with the moldboard made out of wood by his own workmen. By 1814, Jefferson had his plow cast in iron. He wrote to his friend Charles Wilson Peale that "the

Fig. 8-13 Jefferson's moldboard plow

plow was so light that the two small horses or mules draw it with less labor than I have ever seen before necessary. It does beautiful work and is approved by everyone." [32] [Fig. 8-13]

Mules: Although Jefferson continued using oxen for work on his farms throughout his lifetime, their numbers were few, usually just enough for two teams of two animals. He usually had a slightly higher number of work horses than oxen. However, the animal Jefferson came to value over both horses and oxen for farm labor was the mule. Before his presidency, Jefferson stocked his farms with two or three mules, but after the presidency (post-1809), he had about a dozen mules at Monticello and a couple on each of his quarter farms except Poplar Forest (see *Farm Book* pages above). In this practice, he was following the lead of one of his agricultural mentors, the first president, George Washington.

A mule is a cross between a male donkey (or jackass) and a female horse, a mare. Less common but possible is a hinny, which is a cross between a female donkey (a jenny) and a horse (stallion). Both these hybrid animals are usually infertile—they cannot reproduce among themselves. Mules and hinnies look a little like both parents: a donkey with the body of a horse. A mule has a big, heavy head, with long ears and a tail like an ass. It has small, fine-boned legs with small hooves. The hinny, on the other hand, has a smaller body, smaller head, shorter ears and fuller tail, although many experts find it hard to distinguish a mule from a hinny. Mules have been bred more frequently since Roman times because they are stronger and more robust than the hinny. [Fig. 8-14]

In the early years of the United States, George Washington played a pivotal role in promoting the use of mules in agriculture. Some have called him the Father of the American Mule. Washington used many oxen as well as horses on his farm at Mount Vernon, but after the Revolutionary War, he decided that he preferred mules to horses to work his lands because mules "were stronger, more sure-footed, ate less and had more endurance than a horse." They were perceived to be much more resistant to disease than horses. Faster than oxen, their speed under plow was 2.5 mph; not quite like the horse, but more sure-footed and having more stamina. Washington purportedly said, "Horses eat too much, work too little, and die too young." [33]

Although mules were not common in England, southern Europe and France had long traditions of using mules for labor and transportation. Spain had the most admirable mules at the time, using them to draw royal carriages and even for riding. However, such sought-after breeding stock was ferociously protected and not allowed outside the kingdom. Washington used his diplomatic influence to lift embargos so as to be able to import Spanish and later French donkeys in order to breed mules in the United States. The king of Spain, Charles III, upon learning of Washington's plans, and circumventing Spanish export laws, sent him two Andalusian jacks (males) and two jennets (females) as a gift in 1785. [34]

Only one jack made it to Mount Vernon alive. Washington named him Royal Gift and immediately prepared to breed his best mares to him. However, Royal Gift's journey seems to have taken the enthusiasm out of him. For many months he spurned the desirous harem of mares. Washington facetiously wrote of him, "too full of royalty to have anything to do with a plebeian

Fig. 8-14 A mule named Juancito, dubbed the "best mule of Argentina," on an excursion on the Mitre Peninsula, in Tierra del Fuego, Argentina, 2006

race. His late royal master, th' past his grand climacteric, cannot be less moved by female allurements than he is or when prompted, can proceed with more deliberation and majestic solemnity to the work of procreation." Eventually Royal Gift got around to business, and Washington sent him on a triumphant tour of the southern United States to improve the nation's stock of mules, collecting $10 stud fees from the mare owners, and helping to convince others to use mule power in the fields. [35]

A year later, the Marquis de Lafayette sent Washington a smaller Maltese jack, which also began to produce fine riding mules. This jack, called Knight of Malta, was smaller than Royal Gift (his ears only measured 12 inches to Royal Gift's fourteen) but he also did well in Virginia. Crossing these two lines, Washington achieved a jack called Compound that passed on the best of both lines.

In the following letter to Arthur Young, dated December 4, 1788, we can see Washington's plans for mule breeding in the United States:

> I have a prospect of introducing into this Country, a very excellent race of animals, by means of the liberality of the King of Spain. One of the Jacks which he was pleased to present to me (the other perished at sea) is about 15 hands high, his body and limbs very large in proportion to his height; and the Mules which I have had from him appear to be extremely well formed for Service. I have likewise a Jack and two Jennet from Malta, of very good size, which the Marquis de la Fayette sent to me. The Spanish Jack seems calculated to breed for heavy, slow draught; and the other for the saddle or lighter carriages. From these, altogether, I hope to secure a race of extra ordinary goodness, which will stock the country. Their longevity and cheap keeping will be circumstances much in their favor. I am convinced, from the little experiments I have made with ordinary Mules (which perform as much labor, with vastly less feeding than horses) that those of a superior quality will be of the best cattle we can employ for harness. And indeed, in a few years, I intend to drive no other in my carriage: having appropriated for the sole purpose of breeding them, upwards of 20 of my best mares. [36]

Within fifteen years, Washington had replaced many of his horses with mules. From an inventory of 130 horses in 1785, his estate listed only twenty-five by 1799 (at Washington's death). Washington even sold his prized high-bred stud, Magnolia, to Light Horse Harry Lee in 1788, saying, "I am willing to confirm the bargain because it is my intention to breed only mules only.... and I wish to avoid the expense of keeping Magnolia. He is in high health, spirits and flesh and can be delivered in good order." And breed mules he did. Fifteen years after the arrival of Royal Gift, Washington counted fifty-eight mules working the farms at Mount Vernon. [37]

As is well known, mules went on to become the preferred animal for field labor in the South by the nineteenth century and dominated in numbers over the work horse. Mules were used by the vast majority of Southern farmers, but became especially associated with African-American farmers, and the mule-Black farmer image was iconic of the South, of the poor South, until modern times. In general (saddle) horses symbolized authority and wealth, while mules symbolized low status. [38]

For Thomas Jefferson, using mule labor in the fields and for draft purposes was merely another rationalization of scientific agriculture. Jefferson hitched mules to draw heavily loaded wagons and carts long distances, between Monticello and Poplar Forest and between Washington (as president) and Monticello. Usually, the enslaved servants Tom or Phil Evans could transport heavy loads with just three mules (and Jefferson duly noted the approximate weight of the loads in his *Farm Book*). On the return from Washington in 1809, two six-mule teams of mules drew two wagons heavily laden with boxes and goods. Other times Jefferson might order one of his servants to ride a mule and ferry one of his saddle horses north to Philadelphia to exchange for a lame horse. [39]

Jefferson rode a mule once, on a trip over the Alps between France and Italy in April 1787, while on a private tour of the area when he was minister to France. A mule was necessary to scale the alpine peaks, since carriage travel was impossible due to lack of roads that high. However, in the United States one never found Jefferson mounted upon a mule. That mode of transportation was for enslaved people only—or perhaps for small children or young girls. Recall, for example, how one spring President Jefferson wrote his young granddaughter Ann Cary Randolph, asking her to go over to Monticello from

Edgehill, the nearby plantation where she and her family lived, to check on the damage the late frost might have done to Jefferson's peas and figs. He told her that she should mount Midas, a mule, to ride over to Monticello. There must have been horses at Edgehill, but Jefferson must have thought that a mule was safer and more appropriate for a girl. [40]

Jefferson bought his first mules long before Washington began his campaign to encourage mule use in the new United States. In 1773, Jefferson traded two horses, Cuthona and Aron-tyoony, for two mules from Colonel Thomas Mann Randolph. Randolph lived about fifty-five miles southeast of Jefferson at Tuckahoe on the James River, which was on Jefferson's way to Williamsburg or Richmond. He often stopped at the Randolphs' and traded or bought horses and mules. In the years 1780–1781, when Jefferson was governor of Virginia, but also a full-time planter, he bought a series of mules, all of which were named, and which commanded quite a price. He paid Colonel Randolph 2,000 pounds of tobacco for a three-year-old female, Doll Tweezer; he spent 2,000 pounds for a "horse mule" called Rigdumfunnidos from Samuel Miller; and two more three-year-olds, one a "horse mule", Dr. Slop, and one a "mare mule," called Capt. Molly, from James Cocke at 3,000 pounds of tobacco each.[41]

Jefferson was out of the country when Washington sent Royal Gift around the South to breed mules, but when Jefferson was back at Monticello trying to succeed as a planter, during his first retirement from 1794 to 1797, he paid the stud fee and sent seven mares to Thomas Walker's plantation at Castle Hill to breed with his jack (curiously, we don't see a rise in numbers of mules in the *Farm Book* lists for those years). This is the only indication that Jefferson experimented with breeding mules, despite a consistent pattern of buying adult mules from friends and neighbors in Albemarle or surrounding counties (including from Walker). Between 1806 and 1822, his retirement years, Jefferson bought nineteen more mules. Several of these came from traveling mule salesmen from Kentucky, already prime mule-breeding territory. In September 1822, he paid $300 to a William Simms from Kentucky for four mules of the Don Carlos breed. [42]

Mules were often about the same price as the work horses at Monticello, around $50 after 1800. Price seemed to vary by age and perhaps breed. And as with his horses, with each mule he bought, Jefferson made arrangements for payments to be due sixty days to six months to a year in the future. (See material about debt in Chapter 3.) Seemingly, mules were valuable enough that if one strayed, Jefferson was willing to pay tips to enslaved boys to track it down. On at least three occasions a tip ($1) to a young lad for bringing back a mule was carefully noted in the *Memorandum Book*. [43]

In 1857, Jefferson's longtime overseer, Edmund Bacon, was interviewed at length about life at Monticello. He spoke eloquently about Jefferson's fondness for horses. At one point in the interview, Bacon recounted a long story about a Monticello mule named old Dolphin. Bacon claimed that the mule must have been thirty to forty years old, and quite an ugly sight, with long, scraggly hair. He was too old to work, said Bacon, but they "did not like to kill him. . . . He was too old to jump much but he would tear down the fence with his nose and go over the plantation pretty much as he pleased." One time, an old woman was begging for corn meal around the farm, and in a flash of inspiration, Bacon connived to give the old woman the mule to go off to the Blue Ridge in search of corn. Sure enough, he got rid of the old woman and the old mule, and she never came back.

However, six weeks or so after the old woman had gone, Bacon "saw something moving about in the wheat field and, sure enough, there was Dolphin home again." A while later he convinced two Kentucky drovers to take Dolphin away so he wouldn't trouble them "no more." The drovers "sheared off his long hair and trimmed him up so that he looked quite well. They found one in the drove that matched him very well, and went on a few miles, and sold the pair to Hon. Hugh Nelson. He was a Congressman."

Bacon continued:

> It wasn't long before Dolphin was back and I told Mr. Jefferson. He laughed and said, 'you treat him so much better than anybody else will, that he will come back and see you.' When Mr. Nelson's overseer came over for him I asked him how old he supposed he was. He said he could not tell. I then told him his history. He took him off, and we never saw any more of Dolphin. [44]

Although never included in any livestock lists, some donkeys resided at Monticello. Two of Jefferson's great-granddaughters, children of Jefferson's grandson Thomas Jefferson Randolph, wrote down "Memories of what we heard from our parents," including several stories about two donkeys named Jack and Jenny. When their father was a little boy, the donkey Jack was sent off daily with Phil Evans (an enslaved boy) to bring the young Jeff home from school. At the schoolyard, all the schoolmates would sit on Jack's bare back and switch him with a stick until he took off running. When he tired, the donkey would dump the boys onto the ground and gallop home with all in pursuit. The more docile Jenny would be sent to the mill with a bag of corn to mill, grazing around till the meal was ground. Upon her return with Phil, the little donkey would go right into the kitchen to deliver her bag and stay there until she received her reward, a piece of cornbread. Nothing "would induce her to leave the kitchen 'till she got it." [45]

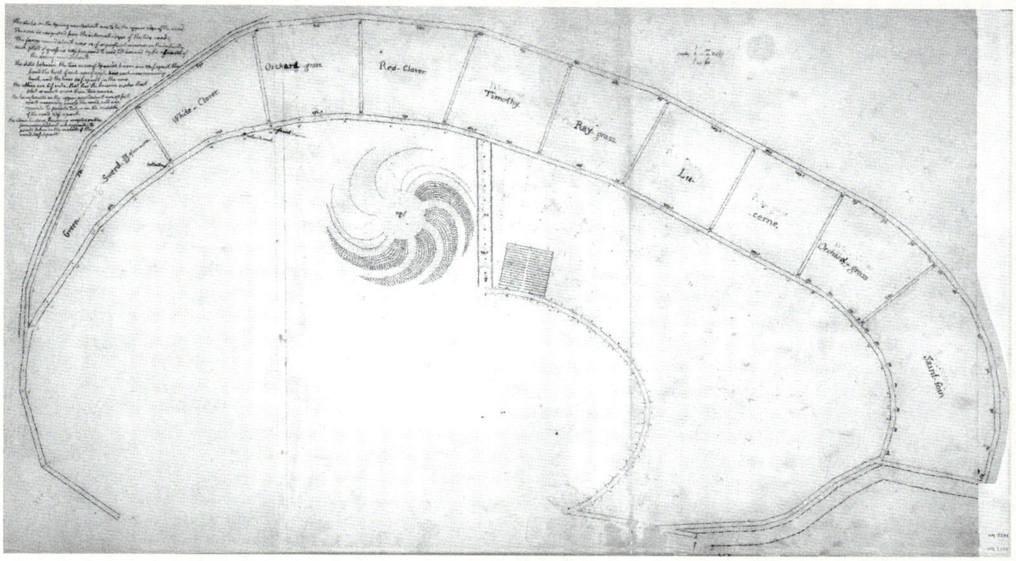

Fig. 8-15 Jefferson's drawing of his *ferme ornée* (ornamental farm), 1790s

Keeping Horses in the Eighteenth and Early Nineteenth Centuries

Horses were necessary work and transportation animals in rural Virginia, and consequently required that the farm or the plantation be adapted to their needs. All horses (both for work and pleasure) were included in the calculations in field planting for support of the farm (food), fencing, dung production, and the location and style of shelter. However, the blooded horses of the Virginia gentry put a special burden on their owners. They were high-maintenance objects, requiring shelter, food, water, care, training, and exercise. As prestige objects (rather than mere laborers), these blooded horses represented their owners in several symbolic ways, and so they had to be kept well fed and well housed and well dressed. Rather than helping the enslaved laborers in their work, enslaved stableboys were assigned to the exclusive care of these horses. Their stables matched the architectural quality of the owners' homes. These are vivid examples of how horses affected human culture as much as human culture affected horses.

Fields, Pastures, and Fences

Although horses can live on 100 percent field pasture if the grass and legumes are nutritious, Jefferson did not pasture his blood horses after 1794. Before the construction of stables at Monticello, Jefferson, like most farmers, let his animals run free in the fields and woods due to lack of fencing. [46]

Jefferson divided all of his plantations into several fields. The names of the fields varied from year to year. At Monticello there were seven to nine different named fields. Although one field, the Deer Park, was partly fenced and contained what Jefferson called "tamed deer," no field was dedicated as merely pasture for stock. Jefferson made two drawings for a *ferme orneé* (ornamental farm). [Fig. 8-15] One plan that he drew in the early 1790s had a field for mares and colts, and separate fields for wagon horses, Chickasaws (work horses), and cows. These small, two-acre fields (pastures) would have been across the road (east) from the stables and on either side of the Farm Road. There is no evidence that this plan was ever implemented. Certainly after a few months these pastures would have been paddocks, or dry lots (i.e., barren of grass). [47]

Building and maintaining fences posed another problem for pasturing horses. Except for the Deer Park, most of the fences up on the mountain were used to keep animals out rather than to keep animals in. For example, after 1804 the vegetable garden was enclosed by a paling fence, [Fig. 8-16] which was designed to keep rabbits out. Nor did Jefferson want animals in the flower gardens and on lawns around the house; in order to keep them off the lawns, he put up a post-and-chain fence and a ha-ha (a kind of sunken fence designed to keep animals out

Fig. 8-16 Paling fence around the vegetable garden at Monticello

of formal gardens, typical of the grand estates of England in the eighteenth century). [Fig. 8-17] There also was a "fence enclosing the top of the mountain at Monticello," and certainly there were gates, at least three from the Thoroughfare (main road from Milton to Charlottesville) to the house, according to Isaac (Granger) Jefferson, the enslaved servant in charge of opening them. The last gate was located at the corner of the stables, 300 yards from the house. Also, dry stone walls were built for enclosures. According to Home in the *Gentleman Farmer* (a book Jefferson owned), a dry-stone wall for horses "cannot be under five feet high"—which would have made it an expensive affair. Although, in 1796, a visitor to Monticello said that Jefferson did not "enclose his fields, and merely divided them by a single row of peach trees." Jefferson's *Farm Book* indicates that he divided some of his fields with wooden rail fences. Because he considered these a "great & perishable work," in the 1800s Jefferson began to plant " 'live fences,' consisting of thorn hedges," especially along the second roundabout. [48]

None of these fences was probably very secure for keeping horses and cows within. In fact, in the eighteenth century, most owners didn't put up fences for their stock. They simply allowed them to graze in the surrounding woods and fields.

Note Anburey's comment about the apparently wild stock that ran in the immense woods in Virginia beyond the reach of their owners. He said, "they have no proprietors, but those on whose lands they are found":

> Most persons who are in possession of any considerable plantation, have what is called a right in the woods, by which they are entitled to a certain proportion of the ewe cattle that run wild, which they can dispose of, or transfer as affixed property; there is no other criterion to ascertain them but by branding, or putting some mark on them; each person differs in this, and they are recorded in the county court, such property is further secured by an act of the assembly, which made it felony, to alter or deface marks. [49]

Jefferson himself referred to this practice when he was in France. He wrote that in America "the inhabitants let their horses go at large in the unenclosed lands … It is therefore easy to steal them & easy to escape." It is not clear if Jefferson branded his animals, but George Washington branded his cows with "G.W.," and the location on the animal indicated on which of his five farms the animal was raised. [50]

Fig. 8-17 Ha-ha fence at Bremo, John Hartwell Cocke's plantation in Fluvanna County, Virginia

Probably due in part to letting the animals run free, horse stealing was quite common.

One of the most common ads in the *Virginia Gazette*, even more evident than announcements of runaway slaves, was for "strayed" horses and other stock. Rewards were offered. In 1780, Thomas Mann Randolph of Tuckahoe offered a reward of $100 for the return of a "blood mare heavy with foal" stolen from his pasture at Dover in Goochland, adding that "there has been 20 valuable horses stolen out of this neighborhood within a few months past." [51]

Advertisements for animals "taken up" (caught and found) by persons obviously hoping for the reward were also common in the broadsheets of the day. The lack of fencing and the consequent straying and taking up of horses may have been one reason Jefferson wrote down detailed descriptions of his horses in his account books or *Farm Book* when he acquired them. This enabled him to claim the horse by its description if it was taken up and advertised by a neighbor or wayside travelers. Jefferson noted many details: age, color, markings, height, price, as well as provenance. However, most of these described horses were also the named blood horses he kept in stables (see below), probably, among other reasons, to avoid their straying. [52] [Fig. 8-18]

The lack of fencing is also indicated in the comment by the Rev. Hugh Jones in 1722, about how ordinary Virginians would spend more time "ranging several Miles in the Woods" to find their horses than they would riding to their destination. Ranging several miles on foot to find a horse seemed to be the norm (if the horse was not stabled). [53]

One consequence of animals loose in the wild (rather than fenced) was that they destroyed crops. For example, Jefferson described the tragic destruction of the three-year-old vineyards planted by his friend and vintner, the Italian Philip Mazzei, at nearby Colle in 1779. Jefferson had worked for years trying to establish vine cuttings and saplings for wine production in Virginia. When Philip Mazzei became his neighbor (buying 400 acres of adjoining land), Mazzei brought over workers and vines from Italy. During the Revolutionary War, while serving the state of Virginia as their agent in Europe, Mazzei rented his home to General Riedesel, an imprisoned Hessian cavalry general, and the commanding officer of captured Hessian troops (fighting for the English), who had been sent to Charlottesville (from the Saratoga, New York campaign) as prisoners of war. Rather than bivouac with his troops, Riedesel was offered Mazzei's more refined situation. Riedesel and his vivacious wife became frequent visitors at Monticello, but Jefferson lamented that "within a week" General Riedesel's horses had "destroyed the whole labor of three or four years" as they used the vineyards for forage. The vineyards fell to ruin, and all Jefferson's and Mazzei's efforts were for naught, owing to the ranging horses. [54] [Fig. 8-19]

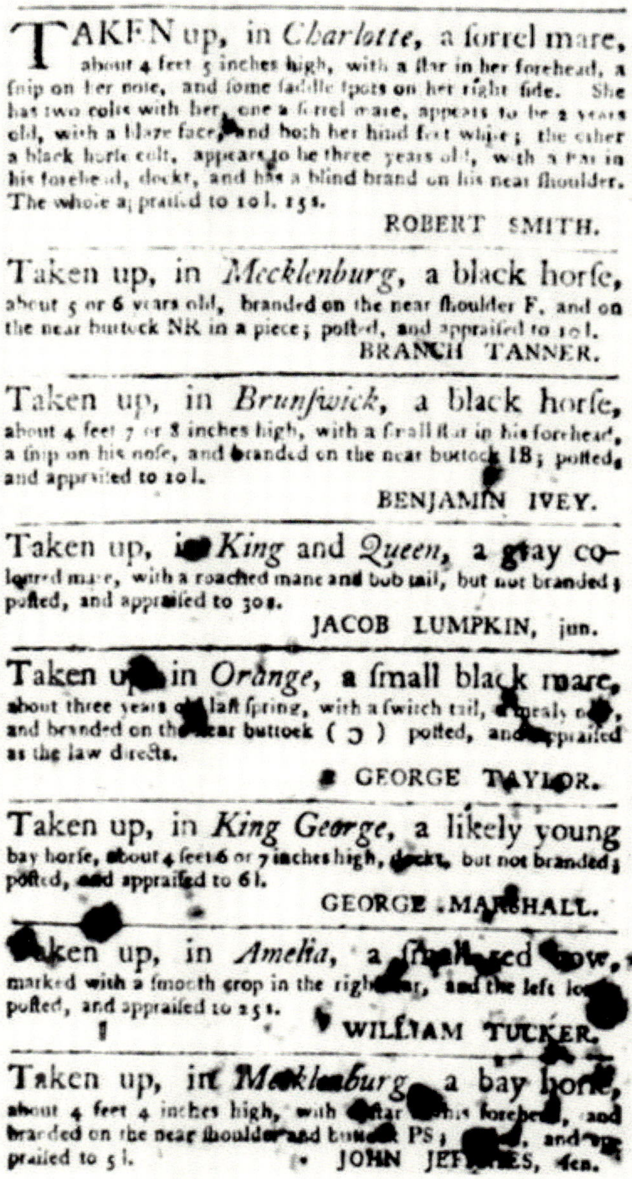

TAKEN up, in *Charlotte*, a ſorrel mare, about 4 feet 5 inches high, with a ſtar in her forehead, a ſnip on her noſe, and ſome ſaddle ſpots on her right ſide. She has two colts with her, one a ſorrel mare, appears to be 2 years old, with a blaze face, and both her hind feet white; the other a black horſe colt, appears to be three years old, with a ſtar in his forehead, docked, and has a blind brand on his near ſhoulder. The whole appraiſed to 10 l. 15 s.
ROBERT SMITH.

Taken up, in *Mecklenburg*, a black horſe, about 5 or 6 years old, branded on the near ſhoulder F, and on the near buttock NR in a piece; poſted, and appraiſed to 10 l.
BRANCH TANNER.

Taken up, in *Brunſwick*, a black horſe, about 4 feet 7 or 8 inches high, with a ſmall ſtar in his forehead, a ſnip on his noſe, and branded on the near buttock IB; poſted, and appraiſed to 10 l.
BENJAMIN IVEY.

Taken up, in *King* and *Queen*, a gray coloured mare, with a roached mane and bob tail, but not branded; poſted, and appraiſed to 30 s.
JACOB LUMPKIN, jun.

Taken up, in *Orange*, a ſmall black mare, about three years old laſt ſpring, with a ſwitch tail, [illegible], and branded on the near buttock (ɔ) poſted, and appraiſed as the law directs.
GEORGE TAYLOR.

Taken up, in *King George*, a likely young bay horſe, about 4 feet 6 or 7 inches high, docked, but not branded; poſted, and appraiſed to 6 l.
GEORGE MARSHALL.

Taken up, in *Amelia*, a [illegible] ſow, marked with a ſmooth crop in the right ear, and the left [illegible] poſted, and appraiſed to 25 s.
WILLIAM TUCKER.

Taken up, in *Mecklenburg*, a bay horſe, about 4 feet 4 inches high, with a ſtar in his forehead, and branded on the near ſhoulder and buttock PS; [illegible], and appraiſed to 5 l.
JOHN JEFFRIES, ſen.

Fig. 8-18 Ads for found ("taken up") horses, *Virginia Gazette*, May 24, 1770, p. 4

Stables (and Barns)

After 1794, most evidence indicates that Jefferson kept his riding and carriage horses in stalls in his stables. His workhorses were probably kept in or near the barns in the fields where they were used for work (plowing, drawing, and threshing) (brood mares may have been pastured—at least at Elkhill in the 1770s, and maybe at Monticello later, too). Today most pleasure horses are pastured full time (with run-ins, or sheds for shelter) or let out to pasture during the day, and put in a stall at night. Only highly bred racehorses and other performers (jumpers and some dressage horses) are kept in stalls at all times—usually to avoid accidents. A stabled horse requires daily exercise or work, along

Fig. 8-19 Vineyards at Colle, in Albemarle County, Virginia

with feed and water. So it may seem strange in the eighteenth century, in rural and lush Albemarle County, that Jefferson stabled his horses, but this was typical for blooded horses. The advantages of stabling a horse are many. [55]

For example, equine historians Raber and Tucker explain:

> A pastured horse requires more than an acre to sustain its nutritional needs. A horse that does not wish to be caught and that has a large space at its disposal can evade the person trying to catch it almost indefinitely, so simply getting one's hands on a pastured horse can be very time-consuming. A horse kept outside always is far dirtier than its stabled counterpart, thus requiring substantial grooming time before it is ready to be used. During the winter months, grooming time is increased by the fact that the horse grows a long, shaggy, greasy coat in order to protect it from the cold and the wet. A horse with a heavy winter coat sweats profusely when worked, so even on an ideal winter day, when the horse has refrained from festooning itself with mud, grooming the dried sweat from the previous day's work out of the horse's long coat requires a substantial amount of additional time and effort. Finally, in cold weather the horse kept outside requires special care after being worked. If the horse is not walked until its sweat has dried completely—called "cooling out"—but is returned to its pasture while still hot and sweating in cold, wet, or windy weather, the chances that it will get sick are quite good. [56]

The main disadvantage of stabling a horse is procuring feed and water, which in fields they can get for themselves for the most part. By the late eighteenth century, books on husbandry advised keeping horses in barns:

> In the first summer, they (colts) may be permitted to run with the mare till Michaelmas, or longer, if the weather continues mild. They should then be weaned, and kept in a stable, with a low rack and manger for their hay and oats.... Colts should be carefully kept from wet and cold; as they are extremely tender, and would be greatly injured by either. During fine weather, however, they may be allowed to pass an hoar [*sic*] or two in the open air, when they should be conducted to the stable. By this treatment, they will acquire a habit of docility. [57]

Jefferson's Stables: An eighteenth-century foreign observer said Virginia agriculturalists built their barns to shelter their crops, not their livestock. "Even then, however, Virginia took rightful pride in her hunters, carriage horses, and racehorses, and stabled them with appropriate care." Most historians insist that a "proper stable was an indispensable building within the Gentleman Farmer's estate." The gentleman's horses were used for transportation and leisurely sporting activities, so a stable helped to keep the horse healthy in a clean and comfortable environment. Moreover, a stable, as a significant building in the estate landscape, would also advertise the gentleman's social status: that he was housing blooded horses. [58]

Most of Jefferson's blooded horses lived in stables, at least in cities and, after 1790, at Monticello. Before that date, there is no record of a building to stable horses on the Mountain at Monticello. Perhaps Jefferson's riding horses were kept with the work horses in barns at the various plantations below. My own horse is kept outside twenty-four hours a day but, as noted above, Jefferson did not designate pastures for horses (although he had cattle, sheep, and deer at Monticello, and the deer, for example, were kept in fenced enclosures). If horses were kept mainly inside (which was the advice of the many *Pocket Farriers* and animal husbandry books of the epoch), they had to be fed 50 percent of their diet in hay, plus some other feed (corn, oats), and, of course, watered.

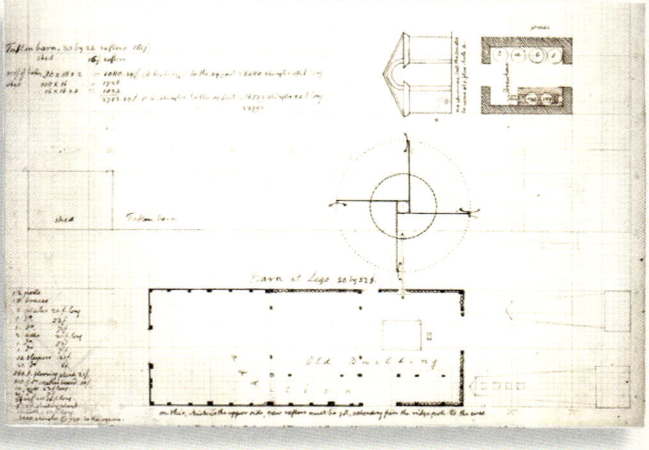

Fig. 8-20 Tufton and Lego barn plan, 1810–1814

As an architect, Jefferson did not ignore the dependencies (called offices) on his plantations. Each of his plantations in Albemarle County had a stable, and/or barn, for storing harvests, machinery, threshing, and work animals. [Fig. 8-20] One crop, tobacco, had its own barns for drying, located near the fields where the crop was grown.

Jefferson's earliest plans for Monticello (1768–1772) included stables under the North Terrace, according to dated drawings. Yet, work on the offices under the North Terrace did not begin until 1803. In fact, no stables (buildings) at Monticello were recorded until 1793. First discussed in letters in 1790 with his overseers, three log buildings equipped with wooden racks and feeding troughs were constructed at the end of Mulberry Row just before Jefferson returned from Philadelphia in 1794. Log stables were common at the time [Fig. 8-21] (although George Washington had stone stables by then at Mount Vernon) and were even recommended by the various contemporary husbandry books. [59]

Later, in 1806, during Jefferson's presidency, the three log stables were enlarged, underwent masonry work, and became the three stone stables (surveyed in 1806), completed by 1809. Eventually, at least on the paper of a survey, these stables appear first as one long building, "105. Feet long and 12. F. wide, one story high," then as a single (backward) L-shaped building, re: 1809 surveys [Fig. 8-22]. It is unclear if the short end of the L that leads away from Mulberry Row (south) is an enclosed addition or merely an open shed added on to the stone building. [60]

There exists a pre-1927 photo of the stone stable, which is the Jeffersonian-era building. The view in the picture is from the vantage point of Mulberry Row and we cannot see the short

Fig. 8-21 Log shed at Edgewood Farm, Clover, Halifax County, Virginia, 1886

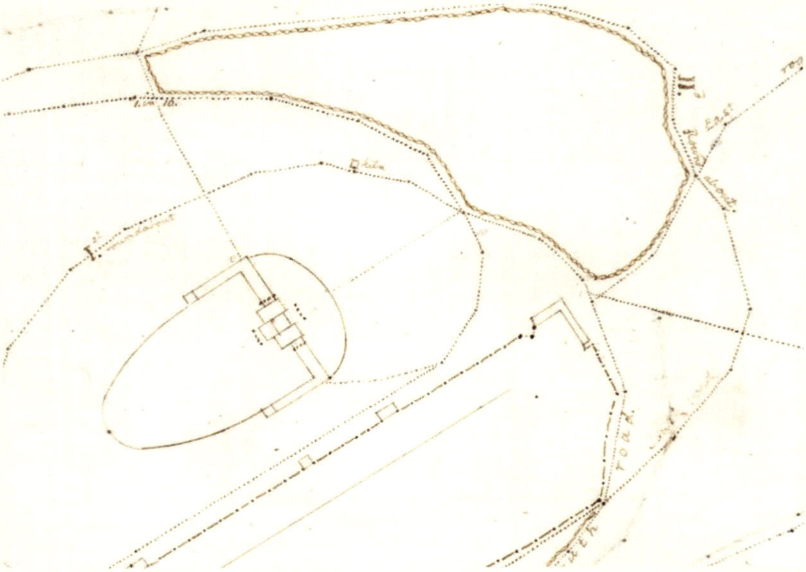

Fig. 8-22 An 1809 Monticello mountaintop plat

side of the L. [Fig. 8-23] In August 1927, a cyclone (tornado) hit the mountain top and badly damaged the Jeffersonian-era stable, taking the roof off the building. Many trees on the mountain also came down. The building was restored in the 1930s with a very different footprint from the pre-1927 photo [Fig. 8-24]. The short end of the L was gone, and the long stone side of the stable on Mulberry Row was shorter. However, at least two of the stone structures (connected by wood siding near the roof line) remained visible. What the interior of the building originally looked like, how many stalls there were for example, or their size, is unknown, because the interior fittings have been lost. Two interior stone walls divided the building in three equal parts. That building (and the 1927 building) was 15½ feet wide (vs. Jefferson's annotation of 12 feet). And the stone foundation was 43½ feet long (vs. Jefferson's 105-foot-long building).

Other Virginia masonry stables (of either stone or brick) of the era show some similarities to the Monticello stables. The brick stables at George Washington's Mount Vernon, built in 1782, are still standing, as are the stables at Shirley Plantation (1740) along the James River, and the coach house at Mount Airy (1758), the Tayloe estate in Richmond County on the Northern Neck. Those eighteenth-century stables in Virginia share a similar tripartite design and follow the dictates of books on animal husbandry of the time. *The Complete Farmer*, published in London in 1769, describes stables that represent state-of-the-art conditions for cleanliness, drainage, ventilation, light, and manure collection. The above-mentioned buildings were rectangular, one- and one-half-story structures with the interior divided into three parts, with a centralized carriage room between two stall rooms, all divided by masonry walls. This created a row of three independent rooms accessible by three doors on the long lateral side of the building. [61]

At Mount Vernon, the stall rooms on either side of the coach room have single doors, while the coach room has double doors. [Fig. 8-25] The stall rooms have several stalls on either side of a central passage. [Fig. 8-26] Windows on the stables at Mount Vernon on the north and east side had louvers for shade as well as for ventilation. The half-story loft above was used to store hay and other feed, with gabled louvered windows for ventilation for the hay. The roofs of all three buildings mentioned above are supported by timber frames, although at Mount Airy the end walls of the loft were also made of timber framing. Some

Fig. 8-23 Stables at Monticello, pre-1927 view

Fig. 8-24 Stables from the back, post-1927 restoration

have closed or open-air sheds attached to the rear of the building.

The placement of eighteenth-century and early-nineteenth-century stables in relation to the central house was often influenced by Renaissance architect Andrea Palladio's *Four Books of Architecture*, which recommended that a stable be located "not too near the master's house ... nor so far off as to be out of sight." The location of the stable had to be convenient to the main house to allow quick access to the horses, yet at a suitable distance so as avoid the animal odors and wastes. [62]

Fig. 8-25 Mount Vernon stables

Jefferson's stone stables exhibit all the above-described characteristics. By 1806, Jefferson had joined his three log stables into a single long masonry building, whose doors were all on the south side of the building (i.e., not along Mulberry Row). The L shape could have been an open shed, like at the back of Washington's stables. The 1927 photo of the Monticello stables shows a second story loft made of wood framing with ventilating windows. The windows conserved in the 1930s reconstruction are the Jeffersonian half-moon type. Jefferson had louvered Venetian blinds in the main house. The stables at Bremo, perhaps influenced by Jefferson, also have louvered windows for ventilation and shade.

In the eighteenth century, stalls were generally small. The horses faced forward and were tied to a ring near the manger. [Fig. 8-27; Fig. 8-28] Box stalls as we know them today (large roomy squares—10 feet by 12 feet—allowing the horse to move around freely in the stall), with a window to the outside, were rare in the eighteenth and early nineteenth century. [63]

In the 1790s, Jefferson visited Governor Penn's stables near Philadelphia, where he took notes on the measurements and accessories of his forward-facing horse stalls. [Fig. 8-29] Jefferson especially noted the nifty hay rack, and slope of the oak floor away from the manger (to carry urine away from the horses' feet). On another page in his notebook, Jefferson commented that he liked Morris's stables better for the light the stall divisions afforded. In his building notebook, he has more notes on the height and rise of the floor under the manger. In 1792, for his first log stable at Monticello he ordered a wooden floor to be built, "& sleepers should be laid so that the end of the slab under the manger may be couple of inches higher than that at the front." [64]

Overseer Bacon claimed that during his years at Monticello, there were thirty-six stalls for horses, although they used only ten of them. Jeff Randolph, Jefferson's grandson, denied there were

Fig. 8-26 Interior of Mt. Vernon stables

Fig. 8-27 James Seymour, *The stables and two famous running horses, belonging to his Grace, the Duke of Bolton*, 1747

Fig. 8-28 Hook, or ring, where horses were tied in the stall, at Bremo

thirty-six stalls, saying there were only about fifteen. But Jeff wanted to deny any extravagance and pretentious consumption on the part of his grandfather (i.e., the implication that the elderly Jefferson, who died deeply in debt, maintained thirty-six horses). It can be assumed that the overseer, a man keenly interested in horses himself, knew exactly how many stalls there were in the several barns of the various quarter-farms of Monticello, at least until he left in 1822. In fact, there was a stable near Bacon's cabin that he may have included in his count (since guest horses were sometimes housed there). Jeff Randolph, who began managing the quarter farms after 1817, may have been referring to the number of stalls towards the very end of Jefferson's life in 1826.[65]

Thus, a question arises about the North Terrace of Monticello. Besides the stone building called a stable at the end of Mulberry Row, were there also stables under the North Terrace of the house? The offices under the North Terrace were not built until 1803 [Fig. 8-30]. During this time, Jefferson was president and only visited Monticello a couple times a year, when he could escape Washington. By the 1930s, the offices under the North Terrace no longer existed. In 1938–1939, the Thomas Jefferson Memorial Foundation undertook a reconstruction of the offices, and modeled them according to early Jefferson plans and drawings. Twelve horse stalls were reconstructed there, using the stables and stalls at Bremo as models. Bremo was a plantation twenty-four miles south of Monticello, in Fluvanna County, belonging to Jefferson's good friend and frequent visitor, John Hartwell Cocke. Some evidence suggests that Bremo was designed (in 1817) with Jefferson influence—the main house is Palladian—and was constructed by Jefferson's master builder, John Nielson.

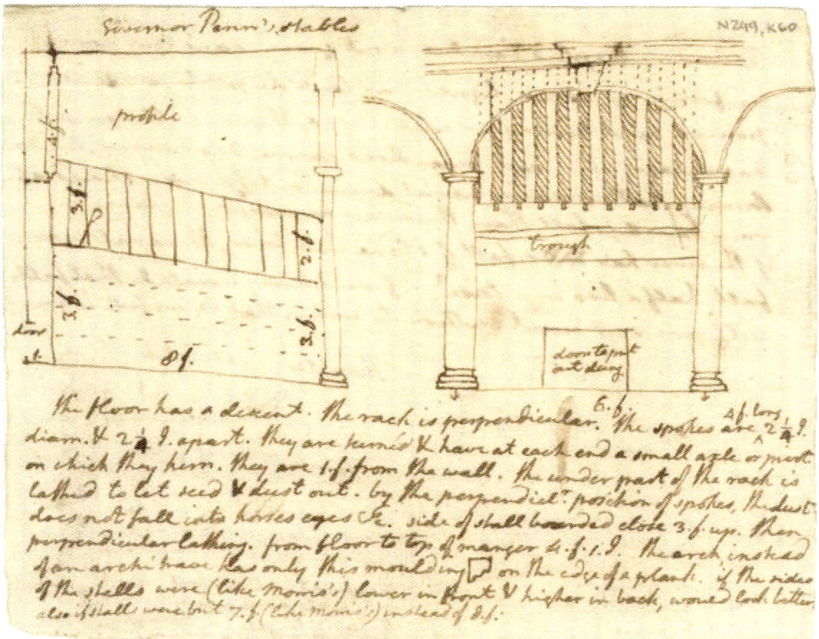

Fig. 8-29 Jefferson's 1778 notes on Governor Penn's stable measurements, in Philadelphia

In the 1930s, the interior of the stables at Bremo was photographed and measured [Fig. 8-31] in order to be replicated under the North Terrace at Monticello. Black-and-white photographs from 1937 show the interior of the Bremo stable in poor and somewhat dilapidated condition. [Fig. 8-32 a, b] Besides the photographs, drawings were made at the time and measurements recorded on these drawings. In the photographs, there were no longer any divisions (walls) between the stalls, but wall fittings indicate the width of each forward-facing stall. Measurements taken then show the stalls to be 5 feet (60 inches) wide and indicate a stall depth of 7 feet (84 inches). The floor plan shows eight stalls on either side of an interior passage, with four stalls on either side of a gateway allowing passage to the other side of the building. [Fig. 8-33]

In 2008, the conditions on the inside of the Bremo stable were almost exactly similar to those in the 1937 photographs. [Fig. 8-34] Measurements confirmed the width between the centers of the remaining fittings (i.e., a single stall width) to be 60 inches. The only hint of stall depth was at one end, where what would have been the right-hand side of a forward-facing stall had a feed room on the other side. The feed-room wall was interrupted with a post with hinges for an entry door (to the feed room). The stall depth to the hinge was 6 feet, 8.5 inches (80.5 inches). [Fig. 8-35]. With the door closed, however, the side of the stall would have been longer. If the 1937 depth measurements are correct, a 5-by-7-foot (60 inches by 84 inches) stall is rather small. [66]

Fig. 8-30 A view of the North Terrace at Monticello shows Ice House, Feed Room, Stables, Coach House, Wash House, and Promenade above. Charlottesville, Virginia, c. 1907–1914.

Fig. 8-31 The stables at Bremo

Yet stalls under the North Terrace at Monticello were even smaller. [Fig. 8-36] My 2008 measurements at Monticello's reconstructed stall under the North Terrace showed a stall that is 52 inches wide and 78 inches deep. *The Gentleman's New Pocket Companion*, an influential horseman's book in the nineteenth century, suggests that a stall should be wide enough— 4.5 to 5 feet (55 inches to 60 inches) wide—so that a horse can

Fig. 8-32 a & b 1937, Grigg photos from inside Bremo stables, 1937

lie down when it needs to. Others say stalls should be at least 6 feet wide (72 inches) (again, so a horse can lie down and stretch its legs). Governor Penn's measurements were 6 feet (72 inches) by 8 feet (96 inches). Why would Jefferson's stalls be so small? Several of Jefferson's horses during these years were 15½ to 16 hands high, which are relatively big and long horses. Could these big horses lie down in a stall only 52 inches wide? Was Jefferson

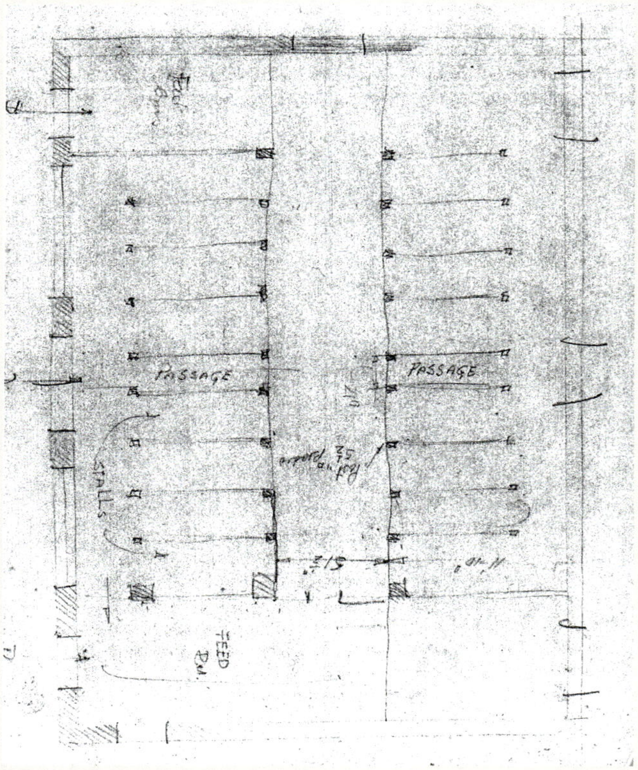

Fig. 8-33 Floor plan, Bremo stables

stuck with this limited space, or were the re-constructionists of the 1930s stuck with this space? Is the re-construction accurate? Were there twelve stalls there? And was the lower part of the North Terrace the main stable for Jefferson's horses? [67]

Various bits of evidence provide clues to an answer. In a March 19, 1802, letter to James Dinsmore, Jefferson said "but as the Northeast building is chiefly for coach houses, the floor must be sunk 9 feet deep below the bottom of the plate to let a coach go under it." Furthermore, an undated Jefferson notebook page, N540, not discovered until the 1940s, lists the number of cells (or partitions) needed under the North Terrace for his carriages and "stranger's carriages" and horses. Given the carriages Jefferson lists, this manuscript most likely dated from the second half of his presidency (because those were the carriages he owned then). Jefferson says there are to be nine cells. In 2000, Monticello's then senior architectural historian, Bill Beiswanger, suggested the following possible partitions under the North Terrace diagrammed in Figure 8-37. (Chariot; Double Phaeton; Single Phaeton; Gig and Sulky; Strangers' Carriages; Strangers' Carriages, Horses, Horses, Storeroom.) [68] [Fig. 8-37]

Another piece of evidence that this space was used primarily for coach houses (and not stables) is a Jefferson note to James Leitch discussing locks needed for various coach rooms, saddle rooms, and stable spaces, which again total nine spaces. Finally, granddaughter Cornelia Jefferson Randolph drew a plan of Monticello after Jefferson's death. She labels the North Terrace:

Fig. 8-34 Interior of Bremo stables, 2008

Fig. 8-35 Stall depth of Bremo stables in 2008—60 inches by 84 inches

Fig. 8-36 Monticello stalls - 52 inches wide and 78 inches deep

"under this terrace carriage house and Ice house." Other family members also differentiate between the stables and coach houses. [69] [Fig. 8-38]

With all of these references, it is possible to conclude that the space under the North Terrace, when it was finally realized in 1803, was dedicated to coaches and vehicles, with perhaps room to stable two to four horses temporarily (guest horses, probably guest coach horses). Although several of the estates described above had a coach room in the center portion of their stable, they also had separate coach houses (Mount Vernon and Mount Airy, for example). As these gentry farmers and planters obtained more and different kinds of coaches, they needed housing for the several vehicles. They also needed housing for their guests' coaches, all of which necessitated additional separate coach houses. [70]

It should be noted that when Jefferson lived in cities, his houses sometimes had their own stable attached, for example, in Paris and in Philadelphia (in the 1790s). Later, as president, Jefferson lived in the president's house in Washington, DC (now known as the White House). At the time the president's house was still under construction. Jefferson had been intimately involved in designing the new city, as well as the White House grounds and dependencies. Jefferson designed and oversaw the building of the original White House terraces, where the stables and coach rooms were located, all of which were burned by the British in 1814. [71]

In other towns, for example in Williamsburg as a student, young Jefferson must have boarded his horse at an outlying farm (there were advertisements in the *Virginia Gazette* for these boarding fields), since a tavern with stable accommodations would have been prohibitively expensive. Jefferson rode a horse back and forth from his mother's home in Shadwell to Williamsburg, but he would not have needed his horse daily in the town itself, since every place in the small capital city was within walking distance.

The architectural plans for the University of Virginia did not include measurements or drawings for horse stables on the plan for the buildings on the Lawn.

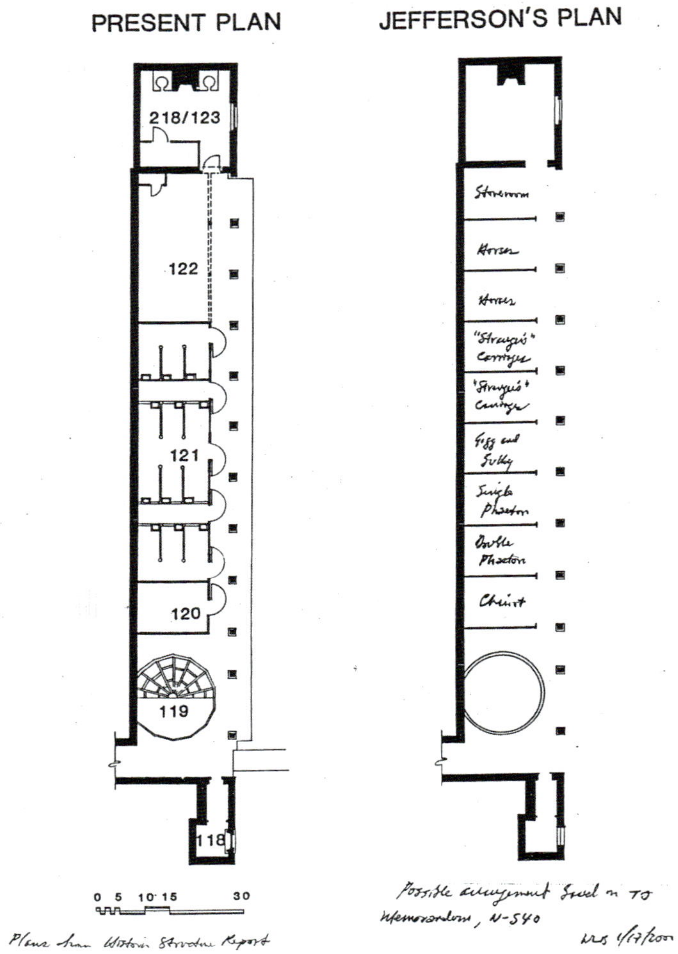

Fig. 8-37 A 1995 comparison by William Beiswanger (at the time, director of restoration at Monticello) of the then current configuration of cells and coach rooms along the east terrace versus Beiswanger's interpretation of Jefferson's handwritten plans only discovered in the 1940s

However, Jefferson wrote of his intention to build stables across the street at the end of the East Range and West Range, with "their front exactly in the range of the line of the future Hotels &c. on the opposite sides of East & West streets." The stables had to be moved about fifty or sixty yards from where originally planned due to the ground falling off in an "unfavorable" way. Arthur Brockenbrough, the first proctor of the University, said the brick work for the stables was begun around June 27, 1825. These stables were for boarding the horses of faculty and staff only. Hacks and other carriages were not to be allowed on the precincts of the Lawn itself. Three other stable buildings were evidently added at the end of the West Range by 1826. [Fig. 8-39] Although the two stables at the end of the Ranges were built of brick, they had apparently been torn down by 1866, as they do not appear on surveys after that date. [72]

Poplar Forest, [Fig. 8-40] Jefferson's octagonal-shaped retreat 100 miles to the south of Monticello, in Bedford County, also had a stable, probably of log construction, to house Jefferson's horses when he was there. The stable was most likely in proximity to the garden and dung pile, since those three things mutually influence each other.

Other examples of eighteenth-century stables are the reconstructions at Colonial Williamsburg. However, officials at Colonial Williamsburg contacted Monticello before reconstructing the stables at the Governor's Palace, [Fig. 8-41], as well as those at the George Wythe House. [Fig. 42] This implies that Colonial Williamsburg officials, perhaps without realizing it, were copying the Bremo-inspired reconstructions at Monticello. Possibly the only extant early-nineteenth-century stable in Virginia is at Ravensworth, constructed in 1805. [Fig. 8-43] Ravensworth mansion was built by William Fitzhugh of Chatham. But the stable was designed by Dr. Thornton in 1805, and Ravensworth was owned then by Bolling Lee. [73]

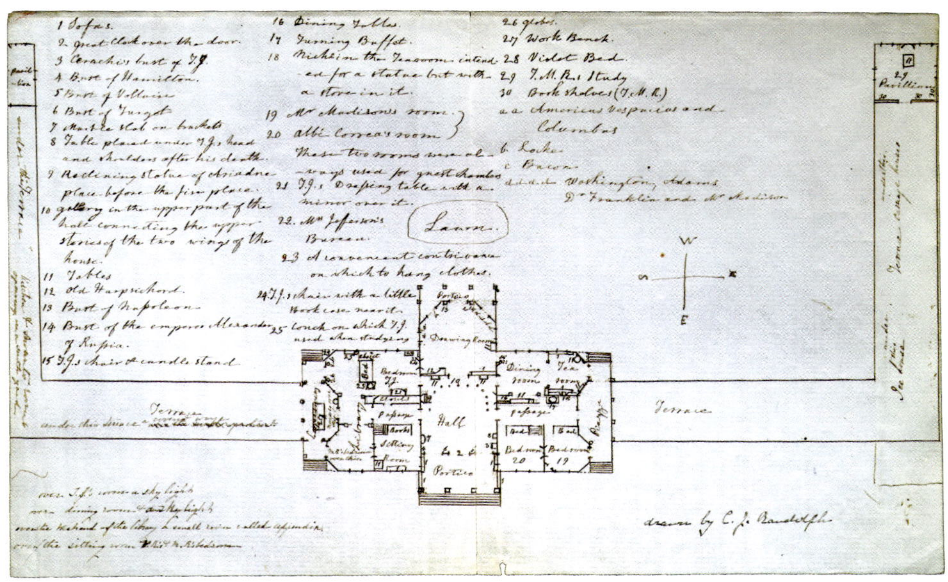

Fig. 8-38 Cornelia's drawing, after Jefferson's death, of Monticello and the terrace buildings, post-1826

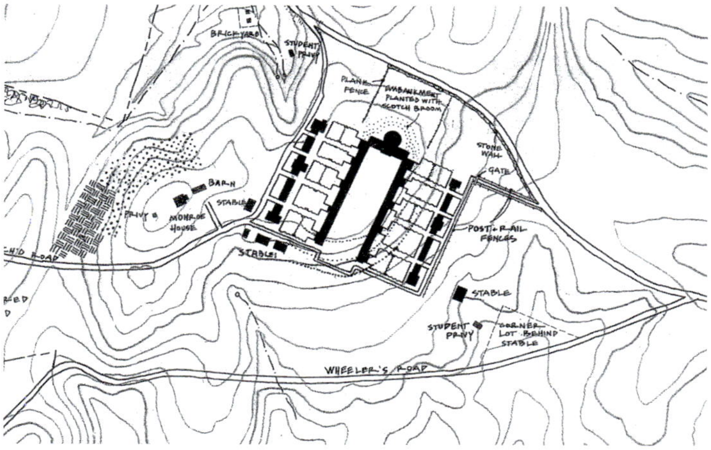

Fig. 8-39 University of Virginia Grounds and stables 1826

Fig. 8-41 The Governor's Palace stables at Colonial Williamsburg

Restoration: In the spring of 2017, Monticello completed a several-year project to restore the Stable and North Wing. Much of the restoration is speculative; the archaeologists who worked on the project told me that the sloping land and earth surrounding the 1930s reconstruction of the Stable had been so disturbed,

Fig. 8-40 The restored Poplar Forest, Thomas Jefferson's home near Bedford, Virginia, in 2009

and a depth of several feet of earth had been removed (for the paving of an adjacent parking lot), that no indication of earlier foundations or soil remained. Although Jefferson's drawings of the Stable were on the 1806 and 1809 surveys, it was never clear if their actual footprints were ever realized. The archaeological team thinks that the building was used for storage and tack, rather than stabling horses. As can be seen by the illustration, [Fig. p-4 on page xii] the two stone stables are now separated by a passageway, rather than being connected (by wood) as in the pre-1927 photo. Up in the North Wing, the individual stalls were dismantled, and carriage housing is now set up there (as indicated by the written Jeffersonian records).

Feed

Horses are grazing animals. Thus, they need a lot of good-quality forage from pasture or hay. In fact, they should consume up to 2.5 percent of their own body weight daily in dry feed (a 1000-pound horse needs twenty-five pounds of food!). Moreover, horses also require up to ten to twelve gallons a day of good, clean water, and salt or a mineral block. When an animal is active or working or used for travel, it

Fig. 8-42 George Wythe's stables behind his house in Colonial Williamsburg

Fig. 8-43 Ravensworth stables, Fairfax, Virginia

may need a supplement of grain (for energy and protein); however, a supplement doesn't replace pasture or hay. In fact, it is safe to feed a horse 100 percent forage along with water and salt; and any feeding ration should be at least 50 percent forage. But the more work a horse does, the more grain supplement it needs.

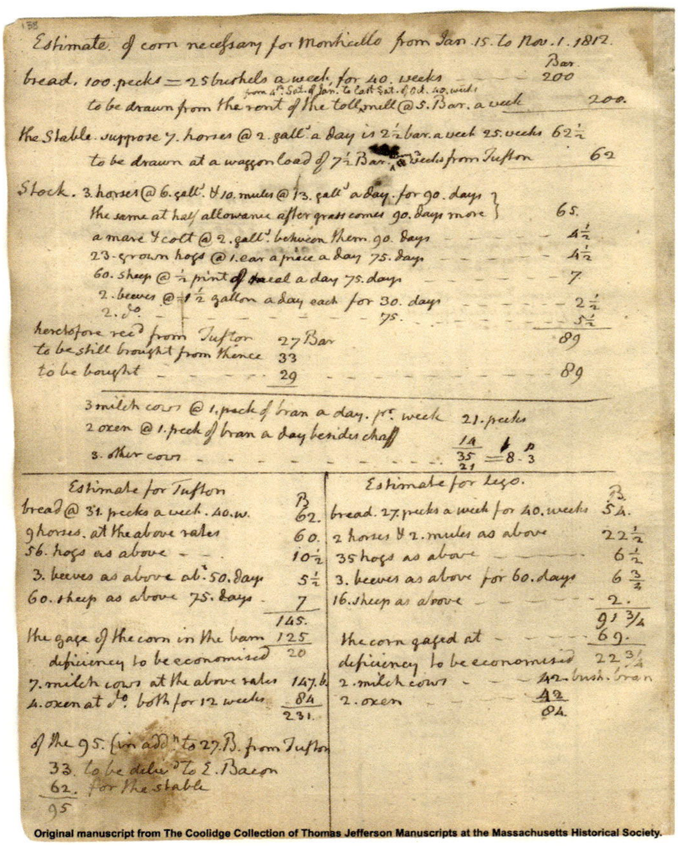

Estimate of corn necessary for Monticello from Jan. 15. to Nov. 1. 1812.

	Bar.
bread. 100. pecks = 25 bushels a week, for 40. weeks (from 4th. Sat. of Jan. to last Sat. of Oct. 40. weeks)	200
to be drawn from the rent of the toll mill @ 5. Bar. a week	200.
the Stable. suppose 7. horses @ 2. gall. a day is 2½ bar. a week 25. weeks	62½
to be drawn at a waggon load of 7½ Bar. [illegible] weeks from Tufton	62
Stock. 3. horses @ 6. gall. & 10. mules @ 13. gall. a day. for 90. days; the same at half allowance after grass comes 90. days more	65.
a mare & colt @ 2. gall. between them 90. days	4½
23. grown hogs @ 1. ear a piece a day 75. days	4½
60. sheep @ ½ pint of meal a day 75. days	7
2. beeves @ 1½ gallon a day each for 30. days	2½
2. do. 75.	5½
	89
heretofore recd from Tufton 27 Bar; to be still brought from thence 33; to be bought 29	89

3 milch cows @ 1. peck of bran a day. pr. week 21. pecks
2 oxen @ 1. peck of bran a day besides chaff 14
3. other cows 35 = 8 - 3
21

Estimate for Tufton

	B
bread @ 31. pecks a week. 40. w.	62.
9 horses. at the above rates	60.
56. hogs as above	10½
3. beeves as above ab. 50. days	5½
60. sheep as above 75. days	7
	145.
the gage of the corn in the barn	125
deficiency to be economised	20
7. milch cows at the above rates	147. b
4. oxen at do. both for 12 weeks	84
	231.

of the 95. (in addn to 27. B. from Tufton)
33. to be deliv. to E. Bacon
62. for the stable
95

Estimate for Lego.

	B.
bread. 27. pecks a week for 40. weeks	54.
2 horses & 2. mules as above	22½
35 hogs as above	6½
3. beeves as above for 60. days	6¾
16. sheep as above	2.
	91¾
the corn gaged at	69.
deficiency to be economised	22¾
2. milch cows	42. bush. bran
2. oxen	42
	84

Original manuscript from The Coolidge Collection of Thomas Jefferson Manuscripts at the Massachusetts Historical Society.

Fig. 8-44 In his *Farm Book*, Thomas Jefferson allowed for livestock feed in his "Estimate of Corn Necessary for Monticello from Jan. 15 to Nov. 1, 1812."

Forages: Forages (or "roughage") are classified as legumes or grasses that can be found in pastures or hay. Hay fields often contain a mix of grasses and legumes. Clover and alfalfa are legumes and are higher in protein and calcium than grasses alone. Horses can graze on forage in pastures or, if kept indoors, can eat hay, which is a dried mixture of grasses and legumes that have been cut in the field and then dried and gathered for storage. Sometimes straw or chaff from cereal grain, which is roughage with little nutritional value, is mixed with grain and fed to animals as a filler. By itself, straw has no nutritional value as feed. Straw is usually used as bedding in stalls to absorb wastes.

Grains: Grains can be given to horses either whole or crushed, as a supplement. Oats and corn are the most common grains for horses. Corn provides twice as much digestible energy as an equal volume of oats and is low in fiber.

Corn as Feed and Food

Jefferson had his garden and orchards, which produced food for his larger extended family and long-term guests. Moreover, many of the enslaved families had their own gardens, which produced enough food to sell the surplus to the Jeffersons on Sunday for some spending money. But the staple crop, corn, was produced out in the larger Monticello fields, others of which were also planted with crops for market (i.e., tobacco and wheat). Corn was grown as food both for people (mainly the enslaved laborers) (120 persons at Monticello in 1794) and animals. The animals that ate corn were horses (39 horses and mules), 22 oxen and cattle, and hogs in 1794, and later sheep (60 in 1812). Having enough corn for both people and animals to make it through at least ten months of the year was so important that the *Farm Book* has several charts showing Jefferson's calculation of the quantity of corn per field, how to distribute it to the various farms, and how many gallons or pecks a day/week each category (people vs. animal) would receive. [Fig. 8-44] "If the supply of corn became deficient, then the food for the plantation became an acute problem." Neither in 1794, 1812, nor 1815 did Monticello produce enough corn to feed its people and stock. In 1794, only a few barrels of corn were bought, but by 1815, 29 barrels were needed, and in 1821, 94.4 barrels (for only 86 persons, 7 horses, 7 mules, 7 oxen & beeves, 93 sheep and 123 pigs). [74]

Evidence About How Jefferson Fed His Horses

Evidence hints that some years, Jefferson allowed his horses and cows to graze for a month or two on the stubble in fields he had planted in grasses or red clover (for fallow cover) after the first cutting. A different practice was in effect in 1796, when a visitor noted that Jefferson cut his clover twice each season, and did not let his cattle graze in his fields. Jefferson probably experimented with different grazing patterns with varying success. Horses were also set out in the surrounding woods. Nevertheless, after 1794 Jefferson's records indicated that most of the year, he was feeding the horses—the work horses and the riding horses—both hay and supplementary corn. [75]

Hay: Jefferson called hay by the term "fodder," or sometimes "provender." Jefferson "used the leaves, tops, shucks, and stalks of corn, clover, Lucerne, vetches, and grasses of various kinds." Lucerne is alfalfa, and vetches are a fodder used for soil improvement, hay, and winter pasture in the South. Jefferson also grew many kinds of grasses on his plantations, with varying success: "bent, blue, couch, crab, Egyptian, fiorin, goose, greensward, guinea, Irish, orchard, panic, Peruvian, ray, rye, sainforn, scury, sweet-scented, and timothy." According to Betts, editor of Jefferson's *Farm Book*, these were the grasses Jefferson cut for hay or let the animals graze upon. "When they flourished, they were cut for hay or left in the meadows and fields for grazing." In 1795, Jefferson and George Washington wrote each other about their disappointment with the use of lucerne as a soil improver. [76]

Red clover soon became a favorite fallow crop for Jefferson. He was convinced that rather than leave his fields completely unplanted in order to "rest them" (i.e., for crop rotations), it was better to cover a fallow field in clover as a nitrogen fixer. Nitrogen is the nutrient most needed for crop growth, and it had been leached from the fields by the tobacco and corn. Certainly, red clover can be used for pastures and hay, and is an excellent soil improvement crop. Moreover, clover, along with Lucerne, is higher in protein, calcium, and energy than grasses and so is an efficient feed for hard-working horses. In July of 1793, before returning to Monticello from Philadelphia, Jefferson wrote his son-in-law Thomas M. Randolph that the introduction of red clover into the rotation of crops would serve, among other things as "horse-food, instead of being eternally on the scramble for [it] as we are in Virginia for the want of winter and summer food." [77]

Under the influence of the agricultural movement occurring in England at the time, Jefferson began with three-year crop rotations and later divided his farms into seven sets of fields for rotation. Production did not increase greatly. Although he grew most of his fodder, Jefferson still had to buy extra from his neighbors almost every year. After all, he was not only feeding his horses, but also hundreds of cattle, sheep, and hogs. But his horses came in for special consideration. On Nov 22, 1767, Jefferson noted in his *Garden Book:* "8 or 10 bundles of fodder are as much as a horse will generally eat thro' the night, 9 bundles x 130. Days = 1170. For the winter." Later in his *Farm Book*, he wrote "an acre of corn yield in blades, tops, & shucks what is equivalent to about 400.lb of blades. 8 or 10 lb. of blades serve a horse a night. Blades are generally put into cocks of about 1000 lb." In Philadelphia, on October 10, 1792, Jefferson jotted down advice from a respected horseman: "Heiltzheimer says that a horse well fed with grain requires 100 lb. hay a week, without grain 130 lb." [78]

Supplementary grain: When Jefferson was traveling and stopped overnight in a tavern with his horses, or when boarding his horses in towns and cities like Staunton, Williamsburg, Philadelphia, or Paris, he paid for "ferrege" (hay) and oats (sometimes corn and rye). Moreover, several books on animal husbandry of the time emphasize how necessary supplementary grains were for any animal that that would be used for travel ("expeditions of long stages"). According to Clark, in a treatise published by William Spotswood, "No man who is acquainted with horses would think of using them on any occasion that required expedition, without preparing their bodies for it, by good feeding [rich dry food, such as oats and beans] and regular exercise." [79]

At home at Monticello, Jefferson gave corn to his horses—both riding horses and work horses—at least nine months a year. (The corn usually ran out by July and until it was harvested a few months later, Jefferson presumably put the horses to pasture on the stubble of the cut clover or alfalfa fields, or he supplemented with other grains). After 1815, Jefferson planted several acres of oats every year. But he also bought oats to use as food for his horses and other stock. [80]

In general, by 1794, the pattern was to feed his riding horses one and a half gallons of corn a day in winter and ("after the grass comes in,") one gallon in summer; his workhorses got two gallons on plowing days, one gallon on days of rest in winter, and half that in summer. In 1821, his saddle horses got two gallons a day for 150 days, while his plantation horse and six mules got one and a half bushels a day for 180 days (till July). Jefferson allowed ten barrels of corn a year for each horse. Compared to today's horses, which work much less—probably many fewer hours—than those of the eighteenth century, one and a half to two gallons of corn is a large amount. After 1809, during his final retirement, Jefferson often had to order Bacon to buy large quantities of corn from other neighbors. Since he never seemed to have enough corn for all his needs, Jefferson was constantly experimenting with other mixtures of high carbohydrate and fibrous food, some of which probably just acted as a filler. [81]

Since Jefferson could not devote more land to pasture or to growing feed for his stock if he wanted to have produce for market (which was the way he was trying to get himself out of debt), he was caught in a vicious circle of needing to buy hay and grain for the farm. So, he looked for ways to reduce his feed expenses by mixing grain with potatoes or pumpkins. [82]

Water: Horses need great quantities of water daily, ten to twelve gallons, whether they are stabled or in pastures. If Jefferson stabled his riding horses and carriage horses (on average seven to ten horses), his hostlers, Jupiter Evans and later Wormley Hughes, must have been kept busy watering the horses. There are several springs on the Mountain, but the well sometimes went dry. The Rivanna River, of course, could be a source of water for stock, but that meant the stock had to be taken to the river (more than a half-hour walk down the mountainside from the main stables). [Fig. 8-45] Evidence points to bringing water to the horses rather than taking them to the river. In a letter written in 1833, granddaughter Virginia Randolph Trist mentions the slave Bagwell Granger "having gone to carry a bucket of water to Brother Jeffs horse." [83]

All the animals at Monticello needed water. Arthur Young's 1770 *Farmer's Guide*, which Jefferson often cited, advised creating at least two "yards" (paddocks) for animals on every large farm. "The mouth of a pond should ever be in each yard, that the cattle may help themselves to water, and not depend in any measure upon the thought and care of servants." Since we have no evidence of animal access to water on Monticello, we can only assume that hostlers had to hand-water the stabled horses daily. [84]

Salt: Horses need salt in their diet, and contemporary horse keepers supply their horses with salt blocks. There is no evidence that Jefferson had salt blocks.

Sources show that farmers were generally aware that their stock needed salt. Isaac (Granger) Jefferson said that he and his father fed the deer in the Deer Park two times a day and "gave 'em salt; got right gentle; come up and eat out of your hand." So we can suppose that Jefferson also procured salt for his other stock, including his horses. Salt was the way of "alluring" wandering animals back to their plantations. Salt was shipped in wagons from the coasts to the interior or brought from salt springs in the western mountains. [85]

Salt was a household necessity, and Jefferson provided lots of it for his extended human "family." Sometimes Jefferson sent an enslaved wagoner to Poplar Forest near Lynchburg to pick up barrels of salt in a small wagon drawn by mules to haul back to Monticello as provisions for the household. In 1814 and 1815, the overseer at Poplar Forest was responsible for procuring salt for both Monticello as well as Bedford. Perhaps he was able to get salt from sources near the springs in western Virginia. [86]

Expenses

Even if horses were allowed to graze freely rather than be stabled, there were nevertheless many hidden costs for the owner. Time and labor were spent rounding up the horse. Often pastures and woods did not produce adequate nutrition, and consequently the owner needed to grow or purchase (and transport) supplemental feed. Moreover, there was more potential for injury out in fields than in a stable. Stabling a horse avoided some of these disadvantages, but stabling also implied other unavoidable expenses: the construction and upkeep of the building itself; the transport and cost of water, feed, and bedding; and daily cleaning of the stall (mucking out). If the owner chose not to perform these daily maintenance tasks himself, there were labor costs for those he chose to hire or assign the work.

Working horses usually require extra grain (for more calories than that supplied by grass and hay). All horses require regular attention from a skilled farrier to trim feet or set shoes.

Horses often need routine exercise to be kept in shape for infrequent use, so unless the owner had the time or desire to exercise all his horses himself, he needed to hire others or assign others to attend to those tasks. Before being used, horses need to be cleaned and groomed, as well as appropriately tacked for use under saddle or to draw a carriage. Later, the animal needs to be untacked and cooled down (often hand walked) before being returned to the stable. Equipment needs to be cleaned and oiled, and then stored properly. Repairs of equipment, tack, and even the stables and fences imply more costs, as does the veterinary care for injured or ill horses. "All things taken into consideration, it is clear that ownership of any type of horse in the early modern period was limited to ... those who could afford not only the initial costs but also all the ongoing expenses of maintenance." The social hierarchy was reflected in the equine hierarchy, even in the mere maintenance of the animals. [87]

Fig. 8-45 The Rivanna River, a possible water source for Jefferson's livestock

Thomas Jefferson's design of the "Rotunda", the library at the heart of the University of Virginia. "South Elevation of the Rotunda, begun 1818, completed March 29, 1819. Ink and pencil drawing."

Postscript

Jefferson's Shadow

I have many personal motivations in writing this book, for I live in Charlottesville and work and ride in Jefferson's shadow.

Jefferson: Our understanding and appreciation of Thomas Jefferson is ever evolving and has at least as much to do with us and our concerns as it does with him and his achievements. Francis D. Cogliano, a historian at the University of Edinburgh, posits five stages of how we view Jefferson. As S. Richard Gard Jr., editor of *Virginia: The UVA Magazine*, presents Cogliano's stages, I find they provide a useful framework to situate myself in Jefferson's shadow. [1]

Stage 1 begins at Jefferson's death (1826) and goes through the Civil War (1865). In this period, Gard writes, "contemporary assessment of Jefferson was partisan, depending on the beholder's views of North vs. South, abolition vs. slavery, Federalism vs. Republicanism." [2]

Stage 2 began with Reconstruction and lasted through the Depression of the 1930s. In this stage, America "lost interest" in Jefferson, writes Gard. "His theories on states' rights, secession and rebellion" and his idealization of an "agrarian, small-government republic" were the antithesis of a "strengthening central government" and the "industrial economy." Jefferson seemed "out of step" with modernizing America. [3]

Stage 3 lasted through World War II and into the Cold War, beginning in 1943 and epitomized by the dedication that year of the Jefferson Memorial. Now "Jefferson became the embodiment of American ideals—liberty, equality, democracy, reason and the overthrow of tyranny," writes Gard. "He was Thomas Jefferson, statesman, philosopher, architect, inventor, the Sage of Monticello." [4]

Gard quotes Cogliano referring to "a third-stage Jefferson, the nonpartisan epitome of American values." Gard notes of the Jefferson of this phase, "If you took your degree from the University up through roughly 1990, that was the Mr. Jefferson you studied, came to know and heard spoken of as if he were in the next room." [5]

The "blind spot" during Stage 3, of course, "was race and, more personally, Jefferson's relationship with Sally Hemings." Most American historians of this period, notes Gard, "asserted what Cogliano describes as a character defense, that Jefferson couldn't have taken an enslaved mistress because it would have been out of character." Stage 3 simply ignored this and celebrated Jefferson's great feats. [6]

Stage 4 dates from the civil rights era, Vietnam, and the post-Watergate rejection of American exceptionalism of the 1960s and 1970s. Now, the author of the words "All men are created equal" was exposed as a slave-owning hypocrite and called to account for his great failings. "For many historians, increasingly concerned with questions of class, gender, and, especially where Jefferson was concerned, race, his limitations seemed more important than his achievements," writes Cogliano, according to Gard. [7]

"An overreliance on source material from Jefferson's white grandchildren gave Stage 3 Jefferson the character of a stately and loving grandfather through all phases of his life," writes Gard. In Stage 4, African American voices in the Jefferson story, especially the Hemings family's oral histories, were finally taken seriously. "In 1998 DNA testing of Jefferson's and Hemings' direct descendants," notes Gard, ". . . resulted in general acceptance that Thomas had fathered Sally's children." [8]

Finally, Gard quotes Cogliano on Stage 5: "A nuanced reassessment of Jefferson that has moved beyond the attack/defense paradigm." Thomas Jefferson, a member of the Virginia ruling class who enslaved Black people, still embodies democracy and equality. What else to do but hold these two contradictory notions at the same time? [9]

The city of Charlottesville has been Jefferson's neighbor, and vice versa, almost since its founding in 1762. Charlottesville lies three miles from Monticello, Jefferson's home. Since Jefferson was born on a farm near here in 1743, he is often considered a native son of Charlottesville. Even so, people in Charlottesville and the surrounding Albemarle County have also probably been influenced by the changing and evolving American views of Thomas Jefferson projected by historians over time.

When I was about twelve years old, in the early 1960s, my family took a trip to Charlottesville, Virginia, and made a visit to Monticello. This was the America of Stage 3. My father was an Army officer stationed at the Pentagon, and we had been living in northern Virginia, in Alexandria, for several years. As a seventh grader, I had studied Virginia history in school; hence, I had heard much about our Founding Fathers. In fact, living in Alexandria, we had visited George Washington's Mount Vernon many times. On our day trip to Charlottesville—a touristic pilgrimage that thousands of Americans continue to make each year—we drove up to Monticello, and later walked the Grounds of the University of Virginia. Forevermore, after that trip, my family and I used to giggle about how everyone in Charlottesville lowered their voices and used the present tense when they spoke about "Mr. Jefferson," as if he were in the next room. In a sense, he was. [10]

It is now more than sixty years later, and I have been living in Charlottesville for the past forty-five years. As a graduate student at the University of Virginia, I worked summer jobs in the vegetable gardens at Monticello. Later, I ended my teaching career as a professor at the University of Virginia. As a longtime

Fig. Post-1. The Rotunda and the Lawn at the University of Virginia

resident of Charlottesville, I often accompany visiting friends and family up to Monticello for tours and have seen how those tours have changed in content and emphasis over the years. Jefferson's home has been the backdrop for many important events in my life, big and small: the Fourth of July naturalization ceremony of my husband; the kick-off of William Jefferson Clinton's inauguration; many years of Kite Day on Montalto; annual Thanksgiving dinners at Tufton (one of the quarter farms, and past home of the former director of gardens at Monticello, Peter Hatch); the wedding engagement of one of my sons in the gardens of Monticello; invitations to talks and tastings on food and wine; Fall Harvest Festivals; scholarly roundtables and presentations of books on Jeffersonian topics at the International Center for Jefferson Studies. In 2008, I was a Fellow at the International Center of Jefferson Studies.

As a professor at the University of Virginia, I walked daily across the Grounds, planned and brought to fruition also by Jefferson, and of which he was so proud. [Fig. Post-1] When my children were young, I took them to trick or treat on the Lawn in the Academical Village. Christmas season begins with the Lighting of the Lawn, a relatively new tradition of illuminating the colonnades of the Lawn with strings of white holiday lights. I celebrated my twenty-fifth wedding anniversary in the Colonnade Club, a Faculty Club on the Lawn (as did my parents many years earlier). Jefferson historians populate the History Department; PhD dissertation defenses take place in the Rotunda,

Fig. Post-2. Statue of Thomas Jefferson, pen in hand, in front of the Rotunda at the University of Virginia

Jefferson's original library, the iconic building that crowns the Lawn. Every May, students and faculty march down the Lawn in Commencement ceremonies. Two of my children graduated from UVA and marched the Lawn, as did their father and I when we received our PhDs. Alumni have been brought to tears when Jefferson's affection and concern for the University is alluded to. It is a campus strewn with Jefferson statues. The most prominent Jefferson statue is the one where he is standing, pen in hand, in front of the Rotunda, Jefferson's replica of the second-century Rotunda in Rome. [Fig. Post-2] In August 2017, this statue was surrounded by University students protecting it from the infamous torch-bearing neo-Nazis and alt-right members who had invaded Charlottesville and marched down the Lawn, chanting slogans reminiscent of Nazi Germany, and who surrounded the students, who were surrounding the statue of Jefferson. [11] [Fig. Post-3]

For those of us who live here, civic life takes place in the city of Charlottesville, once a mile from the University but now enveloping it. Jeffersonia infuses the small city also. In many ways, the city still pays daily homage to Jefferson, just as it did when the citizens heard on July 4, 1826, that Jefferson had died, and they, along with the University students, trudged up the mountain en masse to Monticello, three miles away, to pay their respects. July 4 continues to hold special significance for Charlottesvillians in their celebrations. City architecture is rife with red-brick buildings with porticos and pediments, white-columned facades, classical orders and friezes decorated with dentils and tryglyphs. Octagonal forms, domes, half-moon windows, venetian blinds, and Chinese railings abound in both business and residential buildings in their attempt to reference Thomas Jefferson. In front of City Hall is a statue of the three presidents: Jefferson, Madison, and Monroe (all neighbors). At one end of Main Street (now a pedestrian mall) is a slate monument that serves as a chalkboard and a celebration of the First Amendment and free speech. [12]

Since the local and national events of 2017, Charlottesville has begun to contend with its history and participation in the nefarious institution of slavery and its aftermaths. Statues to Southern Civil War "heroes" have begun to come down. Names of schools and streets named after Jim Crow-leaning officials have been changed. And it has no longer been possible to simply ignore the hypocrisy of the man who enslaved people at the time he wrote, "all men are created equal." Charlottesvillians are now more visibly divided on their views of this sometimes-impenetrable man, Thomas Jefferson. April 13, Jefferson's birthday, is still celebrated as Founder's Day at the University. However, formerly a holiday in the city, since 2017 it is now celebrated as Liberation and Freedom Day. In a desire to be more inclusive of its whole population, the University has slowly but surely changed names on institutions. For example, the Thomas Jefferson Health District has been renamed the Blue Ridge Health District.

Fig. Post-3. American white nationalists march at the University of Virginia ahead of the Unite the Right Rally in Charlottesville on August 11, 2017.

Yet other names remain. One of the principal streets in the center of town is named Jefferson, and other Jefferson streets abound (Jefferson Park, Jefferson Terrace). Other street names are variations of Monticello. Moreover, literally dozens of businesses and institutions incorporate "Jefferson" into their title. Jefferson's words anoint many buildings in Charlottesville, from the regional airport to the gates of the University. Monticello, up on the Mountain, is visible from many parts of

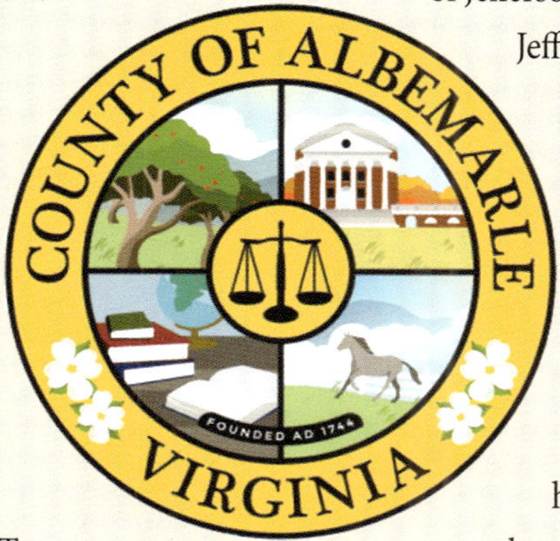

Fig. Post-4. Albemarle County Seal, the Rotunda and horses in the countryside, the Blue Ridge Mountains in the background

the city as well as from the Grounds. With a telescope famously positioned on the North Terrace, Jefferson used to look down upon Charlottesville and the University as it was being built. Now, in 2024, when we gaze back, there is more ambivalence than pure post-World War II Stage 3 celebration.

Political and cultural debates in the media, and elsewhere, are posed in terms of what the speaker or author interprets what Jefferson thought or did with respect to education, religion, free speech, food, horticulture, viticulture, land use, road construction, architecture, landscapes, debt, cosmopolitan perspectives, states' rights, war, women, equal rights, schooling, race relations, and slavery. His writings are mined for his viewpoint and perspectives, as if that should still convince us or repel us today. For many, the written eloquence of Jefferson's thoughts and principles still serve as powerful persuasions. Many other people who live in modern Charlottesville now roll their eyes and renounce Jefferson's influence or veneration. But even in this way we live in his shadow.

Horses: In the surrounding county of Albemarle, more of Jefferson's social history is noted: houses designed by Jefferson, places visited by Jefferson, roads used by Jefferson, and vineyards planted by Jefferson. [Fig. Post-4] As I used to drive to Staunton, a town across the Blue Ridge Mountains to the west, in the Shenandoah Valley, to teach at Mary Baldwin University, for twenty years, I drove on the same road and crossed the same mountain pass that Jefferson had used when he rode horseback to Staunton as a practicing lawyer for four years in the late 1760s. The representative from Albemarle in the Virginia General Assembly in Richmond occupies "Jefferson's seat."

Large estates, both old and new, bounded by white board

Fig. Post- 5. The Albemarle countryside, with the Blue Ridge Mountains behind the grazing horses

fencing, dot the rolling Albemarle countryside. On these estates, with views of the western mountains, horses graze, still symbols of wealth and leisure time. [Fig. Post-5] However, not only the twenty-first-century versions of landed gentry own pleasure horses. Many equestrians reside in Albemarle County: some people board their horses at private stables or farms; others pay fees and take lessons to ride horses. [13] [Fig. Post-6]

Fig. Post-6. The mural at the western entry from Albemarle County into the city of Charlottesville, by Chicho Lorenzo

They all participate in a long tradition of equine culture in the area. Hunt clubs have storied histories; well-known horse shows take place annually; in the fall and

Fig. Post- 7. Foxfield steeplechase races, April 27, 2024

spring the Foxfield Races (steeplechases) are held; [Fig. Post-7] the University sponsors a polo team, and other polo teams and polo fields are located here.[Fig. Post-8] Equestrian experts offer workshops in horse management and dressage; trail riding clubs explore the Blue Ridge Mountains every weekend; breeding farms specialize in certain kinds of horses; nearby county parks reserve trails for horses; veterinarian clinics specialize in equine care; equine masseuses advertise their services; saddle shops and equine-equipment repair shops abound; young people participate and compete in Pony Clubs. The University mascot is the Cavalier, mounted on a bay horse, whose dash into the stadium begins each home football game. [Fig. Post-9]

Fig. Post-9. The Cavalier mascot, also known as Cav Man, the mascot of the Cavaliers, the University of Virginia sports teams

Probably the most compelling of motivations in writing this book is that I myself am a rider of horses. I have been riding and loving these glorious animals since I was four years old. My parents put me on horses on Army posts all over the world, and wherever we were in the states. By the time I was in my twenties, I left the lesson rings and horse shows to ride my horse on trails in the countryside wherever I lived. For the last forty-five years, I have lived in Charlottesville. In this context, I ride my horse on trails through the rolling countryside of Albemarle, in the midst of the cicada sounds in summer, in the festival of glowing colors in fall, in the suddenly clear and crisp vistas of winter, and in forests full of ballerina-like dancing dogwood blossoms in spring. So, it is no wonder that I identified with Jefferson, the trail rider, when he said, "that to old age, the daily ride is among the most cheering of comforts. It renews the pleasurable sensation that we are still in society with beings and the things around us and so delightful and so necessary is this daily revival to me that I would wish to lose that and life together." [14]

Fig. Post-8. Polo at King Family Vineyards in Albemarle County

Given Jefferson's long shadow that extends into activities beyond the political, this book responds to people who want to know more about Thomas Jefferson's involvement with horses and perhaps identify with him as he partnered with a horse to ride trails alone in the forests of Virginia.

endnotes

Timeline of Jefferson's Life

1 Timeline of Jefferson's Life. Accessed June 8, 2021. https://www.monticello.org/site/jefferson/timeline-jeffersons-life..

Prologue—"So Delightful and So Necessary": Jefferson's Daily Revival

1 TJ to WS, April 10, 1824, *Founders Online*.

2 Bear, *Jefferson at Monticello*, 60.

3 Historians point out that Jefferson could never have been master of 5,000 acres and nearly 140 slaves without a horse. Horses sustained his mastery over people and land; Dierksheide to author, August 18, 2021. Edwards, *Horse and Man in Early Modern England*; Raber and Tucker, *The Culture of the Horse*.

4 Kilby, "The Demographics of the U.S. Equine Population," 175-205.

5 "And *The Horse* was bred increasingly for show purposes. So began what we call today the pleasure riding-horse industry."—Derry, Horses in Society, 127, 240. The 9.2 million horses in the US included "horses used for racing, showing, competition, sport, breeding, recreation and work. This includes horses used both commercially and for pleasure," *The Economic Impact of the Horse Industry*. However, the American Horse Council found that *The Horse* population in the United States descended from a high of 9.2 million in 2007 to 7.2 million by 2017, due to significant declines in breeding starting in the 2007–2008 recession. Ibid.; Broadway to author; "1900: *The Horse* in Transition."

6 Currently in Jefferson's Virginia, horses used for trail riding and pleasure include 48.4 percent of horses; *Virginia Equine Survey Report*. In another state, Wisconsin, a 2008 survey found that 78 percent of horses were used primarily for pleasure/trail riding; Trechter et al., *Wisconsin State Horse Council*, 4. Horse owning today in the United States is no longer just a prerogative of the wealthy. The 2005 American Horse Council study found that approximately 34 percent of horse owners have an annual household income of less than $50,000, 46 percent have an income of between $25,000 to $75,000, and 28 percent have an income of over $100,000.

7 The *animal turn* is an "academic focus on animals in new terms and under new premises. Human animal studies start from a genuine interest in the animal and its place in society and manifest a new perception of animals as animal selves, as potential subjects as opposed to mere objects of observation, study and protection," Peters et al., "The Animal Turn"; Ritvo, "On the Animal Turn," 118–122; Feh, "Relationships and Communication in Socially Natural Horse Herds"; Van Dierendonck and Goodwin, "Social Contact in Horses," 28–44.

Introduction: Horses in Thomas Jefferson's World

1 Campbell, *The Horse in Virginia*, 13.

2 Culver, *Blooded Horses of Colonial Days*, 140; Derry, *Horses in Society*, 33.

3 Stong, *Horses and Americans*, 55, writes: "In New England and Pennsylvania horses were bred for hauling and ploughing."

4 Jones, The Present State of Virginia, 45.

5 Stanard, "Racing in Colonial Virginia," 293-294; Culver, *Blooded Horses of Colonial Days*, 147. Horse racing, in all of its forms, was the only spectator sport in existence in the colonies and early Republic until the advent of baseball and basketball after the Civil War.

6 Bulle Rock is considered the first "blood horse" imported in 1737 to Virginia. The Thoroughbred, in fact, is considered the first true breed of horse for which bloodlines and/or pedigrees are recorded in a breed registry. In England, the Thoroughbred registry began in 1791 in the *General Stud Book*. In the United States, it began in 1868/1873 in the Jockey Club's *American Stud Book*. Registries, along with selective breeding, would radically alter animal husbandry in the eighteenth century, and horse breeds, specifically, would proliferate in the new United States during the following nineteenth century.

7 Besides their work horses, gentlemen immersed in eighteenth-century Virginia equine culture had breeding horses (brood mares and studs), carriage horses (teams and single horses), saddle horses, pleasure horses for women (riding sidesaddle), racehorses, horses for foxhunting, parade horses, and war horses.

8 Tillson, "Gentry in Colonial Virginia"; Evans, *A "Topping People."*

9 FFV is not a category used by scholars or historians. Yet it is a very well-known folk category, or social construction, in Virginia, and has been around since at least 1887. The Virginia equine historian Fairfax Harrison borrowed it from the human sphere and applied it to the first blood horses to come to Virginia. Although not in use in the eighteenth century, it does label a recognizable group of colonists. Wikipedia, s.v. "First Families of Virginia," accessed September 15, 2021, https://en.wikipedia.org/wiki/First_Families_of_Virginia.

10 Von Daacke, *Freedom Has a Face*.

11 McLaughlin, *Jefferson and Monticello*, 102.

12 Bear, *Jefferson at Monticello*, 61.

13 Mason, *The Gentleman's New Pocket Farrier*, 14. Jefferson promised his wife on her deathbed that he would never remarry, and he did not. Most historians believe that he maintained a sexual relationship with the enslaved Sally Hemings (Martha Jefferson's half-sister) for thirty-six years, a relationship that produced at least four children who lived to adulthood. See Gordon-Reed, *The Hemingses of Monticello*.

14 Randolph, The Last Days of Jefferson. Dashper, "Learning to Communicate," 99, writes: "The uniquely intimate nature of body-to-body communication that occurs between horse and rider means that the two partners are constantly in action on and with each other, whether they intend to or not." TJ to George Wythe, April 18, 1795; TJ to Benjamin Rush, January 16, 1811.

15 Randolph, *The Last Days of Jefferson*; Bear, *Jefferson at Monticello*, 13, 83.

16 Daniel, "Virginian Reminiscences of Jefferson," 1766–1768.

17 Randall, *Life of Thomas Jefferson*, 1:68–70. These scenes emphasize Jefferson's "oneness" with his steed: embodying the centaur.

18 Randolph, *The Domestic Life of Thomas Jefferson*, 382.

19 Ibid.
Recent literature on horse-rider relationships emphasize mutual communication. According to Dashper, "Learning to Communicate," 99: "Horse riding is a complex mix of intricate inter-species communicating, athletic skill and competence. Horse and rider are constantly communicating with each other, through embodied intra-action, and both also pick up on external cues."

20 Randall, *Life of Thomas Jefferson*, 1:68; Randolph, *The Last Days of Jefferson*.

21 Israel Gillette adopted the surname Jefferson in 1844. A postilion is a person who rides the left-hand horse of a two- or four-horse carriage in place of a driver. Gordon-Reed, *Hemingses of Monticello*, 252. The quote is from an interview Israel gave to the *Pike County (Ohio) Republican*, in December 25, 1873, under the title "Life Among the Lowly, No. 3." However, whatever his own motive, Jefferson was certainly seen from the ground by slaves, white workmen, and family. From the perspective on the ground, Jefferson "on his high horse" was inevitably performing "up" versus "down," superior versus inferior.

22 Randall, *Life of Thomas Jefferson*, 3:538.

23 Ibid., 538-539.

24 TJ to WS, April 10, 1824.

25 Davis and Maurstad, "Meaning of Horses," 5.

Part I: On Their High Horses

Chapter 1: Jefferson in the Saddle

1 Randall, *Thomas Jefferson: A Life*, 1; TJ to WS, April 10, 1824, *Founders Online*.

2 Toddler Tom and his family moved to Tuckahoe for seven years while his father, Peter, served as guardian of the young son of his best friend, Thomas Randolph, who had just died and left his young family without protection.

3 Randall, *Thomas Jefferson: A Life*, 17.

4 Randall, *Life of Thomas Jefferson*, 1:32.

5 Randall, *Thomas Jefferson: A Life*, 29.

6 Ibid., 43. Water travel was the primary means of transportation in the first century after colonization, but the rivers ran east-west in Virginia, and travel inland north and south always had to be by foot or by horse.

7 Randolph, *The Domestic Life of Thomas Jefferson*, 63.

8 TJ to John Barnes, November 11, 1811, in Remarks by Mr. Charles C. Smith at the December Meeting, 1899, of the Society, in Massachusetts Historical Society, *Proceedings of the Massachusetts Historical Society*, 2nd ser., 13:312. Davis & Maurstad, "Meaning of Horses," 5, write: "Equine assisted therapy (EAT) or, more broadly, equine assisted activities, include physical and psychological benefits from riding or just being around horses." Many equine-assisted psychotherapy programs (EAP) exist for sufferers of PTSD (veterans) and other psychological trauma (anxiety, depression, abuse).

9 Bear, *Jefferson at Monticello*, 12; Anburey, *Travels Through the Interior Parts of America*, 409.

10 Poplar Forest was a 5,000-acre plantation a bit beyond Lynchburg.

11 NSV1784; Peden, *Notes on the State of Virginia*.

12 Randolph, *The Domestic Life of Thomas Jefferson*, 74.

13 Randall, *Thomas Jefferson: A Life*, 368.

14 TJ to Peter Carr, August 19, 1785, *Founders Online*.

15 TJ to TMR, August 27, 1786, in TJP.

16 Hailman, *Thomas Jefferson on Wine*, 122.

17 TJ to Madame de Corny, June 30, 1787, in Randolph, *The Domestic Life of Thomas Jefferson*, 129.

18 MB, 639.

19 Randall, *Thomas Jefferson: A Life*, 501.

20 Isaac (Granger) Jefferson, in Bear, *Jefferson at Monticello*, 15. This interview was written down by the interviewer as a brief memoir in the 1840s.

21 TJ to JA, May 27, 1794, in PTJ.

22 TJ to TMR, November 16, 1801, in TJP.

23 Randall, *Life of Thomas Jefferson*, 3:674.

24 Randolph, *The Domestic Life of Thomas Jefferson*, 288.

25 Quoted in Martin, *Thomas Jefferson: Scientist*, 6; Randall, *Thomas Jefferson: A Life*, 569; Rayner, *Life of Thomas Jefferson*, ch. 32.

26 TJ to James Madison, March 17, 1809, in *Founders Online*.

27 TJ to Thaddeus Kosciusko, February 26, 1810, in Randolph, *The Domestic Life of Thomas Jefferson*, 331.

28 TJ to JA, January 21, 1812, in Randolph, *The Domestic Life of Thomas Jefferson*, 355.

29 Randolph, *The Domestic Life of Thomas Jefferson*, 361.

30 TJ to Maria Cosway, October 12, 1786, in PTJ, 10:443-455. The Thoroughfare was the main roadway from Charlottesville, up the mountain, through the gap, and on to Milton further east on the Rivanna River.

31 Randolph, The Last Days of Jefferson.

32 Woolen Mills was one of the earliest textile mill villages in the South; the factory made woolen blankets and was built by the 1830s. Virginia Historical Marker Q-27 about The Farm reads: "A building on the property likely served as headquarters for British Colonel Banastre Tarleton briefly in June 1781. In 1825, Charlottesville lawyer and later University of Virginia law professor, John A. G. Davis, purchased a portion of the original tract and engaged Thomas Jefferson's workmen to design and build this house. It is considered one of the best surviving examples of Jeffersonian residential architecture. Major General George A. Custer occupied the house as his headquarters for a brief time in March 1865."

33 https://www.vocabulary.com/dictionary/hobby; https://www.etymonline.com/word/hobby.

34 TJ to JA, October 12, 1823, in TJP.

35 Randolph, *The Domestic Life of Thomas Jefferson*, 387; Bacon in Bear, *Jefferson at Monticello*, 33; Tucker, *The Life of Thomas Jefferson*, 2:477; Aunt Polly in Daniel, "Virginian Reminiscences of Jefferson."

36 TJ to Dr. Vine Utley, March 21, 1819, in Randolph, *The Domestic Life of Thomas Jefferson*, 371, and TJ to John Adams, June 1, 1822, in ibid., 379.

37 TJ to WS, April 10, 1824, *Founders Online*.

38 TJ to Edmund Bacon, August 18, 1823, *Founders Online*; Randall, *Life of Thomas Jefferson*, 3:538.

39 TJ to William Hamilton, July 1806, in TJP; Randall, *Life of Thomas Jefferson*, 2:375.

40 MJR to ERC, September 18, 1825, *Jefferson Quotes & Family Letters*.

41 Hughes, *The Compleat Horseman*, 5.

42 TJ to Dr. Walter Jones, January 2, 1814, *Founders Online*.

43 MB1997, 1418.

44 One of the most significant books on horsemanship was Henry, Earl of Pembroke's *Military Equitation, or a Method of Breaking horses and Teaching Soldiers to Ride Designed for the Use of the Army*, 1761. Some of these titles on husbandry: J. Bordley's *Essays and Notes on Husbandry and Rural Affairs*, 1799; Richard Bradley's *The Gentleman's and Farmer's Guide for the Increase and Improvement of Cattle, Also the Best Manner of Breeding and Breaking Horses both for Sport and Burden*, 1739; Home's (Ld Kain's) *The Gentleman Farmer*, 1799; Richard Kirwan's *The Manures*, 1796; Charles Estienne's and John Liébault's *Maison Rustique or The Country Farmer*, 1600; Jethro Tull's *Horse-hoeing Husbandry*, 1751; and Arthur Young's *The Farmer's Guide*, 1770. For Jefferson's orders, see TJ to Samuel Pleasants, November 7, 1812, *Founders Online*; MB1997.

45 Sadler and Sadler, *American Stables*, 56; Game, "Riding: Embodying the Centaur," 1-12; Keaveney, "Equines and Their Human Companions," 444–454; Davis and Maurstad, "Meaning of Horses," 6.

46 Weld, *Travels Through the States of North America*, 186.

47 Landry, *Noble Brutes*, 52, notes it wasn't until the end of the nineteenth century, when Italian captain Federico Caprilli proposed a new system of riding and a new scientifically based seat, that stirrups were shortened even more in order to use the flat English saddle on all types of terrain.

48 Advertisements for runaway slaves often described the runaway as wearing a roundabout coat.

49 A description of the spur at Monticello: A pair of U-shaped, silver-colored spurs, missing the spoke wheels. The U terminates with the leather holder for leather straps.

50 Wilson, "Hats." The common round hat had morphed into the top hat, a fashion that lasted the rest of the nineteenth century.

51 Bumstead, "Appearance: Descriptions of Thomas Jefferson"; MB1997, 1508.

52 Bear, *Jefferson at Monticello*, 73; Randall, *Life of Thomas Jefferson*, 1:68.

53 MB1997, 497, 621 982, 1159.

54 TJ to Meriwether Lewis, April 23, 1803, *Founders Online; Virginia Gazette*, 1780.

55 "Historic Structure Report, Mount Vernon Estate and Garden Cultural Landscape Study," 5.

56 So called "bitless bridles" (hackamore, bosal, cavessons) are an inheritance from the Spanish and were not used much in the English colonies.

57 Henry to author; TJ to Davis Durett, December 24, 1812, *Founders Online*; *Virginia Gazette*, 1780.

58 FL, 350.

59 MB1997, 1507.

60 Joseph Fossett (1780–1858) was a member of the privileged Hemings family, and grandson of the matriarch, Elizabeth.

61 William Wertenbacker, second University of Virginia librarian, in Daniel, "Virginian Reminiscences of Jefferson."

62 Cuneo, "Just a Bit of Control," 141–173.

63 TJR in Randall, *Life of Thomas Jefferson*, 3:675.

64 Burstein, *The Inner Jefferson*, 22.

65 TJR in Randall, *Life of Thomas Jefferson*, 3:675.

66 Wormley Hughes, in Randall, *Life of Thomas Jefferson*, 1857, 1:68-70.

67 Byrd, *Jefferson: A Novel*; McCullough, *John Adams*.

68 Randall, *Life of Thomas Jefferson*, 3:538.

69 Ibid.

70 William Wertenbaker, in Daniel, "Virginian Reminiscences of Jefferson."

71 A stallion is a male horse that has not been castrated. A gelding is a male horse that has been castrated.

Chapter 2: Brother Equestrians: Friends, Neighbors, and Family

1 McLaughlin, *Jefferson and Monticello*, 30.

2 Washington earned respect and notice from his role in the French and Indian War (1754–1758).

3 TJ to Dr. Walter Jones, January 2, 1814, in Randolph, The Domestic *Life of Thomas Jefferson*, 356. Alexandria is a few miles north of Mount Vernon on the Potomac River.

4 Lieutenant Colonel Humphreys was an aide-de-camp to George Washington during the Revolution. He wrote a "biography" of Washington while he lived with the Washingtons at Mount Vernon. Ford, "Horsemanship and Hunting"; Campbell, *c*, 9.

5 Haworth, *George Washington: Farmer*.

6 During the Revolution, Washington bought "twenty-seven worn-out army mares" for breeding purposes. Later, as president, he bought thirteen more mares from Lancaster, Pennsylvania, for breeding purposes also. Haworth, *George Washington: Farmer*, chapter 9.

7 The Godolphin Arabian is one of the foundation sires of the Thoroughbred breed. Leonidas's sire was Lloyd's Traveller (1758), by Morton's Traveller (1746) and out of Jenny Cameron (1742).

8 *Virginia Journal*, March 24, 1785. Magnolia was originally called Magnolio.

9 Moreover, Washington told Lee that he wanted to dedicate himself to breeding mules, not horses. "Historic Structure Report, Mount Vernon Estate and Garden Cultural Landscape Study," 5.

10 General T. M. Forman, in Youatt, *The Horse*, 34. Usually a horse from Morocco would be called a Barb (the coast of North Africa is the Barbary Coast), but Ranger is always called an Arabian.

11 Harrison, *Early American Turf-Stock*, 2:160-161. Not everyone believes this story unquestionably. See for example, Wallace, *The Horse of America*.

12 Parkinson, *A Tour in America*, 8–9. Parkinson was an English scientific agriculturalist who had published a book in England called the *Experienced Farmer*. He had contracted with Washington to rent one of his farms, and in 1798 he sailed for Virginia with a cargo of cattle, hogs, and sixteen "blooded" horses, and speculated on making money in America with this fine stock. His plans ultimately fell through, and he returned to England, where he wrote up his impressions of his travels and experiences in America.

13 Haworth, *George Washington: Farmer*, chapter 14.

14 Hunters were usually described as a "combination of the race-horse thorough-bred with one of less blood possessing however more strength and substance with less length of body"; Youatt, *The Horse*, 48. Today we refer to these crosses as warmbloods.

15 According to Cavileer, "George Washington's Horse," they were described by Robert Hunter Jr. in his *Early Descriptions Notebook*, vol. 1, in 1785.

16 Hughes, "First in War." Edwards, *Horse and Man in Early Modern England*, 82-88, says that governing a people was seen to be similar to a rider controlling a horse.

17 Chastellux, *Travels in North America*, 1:111. He was sent in 1779 by the French government as a major general to aid in the American Revolution. While here, he toured America and later wrote a book of his observations. He was a special admirer of Washington but also bonded with Jefferson during a visit to Monticello in 1782.

18 These well-known smallish horses (ponies) have come down to us through children's literature in the books about Misty of Chincoteague by Marguerite Henry. The ponies still live free and wild on the island of Assateague (and formerly Chincoteague, too), one of the barrier islands off the coast of Maryland and Virginia. It is unclear if these horses were remnants of the cargo of a Spanish galleon that sank (and *The Horses* swam to shore and survived), or if they are merely the descendants of horses set free by English settlers. They have been there since the late 1600s. Cavileer, "George Washington's Horse."

19 Haworth, *George Washington: Farmer*, 133.

20 A mule is a hybrid of a male ass (jack) and a female horse (mare).

21 Hur, "Washington's Best Saddle Horse."

22 Haworth, *George Washington: Farmer*, chapter 17.

23 Washington lost ten of his best horses in that fire; "Historic Structure Report, Mount Vernon Estate and Garden Cultural Landscape Study," 5, 7.

24 John Tayloe III was an important Virginia turfman and breeder.

25 The Madisons typically hosted between nine and thirty overnight guests at Montpelier on any given day. James Madison once said he was happy to host his guests, but not so happy to host (and feed) their horses. Johnson, *Jefferson and His Colleagues*, chapter 15 in vol. 15.

26 PTJ, 17:512; MB1997, 2:809, 1245.

27 Jennings, *A Colored Man's Reminiscences of James Madison*, 17.

28 Taylor, *A Slave in the White House*, 72; McCoy, *The Last of the Fathers*, 253.

29 Skinner, *The American Farmer*.

30 The University's first cornerstone was laid in 1817, and the first classes were held in March 1825. TJ to James Madison, February 17, 1826, in TJP.

31 "History of the Land and People of Mount Pleasant."

32 Ibid.

33 JHC to Nicholas Faulcon, April 20, 1803, in "History of the Land and People of Mount Pleasant."

34 "History of the Land and People of Mount Pleasant." Diomeda was a filly from the get of Old Diomed; see Edgar letter in Mackay-Smith, *The Colonial Quarter Race Horse*, 94. See paragraph above about Diomed filly from George Ruffin and see Chapter 5 for information on Diomed.

35 Bremo eventually consisted of three houses: Bremo Recess (the first one in which J. H. Cocke lived), then Lower Bremo and finally Upper Bremo. All three houses exist today and remain in the Cocke family. The Bremo lowlands along the James River are exceptionally fertile. "History of the Land and People of Mount Pleasant."

36 Mackay-Smith, *The Colonial Quarter Race Horse*, 225.

37 Roebuck I was bought from the Virginia-North Carolina border region, the old horse-racing region and quarter-race-horse region. He was a grandson of Old Selim. Young Roebuck also carried the bloodlines of Mark Anthony and Jolly Roger, early important imports; Bishko, "A Spanish Stallion for Albemarle," 150; Mackay-Smith, *The Colonial Quarter Race Horse*, 242. The portrait was a retrospective because it was painted in 1859; "John Hartwell Cocke of Bremo."

38 On May 5, 1817, for example, Cocke wrote in his diary that he left Bremo at 3:45 in the morning and reached Monticello at 8:15; "A Spanish Stallion for Albemarle," 147. There is no citation for this assertion, "When Roebuck died his master had him entombed, standing and in full harness, on the rear lawn at Bremo," but it is ascribed to "family lore" in Barraud, Barraud, *The Story of a Family*, 45.

39 Mackay-Smith, *The Colonial Quarter Race Horse*, 238, 242. Imported Bedford and imported Diomed were the only imported horses that Cocke thought produced fine saddle horses, i.e., comfortable pacers. The others (after the war) only produced speedy racers with uncomfortable trots. See Cocke's letter to *The American Farmer*, February 28, 1823.

40 From a broadsheet that is held in the National Sporting Library, illustrated in Mackay-Smith, *The Colonial Quarter Race Horse*, 241. A landau is a kind of open (convertible) carriage (see Chapter 5).

41 Campbell, *Colonial Caroline*, 417.

42 Harrison, *Roanoke Stud*, 178.

43 Hervey, *Racing in America*, 151.

44 Peters, "Diomed." Weatherby was the editor of the *Racing Calendar* in England, and in 1791 he established the official genealogical record of all English "Thoroughbreds" by publishing the *General Stud Book* (listing pedigrees of racing horses up that that point), and soon became the secretary of the Jockey Club. He established a familial dynasty that ruled British racing for generations.

45 Hervey, *Racing in America*, 177, 180; Harrison, *The Equine F.F.Vs.*, 345; Cohen, "Well Calculated for the Farmer," 383; Rouse, *Planters and Pioneers*, 178. Jefferson's last riding horse, The Eagle, came from Diomed and a Spread Eagle mare of Fearnought blood; and according to one commentator, Fearnought and Stirling "were forefathers of the most famous race-horses in America"; Wingfield, *A History of Caroline County*, 419.

46 Hervey, *Racing in America*, 180.

47 Harrison, *Roanoke Stud*, 178.

48 Craig, "Route to Washington, D.C.

49 TJ to JH, January 12, 1801, PTJ vol. 33. Jefferson was waiting for the outcome of the electoral vote in the Senate from January to March 1801.

50 JH to TJ, January 30, 1801, and TJ to JH, April 17, 1801, both in PTJ vol. 33.

51 Randolph was tangentially involved in a scandalous incident at Bizarre that included a possible affair between a brother-in-law and sister-in-law, a possible aborted fetus, legal accusations, a court case, and unresolved questions. See Kierner, *Scandal at Bizarre*.

52 His voice was thought to be due to a childhood illness. This same illness may have caused him also to be infertile; he never married.

53 Daniels, *The Randolphs of Virginia*, 195; "John Randolph."

54 "Eppes, John Wayles (1773–1823)," Biographical Directory of the United States Congress; Bouldin, *Home Reminiscences of John Randolph*, 117.

55 At one time Randolph owned 383 slaves, all born on Roanoke plantation; "John Randolph." Randolph Macon Woman's College has changed its name to Randolph College.

56 Daniels, *The Randolphs of Virginia*, 174; Bruce, *John Randolph of Roanoke*, 121; Bouldin, *Home Reminiscences of John Randolph*, 102.

57 Mackay-Smith, *The Colonial Quarter Race Horse*, 96. John Randolph of Roanoke was very helpful to Patrick Nisbett Edgar, who published *The American Race-Turf Register*, the first general stud book in the United States, in 1833.

58 Recall that Diomed was imported in 1790 after winning the first Derby at Epsom, and immediately began to improve the bloodlines of horses in America. Daniels, *The Randolphs of Virginia*, 5-6. The teaser stallion prepares the mare to be mounted by the intended stud.

59 Bouldin, *Home Reminiscences of John Randolph*, 26.

60 Eisenberg, *Great Match Race*; Bouldin, *Home Reminiscences of John Randolph*, 26. Johnson was known as the "Napoleon of the Turf."

61 Anburey, *Travels Through the Interior Parts of America*, 359–361.

62 MB1997, 463. For example, Shakespeare was probably the offspring of Fearnought, imported by John Baylor in 1764 (aka Baylor's Shakespeare). Robert Skipwith was another son-in-law of John Wayles. He married Tabitha Wayles, a half-sister of Martha (Wayles) Jefferson. John Wayles was born Jan. 31,

1715, and died May 28, 1773.

63 Kitty Fisher was imported by Carter Braxton in 1759. Jolly Roger (1743, chestnut colt) was imported in 1751 by John Spotswood but later owned by Ralph Wormeley of Rosegill in Middlesex, and was a distinguished sire. He is in many old Virginia pedigrees. He produced two taproot mares (matriarchal Thoroughbred mares). Jefferson's horse Wildair, bought from John Hoomes in 1801, was a son of Syme's Wildair. Harrison, *Early American Turf-Stock*, 1:141.

64 Harrison, *The Equine F.F.Vs.*, 172.

65 Jefferson was in Paris as minister plenipotentiary (ambassador), representing the new United States government, from 1784 to 1789.

66 Ellis, *Thomas Jefferson: A Character Sketch*, 159.

67 Randolph, *The Domestic Life of Thomas Jefferson*, 564; Ellis, *Thomas Jefferson: A Character Sketch*, 159.

68 Bear, *Jefferson at Monticello*, 89.

69 Ibid., 91.

70 Bear, *Jefferson at Monticello*, 91; Randall, *Life of Thomas Jefferson*, 2:225. Perhaps Dromedary and Camel were the same horse, confused by the biographers. Daniels, *The Randolphs of Virginia*, 241.

71 Randall, *Life of Thomas Jefferson*, 3:564.

72 Also Matchless, an unnamed carriage horse (1793), Fitzpartner, Tucappa, and Blucher.

73 Known as the American Saddle Horse and often as the Kentucky Saddle Horse (because it evolved in Kentucky). Harrison, *Early American Turf-Stock*, 1:26; Mackay-Smith, *The Colonial Quarter Race Horse*, 268; Kleber, *The Kentucky Encyclopedia*, 845. Standardbreds race in harness as trotters or pacers.

74 Elizabeth (Wayles) Eppes was one of Martha (Wayles) Jefferson's two surviving half-sisters.

75 His son, Francis, was cared for by a Monticello Hemings slave, Betsy, a gift to Maria from her father at marriage. Francis inherited Poplar Forest from Jefferson. Eppes lost some elections but won others. In all, he served five terms in Congress.

76 Wyatt, "Newmarket of the Virginia Turf," 439, 481. Colonel Francis Eppes was an early member of the House of Burgesses, in 1625.

77 The original imported horse was named Diomed. Jefferson spelled his horses' names as "Diomede." Pierson used "Diomede" in his transcription of the names in his interview with Bacon.

78 Eppes had seen Bell's six-year-old horse when Jefferson's Albemarle neighbor, Dr. Walker, had ridden to Eppington on it; JWE to TJ, July 6, 1800, in PTJ 32:43. Haxhall, Shore and Bell were all members of the Petersburg Jockey Club. Haxall was Bell's brother-in-law. TJ to JWE, April 25, 1801, *Founders Online*; FB1953, 101.

79 Breen, *Tobacco Culture*, 29. Debt in some cultures advertises, trumpets enduring social relations. The challenge to the elite was due to the crash of thetobacco market in the 1760s and the American Revolution.

80 Ibid., 85. Ironically, indebtedness is the antithesis of independence and autonomy.

81 Breen, *Tobacco Culture*, 94; Sloan, *Principle and Interest*, 41.

82 Sloan, *Principle and Interest*, 29; Breen, *Tobacco Culture*, 94, 96, 102, 128.

83 Breen, *Tobacco Culture*, 31. Breen, p. 73, says economic historians discovered that the planters had a naiveté about international market procedures.

84 MB1997, 1296.

85 Ibid., 290.

86 Darlington is another complicated case. Jefferson's son-in-law John Wayles Eppes bought Darlington for Jefferson in 1796 with money from the estate of Jefferson's father-in-law, John Wayles, who died in 1773; MB1997, 941. Jefferson was to credit Wayles's estate for £65, the debts for which Jefferson was responsible. Jefferson never succeeded in repaying these debts in his lifetime. Nevertheless, he "sold" Darlington to Richardson for labor in 1799. MB1997: 94, 279, 299, 1001.

87 MB1997:336, 368, 494. Hylton was an importer of cattle and horses and the comptroller of the port of the James River, Upper District; FB1953, 519. PTJ, 17:512.

88 MB1997:531, 535. Jefferson also sold two of his horses to Thomas Mann Randolph for two mules. The mules were worth more than Jefferson's horses because he had to pay £10 and £15 boot. Ibid., March 1, 1773.

89 TJ to TMR, December 30, 1793, in TJP.

90 MB1997, 1311. Tecumseh became one of a team of four carriage horses for Jefferson's landau. Isaacs's daughter, Julia Ann Isaacs, married Eston Hemings, who was a son of Sally Hemings and Thomas Jefferson, in 1832.

91 This may point to the progressively commercial ethos of the times versus the former mutual interdependence of the agrarian planter economy. MB1997, 762, 809.

92 PTJ, 17:243.

93 MB1997, 1309.

94 JHC to TJ, August 27, 1814, in *Founders Online*. Finally, in October, Jefferson was able to pay the 50£ agreed upon for *The Horse*; FB1999, 107. Breen, *Tobacco Culture*, 103.

95 MB1997:450, 1306.

96 Ibid., 536, 1334.

Chapter 3: Others Who Rode on the Mountain: Women, Workmen and Overseers, Enslaved Servants

1 Stanton, *"Those Who Labor for My Happiness,"* 58.

2 Anna Scott Marks, Jefferson's younger sister and twin of Randolph Jefferson, visited often before she came to live permanently at Monticello upon the death of her husband in 1811.

3 TJ to MJR, April 25, 1803, in FL1966, 244; VRT to NPT, Dec. 3, 1828, in PTJ, 40:273.

4 CJR to VRT, August 17, 1817, in *Jefferson Quotes and Family Letters.*

5 VRT to NPT, Dec. 3, 1828, in *Nicholas Philip Trist Papers.* Dr. Robley Dunglison was a University of Virginia faculty member and Jefferson's attending physician at his death.

6 Randall, *Life of Thomas Jefferson*, 3:340. "Fadladeens" refers to a character in an 1817 poem by Irish poet Thomas Moore, meaning a guardian of a young woman; see "Lalla Rookh."

7 Randall, *Life of Thomas Jefferson*, 1:63. After the death of his third wife, John Wayles took his slave Elizabeth Hemings as his mistress. Six Hemings children were the result of this union, among them Sally Hemings, the mother of several of Thomas Jefferson's children.

8 Sadly, the little boy, John, died at the age of three the summer before she married Jefferson. Written references of Jefferson riding for companionship with other women exist: Maria Cosway in Paris, and his daughters and granddaughters.

9 Randolph, The Domestic *Life of Thomas Jefferson*, 63.

10 TMR to TJ, June 19, 1793, in PTJ, 26:325; TJ to MJR, March 8, 1804, in FL1966, 259.

11 MJE to TJ, May 1, 1791, and TJ to MJE, May 8, 1791, both in FL1966, 80, 82.

12 MJE to TJ, May 29, 1791, in FL1966, 83.

13 TJ to MJR, March 8, 1804, in FL1966, 259; TJ to John Barnes, November 11, 1811, *Founders Online.* The child, also named Maria, survived, but died at three years of age.

14 She and her children became estranged from her husband, Thomas Mann Randolph. She lived at Monticello even while Randolph was governor of Virginia in Richmond (1819–1822).

15 TJ to ARB, May 20, 1803, and ARB to TJ, March 18, 1808, both in FL1966:246, 334.

16 Randall, *Life of Thomas Jefferson*, 3:348.

17 Jefferson actually owned the Natural Bridge; he bought it and 157 acres from King George III in 1774. It stayed in his family until it was sold in 1833.

18 CJR to VRT, August 17, 1817, in *Nicholas Philip Trist Papers.*

19 MJR to ERC, September 18, 1825, in Ellen Wayles Randolph Coolidge Correspondence.

20 Virginia Jefferson (Randolph) Trist to Nicholas Philip Trist, September 19, 1831, *Nicholas Philip Trist Papers.*

21 Virginia Jefferson (Randolph) Trist to Nicholas Philip Trist, September 12, 1833, Nicholas Philip Trist Papers. Carlton had been the home of Anne (Randolph) Bankhead, the oldest Randolph daughter, who had died in 1826, five months before Jefferson. Carlton was about two miles west past Monticello, on the road to Charlottesville.

22 Mackay-Smith, *The Colonial Quarter Race Horse*, 242; Bear, *Jefferson at Monticello*, 16. "The springs" refers to the many hot-water and warm-water springs, high in the western mountains of Virginia and in what is now West Virginia. Although known by the Indians and enjoyed by the white settlers, these springs became sites of resorts for elite Virginia plantation families by the early nineteenth century. Entire families from the sweltering Tidewater and Piedmont, Virginia, would seek the solace of the cooler airs in the mountain and "take the waters" for various ailments. Many of these resorts had quite the social scene as families established themselves there for several weeks, even months at a time. See Lewis, *Ladies and Gentlemen on Display.*

23 Bear, *Jefferson at Monticello*, 114.

24 Martha (Jefferson) Randolph to Ellen Wayles (Randolph) Coolidge, September 18, 1825; Virginia Jefferson (Randolph) Trist to Nicholas Philip Trist, September 12, 1833, Nicholas Philip Trist Papers. A public hack was a kind of simplified, open-sided, smaller and less expensive stagecoach.

25 Randolph, The Domestic *Life of Thomas Jefferson*, 53; Randall, *Life of Thomas Jefferson*, 1:236; Weaver, "The Albemarle of Old." The Italian Mazzei was in Europe at the time.

26 Helliar-Symons, "John Hartwell Cocke and Bremo," 38.

27 Martin, "Thomas Jefferson and Edmund Bacon," 13.

28 MB1997, 521, 1001. Jefferson had bought Darlington from John Wayles Eppes (Jefferson's wife's nephew, then studying law under Jefferson) in 1796 for £65. The following year, Eppes became Jefferson's son-in-law when he married Jefferson's second daughter, Maria.

29 FB1976, 76; FB1999, 152.

30 Martin, "Thomas Jefferson and Edmund Bacon," 3, 6; Bear, *Jefferson at Monticello*, 35.

31 "Edmund Bacon Memoranda Book," 1. Until then, an overseer had lasted about eighteen months in Jefferson's service; Martin, "Thomas Jefferson and Edmund Bacon," 2.

32 Bear, *Jefferson at Monticello*, 83.

33 Ibid., 61. Wormley Hughes was in charge of the stables at that time. Bacon stated that Monticello "had thirty-six stalls for horses, and only used about ten of them for the stock we kept there"; ibid., 114.

34 Bear, *Jefferson at Monticello*, 60, 62. Bacon said they generally worked mules on the plantation.

35 MB1997, 1334; Edmund Bacon Memoranda Book, 9.

36 Non-elites almost always had cash, including slaves. Jefferson often borrowed from his slaves. Martin, "Thomas Jefferson and Edmund Bacon," 17.

37 Bear, *Jefferson at Monticello*, 41.

38 Ibid., 35, 51.

39 Ibid., 35.

40 Skinner, *The American Farmer*.

41 Skinner, "Turf Register. Stud of Mr. Edmund Bacon," 114-115. Bacon also noted who the previous owners had been and the price of each mare.

42 Ibid., 115.

43 This is the stud book for Thoroughbreds in the United States, begun 1868. The *American Studbook* says Edmund Bacon took Duke of Bedford out to Kentucky in 1806. There is no record that Bacon went to Kentucky in 1806, before he started work for Jefferson. Supposedly Bacon's first trip west was in 1818, and his definitive move was in 1822. Perhaps Duke of Bedford was part of Bacon's founding stock. *The Horse* would have been twenty-two years old at that date. Bedford* was out of Mare, by Thornton's Voltaire; Nancy Washington, by Master Stephen*. Sire Line Eclipse. Duke of Bedford sired the unnamed mare who became the fourth dam of both Eliza Bailey (born 1832), a bay filly by Thompson's Columbus, and Jeannettau (born 1840), a chestnut filly by Leviathan*; "Thoroughbred Bloodlines."

44 Jefferson fathered six children with Sally Hemings, four of whom survived to adulthood.

45 McLaughlin, *Jefferson and Monticello*, 127. Presumably McLaughlin means "anonymous" to twenty-first century readers; not necessarily to Jefferson and others at Monticello.

46 "Family" here equates with "household." Some family names were Hern, Evans, Gillette, Granger. Elizabeth (Betty) Hemings had six children with John Wayles, Martha (Wayles) Jefferson's father. Betty's daughter, Sally, had several children with Jefferson himself. Jefferson formally freed seven male slaves, and only two in his lifetime. He allowed two of his "natural children" (Beverly and Harriet) to "walk away" when they came of age; "Enslaved People Who Gained Freedom." See also Gordon-Reed, *The Hemingses of Monticello:* Lewis and Onuf, eds., *Sally Hemings and Thomas Jefferson*, or Stanton, *Free Some Day*.

47 Slaves born on plantations were also sometimes given these names by their families; McLaughlin, *Jefferson and Monticello*, 102.

48 Legal barriers to Black education finally culminated in 1831 in a law that proscribed schools for even free Blacks; Stanton, *Free Some Day*, 98.

49 Randall, *Life of Thomas Jefferson*, 1:70.

50 Hodgson, *Letters from North America*, 320, went on to comment, "The black servants, who drive their master, and mistresses in gigs, generally sit on the step, which has a most unpleasant and unsafe appearance. I was particularly struck with this at Charleston and Savannah."

51 Anburey, *Travels Through the Interior Parts of America*, 359–361.

52 Elkhill was located about twenty-nine miles southeast of Monticello. In total, somewhere between twenty-three to thirty slaves left Jefferson's various plantations with Cornwallis. Originally, Jefferson noted in FB1976, 29, that these people had "fled to the enemy" or "joined the enemy." Years later, in 1788, Jefferson claimed they had been "carried off" by Cornwallis. If they fled, it was presumably to the promise of freedom under the English. When Jefferson claimed his slaves had been carried off, he said, "had this been to give them freedom, he [Cornwallis]would have done right, but it was to consign them to inevitable death from small pox and putrid fever then raging in his camp"; PTJ, 13:363–64. Although many of these slaves died from fevers in the British camps, Jefferson was able to retrieve some. Kranish, *Flight from Monticello*, 292.

53 These slaves would have carried passes from their master; to be off the plantation without a pass was illegal, and they could have been apprehended as runaways. MB1997, 1010.

54 TJ, *A Summary View*, contains the words: "The abolition of domestic slavery is the great object of desire in those colonies where it was unhappily introduced in their infant state"; Stanton, *Free Some Day*, 21.

55 TJ to MJR, August 18, 1783, in FL1966, 123.

56 Helliar-Symons, "John Hartwell Cocke and Bremo," 34. Wilson Cary Nicholas was a protégé of Jefferson's, who lived at Mount Warren in southern Albemarle County. MB1997, 942.

57 Stanton, *Free Some Day*, 21.

58 Ibid., 23.

59 Isaac, *Landon Carter's Uneasy Kingdom*, 25, 206.

60 In those years, horses not kept in barns or stables were allowed to range and graze in the woods, as secure fencing was prohibitively expensive and difficult to maintain. Advertisements about "strayed" animals were constant in the local and state newspapers and gazettes. The "boys" surely knew, of course, that the animal belonged to someone. (See Chapter 10.) Joel Yancey to TJ, December 24, 1818, in Coolidge Collection of Thomas Jefferson Manuscripts.

61 Ibid.

62 Some Jefferson slaves made two or three attempts to leave slavery, were captured and returned once, even twice, before being punished (flogged). Some slaves disappeared and were not pursued, others left one plantation without permission only to turn up at Monticello or the White House to complain of an overseer to Jefferson or to check on the condition of a spouse at the other plantation. See Stanton, *Free Some Day*, for these examples.

63 In this case, the advertisement in the *Virginia Gazette* was submitted by Meriwether Skelton, brother of Martha (Wayles) Jefferson's first husband, Bathurst Skelton. Skelton was searching for a slave, Sanco, sold to Skelton two years previously by Thomas Jefferson. Skelton thought Sanco may have trying to "get to Carolina, as he was heard to say, that he understood a regiment of negros was to be raised there" to fight with the British against the Americans; *Virginia Gazette*, September 14, 1769; June 21, 1780. See also Stanton, *Free Some Day*, 81.

64 It wasn't until a century later that these horses would become known as American Thoroughbreds.

65 Weld, *Travels Through the States of North America*, 106.

66 Morgan, *Slave Counterpoint*, 416, 417.

67 Willie Jones (1741–1801) was known as the "Jefferson of North Carolina." Jones was an American patriot in the Revolutionary War and later became one of the founding fathers of North Carolina. In his role as planter and racehorse breeder, Jones was one of the largest slaveholders in the region. Jones's daughter became the second wife of John Wayles Eppes, after the untimely death of his first wife, Jefferson's second daughter, Maria, in 1804. (See Chapter 9.) Mark and Vaughan, *The South*, 442.

68 Bear, *Jefferson at Monticello*, 20.

69 Stanton, *Free Some Day*, 20.

70 Although Jupiter Evans died in slavery (1799), all three of the Hemings men (Robert and James Hemings and Burwell Colbert) were freed by Jefferson during their lifetimes; Stanton, *Free Some Day*, 27, 127, 140.

71 Evans did not drive Jefferson. (Jefferson usually drove himself if he used a vehicle). Jupiter drove Jefferson's wife and family. Maybe Evans was happy to give up the frequent absences from Monticello, and stay home with his new wife, Sucky, who had just arrived at Monticello in 1774.

72 Randall, *Life of Thomas Jefferson*, 3:510. On TJ's temperament, see Stanton, *"Those Who Labor for My Happiness,"* 112.

73 Stanton, *Free Some Day*, 21. Moreover, it was an illegal and dangerous adventure if they did not have a pass. "Boy" was a term applied to adult Black men also, a way to express racist ideology and mark the inferiority of the Black man (boy = child) to a white man (man = adult).

74 Wormley Hughes was another member of the extended Hemings family. Randall, *Life of Thomas Jefferson*, 1:70.

75 Argent, "Horses, Mourning," 21-30. "[M]utual grooming has become an end in itself, a gesture of 'belonging' and a symbol of the bond between equine companions. Because of this, the grooming of horses by their human owners has a vital significance...In The Horse's mind, [it is] an indication that its human companion is a close friend"; Morris, *Horse Watching*, 56.

76 Randolph, The Domestic *Life of Thomas Jefferson*, 48; Randall, *Life of Thomas Jefferson*, 1:68.

77 Isaac (Granger) Jefferson said, "Jupiter and John drove Mr. Jefferson's coach and four; one of them rode postilion. They rode postilion in those days. Jupiter and John wore caps and gilded bands"; Bear, *Jefferson at Monticello*, 5. This would imply that Jefferson used postilions before Jupiter Evans's death in 1799. During his presidency, Jefferson's chariot was driven by the coachman Dougherty (no postilions). However, the chariot was used mainly for the president's daughter, Martha, and her children, when they were visiting. Jefferson was rarely driven in it.

78 FB1999, 461; TJ to MJR, June 6, 1814, in FL1966, 405.

79 Gordon-Reed, *Thomas Jefferson and Sally Hemings*, 250; Stanton, *Free Some Day*, 96.

80 *Charlottesville Central Gazette*, January 26, 1821.

81 TJ to MJR, July 16, 1801; TJ to MJR, May 14, 1804; TJ to TJR, March 31, 1815, in FL1966, 207, 206, 409. Jefferson left Freeman with *The Horse* on May 14, 1804. Freeman was Jefferson's dining room servant/personal servant at the White House. Jefferson was hiring Freeman at this point; Stanton interview.

82 Bear, *Jefferson at Monticello*, 106; Stanton, *Free Some Day*, 62. Carts were wooden two-wheeled vehicles. Hern's wife, Fanny Gillette, a cook at the White House, and his sister, Edith, lived in Washington in those years. Thus, Hern's mule-cart trips were an excuse for conjugal visits.

Chapter 4 —Equine Gentry: Thorough-Bred, Jefferson's Saddle Horses, 1766 –1826

1 Bear, *Jefferson at Monticello*, 60.

2 TJ to Samuel Clarkson, February 2, 1793, in *Founders Online*. Today the term "purebred" is used for any animal whose pedigree is recognized by a breed registry.

3 All these horses—Barbs, Spanish jennets, English Hobbies—were aterally gaited; they paced and had other lateral intermediate gaits (amble and rack). These are types of horses rather than true breeds.

4 Both sire and dam must trace ancestry to the imported Oriental blood. Russell, *Like Engend'ring Like*; Cassidy, *The Sport of Kings*.

5 Horses are measured in "hands." One hand equals 4 inches.

6 The Thoroughbred's legs are probably too small for its body weight. Leg issues have been constant with this breed, especially in the racing horses.

7 Since 2002, work with horse DNA at Trinity College in Dublin has shown that Thoroughbred horses descend from twenty-eight male ancestors (foundation sires) and to seventy-four foundation mares from the eighteenth and nineteenth centuries; Cunningham and Dooley, "Microsatellite Diversity, Pedigree Relatedness and the Contributions of Founder Lineages to Thoroughbred Horses," 360-364. Recently, studies on the mtDNA reveal it is possible there are only fifteen unique foundation mare lines; Hill et al., "History and Integrity of Thoroughbred Dam Lines."

8 Campbell, *The Horse in Virginia*, 20.

9 Pickrell, "95% of Thoroughbreds Linked to One Superstud."

10 Marguerite Henry, an American, wrote the well-known tale about this horse, *King of the Wind*, which was published in 1948.

11 Regulus was the sire of Fearnought, imported into Virginia in 1764. In fact, the Godolphin Arabian is usually more present in the dam lines in the middle of the pedigree than as a direct sire; Peters, "Godolphin Arabian."

12 Cunningham et al., "Microsatellite Diversity, Pedigree Relatedness and the Contributions of Founder Lineages to Thoroughbred Horses," 360-364.

13 This dual-purpose racehorse and saddle horse became the Virginia Quarter Horse.

14 Harrison, *Early American Turf-Stock*, 2:59.

15 Ibid.

16 "To stand at stud" means that the owner offers his stallion to breed with mares for a fee (the stud fee).

17 "Oriental" is a reference to Arabian horses imported into England.

18 George Jeffreys (1826), Allen Jones Davie (1833), quoted in Mackay-Smith, *The Colonial Quarter Race Horse*, 112, 133.

19 Peters, "Fearnought."

20 Ibid. At Baylor's death he had 100 horses, including 50 thoroughbreds.

21 Harrison, *Early American Turf-Stock*, 2:117.

22 "Diomed's coming to America was doubly epochal. He not only remolded its entire breeding fabric, almost 'at the stroke of the enchanter's wand'—the immediate and sustained success, first of his get and then of his descendants, proved the prime fact in the regeneration of the turf, still laboring under the weight of the Revolutionary disasters, and its rise to new and greater height"; Hervey, *Racing in America*, 167, 177 (quote). Since Diomed was born in 1777, the pedigree connecting is twenty to twenty-three generations in the past, often in several lines. See "Pedigree Online. All Breed Database."

23 Trevathan, *The American Thoroughbred*, 97.

24 Jefferson's life with blooded horses begins only after his marriage to Martha Wayles, in 1772. Because of this marriage into a wealthy Virginia family, Jefferson inherits blooded horses and is able to purchase even more. Thanks to Christa Dierksheide, University of Virginia, for pointing out this relationship; personal communication, August 18, 2021.

25 Jefferson may have bought a couple of retired racehorses, like The General, but he never bought or bred horses to race.

26 When Jefferson arrived in Philadelphia, he had four horses, including The General. It is not clear how many horses were hitched to the phaeton during the trip, two with a riding horse trailing, or three with The General trailing later.

27 Randall, *Life of Thomas Jefferson*, 1:69.

28 Elkhill was land inherited through Jefferson's wife upon the death of her father, John Wayles, in 1774. It lies twenty-nine miles downstream from Monticello at the confluence of the Rivanna and James rivers.

29 This perhaps is an apocryphal story. Lucia Stanton, Monticello historian, reports this embellishment to the escape story that Monticello's enslaved blacksmith shod Jefferson's horse backwards. This is a story that Charles Bullock supposedly heard from Peter Fossett in 1900: "When Col. Tarlton and his men thought Jefferson was coming, he was going in the opposite direction"; Stanton, "The Other End of the Telescope," 148. Recall, Jefferson had broken his wrist in a fall from Caractacus during one morning ride. It took six weeks for the wrist to mend before Jefferson could ride again. McDonnell, "Jefferson, Thomas as Governor of Virginia."

30 TJ to Charles Lilburne Lewis, February 22, 1790, in PTJ, 16:121. Lewis's mother was Thomas Jefferson's mother's sister, Mary Randolph, so in addition to being brothers-in-law, the two were first cousins.

31 Bear, *Jefferson at Monticello*, 13.

32 James Hemings was a son of Elizabeth Hemings, an enslaved woman, whose family was inherited by Thomas and Martha from Martha's father, John Wayles.

33 He often wrote about sitting in the Tuileries Garden and watching the completion of the construction on the embankment on the other side of the Seine of a neo-classical house, the Hotel de Salm, which Jefferson thought was an example of architectural beauty. TJ to Peter Carr, August 19, 1785, in *Founders Online*.

34 TJ to Rayneval, March 3, 1786, and TJ to William S. Smith, June 4, 1786, in PTJ 9:313, 605; MB1997, April 1, 1786, 617, and April 14, 1786, 621.

35 The Grand Stables are 186 meters long. Later, after the French Revolution, as racehorses began to be bred in France, the Chantilly Grand Stables became the site of a famous race course, still used today.

36 Landry, *Noble Brutes*, 38.

37 As described earlier, smallish indigenous English horses (mares) were crossed with imported Oriental, or Arab, stallions. Landry, "Learning to Ride in Early Modern Britain"; Nash, " 'Honest English Breed,' 245272).

38 A martingale is a piece of tack used for head carriage to keep a horse from throwing its head back too high and hitting the rider in the face. MB1997, 635, 639. Maria Cosway was an Anglo-Italian artist, composer, musician, and society hostess. Despite being married to a painter of miniatures, Richard Cosway, Maria, when introduced to Jefferson in Paris, spent several weeks in his company, exploring art exhibits and architecture in the city gardens and countryside together. Although she may have been a romantic interest for Jefferson, Cosway returned to England after six weeks, and their relationship effectively ended (although they continued to write each other periodically the rest of their lives).

39 WS to TJ, May 14, 1787, in PTJ, 2:362.

40 Jefferson's "family" had now expanded to include not only daughter Martha and the enslaved James Hemings, but also Jefferson's younger daughter, Mary (henceforth known as Maria), accompanied by her enslaved caretaker, James's sister, the fourteen-year-old Sally Hemings. Mary had originally been left behind in Virginia in the care of an aunt, too young to travel abroad with her father. By 1787, Maria and Sally were sent to France to be with Jefferson. WS to TJ, November 25, 1789, in PTJ 15:558; MB1997, 635 n. 47.

41 A horse with intermixed white and colored hairs of any color is usually called a roan. Except for white markings under the control of other genes, the head, mane, tail, and lower legs are dark. There are bay or strawberry roans (chestnut base coat), red roans (on a bay coat), and blue roans (on a black coat).

42 Harrison, *Early American Turf-Stock*, 2:572.

43 See Chapter 7 for the rumor that in his racing days, Tarquin had raced against and had beaten George Washington's favorite horse, Magnolia. MB1997, 638.

44 TJ to TMR, Dec. 30, 1793, in TJP; FB1953, 96-97.

45 TMR to TJ, November 14, 1793, in PTJ, 27:378; TJ to TMR, November 24, 1793, in PTJ, 28:431.

46 TJ to TMR, December 30, 1793, in PTJ, 27:637.

47 MB1997, 941. John Wayles Eppes married Maria Jefferson on October 13, 1797.

48 TJ to TMR, April 18, 1798, in PTJ, 30:283. Randolph lived across the Rivanna River at Edgehill.

49 TMR to TJ, April 29, 1798, in PTJ, 30:313.

50 MB1997, 1001.

51 Young Kitty Fisher was got by Jolly Roger, one of the early, distinguished English imports (1750) by Ralph Wormeley of Rosegill, and her dam was Kitty Fisher, a mare imported (1759) by Carter Braxton of Elsing Green; Harrison, *The Equine F.F.Vs.*, 60, 149; Harrison, *Early American Turf-Stock*, 1:141.

52 Jefferson also owned several horses of Diomed blood after 1808.

53 JH to TJ, Letter, January 5, 1801, in *Founders Online*; TJ to JH, Washington, Jan. 12, 1801, in TJP.

54 TJ to JH, April 17, 1801, in *Founders Online*.

55 Randolph, The Domestic *Life of Thomas Jefferson*, 276.

56 TJ to JWE, August 7, 1804, in Randolph, The Domestic *Life of Thomas Jefferson*, 309. A Wm. Farris from the Shenandoah Valley of Virginia went out to Kentucky after 1800 and was an important breeder of Thoroughbred horses there; Johnson, *A History of Kentucky and Kentuckians*, 1119.

57 Wormley Hughes, quoted in Randall, *Life of Thomas Jefferson*, 1:70.

58 TJ to JWE, May 27, 1805, in MB1997, 2:1154.

59 TJ to TMR, May 24, 1807, in *Founders Online*.

60 Randall, *Life of Thomas Jefferson*, 1:69.

61 Meade was good friends with another important breeder (and Jefferson relative), John Randolph of Roanoke. Meade served in the American Revolution and later in the Virginia House of Delegates and the Virginia State Senate. The Meade home was known as the Hermitage. Brandon's pedigree traces back to Jenny Morris in Allycroker's pedigree (Jefferson's main broodmare).

62 MB1997, 1381; Randall, *Life of Thomas Jefferson*,1:69. Dropping the post-vowel /r/ is common is several American (and English) regional accents.

63 Bear, *Jefferson at Monticello*, 61.

64 National Register of Historic Places Registration Form: Oaklands (Malvern Farm), Section 8, 3. Jefferson probably bought the offspring of one of those mares. In 1813 Jefferson wrote in his account book that he bartered a gold watch with Sam Carr (Jefferson's nephew through his sister Martha) for a six-year-old red bay horse "got by Nosley"; Dec. 27, 1813, in MB1997, 1296. Harrison, *Early American Turf-Stock*, 2:390.

65 Jefferson was going to his retreat at Poplar Forest in Bedford County.

66 JHC to TJ, April 19, 1814, in Cocke Family Papers.

67 Bear, *Jefferson at Monticello*, 62.

68 Wills, *Mr. Jefferson's University*, 134.

69 Randall, *Life of Thomas Jefferson*, 1:69.

70 Cornelia was twenty-six years old at the time. MJR to ERC, September 18, 1825, in Jefferson Quotes and Family Letters.

71 Randall, *Life of Thomas Jefferson*, 3:538.

72 Ibid.. 1:69. Jefferson's grandson, Thomas Jefferson "Jeff" Randolph, had been stabbed by Jeff's own brother-in-law, Charles Lewis Bankhead, in Charlottesville. That incident took place on February 1, 1819; Crawford, *Twilight at Monticello*, xv. Jefferson did not buy The Eagle until November 1820, so *The Horse* he used in his dash down the mountain to rescue Jeff could not have been The Eagle. Family members must have been mistaken when they recalled for Randall that it was The Eagle that the elderly Jefferson rode that evening.

73 Randall, *Life of Thomas Jefferson*, 3:538.

74 Anthropomorphism is the attribution of human traits, emotions, or intentions to non-human entities.

75 Argent, "Toward a Privileging of the Nonverbal Communication, Corporeal Synchrony, and Transcendence in Humans and Horses," 111-128; Argent, "Horses, Mourning," 23; Hearne, Adam's Task, 149.

76 Various members of Jefferson's family stayed at Monticello until it was sold in 1831. Edgehill was Randolph family land on the other side of the Rivanna River from Monticello.

77 Margaret Smith Randolph (March 17, 1816–December 20, 1842) and Wilson Cary Randolph (October 26, 1834–April 26, 1907) were both children of Thomas Jefferson Randolph, Jefferson's oldest grandson. Margaret Smith Randolph to Wilson Cary Randolph, July 7, 1841, in Edgehill-Randolph Papers, 1749.

78 Bear, *Jefferson at Monticello*, 60; Mason, *The Gentleman's New Pocket Farrier*, 22.

79 TMR to TJ, June 19, 1793, in PTJ, 26:325.

80 Mason, *The Gentleman's New Pocket Farrier*, 72. Today a horse's physical and mental peak is considered between twelve and fifteen years old.

81 In eighteenth-century Virginia, "horse" referred to a four-year-old unneutered male animal, a stallion. "Mare" referred to a four-year-old female horse. "Colt" and "filly" referred to animals between one and four years old, male and female respectively. "Foal" refers to a newborn.

82 Some present-day laterally gaited breeds are the Paso Finos of Cuba, Puerto Rico, Columbia, and Peru; the Campolinas of Brazil; and in the United States, Rocky Mountain and Kentucky Mountain Horses.

83 For example, the American Saddlebred and Tennessee Walking Horse.

84 Haworth, *George Washington: Farmer*, 3.

85 Anburey, *Travels Through the Interior Parts of America*, 410. In England, riders use the expression "to rise to the trot," whereas in the United States the expression is "to post." In the rapid two-beat diagonal gait of the trot, *The Horse*'s back rises and falls, making it very uncomfortable for the rider to sit, espe-

cially over long distances (as compared to the pace or amble of the gaited horses). Rising up (and down) in the stirrups in rhythm with *The Horse* is more comfortable for the rider. But rising to the trot had to be taught to and practiced by new riders and took many years to become commonplace after the introduction of the new trotting blooded"horses, the soon-to-be-called Thoroughbreds. It also required that the rider shorten the stirrups in order to rise. If the stirrups were left longer, as was the fashion, as in manège (dressage), one couldn't rise off the saddle.

86 Weld, *Travels Through the States of North America*, 186–187.

87 Postilions and post-coaches are explained in Chapter 6. J. S. Skinner, quoted in Bishko, "A Spanish Stallion for Albemarle," 174.

88 MB1997, 94, 279.

89 Mackay-Smith, *The Colonial Quarter Race Horse*, 8, 133.

90 Recall that it was common to name a horse after its sire, i.e., Dandridge's Fearnought, Gay's Fearnought, Bland's Fearnought. It is like carrying on an important last name. Note that the dam is often referred to as a Janus mare or a Diomed mare.

91 MJE to TJ, May 29, 1791, in FL1966, 83.

92 J. H. Cocke included Fearnought with Janus as part of the "good old stocks of saddle and harnass" horses. He also said that a "fine saddle horse" could be found "now and then [of] a Diomed or Bedford cross"; letter, *American Farmer*, Feb. 28, 1823, cited in Mackay-Smith, *The Colonial Quarter Race Horse*, 229.

93 Holmes, *Thomas Jefferson Treats Himself*, 81; TJ to John Barnes, November 11, 1818, Remarks by Mr. Charles C. Smith at the December Meeting, 1899, of the Society, in Massachusetts Historical Society, *Proceedings of the Massachusetts Historical Society*, 2nd ser., 13:312.

94 Burstein, *The Inner Jefferson*, 31, 32. Jefferson also used toponyms from the epic to name some of his land parcels: Lego, Morven. The authenticity of these poems was under attack from the very beginning of Macpherson's publication. The Irish claimed he was stealing their own Celtic production and heritage. Others accused Macpherson of adding his own compositions, if not inventing the whole cycle.

95 Oroonoko was also the name of a kind of tobacco cultivated in the South.

96 In the Treaty of Lancaster, the various Iroquois tribes "sold" lands to the west (i.e., West Virginia and Ohio) to the representatives of Virginia, Maryland, and Pennsylvania. Hodgson, *Letters from North America*, 1:320.

97 Larson, *A Magnificent Catastrophe*, 70.

98 Molnar, *Songs from the Williamsburg Theatre*, vii. Peggy Woffington died in 1760, before *The Beggar's Opera* opened in Williamsburg.

99 Nelson-Burns, "Ally Croaker."

100 Molnar, *Songs from the Williamsburg Theatre*, ix, 153; MB1997, 234.

101 Neighbor and closest friend James Madison named his final saddle horse Liberty.

Chapter 5. Carriage Horses, Carriages, and Roads

1 Randall, *Life of Thomas Jefferson*, 1:68; Bear, *Jefferson at Monticello*, 5; Randall, *Thomas Jefferson: A Life*, 90.

2 Bear, *Jefferson at Monticello*, 61.

3 Tarr, *The History of the Carriage*, 238.

4 Bear, *Jefferson at Monticello*, 5. In his *Farm Book*, Jefferson had written Gustavus was foaled in 1762, but later in 1773 in his *Account Book*, Jefferson rectified this: "On accurate settlement of Gustavus's age with F. Willis we find he was foaled in the spring of 1763"; FB1999, 89.

5 Harrison, *Early American Turf-Stock*, 2:8.

6 Jefferson's Crab's dam was noted as a Crab mare. In other words her sire was Crab imported quite early on in 1746 to Carter's stud at Shirley; Harrison, *The Equine F.F.Vs.*, 58. Sprightly was another imported horse. A chestnut horse, foaled in 1768 and brought to Maryland in 1773, Sprightly stood at stud all over Virginia, Maryland, and Pennsylvania; Harrison, *Early American Turf-Stock*, 2:197. MB1997, 1:531.

7 Alexander Spotswood (1751–1818) was the grandson of Alexander Spotswood (1676–1740), the governor of Virginia from 1710 to 1722. The grandson would serve in the Revolutionary War and was appointed general. He was a close friend and neighbor to George Washington.

8 Crews, "Comfort, Economy, Style," 86.

9 "Colonial Roads and Wheeled Vehicles," 37–42.

10 Berkebile, *Carriage Terminology*, 213. Jefferson and Martha were married at the Forest, Martha's father's home on the James River down in the Tidewater area. After the wedding they traveled to Monticello in Albemarle County in the phaeton. Because of a tremendous snowstorm, the young couple was forced to abandon the phaeton and ride the final miles of the journey on horseback.

11 The term phaeton for a carriage is believed to have come from the French in the early eighteenth century; Berkebile, *Carriage Terminology*, 213.

12 For taxes in 1773, Jefferson listed one chariot and one phaeton; FL1999, 461.

13 Goodwin, *Wheeled Carriages in Eighteenth Century Virginia*, clii; Berkebile, *Carriage Terminology*, 84.

14 Berkebile, *Carriage Terminology*, 84.

15 Large-scale coach manufacturing began in the United States in New Hampshire in 1813; Tarr, *The History of the Carriage*, 271. For 1782 taxes, Jefferson claimed one chariot and one chair; FB1999, 461; MB1997, 1:518. Also see MB1997, 535 (Sept. 30, 1783).

16 A postilion is a person who rides the left-hand horse of a two- or four-horse carriage in place of a driver.

17 MB1997, 630.

18 WS to TJ, May 14, 1787, in PTJ, 11:362.

19 MB1997, 630. Jefferson thought he was returning temporarily, and would soon come back to France after making the appropriate arrangements for his daughters to stay in Virginia. Although Jefferson took four of his carriages home with him, he left two for Short to dispose of.

20 Changing horses at each stage began in 1734.

21 While in England, Jefferson ordered some plated carriage harness sets (the plated harness arrived to France later that November) Jefferson also bought, besides the harness sets, a saddle and bridle and riding boots. Finally, he was ready to own his own horses back in Paris.

22 Mazzei, *Memoirs of the Life and Peregrinations of the Florentine, Philip Mazzei,* 296n.

23 Berkebile, *Carriage Terminology*, 64; Tarr, *The History of the Carriage*, 243; TJ to William Stephens Smith, August 9, 1786, in PTJ, 10:211.

24 Tarr, *The History of the Carriage*, 243.

25 Ibid.

26 Günther, *The Casanova Tour*, part 2. The mail-coach system was established in 1784.

27 Landry, "Learning to Ride in Early Modern Britain," 329–349. Although in England this is still referred to as "rising to the trot," in America it is called "posting" (the verb is "to post").

28 MB1997, 613–623.

29 Adams, "The Coach Motif in Eighteenth-Century Fiction," 17–26.

30 Hailman, *Thomas Jefferson on Wine*, 102.

31 TJ to Samuel Clarkson, February 2, 1793, PTJ, 25:13.

32 Ibid. Jefferson may have regretted selling Brimmer so soon because a week later, Joseph, one of Jefferson's servants, took a ride on another horse, Matchless, a fierce-tempered horse who ran away with Joseph, impaled himself on the shaft of a cart, and died. At that point, Jefferson was left with his "old pair," probably Romulus and Remus, and Tarquin.; TJ to TMR, Feb. 18, 1793, in PTJ, 25:230.

33 TJ to TMR, August 7, 1791, in TJP; TJ to MJE, July 16, 1801, in Randolph, The Domestic *Life of Thomas Jefferson*, 279. After her husband's death, Mrs. Marks moved permanently to Monticello.

34 For taxes in 1794 and 1800, Jefferson listed only one phaeton; FB1999, 461.

35 JA to TJ, February 20, 1801, in PTJ, 33:23.

36 Note to JA to TJ, February 20, 1801, in PTJ, 33:23n.

37 The 1800 election had been thrown into the House of Representatives over a technicality about president versus vice president. Jefferson had beaten Adams but had technically tied with Aaron Burr, his running mate. The House of Representatives took two months and 36 ballots to confirm Jefferson as president. The chariot did not arrive until late September 1801.

38 TJ to JWE, January 19, 1801, in PTJ, 32:489; JWE to TJ, March 18, 1801, in PTJ, 33:350.

39 MB1997, 1038.

40 TJ to JWE, June 4, 1808, in "Some Family Letters of Thomas Jefferson," 576.

41 JWE to TJ, April 18, 1801, in PTJ, 33:610–611.

42 JWE to TJ, April 18, 1801, in PTJ, 33:610. The visitor was Jefferson's Albemarle neighbor Dr. Walker, visiting in the Petersburg area; JWE to TJ, July 6, 1800, in PTJ, 32:43.

43 JWE to TJ, March 18, 1801, in PTJ, 33:350; EB1953, 10.

44 JWE to TJ, March 18, April 18, 1801, in PTJ, 33:350, 610.

45 FB1999,102.

46 TJ to MJR, May 14, 1804, in Jefferson, *Autograph letters Signed.*

47 TJ to JWE, April 25, 1801, in PTJ, 33:641.

48 TJ to JWE, June 17, 1801, in FB1999, 102.

49 Jefferson, "Monticello: icehouse, coachrooms, etc.," *Thomas Jefferson Papers.*

50 Berkebile, *Carriage Terminology*, 265.

51 TJ to Enoch Edwards, March 30, 1801, in PTJ, 33:500–501.

52 Jefferson sold the chariot for $500 to Dr. Elzey, March 10, 1809, just before he left Washington, DC, upon his retirement from the presidency; MB1997, 1242.

53 TJ to MJR, June 18, 1802, in *Founders Online.*

54 TJ to Enoch Edwards, July 9, 1801, in PTJ, 34:530.

55 Bear, *Jefferson at Monticello*, 61.

56 JWE to TJ, September 5, 21, 1808, in FB1999, 104, 105; Bear, *Jefferson at Monticello*, 60.

57 FL1966, 350; Bear, *Jefferson at Monticello*, 61.

58 Bear, *Jefferson at Monticello*, 41.

59 MB1997, 1308.

60 Bear, *Jefferson at Monticello*, 61.

61 Ibid.; Thomas Jefferson Foundation, "Sally Hemings's Children: Eston Hemings." Tecumseh, the famous Native American leader of the Shawnee, died defending his homeland from the Americans in 1813. The respect his enemies felt for him is proved by the many times his name was given to towns, ships, and people.

62 FB1999, 461; TJ to Enoch Edwards, July 9, 1801, in *Founders Online*.

63 There were eventually two main types of landau: a square type with an angular body, and a rounded or canoe-shaped vehicle; Smith, *A Dictionary of Horse-Drawn Vehicles*, 103. Jefferson's was the canoe-shaped type.

64 Bacon, quoted in Bear, *Jefferson at Monticello*, 102; FB1999, 462; Israel Gillette in Stanton, *Free Some Day*, 93, and in Gordon-Reed, *Thomas Jefferson and Sally Hemings*, 249. Rattinet is a light woolen cloth.

65 For taxes in 1815, 1816, and 1817, Jefferson listed one gig and one landau; FB1999, 461. CJR to VRT, August 17, 1817, in Family Letters.

66 Mrs. Marks, Jefferson's sister and a semi-permanent guest at Monticello at the time, had started out in the gig to visit her other brother, Randolph, who was sick, at Snowdon in Buckingham County. After going about seven miles south, Bedford took ill, and Mrs. Marks decided to turn around. Bedford died that very night; TJ to TJR, March 31, 1815, in FL1966, 409.

67 MB1997, 2:1305.

68 Harrison, *Early American Turf-Stock*, 2:302, 303. In 1808, when Jefferson's Bedford would have been bred, imported Bedford would have been at John Avery's in Brunswick County, Virginia. Bacon retired from Jefferson's service in 1822 and went to Kentucky, where he became a successful planter and stock breeder.

69 FL1966, 409. Jefferson had previously used his Chickasaws to drive Martha (another female) to Washington for a visit; TJ to MJR, April 23, 1803, in FL1966, 244. Snowden was Randolph Jefferson's home, south of the James River in Buckingham County. Randolph was Anna Scott's twin brother and Thomas Jefferson's younger brother. He was ill at the time. Tufton was one of Jefferson's quarter-farms at Monticello.

70 MB1997, 1307.

71 Randolph, The Domestic *Life of Thomas Jefferson*, 278.

72 TJ to Enoch Edwards, April 18, 1801, in PTJ, 33:609.

73 TJ to William Stephens Smith, July 9, Aug. 9, 1786 in PTJ, 10:115, 211; TJ to John Trumbull, September 10, 1788, in PTJ, 13:597.

74 Bear, *Jefferson at Monticello*, 5; Daniel, "Virginian Reminiscences of Jefferson," 1766.

75 Wormley Hughes, a Monticello slave, was a door-yard servant and later Jefferson's gardener. By the time of the interview in 1851, Hughes was a free man; Randall, *Life of Thomas Jefferson*,1:69, 3:332.

76 Workers of the Writers' Program, *Virginia: A Guide to the Old Dominion*.

77 England had a quite well-developed road system, and post-chaise transportation was quite common by the late seventeenth century; Edwards, *Horse and Man in Early Modern England*. Hugh Jones, quoted in "Colonial Roads and Wheeled Vehicles," 39; Pawlett, *A Brief History of the Roads of Virginia*, 9. Berkeley was governor of Virginia, appointed by the king, 1641–1652 and 1660–1677.

78 TJ to Richard Richardson, April 22, 1800, in PTJ, 31:536–37. Three Notch'd Road (or Three Chopt Road) received its name from the three ax chops in the tree made by settlers to blaze the trail (over an old Indian trail). Three Notch'd Road was finally superseded in the 1930s by Route 250. In the 1960s, Interstate 64 was built paralleling Route 250.

79 Pawlett, "A Brief History of the Roads of Virginia," 7, 15; Workers of the Writers' Program, *Virginia: A Guide to the Old Dominion*.

80 Workers of the Writers' Program, *Virginia: A Guide to the Old Dominion*.

81 TJ to TMR, March 28, 1790, in Randolph, The Domestic *Life of Thomas Jefferson*, 175.

82 TJ to MJR, May 14, 1804, in AD1995, 259–260.

83 TJ to John Page, May 1766, in Randall, *Thomas Jefferson: A Life*, 86.

84 TJ to MJR, Oct. 12, 1807, in AD1995, 311.

85 JWE to TJ, November 17, 1797, in PTJ, 29:572; CJR to VRT, July 28, 1821, in Stanton, *Free Some Day*, 94.

86 Randall, *Life of Thomas Jefferson*, 1:522.

87 Carter's Mountain was the taller mountain, beside Monticello. Jefferson refers to it as Montalto. The roundabouts were four roads that Jefferson had built that encircled his house on the Mountain, each at a different contour level. Other diagonal roads connected the contour roundabouts at different points. They also made the ascent to the main house gentler. Margaret Bayard Smith was a writer, Washington socialite, and the wife of John Bayard, editor of the *National Intelligencer*, a newspaper supported by Jefferson when the government moved to Washington.

Chapter 6. Sport: Foxhunting and Horse Racing

1 TJ to TJR, November 24, 1808, in MB1997, 12:196.

2 John Page quoted in Maxwell, *The Virginia Historical Register and Literary Note-book*, 150–151.

3 Jones, "Fox Hunting in America," 62.

4 TJ to ERC, October 25, 1808, in FL1966, 354.

5 Jones, "Fox Hunting in America," 62.

6 Landry, *Noble Brutes*, 43. The "forward seat" was not "invented" until the end of the nineteenth century by the Italian Federico Caprilli. The "broken" snaffle bit was considered less "oppressive" than the curb bit.

7 Landry, "Learning to Ride in Early Modern Britain," 329–349.

8 Jones, "Fox Hunting in America," 62.

9 Ibid.

10 Washington not only hunted foxes. He notes hunting ducks (and which kind) and catching fish too. Washington et al., *The Diaries of George Washington*, 44; Smucker, "A Fowler and a Fisher."

11 Jones, "Fox Hunting in America," 62.

12 Ibid.

13 Ibid.; Masters of Foxhounds Association website, http://www.mfha.com/foxhunting-history.html.

14 Masters of Foxhounds Association website, http://www.mfha.com/foxhunting-history.html.

15 The role of "whipper-in" in hunts has inspired some parliamentary systems (including the Westminster System and the US Congress) to use the term "whip" for a member who enforces party discipline and ensure the attendance of other members at important votes.

16 "Fox hunting," Wikipedia, https://en.wikipedia.org/wiki/Fox_hunting.

17 Ibid.

18 Fox populations in England are still quite high, and as the English consider the fox vermin, the object is to kill the fox.

19 Mackay-Smith, "Chronicle Commentary." The first recorded steeplechase took place in County Cork, Ireland, in 1752 (as a race to the church steeple) and then spread to England. The first recorded steeplechase in America was the Maryland Hunt Cup in 1894.

20 Harness racing of pacing horses developed in the northern colonies, especially New York.

21 Breen, "Horses and Gentlemen," 249; Mackay-Smith, *The Colonial Quarter Race Horse*, 4, 57. Mackay-Smith, ibid., 5, wrote that the first horses were imported into Virginia from Ireland in 1621. These paths were from 10 to 24 feet wide. The quarter races between two horses remind me of informal drag races between two cars in many rural areas.

22 Mackay-Smith, *The Colonial Quarter Race Horse*, 58; Breen, "Horses and Gentlemen," 250. A 1713 Virginia law allowed only land-owning men to own horses or mares for breeding; Johnson and Crookshanks, *Virginia Horseracing: Triumphs of the Turf*, 24.

23 Hervey, *Racing in America*, 24.

24 Ibid., 22–23.

25 Breen, "Horses and Gentlemen"; Breen, *Tobacco Culture*, 1985.

26 Breen, "Horses and Gentlemen," 252; Morgan, *Slave Counterpoint*, 416.

27 Breen, "Horses and Gentlemen," 254.

28 Henrico Records, 1677–1699, 181, quoted in Mackay-Smith, *The Colonial Quarter Race Horse*, 63.

29 Anburey, *Travels Through the Interior Parts of America*, 2:393. Jefferson was living at Monticello at this time, but he probably did not attend these races near his home, because from May 4 to May 20, 1779, he was attending the assembly in Williamsburg; MB1997, 445.

30 Smyth, *A Tour of the United States of America*, 22–23.

31 Mackay-Smith, *The Colonial Quarter Race Horse*, xxi, xxx.

32 Bringing horses across the sea from England was an incredibly expensive affair at the time. After one paid for the horse, the trip in the ship on the high ocean might last three months, and included all the necessary provisions of hay and water, plus an attendant groom. Land transportation, stabling, and feed were also a necessary part of the calculations. This "bottom," or endurance, bred for in these horses also served to help them race across the countryside for three to four hours during a foxhunt. The first racetrack in the colonies was set up in Jamaica, New York, in 1655.

33 The *Virginia Gazette* was a newspaper founded in 1736 at Williamsburg, Virginia. Old fields were fields no longer cultivated. In other words, fields exhausted by successive planting of tobacco and now, although cleared of woods and trees, no longer in use, perfect places for the circular race course; Mackay-Smith, *The Colonial Quarter Race Horse*, 71. Today, the longest race for Thoroughbred racing horses in the United States is the mile-and-a-half Belmont.

34 Weld, *Travels Through the States of North America*, 106. One stone equals 14 pounds. The plural of stone is stone.

35 Gill, "A Sport Only for Gentlemen."

36 Smyth, *A Tour of the United States of America*, 21-22. Newmarket is an important racing center in England.

37 Anburey, *Travels Through the Interior Parts of America*, 2:394–95.

38 Harrison, *Early American Turf-Stock*, 1:370, 2:559. Fifty stallions and thirty mares were imported into Virginia by 1774.

39 Janus, whose blood runs in many great Thoroughbreds and Quarter Horses, as well as other breeds, was imported earlier in 1756. Janus was more famous for his quarter-racing progeny than for his distance racers.

40 In England, the Jockey Club was founded in 1752 as the governing body of racing there. Some claim that the Rev. James Blair, founder of the College of William and Mary, founded the first Jockey Club in Williamsburg. In Maryland, there were race courses at Marlborough, Joppa, Chestertown, Elkridge, and Williamstadt; Fisher, *Men, Women and Manners in Colonial Times*, 208. After their wedding in 1772, Jefferson and his new wife, Martha, got as far as Blenheim on their way to Monticello before leaving their carriage and pushing on in a snowstorm on horseback. Later, in 1781, Jefferson rendezvoused with his family there after escaping British troops who had arrived at Monticello to capture him.

41 Renau, *Jockeys, Belles and Bluegrass Kings*; Hotaling, *The Great Black Jockeys*. Jefferson's authorization of the military to seize citizens' horses was a very unpopular order with horse-owning Virginians.

42 Diomede, Peacemaker, and The Eagle.

43 MB1997, 147.

44 Ibid., 1087.

Chapter 7. Breeding Horses (1772–1782): Improving the Breed

1 Bishko, "A Spanish Stallion for Albemarle," 146.

2 Recall, the term FFVs is a social category applied retrospectively to this group of people; "First Families of Virginia," Wikipedia.

3 Williams, "Rival First Families of Virginia," 277.

4 Harrison, *The Equine F.F. Vs.*; Fithian, *Journal and Letters of Philip Vickers Fithian*, 233. The emergence of the gracious lifestyle was based on the increase in profits from tobacco at this time.

5 Fithian, *Journal and Letters of Philip Vickers Fithian*, 127. John Tayloe II (1721–1779) was an important importer of English racehorses, and his home, Mount Airy in Richmond County, Virginia, housed one of the largest stud farms in the state at the time, plus a one-mile racetrack.

6 "Non-alienable" means that the previous owner's status and reputation added to the prestige and value of *The Horse*. In essence, the previous owner remained as part of the horse

7 John Wayles (1715–1773) was a successful planter whose home was The Forest, in Charles City County. He also imported slaves for profit.

8 FB1999, 7. Jefferson already had inherited twenty slaves from his own father. Elkhill and Willis Creek were lands on the James River (at the confluence of the Rivanna) about twenty-nine miles southeast of Monticello. Elkhill, on the north side, is in Goochland County; Willis Creek, on the south side, is in Cumberland County. Poplar Forest is located southwest of Lynchburg, in Bedford and Campbell counties.

9 Although Jefferson did buy retired racehorses on several occasions (The General, Tarquin, and Brimmer). Nor did Jefferson try to make money by breeding horses for sale and profit. Although he bred horses at his inherited plantation at Elkhill in the 1770s, and did charge stud fees for his favorite riding horse, Caractacus, in the 1780s, Jefferson never commercialized his breeding program.

10 Jefferson's father-in-law, John Wayles, died in May 1773. After Wayles's will was probated, Jefferson, through his wife, Martha, inherited much wealth, doubling his land holdings and the number of his slaves. Many of the horses listed at the beginning of the *Farm Book* were inherited from Wayles. Only a few of these horses resided at Monticello. Others, mostly his breeding stock, were still on Wayles's lands, at Elkhill and Bedford.

11 MB1997, 375, 438, 450, 494; *Farm Book*, 1774-1824, 2, in Thomas Jefferson Papers: An Electronic Archive. Colonel Thomas Mann Randolph was kin—Jefferson's second cousin; he was the son of Jefferson's mother's cousin—and was later the father of Jefferson's son-in-law Thomas Mann Randolph Jr.

12 Cassidy, The Sport of Kings, 147. Of course, genetically, this is not true. Both dam and sire contribute 50 percent of the genetic material. But note the mythological tracing of all Thoroughbred lines to three male stallions. There is no mention of female origins.

13 There are thirty-nine so-called American foundation mares, or matriarchs, of the American Thoroughbred breed. These are the female taproot lines (from dam to grand dam, etc.) that produced the most racing winners; Peters, "Historic Dams." Matthes, "Foundation Matriarchs of the Thoroughbred"; Harrison, *Early American Turf-Stock*, 2:70.

14 *Farm Book*, 1774-1824, 1, in *Thomas Jefferson Papers: An Electronic Archive.*

15 Secretary John Carter (ca. 1695–1742) was the eldest son of Robert "King" Carter (1663–1732), one of the wealthiest men and the largest landholder in the colony. John Carter was secretary of the colony from 1722 until 1742, when he died; Evans, "John Carter (1695 or 1696–1742)," *Encyclopedia Virginia.*

16 Archibald Cary (1721–1787) was a public figure and politician in Virginia, who eventually strongly supported independence and even funded the Virginia militia during the Revolution. He owned an iron mill but also imported several Thoroughbred horses from England. Although a slave owner, he was well known for his stand against slavery, as well as his antagonism against Baptists.

17 MB1997, 463.

18 William Byrd III (1728–1777) inherited the family land at Westover on the James, but being an inveterate gambler, he lost the family fortune, made bad investments, and eventually, deep in debt, sold the family estate.

19 Another important (Old) Fearnought son was Syme's Wildair, sire of Jefferson's horse while Jefferson was president, Wildair.

20 NSV, 294.

21 Cohen, "Well Calculated for the Farmer," 379, 381.

22 Richard Anderson (1747–1793) was an Albemarle neighbor and married to Ann Meriwether.

23 There is evidence of mule breeding, which is covered in Chapter 9.

24 MB1997, 510. Tuckahoe was the home of Colonel Thomas Mann Randolph, where Jefferson had lived with his family as a child, while his father, Peter, served as guardian of the orphaned Thomas.

25 Britton, *Jefferson: A Monticello Sampler*, 24.

26 Dian subsequently bred a line of important American racehorses; Mackay-Smith, *The Colonial Quarter Race Horse*, 259.

27 Tarleton planned to cover the seventy miles to Charlottesville in twenty-four hours, an impressive feat.

28 Kranish, *Flight from Monticello*, 176. Imagine if Tarleton had succeeded in capturing the governor of Virginia, the author of the Declaration of Independence, and the Virginia legislators, three of whom had signed the Declaration! Stuart G. Gibbony, president of the Thomas Jefferson Memorial Foundation, said of Jack Jouett in 1926: "But for Captain Jack Jouett's heroic ride, there would have been no Yorktown and the Revolutionists would have been only unsuccessful rebels. A fitting tribute to a gallant Patriot"; Moran, "Jack Jouett of Virginia: The Other Ride."

29 Wilson, "Jack Jouett's Ride."

30 Dabney, "Jack Jouett's Ride."

31 Kranish, *Flight from Monticello*, 283. Kranish, p. 293, notes that Jefferson had not visited this property in eight years. Jack Jouett himself was almost

detained by Tarleton's men but was able to elude capture. The legislature recognized his feat by voting to award him "a pair of pistols and a sword as symbols of gratitude"; Wilson, "Jack Jouett's Ride," 2–3. But Jack didn't stay in Virginia. The following year, he married his childhood sweetheart, Sallie Robards, for whom his fleet and vigorous mare was named, and moved to Kentucky, settling in Mercer County and later in Woodford County, where he and Sallie raised twelve children. Jouett became an important politician in the new state of Kentucky, as well as a successful planter, and pioneered live-stock breeding by importing blooded horses from England—"in the bluegrass where today great racing stables raise swift colts for the Derby"; Dabney, "Jack Jouett's Ride."

32 TJ to William Gordon, July 16, 1788, in Randall, *Thomas Jefferson: A Life*, 339.The number of freed slaves is under dispute. Much later, in 1799, Jefferson sold his Elkhill lands to help pay off his mounting debts.

33 Kranish, *Flight from Monticello*, 270, 274.

34 TJ to Marquis de Lafayette, May 29, 1781, in PTJ, 6:35. The Marquis de Lafayette (1757–1834), a French aristocrat, served in the Continental army under George Washington and was instrumental in the surrender of Gen. Cornwallis at Yorktown. An aide to Lafayette reported to the government that "his force had sixty cavalry horses, while the British had five hundred"; Kranish, *Flight from Monticello*, 270.

35 Randall, *Thomas Jefferson: A Life*, 340.

36 In Notes on the State of Virginia, two of the chapters called "Queries" dealt with the issue of human chattel slavery in the United States. There Jefferson voiced his opposition to slavery, but also tried to justify it in awkward and inelegant terms. This degeneration theory was put forth by the French naturalist Georges Louis Leclerc, comte de Buffon, in his authoritative *Histoire Naturelle*.

37 NSV1832, 177.

38 Jefferson, *Autobiography*.

39 Randolph, *The Domestic Life of Thomas Jefferson*, 63.

40 WTJ1903, 199; Crawford, *Twilight at Monticello*, 155.

41 Niemcewicz, *Under Their Vine and Fig Tree*, 47.

42 Animals (sheep) that were strays and ownerless were thus claimed by the thirteenth-century Mesta, a Spanish organization of transhumanist sheep owners; Dobie, *The Mustangs*, 94. Pike is quoted in ibid., 95. When Cortez landed in Mexico in 1519, he brought the first horses seen on the continent in 10,000 years.

43 Over time, English horses were purposely introduced into the herds of Colonial Spanish stock: draft, Thoroughbreds, Morgan, and other types, often in order to try and create a bigger horse; Sponenberg, "North American Colonial Spanish Horse Update." Most of those horses were recorded as killed or eaten. Furthermore, the Spanish rode only stallions, so there were no mares for breeding; Chard, "Did the First Spanish Horses Landed in Florida and Carolina Leave Progeny?" 90–106. Davis, "The Spanish Horse in the East." Native American horse culture effectively disappeared after the last Indian war in 1889. Protection of modern mustangs was increased further by the Wild Free-Roaming Horse and Burro Act of 1971.

44 Flores, "Bringing Home All the Pretty Horses." Size may have as much to do with marginal nutrition as with essential "type."

45 Sponenberg, "North American Colonial Spanish Horse Update."

46 Flores, "Bringing Home All the Pretty Horses," 10.

47 TJ to Philip Nolan, June 24, 1798, in PTJ, 1950.

48 Gale, "Cantonment Wilkinsonville"; Flores, "Bringing Home All the Pretty Horses," 10.

49 Besides the Lewis and Clark expedition, President Jefferson sent another expedition to the West, this time to the Southwest (Spanish territory). Known as the Grand Expedition, just as it started out in 1806, it was confronted by a huge Spanish force and turned back.

50 The capture of merchant ships occurred after the US lost British protection at the end of the Revolution.

51 *Universal Gazetteer*, quoted in Harrison, *Early American Turf-Stock*, 1:323–324.

52 *National Intelligencer*, October 17, 1806, in Harrison, *Early American Turf-Stock*, 1:323–324.

53 *National Intelligencer*, December 15, 1806, in Harrison, *Early American Turf-Stock*, 1:323–324.

54 "American Foundation Mares." Sir Archie, from the get of imported Diomed, is perhaps Diomed's most famous son. Sir Archie is sometimes called the "Godolphin Arabian of the Americas" for the number of Thoroughbred race winners that he sired, truly the foundation sire of American distance strains; Mackay-Smith, *The Colonial Quarter Race Horse*, 92. Sir Archie was originally named Robert Burns, but John Tayloe III changed his name in honor of his friend who owned a half interest in *The Horse*, Archibald Randolph (a Jefferson cousin). William Ransom Johnson, "the Napoleon of the Turf," once owned Sir Archie and described him as "the best horse I ever saw." Sir Archie stood at stud in the racehorse region for more than twenty years, 1810–1833; "US Thoroughbreds Rise to New Heights by 1800."

55 Nowlan, *The American Presidents, Washington to Tyler*, 178. Not all members of the society were necessarily from Albemarle County.

56 The Andalusian horse was considered to be another Oriental type. The Andalusian horse has a long breeding history in southern Spain (since the thirteenth century), and MtDNA evidence shows that it shared genes with the Barb of North African. Bishko, "A Spanish Stallion for Albemarle," 157, 177.

57 Ibid., 146.

58 Ibid., 168; Skinner, *The American Farmer*; *The American Farmer*, II, no. 30 (October 20, 1820), 238–239, quoted in Bishko, 171. Spanish law prohibited selling the Andalusian breed outside of Spain.

59 Jones quoted in Skinner, *The American Farmer*.

60 Cocke, J. H., letter, Feb. 28, 1823 issue of the *American Farmer*, in Mackay-Smith, *The Colonial Quarter Race Horse*, 235; TJ to TMR, December 30, 1793, in PTJ638.

61 Bishko, "A Spanish Stallion for Albemarle," 149.

62 Letter in the Feb. 28, 1823 issue of *the American Farmer*, in Mackay-Smith, *The Colonial Quarter Race Horse*, 234. A garron is a much-despised and small horse in Scotland and Ireland, a Highland pony.

63 Bishko, "A Spanish Stallion for Albemarle," 150.

64 Cocke, J. H., letter, Feb. 28, 1823 issue of *the American Farmer*, in Mackay-Smith, *The Colonial Quarter Race Horse*, 235.

65 Ibid.

66 Mackay-Smith, *The Colonial Quarter Race Horse*, 234.

67 Mackay-Smith, *The Colonial Quarter Race Horse*, 239. Roebuck I was bought from the Virginia-North Carolina border region, the old horse racing region and quarter racehorse region.

68 Part of an advertisement for Randolph's stallion, Rinaldo, published in the *Richmond Enquirer*, Feb. 21, 1832, in Mackay-Smith, *The Colonial Quarter Race Horse*, 113. John Randolph of Roanoke was a cousin of Jefferson's, a politician, and the biggest breeder of horses in the 1820s. (See Chapter 8.)

69 His horses measured from 14.3 hands in 1778 to 16 hands in 1820.

Chapter 8. The Livestock: Work Horses, Chickasaws, and Mules

1 FB1999, 109.

2 On the modern counterparts, Campbell, *Horse in Virginia*, 16. A "pony" is defined as 14 hands and under. A horse measures 14.1 hands and above. These first English horses were present in the British Isles by the thirteenth century. They were similar types, associated with different geographic locales. Hobbies as pacers were especially comfortable to ride, so much so that they were often used for recreational riding, from whence comes the term "a hobby." The child's toy horse, the hobby horse, was inspired by this Irish type.

3 The American Thoroughbred Stud Book was established in 1896.

4 John Syme to TJ, Sept. 2, 1792, in PTJ, 24:340. John Syme was the half-brother of Patrick Henry, and also a respected horse breeder in Virginia. It was his horse, Wildair (Syme's Wildair) that was the sire of Jefferson's Wildair during his presidency.

5 TJ to JA, October 12, 1823, in *Founders Online*.

6 Although previously indigenous to the Americas, primitive horses had become extinct 10,000 years earlier; Clutton-Brock, *Horse Power*, 142. The Spanish horse was sometimes called the Iberian horse.

7 "Jennet" comes from the Spanish word *ginete*, which means jockey. Originally it referred to a light cavalryman who rode *a la ginete*, or with his legs tucked up.

8 Known outside of Spain as Andalusians, these horses within Spain were referred to as the "Spanish breed" (*raza Española*) or "pure Spanish breed" (*pura raza Española*, or PRE); Altamirano, *Historia y origen del caballo español*. National Purebred Spanish Breeders' Association of Spain. Today, most Andalusian horses are gray or bay in color.

9 Sponenberg, "North American Colonial Spanish Horse Update."

10 Dobie, *The Mustangs*, 97-99; Chard, "Did the First Spanish Horses Landed in Florida and Carolina Leave Progeny?"; Sponenberg, "North American Colonial Spanish Horse Update."

11 The Chickasaw is currently a protected heritage breed in the following registries: Horse of the Americas, Spanish Mustang Registry, and the Spanish Barb Breeders Association, and recognized as a Colonial Spanish Horse. These registries included geographically distinct, many-named types. Some Native American tribal groups currently breed herds that continue to conserve distinct strains of the Colonial Spanish Horse. In the Southeast, the Banker ponies on the Outer Banks of Virginia and the Carolinas (Hatteras, Shackelford, Corolla, and Ocracoke), the Marsh Tackies, and the Florida Cracker pony all may be Colonial Spanish Horse descendants; Sponenberg, "North American Colonial Spanish Horse Update."

12 TJ to MJR, April 23, 1803, in FL1966, 244; Bear, *Jefferson at Monticello*, 106.

13 Mackay-Smith, *The Colonial Quarter Race Horse*, xxxi. The American Quarter Horse claims ancestry from the F.A.Q.R.H., or colonial Virginia Quarter Horse. The American Quarter Horse was not established as a breed until 1940, but it traces important foundation studs back to Janus and other Virginia horses in the eighteenth century; American Quarter Horse Association.

14 Lemon, "The Chickasaw Horse"; American Quarter Horse Association.

15 Patrick Nisbett Edgar, quoted in Mackay-Smith, *The Colonial Quarter Race Horse*, 112; American Quarter Horse Association website.

16 Some of the first broodmares that Jefferson inherited from his father-in-law had written physical descriptions in the *Farm Book* but no name, just a number, e.g., #11 very old mare at Willis Creek, or ##14, born 1773, black mare at Elkhill; FB1999, 7. MB1997, 753.

17 FB1999, 33, 132.

18 Bear, *Jefferson at Monticello*, 62.

19 TJ to TJR, March 31, 1815, in FL1966, 409.

20 MB1997, 1359. The *Virginia Gazette* was a kind of broadsheet newspaper published weekly in Williamsburg (by various publishers) from 1736 to 1780.

21 *Virginia Gazette*, September 14, 1769.

22 GFB1987, 72. The principal overseer from 1806 to 1822, Edmund Bacon, who owned several horses while he worked at Monticello, also had a horse stable near his cabin on Monticello.

23 MB1997, 944.

24 Thweatt was a brother-in-law to Jefferson's son-in-law John Wayles Eppes, having married Eppes's sister, Mary.

25 FB1999, 33,132.

26 The sub-title of *Horse-hoeing husbandry* further explains the purpose of the book: or, *An essay on the principles of vegetation and tillage. Designed to introduce a new method of culture; whereby the produce of land will be increased, and the usual expence lessened. Together with accurate descriptions and cuts of the instruments employed in it.*

27 FB1999, 109. George Washington was an innovator in this regard. He had a sixteen-sided threshing barn built (in 1792) to collect the wheat more hygienically.

28 GFB1987, 321.

29 Home, *The Gentleman Farmer,* 26–36.

30 Ibid.

31 Clutton-Brock, *Horse Power,* 154; TJ to Enoch Edwards, April 18, 1801, in PTJ, 33:609.

32 TJ to Charles Willson Peale, March 21, 1815, in Martin and Stanton, "Moldboard Plow."

33 Mount Vernon Ladies Association, "Heritage Breed Animals"; Hauer, *The Natural Superiority of Mules,* 26.

34 This was typical of all highly valued flora and fauna native to certain national locales. Recall that Arab-type horses often had to be smuggled into England. Jefferson himself "stole" rice seed while he was on a private trip in Italy while serving as ambassador to France in 1787. Mules were highly valued in Spain, used for riding and pulling even royal coaches. The Spanish king wanted to keep his monopoly on the asses that produced mules.

35 Hauer, *The Natural Superiority of Mules,* 26.

36 Young was an English agriculturalist and leader in introducing modern methods of agriculture into England. He published widely and was read by Washington and Jefferson; Washington, *The Papers of George Washington Digital Edition.*

37 Cavileer, "George Washington's Horse." The sale of Magnolia meant that Washington gave up the stud fees that added to the estate's income when friends and neighbors brought their mares to Mount Vernon for a season with Magnolia.

38 Garrett, "Mules in Southern Agriculture," 584.

39 GFB1987, 319; Bear, *Jefferson at Monticello,* 106; TJ to TMR, August 11, 1792, in PTJ, 26:657.

40 MB1997, 661; TJ to ARB, May 20, 1803, in FL1966, 246.

41 MB1997, 500, 503, 507. Rugdum Funnidos was the fun-loving lord-in-waiting in Henry Carey's burlesque of 1734, *Chrononhotonthologos*; MB 1997, 503.

42 MB1997, 924, 958.

43 Ibid., 498, 502, 925.

44 Edmund Bacon, in Bear, *Jefferson at Monticello,* 77–78.

45 Harrison and Burke, "Monticello's Child Life."

46 While in Philadelphia in 1776 and again in the 1790s, Jefferson paid for pasturage of his horses.

47 FB1999, 336.

48 FB1953, 78; Bear, *Jefferson at Monticello,* 15; Home, *Gentleman Farmer,* 250; Randall, The *Life of Thomas Jefferson,* 2:305."The fences and enclosures in this province are different from those to the northward; here they are composed of what is termed fence rails. From a mode of constructing these enclosures in a zig zag form, the New-Englanders have a saying, when a man is in liquor, he is making Virginia fences"; Anburey, *Travels Through the Interior Parts of America.* The visitor was the Duke de la Rochefoucauld-Liancourt.

49 Anburey, *Travels Through the Interior Parts of America,* 9.

50 ODM, June 22; Haworth, *George Washington: Farmer,* 9.

51 Harrison, *The Equine F.F. Vs.,* 172.

52 Finding, or taking up, a strayed animal came with the costs of providing for it. Recall one of the reasons the rich and wealthy had horses while the commoner didn't was the expense involved.

53 Jones, *The Present State of Virginia,* 35.

54 TJ to Albert Gallatin, January 25, 1793, in PTJ, 25:92. The Colle vineyards have been replanted and renamed the Jefferson Vineyards, and finally have successfully been producing wine since 1986.

55 Or in summer, kept in during the day and let out in the cooler night.

56 Raber and Tucker, *The Culture of The Horse,* 6-7, n7.

57 Willich, *The Domestic Encyclopaedia.*

58 Sadler and Sadler, *American Stables,* 34; "Historic Structure Report, Mount Vernon Estate and Garden Cultural Landscape Study," 7.

59 In this drawing (N-56), Jefferson gave the measurement for several stalls: 8 at 5'x 7', 3 at 6' x 7' and 3 at 5' 9 2/3" x 6'; Jefferson, "Monticello: dependencies (plan), recto, before 4 August 1772." Mulberry Row is the 1,000-yard street running east-west, and was the center of plantation work life. A series of shops, yards, and slave dwellings lined this row, which was set at a lower level than the mansion, and thus out of sight. Most were temporary buildings, although the stable (placed farther north on the row than other buildings and next to the house gate where the South Road intersected it) was one of two buildings made of stone.

60 FB1976, 78.

61 "Historic Structure Report, Mount Vernon Estate and Garden Cultural Landscape Study." This was the third stable building built in the same place. Building of brick or stone is a fireproofing method, an added expense affordable only by the wealthy. Washington's second (log) stable was destroyed by fire in 1781. Shirley's is the oldest masonry stable in Virginia.

62 Sadler and Sadler, *American Stables*, 35. Of course, although not all eighteenth-century colonial planters owned or had even read Palladio's books, they were probably familiar with the ideal Palladian principles of balance and symmetry currently reigning in English country estate tastes. Jefferson owned the books after 1764.

63 Ibid., 43.

64 Jefferson, "Philadelphia: latch, stalls, cart, and doors," and "Monticello: building notebook," 39; TJ to TMR, October 12, 1792, in FB1999, 79.Governor Morris's house in Philadelphia was where President Washington lived at this time.

65 Bear, *Jefferson at Monticello*, 114; Randolph, *The Last Days of Jefferson*.

66 Other aspects of the Bremo stalls approximate Jefferson's drawings of Governor Penn's stables in Philadelphia, especially the hay racks with the spokes that spin (easier on a horse's mouth when pulling hay from the rack).

67 Mason, *The Gentleman's New Pocket Companion*, 51; Clark, *A Treatise on the Prevention of Diseases Incidental to Horses*, 15. On his drawing of Penn's stables, Jefferson writes that "if stalls were but 7.f. (like Morris's) instead of 8.f., [they] would look better"; Jefferson, "Philadelphia: stables, railing, and latch, recto." Regarding *The Gentleman's New Pocket Companion*, "The true merit and value of the work was such that for three generations it was the standard manual for *The Horse*men of the country"; Robb, "Richard Mason of Surry County, Virginia," 73.

68 TJ to James Dinsmore, March 19, 1802, in *Founders Online*; Jefferson, *Thomas Jefferson's Architectural Drawings*, drawing N540. James Dinsmore was one of Jefferson's resident paid workmen, a master builder.

69 TJ to James Leitch, June 23, 1809, in *Founders Online*; Stein, *Worlds of Thomas Jefferson at Monticello*; VRT to NPT, Sept. 12, 1833, in Nicholas Philip Trist Papers #2104.

70 As the eighteenth century wore on and roads improved, ownership of carriages and other two- and four-wheeled vehicles became more common.

71 Sadler and Sadler, *American Stables*, 59.

72 TJ to Arthur S. Brockenbrough, June 27, 1825, in The Papers of the Proctor of the University of Virginia, 1817-1828 (Arthur Spicer Brockenbrough); "Uva Cultural Landscape Survey, 1817–1826."

73 Dr. William Thornton was an early American painter and architect. He was the principal designer of the US capitol building and many other civic buildings as well as residential houses in Washington, DC.

74 FB:44 in GFB1987, 272–273; FB:138 in ibid., 410; FB:138 in ibid., 411; FB:167 in ibid., 470. And GB1999 or FB1999, 228.

75 Randall, *Life of Thomas Jefferson*, 3:305. Explaining the rotation of crops in the seven proposed fields, Jefferson wrote, "6th. Cut the first crop of clover & pasture the 2d. 7th. Pasture the 1st crop, and cut the 2d. this change gives spring pasture and eases the mowing. 8th. Pasture"; TJ to TMR, July 28, 1793, PTJ, 26:577. It is not clear if this plan was ever implemented. Duke de la Rochefoucauld-Liancourt, president of the National Assembly of France, then in exile in the United States, was a visitor to Monticello on June 22, 1796.

76 FB1953, 244, 246; TJ to George Washington, September 12, 1795, in *Founders Online*. Jacqueline Ambler (1742–1798) wrote an important pamphlet on Lucerne in 1800, *A Treatise on the Culture of Lucerne*. Ambler, a native of Yorktown, and secretary of Virginia, married Rebecca Burwell and became the father-in-law of John Marshall. Rebecca was Jefferson's first love.

77 TJ to TMR, July 28, 1793, PTJ, 27:577.

78 GFB1987, 51; FB1953, 91; MB1997, 881; FB1976, 244.

79 Clark, *A Treatise on the Prevention of Diseases Incidental to Horses*, 35, 38, 201.

80 FB1976, 227.

81 FB:138 in GFB1987, 410; FB:44 in ibid., 272; FB:167 in ibid., 470. Also FB1999, 110.

82 Jefferson never discussed selling land or slaves to pay down his mounting debts.

83 VRT to NPT, September 12, 1833, in Nicholas Philip Trist Papers #2104.

84 Young, *Farmer's Guide in Hiring and Stocking Farms*, 36. Although Jethro Tull was probably the instigator of the "scientific" agricultural revolution in England, another English agriculturalist, Arthur Young, became a very important reference for Virginia plantation owners such as George Washington and Thomas Jefferson, who corresponded with him and exchanged results of his advice with each other.

85 Bear, *Jefferson at Monticello*, 21; Anburey, *Travels Through the Interior Parts of America*, 22–23.

86 FB1999, 186; McEwan, *Thomas Jefferson, Farmer*, 120.

87 Raber and Tucker, *The Culture of The Horse*, 6–7.

Postscript: Jefferson's Shadow

1 Cogliano's stages appear in *Thomas Jefferson's Lives: Biographers and the Battle for History*, a 2019 collection of essays edited by Robert M. S. McDonald, in a chapter titled "Merrill Peterson and the Apostle of Freedom: Thomas Jefferson and the New Nation." For my purposes, I relied on the analysis by S. Richard Gard, Jr., "The Jefferson Progression," of Cogliano's stages, of McDonald's book, and of other books about Jefferson. Gard is the editor of *Virginia: The UVA Magazine*, where his article appeared in 2019. It is unpaginated in its web version. See the bibliography for the full citation and the URL.

2 Gard, "The Jefferson Progression."

3 Ibid.

4 Ibid.

5 Ibid.

6 Ibid.

7 Ibid.

8 Ibid.

9 Ibid.

10 In those days, we didn't get past the Civil War in our Virginia history class.

11 "Grounds" is the term used (by Jefferson) instead of "campus."

12 The Charlottesville Metropolitan Statistical Area in Virginia had a 2020 population of about 235,000 people.

13 Albemarle has the third largest population of horses after two counties in northern Virginia near Middleburg.

14 TJ to William Short, April 10, 1824, *Founders Online*.

Credits

■ **Prologue:** **Fig. P-1** ©Thomas Jefferson Foundation at Monticello. **Fig. P-2** ©Thomas Jefferson Foundation at Monticello. **Fig. P-3** ©Thomas Jefferson Foundation at Monticello. **Fig. P-4** Photo by author. **Fig. P-5** ©Thomas Jefferson Foundation at Monticello. **Fig. P-6** ©Thomas Jefferson Foundation at Monticello. **Fig. P-7** Photo by author. **Fig. P-8** https://www.eekwi.org/animals/mammals/white-tailed-deer Environmental Education for Kids. Wisconsin. **Fig. P-9** ©Thomas Jefferson Foundation at Monticello. **Fig. P-10** Photo by author. **Fig. P-11** ©Thomas Jefferson Foundation at Monticello.

■ **Introduction:** **Fig. I-1** © The Albert and Shirley Small Special Collection Library, University of Virginia. **Fig. I-2** Wikimedia Commons contributors, "File:Cabriolet (PSF).jpg," Wikimedia Commons, https://commons.wikimedia.org/w/index.php?title=File:Cabriolet_(PSF).jpg&oldid=845145270 (accessed October 22, 2024) . Source: Archives of Pearson Scott Foresman donated to the Wikimedia Foundation. **Fig. I-3** © The Albert and Shirley Small Special Collection Library, University of Virginia. **Fig. I-4** © The Albert and Shirley Small Special Collection Library, University of Virginia. **Fig. I-5** By Makarova Viktoria. Fig. I-6. By Tosca Suto, Equine Fotographie.

■ **Chapter 1:** Facing page: Gentleman on a Grey Horse is a painting by George Stubbs,1781. Several online platforms offer information and reproductions of the painting, but it is in a private collection: the Collection of Mr. and Mrs. Paul Mellon. (www.trintiyhousepaintings.com, 2017), accessed December 1, 2019. **Fig. 1-1** Massachusetts Historical Society (MHiS), Coolidge Collection 1803. **Fig. 1-2** ©Thomas Jefferson Foundation at Monticello. **Fig. 1-3** Photo by author. **Fig. 1-4** Painting in the Fralin Museum, University of Virginia, gift of Thomas Fortune Ryan. Wikimedia Commons contributors, "File:Frederic Edwin Church - The Natural Bridge, Virginia.jpg," Wikimedia Commons, https://commons.wikimedia.org/w/index.php?title=File:Frederic_Edwin_Church_-_The_Natural_Bridge,_Virginia.jpg&oldid=853995849 (accessed October 19, 2024). **Fig. 1-5** Virginia Museum of Fine Arts. https://vmfa.museum/piction/6027262-8090011/. **Fig. 1-6** © Thomas Jefferson Foundation at Monticello. **Fig.1-7** [Pdf] Retrieved from the Library of Congress, https://www.loc.gov/item/12019922/. **Fig. 1-8** Wikimedia Commons contributors, "File:Centaure Malmaison crop.jpg," Wikimedia Commons, https://commons.wikimedia.org/w/index.php?title=File:Centaure_Malmaison_crop.jpg&oldid=852460997 (accessed October 19, 2024). Author: Clicgauche. **Fig. 1-9** eBook; Online UVA Library Catalog. Shaw-Shoemaker Digital Edition. **Fig. 1-10** https://jp.pinterest.com/pin/121667627411353580/. **Fig. 1-11** ©Thomas Jefferson Foundation at Monticello. **Fig. 1-12** Wikimedia Commons contributors, "File:Pierre Sériziat - Jacques-Louis David - Musée du Louvre Peintures RF 1281.jpg," Wikimedia Commons, https://commons.wikimedia.org/w/index.php?title=File:Pierre_S%C3%A9riziat_-_Jacques-Louis_David_-_Mus%C3%A9e_du_Louvre_Peintures_RF_1281.jpg&oldid=672347443 (accessed October 19, 2024). Photo by Shonagon. 2022-04-19. **Fig. 1-13** Photo by author. **Fig. 1-14** Photo by author. **Fig. 1-16** © biodiversitylibrary.org. **Fig. 1-17** © biodiversitylibrary.org. **Fig. 1-18** Wikimedia Commons contributors, "File:Curb and bradoon.jpg," Wikimedia Commons, https://commons.wikimedia.org/w/index.php?title=File:Curb_and_bradoon.jpg&oldid=872027523 (accessed October 19, 2024). **Fig. 1-19** © biodiversitylibrary.org.

■ **Chapter 2:** Facing photo: Wikimedia Commons contributors. File: Portrait-of-george-washington-taking-the-salute-at-trenton-john-faed.jpg [Internet]. Wikimedia Commons; 2023 Mar 15, 08:53 UTC [cited 2024 Dec 17]. Available from: https://commons.wikimedia.org/w/index.php?title=File:Portrait-of-george-washington-taking-the-salute-at-trenton-john-faed.jpg&oldid=741096589. **Fig. 2-1** National Portrait Gallery of the Smithsonian Institution. Gift of the Donald W. Reynolds Foundation; source: https://npg.si.edu/object/npg_NPG.2001.13. **Fig. 2-2** Library of Congress Prints and Photographs Division Washington, D.C. **Fig. 2-3** Mount Vernon Ladies' Association, Encyclopedia Virginia. **Fig. 2-4** Wikimedia Commons contributors, "File:Washington and Lafayette at Valley Forge.jpg," Wikimedia Commons, https://commons.wikimedia.org/w/index.php?title=File:Washington_and_Lafayette_at_Valley_Forge.jpg&oldid=767084794 (accessed October 21, 2024). Source: Library of Congress Prints and Photographs Division Washington, D.C, item 9179220. **Fig. 2-5** 1. Wikimedia Commons contributors, "File: USA-Washington Circle Park.JPG," Wikimedia Commons, https://commons.wikimedia.org/w/index.php?title=File:USA-Washington_Circle_Park.JPG&oldid=711167222, (accessed October 21, 2024), Author: Ingfbruno - Own work. 2. Wikimedia Commons contributors, "File:George Washington Statue - Capitol Hill Richmond (VA) 2013 (8759158238).jpg," Wikimedia Commons, https://commons.wikimedia.org/w/index.php?title=File:George_Washington_Statue_-_Capitol_Hill_Richmond_(VA)_2013_(8759158238).jpg&oldid=896408966 (accessed October 21, 2024).3. Wikimedia Commons contributors, "File:George Washington hoch zu Ross am Union Square - panoramio.jpg," Wikimedia Commons, https://commons.wikimedia.org/w/index.php?title=File:George_Washington_hoch_zu_Ross_am_Union_Square_-_panoramio.jpg&oldid=876636517 (accessed October 24, 2024),Martin Furtschegger, 2012. **Fig. 2-6** Wikimedia Commons contributors, "File:James Madison 1816.jpg," Wikimedia Commons, https://commons.wikimedia.org/w/index.php?title=File:James_Madison_1816.jpg&oldid=929011831 (accessed October 20, 2024). **Fig. 2-7** Wikimedia Commons contributors, "File: James Madison's Montpelier.jpg," Wikimedia Commons, https://commons.wikimedia.org/w/index.php?title=File:James_Madison%27s_Montpelier.jpg&oldid=497392440 (accessed October 20, 2024). White House Collection. The White House Historical Association. **Fig. 2-8** University of Virginia Library, John Hartwell Cocke Papers (MSS 640). **Fig. 2-9** Photo by the author. **Fig. 2-10** Photo by the author. **Fig. 2-11** Wikimedia Commons contributors, "File:John Hartwell Cocke by Edward Troye, 1859.jpg," Wikimedia Commons, https://commons.wikimedia.org/w/index.php?title=File:John_Hartwell_Cocke_by_Edward_Troye,_1859.jpg&oldid=834685550 (accessed October 21, 2024). Source: The White House Historical Association (White House Collection). Gift of the Charles W. Engelhard Foundation. Public Domain. **Fig. 2-12** Wikimedia Commons contributors, "File:The Mansion, Bowling Green, Caroline County, Virginia.jpg," Wikimedia Commons, https://commons.wikimedia.org/w/index.php?title=File: The_Mansion,_Bowling_Green,_Caroline_County,_Virginia.jpg&oldid=669936415 (accessed October 21, 2024). Source: Library of Congress Prints and Photographs Division Washington, D.C. 20540 USA. **Fig. 2-13** Wikipedia, Source:

American Historical and Literary Antiquities, By John Jay Smith and John F. Watson, 1861. https://en.wikipedia.org/wiki/File:Autographed_portrait_of_John_Randolph.jpg (accessed October 21, 2024). **Fig. 2-14** Wikimedia Commons contributors, "File:SirArchy1.jpg," Wikimedia Commons, https://commons.wikimedia.org/w/index.php?title=File:SirArchy1.jpg&oldid=592582217 (accessed October 21, 2024), Source: Frank Forester's Horse and Horsemanship of the United States Volume One published 1857, J. C. Buttre d. 1893. **Fig. 2-15** Wikimedia Commons contributors, "File:American Eclipse (USA).jpg," Wikimedia Commons, https://commons.wikimedia.org/w/index.php?title=File:American_Eclipse_(USA).jpg&oldid=790427913 (accessed October 21, 2024). Source: Gooreen collection. **Fig. 2-16** Wikimedia Commons contributors, "File:Tuckahoe Plantation Whole House.jpg," Wikimedia Commons, https://commons.wikimedia.org/w/index.php?title=File:Tuckahoe_Plantation_Whole_House.jpg&oldid=506346409 (accessed October 26, 2024). Author, James Shelton32. **Fig. 2-17** Wikimedia Commons contributors, "File:Thomas Mann Randolph.jpg," Wikimedia Commons, https://commons.wikimedia.org/w/index.php?title=File:Thomas_Mann_Randolph.jpg&oldid=903366280 (accessed October 21, 2024)., author not attributed. **Fig. 2-18** Virginia Department of Historic Resources, photo credit, Calder Loth/ 2007. **Fig. 2-19** Virginia Argus, 1799, Chronicling America, Library of Congress. loc.gov/lccn/sn84024710/1799-05-24/ed-1/seq-1/. **Fig. 2-20** Wikimedia Commons contributors, "File:John Wayles Eppes, head-and-shoulders portrait, facing left LCCN92512624.tif," Wikimedia Commons, https://commons.wikimedia.org/w/index.php?title=File:John_Wayles_Eppes,_head-and-shoulders_portrait,_facing_left_LCCN92512624.tif&oldid=683417494 (accessed October 21, 2024). Courtesy of the U.S Senate Historical Office. **Fig. 2-21** National Park Service, /www.nps.gov/articles/eppington.htm, Courtesy of Virginia Department of Historic Resources.

■ **Chapter 3.** Facing photo: The Historic New Orleans Collection© Historic New Orleans Collection /Bridgeman Images. **Fig. 3-1.** © Colonial Williamsburg. **Fig. 3-2** Photo by author. **Fig. 3-3** © Colonial Williamsburg. **Fig. 3-4** Wikimedia Commons contributors, "File:Horsemanship for women (IA Horsemanshipwom00Mead).pdf," Wikimedia Commons, https://commons.wikimedia.org/w/index.php?title=File:Horsemanship_for_women_(IA_Horsemanshipwom00Mead).pdf&oldid=871462821 (accessed October 26, 2024). Image from book Horsemanship for Women by Theodore Hoe Mead, 1887, p. 97. **Fig. 3-5** Wikimedia Commons contributors, "File:Martha Jefferson Randolph portrait.jpg," Wikimedia Commons, https://commons.wikimedia.org/w/index.php?title=File:Martha_Jefferson_Randolph_portrait.jpg&oldid=543942646 (accessed October 21, 2024), Source: https://classroom.monticello.org/media-item/martha-jefferson-randolph/. **Fig. 3-6** ©Thomas Jefferson Foundation at Monticello. **Fig. 3-7** ©Thomas Jefferson Foundation at Monticello **Fig. 3-8** Wikimedia Commons contributors, "File:Portrait of Thomas Jefferson Randolph.jpg," Wikimedia Commons, https://commons.wikimedia.org/w/index.php?title=File:Portrait_of_Thomas_Jefferson_Randolph.jpg&oldid=645602613 (accessed October 21, 2024), Source: http://classroom.monticello.org/kids/gallery/image/109/Thomas-Jefferson-Randolph/. **Fig. 3-9** Wikimedia Commons contributors, "File:Edmund Bacon.JPG," Wikimedia Commons, https://commons.wikimedia.org/w/index.php?title=File:Edmund_Bacon.JPG&oldid=217380545 (accessed October 21, 2024), Source: National Gallery, image of photo, photo touch up by Gwillhickers. **Fig. 3-10** Founders Online, National Archives, accessed September 29, 2019, Original source: The Papers of Thomas Jefferson, vol. 1, 1760–1776, ed. Julian P. Boyd. Princeton: Princeton University Press, 1950, p. 33. **Fig. 3-11** in A. Mackay-Smith's The Colonial Quarter Race Horse, 1983, title page. **Fig. 3-12** Wikimedia Commons contributors, "File:Isaac Jefferson c1845.jpg," Wikimedia Commons, https://commons.wikimedia.org/w/index.php?title=File:Isaac_Jefferson_c1845.jpg&oldid=872882662 (accessed October 21, 2024). Source: Tracy W. McGregor Library of American History, Special Collections, University of Virginia Library, photograph of unattributed daguerreotype, circa 1845. **Fig. 3-13** Wikimedia Commons contributors, "File:Postilion.png," Wikimedia Commons, https://commons.wikimedia.org/w/index.php?title=File:Postilion.png&oldid=710709146 (accessed October 21, 2024). Rogers, Fairman. A Manual of Coaching. Philadelphia, London, J. B. Lippincott company, 1900. Source: books.google.com/books. End picture: © Colonial Williamsburg.

■ **Chapter 4:** Facing photo: Wahoo Photos. **Fig. 4-1** Internet Archive, Contributor: University of California Libraries, https://archive.org/details/anhistoryofearth03goldrich/page/n5/mode/2up. **Fig. 4-2** Wikimedia Commons contributors, "File:Barb Horse tbourida Morocco.jpg," Wikimedia Commons, https://commons.wikimedia.org/w/index.php?title=File:Barb_Horse_tbourida_Morocco.jpg&oldid=836019963 (accessed October 21, 2024). Photographer: Houssain tork , 2019. **Fig. 4-3** Wikimedia Commons contributors, "File:George Townly Stubbs - Warren Hastings on his Arabian Horse - Google Art Project.jpg," Wikimedia Commons, https://commons.wikimedia.org/w/index.php?title=File:George_Townly_Stubbs_-_Warren_Hastings_on_his_Arabian_Horse_-_Google_Art_Project.jpg&oldid=494943212 (accessed October 21, 2024)Collection: Yale Center for British Art, , photographer: JwH7FQRYsTruxA **Fig. 4-4** Wikimedia Commons contributors, "File:George Stubbs - Molly Long-legs with her Jockey - Google Art Project.jpg," Wikimedia Commons, https://commons.wikimedia.org/w/index.php?title=File:George_Stubbs_-_Molly_Long-legs_with_her_Jockey_-_Google_Art_Project.jpg&oldid=684281050 (accessed October 21, 2024).Collection: Walker Art Gallery, Source: Google Cultural Institute. **Fig. 4-5** Wikimedia Commons contributors, "File:Byerly Turk.jpg," Wikimedia Commons, https://commons.wikimedia.org/w/index.php?title=File:Byerly_Turk.jpg&oldid=840219367 (accessed October 21, 2024). Unidentified location. **Fig. 4-6** Wikimedia Commons contributors, "File:Darley Arabian.jpg," Wikimedia Commons, https://commons.wikimedia.org/w/index.php?title=File:Darley_Arabian.jpg&oldid=885614528 (accessed October 26, 2024). Collection: National Trust Collections.org,uk, Object/169581.1, Original source: User:Breda~enwiki, 2005. **Fig. 4-7** Wikimedia Commons contributors, "File:Godolphin Arabian.jpg," Wikimedia Commons, https://commons.wikimedia.org/w/index.php?title=File:Godolphin_Arabian.jpg&oldid=769946740 (accessed October 21, 2024). Collection: unknown, Photographer: unknown. https://commons.wikimedia.org/wiki/File:Godolphin_Arabian.jpg. **Fig. 4-8** From Maryland's First Famed Horses, , Ellen Moyer, What's Up Media Magazine, May, 06, 2022. On-line, https://whatsupmag.com/culture/marylands-first-famed-horses/. **Fig. 4-9** Rockefeller Library (Digital) Collection, Colonial Williamsburg, Virginia Gazette, Purdie and Dixon, May 24, 1770, p. 4. **Fig. 4-10** Wikimedia Commons contributors, "File:Diomed by John Nost Sartorius 1777.jpg," Wikimedia Commons, https://commons.wikimedia.org/w/index.php?title=File:Diomed_by_John_Nost_Sartorius_1777.jpg&oldid=940776334 (accessed October 21, 2024)., Source: Pinterest,. **Fig. 4-11** Thomas Jefferson Papers, Farm

Book, (inside front cover), MHiS. **Fig. 4-12** Wikimedia Commons contributors, "File:François Nicolas Martinet, Site of Hotel d'Langeac, Jefferson's residence in Paris - Lehigh University Library.jpg," Wikimedia Commons, https://commons.wikimedia.org/w/index.php?title=File:Fran%C3%A7ois_Nicolas_Martinet,_Site_of_Hotel_d%27Langeac,_Jefferson%27s_residence_in_Paris_-_Lehigh_University_Library.jpg&oldid=498129757 (accessed October 22, 2024). Source: Lehigh University Libraries, Courtesy of the BibliothÃ¨que Nationale. **Fig. 4-13** Wikimedia Commons contributors, "File:Chantilly (60), Grandes écuries.jpg," Wikimedia Commons, https://commons.wikimedia.org/w/index.php?title=File:Chantilly_(60),_Grandes_%C3%A9curies.jpg&oldid=854183560 (accessed October 22, 2024).Photographer: P. poschadel 2011. **Fig. 4-14** Wikimedia Commons contributors, "File:KochCourbette.jpeg," Wikimedia Commons, https://commons.wikimedia.org/w/index.php?title=File:KochCourbette.jpeg&oldid=930757240 (accessed October 22, 2024). Source/Photographer aus Die Reitkunst im Bilde. **Fig. 4-15** Wikimedia Commons contributors, "File:Rejoneador.jpg," Wikimedia Commons, https://commons.wikimedia.org/w/index.php?title=File:Rejoneador.jpg&oldid=444670818 (accessed October 22, 2024). Author : VeredKurlender, 21 August 2006. **Fig. 4-16** Wikimedia Commons contributors, "File:The horse wrangler.tif," Wikimedia Commons, https://commons.wikimedia.org/w/index.php?title=File:The_horse_wrangler.tif&oldid=869848886 (accessed October 22, 2024)... Source: Library of Congress, https://www.loc.gov/pictures/item/2004667149/. Photographer, Erwin E. Smith, 1910. **Fig. 4-17** Wikimedia Commons contributors, "File:James Ogilvie Fairlie (Portrait by John E. Ferneley, c. 1840).PNG," Wikimedia Commons, https://commons.wikimedia.org/w/index.php?title=File:James_Ogilvie_Fairlie_(Portrait_by_John_E._Ferneley,_c._1840).PNG&oldid=901726392 (accessed October 22, 2024) Source: Clan MacFarlane Geneology, TNG Website. **Fig. 4-18** Wikimedia Commons contributors, "File:The Hunt in Full Cry) by John E. Ferneley, Sr..jpg," Wikimedia Commons, https://commons.wikimedia.org/w/index.php?title=File:The_Hunt_in_Full_Cry)_by_John_E._Ferneley,_Sr..jpg&oldid=931697386 (accessed October 22, 2024). source/Photographer: Berger collection, id #22, Denver, Colorado. **Fig. 4-19** Wikimedia Commons contributors, "File:Red roan Quarter Horse.jpg," Wikimedia Commons, https://commons.wikimedia.org/w/index.php?title=File:Red_roan_Quarter_Horse.jpg&oldid=854318745 (accessed October 22, 2024)., Source: Betty Wills (Atsme), 2014. **Fig. 4-20** Mathew Tucker, Bettmann / Bettmann Archive (2017). https://www.buzzfeed.com/matthewtucker/in-pictures-presidential-inaugurations-through-american-hist. **Fig. 4-21** Virginia Department of Historic Resources. NRHP reference number 95000974, listing date 1995. https://www.dhr.virginia.gov/historic-registers/002-0092/. **Fig. 4-22** Wikimedia Commons contributors, "File:University of Virginia 1856 (Bohn) color.jpg," Wikimedia Commons, https://commons.wikimedia.org/w/index.php?title=File:University_of_Virginia_1856_(Bohn)_color.jpg&oldid=900855017 (accessed October 22, 2024)., Source: PBS website "View of the University of Virginia, author: Edward Sachse., 1856, published by Casimir Bond, Washington, D.C. and Richmond, VA. **Fig. 4-23** ©Thomas Jefferson Foundation at Monticello. https://virginiachronicle.com/?a=d&d=RE18261103.1.3&e=-------en-20--1--txt-txIN------. **Fig. 4-24** Gunston Hall Farms, Kentucky, full service thoroughbred facility. http://gunstonhallfarm.net/kentucky/wp-content/uploads/2016/08/gunston-hall-farm-horse-800x600.jpg. **Fig. 4-25** Original manuscript from MHIS ,Coolidge Collection. Thomas Jefferson Manuscripts. **Fig. 4-26** Original manuscript from MHIS, Coolidge Collection Thomas Jefferson Manuscripts, 1781-1797. **Fig. 4-27** Wikimedia Commons contributors, "File:She-wolf suckles Romulus and Remus.jpg," Wikimedia Commons, https://commons.wikimedia.org/w/index.php?title=File:She-wolf_suckles_Romulus_and_Remus.jpg&oldid=902066497 (accessed October 22, 2024)., Collections: Capitoline Museums, location: Palazzo dei Conservatori, Hall of the She-Wolf, Source/Photographer: Wilfredo Rafael Rodriguez Hernandez, retouched, 2024., **Fig. 4-28** Wikimedia Commons contributors. File:Ossian. Den gamle blinde skotske barde synger til harpen sin svanesang.jpg [Internet]. Wikimedia Commons; 2024 Oct 15, 02:51 UTC [cited 2024 Oct 22]. Available from: https://commons.wikimedia.org/w/index.php?title=File:Ossian._Den_gamle_blinde_skotske_barde_synger_til_harpen_sin_svanesang.jpg&oldid=942923749 Collection: Statens Museum for Kunst, Source/Photographer: , **Fig. 4-29** The British Library. Print made by: Guillaume Philippe Benoist, 1757https://www.britishmuseum.org/collection/object/P_1874-1010-80, **Fig. 4-30** Wikimedia Commons contributors, "File:MANTE(1800) p1.063 CARACTACUS, KING OF THE BRITENS.jpg," Wikimedia Commons, https://commons.wikimedia.org/w/index.php?title=File:MANTE(1800)_p1.063_CARACTACUS,_KING_OF_THE_BRITENS.jpg&oldid=933817166 (accessed October 22, 2024) Collection: British Library. Source: Mechanical Curator collection. **Fig. 4-31** Wikimedia Commons contributors, "File:Gustavus Adolphus at the Battle at Breitenfeld.jpg," Wikimedia Commons, https://commons.wikimedia.org/w/index.php?title=File:Gustavus_Adolphus_at_the_Battle_at_Breitenfeld.jpg&oldid=935321856 (accessed October 26, 2024). Collection: unknown, Source/Photographer: Uploaded by: sv:User:Den fjättrade ankan **Fig. 4-32** Wikimedia Commons contributors, "File:Del av hjälm vendel vendeltid möjligen oden.jpg," Wikimedia Commons, https://commons.wikimedia.org/w/index.php?title=File:Del_av_hj%C3%A4lm_vendel_vendeltid_m%C3%B6jligen_oden.jpg&oldid=907467049 (accessed October 22, 2024). Source: Oscar Montelius, Om lifvet i Sverige under hednatiden (Stockholm 1905) s.98. **Fig. 4-33** Wikimedia Commons contributors, "File:Southerne Oroonoko 1776 performance.jpg," Wikimedia Commons, https://commons.wikimedia.org/w/index.php?title=File:Southerne_Oroonoko_1776_performance.jpg&oldid=633161826 (accessed October 22, 2024). Source: scan of public domain document. Doc. published 23 November 1776. Author: unknown. **Fig. 4-34** Wikimedia Commons contributors, "File:Tecumseh02.jpg," Wikimedia Commons, https://commons.wikimedia.org/w/index.php?title=File:Tecumseh02.jpg&oldid=902258092 (accessed October 22, 2024). Source: Gift of J. Ross Robertson in Toronto Public Library. **Fig. 4-35** Wikimedia Commons contributors, "File:Jakobinerklub.jpg," Wikimedia Commons, https://commons.wikimedia.org/w/index.php?title=File:Jakobinerklub.jpg&oldid=657758504 (accessed October 22, 2024). Source: Paris, BnF, département des estampes et de la photographie. Collection: Bibliothèque nacionale de France, Source/Photographer: Gallica Digital Library. **Fig. 4-36** Wikimedia Commons contributors, "File:The Beggar's Opera MET DP825185.jpg," Wikimedia Commons, https://commons.wikimedia.org/w/index.php?title=File:The_Beggar%27s_Opera_MET_DP825185.jpg&oldid=651688314 (accessed October 22, 2024). Collection: Metropolitan Museum of Art, Credit: Harris Brisbane Dick Fund, 1932, Source/Photographer: https://www.metmuseum.org/art/collection/search/399370, **Fig. 4-37** Wikimedia Commons contributors, "File:Margaret ('Peg') Woffington by John Lewis.jpg," Wikimedia Commons, https://commons.wikimedia.org/w/index.php?title=File:Margaret_(%27Peg%27)_Woffington_by_John_Lewis.jpg&oldid=838598858 (accessed October 22, 2024). Source/

Photgrapher1./3. National Portrait Gallery, London, **Fig. 4-38** © Colonial Williamsburg. **Fig. 4-39** © Colonial Williamsburg. **Fig. 4-40** Flickr, Author: Bob bob194156, CC BY 2.0, taken on August 3, 2013. https://www.flickr.com/photos/23295039@N02/12075049824/. **Fig. 4-41** Wikimedia Commons contributors, "File:Great Seal of the United States (obverse).svg," Wikimedia Commons, https://commons.wikimedia.org/w/index.php?title=File:Great_Seal_of_the_United_States_(obverse).svg&oldid=935059074 (accessed October 22, 2024). Author: US Government, Source: Extracted from PDF version of Our Flag, this file 2007.

■ **Chapter 5:** Facing photo: Wikimedia Commons contributors, "File:Coach House wide view - Stables - Mount Vernon.jpg," Wikimedia Commons, https://commons.wikimedia.org/w/index.php?title=File:Coach_House_wide_view_-_Stables_-_Mount_Vernon.jpg&oldid=894420101 (accessed December 17, 2024). Author : Tim Evanson 2014. **Fig. 5-1** © Colonial Williamsburg. **Fig. 5-2** Internet Archive, in One Hundred Years' Progress of the United States 1871, Flint, et al., p. 364, https://archive.org/details/onehundredyearsp00flinrich/page/364/mode/2up **Fig. 5-3** The Carriage Journal, 14, no. 2 (Autumn 1976), "The President's Phaeton," possibly by Max Terrier, p. 63. Google Books. Com **Fig. 5-4** 1806, https://static.lib.virginia.edu/rmds/nichols/source/n532ar.html. **Fig. 5-5** © Colonial Williamsburg. **Fig. 5-6** © Colonial Williamsburg. **Fig. 5-7** Wikimedia Commons contributors, "File:George Stubbs 003.jpg," Wikimedia Commons, https://commons.wikimedia.org/w/index.php?title=File:George_Stubbs_003.jpg&oldid=884558926 (accessed October 22, 2024). Collection: National Gallery, Source: The Yorck Project (2002) 10.000 Meisterwerke der Malerei. **Fig. 5-8** Wikimedia Commons contributors, "File:Cabriolet (PSF).jpg," Wikimedia Commons, https://commons.wikimedia.org/w/index.php?title=File:Cabriolet_(PSF).jpg&oldid=845145270 (accessed October 22, 2024) . Source: Archives of Pearson Scott Foresman donated to the Wikimedia Foundation, author: Pearson Scott Foresman. **Fig. 5-9** Wikimedia Commons contributors, "File:Mail Changing Horses - James Pollard.png," Wikimedia Commons, https://commons.wikimedia.org/w/index.php?title=File:Mail_Changing_Horses_-_James_Pollard.png&oldid=489940461 (accessed October 22, 2024). Source: Corel Professional Photos. **Fig. 5-10** Wikimedia Commons, contributors, "File:Carter braxton old.jpg," https://commons.wikimedia.org/w/index.php?title=File:Carter_braxton_old.jpg&oldid=849373267 (accessed October 3, 2024). **Fig. 5-11** Original manuscript from MHIS, Coolidge Collection. Thomas Jefferson Manuscripts, N540. **Fig. 5-12** Internet Archive, A treatise on carriages, by Felton, William; Debrett, John, 1796, p. 131, Contributor: Getty Research Institute. **Fig. 5-13** Auction house: https://www.invaluable.com/auction-lot/gilt-harris-style-horse-drawn-sulky-weather-vane--59-c-bdf4301930. **Fig. 5-14.** Drawing by Edwin Tunis, in Wheels a Pictorial History, written and illustrated by Edwin Tunis, New York : Crowell 1977, p. 44. Contributor: Internet Archive, https://archive.org/details/wheelspictorialh00tuni/page/44/mode/2up. **Fig. 5-15** Photo by author. **Fig. 5-16** The Thomas Jefferson Papers at the Library of Congress, Manuscript Division, 1801-07-09 , http://hdl.loc.gov/loc.mss/mtj.mtjbib010276. **Fig. 5-17** University of Virginia Library, Nichols Collection, a. https://static.lib.virginia.edu/rmds/nichols/source/n532av.html, and b. https://static.lib.virginia.edu/rmds/nichols/source/n532b.html. **Fig. 5-18** ©Thomas Jefferson Foundation at Monticello. **Fig. 5-19** Photo by author. **Fig. 5-20.** Drawing by Edwin Tunis, in Wheels a Pictorial History, written and illustrated by Edwin Tunis, New York : Crowell 1977, p. 41. Contributor: Internet Archive, https://archive.org/details/wheelspictorialh00tuni/page/40/mode/2up. **Fig. 5-21** a. and b. Original manuscript from MHIS, Coolidge Collection. Thomas Jefferson Manuscripts. 1802. 533. **Fig. 5-22.** Photo by author. **Fig. 5-23.** ©Thomas Jefferson Foundation at Monticello. **Fig. 5-24** a .Wikimedia Commons contributors, "File:Sketch plan for landscaping the grounds of the President's House, ca. 1802-05. LOC 88693237.tif," Wikimedia Commons, https://commons.wikimedia.org/w/index.php?title=File:Sketch_plan_for_landscaping_the_grounds_of_the_President%27s_House,_ca._1802-05._LOC_88693237.tif&oldid=838513650 (accessed October 22, 2024). United States Library of Congress's Geography & Map Division, under the digital ID g3852w.ct002310. b. Original manuscript from MHIS Coolidge Collection. Thomas Jefferson Manuscripts **Fig. 5-25** Photo by author. **Fig. 5-26.**Wisconsin Historical Society, b & w photographic print, 1898, Image ID 40237.Page 127. © Colonial Williamsburg.

■ **Chapter 6:** Facing photo: What's Up Media, "Maryland's First Famed Horses," Ellen Moyer, May 5, 2022. Painting by William Wilson, On-line, https://whatsupmag.com/culture/marylands-first-famed-horses/and http://www.marylandracingart.com/selimamatchracepage.html. (accessed October 27, 2024). **Fig. 6-1** In Philadelphia Museum of Art, Credit line: Purchased with the W. P. Wilstach Fund, the John D. McIlhenny Fund, and gifts (by exchange) of Samuel S. White 3rd and Vera White, Mrs. R. Barclay Scull, and Edna M. Welsh, 1984 . Accession Number. W1984-57-1 https://philamuseum.org/collection/object/104512 . **Fig. 6-2** https://www.christies.com/lot/lot-john-frederick-herring-snr-over-the-gate-5956425/ **Fig. 6-3** Wikimedia Commons contributors, "File:William Ward - Fox Hunting, Raby Pack - The Earl of Darlington's Fox Hounds in Their Kennel - B1985.36.302 - Yale Center for British Art.jpg," Wikimedia Commons, https://commons.wikimedia.org/w/index.php?title=File:William_Ward_-_Fox_Hunting,_Raby_Pack_-_The_Earl_of_Darlington%27s_Fox_Hounds_in_Their_Kennel_-_B1985.36.302_-_Yale_Center_for_British_Art.jpg&oldid=856481107 (accessed October 22, 2024). **Fig. 6-4** Wiki Art, 17771, Private collection, public domain. https://www.wikiart.org/en/george-stubbs/a-bay-hunter-with-two-spaniels. **Fig. 6-5** Mount Vernon emuseum. Collection, 1856, Printer William Pate, Publisher G. P. Putman & Co., Credit: Gift of Mr. and Mrs. Robert B. Gibby, Object Number WB-2C1/B1984. https://emuseum.mountvernon.org/objects/12166/washington-and-fairfax--field-sports;jsessionid=211E6F258797FD05A04A4FE305ABCE55. **Fig. 6-6** Fine Art America, https://fineartamerica.com/featured/fox-hunting-going-into-cover-henry-thomas-alken.html?product=art-print, The National Sports of Great Britain: Fifty Engravings With Descriptions by Henry Thomas Alken, Published by London: Printed for Thomas M'Lean, 1825. **Fig. 6-7** John Ward Dunsmore Collection at the Fraunces Tavern Museum in New York City, Catalogue Number 1936.02.024, Credit line: Gift of George A. Zabriskie Memorial, 1936. https://fraunces tavern.pastperfectonline.com/webobject/EB0C37BF-E589-42DA-BFCC-599733844237. **Fig. 6-8** Wikimedia Commons contributors, "File:Herring The Kill.jpg," Wikimedia Commons, https://commons.wikimedia.org/w/index.php?title=File:Herring_The_Kill.jpg&oldid=860642315 (accessed October 22, 2024). Source: COREL photo CD, Masters I. **Fig. 6-9** https://www.pinterest.com/pin/411516484677777770/. **Fig. 6-10** Montpelier Hunt Races, September 2023. Facebook page: Montpelier Hunt Races, https://www.facebook.com/photo/?fbid=623379173234528&set=gm.634153978806664 **Fig. 6-11** emuseum, Colonial Williamsburg, Credit line:

Gift of Abby Aldrich Rockefeller, Object number1933.305.2. https://emuseum.history.org/objects/58097/birth-record-for-samual-asay-18061891. **Fig. 6-12** Fig. 6-12 Ruidoso Downs Race Track & Casino, Ruidoso, NM, the All-American Futurity, Sept. 8, 2020, Midland Reporter Telegram, https://www.mrt.com/sports/article/Whistle-Stop-Cafe-wins-All-American-Futurity-in-15548861.php **Fig. 6-13** Wikimedia Commons contributors, "File:Le Derby de 1821 à Epsom - Théodore Géricault - Musée du Louvre Peintures MI 708 - photo 2.jpg," Wikimedia Commons, https://commons.wikimedia.org/w/index.php?title=File:Le_Derby_de_1821_%C3%A0_Epsom_-_Th%C3%A9odore_G%C3%A9ricault_-_Mus%C3%A9e_du_Louvre_Peintures_MI_708_-_photo_2.jpg&oldid=852731722 (accessed October 31, 2024). Source: The Yorck Project (2002), Meisterwerke der Malerei. **Fig. 6-14** Rockefeller Library Collections, Colonial Williamsburg, Virginia Gazette, March 22, 1770, pg.4, https://research.colonialwilliamsburg.org/DigitalLibrary/va-gazettes/VGSinglePage.cfm?issueIDNo=70.PD.06&page=4&res=LO. **Fig. 6-15** 141st "Run for the Roses: Kentucky Derby 2015: American Pharoah Wins a Close Race." NYT, Section SP, Page 1. photo by Andrew Hancock. https://www.nytimes.com/slideshow/2015/05/02/sports/DERBY.html. **Fig. 6-16** Claiborne Farm, Face Book, posted: March 30, 2024. Happy Birthday Big Red. Claiborne Farm photograph. https://www.facebook.com/photo/?fbid=807340841433722&set=a.550917317076077. Source/Photographer: Dell Hanncock.

Chapter 7: Facing photo: © Colonial Williamsburg **Fig. 7-1** Wikimedia Commons contributors, "File:John Wootton - Portrait of a Man on Horseback - Google Art Project.jpg," Wikimedia Commons, https://commons.wikimedia.org/w/index.php?title=File:John_Wootton_-_Portrait_of_a_Man_on_Horseback_-_Google_Art_Project.jpg&oldid=774353621 (accessed October 22, 2024). References: Yale Center for British Art, ID: 1665697, Source/Photographer: -AEZ8f-FhTbE4w at Google Cultural Institute. **Fig. 7-2** Original manuscript from MHIS, Coolidge Collection. Thomas Jefferson Manuscripts. Thomas Jefferson Papers, Farm Book, (inside front cover). **Fig. 7-3** Rockefeller Library Collections, Colonial Williamsburg , Virginia Gazette, April 04, 1766, p. 3, https://research.colonialwilliamsburg.org/DigitalLibrary/va-gazettes/VGSinglePage.cfm?issueIDNo=66.PD.06&page=3&res=LO **Fig. 7-4** Wikimedia Commons contributors, "File:Shirley Plantation 2006.jpg," Wikimedia Commons, https://commons.wikimedia.org/w/index.php?title=File:Shirley_Plantation_2006.jpg&oldid=663847873 (accessed October 22, 2024)., Author: Yellowute at en.wikipedia , 2007, **Fig. 7-5** Rockefeller Library Collections, Colonial Williamsburg, Virginia Gazette, April 18, 1766, p. 1, https://research.colonialwilliamsburg.org/DigitalLibrary/va-gazettes/VGSinglePage.cfm?issueIDNo=66.PD.08 **Fig. 7-6** Rockefeller Library Collections, Colonial Williamsburg, Virginia Gazette, April 16, 1772, p. 3, https://research.colonialwilliamsburg.org/DigitalLibrary/va-gazettes/VGSinglePage.cfm?issueIDNo=72.PD.18 **Fig. 7-7** Wikimedia Commons contributors, "File:WestoverPlantationSEGL.jpg," Wikimedia Commons, https://commons.wikimedia.org/w/index.php?title=File:WestoverPlantationSEGL.jpg&oldid=670777410 (accessed October 22, 2024). Photographer/Author: Stephen Lea, 2006. **Fig. 7-8** ©Thomas Jefferson Foundation at Monticello. **Fig. 7-9** Wikimedia Commons contributors, "File:Banastre-Tarleton-by-Joshua-Reynolds.jpg," Wikimedia Commons, https://commons.wikimedia.org/w/index.php?title=File:Banastre-Tarleton-by-Joshua-Reynolds.jpg&oldid=816238047 (accessed October 22, 2024). Collection: National Gallery, Accession Number: NG5985 (National Gallery) **Fig. 7-10** Wikimedia Commons contributors, "File:Jack jouett silhouette.jpg," Wikimedia Commons, https://commons.wikimedia.org/w/index.php?title=File:Jack_jouett_silhouette.jpg&oldid=353063616 (accessed October 22, 2024), Source: **Fig. 7-11** Wikimedia Commons contributors, "File:First Marquis of Cornwallis.jpg," Wikimedia Commons, https://commons.wikimedia.org/w/index.php?title=File:First_Marquis_of_Cornwallis.jpg&oldid=848554207 (accessed October 22, 2024). painting, c. 1795, Collection: Guildhall Art Gallery, Source/Photographer: First Foot Guards. **Fig. 7-12** Wikimedia Commons contributors, "File:Gilbert du Motier Marquis de Lafayette.PNG," Wikimedia Commons, https://commons.wikimedia.org/w/index.php?title=File:Gilbert_du_Motier_Marquis_de_Lafayette.PNG&oldid=808451063 (accessed October 22, 2024). oil on canvas, 1834. Collection: Palace of Versailles, Accession number MV 2346; INV 3424; LP 471, **Fig. 7-13** Wikimedia Commons contributors, "File:LaMirage body07.jpg," Wikimedia Commons, https://commons.wikimedia.org/w/index.php?title=File:LaMirage_body07.jpg&oldid=487228424 (accessed October 22, 2024). Author: Trescastillos, 2007. **Fig. 7-14** Illumiseen, "The 8 Fastest Horses in the World | Who Leads the Race?" July 09, 2020, https://www.illumiseen.com/blogs/news/the-8-fastest-horses-in-the-world-who-leads-the-race **Fig. 7-15** Photo by author. **Fig. 7-16** Wikimedia Commons contributors, "File:Fred E. Miller-Spotted Rabbit (Crow tribe) on horseback, Montana.jpg," Wikimedia Commons, https://commons.wikimedia.org/w/index.php?title=File:Fred_E._Miller-Spotted_Rabbit_(Crow_tribe)_on_horseback,_Montana.jpg&oldid=674975152 (accessed October 22, 2024), Author: Fred E. Miller, Source: Newsdesk.si.edu. **Fig. 7-17** Wikimedia Commons contributors, "File:Andalusier 1 voll versammelt.jpg," Wikimedia Commons, https://commons.wikimedia.org/w/index.php?title=File:Andalusier_1_voll_versammelt.jpg&oldid=805167999 (accessed October 22, 2024). Author: BS Thurner Hof, 2 March 2005, **Fig. 7-18** Wikimedia Commons contributors, "File:WELBECK Le Superbe Cheval De Spanie.jpg," Wikimedia Commons, https://commons.wikimedia.org/w/index.php?title=File:WELBECK_Le_Superbe_Cheval_De_Spanie.jpg&oldid=939540388 (accessed October 22, 2024). engraving, reprinted 1743, Source/Photographer: Welbeck Le Superbe Cheval de Spanie at beinecke.library.yale.edu. **Fig. 7-19** In The Gentleman's New Pocket Companion, R .Mason, 1883, Title page and p. 22. https://www.google.com/books/edition/The_Gentleman_s_New_Pocket_Farrier/TWUCAAAAYAAJ?hl=en&gbpv=1 **Fig. 7-20** Seen in Alexander McKay-Smith, The Colonial Race Horse, (1983: 238), in John Page Elliot Collection.

Chapter 8: Facing page: photo by author. **Fig. 8-1** Wikimedia Commons contributors, "File:Connemara Ponies (209943565).jpeg," Wikimedia Commons, https://commons.wikimedia.org/w/index.php?title=File:Connemara_Ponies_(209943565).jpeg&oldid=867522184 (accessed October 15, 2024). **Fig. 8-2** Wikimedia Commons contributors, "File:Fell pony.jpg," Wikimedia Commons, https://commons.wikimedia.org/w/index.php?title=File:Fell_pony.jpg&oldid=917571428 (accessed October 15, 2024). **Fig. 8-3** Ad for horse riding holiday in Southern Spain. For Globetrotting. https://www.globetrotting.com.au/horse-riding-holidays/andalusia-spain/. **Fig. 8-4** Wikimedia Commons contributors, "File:Chestnut Paso Fino.jpg," Wikimedia Commons, https://commons.wikimedia.org/w/index.php?title=File:Chestnut_Paso_Fino.jpg&oldid=855731277 (accessed October 15, 2024). **Fig. 8-5** Wikimedia Commons contributors, "File:Remington A cracker cowboy.jpg,"

Wikimedia Commons, https://commons.wikimedia.org/w/index.php?title=File:Remington_A_cracker_cowboy.jpg&oldid=770079848 (accessed October 15, 2024). **Fig. 8-6** Photo by author. **Fig. 8-7** Rockefeller Library (Digital) Collection, Colonial Williamsburg, Virginia Gazette, Purdie and Dixon, May 24, 1770, p. 3, https://research.colonialwilliamsburg.org/DigitalLibrary/va-gazettes/VGSinglePage.cfm?issueIDNo=70.PD.11&page=3&res=LO . **Fig. 8-8** Wikimedia Commons contributors, "File:Jethro Tull seed drill (1762).png," Wikimedia Commons, https://commons.wikimedia.org/w/index.php?title=File:Jethro_Tull_seed_drill_(1762).png&oldid=505512486 (accessed October 15, 2024). **Fig. 8-9** © Colonial Williamsburg. **Fig. 8-10** Wikimedia Commons contributors, "File:Shire.jpg," Wikimedia Commons, https://commons.wikimedia.org/w/index.php?title=File:Shire.jpg&oldid=860073828 (accessed October 15, 2024). **Fig. 8-11** © Colonial Williamsburg. **Fig. 8-12** Small Farmer's Journal, on-line, "Plowing with the Single Horse," by Lynn R.Miller of Singling Horse Ranch, n.d., https://smallfarmersjournal.com/plowing-with-the-single-horse/. **Fig. 8-13** ©Thomas Jefferson Foundation at Monticello. **Fig. 8-14** Wikimedia Commons contributors, "File:Juancito.jpg," Wikimedia Commons, https://commons.wikimedia.org/w/index.php?title=File:Juancito.jpg&oldid=739317901 (accessed October 15, 2024). **Fig. 8-15** American Presidential and Founders Papers, Huntington Digital Library, N197. Huntington Library, California. **Fig. 8-16** ©Thomas Jefferson Foundation at Monticello. **Fig. 8-17** Photo by author. **Fig. 8-18** Rockefeller Library (Digital) Collection, Colonial Williamsburg, Virginia Gazette, Purdie and Dixon, May 24, 1770, p. 4. **Fig. 8-19** Northern Virginia Magazine, 0nline, "The Head Winemaker at Jefferson Vineyards Is Producing Award-Winning Vino," Ashley Davidson, August 29, 2022 . https://northernvirginiamag.com/food/drinks/2022/08/29/jefferson-vineyards-virginia-wine-festival/. **Fig. 8-20** Original manuscript from MHiS, Coolidge Collection. Thomas Jefferson Manuscripts, N 298 K 1976 [electronic edition]. http://www.thomasjeffersonpapers.org/. **Fig. 8-21** Historic American Buildings Survey, Creator. Edgewood Farm, Stable, West side of State Route 600, .8 mile north of State Route 778, Clover, Halifax County, VA. Halifax County Virginia Clover, Documentation Compiled After. Photograph. https://www.loc.gov/item/va1893/. 1933. **Fig. 8-22** Original manuscript from MHiS, Coolidge Collection. Thomas Jefferson Manuscripts, N225; K169 [electronic edition]. http://www.thomasjeffersonpapers.org/ **Fig. 8-23** Stable from the west, Accession/file number, none, ca 1925-27, image creator: unk, Location: Robert H. Smith International Center for Jeffeson Studies, Monticello, Va., accessed, by author as a Fellow, 2008. **Fig. 8-24** Stables from the South, Accession/file number: Acc. 68-24, ca 1929-34, image creator: unk, image of stable after it was restored in 1929. Location, Robert H. Smith International Center for Jeffeson Studies, Monticello, Va. , accessed, by author as a Fellow, 2008. **Fig. 8-25** Photo by author. **Fig. 8-26** Photo by author. **Fig. 8-27** Wikimedia Commons contributors, "File:James Seymour - The Stables and Two Famous Running Horses belonging to His Grace, the Duke of Bolton - Google Art Project.jpg," Wikimedia Commons, https://commons.wikimedia.org/w/index.php?title=File:James_Seymour_-_The_Stables_and_Two_Famous_Running_Horses_belonging_to_His_Grace,_the_Duke_of_Bolton_-_Google_Art_Project.jpg&oldid=758941900 (accessed October 15, 2024). **Fig. 8-28** Photo by author. **Fig. 8-29** Philadelphia: stables, railing, and latch, recto, [probably 1778], by Thomas Jefferson. N249; K60 [electronic edition]. Thomas Jefferson Papers: An Electronic Archive. Boston, Mass. MHiS, 2003. http://www.thomasjeffersonpapers.org/. **Fig. 8-30** Digital collections, University of Maryland, North Terrace Building, Monticello, Charlottesville, Virginia, circa 1907-1914, https://digital.lib.umd.edu/resultsnew/id/umd:65788 https://hdl.handle.net/1903.1/8046 **Fig. 8-31** Photo by author. **Fig. 8-32** a and b photos (inside Bremo stables, 1937) Grigg & Johnson, Architects, file, Bremo Stables "Monticello", 2/21/38, Number 787, Robert H. Smith International Center for Jeffeson Studies, Monticello, Va, accessed, by author as a Fellow, 2008. **Fig. 8-33** (floor plan Bemo stables, 1937) Grigg & Johnson, Architects, file, Bremo Stables "Monticello", 2/21/38, Number 787, Robert H. Smith International Center for Jeffeson Studies, Monticello, Va, accessed, by author as a Fellow, 2008. Fig. 8-34. Photo by author. **Fig. 8-35** Photo by author. **Fig. 8-36** Photo by author. **Fig. 8-37** ©Thomas Jefferson Foundation at Monticello. Nichols 540, KM-3. **Fig. 8-38** ©Thomas Jefferson Foundation at Monticello. **Fig. 8-39** © UVA Cultural Landscape maps, 1817-1826, University of Virginia Facilities Management, Resources Center."Earliest Map" 00082057. **Fig. 8-40** Wikimedia Commons contributors, "File:PoplarForest.jpg," Wikimedia Commons, https://commons.wikimedia.org/w/index.php?title=File:PoplarForest.jpg&oldid=536368764 Author: Warfieldian, 2009, (accessed October 18, 2024). **Fig. 8-41** Photo by author. **Fig. 8-42** Photo by author. **Fig. 8-43** Library of Congress Prints and Photographs Division, created: Historic American Buildings Survey, creator compiled after 1933. https://www.loc.gov/resource/hhh.va0405.photos/?sp=10 Survey HABS VA-105 **Fig. 8-44** Original manuscript from MHiS, Coolidge Collection. Thomas Jefferson Manuscripts, Farm Book (1774-1824), p. 138. **Fig. 8-45** ©Thomas Jefferson Foundation at Monticello.

■ **Postscript:** Facing photo: Wikimedia Commons contributors, "File:University of Virginia Rotunda 1819 draft.jpg," Wikimedia Commons, https://commons.wikimedia.org/w/index.php?title=File:University_of_Virginia_Rotunda_1819_draft.jpg&oldid=739202442 (accessed January 10, 2025), Thomas Jefferson, Source: https://www.loc.gov/exhibits/jefferson/images/vc77.jpg. **Fig. Post-1** University of Virginia, University Communications; images are available for general use. **Fig. Post-2** Wikimedia Commons contributors, "File:Close view of Statue and Rotunda at University of Virginia.jpg," Wikimedia Commons, https://commons.wikimedia.org/w/index.php?title=File:Close_view_of_Statue_and_Rotunda_at_University_of_Virginia.jpg&oldid=862363181 (accessed October 19, 2024). Author: BestbudBrian. **Fig. Post-3** Reuters/by Stephanie Keith. In The Atlantic, "Charlottesville was only a Preview," by James Loeffler, Dec. 23, 2021. https://www.theatlantic.com/ideas/archive/2021/12/why-charlottesville-matters/621096/. **Fig. Post-4** The Daily Progress, 2/22/2019, online article, Albemarle Upgrades GIS Mapping Tool, DP Staff. **Fig. Post-5** Wahoo photography. **Fig. Post-6** Photo by author. **Fig. Post-7** The Daily Progress. By Cal Cary. Fig. **Post-8** Photo by author. **Fig. Post-9** Wikimedia Commons contributors, "File:Cav Man UVa canters 2009.jpg," Wikimedia Commons, https://commons.wikimedia.org/w/index.php?title=File:Cav_Man_UVa_canters_2009.jpg&oldid=851863346, (accessed October 19, 2024), Author: Karen Blaha. **Fig. Post-10** Photo by author.

Bibliography

Thomas Jefferson's Writings

Followed by abbreviated citations when used

Jefferson, Thomas. *Autobiography*. 1821. Liberty Online! http://libertyonline.hypermall.com/Jefferson/Autobiography.html#return. Accessed June 8, 2021. (abbreviated as A1821)

Collection of Autograph Letters Signed: Philadelphia, Washington, etc., to his daughter Martha, 1784 Jan. 15-1819 Aug. 24. The Morgan Library & Museum, New York.

Family Letters of Thomas Jefferson. Edited by Edwin Morris Betts and James Bear, Jr. Charlottesville: University of Virginia Press, 1966. (abbreviated as FL1966)

Garden and Farm Books of Thomas Jefferson. Edited by Robert C. Baron. Golden, Colorado: Fulcrum, 1987. (abbreviated as GFB1987)

Jefferson's Memorandum Books: Accounts, with Legal Records and Miscellany, 1767–1826. Edited by James A. Bear, Jr., and Lucia C. Stanton. Princeton: Princeton University Press, 1997. (abbreviated as MB1997)

"Jefferson's Observations on Démeunier's Manuscript." June 22, 1786. Founders Online. http://founders.archives.gov/documents/Jefferson/01-10-02-0001-0005. (abbreviated as ODM)

"Monticello: building notebook." Identification numbers N113; K84. Thomas Jefferson Papers, Massachusetts Historical Society.

"Monticello: dependencies (plan)," recto, before 4 August 1772. Identification numbers N56; K31. Thomas Jefferson Papers, Massachusetts Historical Society.

"Philadelphia: latch, stalls, cart, and doors," recto, probably 1778. Identification numbers N250; K61. Thomas Jefferson Papers, Massachusetts Historical Society.

Notes on the State of Virginia. Paris: T. Jefferson, 1784. http://search.lib.virginia.edu/catalog/uva-lib:710304. (abbreviated as NSV1784)

Notes on the State of Virginia. Boston, Lilly and Wait, 1832. https://www.loc.gov/item/03004902/. (abbreviated as NSV1832)

Papers of Thomas Jefferson. Edited by Julian P. Boyd. Princeton: Princeton University Press, 1950. (abbreviated as PTJ)

"Some Family Letters of Thomas Jefferson." *Scribner's Magazine* 36 (1904): 573–586. (abbreviated as FL1904)

Summary View of the Rights of British America. Williamsburg: Printed by Clementina Rind, 1774.

Thomas Jefferson, Political Writings. Edited by Joyce O. Appleby and Terence Ball. New York: Cambridge University Press, 1999. (abbreviated as PW1999)

Thomas Jefferson's Architectural Drawings. Chapel Hill: Thomas Jefferson Foundation, 1995. (abbreviated as AD1995)

Thomas Jefferson's Farm Book. Edited by Edwin Morris Betts. Chapel Hill: University of North Carolina Press, 1953. (abbreviated as FB1953)

Thomas Jefferson's Farm Book. Edited by Edwin Morris Betts. Charlottesville: University of Virginia Press, 1976. (abbreviated as FB1976)

Thomas Jefferson's Farm Book. Edited by Edwin Morris Betts. Charlottesville: Thomas Jefferson Memorial Foundation, Inc., 1999. (abbreviated as FB1999)

Thomas Jefferson's Farm Book. Edited by Edwin Morris Betts. Charlottesville: Thomas Jefferson Memorial Foundation, Inc., 1999. (abbreviated as GB1999)

Thomas Jefferson's Scrapbooks: Poems of a Nation, Family, and Romantic Love Collected by America's Third President. Edited by Jonathan Gross. Hanover, New Hampshire: Steerforth Press, 2006. (abbreviated as SCR)

Writings of Thomas Jefferson. Edited by Andrew A. Lipscomb and Albert Ellery Bergh. New York: Thomas Jefferson Memorial Association of the United States, 1903. (abbreviated as WTJ1903)

Retirement Series Digital Archive. Thomas Jefferson Foundation, Inc. http://tjrs.monticello.org. (abbreviated as RSDA)

Thomas Jefferson Papers, 1606 to 1827. Series 1: General Correspondence, 1651–1827. Manuscript Division. Library of Congress. https://www.loc.gov/collections/thomas-jefferson-papers/. (abbreviated as TJP)

Thomas Jefferson Papers: An Electronic Archive. Massachusetts Historical Society. http://www.thomasjeffersonpapers.org/. (abbreviated as TJPEA)

Thomas Jefferson's Architectural Drawings (electronic edition). Thomas Jefferson Papers. Massachusetts Historical Society. http://www.masshist.org/thomasjeffersonpapers/arch/. See particularly drawings N56, N113, N249, N250, N540. (abbreviated as ADEE)

Manuscript Collections

Cocke Family Papers. Special Collections. University of Virginia Library.

Coolidge Collection of Thomas Jefferson Manuscripts. Massachusetts Historical Society.

Edgehill-Randolph Papers, 1749 (1790-1850) 1886. Special Collections. University of Virginia Library.

Founders Online. National Archives. http://founders.archives.gov.

Nicholas Philip Trist Papers, 1765–1903. Southern Historical Collection. Wilson Library, University of North Carolina at Chapel Hill.

Papers of the Proctor of the University of Virginia, 1817–1828 (Arthur Spicer Brockenbrough). Special Collections. University of Virginia Library.

Books, Articles, and Other Sources

Adams, Percy G. "The Coach Motif in Eighteenth-Century Fiction." *Modern Language Studies* 8, No. 2 (Spring 1978): 17–26.

Altamirano, J. C. *Historia y Origen del Caballo Español (1567–1800) (History and Origins of the Spanish Horse (1567–1800)*. Málaga: Ediciones Ecuestres, 2005.

Ambler, Jacquelin. *A Treatise on the Culture of Lucerne*. Richmond, Virginia: Printed by T. Nicolson, 1800.

American Farmer: Devoted to Agriculture, Horticulture and Rural Life. Baltimore: Printed for J. S. Skinner by J. Robinson, 1819–1834.

"American Foundation Mares." Thoroughbred Heritage. Historic Dams. http://www.tbheritage.com/HistoricDams/AmFoundationMares.html, 2005.

American Horse Council Foundation. *The Economic Impact of the Horse Industry on the United States National Report*. 2005. http://www.horsecouncil.org/product/2005-the-economic-impact-of-the-horse-industry-on-the-united-states-national-report/.

American Quarter Horse Association. https://www.aqha.com/.

American Turf Register and Sporting Magazine. Baltimore: J. S. Skinner, 1829–1844.

Anburey, Thomas. *Travels Through the Interior Parts of America in a Series of Letters 1776–1781*. London: William Lane, Leadenhall Street, 1789.

Argent, Gala. "Toward a Privileging of the Nonverbal Communication, Corporeal Synchrony, and Transcendence in Humans and Horses," in Julie A. Smit & Robert W. Mitchell, eds., Experiencing *Animal Minds: An Anthology of Animal Human Encounters*. New York: Columbia University Press, 2012.

"Horses, Mourning—Interspecies Embodiment, Belonging, and Bereavement in the Past and Present," in Margo DeMello, ed., *Mourning Animals: Rituals and Practices Surrounding Animal Death (The Animal Turn)*. East Lansing: Michigan State University Press, 2016.

Bacon, Edmund. "Memoranda Book, 1802–1822." Special Collections, University of Virginia Library, Charlottesville.

Barraud, E. M. *Barraud, the Story of a Family*. London: The Research Publishing Co., 1967.

Bear, James A., Jr., ed. *Jefferson at Monticello: Recollections of a Monticello Slave and of a Monticello Overseer*. Charlottesville: University Press of Virginia, 1967.

Berkebile, Don H. *Carriage Terminology: An Historical Dictionary*. Washington, D.C.: Smithsonian Institution Press, 1978.

Bishko, Lucretia Ramsey. "A Spanish Stallion for Albemarle," *Virginia Magazine of History and Biography* (April 1968): 146–180.

Bordley, J. B. *Essays and Notes on Husbandry and Rural Affairs*. Philadelphia: Budd and Bartram, for Thomas Dobson, at the Stone House, no. 41, South Second Street, 1801.

Bouldin, Powhatan. *Home Reminiscences of John Randolph, of Roanoke*. Richmond, Virginia: Clemmitt & Jones, Printers, 1876.

Bradley, Richard. *The Gentleman's and Farmer's Guide for the Increase and Improvement of Cattle, Also the Manner of Breeding and Breaking Horses, Both for Sport and Burden*. London: R. Bradley, 1739.

Braudel, Fernand. *Civilization and Capitalism, 15th–18th Century.* Translated by Siân Reynold. New York: Harper & Row, 1981.

Breen, T. H. "Horses and Gentlemen: The Cultural Significance of Gambling among the Gentry of Virginia." *William and Mary Quarterly 34*, No. 2 (April 1977): 239–257.

Tobacco Culture: The Mentality of the Great Tidewater Planters on the Eve of Revolution. Princeton: Princeton University Press, 1985.

Britton, Rick. *Jefferson: A Monticello Sampler.* Buena Vista, Virginia: Mariner Publishing, 2008.

Bruce, William Cabell. *John Randolph of Roanoke, 1773–1833; A Biography Based Largely on New Material.* New York: G. P. Putnam's Sons, 1922.

Bumstead, S. A. "Appearance: Descriptions of Thomas Jefferson." August 23, 1822. Jefferson Library Information File. Jefferson Library, Charlottesville.

Burstein, Andrew. *The Inner Jefferson: Portrait of a Grieving Optimist*. Charlottesville: University of Virginia Press, 1995.

Byrd, Max. *Jefferson: A Novel.* New York: Bantam Books, 1993.

Byswanger, Willian L. Personal communication, April 2008.

Campbell, Julie A. *The Horse in Virginia: An Illustrated History.* Charlottesville: University of Virginia Press, 2010.

Campbell, Thomas Elliott. *Colonial Caroline: A History of Caroline County, Virginia.* Richmond, Virginia: Dietz Press, 1954.

Cassidy, Rebecca. *The Sport of Kings: Kinship, Class, and Thoroughbred Breeding in Newmarket.* Cambridge: Cambridge University Press, 2002.

Cavileer, Sharon. "George Washington's Horse." Equine Network/Equisearch.com. http://www.equisearch.com/horses_riding_training/travel/eqmtvernon2213/, 2002. Accessed June 8, 2021.

Chard, Thornton. "Did the First Spanish Horses Landed in Florida and Carolina Leave Progeny?" *American Anthropologist* 42, no. 1 (January–March 1940): 90–106.

"Three Centuries, Three Statesmen: Patrick Henry, John Randolph, David K. E. Bruce." Exhibit. Charlotte County Visitors' Center and Museum of Charlotte County (Virginia). http://charlotteva.com/museum/john_randolph.html. Accessed June 8, 2021.

Charlottesville Central Gazette.

Chastellux, F. J. *Travels in North America in the Years 1780, 1781 and 1782.* 2 vols. Translated by Howard C. Rice Jr. Chapel Hill: University of North Carolina Press for the Institute of Early American History and Culture, 1963.

Clark, J. *A Treatise on the Prevention of Diseases Incidental to Horses, from Bad Management in Regard to Stables, Food, Water, Air, and Exercise. To Which are Subjoined, Observations on Some of the Surgical and Medical Branches of Farriery.* Philadelphia: Printed by William Spotswood, 1791.

Clutton-Brock, Juliet. *Horse Power: A History of the Horse and Donkey in Human Societies.* London: Natural History Museum, 1992.

Cocke, J. H. Letter. *American Farmer* (February 28, 1823). In MacKay-Smith, *The Colonial Quarter Race Horse:* 235.

Cohen, Kenneth. "Well Calculated for the Farmer: Thoroughbreds in the Early National Chesapeake, 1790–1850." *Virginia Magazine of History and Biography* 115, no. 3 (2007): 370–411.

"Colonial Roads and Wheeled Vehicles." *William and Mary College Quarterly* 8, no. 1 (July 1899): 37–42.

Craig, Bryan. "Route to Washington, D.C." Thomas Jefferson Encyclopedia. May 31, 2007. https://www.monticello.org/site/research-and-collections/route-washington-dc.

Crawford, Alan Pell. *Twilight at Monticello: The Final Years of Thomas Jefferson.* New York: Random House, 2008.

Crews, Ed. "Captain Jack Jouett's Ride to the Rescue: Did Virginia's Paul Revere Spare Thomas Jefferson the Acquaintance of a British Hangman?" *Journal of the Colonial Williamsburg Foundation* 28, no. 3 (Summer 2006): 66–71.

———. (2007). "Comfort, Economy, Style: The Virtues of the Riding Chair." *Journal of the Colonial Williamsburg Foundation* 29, no. 4 (Autumn 2007): 84–88.

Culver, Francis Barnum. *Blooded Horses of Colonial Days: Classic Horse Matches in America Before the Revolution.* Baltimore: Published by the author, 1922.

Cuneo, Pia F. "Just a Bit of Control: The Historical Significance of Sixteenth- and Seventeenth-Century German Bit-Books." In *The Culture of the Horse: Status, Discipline, and Identity in the Early Modern World,* edited by Karen Raber & Trena J. Tucker, 141–173. New York: Palgrave Macmillan, 2005.

Cunningham, E. P., and J. J. Dooley, R. K. Splan, and D. G. Bradley. "Microsatellite Diversity, Pedigree Relatedness and the Contributions of Founder Lineages to Thoroughbred Horses." *Animal Genetics* 23, vol. 6 (December 2001): 360–364.

Dabney, Virginius. "Jack Jouett's Ride." *American Heritage Magazine* 13, no. 1 (December 1961). https://www.americanheritage.com/jack-jouetts-ride.

Daniel, Frederick. "Virginian Reminiscences of Jefferson." *Harper's Weekly* 48, no. 2500 (November 19, 1904): 1766–1768.

Daniels, Jonathan. *The Randolphs of Virginia.* Garden City, New York: Doubleday, 1972.

Dashper, Katherine. "Learning to Communicate: The Triad of (Mis)Communication in Horse Riding Lessons." In *The Meaning of Horses: Biosocial Encounters*, edited by Dona Lee Davis and Anita Maurstad, 87–101. New York: Routledge, 2016.

Davis, B. J. "The Spanish Horse in the East." Horse of the Americas. http://www.horseoftheamericas.com. 2010. Accessed June 8, 2021.

Davis, Dona Lee and Anita Maurstad. "Meaning of Horses." In *The Meaning of Horses: Biosocial Encounters,* edited by Dona Lee Davis and Anita Maurstad, 1-20. New York: Routledge, 2016.

Denhardt, Robert M. *Foundation Dams of the American Quarter Horse.* Norman: University of Oklahoma Press, 1995.

Derry, Margaret E. *Horses in Society: A Story of Animal Breeding and Marketing Culture, 1800–1920.* Toronto: University of Toronto Press, 2006.

Dobie, J. Frank. *The Mustangs.* Lincoln: University of Nebraska Press, 2005.

Edwards, Peter. *Horse and Man in Early Modern England.* London: Continuum, 2007.

Eisenberg, John. *Great Match Race: When North Met South in American's First Sport Spectacle.* Boston: Houghton Mifflin, 2006.

Ellis, Edward S. *Thomas Jefferson: A Character Sketch.* Chicago: The University Association, 1898.

Encyclopedia Virginia. http://www.encyclopediavirginia.org.

"Enslaved People Who Gained Freedom." https://www.monticello.org/research-education/thomas-jefferson-encyclopedia/slaves-who-gained-freedom.

"Eppes, John Wayles (1773–1823)." *Biographical Directory of the United States Congress.* https://bioguide.congress.gov/search/bio/E000197.

Estienne, Charles, and John Liébault. *Maison Rustique, or, The Countrie Farme.* Translated by Richard Surflet. Printed at London by Edm. Bollifant, for Bonham Norton, 1600.

"Eston Hemings Jefferson." Thomas Jefferson Encyclopedia. https://www.monticello.org/research-education/thomas-jefferson-encyclopedia/eston-hemings-jefferson.

Etymonline.com. https://www.etymonline.com/word/hobby.

Evans, Emory G. A *"Topping People": The Rise and Decline of Virginia's Old Political Elite,* 1680–1790. Charlottesville: University of Virginia Press, 2009.

——— and *Dictionary of Virginia Biography.* "John Carter (1695 or 1696–1742)." *Encyclopedia Virginia.* https://encyclopediavirginia.org/entries/carter-john-1695-or-1696-1742. December 22, 2021.

Family Letters Project. Thomas Jefferson's Monticello. http://familyletters.dataformat.com/PrintText.aspx?entry_id=207. Accessed June 8, 2021.

Feh, Claudia. "Relationships and Communication in Socially Natural Horse Herds," in *The Domestic Horse: The Origins, Development and Management of its Behaviour,* edited by Daniel S. Mills and Sue M. McDonnell. Cambridge: Cambridge University Press, 2005.

"First Families of Virginia." Wikipedia. https://en.wikipedia.org/wiki/First_Families_of_Virginia

Fisher, Sydney George. *Men, Women and Manners in Colonial Times.* Philadelphia: J. B. Lippincott Co., 1898.

Fithian, Philip Vickers. *Journal and Letters of Philip Vickers Fithian, 1773–1774: A Plantation Tutor of the Old Dominion.* Edited by Hunter Dickinson Farish. Williamsburg: Colonial Williamsburg, 1943.

Fitzhugh, William. *William Fitzhugh and His Chesapeake World, 1676–1701: The Fitzhugh Letters and Other Documents.* Edited by Richard Beale Davis. Chapel Hill: Published for the Virginia Historical Society by the University of North Carolina Press, 1963.

Flores, Dan. "Bringing Home All the Pretty Horses: The Horse Trade in the Early American West, 1785–1825." *Montana: The Magazine of Western History* 58 (Summer 2008): 3–21, 94–6.

Ford, Paul Leicester. "Horsemanship and Hunting." *The True George Washington.* Philadelphia: J. B. Lippincott, 1896. http://www.infoplease.com/t/history/true-washington/horsemanship.html.

"Fox hunting." Wikipedia. https://en.wikipedia.org/wiki/Fox_hunting. 2017.

"Free Workers Employed at Monticello." https://www.monticello.org/slavery/the-plantation/free-workers/.

Gale, Kira. "Cantonment Wilkinsonville, a 200-Year-Old Secret Military Base in Southern Illinois is Revealed: Lewis and Clark Expedition Members Were Posted There." In *Lewis and Clark Road Trips: Exploring the Trail Across America.* Omaha, Nebraska: River Junction Press, 2006.

Game, Ann. "Riding: Embodying the Centaur." *Body & Society* 7, no. 4 (December 2001): 1–12.

Gard, S. Richard, Jr. "The Jefferson Progression: How Historians Keep Changing their View of the Founder." *Virginia: The UVA Magazine* (Winter 2019). https://uvamagazine.org/articles/historians_write_about_a_different_jefferson_now.

Garrett, Martin A., Jr. "Mules in Southern Agriculture: Revisited." *Journal of Agriculture and Applied Economics* 33, no. 3 (December 2001), 1–8.

Gill, Harold B., Jr. "A Sport Only for Gentlemen." *Colonial Williamsburg Journal* 20, no. 1 (Autumn 1997): 49–53.

Goodwin, Mary R. M. *Wheeled Carriages in Eighteenth-Century Virginia*. Williamsburg, Virginia: Colonial Williamsburg, Inc., 1959.

Gordon-Reed, Annette. *Thomas Jefferson and Sally Hemings: An American Controversy.* Charlottesville: University Press of Virginia, 2007.

The Hemingses of Monticello: An American Family. New York: W.W. Norton & Company, 2008.

Günther, Pablo. *The Casanova Tour: A Handbook for the Use of the Private Travelling Carriage in Eighteenth Century Europe and America.* E-book: 1995–2019. https://giacomo-casanova.de/catour1.htm.

Hailman, John R. *Thomas Jefferson on Wine.* Jackson: University Press of Mississippi, 2006.

Harness, Cheryl. *Thomas Jefferson*. Washington, D.C.: National Geographic Children's Books, 2004.

Harris, Susan E. *Horse Gaits, Balance and Movement*. New York: Howell Book House, 1993.

Harrison, E. W. R., and Burke, M. J. T. "Monticello's Child Life." Unpublished manuscript, 1888. Thomas Jefferson Foundation.

Harrison, Fairfax. *The Equine F.F.Vs., A Study of the Evidence for the English Horses Imported into Virginia Before the Revolution.* Richmond, Virginia: Old Dominion Press, 1928.

Roanoke Stud, 1795–1833. Richmond, Virginia: Old Dominion Press, 1930.

Early American Turf-Stock, 1730–1830; Being a Critical Study of the Extant Evidence for the English, Spanish and Oriental Horses and Mares to Which Are Traced the Oldest American Turf Pedigrees. 2 vols. Richmond, Virginia: Old Dominion Press, 1934.

Hauer, John. *The Natural Superiority of Mules.* Guilford, Connecticut: Lyons Press, 2005.

Haworth, Paul Leland. *George Washington: Farmer; Being an Account of His Home Life and Agricultural Activities*. Indianapolis: Bobbs-Merrill, 1915. https://www.gutenberg.org/ebooks/11858.

Hearne, Vicki. *Adam's Task: Calling Animals by Name.* Skyhorse Publishing, 2007.

Helliar-Symons, Catherine. "John Hartwell Cocke and Bremo: A Study of Plantation Life." Master's thesis, University of Wales, 2003.

Hemings, Madison. "Life Among the Lowly, No. 1." March 13, 1873. *Encyclopedia Virginia*. https://encyclopediavirginia.org/entries/life-among-the-lowly-no-1-by-madison-hemings-march-13-1873/.

Henry, Joyce. Colonial Williamsburg Foundation. Personal communication, 2008.

Hervey, John. *Racing in America: 1665–1865*. New York: The Jockey Club, 1944.

Hill, E. W., and D. G. Bradley, M. Al-Barody, O. Ertugrul, R. K. Splan, I. Zakharov, and E. P. Cunningham. "History and Integrity of Thoroughbred Dam Lines Revealed in Equine mtDNA Variation." *Animal Genetics* 33, no. 4 (August 2002): 287–294.

"Historic Structure Report, Mount Vernon Estate and Garden Cultural Landscape Study." John Milner Associates, Rivanna Archaeological Consulting, 2004.

"History of the Land and People of Mount Pleasant." Mount Pleasant Plantation. http://mountpleasantplantation.com. Accessed June 8, 2021.

Hodgson, Adam. *Letters from North America, Written During a Tour in the United States and Canada.* London: Printed for Hurst,

Robinson, & Co., 1824.

Holmes, John M. *Thomas Jefferson Treats Himself: Herbs, Physicke, and Nutrition in Early America.* Fort Valley, Virginia: Loft Press, 1997.

Home, Francis. *The Principles of Agriculture and Vegetation.* London: Printed for A. Miller, 1762.

Home, Henry, Lord Kames. *The Gentleman Farmer: Being an Attempt to Improve Agriculture by Subjecting it to the Test of Rational Principles.* Edinburgh: Printed for W. Creech, Edinburgh, and T. Cadell, London, 1776.

Hotaling, Edward. *The Great Black Jockeys: The Lives and Times of the Men Who Dominated America's First National Sport.* New York: Forum Press, 1999.

Hughes, Charles. *The Compleat Horseman, or the Art of Riding Made Easy.* London: F. Newbury, 1772.

Hughes, Hillary. "First in War, First in Peace, and First in the Hearts of His Countrymen." https://www.mountvernon.org/library/digitalhistory/digital-encyclopedia/article/first-in-war-first-in-peace-and-first-in-the-hearts-of-his-countrymen.

Hur, Ben. "Washington's Best Saddle Horse." *Western Horseman* (January/February 1946).

Isaac, Rhys. *Landon Carter's Uneasy Kingdom: Revolution and Rebellion on a Virginia Plantation.* Oxford: Oxford University Press, 2004.

Jefferson, Thomas, to Edmund Bacon. August 18, 1823. *Founders Online.* National Archives. http://founders.archives.gov/documents/Jefferson/98-01-02-3708.

"Jefferson Quotes and Family Letters." Thomas Jefferson's Monticello. https://tjrs.monticello.org/letter/1003.

Jennings, Paul. *A Colored Man's Reminiscences of James Madison.* Brooklyn: George C. Beadle, 1865. http://docsouth.unc.edu/neh/jennings/menu.html.

"John Hartwell Cocke of Bremo." https://library.whitehousehistory.org/fotoweb/archives/5017-Digital-Library/Main%20Index/Artwork/484.tif.info.

"John Randolph." Exhibit. Museum of Charlotte County (Virginia). http://www.charlotteva.com/museum/john_randolph.html. Accessed June 8, 2021.

Johnson, Allen. *Jefferson and His Colleagues; A Chronicle of the Virginia Dynasty.* Yale University Press, 1921. "Chapter XV: The End of an Era." Project Gutenberg. 2002. https://ia800203.us.archive.org/2/items/jeffersonandhisc03004gut/jandc10.txt.

Johnson, E. Polk. *A History of Kentucky and Kentuckians; The Leaders and Representative Men in Commerce, Industry and Modern Activities.* Chicago: Lewis Publishing Co., 1912.

Johnson, Virginia C., and Barbara Crookshanks. *Virginia Horseracing: Triumphs of the Turf.* Charleston, South Carolina: The History Press, 2008.

Johnston, Caryl. *The Thoroughbred Colt: Identity and Moral Will in a Southern Family.* Bryn Mawr, Pennsylvania: Buy Books on the web.com, 1999.

Jones, Caroline. "Fox Hunting in America." *American Heritage* 24, vol. 6 (October 1973).

Jones, Hugh. *The Present State of Virginia; from Whence is Inferred a Short View of Maryland and North Carolina.* 1865.

Kames, Henry Home. *The Gentleman Farmer; Being an Attempt to Improve Agriculture, by Subjecting It to the Test of Rational Principles.* Edinburgh: Printed for W. Creech and T. Cadell, 1776.

Keaveney, Susan M. "Equines and Their Human Companions." *Journal of Business Research* 61, no. 5 (May 2008): 444–454.

Kierner, Cynthia A. *Scandal at Bizarre: Rumor and Reputation in Jefferson's America.* Charlottesville: University of Virginia Press, 2004.

Kilby, Emily R. "The Demographics of the U.S. Equine Population." In *The State of the Animals IV: 2007,* edited by Deborah J. Salem and Andrew N. Rowan, 175-205. Washington, D.C: Humane Society Press, 2007.

Kirwan, Richard. *Elements of Mineralogy.* 2nd edition. Dublin: Printed by R. E. Mercier and for P. Elmsly, London, 1796.

Kleber, John E. *The Kentucky Encyclopedia.* Lexington: University Press of Kentucky, 1992.

Kranish, Michael. *Flight from Monticello: Thomas Jefferson at War.* Oxford: Oxford University Press, 2010.

"Lalla Rookh." https://www.bartleby.com/library/readersdigest/1156.html.

Landry, Donna. "Learning to Ride in Early Modern Britain, or, The Making of the English Hunting Seat." In *The Culture of the Horse: Status, Discipline, and Identity in the Early Modern World,* edited by Karen Raber & Trena J. Tucker, 329–349. New York: Palgrave Macmillan, 2005.

Noble Brutes: How Eastern Horses Transformed English Culture. Baltimore: Johns Hopkins University Press, 2008.

Larson, Edward J. *A Magnificent Catastrophe: The Tumultuous Election of 1800.* New York: Free Press, 2008.

Latchford, Benjamin, and Juan Segundo. *The Loriner: Opinions and Observations on Bridle-bits and the Suitable Bitting of Horses, with Illustrations*. London: Nichols, Son, & Co., 1871.

Lemon, Holmes Willis. "The Chickasaw Horse: Grandfather to Quarterhorse." Chickasaw Times (April-May-June 1977). http://www.chickasaw.net/history_culture/index_681.htm. Accessed June 8, 2021.

Lewis, Charlene M. Boyer. *Ladies and Gentlemen on Display: Planter Society at the Virginia Springs, 1790–1860.* Charlottesville: University Press of Virginia, 2001.

Lewis, Jan Ellen, and Peter S. Onuf, eds. *Sally Hemings and Thomas Jefferson: History, Memory, and Civic Culture*. Charlottesville: University Press of Virginia, 1999.

Lucas, Ann M. "Road to Monticello." Thomas Jefferson Encyclopedia. https://www.monticello.org/site/house-and-gardens/road-monticello, 1996.

Mackay-Smith, Alexander. *The Colonial Quarter Race Horse: America's First Breed of Horses, America's Native Breed of Running Horses, the World's Oldest Breed of Race Horses, Prime Source of Short Speed.* Richmond: Whittet & Shepperson, 1983.

"Chronicle Commentary." *The Chronicle of the Horse* 55, no. 38 (September 18, 1992), reprinted in "Mission Statement," Hickory Creek Hunt, Fort Worth, Texas. http://www.hickorycreekhunt.com/missionstatement/.

"Margaret Bayard Smith's Account of a Visit to Monticello." July 29–August 2, 1809. https://founders.archives.gov/documents/Jefferson/03-01-02-0315.

Mark, Rebecca, and Rob C. Vaughan, eds. *The South: The Greenwood Encyclopedia of American Regional Cultures.* Westport, Connecticut: Greenwood Press, 2004.

Martin, Edwin T. *Thomas Jefferson: Scientist*. New York: H. Schuman, 1952.

Martin, Russell L. "Thomas Jefferson and Edmund Bacon: Two American Farmers." *Magazine of Albemarle County History* 50 (1992): 1–27.

and Lucia C. Stanton. "Moldboard Plow." Thomas Jefferson Encyclopedia. https://www.monticello.org/research-education/thomas-jefferson-encyclopedia/moldboard-plow/, October 1988.

Mason, Richard. *The Gentleman's New Pocket Companion: Comprising a General Description of the Noble and Useful Animal the Horse.* Petersburg, Virginia: Printed by John Dickson, 1811.

The Gentleman's New Pocket Farrier: Comprising a General Description of the Noble and Useful Animal the Horse. Richmond: Peter Cottom, 1820.

Massachusetts Historical Society. *Proceedings of the Massachusetts Historical Society*. Second series (13). https://archive.org/stream/proceedingsofmas213mass/proceedingsofmas213mass_djvu.txt. 1899, 1900.

Masters of Foxhounds Association of North America. http://www.mfha.com/foxhunting-history.html. Accessed June 8, 2021.

Matthes, C. A. "Foundation Matriarchs of the Thoroughbred." http://www.stallionsoftware.com/amfam1.htm.

Maxwell, William, ed. *The Virginia Historical Register and Literary Note-book, Vol. III, for the Year 1850.* Richmond: Macfarland & Fergusson, 1850: 150-151.

Mazzei, Filippo. *Memoirs of the Life and Peregrinations of the Florentine, Philip Mazzei, 1730–1816.* Translated by Howard Rosario Marraro. New York: Columbia University Press, 1942.

McCoy, Drew. *The Last of the Fathers: James Madison and the Republican Legacy.* Cambridge: Cambridge University Press, 1989.

McCullough, David G. *John Adams.* New York: Simon & Schuster, 2001.

McDonald, Robert M. S. *Thomas Jefferson's Lives: Biographers and the Battle for History.* Charlottesville: University of Virginia Press, 2019.

McDonnell, Michael. "Jefferson, Thomas as Governor of Virginia." *Encyclopedia Virginia.* https://encyclopediavirginia.org/entries/jefferson-thomas-as-governor-of-virginia/. December 7, 2020; September 25, 2021.

McEwan, Barbara. *Thomas Jefferson, Farmer.* Jefferson, North Carolina: McFarland, 1991.

McLaughlin, Jack. *Jefferson and Monticello: The Biography of a Builder.* New York: Holt & Co., 1988.

Molnar, John W. *Songs from the Williamsburg Theatre: A Selection of Fifty Songs Performed on the Stage in Williamsburg in the Eighteenth Century.* Charlottesville: University Press of Virginia, 1972.

Moore, Virginia. *Virginia Is a State of Mind.* New York: E. P. Dutton & Co, 1944.

Moran, Donald Norman, ed. "Jack Jouett of Virginia: The 'Other Ride.'" *The Valley Compatriot.* (1984).

Morgan, Philip D. *Slave Counterpoint: Black Culture in the Eighteenth-Century Chesapeake and Lowcountry.* Chapel Hill: Published for the Omohundro Institute of Early American History and Culture, Williamsburg, Virginia, by the University of North Carolina Press, 1998.

Morris, Desmond. *Horse Watching.* New York: Crown, 1988.

Morton, Louis. *Robert Carter of Nomini Hall: A Virginia Tobacco Planter of the Eighteenth Century.* Williamsburg: Colonial Williamsburg, Inc., 1941.

Mount Vernon Ladies Association. "Sixteen-sided Barn." 2010. http://www.mountvernon.org/learn/explore_mv/index.cfm/sss/76. Accessed June 8, 2021.

"Heritage Breed Animals." 2010. http://www.mountvernon.org/learn/explore_mv/index.cfm/ss/33/. Accessed June 8, 2021.

Nash, Richard. " 'Honest English Breed': The Thoroughbred as Cultural Metaphor." In *The Culture of the Horse: Status, Discipline, and Identity in the Early Modern World,* edited by Karen Raber & Trena J. Tucker, 245–272. New York: Palgrave Macmillan, 2005.

National Intelligencer. October 17, December 15, 1806.

National Purebred Spanish Breeders' Association of Spain (ANNCE). https://www.ancce.es/en/. Accessed June 8, 2021.

National Register of Historic Places Registration Form. Oaklands (Malvern Farm). 1995. https://www.dhr.virginia.gov/wp-content/uploads/2018/04/002-0092_Malvern_1995_Final_Nomination.pdf

Nelson-Burns, Lesley. "Ally Croaker." *Folk Music of England, Scotland, Ireland, Wales and America.* http://www.contemplator.com/england/croaker.html, 1996.

New York Times, April 13, 1879.

Nichols, Frederick Doveton, and Ralph E. Griswold. *Thomas Jefferson: Landscape Architect*. Charlottesville: University Press of Virginia, 1978.

Niemcewicz, Julian Ursyn. *Under Their Vine and Fig Tree; Travels Through America in 1797–1799, 1805, With Some Further Account of Life in New Jersey.* Translated and edited by Metchie J. E. Budka. Elizabeth, New Jersey: Grassman Publishing Company, 1965.

"1900: The Horse in Transition." Exhibit. International Museum of the Horse. http://www.imh.org/exhibits/online/1900-horse-transition-overview. Accessed June 8, 2021.

Nowlan, Robert A. *The American Presidents, Washington to Tyler: What They Did, What They Said.* Jefferson, North Carolina: McFarland & Company, 2012.

Parkinson, Richard. *A Tour in America in 1798, 1799, and 1800: Exhibiting Sketches of Society and Manners.* London: J. Harding & J. Murray, 1805.

Pawlett, Nathaniel Mason. "A Brief History of the Roads of Virginia, 1607–1840." Charlottesville: Virginia Highway & Transportation Research Council, 1977.

Peden, William, ed. *Notes on the State of Virginia*. Chapel Hill: University of North Carolina Press; Williamsburg, Virginia: Published for the Institute of Early American History and Culture, 1955.

"Pedigree Online. All Breed Database." http://www.allbreedpedigree.com/.

Peters, Anne. "Diomed." Thoroughbred Heritage: Portraits. http://www.tbheritage.com/Portraits/Diomed.html. 2005.

"Fearnought." Thoroughbred Heritage. http://www.tbheritage.com/Portraits/Fearnought.html. 2005.

"Godolphin Arabian." Thoroughbred Heritage. http://www.tbheritage.com/Portraits/GodolphinArabian.html. 2005.

"Historic Dams." Thoroughbred Heritage. http://www.tbheritage.com/HistoricDams/FamilyNumbers.html. 2005.

Peters, Anne, Saskia Stucki, and Livia Boscardin. "The Animal Turn—What Is It and Why Now?" *Verfassungblog on Matters Constitutional* (blog), April 14, 2014. https://verfassungsblog.de/the-animal-turn-what-is-it-and-why-now/.

Pickrell, John. "95% of Thoroughbreds Linked to One Superstud." *New Scientist* 14, no. 36 (September 6, 2005). https://www.newscientist.com/article/dn7941-95-of-thoroughbreds-linked-to-one-superstud/.

Raber, Karen, and Treva J. Tucker, eds. *The Culture of the Horse: Status, Discipline, and Identity in the Early Modern World.* New York: Palgrave Macmillan, 2005.

Randall, Henry S. *The Life of Thomas Jefferson.* 3 vols. New York: Derby & Jackson, 1857.

Randall, Willard Sterne. *Thomas Jefferson: A Life.* New York: H. Holt, 1993.

Randolph, Martha Jefferson to Ellen W. Randolph Coolidge. September 18, 1825. http://tjrs.monticello.org/letter/1003.

Randolph, Sarah Nicholas. *The Domestic Life of Thomas Jefferson.* New York: Harper & Brothers, 1871.

Randolph, Thomas Jefferson. *The Last Days of Jefferson.* Richmond: Jeffersonian Print, 1873.

Rayner, B. L. *Life of Thomas Jefferson.* Boston: Lilly, Wait, Colman, & Holden, 1834.

Renau, Lynn S. *Jockeys, Belles and Bluegrass Kings.* Louisville, Kentucky: Herr House Press, 1995.

Ritvo, Harriet. "On the Animal Turn." *Daedalus* 136 (2007): 118–122.

Rives, Judith Page Walker. "The Autobiography of Judith Page Walker Rives." Rives-Troubetzkoy Papers. Special Collections. University of Virginia Library.

Robb, Seymour. "Richard Mason of Surry County, Virginia." *William and Mary Quarterly* 15, no. 1 (January 1935): 73-75.

Rothman, Joshua D. " 'Notorious in the Neighborhood': An Interracial Family in Early National and Antebellum Virginia." *Journal of Southern History* 67, no. 1 (February 2001): 73-114.

Rouse, Parke, Jr. *Planters and Pioneers: Life in Colonial Virginia.* New York: Hastings House, 1968.

Rozbicki, Michal J. *The Complete Colonial Gentleman: Cultural Legitimacy in Plantation America.* Charlottesville: University Press of Virginia, 1998.

Russell, Nicholas. *Like Engend'ring Like: Heredity and Animal Breeding in Early Modern England.* Cambridge: Cambridge University Press, 1986.

Sadler, Julius Trousdale, and Jacquelin J. D. Sadler. *American Stables: An Architectural Tour*. Boston: New York Graphic Society, 1981

Skinner, John S., ed. *The American Farmer* 4, vol. 40 (December 27, 1822): 313.

"Turf Register. Stud of Mr. Edmund Bacon." *American Turf Register and Sporting Magazine* (January-February 1839): 114-115. https://archive.org/details/americanturfregi10skin.

Sloan, Herbert E. P*rinciple and Interest: Thomas Jefferson and the Problem of Debt.* Charlottesville: University Press of Virginia, 1995.

Smith, D. J. M. *A Dictionary of Horse-drawn Vehicles.* London: J.A. Allen, 1988.

Smucker, Philip G. "A Fowler and a Fisher." https://www.mountvernon.org/george-washington/athleticism/hunting-fishing.

"Some Family Letters of Thomas Jefferson." *Scribner's Magazine* 36 (1904): 573-586.

Sponenberg, Phillip. "North American Colonial Spanish Horse Update." Center for America's First Horse. http://www.centerforam-ericasfirsthorse.org/north-american-colonial-spanish-horse.html, July 2011.

Stanard, W. G. "Racing in Colonial Virginia," *The Virginia Magazine of History and Biography* 2, no. 3 (January 1895): 293–305. http://www.jstor.org/stable/4241820.

Stanton, Lucia C. *Free Some Day: The African-American Families of Monticello.* Charlottesville: Thomas Jefferson Foundation, 2000.

Personal interview. February 7, 2008.

"Slaves Who Gained Freedom." Thomas Jefferson's Monticello. https://www.monticello.org/site/plantation-and-slavery/slaves-who-gained-freedom, 1999. Accessed June 8, 2021.

"The Other End of the Telescope: Jefferson Through the Eyes of His Slaves." *William and Mary Quarterly* 57, no. 1 (January 2000): 139–152.

"Those Who Labor for My Happiness": Slavery at Thomas Jefferson's Monticello. Charlottesville: University of Virginia Press, 2012.

Stein, Susan R. *Worlds of Thomas Jefferson at Monticello*. Charlottesville: H. N. Abrams, in association with the Thomas Jefferson Memorial Foundation, Inc., 1993.

Stong, Phil. *Horses and Americans*. New York: Frederick A. Stokes, 1939.

Stuart, John Ferdinand Smyth. *A Tour of the United States of America: Concerning an Account of the Present State of that Country.* London: G. Robinson, 1784.

Tarr, Laszlo. *The History of the Carriage.* New York: Arco Publishing Co., 1969.

Taylor, Elizabeth Dowling. *A Slave in the White House: Paul Jennings and the Madisons.* New York, New York: St. Martin's Press, 2012.

"Thomas Jefferson and Sally Hemings: A Brief Account." Thomas Jefferson's Monticello. https://www.monticello.org/site/plantation-and-slavery/thomas-jefferson-and-sally-hemings-brief-account, 2008.

"Thoroughbred." Wikipedia. http://en.wikipedia.org/wiki/Thoroughbred, 2016.

"Thoroughbred Bloodlines." Early Studbook Index. http://www.bloodlines.net/TB/Studbook/EarlyD.htm, 2008.

Tillson, Albert H. "Gentry in Colonial Virginia." *Encyclopedia Virginia*. http://www.EncyclopediaVirginia.org/Gentry_in_Colonial_

Virginia, December 6, 2012.

“Timeline of Jefferson’s Life.” Thomas Jefferson’s Monticello. https://www.monticello.org/site/jefferson/timeline-jeffersons-life.

Trechter, David, Shelly Hadley, Denise Parks, and James Janke. (2008). “Wisconsin State Horse Council General Population Survey and Horse Owners’ Survey Report.” 2008. PDF at https://minds.wisconsin.edu/handle/1793/35365.

Trevathan, Charles E. *The American Thoroughbred.* New York: Macmillan, 1905.

Tucker, George. *The Life of Thomas Jefferson: Third President of the United States.* 2 vols. Philadelphia: Carey, Lea and Blanchard, 1837.

Tull, Jethro. *Horse-hoeing Husbandry, or, An Essay on the Principles of Vegetation and Tillage.* London: Jethro Tull, 1751.

“US Thoroughbreds Rise to New Heights by 1800.” Exhibition. International Museum of the Horse. https://www.imh.org/exhibits/past/legacy-of-the-horse/us-thoroughbreds-rise-new-heights-1800/.

“Uva Cultural Landscape Survey, 1817–1826.” University of Virginia Facilities Management Cultural Resource Center.

Van Dierendonck, Machteld C., and D. Goodwin. “Social Contact in Horses: Implications for Human-Horse Interactions,” in Machteld C. van Dierendonck, ed., *The Importance of Social Relations in Horses.* Utrecht: Universitat Utrecht, 2006.

Virginia Field Office of the National Agricultural Statistics Service. “Virginia Equine Survey Report.” 2006. https://www.nass.usda.gov/Statistics_by_State/Virginia/Publications/Equine/equine2007full.pdf.

Virginia Gazette, 1736–1780. http://research.history.org/DigitalLibrary/va-gazettes/.

Virginia Historical Marker Q-27. https://vcris.dhr.virginia.gov/HistoricMarkers/.

Virginia Journal. March 24, 1785.

Vlach, John Michael. *Back of the Big House: The Architecture of Plantation Slavery.* Chapel Hill: University of North Carolina Press, 1993.

Vocabulary.com. https://www.vocabulary.com/dictionary/hobby.

Von Daacke, Kirt. *Freedom has a Face: Race, Identity, and Community in Jefferson’s Virginia.* Charlottesville: University of Virginia Press, 2012.

Wallace, John Hankins. *The Horse of America in His Derivation, History and Development.* New York: J. H. Wallace, 1897.

Washington, George. *The Papers of George Washington Digital Edition.* Charlottesville: University of Virginia Press, Rotunda. http://rotunda.upress.virginia.edu/founders/GEWN.html.

Donald Jackson and Dorothy Twohig. *The Diaries of George Washington.* Charlottesville: University Press of Virginia, 1976–1979.

Weaver, J. C. “The Albemarle of Old.” *New River Notes.* http://www.newrivernotes.com/topical_books_xxxx_virginia_thealbemarleofold.htm. 2001. Accessed June 8, 2021.

Weld, Isaac. *Travels Through the States of North America and the Provinces of Upper and Lower Canada, During the Years 1795, 1796, and 1797.* London: J. Stockdale, 1799.

Wharton, Anne Hollingsworth. *Martha Washington.* New York: C. Scribner’s Sons, 1897.

“What’s an American Quarter Horse? The History of the World’s Most Popular Breed.” http://www.aqha.com/horse/index.html. July 30, 2010.

Williams, Alfred B. “Rival First Families of Virginia.” *William and Mary College Quarterly Historical Magazine* Vol. XXIII (January 9, 1921):277.

Willich, A. F. M. *The Domestic Encyclopaedia: Or a Dictionary of Facts and Useful Knowledge.* London: B. McMillan, 1802–1806.

http://chestofbooks.com/reference/The-Domestic-Encyclopaedia-Vol2/Horse.html.

Wills, Garry. *Mr. Jefferson's University.* Washington, D.C.: National Geographic, 2002.

Wilson, Gaye. "Hats." Thomas Jefferson Encyclopedia. https://www.monticello.org/site/research-and-collections/hats. February 2001.

"Jack Jouett's Ride." https://www.monticello.org/site/research-and-collections/jack-jouetts-ride. September 5, 2006.

Wingfield, Marshall. *A History of Caroline County, Virginia, from its Formation in 1727 to 1924.* Baltimore: Reprinted for Clearfield Co. Inc. by Genealogical Publishing Co. Inc. 2005.

Workers of the Writers' Program of the Work Projects Administration in the State of Virginia. *Virginia: A Guide to the Old Dominion.* Richmond: Virginia State Library and Archives, 1992.

Wyatt, Edward A. "Newmarket of the Virginia Turf." *William and Mary Quarterly* 17, no. 4 (October 1937): 481–495.

Youatt, William. *The Horse.* Philadelphia: Blanchard and Lea, 1853.

Young, Arthur. *Farmer's Guide in Hiring and Stocking Farms.* Dublin: For Exshaw, Saunders, Sleater, Chamberlaine, Potts, Williams, Hoey, Milliken, Porter and Walker, 1770.

Index

Horses